AF592657

INDIGO

Dictionary of PHILOSOPHY

INDIGO COMPANIONS comprise of quality reference Dictionaries which are comprehensive, latest, and published with finest production techniques, compiled by a trained team of experts especially for this series.

INDIGO COMPANIONS available (or to be published shortly) are:

INDIGO DICTIONARY OF FINANCE

INDIGO DICTIONARY OF BUSINESS

INDIGO DICTIONARY OF ABBREVIATIONS

INDIGO DICTIONARY OF ANTHROPOLOGY

INDIGO DICTIONARY OF LITERATURE

INDIGO DICTIONARY OF LANGUAGES

INDIGO DICTIONARY OF INSURENCE

INDIGO DICTIONARY OF ASTROLOGY

INDIGO DICTIONARY OF POLITICS

INDIGO DICTIONARY OF SOCIOLOGY

INDIGO DICTIONARY OF MATHEMATICS

INDIGO DICTIONARY OF BIOLOGY

INDIGO DICTIONARY OF PHYSICS

INDIGO DICTIONARY OF CHEMISTRY

INDIGO DICTIONARY OF LINGUISTICS

INDIGO

Dictionary of PHILOSOPHY

the most comprehensive, authoritative, and up-to-date work available

INDIGO BOOKS

AN
INDIGO BOOK
PUBLISHED BY INDIGO BOOKS
Paperback division of
COSMO PUBLICATIONS,
24-B, Ansari Road, Darya Ganj,
New Delhi 110 002, India.

INDIGO BOOKS and
COSMO PUBLICATIONS
are wholly owned subsidiaries of
GENESIS PUBLISHING PVT. LTD.,
New Delhi, India

INDIGO DICTIONARY OF PHILOSOPHY

Copyright © 2002 INDIGO BOOKS

First INDIGO Edition 2002

ISBN 81-291-0009-6

This book is sold subject to the condition that it shall not, by way of trade or otherwise, be lent, re-sold, hired out or otherwise circulated without the publisher's prior consent in any form of binding or cover other than that in which this is published and without a similar condition including this condition being imposed on the subsequent purchaser.

ALL RIGHTS RESERVED

PRINTED AND BOUND IN INDIA

PREFACE

For bringing some of the finest reference Dictionaries in several subject areas the publishers set themselves the following rules :

1. Every explanation must be clear to a person who knows little or nothing about the particular subject, and must be made if possible with as many cross-references as possible; but references to additional information may be given at the end. (*Entries were tested and rewritten as many as ten times to comply with this.*)

2. Every explanation must be of such length as is necessary to give an adequate idea of the meaning (sometimes a page, or more may be necessary); but this book is not an encyclopaedia: it deals with words not subjects.

3. Words should not be included which are adequately explained by an ordinary dictionary (but certain defining words are included).

4. No word may be omitted because it is too difficult to explain, but only because the explanation would take more space than is justified by its importance.

5. The matter to be digitally set by using latest composing techniques so as to bring to the readers pages which are crisp and put least amount of strain.

6. Not to fill-up the pages with useless material or entries which are no longer valid to the topic. The focus should be on current usage and to include sub-areas wherever necessary that infringe upon the main subject.

The readers and users of this Dictionary may send their comments, observations, and suggestions to the publishers. These will not only be incorporated, if found valid, in futur0e editions but will also help in making further improvements.

A Posteriori (Latin, "from what comes after"), relating to that which is known through experience, a central concept in epistemology. Those who argue that a posteriori knowledge is the only true knowledge, advocates of empiricis m, insist that all we can ever know is that which is accessible to us through experience, mainly sense perception. They therefore deny the plausibility of a priori knowledge as being untestable and thus worthless. David Hume, for example, developed his empirical scepticism to the extent that he denied the existence of the self, claiming that it was unknowable and that human beings were "bundles of perceptions".

While rationalist philosophers can allow for the existence of both a priori and a posteriori knowledge, empiricists deny the validity of a priori knowledge completely. That is not, however, to deny the validity of analytic truths (for example, the statement "all brown dogs are dogs" is necessarily true, regardless of any real experience of brown dogs), which can be known by virtue of the meaning of the words alone. But such truths are viewed on a different level from the real pursuits of epistemology: John Locke described them as "trifling", and John Stuart Mill as "merely verbal" because they offer no new knowledge.

A Priori (Latin, "from what comes before"), in philosophy, relating to knowledge that is acquired irrespective of experience, that is, by deductive reasoning alone. A priori knowledge is central to certain branches of epistemology, especially to rationalist theories. René Descartes, for example, posited the reason as a faculty independent of experience, and argued for an innate, or a priori, knowledge of the self in his famous statement *Cogito, ergo sum* ("I think, therefore I am"), which became the starting point for further of his investigations.

On the other hand, the existence of a priori knowledge is denied by the empiricists, such as David Hume and John Locke, who argue that only that which comes through experience (that is, a posteriori) can truly be said to be knowable. The existence of a priori knowledge has been a fundamental concern in arguments relating to the existence of God. Many philosophers have argued that to deny a priori knowledge is to make it impossible to prove the existence of God as He is not outwardly perceivable.

The existence of a priori truths is often appealed to in ethics, that is to say, that the fundamental moral ideals can be arrived at by the use of reason.

Abduction, the process of inference to the best explanation. The term is sometimes used to mean just the generation of hypotheses to explain observations or conclusions, but the former definition is more common both in philosophy and computing.

The notion was first introduced by Peirce in an attempt to classify a certain form of syllogism.

Abductive inferences are of the following form:

i) All beans from this bag are white
ii) These beans are white.
iii) Therefore, these beans are from this bag.

This inference results in an explanation of the observation in the second premise.

The semantics and the implementation of abduction cannot be reduced to those for deduction, as explanation cannot be reduced to implication.

Though this method of reasoning is not logically valid as the beans may be from a different source, Peirce argues that scientists regularly engage in this sort of inferential reasoning. Though scientific hypo-theses are not valid by virtue of how they are abducted, abductive reasoning was thought to constitute "a logic of discovery" in one of Peirce's four steps of scientific investigation. These steps are:

1) observation of an anomaly
2) abduction of hypotheses for the purposes of explaining the anomaly
3) inductive testing of the hypotheses in experiments
4) deductive confirmation that the selected hypothesis predicts the original anomaly

Abduction is currently thought not to be wellunderstood and Peirce's formulation has been criticised as being restricted to language-like mediums (Shelley, 1996). It should be noted that for Peirce, abduction was restricted to the generation of explanatory hypotheses.

The more general characterisation of abduction as inference to the best explanation is a more recent interpretation.

Applications include fault diagnosis, plan formation and default reasoning.

Negation as failurein logic programming can both be given an abductive interpretation and also can be used to implement abduction. The abductive semantics of negation as failure leads naturally to an argumentation—theoretic interpretation of default reasoning in general.

References: Peirce, C. (1958) Volume 2, paragraph 511, 623; Volume 5, paragraph 270. In Hartshoren and Weiss. Levesque (1989). A knowledge level account of abduction. In Sridharan 1989 pp. 1061-1067. Shelley, C. (1996) Visual abductive reasoning in archaeology. Philosophy of Science Association, 63. 278-301.

Abelard Peter, French scholastic logician (1079-1142) whose sexual relationship with his teenaged student provoked the vengeful anger of her uncle, Fulbert, in 1118. Despite the many distractions of the turbulent life he described in *Historia Calamitatum Mearum* (The *History of my Misfortunes*), Abelard embarked on a monastic career of detached contemplation marked by intellectual independence from both traditional authorities and contemporaneous fashions. In commentaries on the logic of Aristotle and his own Dialectica, Abelard invented a novel solution to the problem of universals that rejected both realism and nominalism in their most extreme forms. Only individual things exist for Abelard, but general terms have universal applicability to things whose common features are known by a process of mental abstraction. Abelardalso wrote on the difficulties involved in scriptural interpretation in *Sic et Non* (For and Against) and on the importance of human intentions for theological ethics in *Scito te Ipsum* (Know Thyself).

Recommended Reading: Five Texts on the Mediaeval Problem of Universals, ed. by Paul Vincent Spade (Hackett,

1994); John Marenbon, The Philosophy of Peter Abelard (Cambridge, 1999); Letters of Abelard and Heloise, ed. by Betty Radice (Penguin, 1998).

Absolute, the solitary, uniquely unconditioned, utterly independent, and ultimately all-encompassing being that comprises all of reality according to such Romantic idealists as Schelling, and Hegel. British philosopher F.H. Bradley emphasized that the Absolute must transcend all of the contradictory appearances of ordinary experience, while American Josiah Royce took the Absolute to be a spiritual entity whose self-consciousness is reflected only imperfectly in the totality of human thought.

Absolute, term used to denote that which is in no way dependent on or limited by anything else. Thus, in ethics an absolute value is one that is good in itself rather than useful as a means to obtaining something else, and an absolute principle is one that permits of no exceptions. In political theory an absolute right is a right that society cannot take away from an individual.

In theology and metaphysics the term *Absolute* usually refers to God. According to the Dutch philosopher Baruch Spinoza, God is absolute; that is, unlimited, because by his very concept nothing can limit God. All other existing things exist through this absolute substance. The German philosopher Immanuel Kant defined the Absolute as an all-encompassing totality and argued that scientific knowledge of such a being is impossible. This position was also adopted by the British philosophers Herbert Spencer and Sir William Hamilton. The Absolute figures again as the central concept in the philosophies of the 19th-century German idealists. In particular, the German philosopher G. W. F. Hegel regarded the Absolute as a spiritual process that realizes itself through rationality alone, because only through the use of logic can reality be recognized. He maintained, as did the British idealist philosophers Bernard Bosanquet, Francis Herbert Bradley, and Thomas Hill Green, that all knowledge is indirectly and incompletely knowledge of the Absolute. The American idealist philosopher Josiah Royce identified the Absolute with a so-called *cosmic community;* his system of philosophy came to be known as absolute idealism.

Absolute consistency, A system S is absolutely consistent *iff* at least ne *wff* of the formal language of S is not a theorem.

Absolute inconsistency, A system is absolutely inconsistent *iff* all its *wff* S are theorems.

Absolutism, the belief that there is one and only one truth. Those who espouse absolutism usually also believe that they know or have access to what this absolute truth is. In ethics, absolutism is usually contrasted to relativism. See also authoritarianism in political theory.

Absorption, a rule of inference of the form:

$$p \rightarrow q$$
$$p \rightarrow (p \& q)$$

Example: "If Mary comes to the party, then so will George. Therefore, if Mary comes to the party, then both Mary and George will." As a simple truth-table shows, any argument of this form is valid.

Abstract class, In object-oriented programming, a class designed only as a parent from which sub-classes may be derived, but which is not itself suitable for instantiation. Often used to "abstract out" incomplete sets of features which may then be shared by a group of sibling sub-classes which adddifferent variations of the missing pieces.

Abstract interpretation, A partial execution of a program which gains information about its semantics (*e.g.* control structure, flow of information) without performing all the calculations. Abstract interpretation is typically used by compilers to analyse programs in order to decide whether certain optimisations or transfor-mations are applicable.

The objects manipulated by the program (typically values and functions) are represented by points in some domain. Each abstract domain point represents some set of real ("concrete") values.

For example, we may take the abstract points "+", "0" and "–" to represent positive, zero and negative numbers and then define an abstract version of the multiplication operator, *#, which operates on abstract values:

*#	+	0	–
+	+	0	–
0	0	0	0
–	–	0	+

An interpretation is "safe" if the result of the abstract operation is a safe approximation to the abstraction of the concrete result. The meaning of "a safe approximation" depends on how we are using the results of the analysis.

If, in our example, we assume that smaller values are safer then the "safety condition" for our interpretation (#) is

a# *# b# <= (a * b) #

where a# is the abstract version of a etc.

In general an interpretation is characterised by the domains used to represent the basic types and the abstract values it assigns to constants (where the constants of a language include primitive functions such as *). The interpretation of constructed types (such as user defined functions, sum types and product types) and expressions can be derived systematically from these basic domains and values.

A common use of abstract interpretation is strictness analysis. See also standard interpretation.

Abstraction, 1. Generalisation; ignoring or hiding details to capture some kind of commonality between different instances. Examples are abstract data types (the representation details are hidden), abstract syntax (the details of the concrete syntax are ignored), abstract interpretation (details are ignored to analyse specific properties).

2. Parameterisation, making something a function of something else. Examples are lambda abstractions (making a term into a function of some variable), higher-order functions (parameters are functions), bracket abstraction (making a term into a function of a variable).

Opposite of concretisation.

The process of forming a general concept by omitting distinguishing features from the notions of particular things, or the endresult of that process. Introducedby Peter Abelard as part of his solution to the problem of universals, abstraction became crucial for Locke's account of our use of general terms. Thus, for example, the idea of "green" could in principle be derived by abstracting from one's specific experiences of a summer lawn, the leaves of trees, and emeralds. Berkeley, on the other hand, argued that abstract ideas in this sense are impossible because every sensible idea has only particular content.

Recommended Reading: Berkeley on Abstraction and Abstract Ideas, ed. by Willis Doney (Garland, 1993); Roger Teichmann, Abstract Entities (St. Martin's, 1992).

Abstractionism, 1) in metaphysics see idealism.

2) in aesthetics, see modernism, also called abstract expressionism.

Absurd, Contrary to reason or beyond the limits of rationality; paradoxical, nonsensical, or meaningless. According to Camus, Sartre, and other existentialists, absurdity is an inescapable consequence of any sensitive effort to live in the face of an indifferent reality. The human tendency to desire most passionately what we can never have is absurd in this sense. *Recommended Reading*: Donald A. Crosby, Specter of the Absurd: Sources and Criticisms of Modern Nihilism (SUNY, 1988); Richard E. Baker, The Dynamics of the Absurd in the Existentialist Novel (Peter Lang, 1993); Martin Esslin, The Theatre of the Absurd (Viking, 1992).

Abunaser, Latinized form of the name of Persian philosopher al-Farabi.

Accent fallacy of, An informal fallacy that arises from the ambiguity produced by a shift of emphasis in spoken or written language. Example: "Joan said that she never wants to see another Demi Moore movie, so we won't show her another one; we'll just play this same one over and over again". In such instances, an uninflected reading of the premise often provides no reason at all for believing the conclusion.

Acceptance testing, Formal testing conducted to determine whether a system satisfies its acceptance criteria and thus whether the customer should accept the system.

Accident, A feature that something happens to have but might have existed without having, since this feature is no part of the very nature of the thing, in contrast to the essence without which the thing could not be at all.

Accidentalism, the position according to which some events are accide-ntal, that is, either they are not predictable or they lack a cause. Accidentalism is part of some defenses of the freedom of the will (see libertarianism). See also indeterminism.

Accident fallacy of, (Lat. a dicto simpliciter ad dictum secundum quid) the informal fallacy of applying a generally reliable rule to a particular case without considering the qualifying features that make it an exception to the rule. Example: "Since authors of best-selling books usually appear on television talk shows, and the Pope is in fact the author of a best-selling book, it follows that the Pope will soon appear on a television talk show". Unlimited applicability to every instance would follow syllogistically only from a genuinely universal proposition, the truth of which is often difficult to defend. Merely probable guidelines are easier to establish as "rules of thumb", but do not deserve to be applied so indiscriminately.

Accuracy, How close to the real value a measurement is. Compare precision.

Aconsciousness, access consciousness

Acronym, An identifier formed from some of the letters (often the initials) of a phrase and used as an abbreviation.

Action, that which an agent or actor A does, in contrast to that which merely happens to A or to A's parts.

Action theory, branch of philosophy concerned with the analysis and explanation of what human beings do. Understanding the relation between choice or volition and the performance of an action seems crucial for the ascription of responsibility in ethics.

Recommended Reading: Readings in the Theory of Action, ed. By Norman S. Care and Charles Landesman (Indiana, 1968); The Philosophy of Action, ed. by Alfred R. Mele (Oxford, 1997); Philosophical Perspectives: Action Theory and Philosophy, ed. by James E. Tomberlin (Ridgeview, 1990).

Active object, An object each instance of which has its own thread running as well as its own copies of the object's instance variables.

Actor, 1. In object-oriented programming, an object which exists as a concurrent process.

2. In Chorus, the unit of resource allocation.

Act - rule utilitarianism, Distinction between ways of applying the greatest happiness principle for moral evaluation on utilitarian grounds. Act-utilitarianism supposes that each particular action should be evaluated solely by references to its own consequences, while rule-utilitarianism considers the consequences of widespread performance of similar actions. The actutilitarian asks, "How much pleasure or pain would result if I did this now?" The rule-utilitarian asks, "What pleasure or pain would result if everyone were always to do this?" Since the answers to these questions may be quite different, they may lead to distinct recommendations about moral conduct. Although Mill noted that reliance on moral rules may be of practical use in decisionmaking, he argued that their influence should remain defeasible in particular circumstances. *Recommended Reading*: J. J. C. Smart and Bernard Williams, Utilitarianism: For and Against (Cambridge, 1973).

Actual, what really is the case, as opposed to what's possible (could be the case) and to what's necessary (must be the case); all of which are opposed to what's impossible (can't be the case). Concerning the latter "opposition": the categories possible and impossible are jointly exhaustive(everything is either one or the other). Concerning the former "opposition": necessity, actuality, and possibility are not mutually exclusive: everything necessary is also actual (what must be the case is the case) and everything actual is possible (whatever is possible). In other words, necessity entails actuality, and actuality entails possibility. (Also see contingent.)

Actuality-potentiality, (Gr. energeia /dynamis) Aristotle's distinction between what really is the case and what merely has the power to change or come to be the case. Thus, for example, this fresh acorn is actually a seed but only potentially an oak tree.

Adaptive learning, (Or "Hebbian learning") Learning where a system programs itself by adjusting weights or strengths until it produces the desired output.

Addams Jane, American pragmatist and social worker (1860-1935). Concerned by the dismal living conditions endured by women, minorities, and the working poor, Addams established Hull House in Chicago as a social settlement in 1889 and campaigned tirelessly for women's suffrage, world peace, and economic justice. Her address to the Chicago Liberty Meeting, Democracy or Militarism (1899) and the pamphlet Why Women Should Vote (1909) are representative expressions of her belief that women properly exert a pacifistic influence on American political life. Her writings on social issues include Democracy and Social Ethics (1902), Newer Ideals of Peace (1907), A New Conscience and an Ancient Evil (1911), Twenty Years at Hull House (1912), The Larger Aspects of the Women's Movement (1914), and Women, War, and Suffrage (1915). Addams shared the 1931 Nobel Prize for peace. *Recommended Reading*: Allen F. Davis, American Heroine (Ivan R. Dee, 2000); Mary Jo Deegan, Jane Addams and the Men of the Chicago School, 1892-1918 (Transaction, 1990).

Addition, a rule of inference of the form:

$$\frac{p}{p \vee q}$$

Example: "It is raining. Therefore, either it is raining or the sun is shining." Although its use in ordinary thought is notably rare, this pattern of reasoning serves a vital role in the construction of formal proofs in many systems of logic.

Additive, A function *f*: *X* -> *Y* is additive if for all *Z* <= *X f* (lub *Z*) = lub [*f z*: *z* in *Z*] [*f* "preserves (lub) *s*"]. All additive functions defined over [cpo]s are continuous.

Ad hoc, Contrived purely for the purpose in hand rather than planned carefully in advance. *E.g.* "We didn't know what to do about the sausage rolls, so we set up an ad-hoc committee".

Ad hominem argument, (argument against the person) the informal fallacy of supposing that a proposition should be denied because of some disqualifying features of the person who affirms it. This fallacy is the mirror image of the appeal to authority. In its abusive form, ad hominem is a direct (and often inflammatory) attack on the appearance, character, or personality of the individual. *Example*: "Jeremy claims that Susan was at the party, but since Jeremy is the kind of person who has to ride to work on the city bus, it must be false that she was there." A circumstantial ad hominem accuses the person of having an alternative motive for defending the proposition or points out its inconsistency with the person's other views. Tuquoque [the ("so do you" fallacy)] uses a similar method in response to criticism of a position already held. *Recommended Reading*: Douglas Walton, Ad Hominem Arguments (Alabama, 1998).

Adiaphora, Greek term used by the classical Stoics to designate actions that are morally indifferent. On this view, we have no direct obligation either to perform or to avoid such actions, even when they might indirectly affect our general well-being. Thus, for example, although there is no duty to preserve one's own health, doing so is advisable, since it will probably feel good and improve one's capacity for doing what is right. Pyrrho, Carneades, and other Skeptics, on the other hand, argued that there can be no coherent reason for preferring beneficial acts unless they are themselves virtuous. *Recommended Reading*: F. E. Peters, Greek Philosophical Terms:A Historical Lexicon (NYU, 1967).

Adler Alfred, Austrian psychiatrist (1870-1937); author of such books as Studie ueber Minderwertigkeit von Organen (Study of Organ Inferiority and its Psychical Compensation) (1907), Praxis und Theorie der Individual psychologie (Practice and Theory of Individual Psychology) (1918), and Der Sinn des Lebens (What Life Should Mean to You) (1934). Influenced by the philosophy of Hans Vaihinger, Adler's "individual psychology" focussed on the efforts people invariably make in order to compensate for their (self-perceived) inferiority to others, whether it originally arose from a specific physical defect, relative position in the family constellation, particular experiences of humiliation, or a general lack of social feeling for others. *Recommended Reading*: Individual Psychology of Alfred Adler: A Systematic Presentation in Selections from His Writings (Harpercollins, 1989); Super-iority and Social Interest: A Collection of Later Writings, ed. by Heinz L. Ansbacher and Rowena R. Ansbacher (Norton, 1979); and Harold H. Mosak and Michael Maniacci, A Primer of Adlerian Psychology: The Analytic-Behavioral-Cognitive Psychology of Alfred Adler (Brunner/ Mazel, 1999).

Adorno Theodor Wiesengrund, German musicologist, social critic, and political philosopher (1903-1969); author of Philosophie der neuen Musik (The Philosophy of Modern Music) (1949) and Noten zur Literatur (Notes to Literature) (1958-74). A leading member of the Frankfurt school, Adorno traced the development and failure of Western reliance on reason in Dialektik der Aufklaerung (Dialectic of Enlightenment) (1947). In The Authoritarian Personality (1951) Adorno described the ways conformity to the demands of social propriety imposes paradox and contradiction on the lives of in-dividual human beings. Negative Dialektik (Negative Dialectics) (1966) openly defends the critical task of exposing, dissolving, and undermining the harmful influence of rigid conceptual schemes. *Recommended Reading*: The Adorno Reader, ed. by Brian O'Connor (Blackwell, 2000); Simon Jarvis, Adorno: A Critical Introduction (Routledge, 1998); Martin Jay, Adorno (Harvard, 1984); Hauke Brunkhorst, Adorno and Critical Theory (U of Wales, 1999); The Actuality of Adorno: Critical Essays on Adorno and the Postmodern, ed. by Max Pensky (SUNY, 1997).

Aesthetic, branch of philosophy that studies beauty and taste, including their specific manifestations in the tragic, the comic, and the sublime. Its central issues include questions about the origin and status of aesthetic judgments: are they objective statements about genuine features of the world or purely subjective expressions of personal attitudes; should they include any reference to the intentions of artists or the reactions of patrons; and how are they related to judgments of moral value? Aesthetics is a significant component of the philosophical work of Plato, Aristotle, Kant, and Santayana. *Rec-*

ommended Reading: A Companion to Aesthetics, ed. by David Cooper, Crispin Sartwell, and Joseph Margolis (Blackwell, 1995); Aesthetics, ed. by Patrick Maynard and Susan Feagin (Oxford, 1998); Anne D. R. Sheppard, Aesthetics: An Introduction to the Philosophy of Art (Oxford, 1987).

Aesthetics, branch of philosophy concerned with the essence and perception of beauty and ugliness. Aesthetics also deals with the question of whether such qualities are objectively present in the things they appear to qualify, or whether they exist only in the mind of the individual; hence, whether objects are perceived by a particular mode, the aesthetic mode, or, instead, whether the objects have, in themselves, special qualities—aesthetic qualities. Aesthetics also asks if there is a difference between the beautiful and the sublime.

Criticism and the psychology of art, although independent disciplines, are related to aesthetics. The psychology of art is concerned with such elements of the arts as human responses to colour, sound, line, form, and words, and with the ways in which the emotions condition such responses. Criticism confines itself to particular works of art, analysing their structures, meanings, and problems, comparing them with other works, and evaluating them. The distinction between aesthetics and critical theory is somewhat harder to specify. However, it may be said that where the former treats art as an autonomous domain of philosophical enquiry, the latter tends to draw upon various other disciplines (for example, sociology, linguistics, and psychoanalysis) in the search for illuminating methods and ideas.

The term "aesthetics" was introduced in 1753 by the German philosopher Alexander Gottlieb Baumgarten, but the study of the nature of beauty had been pursued for centuries. In the past it was chiefly a subject for philosophers. Since the 19th century, artists have also contributed their views.

Classical Theories: The first aesthetic theory of any scope is that of Plato, who believed that reality consists of archetypes, or forms, that are beyond the bounds of human sensation and are the models for all things that exist in human experience. The objects that human beings can experience are examples, or imitations, of those forms. The philosopher's job is to reason from the object experienced to the reality it imitates, while the artist copies the experienced object, or uses it as a model for the work. Thus, the artist's work is an imitation of what is itself an imitation.

Plato's thinking had a marked ascetic strain. In his *Republic,* he went so far as to banish some types of artists from his ideal society because he thought their work encouraged immorality or portrayed base characters, and that certain musical compositions caused laziness or incited people to immoderate actions.

Aristotle also spoke of art as imitation, but not in the Platonic sense. One could imitate "things as they ought to be", he wrote, and "art partly completes what nature cannot bring to a finish". The artist separates the form from the matter of some objects of experience, such as the human body or a tree, and imposes that form on another matter, such as canvas or marble. Thus, imitation is not just copying an original model, nor is it devising a symbol for the original; rather, it is a particular representation of an aspect of things, and each work is an imitation of the universal whole.

Aesthetics was inseparable from morality and politics for both Aristotle and Plato. The former wrote about music in his *Politics,* maintaining that art affects human character, and hence the social order. Because Aristotle held that happiness is the aim of life, he believed that the major function of art is to provide human satisfaction. In the *Poetics,* his great work on the principles of drama, Aristotle argued that tragedy stimulates the emotions of pity and fear, which he considered ordinarily morbid and unhealthy, to such an extent that by the end of the play the spectator is purged of them. This catharsis makes the audience psychologically healthier and thus more capable of happiness. Neo-Classical drama since the 17th century has been greatly influenced by Aristotle's *Poetics.* The works of the French dramatists Jean-Baptiste Racine, Pierre Corneille, and Molière, in particular, advocate its doctrine of the three unities: time, place, and action. This concept dominated literary theories up to the 19th century.

Other Early Approaches: The 3rd-century philosopher Plotinus, born in Egypt and trained in philosophy at Alexandria, although a Neoplatonist, accorded far more importance to art than did Plato. In Plotinus' view, art reveals the form of an object more clearly than is possible in ordinary experience, and raises the soul to contemplation of the universal. According to Plotinus, the highest moments of life are mystical, which is to say that the soul is united, in the world of forms, with the divine, which Plotinus spoke of as "the One". Aesthetic experience comes closest to mystical experience, for one loses oneself while contemplating the aesthetic object.

Art in the Middle Ages was primarily an expression of religion, with aesthetic principles based largely on Neoplatonism. During the Renaissance in the 15th and 16th centuries, art became more secular, and aesthetics Classical rather than religious. The great impetus to aesthetic thought in the modern world occurred in Germany during the 18th century. In his *Laokoon* (1766) the German critic Gotthold Ephraim Lessing argued that art is self-limiting and reaches its height only when these limitations are recognized. The German critic and Classical archaeologist Johann Joachim Winckelmann maintained that, in accordance with the ancient Greeks, the best art is impersonal, expressing ideal proportion and balance rather than its creator's individuality. The German philosopher Johann Gottlieb Fichte considered beauty a moral virtue. In creating a world in which beauty, as much as truth, is an end, the artist foreshadows the absolute freedom that is the goal of human will. For Fichte, art is individual, not social, but it fulfils a great human purpose.

Modern Aesthetics: The 18th-century German philosopher Immanuel Kant was concerned with judgements of taste. Objects can be judged beautiful, he proposed, when they satisfy a disinterested desire: one that does not involve personal interests or needs. It follows from this that beautiful objects have no specific purpose and that judgements of beauty are not expressions of mere personal preference but are universal. Although one cannot be certain that others will be satisfied by objects he or she judges to be beautiful, one can at least say that others ought to be satisfied. The basis for one's response to beauty, therefore, exists in the structure of one's mind. Kant's theory suggests how judgements might be reconciled—or aesthetic valuations harmonized—through the appeal to a realm of shared appr-eciation beyond the mere vagaries of individual taste. Art should give the same disinterested satisfaction as natural beauty. Paradoxically, art can accomplish one thing nature cannot: it can offer ugliness and beauty in one object. A fine painting of an ugly face is still beautiful.

According to the 19th-century German philosopher G. W. F. Hegel, art, religion, and philosophy are the bases of the highest spiritual development. Beauty in nature is everything that the human spirit finds pleasing and congenial to the exercise of spiritual and intellectual freedom. Certain things in nature can be made more congenial and pleasing, and it is these natural objects that are reorganized by art to satisfy aesthetic demands.

The German philosopher Arthur Schopenhauer believed that the forms of the universe, like the eternal Platonic forms, exist beyond the worlds of experience, and that aesthetic satisfaction is achieved by contemplating them for their own sakes, as a means of escaping the painful world of daily experience.

Fichte, Kant, and Hegel are in a direct line of development. Schopenhauer attacked Hegel but was influenced by Kant's view of disinterested contemplation. The German philosopher Friedrich Nietzsche followed Schopenhauer at first, then disagreed with him. Nietzsche concurred that life is tragic, but thought that this should not preclude acceptance of the tragic with joyous affirmation, the full realization of which is art. Art confronts the terrors of the universe and is therefore only for the strong. Art can transform any experience into beauty, and by so doing transforms its horrors in such a way that they may be contemplated with enjoyment.

Although much of modern aesthetics is rooted in German thought, German thinking was subject to other Western influences. Lessing, a founder of German Romanticism, was affected by the aesthetic writings of the British statesman and aesthetic theorist Edmund Burke.

Aesthetics and Art: Traditional aesthetics in the 18th and 19th centuries was dominated by the concept of art as imitation of nature. Novelists such as Jane Austen and Charles Dickens in Britain and dramatists such as Carlo Goldoni in Italy and Alexandre Dumas *fils* (the son of Alexandre Dumas *père*) in France presented realistic accounts of middle-class life. Painters, whether Neo-Classical, such as Jean Auguste Dominique Ingres, Romantic, such as Eugène Delacroix, or Realist, such as Gustave Courbet, rendered their subjects with careful attention to lifelike detail.

In traditional aesthetics it was also frequently assumed that works of art are useful as well as beautiful. Paintings might commemorate historical events or encourage morality. Music might inspire piety or patriotism. Drama, especially in the hands of Dumas and the Norwegian Henrik Ibsen, might serve to criticize society and so lead to reform.

In the 19th century, however, avant-garde concepts of aesthetics began to challenge traditional views. The change was particularly evident in painting. French Impressionists, such as Claude Monet, denounced academic painters for depicting what they thought they should see rather than what they actually saw—that is, the surfaces of many colours and wavering forms caused by the distorting play of light and shadow as the Sun moves.

In the late 19th century, Post-Impressionists such as Paul Cézanne, Paul Gauguin, and Vincent van Gogh were more concerned with the structure of a painting and with expressing their own psyches than with representing objects in the world of nature. In the early 20th century this structural interest was developed further by Cubist painters such as Pablo Picasso, and the Expressionist concern was reflected in the work of Henri Matisse and other Fauvists and by the German Expressionists such as Ernst Ludwig Kirchner. The literary aspects of Expressionism can be seen in the plays of August Strindberg, a Swede, and Frank Wedekind, a German.

Closely connected with these relatively non-representational approaches to art was the principle of "art for art's sake", which was derived from Kant's view that art has its own reason for being. The phrase was first used by the French philosopher Victor Cousin in 1818, and this doctrine, sometimes called aestheticism, was espoused in England by the critic Walter Horatio Pater, by the Pre-Raphaelite painters, and by the expatriate American painter James Abbott McNeill Whistler. In France it was the credo of such Symbolist poets as Charles Baudelaire. Indeed, the "art for art's sake" principle underlies most of avant-garde Western art of the 20th century.

Major Contemporary Influences: Four philosophers of the late 19th and early 20th centuries have been the primary influences on present-day aesthetics. In France Henri Bergson defined science as the use of intelligence to create a system of symbols that supposedly describes reality but actually falsifies it. Art, however, is based on intuition, which is a direct apprehension of reality unmediated by thought. Thus, art cuts through conventional symbols and beliefs about people, life, and society and confronts one with reality itself.

In Italy the philosopher and historian Benedetto Croce also exalted intuition, but he believed that it was the immediate awareness of an object that somehow gave that object form; that is, the apprehension of things before one reflects about them. Works of art are the expression, in material form, of such intuitions; beauty and ugliness, however, are not qualities of the works of art but qualities of the spirit expressed intuitively in these works of art.

The American philosopher and poet George Santayana argued that when one takes pleasure in a thing the pleasure may be regarded as a quality of the thing itself, rather than as a subjective response to it. Just as one may characterize some human act as good in itself, instead of calling it good merely because one approves of it, so one may say that some object is beautiful, not merely that one's aesthetic delight in its colour and form leads one to call it beautiful.

John Dewey, the American educator and philosopher, viewed human experience as disconnected, fragmentary, full of beginnings without conclusions, or as subject to forms of purely instrumental (means to end) manipulation. Those exceptional experiences that flow from their beginnings to consummations are aesthetic. Aesthetic experience is enjoyment for its own sake, is complete and self-contained, and is terminal, not merely instrumental to other purposes.

Marxism and Freudianism: Two powerful movements, Marxism in the fields of economics and politics and Freudianism in psychology, have rejected the art-for-art's sake principle and reasserted art's practical uses. Marxism treats art as an expression of the underlying economic relations in society, and proponents maintain that art is great only when it is "progressive", that is, when it supports the cause of the oppressed classes or (in the case of Communist regimes) the values of the society in which it is created.

Sigmund Freud believed the value of art to lie in its therapeutic use: it is by this means that both the artist and the public can reveal hidden conflicts and discharge tensions. Fantasies and daydreams, as they enter into art, are thus transformed from an escape from life into ways of meeting it. In the Surrealist movement in painting and poetry, the unconscious is used as a source of material. The stream of consciousness technique of fiction, notably in the novels of Virginia Woolf and James Joyce, was derived not only from Freud's work but partly from *The Principles of Psychology* (1890) by the American philosopher and psychologist William James and partly from the French novel *We'll to the Woods No More* (1887; trans. 1957) by Edouard Dujardin.

Existentialism: More recently, the French philosopher and writer Jean-Paul Sartre advocated a form of existentialism in which art is seen as an expression of the freedom of the individual to choose, and as such demonstrates the individual's responsibility for his or her choices. Despair, as reflected in art, is not an end but a beginning, because it overcomes the pretexts, alibis, and self-evasions behind which people ordinarily shelter, thus opening the way for genuine freedom.

Aestheticism, the position according to which the highest values (including the highest ethical values) are ultimately aesthetic values. The idea is often associated with nineteenth-century romanticism and personally with Friedrich Schiller, author of The Aesthetic Education of Man, and with Friedrich Nietzsche, both of whom sometimes exhorted their readers to "make your life a work of art".

Aesthetics, the philosophy of art. The study of contemplation or appreciationof the (nature of) artistic value of beauty.

Affirmative action, a policy of providing reverse preferences favo-ring members of classes previously disadvantaged to compensate victims of previous racial and sexual discrimination, to remedy lingering effects of such discrimination, or to combat ongoing institutionalized and unintentional discriminatory practices.

Affirmative conclusion from negative premise, the formal fallacy committed in a categorical syllogism that violates a syllogistic rule by having an affirmative conclusion derived from at least one negative proposition as a premise. Example: "All senators are eligible to vote on legislation, but no homeless people are senators, so all homeless people are eligible to vote on legislation." The problem with any such reasoning is that the exclusion of one class from another cannot provide deductively certain grounds for the inclusion of either of these classes with another.

Affirmative proposition, a statement whose propositional quality is determined by its assertion that some or all members of one class of things are also included as members of some other class. Examples: "All spaniels are dogs." and "Some children are people who play word games." The first affirms that every spaniel also belongs to the class of dogs, while the latter affirms that there is at least one member commonly included among both children and people who play word games.

Affirming the alternative, a fallacious inferencehaving the form:

p v q
p
~ q

Example: "The softball team will win either Tuesday's game or Thursday's. It will win Tuesday's game. Therefore, it will not win Thursday's game". Arguments of this form should not be confused with legitimate applications of Disjunctive Syllogism. The logical relation of disjunction expressed by the symbol "V" purposefully allows for the possibility that both of its terms are true propositions. In order to exclude that possibility, one must explicitly declare that one or the other of the terms is true, but not both, using the form:

$(p \vee q) \; \& \sim (p \; \& \; q)$.

Affirming the consequent, a fallacy having the form:

p -> *q*
q
p

Example: "If Dole had been elected President in 1996, then he would no longer be a Senator. Dole is no longer a Senator. Therefore, Dole was elected President in 1996." Arguments of this form should not be confused with a legitimate instance of Modus Ponens.

Afortiori, "to the stronger," or "even more so. "We are bound to accept an a fortiori claim because of our prior acceptance of a weaker application of the same reasoning or truth. Thus, for example: Frank can't run to the store in less than five minutes, and the restaurant is several blocks further away than the store. Thus, a fortiori, Frank can't run to the restaurant in less than five minutes.

Agent, the person who performs an action. Ethical conduct is usually taken to presuppose the possibility that individual human agents are capable of acting responsibly. *Recommended Reading*: Hugh J. McCann, The Works of Agency: On Human Action, Will, and Freedom (Cornell, 1998); Relational Autonomy: Feminist Perspectives on Autonomy, Agency, and the

Social Self, ed. by Catriona MacKenzie and Natalie Stoljar (Oxford, 2000); Carol A. Rovane, The Bounds of Agency (Princeton, 1997).

In the client-server model, the part of the system that performs information preparation and exchange on behalf of a client or server. Especially in the phrase "intelligent agent" it implies some kind of automatic process which can communicate with other agents to perform some collective task on behalf of one or more humans.

Aggregate type, A data type composed of multiple elements. An aggregate can be homogeneous (all elements have the same type) *e.g.* an array, a list in a functional language, a string of characters, a file; or it can be heterogeneous (elements can have different types) *e.g.* a structure. In most languages aggregates can contain elements which are themselves aggregates. *e.g.* a list of lists. See also union.

Aggregation, A composition technique for building a new object from one or more existing objects that support some or all of the new object's required interfaces.

Agnosticism, the position according to which one cannot (or should not) take either a positive or a negative stance with respect to the existence of God. Agnosticism takes a wait-and-see attitude towards the existence of God. It is often based on skepticism, which argues that one cannot know whether God exists, although this can also lead to fideism. It may be accompanied with a further conviction that one need not care whether God exists or not. It should not be confused with atheism, which argues against the existence of God.

Belief that human beings do not have sufficient evidence to warrant either the affirmation or the denial of a proposition. The term is used especially in reference to our lack of knowledge of the existence of god.

Recommended Reading: Clarence Darrow, Why I Am an Agnostic and Other Essays (Prometheus, 1994); Bertrand Russell, Why I Am Not a Christian, and Other Essays on Religion and Related Subjects (Simon & Schuster, 1977).

Agnosticism, doctrine that the existence of God and other spiritual beings is neither certain nor impossible. The term, derived from the Greek *agnostikos* ("not knowing"), was introduced into English in the 19th century by the British biologist Thomas Henry Huxley. The agnostic position is distinct from both theism, which affirms the existence of such beings, and atheism, which denies their existence.

Although usually regarded as a form of scepticism, agnosticism is more limited in scope, for it denies the reliability only of metaphysical and theological beliefs rather than of all beliefs. The basis of modern agnosticism lies in the works of the Scottish philosopher David Hume and the German philosopher Immanuel Kant, both of whom pointed out logical fallacies in the traditional arguments for the existence of God and of the soul. Like agnosticism, empiricism, also known as logical positivism, rejects both atheism and theism, and maintains that metaphysical statements are meaningless.

Agreement method of, one of Mill's Methods for discovery of causalrelationships. If a specific antecedent circumstance is found to be present on every occasion on which a phenomenon occurs, it may be inferred to be the cause of that phenomenon. *Example*: "It snowed in October only three times during the past seventeen years, and each time was during an "El Nin~o" year, so the warm Pacific waters probably caused our early snows." *Recommended Reading*: John Stuart Mill, System of Logic (Classworks, 1986).

AI, artificial intelligence

Aisthaesis, Greek term for sense perception, the epistemic significance of which was vigorously debated. The Eleatics argued that mere sensation is inferior to noesis, while Empedocles and the Atomists regarded it as a vital connection with the natural world. Plato took perception to be unreliable as a source of knowledge, since it deals only with temporal objects. For Aristotle, on the other hand, aisthaesis is a basic activity of living organisms, through which they acquire information about material things. *Recommended Reading*: F.E. Peters, Greek Philosophical Terms: A Historical Lexicon (NYU, 1967).

Aition, the most general Greek term for cause or responsibility, used by Aristotle especially in reference to any one of the four kinds of answer it is legitimate to give in response to any "Why...?" question. *Recommended Reading*: F.E. Peters, Greek Philosophical Terms: A Historical Lexicon (NYU, 1967).

Aka, also known as.

Akrasia, literally, "bad mixture," the Greek term for the character flaw of incontinence or weakness of the will, the condition in which an agent is unable to perform actions that are known to be right. Although Socrates apparently held that doing good follows directly from knowing what is good, Aristotle believed akratic human behavior to be commonplace, and offered an extended account of its origin and consequences. *Recommended Reading*: Alfred R. Mele, Irrationality: An Essay on Akrasia, Self-Deception, and Self-Control (Oxford, 1992); Justin Gosling, Weakness of the Will (Routledge, 1990).

AL, Artificial Life

Albert the Great, German Dominican philosopher and Bishop of Ratisbon (1206-1280). Revered by his contemporaries as "doctor universalis" for the breadth of his philosophical knowledge, Albert tried to synthesize many disparate philosophical positions from the tradition but also encouraged empirical study as a source of knowledge of the natural world. He is remembered chiefly as the teacher and colleague who encouraged Thomas Aquinas to apply Aristotelian arguments to Christian thought.

Alexander Samuel, Australian-English philosopher (1859-1938). Alexander defended perceptual realism as an alternative to the idealism of his contemporaries. His theory regarding the "emergent evolution" of mind within the natural order, proposed in Space, Time, and Deity (1920), was similar in many respects to the views of Henri Bergson. Alexander also developed a thorough axiology in Beauty and other Forms of Value (1933). During his tenure at Manchester, Alexander helped Zionist colleague Chaim Weizmann secure the Balfour agreement, an initial step toward creation of the modern state of Israel. *Recommended Reading*: Samuel Alexander, Collected Works

(Thoemmes, 2000); Samuel Alexander, Philosophical and Literary Pieces (Ayer, 1940).

Algazel, Latinized name of al-Ghazàli.

Algorithm, A detailed sequence of actions to perform to accomplish some task. Named after an Iranian mathematician, Al-Khawarizmi.

Technically, an algorithm must reach a result after a finite number of steps, thus ruling out brute force search methods for certain problems, though some might claim that brute force search was also a valid (generic) algorithm. The term is also used loosely for any sequence of actions (which may or may not terminate).

Alias, 1. A name, usually short and easy to remember and type, that is translated into another name or string, usually long and difficult to remember or type. Most command interpreters (*e.g.* Unix's csh) allow the user to define aliases for commands, *e.g.* "alias l ls -al". These are loaded into memory when the interpreter starts and are expanded without needing to refer to any file.

2. One of several alternative hostnames with the same Internet address. *E.g.* in the Unix hosts database (/etc/hosts or NIS map) the first field on a line is the Internet address, the next is the official hostname (the "canonical name" or "CNAME") and any others are aliases.

Hostname aliases often indicate that the host with that alias provides a particular network service such as archie, finger, FTP, or World-Wide Web. The assignment of services to computers can then be changed simply by moving an alias from one Internet address to another, without the clients needing to be aware of the change.

Aliasing, 1. When several different identifiers refer to the same object. The term is very general and is used in many contexts. See alias, aliasing bug, antialiasing.

2. (Or "shadowing") Where a hardware device responds at multiple addresses because it only decodes a subset of the address lines, so different values on the other lines are ignored.

Alienation, (Ger. Entaeusserung or Entfremdung) extreme separation from one's own nature, from the products of one's labor, or from social reality, which often results in an indifference or outright aversion toward some aspects of life that might otherwise be attractive and significant. Hegel introduced the term, pointing out that human life, unless comprehended through the Absolute, easily becomes estranged from the natural world. Feuerbach, on the other hand, emphasized the dangerous practical consequences of an extreme detachment from one's own nature and activities.

Marx carried this line of thought further, by noting that conditions in a capitalist society make it impossible for workers to live meaningfully in relation to each other, to the products of their labor, or even to themselves. Simone de Beauvoir and other feminist thinkers point out that women in a patriarchal culture undergo additional forms of alien-ation when they are pervasively treated as the objects of male sexual desire and effectively coerced into submitting to male-based political, social, and intellectual norms. *Recommended Reading*: Istvan Meszaros, Marx's Theory of Alienation (Merlin, 1986); Bertell

Ollman, Alienation: Marx's Conception of Man in Capitalist Society (Cambridge, 1977); Arthur G. Neal and Sara F. Collas, Intimacy and Alienation: Forms of strangement in Female/Male Relationships (Garland, 2000).

Alife, artificial life

A-Life, artificial life

Alpha-categoricity, A first order theory is alpha-categorical *iff* (1) it has a normal model of cardinality alpha and (2) any two normal models of cardinality alpha are isomorphic.

Alpharabius, Latinized name of al-Farabi.

Alternation, Logical relation holding between propositions at least one of which is true; see: disjunction.

Alternative occurrence, the complex event comprising the occurrence of one or the other (or both) of its constituent events. The probability of an alternative occurrence may be calculated by the formula: $P(A \vee B) = P(A) + P(B) - P(A \& B)$. Thus, for example, the chances of getting "heads" at least once in two flips of a coin are equal to the chances of getting "heads" on the first toss (1/2) plus the chances of getting "heads" on the second toss (1/2) minus the chances of getting "heads" both times (1/4), or 3/4. *Recommended Reading*: Richard Lowry, The Arch-itecture of Chance: *An Introduction to the Logic and Arithmetic of Probability* (Oxford, 1989); Ian Hacking, *An Introd-uction to Probability and Inductive Logic* (Cambridge, 2001); Donald Gillies, Philosophical Theories of Probability (Routledge, 2000).

Althusser Louis, Algerian-French social philosopher (1918-1990). In Pour Marx (For Marx) (1965), Lénin et la philosophie (Lenin and Philosophy) (1969), and Lire le Capital (Reading Capital) (1970), Althusser offered a structuralist re-interpretation of the later work of Marx. According to Althusser, social organization is determined wholly by ideological consequences expressed in economic and political power, enforced in home and family as well as in the workplace. The differential roles to which individuals are assigned in a society, he argued, are clearly signified not only by the presence of particular notions in its cultural paradigms, but even more dram-atically by the absence of others. Elements d'autocritique (Essays in Self-Criticism) (1974) includes retractions from many of these central themes. *Recommended Reading*: Althusser: A Critical Reader, ed. By Gregory Elliott (Blackwell, 1994).

Altruism, devotion to the welfare of others. Altruism is the English form of the French word *altruisme* created by the 19th-century French philosopher and sociologist Auguste Comte from the Italian *altrui,* meaning "of or to others". The word has gradually come into more general use. In philosophy altruism describes a theory of conduct that aspires to the good of others as the ultimate end for any moral action. In theories of ethics altruism is the antithesis of egoism (self-interest).

Altruism, selfless concern for other people purely for their own sake.. Altruism is usually contrasted with selfishness or egoism in ethics. As a theoretical position, it is the view according to which the happiness of others ought to be given greatest importance in the agent's ethical decisions. Altruism could give rise to forms of eudaimonism, *e.g.* when there is only one individual, the agent, involved, or when the agent's happines coincides with the happiness of all the others. In practice, eudaimonism is always a kind of individualism or egoism. Some forms of altruism put the emphasis more on duty or moral law rather than on the actual interests of other people, for example Kantianism and various other forms of deontologism. Obviously, altruistic forms of utilitarianism and pragmatism put a practical emphasis on consequences (see consequential-ism), that is, on helping or having regard for the welfare of other people, rather than on some sort of abstract formulation like "moral law". Altruism is often taken to be a positive thing, especially by the average citizen. However, one has to tread carefully here, because in this common usage, "altruism" does not always refer to self-sacrifice, but sometimes only to an attitude of benevolence toward others (for example, dictionaries often define "altruistic" as "benevolent"). As always, but especially in this case, it is best to get the other person to clarify what he means before you "go on the offensive". Technical philosophical definitions do not always agree with any given individual's understanding of altruism. (References from collectivism, communism, consequentialism, eontologism, hedonism, humanism, and utilitarianism). *Recommended Reading*: Thomas Nagel, The Possibility of Altruism (Princeton, 1979); Altruism, ed. by Jeffrey Paul, Ellen F. Paul, and Fred D. Miller, Jr. (Cambridge, 1993); Matt Ridley, The Origins of Virtue: Human Instincts and the Evolution of Cooperation (Penguin, 1998).

Ambiguity, the presence of two or more distinct meanings for a single word or expression. In itself, ambiguity is a common, harmless, and often amusing feature of ordinary language. When unnoticed in the context of otherwise careful reasoning, however, it can lead to one of several informal fallacies. *Example*: "I'll give you a ring tomorrow." could signify either the promise of a gift of jewelry or merely an intention to telephone. Note the difference between ambiguity and vagueness. *Recommended Reading*: Israel Scheffler, Beyond the Letter: A Philosophical Inquiry into Ambiquity, Vagueness and Metaphor in Language (Routledge, 1981); Douglas Walton, Fallacies Arising from Ambiguity (Kluwer, 1996).

Amoral, having no bearing on, declining to be influenced by, or making no reference to, moral values or judgments.

Amphiboly, the informal fallacy that can result when a sentence is ambiguous because of its gramma-tical structure, even if al of its terms are clear. Example: "One morning in Africa, Captain Spaulding shot an elephant in his pajamas. Therefore, it is dangerous for large animals to wear human clothing."

Analog, American spelling of analogue.

Analogy, a systematic comparison between usually two structures that relies on properties of, and relations between, features (usually entities) of a source structure to infer properties of, and relations between, features (usually entities) of a target structure.

Analogy is an important methodo of reasoning, contributing to such cognitive tasks as explanation, planning, and decision making. Analogical arguments are sometimes used in philosophy, for example to argue that there exist other minds analogous to one's own. In artificial intelligence, analogy is often called case-based reasoning.

References: Gentner, D., Markman, A. B. (1997). Structure mapping in analogy and similarity. American Psychologist, 52, 45-56. Holyoak, K. J., Thagard, P. (1995). Mental leaps: Analogy in creative thought. Cambridge, MA: MIT Press/Bradford Books. Kolodner, J. (1993). Case-based reason-ing. San Mateo, CA: Morgan Kaufmann. Paul Thagard Chris Eliasmith—[Dictionary of hilosophy of Mind], similarity in several respects between discrete cases. A logical argument by analogy relies upon an inductive inference from the supposition that things are similar is certain known respects to the likelihood that they are also similar in some further unknown respect. Example: "Jennifer enjoys listening to the music of Beethoven, Mahler, and Bartok. Susan and Harold also like Beethoven, Mahler, and Bartok. Chris enjoys listening to Beethoven and Mahler. Therefore, Chris would probably like the music of Bartok, too." The degree of reliability achieved by such an argument depends upon the extent and nature of the similarities that hold between the instances in its premises and the new case in its conclusion. *Recommended Reading*: G.E.R. Lloyd, Polarity and Analogy: Two Types of Argumentation in Early Greek Thought (Hackett, 1992); Ralf M. W. Stammberger, On Analogy: An Essay Historical and Systematic (Peter Lang, 1995).

Analysis, process of breaking up a complex concept or expression in order to reveal its simpler constituents, thereby elucidating it implicit meaning. The significance and value of this method is challenged by the paradox that analyses seem bound either to be inadequate or incorrect (if they propose major revisions in our understanding) but trivial and uninformative (if they do not).

Analytic, true by definition, or the denial of which would lead to a contradiction. Example: "all triangles have three angles" and "all bachelors are unmarried males". Some philo-sophers have maintained that all the truths of mathematics are analytic, and that all necessary and a priori truths are analytic. Contrast term: synthetic. Kant coined this terminology and stressed this distinction. Many contemporary analytic philosophers, following Quine, deny its cogency. based on,

Analytic and Linguistic Philosophy, 20th-century philosophical movement, dominant in Britain and the United States since World War II, that aims to clarify language and analyse the concepts expressed in it. Versions of the movement have been given a variety of designations, including "linguistic analysis", "logical empiricism", "logical positivism", "Cambridge analysis", and "Oxford philosophy". The last two labels are derived from the English universities where this philosophical method has been particularly influential. Although no specific doctrines or tenets are accepted by the movement as a whole, analytic and linguistic philosophers mostly agree that the proper activity of philosophy is clarifying language, or, as some prefer, clarifying concepts. The aim of this activity is to settle philosophical disputes and resolve philosophical problems, which, it is often argued, originate in linguistic confusion.

Approaches: A considerable diversity of views exists among analytic and linguistic philosophers regarding the nature of conceptual or linguistic analysis. Some are primarily concerned with clarifying the meaning of specific words or phrases as an essential step in making philosophical assertions clear and unambiguous. Others are more concerned with determining the general conditions that must be met for any linguistic utterance to be meaningful; their intent is to establish a criterion that will distinguish between meaningful and nonsensical sentences. Still other analysts are interested in creating formal, symbolic languages that are mathematical in nature. Their claim is that philo-sophical problems can be more effectively dealt with once they are formulated in a rigorous logical language.

By contrast, many philosophers associated with the movement have focused on the analysis of ordinary, or natural, language. Difficulties arise when concepts such as time and freedom, for example, are considered apart from the linguistic context in which they normally appear. Attention to language as it is ordinarily used is the key, it is argued, to resolving many philosophical puzzles.

Early History: Linguistic analysis as a method of philosophy is as old as the Greeks. Several of the dialogues of Plato, for example, are specifically concerned with clarifying terms and concepts. Nevertheless, this style of philosophizing has received dramatically renewed emphasis in the 20th century. Influenced by the earlier British empirical tradition of John Locke, George Berkeley, David Hume, and John Stuart Mill and by the writings of the German mathematician and philosopher Gottlob Frege, the 20th-century English philosophers G. E. Moore and Bertrand Russell became the founders of this contemporary analytic and linguistic trend. As students together at the University of Cambridge, Moore and Russell rejected Hegelian Idealism, particularly as it was reflected in the work of the English metaphysician Francis Herbert Bradley, who held that nothing is completely real except the Absolute. In their opposition to idealism and in their commitment to the view that careful attention to language is crucial in philosophical inquiry, they set the mood and style of philosophizing for much of the 20th-century English-speaking world.

For Moore, philosophy was first and foremost analysis. The philosopher's task involves clarifying puzzling propositions or concepts by indicating less puzzling propositions or concepts to which the originals are held to be logically equivalent. Once this task has been completed, the truth or falsity of problematic philosophical assertions can be determined more adequately. Moore was noted for his careful analyses of such puzzling philosophical claims as "time is unreal", analyses that then helped him determine the truth of such assertions.

Russell, strongly influenced by the precision of mathematics, was concerned with developing an ideal logical language that would accurately reflect the nature of the world. Complex propositions, Russell maintained, can be resolved into their simplest components, which he called atomic propositions. These propositions refer to atomic facts, the ultimate constituents of the universe. The metaphysical view that the universe is composed of such atomic facts, and the insistence that meaningful propositions must correspond to these facts make up what Russell called logical atomism. His interest in the structure of language also led him to distinguish between the grammatical form of a proposition and its logical form. According to Russell, the statements "John is good" and "John is tall" have the same grammatical form but different logical forms. Failure to recognize this would lead one to treat the property "goodness" as if it were a characteristic of John in the same way that the property "tallness" is a characteristic of John. Such failure results in philosophical confusion.

Wittgenstein and the Logical Positivists: Russell's work in mathematics attracted to Cambridge the Austrian philosopher Ludwig Wittgenstein, who became a central figure in the analytic and linguistic movement. In his first major work, *Tractatus Logico-Philosophicus* (1921; trans. 1922), in which he first presented his theory of language, Wittgenstein argued that "all philosophy is a 'critique of language'" and that "philosophy aims at the logical clarification of thoughts". The results of Wittgenstein's analysis resembled Russell's logical atomism. The world, he argued, is ultimately composed of simple facts, which it is the purpose of language to picture. To be meaningful, statements about the world must be reducible to linguistic utterances that have a structure similar to the simple facts pictured. In this early Wittgensteinian analysis, only propositions that picture facts—the propositions of science—are considered factually meaningful. Metaphysical, theological, and ethical sentences are judged to be factually meaningless.

Influenced by Russell, Wittgenstein, Ernst Mach, and others, a group of philosophers and mathematicians in Vienna in the 1920s initiated the movement known as logical positivism. Led by Moritz Schlick and Rudolf Carnap, the Vienna Circle initiated one of the most important chapters in the history of analytic and linguistic philosophy. According to the positivists, the task of philosophy is the clarification of meaning, not the discovery of new facts (the job of science) or the construction of comprehensive accounts of reality (the misguided pursuit of traditional metaphysics).

The positivists divided all meaningful assertions into two classes: analytic propositions and empirically verifiable ones. Analytic propositions, which include the propositions of logic and mathematics, are statements the truth or falsity of which depend altogether on the meanings of the terms constituting the statement. An example would be the proposition "two plus two equals four". The second class of meaningful prop-ositions includes all statements about the world that can be verified, at least in principle, by sense experience. Indeed, the meaning of such propositions is identified with the empirical method of verification. This verifiability theory of meaning, the positivists concluded, would demonstrate that scientific state-ments are genuine factual claims and that metaphysical, religious, and ethical sentences are factually empty. The ideas of logical positivism were made popular in England by the publication of *Language, Truth and Logic* by A. J. Ayer in 1936. In the field of ethics, the logical positivists argued that although ethical statements had no factual content, they served to express the emotions of the speaker. This theory, known as the emotivist theory of ethics, had its roots in Hume's philosophy.

Ordinary Language Philosophy: The positivists' verifiability theory of meaning came under intense criticism from philosophers such as the Austrian-born British philosopher Karl Popper. Eventually this narrow theory of meaning yielded to a broader understanding of the nature of language. Again, an influential figure was Wittgenstein. Repudiating many of his earlier conclusions in the *Tractatus*, he initiated a new line of thought culminating in his posthumously published *Philosophical Investigations* (1953; trans. 1953). In this work, Wittgenstein argued that once attention is directed to the way language is actually used in ordinary discourse, the variety and flexibility of language become clear. Linguistic utterances do much more than simply picture facts. For example, language is used to ask questions, give orders, express attitudes, and so on.

This recognition led to Wittgenstein's influential concept of language games. The scientist, the poet, and the theologian, for example, are involved in different language games. Moreover, the meaning of a proposition must be understood in its context, that is, in terms of the rules of the language game of which that proposition is a part. Philosophy, concluded Wittgenstein, is an attempt to resolve problems that arise as the result of confusion as to how language works, and the key to the resolution of such problems is ordinary language analysis and the proper use of language.

The idea that the key to the solution of philosophical problems is the analysis of ordinary language became the central tenet of the version of analytic and linguistic philosophy known as ordinary language philosophy, or sometimes simply as linguistic philosophy, which became dominant in Britain in the 1950s and 1960s. Important figures associated with ordinary language philosophy include the British philosophers Gilbert Ryle, John Langshaw Austin, and P. F. Strawson.

According to Ryle, the task of philosophy is to restate "systematically misleading expressions" in forms that are logically more accurate. He was particularly concerned with statements the grammatical form of which suggests the existence of non-existent objects. For example, Ryle is best known for his analysis of mentalistic language in *The Problem of Mind* (1949), language that misleadingly suggests that the mind is an entity in the same way as the body.

Austin maintained that one of the most fruitful starting points for philosophical inquiry is attention to the extremely fine distinctions drawn in ordinary language. His analysis of language eventually led to a general theory of speech acts, that is, to a description of the variety of activities that an individual may be performing when something is uttered.

Strawson is known for his analysis of the relationship between formal logic and ordinary language. The complexity of the latter, he argued, is inadequately represented by formal logic. A variety of analytic tools, therefore, is needed in addition to logic in analysing ordinary language.

The American philosopher Willard van Orman Quine also highlighted the importance of ordinary language. He argued that there is a close connection between language and ontology, in that the use of a particular language system commits one to the existence of certain things. For Quine, the justification for speaking one way rather than another is a thoroughly pragmatic one.

In ethics, the analytic philosophers of the 1950s and 1960s again concentrated on the analysis of ordinary language: in this case, moral language. For example, the British philosopher Richard M. Hare argued in *The Language of Morals* (1952) that moral language is inherently prescriptive, so that to use a moral term is always to give other people some kind of order, and that it is also always inherently universalizable, so that to apply a moral term to an act is always to commit oneself to applying the same term to similar acts done by other people in similar circumstances.

Analytical Machine, Analytical Engine

Analytic philosophy, twentieth-century methods of philosophizing, generally characterized by the careful effort to uncover logical and philosophical suppositions concealed beneath the superficial structure of statements in ordinary uses of language, pursuit of clarity in the treatment of genuine philosophical issues, and a deep respect for the achievements of natural science. In a variety of distinct forms, philosophical analysis was practiced by Moore, Russell, Wittgenstein, the logical positivists, Ryle, Austin, Bergmann, and Quine. Greatly influential in England and America, analytic philosophy is sometimes criticized for its excessive professionalization of the discipline. *Recommended Reading*: James Baillie, Contemporary Analytic Philosophy (Prentice-Hall, 1996); Michael Dummett, Origins of Analytical Philosophy (Harvard, 1996); Avrum Stroll, Twentieth-Century Analytic Philosophy (Columbia, 2000).

Analytic-synthetic, distinction between judgments or propositions. A judgment is analytic if the concept of its predicate is already contained in that of its subject; if the concepts of its subject and predicate are independent, it is synthetic. Alternatively, a proposition is analytic if it is true merely by virtue of the meaning of its terms or tautolo-gous; otherwise, it is synthetic. For example: "Golden retrievers are dogs" is analytic. "Dogs enjoy chasing squirrels" is synthetic. Empiricists generally suppose that this distinction coincides with the a priori/a posteriori and necessary contingent disti-nctions, while Kant held that synthetic a priori judgments are possible. Quine has gued that no strict distinction can be maintained, since the analyticity of any proposition can be denied, with suitable revisions of the entire system of language in which it is expressed. *Recommended Reading*: Analyticity: Selected Readings, ed. By James F. Harris, Jr. and Richard H. Severens (Quadrangle, 1970); Arthur Pap, Semantics and Necessary Truth (Yale, 1958); and Willard V. Quine, From a Logical Point of View: Nine Logico-Philosophical Essays (Harvard, 1980).

Anamnaesis, psyche, learning; a Greek term for recollection as a source of human knowledge. Socrates himself may have argued that recollection establishes mathematical truths independently of sensory experience (Gk. *aisthaesis*). In the mature philosophy of Plato, however, our ability to recollect the immutable form (Gk. *eidos*) is taken to provide direct evidence of the pre-existence of the human soul (Gk. *psychae*).

Recommended Reading: Dominic Scott, Recollection and Experience: Plato's Theory of Learning and Its Successors (Cambridge, 1995); F.E. Peters, Greek Philosophical Terms: A Historical Lexicon (NYU, 1967).

Anankae, Greek word for the logical or causal necessity of anything cannot be otherwise than as it is. According to Aristotle, for example, the efficient cause of a thing produces its effect and the conclusion of a valid syllogism produces its conclusion with anankae. *Recommended Reading*: F.E. Peters, Greek Philosophical Terms: A Historical Lexicon (NYU, 1967).

Anarchism, anarchism was a sometimes violent political movement around the turn of the century, but the word also describes a moral-political ideal of a society untouched by relations of power and domination among human beings. This moral ideal has most often expressed itself in what is the technical meaning of the term, namely the "total absence of government". Anarchism, in this sense, differs from the position of classical liberalism or libertarianism in politics (which upholds not a lack of government but limited government), but in its moral sense (the abolition of force and domination from human relations) it is consonant with a rational ethics. Note, however, that this ethical aspect is overshadowed in popular understanding by the political aspect, and by the former political movement. (*Reference* from pacifism. *Recommended Reading*: Peter Kropotkin, The Conquest of Bread (Black Rose, 1989); Todd May, The Political Philosophy of Poststructuralist Anarchism (Penn. State, 1994); Michael Taylor, Community, Anarchy and Liberty (Cambridge, 1983); Robert Paul Wolff, In Defense of Anarchism (California, 1998).

Anaxagoras of Clazomenae, Presocratic philosopher (500-428 B.C.) who taught at Athens, leaving fragments of his philosophical work. Despite his rejection of a fundamental distinction between appearance and reality and adoption of an atomistic natural philosophy, Anaxagoras was the first philosopher in the estern tradition to draw a substantial distinction between inert and chaotic matter on the one hand and mind as an active principle and source of order on the other hand. *Recommended Reading*: Malcolm Schofield, An Essay on Anaxagoras (Cambridge, 1980).

Anaximander, presocratic philosopher (611-547 B.C). According to fragmentary reports from other philosophers, Anaximander spec-ulated that all matter results from the distillation of hot, cold, dry, and wet elements from apeiron (the Boundless), an infinite, intelligent, living whole. Examination of fossil evidence persuaded Anaximander that living beings develop from simpler to more complex forms over time. *Recommended Reading*: Charles H. Kahn, Anaximander and the Origins of Greek Cosmology (Hackett, 1994); . Paul Seligman, The Apeiron of Anaximander;

A Study in the Origin and Function of Metaphysical Ideas (Greenwood, 1974).

Anaximenes, Presocratic philosopher (*c.* 550 B.C). In fragmentary reports from other philosophers, Anaximenes is said to hold that condensation and evaporation of vapor or mist produces the physical world of earth, water, and fire.

Andreia, the Greek term for bravery or courage (from andreios—"manly" or "stubborn"). According to Plato, this is the virtue properly exemplified by soldiers in the ideal state. *Recommended Reading*: Walter T. Schmid, On Manly Courage: A Study of Plato's Laches (Southern Illinois, 1992).

Angst, German word for the anxiety or anguish produced by an acute awareness of the implications of human freedom. An important notion for existentialist philosophers, including especially Kierkegaard and Heidegger. *Recommended Reading*: Martin Heidegger, Being and Time, tr. by Joan Stambaugh (SUNY 1997); Soren Kierkegaard, The Concept of Anxiety, ed. by Albert B. Anderson (Princeton, 1981); James Leonard Park, Existential Anxiety: Angst (Existential Books, 1996).

Anima, Latin term for wind, breath, life. Thus, for Descartes and other philosophers, the rational soul of any human being.

Animal rights, the ontological status accorded to non-human animals has obvious consequences for the morality of our willingness to use them for our own purposes. Kant argued that animals do not qualify as members of the kingdom of ends among whom morality properly holds, while Bentham supposed that the evident pleasure and pain experienced by animals deserve to be included in any utilitarian calculation. More recently, Mary Midgley makes concern for animals central to moral philosophy, Peter Singer shows that mistreatment of animals is the result of a morally indefensible 'speciesism,' and Tom Regan argues that animals are entitled to basic rights. *Recommended Reading*: Mary Midgley, Animals and Why They Matter (Georgia, 1998); Tom Regan, The Case for Animal Rights (California, 1985); Peter Singer, Animal Liberation (Avon, 1991); Richard Alan Young and Carol J. Adams, Is God a Vegetarian? Christianity, Vegetarian-ism, and Animal Rights (Open Court, 1998); Michael P. T. Leahy, Against Liberation: Putting Animals in Perspective (Routledge, 1994).

Animals, many philosophers of the Western tradition have considered the relationship between human beings and other species of animals. Although some have been impressed with the obvious similarities in organic structure and behavior, most have tried to draw a clear distinction between the two. Only recently have a few taken seriously the extent of our moral obligations to fellow sentient beings. Plato, Aristotle, Augustine, and Aquinas all supposed that the ability to reason makes human souls uniquely superior to those of all other beings. Descartes regarded it as a consequence of mind-body dualism that non-human animals are mere machines incapable of thought of any sort. But Locke, E/tienne de Condillac, and Bayle noticed that many of the capacities and activities exhibited by animals are similar to those of human beings, and La Mettrie argued that purely mechanistic explanations could be given for both human and animal behavior. *Recommended* Reading: Leonora Cohen

Rosenfield, From Beast-Machine to Man-Machine: Animal Soul in French Letters from Descartes to La Mettrie (New York, 1941); Marc D. Hauser, Wild Minds: What Animals Really Think (Holt, 2000).

Animism, belief that everything in the universe (or the universe itself) has some kind of soul or is a living being. *Recommended Reading*: Edward Clodd, Animism: The Seed of Religion (Holmes, 1993). See also panpsychism.

Annealing, simulated annealing

Anomalous monism, the view put forward by Donald Davidson that all mental events are identical to physical events, and that the only laws that govern the relations between events are physical, not psychological, laws.

References: Anomalous Monism Biblio Davidson. D. (1970). Mental Events. In (L. Foster and J. Swanson, eds.) Experience and Theory. Humanities Press. Reprinted in Davidson (1980) Essays on Actions and Events. Oxford: Oxford University Press. See monism, supervenience, token identity thesis, physicalism Pete Mandik Chris Eliasmith

Anscombe G.E.M., (Gertrude Elizabeth Margaret) English philosopher (1919-2001), who edited and translated much of the work of Wittgenstein after his death. She has also written extensively on human action and ethics, most notably in Intentions (1957) and her Collected Papers (1981). *Recommended Reading*: Logic, Cause and Action: Essays in Honour of Elizabeth Anscombe, ed. by G.E.M. Anscombe and Roger Teichmann (Cambridge, 2000).

Anselm-Anselm of Canterbury, although born at Aosta in Alpine Italy and educated in Normandy, Anselm (1033-1109) became a Benedictine monk, teacher, and abbot at Bec and continued his ecclesiastical career in England. Having been appointed the second Norman archbishop of Canterbury in 1093, Anselm secured the Westminster Agreement of 1107, guaranteeing the (partial) independence of the church from the civil state. In a series of short works such as De Libertate Arbitrii (On Free Will), De Casu Diaboli (The Fail of the Devil), and Cur Deus Homo (Why God became Man), Anselm ropounded a satisfaction theory of the atonement, upon which the incarnation promises relief from the strict demands of divine justice. He defended a notion of the relation between philosophy and theology that, like Augustine's, emphasized the methodological priority of faith over reason, since truth is to be achieved only through "fides quaerens intellectum" ("faith seeking understanding"). Anselm's combination of Christianity, neoplatonic metaphysics, and Aristotelean logic in the form of dialectical question-and answer was an important influence in the development scholasticism during the next several centuries. As a philosopher, Anselm is most often remembered for his attempts to prove the existence of god: In De Veritate (Of Truth) he argued that all creatures owe their being and value to god as the source of all truth, to whom a life lived well is the highest praise. In the Monologion he described deity as the one most truly good thing, from which all real moral values derive and whose existence is required by the reality of those values. Most famously, in the Proslogion (Addition), Anselm proposed the famous Ontological Argument, according to which god is understood as "aliquid quod maius non cogitari potest" ("that than which nothing greater can be conceived"). The being so conceived must necessarily exist in reality as well as in thought, he argued, since otherwise it would in fact be possible to conceive something greater—namely, something exactly similar except that it really does exist. Thus, at least for Anselmian believers guided by a prior faith, god must truly exist as the simple, unified source of all perfections, a reality that excludes corruption, imperfection, and deception of every sort.

Recommended Reading. Primary sources: Sancti Anselmi opera omnia (Schmitt, 1938-61); Anselm of Canterbury: The Major Works, edited by Brian Davies and G. R. Evans (Oxford, 1998). Additional on-line information about Anselm includes: The thorough collection of resources at Episteme Links.com. R.J. Kilcullen's lectures on the Monologion and the Proslogion. Thomas Williams's article in The Stanford Encyclopedia of Philosophy. Marilyn McCord Adams's article in The Oxford Companion to Philosophy. Also see: credo ut intelligam, medieval philosophy, the ontological argu-ment, and scholasticism. A paper on Anselm's Proof from Gyula Klima.

Antecedent, the element that states the prior condition in any conditional statement. For example, "It doesn't rain" is the antecedent in both "If it doesn't rain, then we'll have a picnic" and "It will reach ninety degrees today if it doesn't rain." In a true material implication, the truth of its antecedent is incompatible with the falsity of its consequent.

Anthony Susan Brownell, American political activist (1820-1906). As head of the American Woman Suffrage Association and editor of the radical newspaper, The Revolution, Anthony campaigned vigorously for the abolition of slavery the rights of women. Having cast a ballot in the election of 1872, Anthony was arrested and fined; despite her tireless efforts, she did not live to see widespread 'adoption of women's right to vote. *Recommended Reading*: The Elizabeth Cady Stanton-Susan B. Anthony Reader: Correspondence, Writings, Speeches, ed. By Ellen Carol Dubois and Gerda Lerner (Northeastern, 1992); Geoffrey C. Ward, Martha Saxton, Ann D. Gordon, Ellen Carol Dubois, and Paul Barnes, Not for Ourselves Alone: The Story of Elizabeth Cady Stanton and Susan B. Anthony: An Illustrated History (Knopf, 1999).

Anthropic principle, belief that the existence of human life entails certain features of the physical world. In a minimal form, this view merely points out that we would not be here to observe natural phenomena were they not compatible with our existence. Stronger versions of the anthropic principle, however, seem to rely upon the idealistic notion that the universe could not exist without intelligent observers. *Recommended Reading*: John D. Barrow and Frank J. Tipler, The Anthropic Cosmological Principle (Oxford, 1988); Errol E. Harris, Cosmos and Theos: Ethical and Theological Implications of the Anthropic Cosmological Principle (Humanity, 1992).

Anthropomorphism, attribution of human characteristics to non-human things. Thus, an anthropomorphic religion treats god as a personal being, and anthropomorphic natural theories may suppose that plants, animals, or the earth itself think and feel in the same ways that we do. *Recommended Reading*: Eileen Crist, Images of Animals: Anthropo-morphism and Animal Mind (Temple, 2000); Anthropomorphism, Anecdotes, and Animals, ed. by Robert W. Mitchell, Nicholas S. Thompson, and H. Lyn Miles (SUNY, 1996).

Antinomy, Kant believed that when reason goes beyond possible experience it often falls into various antinomies, or equally rational but contradictory views. Reason cannot here play the role of establishing rational truths because it goes beyond possible experience and becomes transcendent. *E.g.* Kant thought that one could reason from the assumption that the world had a beginning in time to the conclusion that it did not, and vice versa. This was part of Kant's critical program of determining limits to science and philosophical inquiry.

Antisthenes, Greek philosopher, friend of Socrates, and founder of cynicism (445-360 B.C.). Fragmentary reports suggest that Antisthenes denied the possibility of contradiction and supposed that the wise can never act foolishly. *Recommended Reading*: The Cynics: The Cynic Movement in Antiquity and Its Legacy, ed. by R. Bracht Branham and Marie Odile Goulet-Caze (California, 2000).

Antisymmetric, A relation R is antisymmetric if, for all x and y, $x R y$ and $y R x => x = y$.

I.e. no two different elements are mutually related.

Partial orders and total orders are antisymmetric. If R is also symmetric ($x R y => y R x$) then $x R y => x = y$. *I.e.* different elements are not related.

Antitheorem, A *wff* whose negation is a theorem. (This is a new term not yet widely used; I include it here to help it catch on.)

Apodeictic, the characteristic feature of any proposition that states what is necessary (or impossible), perfectly certain (or inconceivable), or demonstrably true (or false). See: Problematic/ Assertoric / Apodeictic.

Apodosis, implication

Aporia, Greek term for a difficulty or puzzle (literally, "with no pathway"). Aristotle commonly used this term to signify a group of individually plausible but collectively inconsistent statements. The reconciliation of such statements by considering alternative solutions, he supposed, is the chief business of philosophy.

Aposteriori, a sentence, proposit-ion, thought, or judgement is a posteriori (literally "after") if its truth is dependent on how our actual expe-rience (experiment and observation) turns out. Many have thought that the truths of the empirical, or nonmathematical, sciences are entirely a posteriori, though the rationalists and some recent philosophers such as S. Kripke and N. Chomsky seem to deny this. Some take synthetic and a posteriori to be equivalence. Compare a priori

Appearance-reality, distinction between the way things seem to be and the way they are. The merely apparent is often supposed to be internal, subjective, or temporal, but available for direct awareness, whereas the the real is supposed to be external, objective, or eternal, but known only inferentially. Drawn in different terms and applied in various contexts, the distinction is important in the philosophies of Plato, Dçscartes, Kant, and Bradley. *Recommended Reading*: Julius Moravcsik, Plato and Platonism: Plato's Conception of Appearance and

Reality in Ontology, Epistemology, and Ethics, and Its Modern Echoes (Blackwell, 2000); John W. Yolton, Realism and Appearances: An Essay in Ontology (Cambridge, 2000).

Apperception, Self-conscious awareness (as opposed to sensory perception of external objects), including especially the operation of the will, in the philosophy of Leibniz and Kant. *Recommended Reading*: Mark Kulstad, Leibniz on Apperception, Consciousness and Reflection (Philosophia Verlag, 1991).

Appiah Kwame Anthony, African American philosopher whose work on the foundations of probabalistic semantics is exemplified in Assertions and Conditionals (1985) and Truth in Semantics (1986). He is also the author of In My Father's House: Africa in thePhilosophy of Culture (1992), a discussion of the influence of racial concepts on the development of African literature and art, and Color Conscious: The Political Morality of Race (1996). A native of Ghana, Appiah is Past President of the Society for African Philosophy in North America.

Applied ethics, branch of ethics that considers the practical application of ethical principles to specific issues of social or personal concern. *Recommended Reading*: Peter Singer, Applied Ethics (Oxford, 1986); Peter Singer, Practical Ethics (Cambridge, 1993); Anthony Weston, A 21st Century Ethical Toolbox (Oxford, 2000).

A priori, a sentence, proposition, thought or judgement is a priori (literally "before") if its truth is not dependent on how our actual experience (experiment and observation) happens to turn out. Some a priori truths (axiomsor first principles) are held to be directly intuited; the rest are supposed to be deducible from these. Euclid's geometry provides the model for this traditional conception. With a posteriori knowledge or statements, on the other hand, justification does invoke sensory experience either directly via perception or indirectly via induction. Many have thought that the truths of logic and mathematics are a priori, though J. S. Mill and W. V. O. Quine might be thought to maintain the contrary position. Some equate a priori and analytic. The ontological argument for the existence of God is deemed a priori. based on, distinction among judgments, propositions, ideas, arguments, or kinds of knowledge. In each case, the a priori is taken to be independent of experience, which the a posteriori presupposes. An a priori argument, then, is taken to reason deductively from abstract general premises, while an a posteriori argument relies upon specific information derived from sense perception. The necessary truth of an a priori proposition can be determined by reason alone, but the contingent truth of an a posteriori proposition can be discovered only by reference to some matter of fact. Thus, for example: "3 + 4 = 7" is known a priori. "Chicago is on Lake Michigan." is known a posteriori. Rationalists typically emphasize the importance of a priori ideas and arguments as the foundation of all knowledge. Kant held that synthetic a priori judgments are preconditions of experience and form the basis for mathematics and science. Empiricists, on the other hand, usually hold that all a priori propositions are merely analytic, so that we must rely on a posteriori propositions for significant knowledge of the world. Kripke challenges even the identification of this distinction with that between the necessary and the contingent. *Recommended Reading*: Immanuel Kant, Prolegomena to Any Future Metaphysic (Hackett, 1977); New Essays on the A Priori, ed. by Paul Boghossian and Christopher Peacocke (Oxford, 2000); A Priori Knowledge, ed. by Albert Casullo (Dartmouth, 1999); Robert Greenberg, Kant's Theory of a Priori Knowledge (Penn. State, 2001).

A proposition, In the traditional notation for categorical logic, a proposition that is both universal in quantity and affirmative in quality. Example: "All dogs are mammals." Such a proposition affirms of each and every dog that it is also a mammal. Its contradictory is an "O" proposition with the same subject and predicate terms.

Aquinas Thomas, Born to an aristocratic family living in Rocc-asecca, Italy, Thomas Aquinas (1224-1274) joined the Dominican order while studying philosophy and theology at Naples. Later he pursued additional studies in Paris and Koeln, where he was exposed to Aristotelean thought by Albert the Great and William of Moerbeke. During the rest of his life, he taught at Paris and Rome, writing millions of words on philosophical and theological issues and earning his reputation among the scholastics as "the angelic doctor." Aquinas developed in massive detail a synthesis of Christianity and Aristotelian philosophy that became the official doctrine of Roman Catholic theology in 1879. De Ente et Essentia (On Being and Essence) includes a basic statement of Aquinas's metaphysical position. His literary activity stopped abruptly as the result of a religious experience a few months before his death. Although he wrote many commentaries on the works of Aristotle and a comprehensive Summa de Veritate Catholicae Fidei contra Gentiles (Summa Contra Gentiles) (1259-1264) Aquinas's unfinished Summa Theologica (1265-1273) represents the most complete statement of his philosophical system. The sections of greatest interest for survey courses include his views on the nature of god, including the five ways to prove god's existence, and his exposition of natural law. Although matters of such importance should be accepted on the basis of divine revelation alone, Aquinas held, it is at least possible (and perhaps even desirable) in some circumstances to achieve genuine knowledge of them by means of the rigorous application of human reason. As embodied souls (hylomorphic composites), human beings naturally rely on sensory information for their knowledge of the world. Reading hint: Although the rigidly formal structure of the Summa articles can be rather confusing to a modern reader, the central portion beginning with the words, "I answer that..." is always a direct statement of Aquinas's own position. *Recommended Reading*. Primary sources: Opera omnia (Rome, 1882-); Thomas Aquinas, Selected Writings, ed. by Ralph McInerny. (Penguin, 1999); Thomas Aquinas, Selected Philosophical Writings, tr. By Timothy McDermott (Oxford, 1998); Thomas Aquinas, Summa Theologiae: A Concise Translation, ed. by Timothy McDermott (Christian Classics, 1997); An Aquinas Reader, ed. by Mary T. Clark (Fordham, 2000); Thomas Aquinas, On Law, Morality, and Politics, ed. By William P. Baumgarth and

Richard J.Regan, S.J. (Hackett, 1988). Secondary sources: Etienne Gilson, The Philosophy of St. Thomas Aquinas (Dorset, 1981); The Cambridge Companion to Aquinas, ed. by Norman Kretzmann and Eleonore Stump (Cambridge, 1993); Ralph McInerny, St. Thomas Aquinas (Notre Dame, 1982); The Christian Philosophy of St. Thomas Aquinas, by Etienne Gilson, tr. by I. T. Shook (Notre Dame, 1994); Ralph McInerny, Ethica Thomistica: The Moral Philosophy of Thomas Aquinas (Catholic University of America, 1997); Guide to Thomas Aquinas by Josef Pieper (Ignatius, 1997). Additional on-line information about Aquinas includes: Daniel J. Kennedy's extremely thorough treatment of Aquinas and treatise on his relation to medieval thought at The Jacques Maritain Center. The thorough colle-ction of resources at Episteme Links.com. Alexander Broadie's article in The Oxford Companion to Philosophy. Also see: concupiscence, the cosmological argument, the first cause argument, the five ways, human nature, medieval philosophy, moral philosophy, neo-Thomism, ratiocination,philosophy of reli-gion, scholasticism, suicide, Thomism, analytical Thomism, traversal of the infinite, and just war. An article in The Internet Encyclopedia of Philosophy. The excellent bibliography prepared by ThÈrÈsa Bonin. Walter Farrell's masterly Companion to the Summa.

Archae, Greek term for beginning or ultimate principle. The Milesian philosophers looked for a single material stuff of which the entire universe is composed, while Empedocles identified no fewer than four elements whose mixture makes up ordinary things. For both Plato and Aristotle, however, the arch most worth seeking would be an originating power from which the material order flows and upon which theoretical knowledge of its nature might be grounded logically. *Recommended Reading*: F. E. Peters, Greek Philosophical Terms: A Historical Lexicon (NYU, 1967).

Archimedes, Sicilian geometrician (287-212 BCE) who calculated an accurate value for *p*, demonstrated the relationship between the volume of spheres and cylinders, discovered methods for determining the center of gravity of plane figures, and provided a foundation for the science of hydrostatics. Archimedes also invented many ingenious machines, including a pump for raising water, effective levers and compound pulleys, and a mechanical plane-tarium. He died defending Syracuse against a Roman seige during the second Punic war. *Recommended Reading*: E. J. Dijksterhuis, Archimedes (Princeton, 1987).

Arendt Hannah, German-American political philosopher (1906-1975). Althoughshe had studied with Jaspers and Heidegger in Heidelberg, Arendt fled Germany in 1933 and, from her new home in the United States, wrote powerfully about the anti-Semitism of the Nazi regime, describing its emergence as an instance of "the eerie banality of [evil" in Eichmann in Jerusalem: A Report on the Banality of Evil (1963). Arendt's The Origins of Modern Totalitarianism (1951) decried the concentration of political power engendered by imperialism of every sort. In The Human Condition (1958), On Revolution (1963), and The Life of the Mind (1978), however, she expressed a profound skepticism about the prospect that philosophical thought could significantly influence the individual actions that determine the political structure of human culture. *Recom-*

mended Reading: The Portable Hannah Arendt, ed. By Peter Baehr (Penguin, 2000); Hannah Arendt/Karl Jaspers Correspondence 1926-1969, ed. by Lotte Kohler and Hans Saner (Harcourt Brace, 1993); Margaret Canovan, Hannah Arendt: A Reinterpretation of Her Political Thought (Cambridge, 1994); Feminist Interpretations of Hannah Arendt, ed. By Bonnie Honig (Penn. State, 1995); and Dana Richard Villa, Arendt and Heidegger (Princeton, 1995).

Ares, Greek god of destruction, slaughter, and war, later called Mars by the Romans. Hence, for poets and philosophers, a symbol of strife and discord generally.

Aretae, the Greek word for "excellence" or "virtue". For the Greeks, this was not limited to human beings. A guitar, for example, has its arete" in producing harmonious music, just as a hammer has its excellence or virtue in pounding nails into wood well. So, too, the virtue of an Olympic swimmer is in swimming well, and the virtue of a national leader lies in motivating people to work for the common good.

Greek word for unique excellence or skill of any sort; hence, especially, moral virtue. Socrates supposed that aretae can be identified with knowledge of the good, but Plato distinguished four distinct virtues as crucial components of the perfect state or person. Aristotle maintained that moral aretae is invariably found as the mean between vicious extremes. *Recommended Reading*: F. E. Peters, Greek Philosophical Terms: A Historical Lexicon (NYU, 1967).

Arg, argument

Argument,

1. a. an inference
   b. input to a function
   c. a subject-term for a predicate.

See also corresponding argument

2. ("arg" or parameter) A value or referencepassed to a function, procedure, subroutine, command or program, by the caller. For example, in the function:

square(x) = x * x

x is the formal argument and in the call

y = square(3+3)

3+3 is the actual argument. This will execute the function square with x having the value 6.

There are many different conventions for passing arguments to functions and procedures including call-by-value, call-by-name, call-by-need. These affect whether the value of the argument is computed by the caller or the callee (the function) and whether the callee can modify the value of the argument as seen by the caller (if it is a variable).

Arguments to a program are usually given after the command name, separated by spaces, *e.g.*:

cat myfile yourfile hisfile

Here "cat" is the command and "myfile", "yourfile", and "hisfile" are the arguments.

Argument form, *f*, the general logical structure of an argument considered apart from any of its specific content. In categorical logic, an argument form is any one of the 256 distinct varieties of categorical syllogism. In the propositional calculus, an argument form is a set of two or more statement forms such that the substitution of an actual statement for each of its statement variables would result in an argument.

Argument from evil, argument from the existence of evil to the non existence of an omnipotent, omniscient and perfectly benevolent being such as God is supposed to be. Since evil exists, it's argued, either God can't prevent it (and so, is not omnipotent) or doesn't know about it (and so, is not omniscient) or doesn't wish to remove it (and so, is not perfectly benevolent). Contrast: teleological argument.

Argumentum,...ad baculum: see appeal to force...ad hominem: see ad hominem argu ment...ad ignorat-iam: see appeal to ignorance...ad misericordiam: see appeal to pity...ad populum: see appeal to emotion...ad verecundiam: see appeal to authority.

Argumentum ad populum, emotion appeal

Aristippus, ethics, pleasure, cynism, wisdom, happiness. North African philosopher (435-356 B.C). Originally a student of Socrates, Aristippus (and his eponymous grandson) established the Cyrenaic school of philosophy, according to which sensual pleasure in the present moment, tempered only by mode-ration, is the genuine good for human life.

Aristocracy, political theory that advocates the rule of "the best" whom it identifies, generally, with a hereditary upper class. Contrast: autocracy, democracy, oligarchy.

Aristotelianism, A tradition, dating from the medieval period, concerned with promoting and defending significant portions of the philosophy of Aristotle.

Aristotelian logic, traditional categorical logic, as developed originally in the Organon of Aristotle.

Aristotle, born at Stagira in northern Greece, Aristotle (384-322 B.C.) was the most notable product of the educational program devised by Plato; he spent twenty years of his life studying at the Academy. When Plato died, Aristotle returned to his native Macedonia, where he is supposed to have participated in the education of Philip's son, Alexander (the Great). He came back to Athens with Alexander's approval in 335 and established his own school at the Lyceum, spending most of the rest of his life engaged there in research, teaching, and writing. His students acquired the name "peripatetics" from the master's habit of strolling about as he taught. Although the surviving works of Aristotle probably represent only a fragment of the whole, they include his investigations of an amazing range of subjects, from logic, philosophy, and ethics to physics, biology, psychology, politics, and rhetoric. Aristotle appears to have thought through his views as he wrote, returning to significant issues at different stages of his own development. The result is less a consistent system of thought than a complex record of Aristotle's thinking about many significant issues. The aim of Aristotle's logical treatises (known collectively as the Organon) was to develop a universal method of reasoning by means of which it would be possible to learn everything there is to know about reality. Thus, the Categories proposes a scheme for the description of particular things in terms of their properties, states, and activities. On Interpretation, Prior Analytics, and Posterior Analytics examine the nature of deductive inference, outlining the system of syllogistic reasoning from true propositions that later came to be known as categorical logic. Though not strictly one of the logical works, the Physics contributes to the universal method by distinguishing among the four causes which may be used to explain everything, with special concern for why things are the way they are and the apparent role of chance in the operation of the world. In other treatises, Aristotle applied this method, with its characteristic emphasis on teleological explanation, to astronomical and biological explorations of the natural world. In Metaphysics Aristotle tried to justify the entire enterprise by grounding it all in an abstract study of being qua being. Although Aristotle rejected the Platonic theory of forms, he defended his own vision of ultimate reality, including the eternal existence of substance. On The Soul uses the notion of a hylomorphic composite to provide a detailed account of the functions exhibited by living things—vegetable, animal, and human—and explains the use of sensation and reason to achieve genuine knowledge. That Aristotle was interested in more than a strictly scientific exploration of human nature is evident from the discussion of literary art (particularly tragedy) in Poetics and the methods of persuasion in the Rhetoric. Aristotle made several efforts to explain how moral conduct contributes to the good life for human agents, including the Eudemian Ethics and the Magna Moralia, but the most complete surviving statement of his views on morality occurs in the Nicomachean Ethics. There he considered the natural desire to achieve happiness, described the operation of human volition and moral deliberation, developed a theory of each virtue as the mean between vicious extremes, discussed the value of three kinds of friendship, and defended his conception of an ideal life of intellectual pursuit. But on Aristotle's view, the lives of individual human beings are invariably linked together in a social context. In the Politics he speculated about the origins of the state, described and assessed the relative merits of various types of government, and listed the obligations of the individual citizen. He may also have been the author of a model Constitution of Athens, in which the abstract notion of constitutional government is applied to the concrete life of a particular society.

Recommended Reading: Primary sources: Aristotelis opera, ed. by I. Bekker (Prussian Academy, 1831-70); The Complete Works of Aristotle, ed. by Jonathan Barnes. (Princeton, 1984)—vol. 1: includes the logical works, Physics, treatises on astronomy and animals, and Of the Soul—vol. 2: includes additional scientific treatises, Metaphysics, the works on ethics, Politics, Rhetoric, and Poetics. Basic Works of Aristotle, ed. by Richard McKeon (Random House, 1941); Aristotle: Introductory Readings, tr. by Terence Irwin and Gail Fine (Hackett, 1996); Nichomachean Ethics, tr. By Terence Irwin (Hackett, 1985). Secondary sources: The Cambridge Companion to Aristotle, ed. by Jonathan Barnes (Cambridge, 1995); Aristotle the Philosopher, ed. by J.L. Ackrill (Oxford, 1981); Henry Veatch, Aristotle, a Contemporary Appreciation (Indiana, 1974); Jonathan Lear, Aristotle: The Desire to Understand (Cambridge, 1998); Feminist Interpretations of Aristotle, ed. by Cynthia A. Freeland (Penn. State, 1998); Kenneth McLeish, Aristotle (Routledge,

1999); Joseph Owens, Doctrine of Being in the Aristotelian Metaphysics (Pontifical Institute, 1978); Essays on Aristotle's De Anima, ed. by Martha Nussbaum and Amelie Rorty (Clarendon, 1996); John M. Cooper, Reason and Emotion (Princeton, 1998); Sarah Broadie, Ethics with Aristotle (Oxford, 1995); Aristotle's Ethics: Critical Essays, ed. by Nancy Sherman (Rowman & Littlefield, 1999); J. O. Urmson, Aristotle's Ethics (Blackwell, 1988); Anthony Kenny, Aristotle's Theory of the Will (Yale, 1979); Fred D. Miller, Jr., Nature, Justice, and Rights in Aristotle's Politics (Oxford, 1997). Additional on-line information about Aristotle includes: Richard Hooker's excellent treatment.

Arithmetic, formal system of, A first-order theory with a finite alphabet, and only finitely long wffs which, on its intended interpretation (1) contains theorems that express truths of number theory, and (2) permits the construction of a term to denote any natural number.

Arithmetisation, A generalized form of Goedel numbering in which distinct numerals Are assigned to distinct symbols in the alphabet of a formal language. As a result every *wff* of the language can be re-expressed as a Numeral concatenating all the numerals for its component symbols). When done well, there can easily be an effective method for translating wffs into numerals and vice versa.

Arity, The number of arguments a function or operator takes. In some languages functions may have variable arity which sometimes means their last or only argument is actually a list of arguments.

Armstrong David M., Australian philosopher (1926-). In Perception and the Physical World (1961) and A Materialist Theory of Mind (1968). Armstrong strictly defends the identity of mental events with states of the brain. Armstrong also argues for the objective reality of qualities and relations in Universals and Scientific Realism (1978) and Universals (1989). *Recommended Reading*: D. M. Armstrong, A World of States of Affairs (Cambridge, 1997) and Ontology, Causality, and Mind: Essays in Honor of D. M. Armstrong, ed. by John Bacon, Keith Campbell, and Lloyd Reinhardt (Cambridge, 1993).

Arnauld Antoine, French theologian and philosopher (1612-1694). Influential as co-author (with Pierre Nicole) of La logique, ou l'art de penser (The "Port-Royal" Logic) (1662), Arnauld was active in the seventeenth-century French philosophical community that also included Mersenne and Pascal. Arnauld wrote the fourth set of Objections that were published along with Descartes's Meditations (1641), criticized the occasionalist philosophical system and theological views of Malebranche in Traite de vraies et fausses idees (On True and False Ideas) (1683), and engaged in a lengthy correspondence with Leibniz. *Recommended Reading*: Steven Nadler, Arnauld and the Cartesian Philosophy of Ideas (Princeton, 1989).

Arrow Kenneth Joseph, American economist and social theorist (1921). In Social Choice and Individual Values (1951). Arrow introduced the general impossibility theorem, which shows that the rationally collective preference of a group cannot always be derived from the transitive preferences of its individual members. (This point is often illustrated with instances of the voting paradox.) Arrow won the Nobel Prize in Economic Sciences in 1972. *Recommended Reading*: Kenneth Joseph Arrow, The Limits of Organization (Norton, 1974) and Markets, Information, and Uncertainty: Essays in Economic Theory in Honor of Kenneth J. Arrow, ed. by Graciela Chichilnisky (Cambridge, 1999).

Artificial Intelligence (AI), the study of how to make computers do things that minds can do. These include many things not normally thought of as intelligent, such as moving without bumping into obstacles, or gaining information about an environment through vision. Humans share these capacities, and also the ability to learn from experience, with many other animals. Only humans, however, have language. The intellectual aspects of intelligence depend on language. Much work in AI models intellectual tasks, as opposed to the sensory, motor, and adaptive abilities possessed by all mammals. Most AI systems are programs, existing only inside the computer. Others are robots, controlled either by a program or (in "situated" robots) by engineered reflexes.

Scope of Artificial Intelligence: AI programs can do many different things. They can play games, predict share values, interpret photographs, diagnose diseases, plan travel itineraries, translate languages, take dictation, draw analogies, help design complex machinery, teach logic, make jokes, compose music, do drawings, and learn to do tasks better. Some of these things they do well. Expert systems can make medical diagnoses as well as, or better than, most human doctors. The world chess champion Garry Kasparov was beaten by a program in 1997, computers often predict share prices better than humans, and some AI-generated music sounds like compositions by famous composers. Other things, they do rather badly. Their translations are imperfect, but good enough to be understood. Their dictation is reliable only if the vocabulary is predictable and the speech unusually clear. And their jokes are poor, although some are found funny by children. To match everything that people can do, they would need to model the richness and subtlety of human memory and common sense. Moreover, programs do only one thing, whereas people do many things.

AI robots, although more flexible than industrial robots, are similarly limited. Very few can avoid obstacles smoothly, or move across uneven surfaces without falling over. Robots that plan their actions beforehand are vulnerable to unexpected environmental changes. Even if a robot performs successfully, it cannot undertake a wide variety of tasks. And its success often requires simplification of the environment: floor-cleaning robots are useful only if the floor is uncluttered. Neve-rtheless, AI-robots can do boring, dirty, or dangerous jobs, sometimes in places that humans cannot reach.

Purposes of Artificial Intelligence: AI developers have one or both of two motivations: technological and psychological. Some want to make their computers do a useful task, without caring just how they do it. These may include methods that people cannot match, such as sensitivity to ultraviolet light, or an exhaustive search ahead through all the legal chess moves for several steps. Others want to learn about human minds (or brains). They see their programs as psychological theories, and avoid methods that humans cannot use.

Psychologists can be helped by AI because they must state their theories very clearly to express them as programs. If the program fails to produce the intended results, then the theory must be mistaken, but the computer run may indicate where the mistake is. If the program succeeds, it does not follow that people think in the same way: only psychological (or neurophysiological) evidence can confirm that.

AI is used by financial institutions, scientists and medical practitioners, design engineers, public transport schedulers, planning authorities, government departments, and security services, among many others. AI techniques are also applied in systems used to browse the Internet and online news and wire services. In the home, AI systems can provide guidance on gardening, travel, car maintenance, and many other matters; and AI robots are being developed to assist the disabled.

Artificial Intelligence and Real Intelligence: The question, "Is artificial intelligence possible?" is ambiguous. It may mean "Can AI programs actually produce results that resemble human behaviour?" This is a scientific question. The answer at present is yes, at least in some cases. Whether it would also be true to say that this is so in all cases is not yet known. Some things that most people assume computers could never do are already possible. AI programs can compose aesthetically appealing music, draw attractive pictures, and even play the piano "expressively". Other things are more elusive: producing perfect translations of a wide range of texts; making fundamental, yet aesthetically acceptable, transformations of musical style; producing robots that move nimbly over rough ground, swim across rivers, or climb mountains. It is controversial whether these things are merely very difficult in practice, or impossible in principle.

Alternatively, "Is artificial intelligence possible?" may mean "Could any program (or robot), no matter how humanlike its performance, really be intelligent?" This question involves highly controversial issues in the philosophy of mind, including the importance of embodiment and the nature of intentionality and consciousness. Some philosophers and AI researchers argue that intelligence can arise only in bodily creatures sensing and acting in the real world. If this is correct, then robotics is essential to the attempt to construct truly intelligent artefacts. If not, then a mere AI program might be intelligent.

The celebrated mathematician and computer scientist Alan Turing proposed what is now called the Turing Test as a way of deciding whether a machine is intelligent. He imagined a person and a computer hidden behind a screen, communicating by electronic means. If we cannot tell which one is the human, we have no reason to deny that the machine is thinking. That is, a purely behavioural test is adequate for identifying intelligence (and consciousness). The philosopher John Searle has expressed a different view. He admits that a program might produce replies identical to those of a person, and that a programmed robot might behave exactly like a human. But he argues that a program cannot understand anything it "says". It is not actually saying (asserting) anything at all, merely outputting meaningless symbols that it has manipulated according to purely formal rules. Lacking understanding (intentionality), it is all syntax and no semantics. But human beings can ascribe meaning to its empty symbols, because our brains can somehow (Searle does not say how) cause intentionality, whereas metal and silicon cannot. There is no consensus, in either AI or philosophy, as to which theory, that of Turing or that of Searle, is right.

Whether an AI system could be conscious is an especially controversial topic. The concept of consciousness itself is illunderstood, both scientifically and philosophically. Some people think it obvious that any robot, no matter how superficially humanlike, must be zombie-like. But others think it obvious that a robot whose functions matched the relevant functions of the brain (whatever those may be) would inevitably be conscious. The answer has moral implications: if an AI system were conscious, it would arguably be wrong to "kill" it, or even to use it as a "slave".

Artificial intelligence, (AI) The subfield of computer science concerned with the concepts and methods of symbolic inference by computer and symbolic knowledge representation for use in making inferences.

AI can be seen as an attempt to model or simulate aspects of human cognition on computers. Thus Minsky defined it as "The science of making machines do things that would require intelligence if done by people" (1968). It is also sometimes defined as trying to solve by computer any problem that a human can solve faster.

Two examples of AI problems are computer vision (building a system that can understand images as well as a human) and natural language processing (building a system that can understand and speak a human language as well as a human). These may appear to be modular, but all attempts so far (2001) to solve them have foundered on the amount of context information and "intelligence" they seem to require.

The birth of AI was at the Dartmouth Summer Research Project on Artificial Intelligence organised by John McCarthy in 1956. However, researchers had been working on problems related to machine intelligence decades earlier. The early years of AI were dependent on symbolic models of cognitive processing which are formally equivalent to the Turing machine and thus computable (algorithmically calculable). The Physical Systems Symbol Hypothesis of Newell and Simon formalised the commitments of this sort of approach to machine intelligence.

References: Introduction to AI (Cogsci Dictionary) Foundational Questions in AI Minsky, M.L., ed. (1968). Semantic information processing. Cambridge, MA: MIT Press. Newell, A (1990). Unified theories of cognition. Cambridge, MA: Harvard University Press. Turing, A.M. (1950). Computing machinery and intelligence. Mind. 59: 433-460. ACM SIGART. U Cal Davis. CMU Artificial Intelligence Repository. See also AI-complete, artificial life, connectionism, fuzzy computing, genetic programming, neats vs. scruffies, neuralnetwork, symbolicism Based on and Chris Eliasmith—[Dictionary of Philosophy of Mind]

Scientific research aimed at building machines capable of performing a variety of functions as well as (or better than) human agents do. Although early efforts focused on symbolic manipulation and linguistic representation, most now use the notion of parallel distributed processing for the construction of a quasineural network that recognize and associate patterns. Hopes (or fears) of the success of this discipline often give rise to philosophical questions about whether purely physical systems can adequately support consciousness, perception, and mind. *Recommended Reading*: The Simulation of Human Intelligence, ed. by Donald Broadbent (Blackwell, 1993); Jack Copeland, Artificial Intelligence: A Philosophical Introduction (Blackwell, 1993); Daniel C. Dennett, Brainchildren: Essays on Designing Minds, 1984-1996 (Bradford, 1998); and Semantic Information Processing, ed. by Marvin L. Minsky (MIT, 1969).

Artificial Life, (a-life) The study of synthetic systems which behave like natural living systems in some way. Artificial Life complements the traditional biological sciences concerned with the analysis of living organisms by attempting to create lifelike behaviours within computers and other artificial media. Artificial Life can contribute to theoretical biology by modelling forms of life other than those which exist in nature. It has applications in environmental and financial modelling and network communications.

There are some interesting implementations of artificial life using strangely shaped blocks. A video, probably by the company Artificial Creatures who build insect-like robots in Cambridge, MA (USA), has several mechanical implementations of artificial life forms. See also Evolutionary Computing, Life. [Christopher G. Langton (Ed.), "Artificial Life", Proceedings Volume VI, Santa Fe Institute Studies in the Sciences of Complexity. Addison-Wesley, 1989].

Artificial neural network, (ANN, commonly just "neural network" or "neural net") A network of many very simple processors ("units" or "neurons"), each possibly having a (small amount of) local memory. The units are connected by unidirectional communication channels ("connections"), which carry numeric (as opposed to symbolic) data. The units operate only on their local data and on the inputs they receive via the connections.

A neural network is a processing device, either an algorithm, or actual hardware, whose design was inspired by the design and functioning of animal brains and components thereof.

Most neural networks have some sort of "training" rule whereby the weights of connections are adjusted on the basis of presented patterns. In other words, neural networks "learn" from examples, just like children learn to recognise dogs from examples of dogs, and exhibit some structural capability for generalisation.

Neurons are often elementary nonlinear signal processors (in the limit they are simple threshold discriminators). Another feature of NNs which distinguishes them from other computing devices is a high degree of interconnection which allows a high degree of parallelism. Further, there is no idle memory containing data and programs, but rather each neuron is preprogrammed and continuously active.

The term "neural net" should logically, but in common usage never does, also include biological neural networks, whose elementary structures are far more complicated than the mathematical models used for ANNs. See Aspirin, Hopfield network, McCulloch-Pitts neuron.

Asceticism, the position according to which the pleasures of this world should be renounced, usually for the sake of some "higher" purpose like intellectual discipline or mystical insight. The doctrine is often connected with the mind-body dichotomy, as it consists of an extreme emphasis on the mind and the pleasures of thought (somewhat akin to psychological rationalism). For the opposite view, see sensualism. (References from Buddhism, Cynicism, Kantianism, Pythagoreanism, sensualism, and spiritualism.)

Asceticism (Greek, *askesis,* "exercise"), practice of selfdenial and renunciation of worldly pleasures in order to attain a higher degree of spirituality, intellectuality, or self-awareness. Among the ancient Greeks, the term originally denoted the training practised by athletes and soldiers. In Greek philosophy, the adherents of Cynicism and Stoicism adopted the practice of mastering desire and passion. Asceticism is practised to some extent by the adherents of every religion. It often requires abstinence from food, drink, or sexual activity, as in fasting or celibacy, and may also require physical pain or discomfort, such as endurance of extreme heat or cold or self-punishment, as in sufism or as practised by the flagellants. Asceticism may require withdrawal from the material world to a life of meditation, as in the practice of Yogâ. *See also* Buddhism; Hinduism; Monasticism; Penance.

Aspectual shape, Similar to the notion of sense introduced by John Searle in 1992.

Assent, make a judgment. For many philosophers of the modern period, assent is the mental act of accepting the truth of a statement, whether or not one has adequate evidence for knowing it.

Assertion, 1. An expression which, if false, indicates an error. Assertions are used for debugging by catching can't happen errors.

2. fact or rule added to the database by the program at run time. This is an extralogical or impure feature of logic programming languages.

Assertoric, a proposition stating that something actually is the case, rather than necessary or merely possible. See: problematic / assertoric / apodeictic.

Assignment, Storing the value of an expression in a variable. This is commonly written in the form "$v = e$". In Algol the assignment operator was ":=" (pronounced "becomes") to avoid mathematicians qualms about writing statements like $x = x + 1$.

Assignment is not allowed in functional languages, where an identifier always has the same value.

See also referential transparency, single assignment, zero assignment.

Assignment problem, (Or "linear

assignment") Any problem involving minimising the sum of $C(a, b)$ over a set P of pairs (a, b) where a is an element of some set A and b is an element of set B, and C is some function, under constraints such as "each element of A must appear exactly once in P" or similarly for B, or both.

For example, the *a's* could be workers and the *b's* projects.

The problem is "linear" because the "cost function" $C()$ depends only on the particular pairing (a, b) and is independent of all other pairings.

Associated propositional formula, *A* wff *A* of propositional logic created from a wff *B* of predicate logic by (1) removing the quantifiers from *B*, and (2) replacing each predicate symbol (and its arguments) in *B* with a propositional symbol. Notation: B^prop = p.

Association, a rule of replacement of the forms:

$$(p \vee (q \vee r)) = ((p \vee q) \vee r)$$

$$(p \,\&\, (q \,\&\, r)) = ((p \,\&\, q) \,\&\, r)$$

Example: "Harold is over 21, and so are Jane and Kelly." Is equivalent to "Harold and Jane are over 21, and so is Kelly." The associativity of both disjunction and conjunction can be demonstrated by truth-table analysis.

Associationalism, psychological theory of knowledge which holds that all of our concepts come about through the association of images. David Hume is often called the first associationalist, but the idea enjoyed its great heyday in the late nineteenth century in tandem with sensationalism.

Association of ideas, presumed regularities in the co-existence or succession of particular mental contents. Noted as unreliable by Locke, the process of association became a central feature of human thought in the philosophy of Hume and Mill and in the psychology of Skinner.

Assumption, a proposition accepted without proof or evidence as the basis for some further conclusion.

Ataraxia, The Greek term used by Pyrrho and Epicurus for tranquillity, or the freedom from disturbance and pain that characterizes a balanced mind and constitutes its first step toward the achievement of pleasure (Gk. haedonae).

Atheism, the belief that, or the philosophical position according to which, God, gods, deities, and supernatural powers do not exist. In this respect it is similar to secularism and opposed to any variety of theism. In the last two centuries, some of the most influential atheistic hilosophers have been Karl Marx, Friedrich Nietzsche, Bertrand Russell, and Jean-Paul Sartre. Atheism is to be contrasted with agnosticism, which takes a doubtful attitude towards the existence of God(s) but does not proclaim disbelief. Ponularly, atheism is often taken to imply a lack of any ideals or values whatsoever (see immoralism), but this connotation rests on the controversial assumption that religious or supernatural values are the only real values. (References from agnosticism, secularism, and theism.)

Atheism (Greek, *a,* "not"; *theos,* "god"), doctrine that denies the existence of deity. Atheism differs distinctly from agnosticism, the doctrine that the existence of deity can neither be proved nor disproved. Many people have incorrectly been called atheists merely because they rejected some popular belief in divinity. To the Romans the early Christians were atheists because they denied the Roman gods. Adherents of various Christian sects have applied the term to anyone unwilling to accept every tenet of their doctrine. Freethinkers, such as the French philosopher and writer Jean-Jacques Rousseau, the French writer Voltaire, or the Anglo-American political philosopher and author Thomas Paine, although subscribing to a form of deism, may frequently be referred to as an atheist. The Sankhya philosophy, one of the great systems of Hindu thought, Buddhism, and Jainism have all been described as atheistic because all deny a personal God.

Atom, 1. In propositional logic, a simple proposition as opposed to a compound proposition or molecule. A wff without connectives.

2. In predicate logic, a wff without quantifiers or connectives.

Atomism, metaphysical or cosmological position according to which reality is fundamentally made up only of indivisible particles, independent, extremely small, self-sufficient atoms (nothing more). According to atomism, a complete description of the universe might be given by specifiying the location and movements of all the atoms composing it. Democritus is the most notable ancient atomist. According to Leibniz monads are "the true atoms." Locke's corpuscular hypothesis is also a version of Atomism.

Attribute, a property or feature possessed by a substance. In the philosophical nomenclature employed by Aquinas and Descartes, attributes are commonly regarded as essential to the substances that have them.

Aufklaerung, German term for Enlightenment, the modern spirit of reliance on reason espoused by such philosophers as Mendelssohn and Kant.

Augustine, philosophy of history, born to a Christian mother and pagan father at Tagaste in North Africa, Augustine (354-430) was a confirmed Manichaean during his early years as a student and teacher of rhetoric at Carthage and Rome. But in Milan, during his early thirties, he began to study Neoplatonic philosophy under the guidance of Ambrose and eventually converted to Christianity. An account of his early life and conversion, together with a reasoned defense of his Neoplatonic principles, may be found in the Confessiones (Confessions) (401). He was named the Christian bishop of Hippo (Annaba, Algeria) in 396, and devoted the remaining decades of his life to the formation of an ascetic religious community. Augustine argued against the skeptics that genuine human knowledge can be established with certainty. His explanation of human nature and agency combined stoic and Christian elements. But it was by reference to the abstract philosophy of Plato that Augustine sought to prove the existence of god. Acknowledging the difficulties of divine control and foreknowledge, he used an analysis of the nature of time to defend human freedom in De Gratia et Libero Aribitrio (On Grace and Free Will). In De Civitate Dei (The City of God) (413-427) Augustine distinguished religion and morality from politics and tried to establish the proper relations among them, arguing for the church's strict independence from (if not its outright superiority to) the civil state. You might be interested in viewing portions of a

Dutch library's copy of a fifteenth-century illuminated manuscript of this text. *Recommended Reading*: Primary sources: Sancti Aurelii Augustini opera omnia (Paris, 1679-1700); The Essential Augustine, ed. by Vernon J.Bourke (Hackett, 1974); Augustine, The Confessions, ed. by Susan B. Varenne (Vintage, 1998); Augustine, City of God, tr. by Marcus Dods (Modern Library, 2000). *Secondary sources*: Henry Chadwick, Augustine (Oxford, 1986); James Wetzel, Augustine and the Limits of Virtue (Cambridge, 1992).

Austin John, British legal theorist (1790-1859). Although he shared many of the utilitarian goals of his friend Bentham, Austin became the foremost representative of legal positivism. He argued in The Province of Jurisprudence Determined (1832) and the unfinished Lectures on Jurisprudence (1863) that, as a matter of practical fact, the law is nothing more than the command of a legitimate sovereign, enforced by the imposition of effective moral sanctions. *Recommended Reading*: Wilfrid E. Rumble, The Thought of John Austin: Jurisprudence, Colonial Reform, and the British Constitution (Athlone, 1985).

Austin John Langshaw, J.L. Austin (1911-1960) was born in Lancaster and educated at Oxford, where he became a professor of philosophy following several years of service in British intelligence during World War II. Although greatly admired as a teacher, Austin published little of his philosophical work during his brief lifetime. Students gathered his papers and lectures in books that were published posthumously, including Philosophical Papers (1961) and Sense and Sensibilia (1962). In "A Plea for Excuses" (1956), Austin explained and illustrated his method of approaching philosophical issues by first patiently analyzing the subtleties of ordinary language. In How to Do Things with Words (1961), the transcription of Austin's James lectures at Harvard, application of this method distinguishes between what we say, what we mean when we say it, and what we accomplish by saying it, or between speech acts involving locution, illocution (or "performative utterance"), and perlocution. *Recommended Reading*: Primary sources: J.L. Austin, How to Do Things with Words (Harvard, 1975); J. L. Austin, Philosophical Papers, ed. by J. O. Urmson and Geoffrey J. Warnock (Oxford, 1990); J.L. Austin, Sense and Sensibilia, ed. by Geoffrey J. Warnock (Oxford, 1962). Secondary sources: G.J. Warnock, J.L. Austin (Routledge, 1991).

Authentication, the verification of the identity of a person or process. In a communication system, authentication verifies that messages really come from their stated source, like the signature on a (paper) letter.

Authenticity, Selfconscious appropriation of the conditions of one's own existence and identity. According to Heidegger, such deliberate reflection about the goals and values of life is the only successful response to the experience of Angst without falling into self-deception. *Recommended Reading*: Michael E. Zimmerman, Eclipse of the Self: The Development of Heidegger's Concept of Authenticity (Ohio, 1986) and Heidegger, Authenticity, and Modernity: Essays in Honor of Hubert L. Dreyfus (MIT, 2000).

Authoritarianism, term used to describe the political practice or philosophical defense of the subordination by force of the wishes and aims of the individual to the interests of the state. Following the usage of Jeanne Kirkpatrick, authoritarianism is sometimes held to involve a less egregious violation of individual rights than totalitarianism. (References from absolutism, collectivism, communism, legalism, and totalitarianism.)

Authority appeal to, (argumentum ad verecundiam). The informal fallacy of claiming that we ought to accept the truth of a proposition because of some personal feature of the individual who affirms it. *Example*: "The former Governor believes that aliens have landed in the Arizona desert, so aliens must have landed in the Arizona desert." *Recommended Reading*: Douglas Walton, Appeal to Expert Opinion: Arguments from Authority (Penn. State, 1997).

Autocracy, one person rule. Where the rulership is hereditary, the government in question is a "monarchy"; where non-hereditary, a "dictatorship." Contrast: Some equate a democracy.

Automata, automaton

Automata theory, automaton

Automatism, the doctrine that all animal activities are mechanistically determined. The view is part of Cartesianism, since Descartes held to a strict determinism in biological affairs. The view is rather extreme, but persists in some circles under different names see, for example, Behaviorism.

Automaton, (Plural automata) A machine, robot, or formal system designed to follow a precise sequence of instructions.

Automata theory, the invention and study of automata, includes the study of the capabilities and limitations of computing processes, the manner in which systems receive input, process it, and produce output, and the relationships between behavioural theories and the operation and use of automated devices.

Autonomy, etymologically, it goes back to the Greek words for "self" and "law." This term is most strongly associated with Immanuel Kant, for whom it meant the ability to give the moral law to oneself. The term may have a weaker and a stronger meaning, depending on the nature of the agent:

1. the ability of an agent A to determine A's course of action. An artificial agent like an applet can be autonomous in this sense.
2. the ability of a human subject S to determine S's own course in life freely.

In this sense autonomy requires freedom.

Autonomy-heteronomy of the will, Kant's distinction between ways of choosing how to act. Autonomous agents are self-legislating; they act according to the categorical imperative of willing only what is universalizable as moral law. Heteronomous agents derive principles of action from outside themselves, by considering the objects or consequences of their choices or being influenced by the will of others. *Recommended Reading*: Immanuel Kant, Grounding for the Metaphysics of Morals, tr. by James W. Ellington (Hackett, 1993); Thomas E. Hill, Jr., Autonomy and Self-Respect (Cambridge, 1991); and Relational Autonomy: Feminist Perspectives on Autonomy, Agency, and the Social Self, ed. by Catriona MacKenzie and Natalie Stoljar (Oxford, 2000).

Avatar, 1. An image representing a

user in a multiuser virtual reality (or VR-like, in the case of Palace) space.

2. (CMU, Tektronix) root, superuser. There are quite a few Unix computers on which the name of the superuser account is "avatar" rather than "root". This quirk was originated by a CMU hacker who disliked the term "superuser", and was propagated through an ex-CMU hacker at Tektronix.

Averroes, Latinized name of the Islamic philosopher Ibn Rushd.

Avicebron, Latinized name of the Jewish philosopher Ibn Gabirol.

Avicenna, Latinized name of Persian philosopher Ibn Sina.

Axiology, branch of philosophy that studies judgments about value, including those of both aesthetics and ethics. *Recommended Reading*: Rem B. Edwards, Formal Axiology And Its Critics (Rodopi, 1995) and Forms of Value and Valuation, ed. by John W. Davis and Rem B. Edwards (Univ. Pr. of Am., 1992).

Axiom, in logic and mathematics, a basic principle that is assumed to be true without proof. The use of axioms in mathematics stems from the ancient Greeks, most probably during the 5th century BC, and represents the beginnings of pure mathematics as it is known today. Examples of axioms are the following: "No sentence can be true and false at the same time" (the principle of contradiction); "If equals are added to equals, the sums are equal"; "The whole is greater than any of its parts". Logic and pure mathematics begin with such unproved assumptions from which other propositions (*theorems*) are derived. This procedure is necessary to avoid circularity, or an infinite regression in reasoning. The axioms of any system must be consistent with one another, that is, they should not lead to contradictions. They should also be independent in the sense that they cannot be derived from one another, and should be few in number. Axioms have sometimes been interpreted as self-evident truths. The present tendency is to avoid this claim and simply to assert that an axiom is assumed to be true without proof in the system of which it is a part.

The terms *axiom* and *postulate* are often used synonymously. Sometimes the word *axiom* is used to refer to basic principles that are assumed by every deductive system, and the term *postulate* is used to refer to first principles peculiar to a particular system, such as Euclidean geometry. Infrequently, the word *axiom* is used to refer to first principles in logic, and the term *postulate* is used to refer to first principles in mathematics.

Axiom, A *wff* that is taken to be true without proof in the construction of a theory or stipulated as unproved premise for the proof of other wffs inside a formal system (compare lemma).

A formula containing variables of the metalanguage which becomes an axiom when its variables are instantiated to wffs of the formal language.

logical axiom,

An axiom that is a logically valid wff of the language of the system. See logical validity

proper axiom,

An axiom that is not a logically valid wff of the language of the system (but is a closed *wff*).

Axiomatic semantics, A set of assertions about properties of a system and how they are effected by program execution. The axiomatic semantics of a program could include pre- and post-conditions for operations. In particular if you view the program as a state transformer (or collection of state transformers), the axiomatic semantics is a set of invariants on the state which the state transformer satisfies.

E.g. for a function with the type:

sort list:: [T] -> [T]

we might give the precondition that the argument of the function is a list, and a postcondition that the return value is a list that is sorted.

One interesting use of axiomatic semantics is to have a language that has a finitely computable sublanguage that is used for specifying pre and post conditions, and then have the compiler prove that the program will satisfy those conditions. See also operational semantics, denotational semantics.

Axiomatic set theory, Set theory, if approached naively, leads to all sorts of problems, the most famous being Russell's paradox. For this reason mathematicians do set theory axiomatically: that is, there is a formal language for talking about sets, and a collection of axioms describing how they behave, and the only legitimate way of drawing conclusions about sets is to use the axioms. There are many different axiomatisations for set theory. Each takes a slightly different approach to the problem of finding a theory that captures as much as possible of the intuitive idea of what a set is, while avoiding the paradoxes that result from accepting all of it.

The main source of trouble in naive set theory is the idea that you can specify a set by saying whether each object in the universe is in the "set" or not. Accordingly, the most important differences between different axiomatisations of set theory concern the restrictions they place on this idea (known as "comprehension").

Zermelo Frankel set theory, the most commonly used axiomatisation, gets round it by (in effect) saying that you can only use this principle to define subsets of existing sets.

NBG (von Neumann-Bernays-Goedel) set theory sort of allows comprehension for all formulae without restriction, but distinguishes between two kinds of set, so that the sets produced by applying comprehension are only second-class sets. NBG is exactly as powerful as ZF, in the sense that any statement that can be formalised in both theories is a theorem of ZF if and only if it is a theorem of ZFC.

MK (Morse-Kelley) set theory is a strengthened version of NBG, with a simpler axiom system. It is strictly stronger than NBG, and it is possible that NBG might be consistent but MK inconsistent.

("New Foundations"), a theory developed by Willard Van Orman Quine, places a very different restriction on comprehension: it only works when the formula describing the membership condition for your putative set is "stratified", which means that it could be made to make sense if you worked in a system where every set had a level attached to it, so that a level-n set could only be a member of sets of level n+1. (This doesn't mean that there are actually levels attached to sets in NF). NF is very different from ZF; for instance, in NF the universe is a set (which it isn't in ZF, because the whole point of ZF is that it forbids sets that are "too large"), and it can be proved that the Axiom of Choice is false in NF!

ML ("Modern Logic") is to NF as NBG is to ZF. (Its name derives from the title of the book in which Quine introduced an early, defective, form of it). It is stronger than ZF (it can prove things that ZF can't), but if NF is consistent then ML is too.

Axiom of Choice, (AC, or "Choice", also called the multiplicative axiom) A controversial axiom of set theory asserting that for a non-empty set *A* of non-empty disjoint sets, there is a set *B* with exactly one member from each of the disjoint sets comprising *A*. Sometimes the axiom is written so as to assert that there is a function for choosing the members of the disjoint sets comprising *A* that will become the members of *B*:

> if *X* is a set, and S is the union of all the elements of *X*, then there exists a function *f*:*X* -> *S* such that for all non-empty sets *x* in *X*, *f*(*x*) is an element of *x*.

In other words, we can always choose an element from each set in a set of sets, simultaneously.

Function *f* is a "choice function" for *X* - for each *x* in *X*, it chooses an element of *x*.

Most people's reaction to AC is: "But of course that's true! From each set, just take the element that's biggest, stupidest, closest to the North Pole, or whatever". Indeed, for any finite set of sets, we can simply consider each set in turn and pick an arbitrary element in some such way. We can also construct a choice function for most simple infinite sets of sets if they are generated in some regular way. However, there are some infinite sets for which the construction or specification of such a choice function would never end because we would have to consider an infinite number of separate cases.

For example, if we express the real number line *R* as the union of many "copies" of the rational numbers, *Q*, namely *Q*, *Q* + *a*, *Q* + *b*, and infinitely (in fact uncountably) many more, where *a, b*, etc. are irrational numbers no two of which differ by a rational, and

$Q+a == q+a$: q in Q

we cannot pick an element of each of these "copies" without AC.

An example of the use of AC is the theorem which states that the countable union of countable sets is countable. *I.e.* if *X* is countable and every element of *X* is countable (including the possibility that they're finite), then the sumset of *X* is countable. This requires AC to be true in general.

Even if one accepts the axiom, it doesn't tell you how to construct a choice function, only that one exists. Most mathematicians are quite happy to use AC if they need it, but those who are careful will, at least, draw attention to the fact that they have used it. There is something a little odd about Choice, and it has some alarming consequences, so results which actually "need" it are somehow a bit suspicious, *e.g.* the Banach-Tarski paradox. On the other side, consider Russell's Attic.

AC is not a theorem of Zermelo Fr"nkel set theory (ZF). Goedel and

Paul Cohen proved that AC is independent of ZF, *i.e.* if ZF is consistent, then so are ZFC (ZF with AC) and ZF(~C) (ZF with the negation of AC). This means that we cannot use ZF to prove or disprove AC.

Axiom of Comprehension, An axiom schema of set theory which states: if $P(x)$ is a property then is a set. *I.e.* all the things with some property form a set.

$$x: P$$

Acceptance of this axiom leads to Russell's Paradox which is why Zermelo set theory replaces it with a restricted form.

Ayer Alfred Jules, English philosopher (1910-1989). After studying with members of the Vienna circle, Ayer published Language, Truth, and Logic (1936), an excellent statement of the central views of logical positivism, including the use of verifiability as a criterion of meaning, the rejection of metaphysics and theology as meaningless, and an emotivist ethical theory. His later works include Foundations of Empirical Knowledge (1940), The Problem of Knowledge (1956), Logical Positivism (1966), and The Central Questions of Philosophy (1972). *Recommended Reading*: The Philosophy of A. J. Ayer, ed. By Lewis Edwin Hahn (Open Court, 1992); Oswald Hanfling, Ayer (Routledge, 1999); and Ben Rogers, A. J. Ayer: A Life (Grove, 2000).

Bachelard Gaston, French philosopher of science (1884-1962); author of Psychoanalyse du feu (Psychoanalysis of Fire) (1937), Le nouvel esprit scientifique (The New Scientific Spirit) (1934), and L'Actualitié de l'histoire des sciences (History of Science) (1951). Rejecting both naive realism and absolute idealism, Bachelard maintained that scientific knowledge emerges from an imaginative interaction between the mind and experimental evidence. His emphasis on discontinuity in the progress of science anticipated portions of the work of Thomas Kuhn. *Recommended Reading*: Mary Tiles, Bachelard: Science and Objectivity (Cambridge, 1985).

Background, a set of nonrepresentational capacities that enable all representing to take place.

The Background includes biological and cultural capacities, skills, stances, assumptions and presuppositions. Introduced in Searle (1978).

1. *Introduction*: It should be noted right off that the hypothesis of the Background is, by Searle's admission, marked by "obscurity" (1991, p. 289), and accordingly, its developing theorisation has involved a number of shifts and clarifications (1992, pp. 186- 187; cf. 1991 generally) since it was first introduced to explain the fixing of literal meaning (1978). The general explanatory function of the Background has remained constant, however, and that is to account for how intentions are grounded and how skills can be applied.

The Background can be seen as one solution to the rule-or representation-grounding problem: how does one prevent an infinite regress in the interpretation of a rule or a representation? Searle's basic argument is that no rule or meaning is self-interpreting; a person needs a contextual understanding in order to arrive at the correct application or interpretation. According to Searle the literal meaning of a sentence underdetermines its truth conditions; our correct literal reading of, *e.g.*, a verb can only be secured given a certain Background in relation to which a clarifying interpretive context can be established (1995, p. 132; 1992, pp. 178-179; 1983, pp. 145-148). The Background, then, functions as the precondition for the intelligibility of representation and intentionality generally.

2. *The Topography and Make-Up of the Background*: Searle has described the Background as consisting of two major divisions which he calls the Deep Background and the Local Background (1983, p. 143-144).

The Deep Background is composed of biological skills and universally human capacities, such as eating, walking, and seeing given patterns of perceptual stimuli as discrete objects.

The Local Background, by contrast, is composed of culturallybound skills and capacities, such as knowing what culturally-specific objects are for, recognising culturally-specific situations as appropriate or inappropriate for certain types of behaviour, and so forth. Within each of these major divisions, Searle further distinguishes between knowing how things are and knowing how to do things (1983, p. 144)—roughly, between presuppositions and stances on the one hand, and skills on the other (see knowledge how). What becomes apparent almost immediately is the sheer hetero-geneity of the items said to make up the Background. Some appear to be entirely physical skills dependent on automatised sequences of motor activity. For example, Searle describes the case of a skier who first learns the basics of balance by being taught certain rules, and who, after having skied enough times, no longer is mindful of those rules but instead lets the learned responses of the body take over (1983, pp. 150-151). At this point the skills required for skiing have become part of the skier's Background; his or her "repeated experiences" have effectively created the right kind of "physical capacities" (1983, p. 150).

Other Background capacities appear to consist in what might be described as habits. These capacities, which seem to belong largely to the Local Background, are characterised as skills and abilities that are "functionally equivalent" to the systems of rules guiding socially-or culturally-situated behaviours and practices, but without involving any "representation or internalisation of those rules" (1995, p. 142). Rather than internalising rules, Searle holds, we "evolve a set of dispositions that are sensitive to the rule structure" (1995, p. 145).

A third category of Background capacities consists of the cognitive capacities inhering in stances, presuppositions, pretheoretical commitments, and the like. One such presupposition or stance, according to Searle, is the sense that objects are solid, which he claims is simply manifested in one's behaviour without one's having to have any belief or conviction about the matter (1992, p. 185). My sitting, walking, and manipulation of objects for instance, are executed in such a way that manifests my taking for granted the solidity of things like tables, chairs, the ground beneath me, and so forth (1992, p. 186; 1983, pp. 142-143). Searle emphasizes that such stances are not beliefs or expectations, but rather are simply presupposed by the agent in performing the actions manifesting them (1992, p. 186; 1983, pp. 156-157).

3. *Is the Background a Form of tacit knowledge?*: There would seem to be a certain amount of ambiguity in the Background. A major source of this ambiguity, as Searle acknowledges, is the difficulty of avoiding terms associated with mental representation per se for describing the Background's nonre-presentational capacities (1983, pp. 156-157). But we might point to another source, and that is the fact that, in at least some cases, the notion of an embodied commitment is liable to explanatory elimination.

At one level, some Background capacities can be described as the automatised effects of our having acquired certain skills (*e.g.*, of grasping objects or walking) under contingent circumstances. To the extent that contingent facts about our learning how to walk (*i.e.*, that we did so on Earth with its solid ground, particular gravitational force, etc. rather than in a weightless environment) have produced the physical habits that afford our walking, we can describe those habits as automatised physical responses to a given environment, and perhaps leave it at that. What is embodied is simply a certain causal history that has left the right kinds of traces in the appropriate neural pathways. While the characterisation of Background capacities in terms of neurophysiological structures is consistent with Searle's thesis (1995, p. 130; 1992, p. 188), it is difficult to see how purely automatised physical skills or habits could qualify as mental.

But to the extent that these physical responses can be associated with properly cognitive commitments regarding the environment, *i.e.*, that it will be reasonably like that in which the physical responses were formed in the first place, we can say that there is an element of expectation involved, if not of hypothesis formation. This raises the possibility that at least some Background capacities can be described as a kind of tacit knowledge or cognitive unconscious in the sense of Reber (1995), which may implicate them as induced abstract generalisations of some sort. That Background stances can be individuated in terms of specific contents would further seem to indicate that they are a kind of tacit knowledge.

Searle's response to the suggestion that the Background's cognitive capacities are a kind of tacit knowledge would probably be that Background capacities are not themselves a form of knowledge (such as beliefs, theories, empirical hypotheses, and so forth) but rather are the preconditions of knowledge. He might further argue—as he in fact does (1983 pp. 156-157)—that though it is very difficult to describe the contents of the Background other than in language that is more appropriate to the description of representational content, Background capacities are not representational. By this he means that Background capacities are not "features of the world independent of the mind" (1991, p. 291). (For Searle, mental representation is defined in terms of such mind-independent features as conditions of satisfaction, and directions of fit and causation).

Still, the case for understanding

some Background items as elements in a cognitive unconscious is compelling. Much of what Searle consigns to the Background does seem to contain information about how the world is, and as with hypotheses is subject to falsification, as in cases of breakdown (1992, pp. 184-185; 1983, p. 155). In addition, a Background at least partly composed of induced generalizations would flesh out the otherwise vague suggestion that the Background is (or contains) a mechanism that is sensitive to the appropriate features of the world, such as socially—or culturally-specific rules (1995, p. 146).

4. *The Background as a Mental Causal Mechanism*: What Searle wants to capture with the postulation of a Background is a causal mechanism that is mental. Not only are Background mechanisms described as "causal structures generally" (1995, p. 129), but as specifically neurophysiological structures (1995, p. 130; 1992, p. 188). While the latter stipulation can be understood to follow from Searle's overall position of "biological naturalism" in regard to mental phenomena (1992, p. 1), it also seems to mean that Background capacities, to the extent that they remain in the Background and do not manifest themselves in intentional states or behaviours, are simply "neurophysiological rather than psychological" (1992, p. 188). Although it is difficult to say for certain, Searle here seems to be saying that the Background as such simply is the capacity for certain neurophysiological events to occur and thus to produce mental events with their associated intentional contents. The relation of this view of the Background to the Background skills described above as automatised motor skills is obscure, as the latter seem more or less independent of the generation of psychological events.

But the postulation of the Background as a physical, causal mechanism also can be interpreted as showing the way out of a difficulty that turns up in a certain class of explanatory theories. These are theories of "practices" such as Bourdieu's, to which Searle's theory of the Background bears some resemblance (1995, p. 132; 1992, p. 177). ("Practices" can be defined, roughly, as consisting in the agreements and regularities, behavioural and otherwise, characterising given social groups and communities.) Such theories, as Turner has pointed out (1995), often suffer from a vagueness regarding "where" practices are located, what kind of entities they may be, and what exact causal role they may play in producing behaviour. By positing a Background that is in people's brains, Searle effectively addresses these issues by redescribing "practices" as ultimately physical mechanisms in individuals, and thus provides the kind of causal explanation that such theories require.

References: Lepore, E. and Van Gulick, R., eds. (1991). John Searle and His Critics. Cambridge, MA, Blackwell. Searle, J. (1978). "Literal Meaning." In Erkenntnis 1, pp. 207-224. Reprinted in Searle (1979). Searle, J. (1979). Expression and Meaning: Studies in the Theory of Speech Acts. New York, Cambridge University Press. Searle, J. (1983). Intentionality: An Essay in the Philosophy of Mind. New York, Cambridge University Press. Searle, J. (1991). "Response: The Background of Intentionality and Action." In Lepore and Van

Gulick (1991). Searle, J. (1992). The Rediscovery of the Mind. Cambridge, MA, MIT Press. Searle, J. (1995). The Construction of Social Reality. New York, Free Press. Turner, S. (1995). The Social Theory of Practices. Chicago, University of Chicago Press. See also intentionality, intentioninaction, implicit memory, tacit knowledge Daniel Barbiero Chris Eliasmith

Back-propagation, (Or "backpropagation") A learning algorithm for modifying a feed-forward neural network which minimises a continuous "error function" or "objective function." Back-propagation is a "gradient descent" method of training in that it uses gradient information to modify the network weights to decrease the value of the error function on subsequent tests of the inputs. Other gradient-based methods from numerical analysis can be used to train networks more efficiently.

Back-propagation makes use of a mathematical trick when the network is simulated on a digital computer, yielding in just two traversals of the network (once forward, and once back) both the difference between the desired and actual output, and the derivatives of this difference with respect to the connection weights.

Backtracking, A scheme for solving a series of sub-problems each of which may have multiple possible solutions and where the solution chosen for one sub-problem may affect the possible solutions of later sub-problems.

To solve the overall problem, we find a solution to the first sub-problem and then attempt to recursively solve the other sub-problems based on this first solution. If we cannot, or we want all possible solutions, we backtrack and try the next possible solution to the first sub-problem and so on. Backtracking terminates when there are no more solutions to the first sub-problem.

This is the algorithm used by logic programming languages such as Prolog to find all possible ways of proving a goal. An optimisation known as "intelligent backtracking" keeps track of the dependencies between sub-problems and only re-solves those which depend on an earlier solution which has changed.

Backtracking is one algorithm which can be used to implement non-determinism. It is effectively a depth-first search of a problem space.

Backward analysis, An analysis to determine properties of the inputs of a program from properties or context of the outputs. *E.g.* if the output of this function is needed then this argument is needed. Compare forward analysis.

Bacon Francis, english politician and philosopher (1561-1626). Bacon became Lord Chancellor of England in 1618, but was driven immediately from office under charges of official corruption. As an early empiricist, he rejected scholastic accounts of the natural world in favor of a new method for achieving knowledge, based exclusively on careful observation and cautious induction, which he described in The Advancement of Learning (1605) and Novum Organum (New Organon) (1620). Bacon warned that effective reasoning must be freed from the "idolatrous" influence of personal interest, human nature, social conventions, and academic philosophy. In The New Atlantis (1626), Bacon described the farreaching social consequences of his epistemological program. Bacon's Essays (1601) address the whole range of his philosophical and social interests. *Recommended Reading*: Selected Philosophical Works, ed. By Rose-Mary Sargent (Hackett, 1999); The Cambridge Companion to Bacon, ed. by Markku Peltonen (Cambridge, 1996); and Stephen Gaukroger, Francis Bacon and the Transformation of Early Modern Philosophy (Cambridge, 2001).

Bacon Roger, english philosopher (1214-1292) who translated many Aristotelean treatises from Arabic into Latin. Although passionately interested in alchemy and magic, Roger defended reliance upon mathematics and experimental methods for the improvement of human knowledge generally and theological understanding in particular in the Opus Maius (Greater Work) (1267) and On Experimental Science (1268). His novel educational doctrines were supposed to violate the condemnation of 1277, and much of Roger's later work, including the Compendium Studii Theologiae (1292) was suppressed. *Recommended Reading*: Roger Bacon's Philosophy of Nature, tr. By David C. Lindberg (St. Augustine, 1997) and Stewart C. Easten, Roger Bacon and His Search for a Universal Science (Greenwood, 1984).

Baculum argumentum ad, see appeal to force.

Bad faith, in the philosophy of Sartre, an effort to avoid anxiety by denying the full extent of one's own freedom. Bad faith, on this view, is an especially harmful variety of self-deception, since it forestalls authentic appropriation of responsibility for ourselves. *Recommended Reading*: Jean-Paul Sartre, Being and Nothin-gness, tr. by Hazel E. Barnes (Washington Square, 1993) and Ronald E. Santoni, Bad Faith, Good Faith, and Authenticity in Sartre's Early Philosophy (Temple, 1995).

Baier Annette, american moral philosopher (1929-). From a thoughtful reading of Hume, Baier derives an ethical stance that emphasizes the importance of membership within a moral community in A Progress of Sentiments: Reflections on Hume's Treatise (1991). In "What Do Women Want in a Moral Theory?" (1983), she argues that the concept of trust provides a vital link between traditional (male) accounts of rational obligation and the equally traditional (female) "ethics of love." Her most recent publications include and Moral Prejudices: Essays on Ethics (1994) and The Commons of the Mind (Open Court, 1997).

Baier Kurt, american moral philosopher (1917-). In The Moral Point of View (1958), Baier argues that practical reasoning that takes into account both individual and social considerations is the appropriate method for deciding "what is the best thing to do" in particular circumstances. Thus, we are moral because it is rational so to be, even when our private interests are outweighed by the welfare of others. *Recommended Reading*: Kurt Baier, The Rational and the Moral Order: The Social Roots of Reason and Morality (Open Court, 1994) and Reason, Ethics, and Society: Themes from Kurt Baier With His Responses, ed. by Kurt Baier and J.B. Schneewind (Open Court, 1996).

Bakunin Mikhail Alexandrovich, Russian philosopher and political anarchist (1814-1876); author of Marxism, Freedom, and the State (1872) and God and the State (1916). Bakunin participated in several European revolutionary movements in an effort to derive practical benefits from the theories of Marx and Proudhon. His philosophical writings emphasized the use of negative arguments as a dialectical method for defining creative results rather than relying upon pseudoscientific theories of government. *Recommended Reading*: The Basic Bakunin: Writings 1869-1871, ed. by Robert M. Cutler (Prometheus, 1992) and Brian Morris, Bakunin: The Philosophy of Freedom (Consortium, 1996).

Banach space, A complete normed vector space. Metric is induced by the norm: $d(x,y) = ||x - y||$. Completeness means that every Cauchy sequence converges to an element of the space. All finitedimensional real and complex normed vector spaces are complete and thus are Banach spaces. Using absolute value for the norm, the real numbers are a Banach space whereas the rationals are not. This is because there are sequences of rationals that converges to irrationals.

Several theorems hold only in Banach spaces, *e.g.* the Banach inverse mapping theorem. All finitedimensional real and complex vector spaces are Banach spaces. Hilbert spaces, spaces of integrable functions, and spaces of absolutely convergent series are examples of infinite-dimensional Banach spaces. Applications include wavelets, signal processing, and radar. [Robert E. Megginson, "An Introduction to Banach Space Theory", Graduate Texts in Mathematics, 183, Springer Verlag, September 1998].

Banach-Tarski paradox, It is possible to cut a solid ball into finitely many pieces (actually about half a dozen), and then put the pieces together again to get two solid balls, each the same size as the original.

This paradox is a consequence of the Axiom of Choice.

Barbara, name given by medieval logicians to any categorical syllogism whose standard form may be designated as AAA-1. *Example*: All finches are birds, and all cardinals are finches, so all cardinals are birds. This most common of all patterns in syllogistic reasoning is one of only fifteen forms that are always valid.

Baroco, name given by medieval logicians to a categorical syllogism whose standard form is AOO-2. Example: All cats are furry mammals, but some housepets are not furry mammals, so some housepets are not cats. This is another of the fifteen forms in which syllogisms are always valid.

Base, radix.

Base class, (Or "superclass") The class from which another class (a "subclass") inherits.

> "base class" is the term used in C++. The term "superclass" is perhaps confusing since objects of the subclass have a superset of the fields of objects in the superclass.
>
> See inheritance.

Bayes Thomas, english clergyman and mathematician (1702-1761). "Bayes theorem," first stated in his Essay towards solving a problem in the doctrine of chances (1764), proposes that evidence confirms the likelihood of an hypothesis only to the degree that the appearance of this evidence would be more probable with the assumption of the hypothesis than without it. *Recommended Reading*: Bradley P. Carlin and Thomas A. Louis, Bayes and Empirical Bayes

Methods for Data Analysis (CRC, 2000); Empirical Bayes and Likelihood Inference, ed. by S. E. Ahmed and N. Reid (Springer Verlag, 2000); and John Earman, Bayes or Bust?: A Critical Examination of Bayesian Confirmation (Bradford, 1992).

Bayle Pierre, although born in France and educated at Toulouse and Geneva, Pierre Bayle (1647-1706) spent most of his life in Holland, as the leading member of an active intellectual community at Rotterdam. The early writings of this French Protestant include a plea for broad political toleration of divergent opinions on religion. His greatest work is the incredibly ambitious Dictionnaire historique et critique (Historical and Critical Dictionary) (1697), which could reasonably be regarded as Western culture's first significant hypertext document. Although its articles about obscure ancient and modern figures sometimes contain little information of direct interest, Bayle used them as the startingpoints for a complex series of endnotes, sidenotes, and footnotes in which he addressed contemporary philosophical nand theological concerns. Bayle's predominant theme was a profound skepticism about human knowledge, derived originally from his admiration of the ancient Pyrrhonists but applied strictly to the new science and philosophy of his own time. He used the fact of animal thinking as evidence against Cartesian efforts to establish the unique status of an immaterial human soul. On the other hand, he also argued that the untenability of the primary / secondary quality distinction poses an insurmountable difficulty for both rationalism and empiricism. On religious matters, Bayle delighted in pointing out contradictions between theological tenets and the self-evident dictates of reason. This declaration of the fundamental irrationality of Christianity, however, left ample room for adherence to a rigorous fideism about god and revelation. Bayle's treatment of such issues posed important challenges for the development of modern thought and were greatly influential on the philosophy of Hume. *Recommended Reading*: Primary sources: Pierre Bayle, Historical and Critical Dictionary: Selections, ed. by Richard H. Popkin and Craig Bush (Hackett, 1991); Pierre Bayle, Political Writings (Cambridge, 2000). Secondary sources: Thomas M. Lennon, Reading Bayle (Toronto, 1999).

Beauty, the characteristic feature of things that arouse pleasure or delight, especially to the senses of a human observer. Thus, "beauty" is the most general term of aesthetic appreciation. Whether judgments about beauty are objective or subjective has been a matter of serious philosophical dispute. *Recommended Reading*: James Kirwan, Beauty (Manchester, 1999) and Philosophies of Art and Beauty, ed. by Hugh Bredin and Liberato Santoro-Brienza (Edinburgh, 2000).

Beauvoir Simone de, born and educated in Paris, Simone de Beauvoir (1908-1986) was among the first women permitted to complete a program of study at the Šcole Normale SupÈrieure. Through her lifelong friendship with Sartre, she contributed significantly to the development and expression of existentialist philosophy. In Le Deuxiëme Sexe (The Second Sex) (1949), de Beauvoir traced the development of male oppression through historical, literary, and mythical sources, attributing its contemporary effects on women to a systematic objectification of the male as a positive norm. This consequently identifies the female as Other, which commonly leads to a loss of social and personal identity, the variety of alienation unique to the experience of women. Her works of fiction focus on women who take responsibility for themselves by making life-altering decisions, and the many volumes of her own autobiography exhibit the application of similar principles in reflection on her own experiences. *Recommended Reading*: Primary sources: Simone De Beauvoir: A Critical Reader, ed. by Elizabeth Fallaize (Routledge, 1998); Simone de Beauvoir, The Second Sex, tr. by H. M. Parshley (Vintage, 1989); The Prime of Life: The Autobiography of Simone de Beauvoir (Marlowe, 1994). Secondary sources: Margaret A. Simons, Beauvoir and the Second Sex: Feminism, Race. and the Origins of Existentialism (Rowman & Littlefield, 1999); Debra B. Bergoffen, The Philosophy of Simone de Beauvoir: Gendered Phenomenologies, Erotic Generosities (SUNY, 1996); Simone de Beauvoir's the Second Sex: New Interdisciplinary Essays, ed. by Ruth Evans (St. Martin's, 1998); Feminist Interpretations of Simone De Beauvoir, ed. by Margaret A. Simons (Penn. State, 1995); Sally Scholz, On De Beauvoir (Wadsworth, 1999). Also see: French philosophy, feminist philosophy, and women in philosophy.

Bedeutung, Frege's German term for the reference of a concept. See Sinn / Bedeutung.

Begging the question, circular reasoning. The "informal fallacy" of (explicitly or implicitly) assuming the truth of the conclusion of an argument as one of the premises employed in an effort to demonstrate its truth. Example: "Since firefighters must be strong men willing to face danger every day, it follows that no woman can be a firefighter." Although arguments of this sort are formally valid because it is impossible for their conclusions to be false if their premises are true, they fail to provide logical support for their conclusions, which have already been accepted without proof at the outset. Known also as petitio principii. *Recommended Reading*: Douglas N. Walton, Begging the Question (Greenwood, 1991).

Begriff, german term for idea or concept.

Behaviourism, the theory according to which mental states can be analysed in terms of observable behaviour or dispositions to engage in such behaviour.

Behaviourism is now widely, but not universally, believed to have been discredited. The recent work of some researchers who focus on the dynamic, interactive, situated behaviour of cognitive systems have been re-exploring ideas central to behaviourism. Historically, behaviourism had two mains forms:

1. Methodological behaviourists, also called "psychological behaviourists', claim that the proper domain of psychology is the study of behaviour. Appeals to unobservable inner states are both method-ologically intractable (*e.g.* the inconsistent first person reports of introspectionists), and unnecessary (we can control and predict behaviour by appeal to external variables that systematically induce behavioural responses as a consequence of conditioning or reinforcement historics). This position was spear-headed by J. B. Watson and most influentially defended by his student, B. F. Skinner. Sometimes

metho-dological behaviourists express agnosticism about the existence of inner mental states, and sometimes they express scepticism, comparing such states to phlogiston, caloric acid, and other posits of discredited theories. Methodological behaviourism dominated American psychology between 1913, when Watson wrote his seminal defence, and 1957, when Chomsky published a devastating review of Skinner's behavioural analysis of language.

2. In its strongest form, philosophical behaviourism, also called 'analytic behaviourism" and "logical behaviourism', is the view that psychological terms can be translated without loss of meaning into behavioural terms. Weakened versions replace translatability with weaker forms of semantic correlation (*e.g.*, co-extensionality), and include neural and other physical terms among those in terms of which mental states can be characterised. Philosophical behaviourism is associated with the Logical Positivists (most notably, Hempel), who endorsed the verifiability principle, according to which the meaning of a term is given by its conditions of verification. Since statements ascribing mental edicates are verified by observing behaviour, behavioural tests enter into the meanings of those mental predicates. A similar position was influentially defended by Ryle. Some subsequent critics of logical positivism continued to endorse their semantically motivated scepticism about inner mental states and their preoccupation with observable behaviour (*e.g.*, Quine and Wittgenstein), but such scepticism waned considerably with the rise of the psychophysical identity theory and functionalism in the 1950s and'60s. *References*: Logical behaviourism Biblio Block, N. (1981). Psychologism and behaviorism. Philosophical Review 90:5-43. Skinner, B.F. (1957). Verbal behavior. New York: Appleton-Century-Crofts. See dynamic system.

Belief, affirmation of, or conviction regarding, the truth of a proposition, especially when one is not (yet) in possession of evidence adequate to justify a claim that the proposition is known with certainty. *Recommended Reading*: Kenneth Malcolm Sayre, Belief and Knowledge: Mapping the Cognitive Landscape (Rowman-Littlefield, 1997) and Michael Williams, Groundless Belief (Princeton, 1999).

Belief revision, The area of theory change in which preservation of the information in the theory to be changed plays a key role.

A fundamental issue in belief revision is how to decide what information to retract in order to maintain consistency, when the addition of a new belief to a theory would make it inconsistent. Usually, an ordering on the sentences of the theory is used to determine priorities among sentences, so that those with lower priority can be retracted. This ordering can be difficult to generate and maintain.

The postulates of the AGM Theory for Belief Revision describe minimal properties a revision process should have.

Bentham Jeremy, English philosopher and political radical (1748-1832). In A Fragment on Government (1776) and An Introduction to the Principles of Morals and Legislation (1789) Bentham outlined an ethical system based on a purely hedonistic calculation of the utility particular actions with a view to the greatest happiness of all, a view later to be defended in modified form by Mill and others. Bentham supposed that consistent application of this principle in social and political life would resolve many difficulties in human conduct, using proportional but perfectly certain punishment to render unacceptably painful to the prospective criminal any behavior that would otherwise be likely to cause injury to others. Bentham's unusual bequest still remains at University College, London. *Recommended Reading*: The Works of Jeremy Bentham, ed. by John Bowring (Thoemmes, 1997); Ross Harrison, Bentham (Routledge, 1999); Essays on Bentham, ed. by H. L. A. Hart (Oxford, 1983); and Gerald J. Postema, Jeremy Bentham: Moral, Political, and Legal Philosophy (Ashgate, 2001).

Berdyaev Nicolai Alexandrovich, ukrainian philosopher (1874-1948) who participated in the Revolution but was exiled to France in 1922. Distressed by totalitarian developments in communism, Berdyaev adopted a religious version of existentialism in which the themes of anxiety and authenticity are conveyed through the medium of traditional Christian mythology about sin and redemption. Vselenskost' i konfessionalism (Universality and Confessionalism) (1933) exemplifies the passionate individualism of this self-styled "believing freethinker," which seldom won institutional approval. *Recommended Reading*: Nicolai Berdyaev, The Bourgeois Mind and Other Essays (Ayer, 1934); Nicolai Berdyaev, Origin of Russian Communism (Michigan, 1960); Nicolai Berdyaev, The Russian Idea (Lindisfarne, 1992); and Howard A. Slaatte, Personality, Spirit, and Ethics: The Ethics of Nicholas Berdyaev (Peter Lang, 1997).

Bergmann Gustav, Gustav Bergmann (1906-1987) studied mathematics, law, and philosophy in his native Vienna and participated in the Vienna Circle discussions of logical positivism. After emigrating to the United States in 1938, Bergmann taught in the Departments of Philosophy and Psychology at the University of Iowa for forty years, where his Philosophy of Science (1957) was the basis for a popular undergraduate course of study. Although he shared many of the substantive convictions of his fellow positivists, Bergmann was more keenly aware than most of the metaphysical commitments presupposed within their ways of thinking. Pursuing methods of philosophical analysis derived from those of Moore, the early Wittgenstein, and Carnap, Bergmann sought to resolve philosophical problems by informally discussing the construction of an "ideal language" whose semantic features would indicate the most fundamental structure of reality. Thus, for Bergmann, the basic question of ontology is: what kinds of things must exist in order for us to devise a formal language in which everything can be perspicuously expressed? In three collections of essays, The Metaphysics of Logical Positivism (1954), Meaning and Existence (1959), and Logic and Reality (1964), Bergmann sharply criticized the philosophical methods and results of his contemporaries, developing an extreme realism that drew him ever further from the mainstream of twentieth-century analysis. His Realism: A Critique of Brentano and Meinong (1967) returned to the work of Brentano and Meinong, significant figures from the turn of the century, for an understanding of philosophical difficulties against the background of which he could best express his own views. The posthumously published New Foundations of Ontology (1992) contains Bergmann's final reflections on the serious issues with which he had been concerned for many decades. Bergmann's contributions to philosophy are explained, honored, and challenged in a collection of essays by his former students and colleagues, The Ontological Turn (1974). *Recommended Reading*: Primary sources: Gustav Bergmann, The Philosophy of Science (Wisconsin, 1966). Gustav Bergmann, The Metaphysics of Logical Positivism (Wisconsin, 1954). Gustav Bergmann, Meaning and Existence (Wisconsin, 1959). Gustav Bergmann, Logic and Reality (Wisconsin, 1964). Gustav Bergmann, Realism: A Critique of Brentano and Meinong (Wisconsin, 1967). Gustav Bergmann, New Foundations of Ontology, ed. by William Heald and Edwin B. Allaire (Wisconsin, 1992). Secondary sources: The Ontological Turn, ed. by Moltke S. Gram and E. D. Klemke (Iowa, 1974).

Bergson Henri, french philosopher (1859-1941). Rejecting sterile mechanistic accounts of the natural world, including those of Darwin and Spencer, Bergson developed an account that emphasized the subjective experience of time as the ground for human freedom in Essai sur les donnÈes immÈdiates de la conscience (Time and Free Will: An Essay on the Immediate Data of Consciousness) (1889), Matiëre et mÈmoire (Matter and Memory) (1896), and The Creative Mind: An Introduction to Metaphysics (1934). In L'Švolution crÈatrice (Creative Evolution) (1907) Bergson argued that thought, creativity, motion, and evolution are all products of a creative impulse (Fr. Èlan vital) that emerges in opposition to material entropy. Bergson won the Nobel Prize for literature in 1927. *Recommended Reading*: Leszek Kolakowski, Bergson (St. Augustine, 2000); F. C. T. Moore, Bergson: Thinking Backwards (Cambridge, 1996); and John Mullarkey, Bergson and Philosophy (Notre Dame, 2000).

Berkeley, George (1685-1753), Irish philosopher and clergyman, generally regarded as the founder of the modern school of idealism. Berkeley held that matter cannot be conceived to exist independent of the mind; the phenomena of sense can be explained only by supposing a deity that continually evokes perception of them in the human mind.

Born in County Kilkenny, Ireland, on March 12, 1685, Berkeley studied at Trinity College, Dublin, where he became a Fellow in 1707. In 1710 he published *The Principles of Human Knowledge*. When it failed to convince people of his theory, he published a more popular version, *The Three Dialogues Between Hylas and Philonous,* in 1713. Both statements of his philosophy were regarded as foolish by his contemporaries. Meanwhile, Berkeley had been ordained a deacon in the Anglican Church of Ireland and became increasingly prominent as a churchman. In 1728 he moved to America to attempt to found a missionary college in Bermuda. Although he abandoned his plan in 1732, he had a great effect on higher education while in America, assisting in the development of Yale and Columbia universities and a number of other schools.

In 1734 he was made Bishop of Cloyne, remaining in this position until his retirement. He died on January 14, 1753.

Berkeley's philosophical theory was developed as an answer to the scepticism and atheism that he felt to be implicit in contemporary philosophy, influenced as it was by John Locke's "way of ideas". Locke had distinguished between the ideas of which people are immediately aware in perception, and the physical objects that are the causes of those ideas. Berkeley argued that, since all that human beings can ever be aware of are ideas (of sight, sound, touch, etc.), any belief in material objects distinct from these ideas (but causing them) is empty speculation, unjustifiable and meaningless. To close the gap that has opened between ideas and physical objects, it must be recognized that, for objects such as tables and trees, being consists in being perceived ("*esse est percipi*"). They do not exist outside of the mind. The difference then, between a real table and a hallucinatory table lies in the orderliness, arrangement, and regularity of the ideas that go together to constitute the real one, but not the other.

Minds, unlike objects such as trees and tables, are active. Their being consists in perceiving, in having ideas. Of the ideas present to the minds, some lie within a person's control (they can be conjured up), while others arise regardless of the will (sights and sounds force themselves on the consciousness). Berkeley argued that those ideas that arise regardless of the will must depend upon some other will, namely the will of God. Thus, what are taken to be material objects that exist beyond the mind are ideas in the infinite mind of God.

The relation between the ideas in God's mind and the corresponding ideas in human minds creates difficulties for Berkeley's philosophy. There cannot, it seems, be one idea, shared between God and people, since God's ideas are so much fuller—unless, that is, people are prepared to admit that there are many things about their own ideas of which they are unaware. If, on the other hand, the ideas in God's mind are different from those in people's minds, the gap that existed in Locke's philosophy—namely that between ideas in consciousness and the physical things that cause them—threatens to re-emerge as a gap between the ideas in consciousness and the ideas in God's mind that also give cause to them. Thus, Berkeley's theory falls into the same trap as that of Locke.

There is also a problem for Berkeley in explaining how it is possible to talk of minds at all, especially since he tends to explain the grasping of meanings as the having of appropriate ideas. Berkeley was aware of the difficulty, but argued that since minds are active and ideas are passive, an (accurate) idea of the mind cannot be formed. He maintained that it is possible to speak meaningfully of minds by forming the appropriate "notion", yet he explains very little about the nature of notions, other than the fact that they are not ideas.

Berkeley's philosophical system produced few followers, despite his claim that it was in accordance with common sense. Nevertheless, his criticisms of arguments for an external world separate from ideas were forceful and have influenced philosophers ever since.

Irish clergyman George Berkeley (1685-1753) completed his most significant philosophical work before turning thirty, during his years as a student, fellow, and teacher at Trinity College, Dublin. Using material from his collegiate notebooks on philosophy, he developed a series of texts devoted to various aspects of a single central thesis: that matter does not exist. In An Essay Towards a New Theory of Vision (1709), for example, he argued that the phenomena of visual sensation can all be explained without presupposing the reality of external material substances; the objects we see are merely ideas in our minds and that of god. Berkeley spent most of his mature years in London, travelling briefly to Rhode Island in the vain hope of securing financial support for a college to be established in Bermuda. He was appointed Anglican bishop of Cloyne in 1734. His later writings, which rarely receive philosophical attention, include: criticisms of Newton's calculus and theory of space in De Motu (1721) and The Analyst (1734); a defence of traditional Christian doctrine in the Alciphron (1734); and, in the interminable Siris (1744), a lengthy disquisition on the presumed benefits to health of "tarwater." It is the earlier immaterialist philosophy, in which he employed strictly empiricist principles in defence of the view that only minds or spirits exist, for which Berkeley is now remembered. He opened A Treatise concerning the Principles of Knowledge (1710) rather technically, with an extended attack on Locke's theory of abstract ideas. The book continues with arguments designed to show that sensible qualities-both secondary and primary can exist only when perceived, as ideas in our minds. Since physical objects are, on Berkeley's view, nothing more than collections of such qualities, these sensible objects, too, are merely ideas. In what he believed to be his most devastating point, Berkeley argued that it is literally inconceivable that anything like a material substance could exist independently of the spirits or active thinking substances that perceive it. Through the rem-ainder of the Principles, Berkeley tried to distinguish his position from that of Malebranche, defended its application to the achievements of modern science, and extolled its beneficial consequences for traditional religion. The same central doctrine, supported by a very similar train of thought, is expressed in different form in Three Dialogoues between Hylas and Philonous (1713). Here Berkeley spoke through Philonous ("Mind-lover"), who tries to convince his reluctant friend Hylas ("Woody") that it is only by rejecting the artificial philosophical concept of material substance that skepticism can be finally defeated and the truths of commonsense secured.

Recommended Reading: Primary sources: The Works of George Berkeley, ed. by A. A. Luce and T. E. Jessop. (London: T. Nelson, 1948-1957); George Berkeley, Principles of Human Knowledge / Three Dialogues Between Hylas and Philonous, ed. by Roger Woolhouse (Penguin, 1988). Secondary sources: Kenneth P. Winkler, Berkeley: An Interpretation (Clarendon, 1994); Geoffrey J. Warnock, Berkeley (Penguin, 1969); Ian C. Tipton, Berkeley: The Philosophy of Immaterialism

(Thoemmes, 1994); David Berman, Berkeley (Routledge, 1999); Berkeley: Critical and Interpretive Essays, ed. by Colin Murray Turbayne (Minnesota, 1982); Douglas M. Jesseph, Berkeley's Philosophy of Mathematics (Chicago, 1993); George J. Stack, Berkeley's Analysis of Perception (Peter Lang, 1992); Margaret Atherton, Berkeley's Revolution in Vision (Cornell, 1990).

Berlin Isaiah, Russian-British historian, diplomat, and political philosopher (1909-1997). In Four Essays on Liberty (1969), Berlin drew an important distinction between the positive freedom to act and the negative freedom from interference in so acting. Societies that differ in their conceptions of liberty, Berlin argued, are likely to exhibit profoundly different social structures. Karl Marx: His Life and Environment (1939) and Historical Inevitability (1954) criticize the philosophy of Marx, with special treatment of his view of history. *Recommended Reading*: Isaiah Berlin, The Crooked Timber of Humanity, ed. by Henry Hardy (Princeton, 1998); The Proper Study of Mankind: An Anthology of Essays, ed. by Roger Hausheer and Noel Annan (Farrar, Strauss, and Giroux, 2000); John Gray, Isaiah Berlin (Princeton, 1997); and The Legacy of Isaiah Berlin, ed. by Mark Lilla, Ronald Dworkin, and Robert Silvers (NY Review, 2001).

Bernstein condition, Processes cannot execute in parallel if one effects values used by the other. Nor can they execute in parallel if any subsequent process uses data effected by both, *i.e.* whose value might depend on the order of execution.

Besant, Annie (1847-1933), British theosophist and nationalist leader in India, born in London. Besant became interested in socialist and freethought movements early on, and wrote pamphlets defending them. She became closely associated with the British social reformer Charles Bradlaugh and later with the Fabian Society. She and Bradlaugh republished an old pamphlet, *The Fruits of Philosophy,* which advocated birth control; for this, they were brought to trial on a charge of obscenity. In 1889 she joined the Theosophical Society, serving as president from 1907 until her death.

Shortly after joining the society Besant moved to India, where she later became a leader of a Hindu nationalist movement. She founded Central Hindu College at Varanasi in 1898 and organized the Indian Home Rule League, becoming president in 1916. She was elected president of the Indian National Congress in 1917, and general secretary of the National Convention of India in 1923. Besant lectured frequently on theosophy and in 1926 travelled widely with her Indian protégé Jiddu Krishnamurti, whom she declared to be the new Messiah. Her works include *Reincarnation* (1892), *The Basis of Morality* (1915), *A World Religion* (1916), and *India, Bond or Free?* (1926).

Bewusstsein, german term for consciousness.

Bivalence principle of, supposition that every proposition must be either true or false. The status of this supposition is controversial, especially with respect to future propositions about human action. Thus, for example, if "I will vacuum the carpet tomorrow." were regarded as already true (or false) today, it would seem that I cannot freely choose whether or not to clean. Note the difference between bivalence and excluded middle. *Recommended Reading*: Ermanno Bencivenga, Logic, Bivalence and Denotation (Ridgeview, 1991).

Blanshard Brand, American philosopher and long-time professor at Yale University (1892-1987). In The Nature of Thought (1939), Blanshard defended absolute idealism and argued that causal necessity is a genuine feature of the natural world. According to Blanshard's Reason and Analysis (Open Court, 1962), the philosophical methods of Anglo-American philosophers during the twentieth century were fundamentally misguided. He also rejected the prevalent non-cognitivism of twentieth-century ethicists by defending a thoroughly naturalistic moral theory in Reason and Goodness (1962). *Recommended Reading*: Brand Blanshard, On Philosophical Style and Philosophy of Brand Blanshard, ed. by Paul Arthur Schilpp (Open Court, 1980).

Blavatsky, Helena Petrovna (1831-1891), Russian-born American leader of the modern religiophilosophical system known as Theosophy. Originally named Helena Hahn, she was born of German parents in Yekaterinoslav (now Dniprope-trovs'k, Ukraine). At the age of 16 she married a much older man but left him after a few months. She spent the next 20 years travelling in Europe, Asia, and the United States, later claiming to have studied for seven years under Hindu mahatmas (masters) in the East. After a narrow escape from drowning at sea, she turned to spiritualism and claimed to possess psychic powers.

In 1873 Madame Blavatsky, as she was always known, went to New York. Within two years she was to become one of the founders—and eventually the central figure—of the Theosophical Society, a small but active international group of occultists who believed in reinc-arnation as the necessary path to the ultimate, inevitable purification of humanity. She became an American citizen, but in 1878 she established a new headquarters in India. Soon she was faced with dissension, charges of chicanery and plagiarism, and considerable notoriety. She maintained to the end of her life, however, that the mahatmas had actually been able to pass on to her their own uncommonly developed spiritual state.

Blavatsky's major works, *Isis Unveiled* (1877) and *The Secret Doctrine* (1888), became the textbooks of the Theosophical Society.

Bocardo, name given by medieval logicians to a categorical syllogism whose standard form has the mood and figure designated as OAO-3. *Example*: Some local jails are not maximum-security prisons, but since all local jails are correctional institutions, it follows that some correctional institutions are not maximum-security prisons. This is one of the fifteen forms of valid syllogism.

Boethius (c. 480-524), Roman philosopher and statesman. Boethius gained the esteem and confidence of Theodoric, King of the Ostrogoths, then the ruler of Rome, and in 510 was made a consul. He was later accused by his enemies of plotting treason, and, although innocent, was imprisoned in Pavia and executed. During his imprisonment he wrote *De Consolatione Philosophiae* (The Consolation of Philosophy, c. 523), a philosophical work that, although written by a non-Christian, contained so many elements of Christian ethics that it was highly regarded in Europe during medieval times. Many translations of the work were made, notably (in England) by King Alfred the Great and by the poet Geoffrey Chaucer. Boethius also wrote treatises on logic that profoundly influenced the terminology of medieval logic; translations and commentaries on the works of Aristotle, from which medieval scholars largely derived their knowledge of the Greek philosopher; and works on music, arithmetic, and theology.

Boethius Anicius Manlius Severinus, Roman logician (480-524). His Com-mentary on the Isagoge of Porphyry (itself a discussion of Aristotle's Categories) carefully distinguished Aristotelean essences from Platonic Forms, setting the basic terms employed in subsequent medieval discussion of the problem of universals. De consolatione philosophiae (The Consolation of Philosophy), written during the imprisonment that preceded his execution, considers the possibility of achieving human happiness despite the inescapable presence of evil, extols the benefits of reason even in the face of misfortune and bad advice, and proposes a compatibilist account of human freedom in the face of divine fore knowledge. *Recom-mended Reading*: Five Texts on the Mediaeval Problem of Universals, ed. by Paul Vincent Spade (Hackett, 1994).

Boetius of Dacia, Swedish Dominican philosopher (1230-1285). Doubts about personal immortality and the espousal of a fideistic account of the relation between faith and reason during his service in Romania resulted in the condemnation of his teachings, along with those of Siger of Brabant and the other radical Aristoteleans. *Recommended Reading*: Boethius of Dacia: On the Supreme Good, on the Eternity of the World, on Dreams, tr. by John F. Wippel (Pontifical Inst., 1987).

Bohr Niels Henrik David, Danish physicist (1885-1962). Although best known for his contributions to atomic theory and quantum mechanics, Bohr also reflected on epistemological issues, defending a sophisticated variety of cultural relativism. Bohr won the Nobel Prize in Physics in 1922. *Recommended Reading*: Dugald Murdoch, Niels Bohr's Philosophy of Physics (Cambridge, 1989); Abraham Pais, Niels Bohr's Times: In Physics, Philosophy, and Polity (Oxford, 1993); and Andrew Whitaker, Einstein, Bohr and the Quantum Dilemma (Cambridge, 1996).

Bolzano Bernard, Austrian mathematician, theologian, and philosopher (1781-1848). In opposition to the idealism of Kant and Hegel, Bolzano maintained that numbers, ideas, and truths all exist independently of the human beings who think about them. His Wissenschaftslehre (1837) and Gr–ssenlehre (1850) offer a philosophical foundation for mathematics, employing a modern theory of classes to define the real numbers. Bolzano's work was a significant influence on that of Husserl, Frege, Lukasiewicz, and Tarski. *Recommended Reading*: Jan Sebestik, Logique et mathÈmatique chez Bernard Bolzano (Paris, 1992).

Bonaventure, Franciscan philosopher and theologian, known also as Giovanni di Fidanza (1221-1274). Following Augustine, Bonaventure held that reason is valuable only in support of faith. Bonaventure's philosophy was predominantly neo-platonic; he accepted Aristotle's philosophical principles only when they could be used in service of his Christian aims, but argued against the eternal reality of the universe. In Itinerarium mentis in deum (The Journey of the Mind to God) (1259) he argued that human beings, as emanations of the deity, embody a footprint (Lat. Vestiguum) of the divine nature. *Recommended Reading*: Etienne Gilson, The Philosophy of St. Bonaventure (Franciscan, 1965).

Boole George, British logician (1815-1864) whose The Mathematical Analysis of Logic (1847) proposed the "Boolean algebra" of propositional connectives representing negation and conjunction. An Investigation into the Laws of Thought (1859) further develops a symbolic system for the expression and evaluation ·of categorical syllog-isms, understood as elements in the logic of classes. *Recommended Reading*: A Boole Anthology: Recent and Classical Studies in the Logic of George Boole, ed. by James Gasser (Kluwer, 2000).

Bordo Susan, American philosopher (1947-). InThe Flight to Objectivity: Essays on Cartesianism and Culture (1987) she explores the masculinization of thought in Cartesian modernism. Bordo's Unbearable Weight: Feminism, Western Culture, and the Body (1993) is a cultural exploration of the significance of social constructions of the human body. Similar themes are explored in Bordo's Twilight Zones: The Hidden Life of Cultural Images from Plato to O.J. (1997) and The Male Body: A New Look at Men in Public and in Private (1999).

Bosanquet Bernard, British philosopher (1848-1923) who defended a modified version of Hegel's absolute idealism in Logic, or the Morphology of Knowledge (1888), The Principle of Individuality and Value (1912), and The Value and Destiny of the Individual (1914). According to Bosanquet, all contradictions are merely apparent and are wholly harmonized as part of the Absolute, a process said to account for the possibility of judgments about beauty in his History of Aesthetics (1892). Bosanquet further argued in The Philosophical Theory of the State (1899) that individual human beings are properly understood only in terms of their social and cultural efforts at transcendence. *Recommended Read-ing*: The Collected Works of Bernard Bosanquet, ed. by William Sweet (Thoemmes, 1999).

Boundless the, the eternal, infinite, undifferentiated stuff from which Anaximander believed the material world to be formed.

Boole George, British logician (1815-1864) whose The Mathematical Analysis of Logic (1847) proposed the "Boolean algebra" of propositional connectives representing negation and conjunction. An Investigation into the Laws of Thought (1859) further develops a symbolic system for the expression and evaluation of catego-rical syllogisms, understood as elements in the logic of classes. *Recommended Reading*: A Boole Anthology: Recent and Classical Studies in the Logic of George Boole, ed. by James Gasser (Kluwer, 2000).

Bordo Susan, American philosopher (1947-). InThe Flight to Objectivity: Essays on Cartesianism and Culture (1987) she explores the masculinization of thought in Cartesian modernism. Bordo's Unbearable Weight: Feminism, Western Culture, and the Body (1993) is a cultural exploration of the significance of social constructions of the human body. Similar themes are explored in Bordo's Twilight Zones: The Hidden Life of Cultural Images from Plato to O.J. (1997) and The Male Body: A New Look at Men in Public and in Private (1999).

Bosanquet Bernard, British philosopher (1848-1923) who defended a modified version of Hegel's absolute idealism in Logic, or the Morphology of Knowledge (1888), The Principle of Individuality and Value (1912), and The Value and Destiny of the Individual (1914). According to Bosanquet, all contradictions are merely apparent and are wholly harmonized as part of the Absolute, a process said to account for the possibility of judgments about beauty in his History of Aesthetics (1892). Bosanquet further argued in The Philosophical Theory of the State (1899) that individual human beings are properly understood only in terms of their social and cultural efforts at transcendence. *Recommended Rea-ding*: The Collected Works of Bernard Bosanquet, ed. by William Sweet (Thoemmes, 1999).

Boundless the, the eternal, infinite, undifferentiated stuff from which Anaximander believed the material world to be formed.

Bound variable, 1. A bound variable or formal argument in a function definition is replaced by the actual argument when the function is applied. In the lambda abstraction x is the

$\backslash x. M$

bound variable. However, x is a free variable of the term M when M is considered on its own. M is the scope of the binding of x.

2. In predicate logic, an individual variable at least one of whose occurrences lies within the scope of a quantifier on the same letter. Because other occurrences may be free, a variable may be both free and bound in the same wffs. to bind a variable to add a quantifier on an individual variable, x, to a wff so that one or more previously free occurrences of x lie inside the scope of that quantifier. See closure, free variable

Bourgeois, in its original designation the term referred to the medieval "middle class" of shopkeepers and artisans. In Communist theory it refers to the capitalist class of owners of the means and forces of production which, as Marx recounts, is historically descended from this medieval middle class. *Contrast*: proletarian. See: communism.

Boyle Robert, English scientist (1627-1692) who discovered the relationship between the temperature, pressure, and volume of a gas and founded The Royal Society. In The Skeptical Chymist (1661) and The Origins of Forms and Qualities (1666), Boyle helped to establish the discipline of chemistry and drew a careful distinction between primary and secondary qualities, later used by his friend Locke. A principled corpuscularian, Boyle defended the reliability of mechanistic philosophy in The Excellency and Grounds of the Corpuscular or Mechanical Philos-ophy (1674) and in extended controversies with Spinoza and Henry More. Boyle employed the teleological argument for god's existence and defended a traditional theology in The Excellence of Theology (1674) and The Christian Virtuoso (1690). *Recommended Reading*: Selected Philosophical Papers of Robert Boyle (Hackett, 1991); Robert Boyle on Natural Philosophy, ed. by Marie Boas Hall (Greenwood, 1980); Peter Alexander, Ideas, Qualities and Corpuscles: Locke and Boyle on the External World; Peter R. Anstey, The Philosophy of Robert Boyle (Routledge, 2000); and Rose-Mary Sargent, The Diffident Naturalist: Robert Boyle and the Philosophy of Experiment (Chicago, 1995).

Bradley Francis Herbert, English philosopher (1846-1924) and absolute idealist. His Ethical Studies (1876) criticized Mill's utilitarianism and defended an ethics of self-realization, understood as the conquest of the bad self by the good. Bradley's metaphysical views, akin to those of Hegel, with a special emphasis on the internal relations of the Absolute are developed at length in Appearance and Reality (1893) and defended in Essays on Truth and Reality (1914). Bradleian metaphysics became the primary target for the anti-idealistic polemics of Moore and Russell. *Recommended Reading*: F. H. Bradley, Writings on Logic and Metaphysics, ed. by James W. Allard and Guy Stock (Oxford, 1994); The Collected Works of F. H. Bradley, ed. by W.J. Mander and Carol Keene (Thoemmes, 1999); Phillip Ferreira, Bradley and the Structure of Knowledge (SUNY, 1999); and W. J. Mander, Perspectives on the Logic and Metaphy-sics of F.H. Bradley (St. Augustine, 1997).

Branch, 1. An edge in a tree. 2. A jump.

Brentano Franz Clemens, German philosopher and psychologist (1838-1917). An early phenomenologist, Brentano proposed the notion that intentionality is the mark of the mental in Psychologie vom empirischen Standpunkt (Psychology from an Empirical Standpoint) (1874). He developed an associated theory of truth in Wahrheit und Evidenz (The True and the Evident) (1930) and applied phenomenological methods to ethical issues in Vom Ursprung sittlicher Erkenntnis (The Origin of Our Knowledge of Right and Wrong) (1889), defending a pluralistic view of objective intrinsic value. *Recommended Reading*: Victor Velarde, On Brentano (Wadsworth, 1999) and Barry Smith, Austrian Philosophy: The Legacy of Franz Brentano (Open Court, 1996).

Broad Charlie Dunbar, English philosopher (1887-1971). Although he criticized the extravagant speculation of absolute idealists like McTaggart in his Examination of McTaggart's Philosophy (1933, 1938), Broad was more willing than his contemporaries Russell and Moore to engage in metaphysical as well as epistemological theorizing. The philosophy of mind expressed in Scientific Thought (1923) and The Mind and its Place in Nature (1925) clearly defended the reality of physical and mental phenomena, including (notoriously) the possibility of genuine parapsychological pheno-mena. *Recommended Reading*: Philosophy of C. D. Broad, ed. by Paul A. Schilpp (Open Court, 1964).

Bruno Giordano, (1548-1600) Italian philosopher of the Renaissance and follower of Nicolas of Cusa. An aposotate Dominican, Bruno tried to incorporate both Copernican astronomy and hermetic mysticism into an atomistic physics. His evident inclination toward pantheism and explicit identification of infinite matter as the eternal substance of the universe in Dell'infinito, universo e mondi (On the Infinite Universe and Worlds) (1584), De Gli Eroici Furori (The Heroic Frenzies) (1585) and De immense et innumerabilibus (1591) earned him the condemnation of the church, which expressed its displeasure by burning him at the stake in Rome. *Recommended Reading*: J. Lewis McIntyre, Giordano Bruno (Kessinger, 1997) and Frances A. Yates, Giordano Bruno and the Hermetic Tradition (Chicago, 1991).

Buber Martin, Austrian-Jewish theologian (1878-1965). In Ich und Du (I and Thou) (1922) Buber suggested that genuinely religious experiences must involve reciprocal intersubjective relations between persons rather than a merely objective apprehension of abstract reality. After emigrating to Israel Buber served as first President of the Academy of Science and Humanities. *Recommended Reading*: Dan Avnon, Martin Buber: The Hidden Dialogue (Rowman-Littlefield, 1998) and Martin Buber and the Human Sciences, ed. by Maurice Friedman and Pat Boni (SUNY, 1996).

Buddhism, individualistic religious and philosophical tradition that originated with the historical Buddha (*c.* 563-483 B.C.) in India and spread throughout the Orient. In this century, it has also spread to America, in the form of Zen Buddhism. Zen is the Japanese name for the form of Buddhism that was most successful in China, Ch'an, which represented a syncretism of Indian Mahayana Buddhism and traditional Chinese beliefs like Confucianism and Taoism. Buddhism, in fact, is quite similar to Taoism: both stress the belief that we cannot trust in the world of appearances and that there is an underlying unity to the universe (see holism); both emphasize a certain level of detachment from worldly affairs (sometimes bordering on asceticism) and the development of a disposition that enables one to enjoy and understand the world. Buddhism transcendentalism puts a great value on ultimate detachment and eternal enlightenment, known as Nirvana. (References from holism, humanism, individualism, Neo-Confucianism, and Taoism.)

Bundle theory, belief that an object comprises only the features or properties it exhibits,without requiring the unifying presence of any unde-rlying substance. Most notably, Hume supposed that the human self or mind is nothing more than a bundle of perceptions linked to each other only by contingent associations.

Buridan Jean, French logician and philosopher who first developed a theory of inertial motion (1295-1356). His commentaries on Aristotle's theory of action made famous the predicament involved in choosing (as must "Buridan's ass") between two equally attractive alternatives. Although he defended nominalism as a solution to the problem of universals, Buridan rejected the extreme version developed by his teacher, Ockham. *Recommended Reading*: Jean Buridan's Logic: The Treatise on Supposition, the Treatise on Consequences, ed. by Peter King (Reidel, 1986) and The Metaphysics and Natural Philosophy of John Buridan, ed. by J. M. M. H. Thijssen and Jack Zupko (Brill, 2000).

Burke Edmund, Irish politician and philosopher (1729-1797). In the early A Philosophical Enquiry into the

Origin of our Ideas of the Sublime and Beautiful (1757) Burke offered an analysis of aesthetic judgment that greatly influenced the work of Kant. Burke's Reflections on the Revolution in France (1790) includes an explicit criticism of the social contract theory, an extended appeal for the preser-vation of established social and political institutions, and the defence of a society ruled by respect for the rights and privileges revealed in traditional value-systems, including established religion. *Recommended Reading*: The Portable Edmund Burke, ed. by Isaac Kramnick (Penguin, 1999); The Enduring Edmund Burke: Bicentennial Essays, ed. by Conor C. O'Brien, Bruce Frohnen, Peter J. Stanlis, and Peter Tann (Intercollegiate, 1997); and Edmund Burke: A Genius Reconsidered, ed. by Roger Scruton (Intercollegiate, 1997).

Butler Joseph, English clergyman and philosopher (1692-1752). Butler's Fifteen Sermons upon Human Nature (1726) attempted to establish human morality in the moderation of self-love by the authority of a divinely-provided conscience, and his The Analogy of Religion, Natural and Revealed, to the Constitution and Course of Nature (1736) defended revealed religion in the face of deistic challenges. *Recommended Reading*: Terence Penelhum, Butler (Routledge, 1986).

Caird Edward, Scottish Hegelian philosopher. Caird (1835-1908) was one of the first generation of 'British idealists,' whose philosophical work was largely in reaction to the then-dominant empiricist and associat-ionist views of Alexander Bain (1818-1903) and J.S. Mill. Best known for his studies of Kant—A Critical Account of the Philosophy of Kant (1877) and The Critical Philosophy of Immanuel Kant (1889)—and Hegel-Hegel (1883), Caird also exercised a strong influence on later idealists such as John Watson and Bernard Bosanquet, particularly concerning the development of an 'evolutionary' account of religion; see his two series of Gifford lectures, The Evolution of Religion (1893), and The Evolution of Theology in the Greek Philos-ophers (1904). (Contributed by Will Sweet.) *Recommended Reading*: The Collected Works of Edward Caird, ed. by Colin Tyler (Thoemmes, 1999).

Cambridge Platonists, an influential group of seventeenth-century English philosophers and latitudi-narian theologians who rejected the tenets of (Oxford-taught) schola-sticism in favor of an eclectic rationalism that employed a neop-latonic metaphysics and placed great emphasis on the role of innate ideas in the acquisition of worthwhile knowledge of reality, while opposing the mechanism of the new science and the atheism to which they feared it might lead. Prominent members of the group included Cudworth, Cumberland, Glanvill, More, Conway and Norris. *Recommended Reading*: The Cambridge Platonists in Philosophical Context: Politics, Metaphysics, and Religion, ed. by G. A. J. Rogers, J. M. Vienne, and Y. C. Zarka (Kluwer, 1997) and Frederick James Powicke, Cambridge Platonists (Greenwood, 1955).

Camenes, name given by medieval logicians to a categorical syllogism whose standard form is AEE-4. *Example*: All first-degree murders are premed-itated homicides, but no premeditated homicides are actions performed in self-defence, so it follows that no actions performed in self-defence are first-degree murders. This is one of the fifteen forms in which syllogisms are always valid.

Camestres, name given by medieval logicians to any categorical syllogism whose standard form may be designated as AEE-2. *Example*: All terriers are dogs, while no cats are dogs, so no cats are terriers. This is another of the fifteen forms of valid syllogism.

Camus Albert, French-Algerian journalist and novelist (1913-1960). Camus explored the practical consequences of existentialist philosophy in his novels, L'Štranger (The Stranger) (1942), La Peste (The Plague) (1947), L'Homme Rëvoltë (The Rebel) (1951), and La Chute (The Fall) (1956). His essay Le Mythe de Sisyphe (Essai sur l'absurde) (The Myth of Sisyphus) (1943) describes the inherent absurdity of human life, a profound meaninglessness that can be mitigated only by moral integrity and social solidarity. Camus was awarded the Nobel Prize in 1957 and died in anautomobile accident three years later. *Recommended Reading*: Olivier Todd and Benjamin Ivry, Albert Camus: A Life (Carroll, 2000); Joseph McBride, Albert Camus: Philosopher and Litterateur (St. Martins, 1992); and Harold Bloom and William Golding, Albert Camus (Chelsea House, 1989).

Canonical, (Historically, "according to religious law")

1. A standard way of writing a formula. Two formulas such as 9 + x and x + 9 are said to be equivalent because they mean the same thing, but the second one is in "canonical form" because it is written in the usual way, with the highest power of x first. Usually there are fixed rules you can use to decide whether something is in canonical form. Things in canonical form are easier to compare.
2. The usual or standard state or manner of something. The term acquired this meaning in computer-science culture largely through its prominence in Alonzo Church's work in computation theory and mathematical logic (see Knights of the Lambda-Calculus).

This word has an interesting history. Non-technical academics do not use the adjective "canonical" in any of the senses defined above with any regularity; they do however use the nouns "canon" and "canonicity" (not "canonicalness"* or "canonicality"*). The "canon" of a given author is the complete body of authentic works by that author (this usage is familiar to Sherlock Holmes fans as well as to literary scholars). "The canon" is the body of works in a given field (*e.g.* works of literature, or of art, or of music) deemed worthwhile for students to study and for scholars to investigate.

The word "canon" derives ultimately from the Greek "kanon" (akin to the English "cane") referring to a reed. Reeds were used for measurement, and in Latin and later Greek the word "canon" meant a rule or a standard. The establishment of a canon of scriptures within Christianity was meant to define a standard or a rule for the religion. The above non-technical academic usages stem from this instance of a defined and accepted body of work. Alongside this usage was the promulgation of "canons" ("rules") for the government of the Catholic Church. The usages relating to religious law derive from this use of the Latin "canon".

Hackers invest this term with a playfulness that makes an ironic contrast with its historical meaning. A true story: One Bob Sjoberg, new at the MIT AI Lab, expressed some annoyance at the incessant use of jargon. Over his loud objections, GLS and RMS made a point of using as much of it as possible in his presence, and eventually it began to sink in. Finally, in one conversation, he used the word "canonical" in jargon-like fashion without thinking. Steele: "Aha! We've finally got you talking jargon too!" Stallman: "What did he say?" Steele: "Bob just used "canonical" in the canonical way."

Of course, canonicality depends on context, but it is implicitly defined as the way *hackers* normally expect things to be. Thus, a hacker may claim with a straight face that "according to religious law" is *not* the canonical meaning of "cano-nical".

Canonicity, The extent to which something is canonical.

Capitalism, economic system in which the principal means of production, distribution, and exchange are in private (individual or corporate) hands and compet-itively operated for profit. A mixed economy combines the private enterprise of capitalism and a degree of state monopoly, as in nationalized industries and welfare services. Most capitalist economies are actually mixed economies, but some (such as the US and Japanese) have a greater share of the economy devoted to free enterprise. The reputation of capitalism, which was quite bad for a while, has recently been on the rise. This is no doubt due mainly to the universal failure of socialism and communism, but credit must also be given to those scholars who have emphasized that what has been traditionally lampooned as evil "capitalism" is in fact the idea of minimal government, which is better described as classical liberalism or libertarianism, which is much more "human" than the twentieth-century authoritarianism and totalitàrianism that supplanted capitalism his-torically. However, some economists insist that capitalism is not a doctrine or theory in political philosophy in the way that Marxism is, because the free market is not an ideology but simply the economic phenomenon that occurs naturally in the absence of political control. References from dialectical materialism and social Darwinism.

Cardinality, The number of elements in a set; intuitively, the set's "size" or "magnitude". Notation: a double bar over the symbol denoting the set; also "|S|" and "card S" when S is the symbol denoting the set. If two sets have the same number of elements (*i.e.* there is a bijection between them) then they have the same cardinality. A cardinality is thus an isomorphism class in the category of sets.

> aleph 0 is defined as the cardinality of the first infinite ordinal, omega (the number of natural numbers).

Cardinality of an interpretation, interpretation

Cardinal number, The cardinality of some set.

Carnap Rudolf, German-American philosopher. A leading logical positivist, Carnap (1891-1970) pro-posed in Der logische Aufbau der Welt (The Logical Structure of the World) (1929) and Logische Syntax der Sprache (The Logical Syntax of Language)

(1934) that all meaningful assertions in a description of reality must be derived from basic statements of experience. Carnap's influential articles "Pseudo-Problems in Philosophy" (1928) and "The Elimi-nation of Metaphysics trough Logical Analysis of Language" (1932) propose that many traditional philosophical disputes amount to little more than differences in poetic rhetoric. His "Empiricism, Semantics, and Ontology" (1950) considers the degree of ontological commitment entailed by linguistic reference to abstract entities. In Meaning and Necessity: A Study in Semantics and Modal Logic (1947) and Logical Foundations of Probability (1950), Carnap tried to devise a purely formal representation of the degree of confirmation to which scientific hypotheses are susceptible. Carnap's notions about the formation of scientific theories are expressed in Philosophical Foundations of Physics (1966). *Recommended Reading*: Alan W. Richardson, Carnap's Construction of the World: The Aufbau and the Emergence of Logical Empiricism (Cambridge, 1997); Bryan G. Norton, Linguistic Frameworks and Ontology: A Re-Examination of Carnap's Metaphilosophy (De Gruyter, 1977); and Philosophy of Rudolph Carnap, ed. by Paul A. Schilpp (Open Court, 1974).

Carneades, Greek philosopher(214-129 B.C.). As leader of the Academy, Carneades advocated a moderate skepticism, which permitted the qualified assertion of probabile judgments. In his own time, Carneades was famous for the ability to develop convincing arguments on both sides of any philosophical dispute. *Recommended Reading*: Edwyn Bevan, Stoics and Skeptics (Ares, 1980).

Carroll Lewis, English logician, mathematician, and author. Charles Lutwidge Dodgson (1832-1898). Carroll's fascination with logical and philosophical puzzles is apparent in the popular books Alice's Adventures in Wonderland (1865) and Through the Looking Glass (1876) as well as in the more technical Games of Logic (1887) and Symbolic Logic (1893). The philosophical paper on "What the Tortoise said to Achilles" (1895) raised a significant issue about the legitimacy of reiterated demands for epistemo-logical justification.

Cartesian coordinates, (After Renee Descartes, French philosopher and mathematician) A pair of numbers, (x, y), defining the position of a point in a two-dimensional space by its perpendicular projection onto two axes which are at right angles to each other. x and y are also known as the abscissa and ordinate.

The idea can be generalised to any number of independent axes.

Cartesian doubt, in his Meditations, Descartes (1596-1650) proposed discarding any kind of belief that could be doubted, that might be false. Initially, he was inclined to doubt all the evidences of his senses (pointing out that it seemed impossible to tell for sure whether he was at any point aswake or asleep). The doubt that Descartes introduced into philosophy has been a characteristic feature as many philosophers since have supposed that we have no secure rational basis for believing in the existence of a world external to our sense experience, etc. private language argument, the

Cartesian interactionist dualism, the view that

1) ontological independence is the criterion for the identification of

substance, that is x = substance iff, for any y different from x, x exists independently of y

2) following (1), strictly speaking, there is only one substance, that is God = substance
3) if x is ontologically dependent only on God, then x = substance in a weak sense
4) the mental and the material are two weak-substances and;
5) both can have causal effects on the other.

Cartesianism, Cartesianism is the name applied in philosophy to the doctrines of Descartes, and to the tradition of modern philosophy that arose out of his thought. In a way, much modern philosophy is just a footnote to, or working out of, Descartes. Some signature ideas and ideals of Cartesianism are dualism and rationalism, a combination of idealism in the spiritual realm and of mechanism in the physical realm. (References from automatism and mechanism.)

Cartesian product, (After Renee Descartes, French philosopher and mathematician) The Cartesian product of two sets A and B is the set *I.e.* the product set contains all possible

$$A \times B = (a, b) \mid a \text{ in } A, b \text{ in } B.$$

combinations of one element from each set. The idea can be extended to products of any number of sets.

If we consider the elements in sets A and B as points along perpendicular axes in a two-dimensional space then the elements of the product are the "Cartesian coordinates" of points in that space. See also tuple.

Cartesian skepticism, 1. sceptical views against the absolute reliability of empiricaland mathematical knowledge.

2. any of a class of sceptical views against empirical knowledge based on the argument that claims to empirical knowledge are defeated by the possibility that we might be deceived insofar as we might be, for example, dreaming, hallucinating, deceived by demons, or brains in vats.

Cassirer Ernst, German neo-Kantian philosopher (1874-1945) who supposed that the fundamental categories of human thought are genuinely a priori, yet develop historically. In his massive Die Philosophie der symbolischen Formen (The Philosophy of Symbolic Forms) (1929) (vol. 1-4), Cassirer suggested that these basic concepts are most clearly revealed in the cultural symbols of language, science, and mythology. *Recommended Reading*: Ernst Cassirer, The Philosophy of the Enlightenment, tr. by J. Pettegrove and F. Koelin (Princeton, 1968) and Ernst Cassirer: A 'Repetition' of Modernity, ed. By Steve G. Lofts and Michael Krois (SUNY, 2000).

Casuistry, approach to ethics that begins by examining a series of concrete cases rather than by trying to deduce the consequences of a moral rule. Although Pascal criticized this method for the excessive, misleading, or harmful cleverness with which it was practiced in his day, it remains a common tool for applied ethics in a theological vein. *Recomm-ended Reading*: The Context of Casuistry, ed. by James F. Keenan, Thomas A. Shannon, and Albert R. Jonsen (Georgetown, 1995) and Richard B. Miller, Casuistry and Modern Ethics: A Poetics of Practical Reasoning (Chicago, 1996).

Categorical imperative, an absolute unconditional command, allowing no exceptions. The commands of morality, according to Kant, are all of this type and are all derivable from a single root imperative—the Categorical Imperative—akin to the Biblical golden rule ("Do unto others as you would have them do unto you"). Kant gives at least two seemingly different formulations of this basic Categorical Imperative. The first formulation says, "Act only on that maxim through which you can at the same time will that it should become universal law" (see maxim). This first formulation speaks more directly to justice, disallowing self-interested favoritism: it deems only those maxims you'd be willing for everyone (not just yourself) to act on to be morally acceptable; those you would be willing to universalize. The second formulation says, "Act in such a way that you always treat humanity, whether in your own person or in the person of any other, never simply as a means, but always at the same time as an end." In this second formulation the appeal seems to be more directly to rights, specifically a right of autonomy or self-deter-mination. What it forbids is using others without their informed consent to achieve one's owns purposes. Whether these two formulations are really equivalent—just saying the same thing in other words—as Kant maintains, is controversial. Contrast: hypothetical imperative.

Categorical logic, the traditional inte-rpretation of the logic of classes developed by Aristotle and the medieval logicians. *Recommended Reading*: Aristotle, Prior Analytics, ed. by Robin Smith (Hackett, 1989) and Jan Lukasiewicz, Aristotle's Syllogistic from the Standpoint of Modern Formal Logic (Clarendon, 1957).

Categorical proposition, a statement of the relationship between two classes, each of which is designated by a categorical term. Within each propo-sition, the subject term occurs before the copula and the predicate term after. There are only four forms of categorical proposition, distinguished by their quantity and quality.

Categorical syllogism, a logical argument consisting of exactly three categorical propositions, two premises and the conclusion, with a total of exactly three categorical terms, each used in only two of the propositions.

Categorical term, a word or phrase that designates a class. Each categorical term divides the world into two parts: the original class and its complement; the things to which the term applies and those to which it does not.

Categoricity of systems, 1. A formal system in general is categorical iff all its models are isomorphic.

2. A first-order theory with identity is categorical iff All its normal models are isomorphic.

See isomorphism of models, model, normal.

Category, predicate; hence, a fundamental class of things in our conceptual framework. In Aristotle's logic specifically, the categories are the ten general modes of being (substance, quantity, quality, relation, place, time, position, possession, doing, and undergoing) by reference to which any individual thing may be described. Following the lead of stoic thought, medieval logicians commonly employed only the first four of these ten, but allowed for additional, syncategorematic terms that belonged to none of them. Kant employed a schematized table of a dozen categories as the basis for our understanding of the phenomenal realm. Gilbert Ryle used the term much more broadly, warning of the category mistakes that occur when we fail to respect the unique features of kinds of things. *Recommended Reading*: F. E. Peters, Greek Philos-ophical Terms: A Historical Lexicon (NYU, 1967) and Aristotle, Categories, ed. By Hugh Tredennick (Harvard, 1938).

A category K is a collection of objects, obj(K), and a collection of morphisms (or "arrows"), mor(K) such that

1. Each morphism f has a "typing" on a pair of objects A, B written f:A->B. This is read 'f is a morphism from A to B'. A is the "source" or "domain" of f and B is its "target" or "co-domain".
2. There is a partial function on morphisms called composition and denoted by an infix ring symbol, o. We may form the "composite" g o f: A -> C if we have g:B->C and f:A->B.
3. This composition is associative: h o (g o f) = (h o g) o f.
4. Each object A has an identity morphism id_A:A->A associated with it. This is the identity under composition, shown by the equations id B o f = f = f o id A.

In general, the morphisms between two objects need not form a set (to avoid problems with Russell's paradox). An example of a category is the collection of sets where the objects are sets and the morphisms are functions.

Sometimes the composition ring is omitted. The use of capitals for objects and lower case letters for morphisms is widespread but not universal. Variables which refer to categories themselves are usually written in a script font.

Category mistake, confusion in the attribution of properties or the classification of things. Thus, to suppose that sleep is furious or that a city is nothing more than its buildings is to commit a category mistake. Ryle maintained that Cartesian dualism arises from the implicit occurrence of just such an error, the supposition that the origins of human behavior must reside in an immaterial substance. *Recommended Reading*: Gilbert Ryle, The Concept of Mind (Chicago, 1984).

Catharsis, cleansing from guilt or defilement; hence, in Aristotle, the elimination of destructive emotions through appreciation of an aesthetic experience. The notion here is that vicariously experiencing strong feelings renders us less likely to be overcome by them in our own lives. *Recommended Reading*: F. E. Peters, Greek Philos-ophical Terms: A Historical Lexicon (NYU, 1967); Aristotle, Poetics, tr. By Malcolm Heath (Penguin, 1997); and Adnan K. Abdulla, Catharsis in Literature (Indiana, 1985).

Cauchy sequence, A sequence of elements from some vector space that converge and stay arbitrarily close to each other (using the norm defined for the space).

Causal functionalism, the view that a physical system realizes a mental state not in virtue of the particular stuff it is made of, but instead in virtue of the causal relations that parts of that system bear to each other. See functionalism.

Causality, in philosophy, relationship of a cause to its effect. The Greek philosopher Aristotle enumerated four different kinds of causes: the material, the formal, the efficient, and the final. The material cause is what anything is made of—for example, brass or marble is the material cause of a given statue. The formal cause is the form, type, or pattern according to which anything is made; thus, the style of architecture would be the formal cause of a house. The efficient cause is the immediate power acting to produce the work, such as the manual energy of the labourers. The final cause is the end or motive for the sake of which the work is produced—that is, the pleasure of the owner. The principles that Aristotle outlined formed the basis of the modern scientific concept that specific stimuli will produce standard results under controlled conditions. Other Greek philosophers, particularly the 2nd-century sceptic Sextus Empiricus, attacked the principles of causality.

Rival Notions: In early modern philosophy, Aristotle's laws of causality were again challenged. The French philosopher and mathematician René Descartes and his school believed that a cause must contain the qualities of the effect or the power to produce the effect. The physical scientists of the 17th and 18th centuries often had a mechanical view of causality, reducing cause to a motion or change followed by another motion or change, with a mathematical equality between measures of motion. The British philosopher David Hume carried to a logical conclusion the contention of Sextus Empiricus that causality is not a real relation, but a fiction of the mind. To account for the origin of this fiction Hume used the doctrine of association.

Hume's explanation of cause led the German philosopher Immanuel Kant to posit cause as a fundamental category of understanding. Kant held that the only knowable objective world is the product of a synthetic activity of the mind. He accepted Hume's sceptical result as far as it concerned the world of things. Dissatisfied, however, with the concept that experience is only a succession of perceptions without any discoverable relationship or coherence, Kant decided that causality is one of the principles of coherence obtaining in the world of phenomena, and that it is universally present there because thought, as part of its contribution to the nature of that world, always puts it there.

The British philosopher John Stuart Mill took up the problem at this point. He denied the fundamental postulate, or principle, of Kant's transcendentalism, namely, that thought is responsible for the order of the world. Mill sought to justify belief in universal causation on empiricist principles; for him, a proposition is meaningful only if it describes what can be experienced.

Modern Directions: *Along with the method of empiricism as the source of all knowledge goes a definition of cause that is widely accepted today. The cause of any event is a preceding event without which the event in question would not have occurred. This is a mechanistic view of causality popular in scientific circles. All previous events would constitute the complete cause.*

Many philosophers deny the ultimate reality, or at least the fundamental validity, of the causal relation. Thus, the American philosopher Josiah Royce maintained that the category of serial order, of which the category of cause is a particular case, is itself subordinate to the ultimate category of purpose. The French philosopher Henri Bergson maintained that ultimate reality or life is not bound by exact causal sequences. It is a process of growth in which the unpredictable, and therefore the uncaused, constantly occurs. No exact repetition happens in real time; and where there is no repetition, there is no cause, for cause means that the antecedent is repeatedly followed by the same consequence.

Cause, whatever is responsible for changes (including the creation and destruction) of things. According to Aristotle causes fall into four types: material cause, the substance a thing is made of; formal cause, the structure or design of the thing; efficient cause, the maker or instigator of the change; and final cause, the purpose or function of it (see teleology). Modern would-be-scientific conceptions of causality generally eschew final causation or teleology Hume argued that all knowledge of causation comes from our actual experience of observed regularities and includes no real knowledge of any objectively necessary conn-ection. See determinism, scientific law.

Cause-effect, distinction between the events involved in a causal relationship, where the occurrence of one (the cause) is supposed to bring about or produce an occurrence of the other (the effect). Although the correct analysis of causation is a matter of great dispute, Hume offered a significant criticism of our inclination to infer a necessary connection from mere regularity, and Mill proposed a set of methods for recognizing the presence of causal relationships. Contemporary philosophers often suppose that a causal relationship is best expressed in the counterfactual statement that if the cause had not occured, then the effect would not have occured either. *Recommended Reading*: Judea Pearl, Causality: Models, Reasoning, and Inference (Cambridge, 2000); Wesley C. Salmon, Causality and Explanation (Oxford, 1997); Evan Fales, Causation and Universals (Routledge, 1990).

Causes the four, Aristotle's distinction in the Physics among four answers to the question of why something is: (1) the material cause is the stuff from which the thing is made; (2) the formal cause is the pattern or structure it has; (3) the efficient cause is the agent that imposed this form on that matter; and (4) the final cause is the purpose for the thing. Thus, for example, the material cause of this chair is the wood out of which it is made, the formal cause is the shape into which it was fashioned, the efficient cause was the carpenter by whom the chair was made, and the final cause is the sitting for the sake of which it was designed. In the case of living beings, Aristotle supposed, the soul is the formal, efficient, and final cause; the body is only the material cause. *Recommended Reading*: Aristotle, The Physics: Books I-IV, tr. By Philip H. Wicksteed and Francis M. Cornford (Harvard, 1986) and Aristotle's Physics: A Collection of Essays, ed. by Lindsay Judson (Clarendon, 1995).

Cavendish Margaret, English philosopher and playwright (1623-1673). Cavendish criticized the natural philosophy of both Hobbes and Descartes in Philosophical Letters (1664), and that of Boyle in Observations upon Experimental Philosophy (1666). Her own view, developed fully in The Grounds of Natural Philosophy (1668), was materialist but not mechanistic, supposing that all matter is imbued with soul. In A True Relation of my Birth, Breeding, and Life (1656) Cavendish commented upon the place of women in seventeenth-century society. *Recommended Reading*: Margaret Cavendish, The Blazing World and Other Writings, ed. by Kate Lilley (Penguin, 1994); Anna Battigelli, Margaret Cavendish and the Exiles of the Mind (Kentucky, 1998).

Celarent, name given by medieval logicians to any categorical syllogism whose standard form may be designated as EAE-1. Example: No cold-blooded animals are furry pets, even though all reptiles are cold-blooded animals; therefore, no reptiles are furry pets. This is one of only fifteen forms of syllogism that are always valid.

Censorship, legal or social practices aiming to bar the creation or dissemination (*e.g.*, the publication or public display) of disapproved forms of artistic expression.

Cohen, Hermann (1842-1918), German Jewish philosopher, one of the founders of the Neo-Kantian school at Marburg. Born in Koswig, he studied at the universities of Breslau and Berlin and graduated from Halle in 1865. He taught at Marburg from 1876 to 1912. Cohen is noted for his commentaries on Immanuel Kant, written over some 40 years, notably his *Kant's Theorie der Erfahrung* (Kant's Theory of Empirical Knowledge, 1871). Other works include *Die Logik der Reinen Erkenntnis* (The Logic of Pure Knowledge, 1902), *System der Philosophie* (A System of Philosophy, 1902-1906), and *Der Begriff der Religion im System der Philosophie* (The Concept of Religion in Systematic Philosophy, 1915).

Cohen's logical refinement of Kant's transcendental method was received with both scepticism and admiration (*see* Transcendentalism). He held that Kant's ethical idealism and Jewish theology are essentially identical, but also that personal religious beliefs are properly outside the jurisdiction of philosophy.

Coherence theory of truth, truth theories

Cesare, name given by medieval logicians to a categorical syllogism whose standard form is EAE-2. Example: Since no truly peaceful nations are places where basic human rights are inadequately defended, while all countries torn by ethnic strife are places where basic human rights are inadequately defended, it follows that no countries torn by ethnic strife are truly peaceful nations. This is one of the fifteen forms of valid syllogism.

Chain of being, belief that existing things can be hierarchically ordered, from least to greatest, in an unbroken series from inanimate particles of matter to the deity. A. O. Lovejoy traced this concrete application of the principle of plenitude from ancient Greek thought through neoplatonism to its influence on early twentieth-century idealism. *Recommended Reading*: Arthur Oncken Lovejoy, The Great Chain of Being: A Study of the History of an Idea (Harvard, 1970).

Chaos, A property of some non-linear dynamic systems which exhibit sensitive dependence on initial conditions. This means that there are initial states which evolve within some finite time to states whose separation in one or more dimensions of state space depends, in an average sense, exponentially on their initial separation. Such systems may still be completely deterministic in that any future state of the system depends only on the initial conditions and the equations describing the change of the system with time. It may, however, require arbitrarily high precision to actually calculate a future state to within some finite precision. ["On defining chaos", R. Glynn Holt and D. Lynn Holt]

Fixed precision floating-point arithmetic, as used by most computers, may actually introduce chaotic dependence on initial conditions due to the accumulation of rounding errors (which constitutes a non-linear system).

Charron Pierre, French theologian (1541-1603). Although De la Sagesse (Of Wisdom) (1601) expressed many themes from the Stoic tradition, Charron shared with Montaigne a profound skepticism about general knowledge of god and the world.

Chinese room, an argument forwarded by John Searle intended to show that the mind is not a computer and how the Turing Test is inadequate.

Searle first formulated this problem in his paper "Minds, brains and programs" published in 1980. Ever since, it has been a mainstay of debate over the possibility of what Searle called "strong AI". Supporters of strong AI believe that a correctly programmed computer is not simply a simulation or model of a mind, it actually would count as a mind. That is, it understands, has cognitive states, and can think. Searle's argument (or more precisely, thought experiment) against this position, the Chinese room argument, goes as follows: Suppose that a computer which behaves as if it understands Chinese. In other words, the computer takes Chinese symbols as input, consults a large look-up table (as all computers can be described as doing), and then produces other Chinese symbols as output. Suppose that this computer performs this task so convincingly that it easily passes the Turing Test. In other words, it convinces a human Chinese speaker that it is a Chinese speaker. All the questions the human asks are responded to appropriately, such that the Chinese speaker is convinced that he or she is talking to another Chinese speaker. The conclusion proponents of strong AI would like to draw is that the computer understands Chinese, just as the person does. Now, Searle asks us to suppose that he is sitting inside the computer. In other words, he is in a small room in which he receives Chinese symbols, looks them up on look-up table, and returns the Chinese symbols that are indicated by the table. Searle notes, of course, that he doesn't understand a word of Chinese. Furthermore, his lack of understanding goes to show, he argues, that computers don't understand Chinese either, because they are in the same situation as he is. They are mindless manipulators of symbols, just as he is—and they don't understand what they're "saying", just as he doesn't. The two most popular replies to this argument (both of which Searle (1980) considers) are the "systems reply" and the 'robot reply'.

Briefly, the systems reply is simply that though Searle himself doesn't understand Chinese in the thought experiment, it is perfectly correct to say that Searle plus look-up table understand Chinese. In other words, the entire computer would understand Chinese, though perhaps the central processor or any other part might not. It is the entire system that matters for attributing unde-rstanding. In response, Searle claims that if we simply imagine the person in the Chinese room to memorize the look-up table, we have produced a counter example to this reply. The robot reply is similar in spirit. The robot reply notes that the reason we don't want to attribute understanding to the room, or a computer as described by Searle is that the system doesn't interact properly with the environment. This is also a reason to think the Turing Test is not adequate for attributing thinking or understanding. If, however, we fixed this problem—*i.e.* we put the computer in a robot body that could interact with the environment, perceive things, move around, etc.—we would then be in a position to attribute understanding properly. In reply, Searle notes that proponents of this reply have partially given up the tenet of AI that cognition is symbol manipulation. More seriously, he proposes that he could be in a Chinese robot, just as easily as a Chinese room,and that he still wouldn't understand Chinese.

References: Harnad (1995). Minds, Machines and Scarle Searle, 1995. Power in the Chinese Room Chinese Room Biblio Introduction to the Chinese Room Searle, J. R. (1980). Minds, brains, and programs. Behavioral and Brain Sciences, 1: 417-24. Also in J. Haugeland (ed) (1997). Mind Design II. MIT Press: Cambridge, M A.

Chisholm Roderick M., American philosopher (1916-1999) who applied the phenomenological methods of Brentano and Meinong to the central issues of epistemology in the analytic tradition in such books as Perceiving: A Philosophical Study (1957), Realism and the Background of Phenomenology (1960), Person and Object: A Metaphysical Study (1976), and Brentano and Intrinsic Value (1986). *Recommended Reading*: Roderick M. Chisholm, A Realistic Theory of Categories: An Essay on Ontology (Cambridge, 1996); The Philosophy of Roderick M. Chisholm, ed. by Lewis Edwin Hahn (Open Court, 1997); and Analysis and Metaphysics: Essays in Honor of R. M. Chisholm, ed. by Keith Lehrer (Kluwer, 1975).

Chomsky Noam Avram, American linguist and philosopher (1928-), author of Syntatactic Structure (1957), Cartesian Linguistics (A chapter in the history of rationalist thought) (1966), Language and Mind (1968), and Knowledge of Language (1986). In opposition to prevalent behaviorism, Chomsky's psycholinguistic approach holds that competence in the use of language reveals innate possession of universal generative grammatical structures that cannot be acquired simply by empirical evidence. Chomsky has also been an out-spoken and thoughtful critic of American foreign policy since the 1960s in such books as American Power and the New Mandarins (1969), Necessary Illusions (1989), and Deterring Democracy (1992). *Recom-*

mended Reading: The Chomsky Reader, ed. by James Peck (Pantheon, 1987).

Christianity, name given to the religion and, later, theology that arose out of the teachings of Jesus, known to believers as "the anointed one", the Christ. The development of Christian doctrine owes much to the Neo-Platonism that was accepted by Augustine. In the late Middle Ages, Thomas Aquinas turned Christian theology more towards Aristotelianism. (References from Buddhism, dualism, pessimism,polytheism, and Thomism)

Chrysippus, primary author of the stoic philosophy (280-207 B.C.). Although none of his many writings survived antiquity, Chrysippus reportedly made significant contributions to the development of logic and ethics. He is generally credited with invention of the propositional calculus and eloquent expression of the doctrine of eternal return. *Recommended Reading*: J. B. Gould, The Philosophy of Chrysippus (Brill, 1997); Brad Inwood, Ethics and Human Action in Early Stoicism (Oxford, 1992); and Stoic Studies (Cambridge, 1996) A. A. Long.

Church Alonzo, American logician and mathematician (1903-); author of Introduction to Mathematical Logic (1956). Building on the work of G–del, Church showed that there can be no systematic decision procedure for the theorems of sophisticated formal systems like arithmetic, since such systems characteristically involve non-recursive formulae for which there is no computable algorithm. *Recommended Reading*: Alonzo Church, A Bibliography of Symbolic Logic (1666-1935) (Association of Symbolic Logic, 1985).

Church-Rosser Theorem, This property of a reduction system states that if an expression can be reduced by zero or more reduction steps to either expression *M* or expression *N* then there exists some other expression to which both *M* and *N* can be reduced. This implies that there is a unique normal form for any expression since *M* and *N* cannot be different normal forms because the theorem says they can be reduced to some other expression and normal forms are irreducible by definition. It does not imply that a normal form is reachable, only that if reduction terminates it will reach a unique normal form.

Church's theorem, If Church's thesis is true, then polyadic predicate logic is undecidable.

Church's thesis, Originally and narrowly, the thesis that all intuitively effective methods are generally recursive (in the sense of this term used in recursive function theory). Due to Alonzo Church, 1935. Cur-rently and more broadly, the thesis that all intuitively effective methods are captured in any one of several formalizations, including recursive function theory, Turing machines, Markov algorithms, the Lambda calculus, and so on. See recursive function theory

Cicero Marcus Tullius, (106-43 B.C.) Roma politician whose philosophical writings primarily translated the work of Greek philosophers into his own polished Latin. Thus, De re publica and De legibus (Of the State and Of the Laws) owe much to dialogues of Plato on political structure. Cicero also relied heavily upon the Stoics for much of his philosophy of nature and ethics, exemplified nicely in Tusculanae disputationes (Disputations at Tusculum) and "The Dream of Scipio." The influence of Aristotle is evident in De officiis (On Duties) and Laelius, sive de Amicitia (Essay on Friendship) (44 B.C.). *Recommended Reading*: Marcus Tullius Cicero, Selected Works, tr. by Michael Grant (Viking, 1960); Cicero the Philosopher: Twelve Papers, ed. by Jonathan Powell (Oxford, 1999); and Neal Wood, Cicero's Social and Political Thought: An Introduction (California, 1991).

Circularity, reasoning that improperly assumes the truth of what is at issue. A circular argument implicitly employs its own conclusion as a premise. A circular definition defines an expression in terms of itself. The problem is that circular reasoning—however accurate—is bound to be uninformative.

Cixous Hélène, Algerian-French philosopher and literary critic (1937). Employing Derrida's methods of deconstruction in Entré l'Écriture (Coming to Writing) (1986) and Le Jeune Née (The Newly Born Woman) (1975), Cixous proposed the creation of literary works by Ècriture féminine, "writing the body" in order to undermine the influence of masculine language. Since the feminine is always regarded as other and inferior in the dichotomies fostered by logocentric patriarchy, Cixous maintains that women can elude male domination only by rejecting the binary oppo-sitions inherent in symbolic lan-guage. By celebrating historically-repressed differences, she believes, victims of repression forge the new identities upon which a genuinely post-colonial and post-patriarchal society might be founded.

Recommended Reading: The Hélène Cixous Reader, ed. by Susan Sellers and Jacques Derrida (Routledge, 1994); Verena Andermatt Conley, Hélène Cixous: Writing the Feminine (Nebraska, 1991); The Body and the Text: Hélène Cixous, Reading and Teaching, ed. by Helen Wilcox, Keith McWatters, Ann Thompson, and Linda R. Williams (St. Martin's, 1991); and Hélène Cixous (Toronto, 1992).

Clarke Samuel, English theologian and philosopher (1675-1729). In an extended correspondence with Leibniz, Clarke defended Newtonian concepts of space and time against Leibniz's relational notions. Clarke's published Discourses Concerning the Unchangeable Obligations of Natural Religion and the Truth and Certainty of Christian Revelation (1705) and Demonstration of the Being and Attributes of God (1711) employed Locke's methods of demonstration against the deists, to prove the existence and nature of god, the human obligation to worship, and the fundamental rules of morality. This view, shared by the Cambridge Platonists, became a target of Hume's criticism of natural religion. *Recommended Reading*: Leibniz and Clarke: Correspondence, ed. by Roger Ariew (Hackett, 2000).

Class, 1. The prototype for an object in an object-oriented language; analogous to a derived type in a procedural language. A class may also be considered to be a set of objects which share a common structure and behaviour. The structure of a class is determined by the class variables which represent the state of an object of that class and the behaviour is given by a set of methods associated with the class.

Classes are related in a class hierarchy. One class may be a specialisation (a "subclass") of another (one of its "superclasses") or it may be composed of other classes or it may use other classes in a client-server relationship. A class may be an abstract class or a concrete class. See also signature.

2. See type class.

3. One of three types of Internet addresses distinguished by their most significant bits.

3. A language developed by the Andrew Project. It was one of the first attempts to add object-oriented features to C.

Class hierarchy, A set of classes and their interrelationships.

One class may be a specialisation (a "subclass" or "derived class") of another which is one of its "supercla-sses" or "base classes".

When a method is invoked on an object it is first looked for in the object's class, then the superclass of that class, and so on up the hierarchy until it is found. Thus a class need only define those methods which are specific to it, and inherits methods from all its superclasses. See also: multiple inheritance.

Classical logic, Non-intuitionistic logic.

Classicism, the word classicism is usually used to describe an emphasis or over-emphasis on past practice, examples, and rules, especially in the making of art. In aesthetics, classicism is usually contrasted historically and philosophically with romanticism. (References from formalism and romanticism).

Class library, A library of reusable classes for use with an object-oriented programming system.

Class method, A kind of method, available in some object-oriented programming languages, that operates on the class as a whole, as opposed to an "object method" that operates on an object that is an instance of the class.

A typical example of a class method would be one that keeps a count of the number of objects of that class that have been created.

Clear and distinct, features of ideas considered as mental entities, without regard for their external relation to objects they are supposed to represent. An idea is clear if its content is precise and detailed; otherwise, it is obscure. An idea is distinct if it can be distinguished from any other idea, confused if it cannot. (Although the two notions are formally distinct, they are commonly supposed to coincide, on the grounds that clarity is a necessary and sufficient condition for distinctness.)Descartes held that the clarity and distinctness of our ideas is a criterion for the truth of what we believe.

Clifford William Kingdon, English mathematician and philosopher (1845-1879). Arguing that belief in uncertain propositions is a public act with moral consequences, Clifford endorsed a wide-ranging agnos-ticism, asserting in "The Ethics of Belief" (1879) that "It is wrong always, everywhere, and for anyone, to believe anything on insufficient evidence."

Clone, 1. An exact copy of a product, made legally or illegally, from docum-entation or by reverse engineering, and usually cheaper.

E.g. "PC clone": a PC-BUS/ISA, EISA, VESA, or PI compatible x86-based microcomputer (this use is sometimes misspelled "klone" or "PClone").

These invariably have much

more bang per buck than the IB PCM they resemble.

E.g. "Unix clone": An operating system designed to deliver a Unix-like environment without Unix licence fees or with additional "mission-critical" features such as support for real-time programming.

2. A clonebot.

Closed term, A term with no free variables.

Closure, 1. In a reduction system, a closure is a data structure that holds an expression and an environment of variable bindings in which that expression is to be evaluated. The variables may be local or global. Closures are used to represent unevaluated expressions when implementing functional programming languages with lazy evaluation. In a real implementation, both expression and environment are represented by pointers. A suspension is a closure which includes a flag to say whether or not it has been evaluated. The term "thunk" has come to be synonymous with "closure" but originated outside functional programming.

2. In domain theory, given a partially ordered set, *D* and a subset, *X* of *D*, the upward closure of *X* in *D* is the union over all *x* in *X* of the sets of all d in *D* such that *x* <= *d*. Thus the upward closure of X in *D* contains the elements of X and any greater element of *D*. A set is "upward closed" if it is the same as its upward closure, *i.e.* any d greater than an element is also an element. The downward closure (or "left closure") is similar but with *d* <= *x*. A downward closed set is one for which any *d* less than an element is also an element.

3. a. *closure of a system*

A system with at least one closed term is closed iff |- At/x implies |- (x)Ax for each closed term t and each 1-wff A. (A 1-wff is a wff with exactly one free variable.) Informally, the system is closed if the fact that A is a theorem when its free variable is replaced with any closed term in the language implies the universal generalization (x)A. It follows from closure that every member of the domain is named by some closed term; hence the domain is countable. See omega-completeness, term, closed, open wff

b. *closure of a wff*

In predicate logic, the binding of all free variables from a wff by placing them within the scope of suitable quantifiers. A closed wff is considered its own closure. The closure of a closure of a wff A is considered a closure of A. Notation: A^c (a closure of wff A). Closed wffs are also called sentences. See bound variable, generalization, instantiation

Closure conversion, The transformation of continuation passing style code so that the only free variables of functions are names of other functions. See also Lambda lifting.

CNF, conjunctive normal form.

Coarse grain, granularity.

Cockburn Catherine Trotter, English philosopher and playwright (1679-1749). She endorsed the philoso-phical methods of Locke in Defense of Mr. Locke's Essay of Human Understanding (1702). In Remarks upon some Writers in the Controversy concerning the Foundation of Moral Virtue and Moral Obligation (1743), Cockburn defended the demonstrably rational morality of Clarke against the promotion of individual self-interest emphasized by

Hobbes, Shaftesbury, and Hutcheson. *Recommended Reading*: The Works of Mrs. Catharine Cockburn (Thoemmes, 1998).

Cogito argument, this argument of Descartes gets its name from the concluding phrase of his first formulation of it (in his Discourse on Method)—cogito ergo sum, "I think therefore I am." In his Meditations on First Philosophy Descartes concludes from the impossibility of doubting his own existence as thinking "that this proposition: I am, I exist, is necessarily true each time I pronounce it, or that I mentally conceive it" (2nd Meditation); my existence as a thinker is thereby assured. This assurance, Descartes thinks, can provide a secure foundation for all scientific know-ledge. See also: method of doubt.

Cognition, the portion of human experience comprising thought, knowledge, belief, and inference (as opposed to sensation, volition, or feeling). *Recommended Reading*: David Braddon-Mitchell and Frank Jackson, The Philosophy of Mind and Cognition (Blackwell, 1996) and Mind As Motion: Explorations in the Dynamics of Cognition, ed. By Robert F. Port and Timothy Van Gelder (MIT, 1998).

Cognitive architecture, A computer architecture involving non-deterministic, multiple inference processes, as found in neural networks. Cognitive architectures model the human brain and contrast with single processor computers.

The term might also refer to software architectures, *e.g.* fuzzy logic. [Origin? Better definition? Reference?]

Cognitive science, the interdisciplinary study which attempts to further our understanding of the nature of thought.

The major contributing disciplines to cognitive science include philosophy, psychology, computer science, linguistics, neuroscience and anthropology.

There are two standard computational approaches to modelling cognitive systems in cognitive science. The first is classicism (or symbolicism) and deals with thought in terms of symbolic processing. The second is known as connectionism and understands thought processes as a set of connections between nodes in a distributed network.

One goal of cognitive science is to design a cognitive architecture on which to build intelligent systems. According to Andy Clark, cognitive science, "sets out to explain the mechanisms implicated in events which are recognizably psychological in nature, such as reasoning, planning, and object recognition." (Clark, 1993).

References: Clark, A. (1993). Associative Engines: Connectionism, Concepts, and Representational Change, Cambridge: M.I.T. Press. Thagard, P. (1996). Mind: Introduction to Cognitive Science. Cambridge, MA. MIT Press.

Cognize, to have access to knowledge that has the properties of knowledge in the ordinary sense, but is not necessarily accessible to consciousness or dependent on warrant or justification.

Cognize is a technical term Chomsky introduces (1980, p. 69) to denote a relation a subject *S* has to *S*' knowledge. Just as *S* can be said to know that *p*, *S* can be said to cognize that *q*, where *p* and *q* stand for propositions representing some state of affairs or another. As such, cognising is said to differ very little from knowing in the ordinary sense. But there are some important features of cognising that set it off from the standard conception of what it is to know something.

Perhaps the most salient feature of cognising is that it is a relation primarily—though apparently not exclusively—associated with unconscious or tacit knowledge. As Chomsky describes it, cognising "has the structure and character of knowledge" in that it is a matter of knowing-that (see knowledge that, which is to say it is propositional and may involve belief (1980, pp. 70; 93-94; 1986, p. 269). What distinguishes cognising per se from ordinary knowing is that in many cases, what is cognised is inaccessible to consciousness (1980, p. 70; 1986, p. 269). However, it would seem that cases of explicit or conscious knowing entail cognising as well. Chomsky states, for example, that when we know that p, we cognize that p (1986, p. 265). What he means is that specific facts that are explicitly known may derive from rules and principles that are (presumably) unconsciously cognised (1986, p. 265). As an example, Chomsky cites the case of a person who, having unconscious knowledge of the binding principles, through deduction (or a similar process) can determine whether or not a pronoun and common noun encountered in the same sentence are coreferring (1986, p. 270). Cognising would thus seem to undergird at least some instances of explicit "knowing that" in important ways.

Despite the apparent fact that what is implicitly cognized often issues in conscious knowledge, it is hypothesised that at least some of what is cognised is inaccessible to conscio-usness in principle. The prototypical example of knowledge that is both cognised and is claimed to be inaccessible to consciousness in principle is a native speaker's knowledge of grammar. Chomsky is careful to point out that to the extent that cognised knowledge is tacit or implicit, it is not the equivalent of knowledge which is conscious but that the holder cannot articulate (1986, p. 271). But although cognising is largely, if not primarily, associated with cognitive structures inaccessible to consciousness, the line between the cognised cognitive unconscious and consciously accessible knowledge is, according to Chomsky, not inviolable. Rather, what is cognised can produce conscious knowledge, as is illustrated by the example of the binding principles' affording explicit knowledge of coreference, described just above. Cognised knowledge is thus not held to be inferentially insulated from ordinary, *i.e.*, conscious, beliefs.

One feature of cognising that sets it apart from many ordinary concepts of knowledge is that what is cognised is held not to consist in warranted or justified belief. Instead, Chomsky holds that cognised knowledge counts as a case of caused belief (1980, pp. 93-95). What this means is that cognised knowledge is caused by triggering experiences, which in at least some instances interact with innate principles to produce specific instances of knowing that p, where p is a cognised content of some sort. A prime example of caused knowledge is of course knowledge of grammar, which Chomsky has long hypoth-esised to arise from the interaction of an innate universal grammar and the triggering experiences afforded by exposure to a particular language. In Chomsky's example, a native English speaker, when exposed to evidence that the phrase "each other" is a reciprocal, will now that this is the case by virtue of the triggering effect such evidence has on the innate principle of opacity (1980, p. 94). but such knowledge does not, on Chomsky's account, stand as justified or warranted; as he puts it, "[e]ven where there is a triggering experience, this does not supply "good reasons" in any useful sense of the term"; (1980, p. 96).

Although the term "cognize" was introduced to dispel certain ambiguities in Chomsky's theory of the nature of human knowledge, some ambiguities seem to remain. It is not always clear, for example, exactly how or even whether cognising differs from knowledge as such. Matters are not helped by Chomsky's statement, after the term is introduced, that he will simply use "know" to mean "cognize" (1980, p. 70), or by his other statements that appear to conflate the two terms.

Nevertheless, the concept does appear to have two main functions. The first is to de-link knowledge from any necessary dependence on justification or warrant, thus fores-talling possible empiricist objections to a theory of knowledge grounded, as Chomsky's is, in content nativism. The second is to provide a covering term encompassing two kinds of knowledge—explicit and implicit—that otherwise might be treated as highly dissimilar and possibly unrelated (or in the case of implicit knowledge, simply dismissed outright).

One plausible interpretation of "cognising" then, is that it denotes an epistemological relation that is

a) neutral in regard to whether or not what is known (or "cognised") is known exp-licitly, and
b) can be fixed independently of justification or warrant.

References: Chomsky, N. (1980). Rules and Representations. New York, Columbia University Press. Chomsky, N. (1986). Knowledge of Language. New York, Praeger. See also tacit knowledge, implicit memory, rules.

Coherence, also cohesiveness, a semantic relation among a number of elements, such as propositions or concepts, that fit together well.

Philosophers have offered coherence theories of truth, know-ledge and ethics. For example, scientific theories can be justified on the basis of how well they cohere internally and externally, with evidence and other beliefs.

Connectionist algorithms have been used to provide computational models of coherence-based inferences, with applications to abduction, impression formation, and analogy.

Coherence is a semantic concept (the meaning or truth of p is compared to the meaning or truth of q), consistency is a syntactical concept (p is compared to not-p). See practical reasoning, connectionism

Collectivism, doctrine in political, or ethical, philosophy which holds that the individual's actions should benefit some kind of wider organized group to which the individual belongs, *e.g.* the members of a certain profession, the state, a community, etc., rather than the (just) the individual himself. Collectivism in political theory can depend on altr-uism in ethics. There are many forms of collectivism in political reality, such as tribalism, communism, socialism, certain forms of trade unionism, authoritarianism, totalitarianism, communalism, and so on. Collect-ivism is a rather technical term, and is not used very often in everyday language. (References from commu-nalism, communism, Hegelianism, holism, individualism, Platonism, socialism, and totalitarianism). Based on [The Ism Book] Edited by Giovanni Benzi

Collingwood Robin George, English philosopher (1889-1943). Influenced by Hegel, Cook Wilson, and Croce, Collingwood explored the implications of idealism for aesthetics and the philosophy of history in Speculum Mentis (1924), Essay on Philosophical Method (1933), The Principles of Art (1938), and The Idea of History (1946). Collingwood proposed that historical unders-tanding be achieved through empa-thetic reconstruction of the thoughts that motivated the actions of historical figures. *Recommended Reading*: Aaron Ridley, Collingwood (Routledge, 1999); Philosophy, History and Civilization: Essays on R. G. Collingwood,ed. by David Boucher (U of Wales, 1996); and William H. Dray, History As Re-Enactment: R. G. Collingwood's Idea of History(Oxford, 1999).

Colour perception theories of, theories of colour perception propose to explain how it is that colours are perceived as properties of physical objects. What proposal one makes depends in turn on what proposal one makes about the nature of colour.

By contrast with theories of colour see colours theories of, which address the problem of the nature of colour, theories of colour perception address the problem: how is it that colours (whatever their nature) are perceived as properties of physical objects? However, the answer one gives to this question about colour perception does depend on one's theory of colour. If one proposes that the colours we perceive physical objects as having are mental qualitative properties of visual states themselves (the proposal about the nature of colour calledsubjectivism), then one must explain how it is that mental qualitative properties are perceived as properties of mind-independent objects. The subjectivist's options seem to be limited to sense datum theories (see sense data) and projectivist theories.

If one proposes that the colours we perceive physical objects as having are properties of physical objects (as is claimed by physicalist and dispositionalist proposals about the constituting nature of colour), then an explanation of how it is colours are perceived as properties of physical objects is relatively straightforward. However, the question remains whether this access is mediated by visual states with mental qualitative properties.

Intentionalist theories of perception claim that visual states of colour are representational states which have no qualitative properties apart from those that they represent. Thus, it holds that the qualitative aspects of colour experience aren't determined by mental qualitative properties of experience itself. Most intentionalists hold physicalism about the nature of colour, which claims that the colours we attribute to physical objects in visual states are physical properties of physical objects. Also, most physicalists (including Smart, Armstrong, Hilbert, Byrne and Hilbert) are intentionalists.

Intentionalism is rejected by most dispositionalists about the nature of colour. According to dispositionalism, the colours we perceive physical objects as having are dispositions of physical objects to produce perceptual responses. The most common version of dispositionalism holds that perceptual responses are visual states of colour characterised in terms of mental qualitative properties, in particular, colour qualia (currently, Peacocke and McDowell; formerly, McGinn and Johnston).

However, even though most dispositionalists reject intentionalism, these theorists do not thereby claim that the colours we perceive physical objects as having are colour qualia them-selves. (If they were to claim this, they would have to explain how qualia are perceived as properties of mind- independent objects—the options would be some version of sense datum theory or projectivism). Rather, Peacocke, for example, claims that the colours we perceive physical objects as having are dispositional properties of physical objects. Colour qualia determine what it's like to experience physical properties of physical objects as colours.

Thompson's answer to the problem of colour perception cannot be easily categorised as intentionalist or non-intentionalist. He addresses the problem from the standpoint of the evolution of colour perception in different species. His answer takes an ecological approach to characterising colour perception.

According to sense datum theories, perceptual states are relations between perceivers and sense data, mental objects that have mental colours and mental shapes. According to Jackson's sense datum theory (which Jackson has by now rejected—see Jackson and Pargetter), physical objects seem to be coloured because coloured sense data are caused by physical objects and the spatial properties of sense data vary as a function of the spatial properties of physical objects. Sense datum theories face difficulties in explaining how sense data, as mental objects, are related to the physical states and in particular the neural states of perceivers. Furthermore, according to Jackson's theory, sense data, which are mental objects, are located in three-dimensional physical space. Jackson's theory faces difficulties in explaining the relation between perceivers and sense data located outside of their bodies in physical space. By contrast with sense datum theories, adverbialist theories claim that perceptual states are relations between perceivers and (actual or nonactual) physical objects rather than sense data, and that perceptual states themselves have mental properties such as mental colours. Mental colours are then held to be identified with, or supervenient on, properties of neural states of perceivers. Most current theories of colour perception which claim that perceptual states have mental colours assume an adverbialist theory of perceptual states of colour.

According to projectivist theories, in colour perception mental colours, characterised as properties of perceptual states rather than sense data, are experienced as properties of mind-independent objects. There are two versions of projectivism, which provide different explanations for how it is that mental colours are experienced as properties of mind-independent objects. According to one, proposed by Boghossian and Velleman, mental colours are experienced as properties of physical objects. But since mental colours are properties of visual states, experiencing mental colours as properties of physical objects involves experiencing properties of mental states as operties of physical objects. Since states are funda-mentally different sorts of things than objects, it's not clear that it even makes sense to hold that we experience properties of mental states as properties of physical objects. According to the other version of projectivism, proposed by McGilvray, we are not aware of physical objects or any of their properties in perception. McGilvray doesn't deny that there are physical objects. Rather, he claims that the spatial properties as well as the colours we're aware of in visual perception are mental qualitative properties of visual states themselves. Thus what we're aware of in visual perception are mind-dependent patches with mental colours and mental shapes. (Alth-ough this claim suggests a sense datum theory, McGilvray explicitly accepts an adverbialist theory of perceptual states.) McGilvray claims that projective representation of colour involves experiencing such mind-dependent colour patches as external to our minds. But if the locations we're aware of in visual experience are never physical locations, the problem now is that it's difficult to characterize these mental locations that McGilvray claims we are aware of. He holds that we can describe mental locations as external to our minds by way of describing them as points in a three-dimensional visual field. However, McGilvray provides no explanation of the relation between perceivers, located in physical space, and the three-dimensional visual field comprised of mental locations, rend-ering mental locations mysterious.

Intentionalist theories of perception claim that visual states of colour are representational states which have no qualitative properties apart from those that they represent. Any proposal about colour perception that claims that visual states of colour have mental qual-itative properties, for example, colour qualia, rejects intentionalism. An objection to intentionalist theories asserts that such theories cannot account for the colours of afterimages. In a recent formulation of this objection, Boghossian and Velleman claim that when we represent an afterimage as an after-image, and not a physical object, what's represented as coloured can't be a physical object, but rather must be a part of the visual field itself. (Although this claim suggests a sense datum theory, Boghossian and Velleman state that their claim is consistent with adverbialism.). Boghossian and Velleman assume that when we represent an afterimage as coloured, then something is represented as coloured. However, it isn't clear that their assumption is correct. We may make the inference that if we represent an afterimage as coloured, then we represent something as coloured. But we can't make the inference that there is something that is represented as coloured, namely, the visual field. Rather, intentionalists would argue that when we represent an afterimage as coloured, we attribute a physical qualitative property to a merely intentional—not an actual—object. What intentional objects are and how physical qualitative properties relate to them is indicated by a theory of intentionality. However, those who accept that visual experiences have mental colours, for example, qualia, may claim that afterimage colours are mental colours. And this may seem to be a more plausible way of acco-unting for afterimage colours.

Thompson addresses the question of how colours are perc-eived as properties of physical objects from the standpoint of the evolution of colour perception in different species. On the basis of comparative studies of the visual systems of different species, Thom-pson claims that different species' colour vision has evolved to perform biological functions which must be described in ecological terms. But how we are to characterize the biological function of colour vision is contr-oversial. (The notion of biological function used in this context is Wright's notion, or some variation on it.). Hilbert addresses the problem of colour perception from the standpoint of computational colour vision, according to which vision involves the processing of infor-mation contained in representations that encode physical properties of objects in the world. A focus of research in computational colour vision is the problem of how a visual system achieves what's called colour constancy. colour constancy is a visual effect in which the colour a physical object looks remains fairly constant despite changes in the light illuminating the object. As it turns out, the constant colours that we perceive physical surfaces as having are correlated with surface refle-ctance. (Surface reflectance is the ratio of reflected to incident light for a surface, where light is measured by its wavelength composition and its intensity at each wavelength.) Hilbert argues that colour constancy shows that the biological function of colour vision is to detect physical object surfaces by way of surface refle-ctance, and thus characterizes the biological function of colour vision in physical terms. By contrast, Thompson offers an alternative characterisation of the biological function of colour vision in ecological terms. Thompson appeals to Mollon's proposal that the biological function of primate colour vision includes promoting the detection of objects in contexts described in ecological terms, for example, the detection of fruit against a back-ground of foliage, or the detection of objects against backgrounds which may include things without surfaces, such as volumes of water or the sky. According to Thompson, comparative colour vision indicates that there are nonhuman species with colour vision, and that for these species the biological function of colour vision cannot be described merely in terms of detecting object surfaces by way of surface reflectances. Hatfield provides further considerations in favour of characterising the bio-logical function of colour vision in ecological terms. Psycho-physics indicates that objects with different surface reflectances can produce perceptions of the same determinate colour (such as teal). Such physically distinct objects are called metamers. If we describe the biological function of colour vision as the detection of object surfaces by way of reflectance properties, then metamerism marks a failure of the visual system. Hatfield points out that if the biological function of colour vision isn't best described as the detection of object surfaces by way of surface reflectance, but rather as, for example, the detection of objects against backgrounds, then it doesn't follow that metamerism marks a failure—the task of detecting fruit against a background of foliage isn't hampered by metamerism. In fact, the detection of objects against backgrounds is better served by a relatively small number of broad colour categories which include starkly contrasting pairs, such as red and green, and yellow and blue. Thompson argues that if the biological function of colour vision is to be described in ecological terms, then colours are relations between perceivers and objects. Thompson supports this claim by citing studies that indicate that species which have evolved in different ecological niches have different categories by which colours are classified as qualitatively identical or similar. But it may be that whereas the colour categories of a species are best explained in terms of ecological relations between members of the species and objects in their environments (over the course of evolution), the colours themselves are nonrelational properties of objects.

References: Armstrong, D. M. (1987). "Smart and the Secondary Qualities" in Metaphysics and Morality: Essays in Honour of J. J. C. Smart, eds. Philip Pettit, Richard Sylvan, and Jean Norman. Oxford: Basil Blackwell, 1-15. Boghossian, Paul A. and J. David Velleman (1989). "Colour as a Secondary Quality" Mind, Vol. 98, No. 389 (January 1989): 81-103. Byrne, Alex and David R. Hilbert (1997). "colours and Reflectances" in Readings on colour, Vol. 1, The Philosophy of colour, eds. Alex Byrne and David R. Hilbert. Cambridge, Mass.: The MIT Press. Hatfield, Gary (1992). "colour Perception and Neural Encoding: Does Metameric Matching Entail a Loss of Information?" in Proceedings of the 1992 Biennial Meeting of the Philosophy of Science Association, Vol. 1, Contributed Papers, eds. David Hull, Micky Forbes, and Kathleen Okruhlik, 492-504. Hilbert, David R. (1992). "What Is colour Vision?", Philosophical Studies, Vol. 68, No. 3 (December 1992): 351-370. Jackson, Frank (1977). Perception: A Representative Theory. Cambridge: Cambridge University Press. Jackson, Frank and Robert Pargetter (1987). "An Objectivist's Guide to Subjectivism about Colour", Revue Internationale de Philosophie, Vol. 41. No. 160 (fascicule 1/1987): 127-141. Johnston, Mark (1992). "How to Speak of the colours" Philosophical Studies, Vol. 68, No. 3 (December 1992): 221-263. McDowell, John (1985). "Values and Secondary Qualities" in Morality and Objectivity: A Tribute to J. L. Mackie, ed. Ted Honderich. London: Routledge & Kegan Paul, 110-129. McGilvray, James A. (1994). "Constant colours in the Head" Synthese, Vol. 100, No. 2 (August 1994): 197-239. McGinn, Colin (1983). The Subjective View: Secondary Qualities and Indexical Thoughts. Oxford: Clarendon Press. Mollon, J. D. (1989). "'Tho" She Kneel'd in That Place Where They Grew..." The Uses and Origins of Primate Colour Vision" Journal of Experimental Biology, Vol. 146 (September 1989): 21-38. Peacocke, Christopher (1984). "colour Concepts and colour Experiences" Synthese, Vol. 58, No. 3 (March 1984): 365- 381. Smart, J. J. C. (1975). "On Some Criticisms of a Physicalist Theory of colours" in Philosophical Aspects of the Mind-Body Problem, ed. Chungying Cheng. Honolulu: University of Hawaii Press, 54-63. Thompson, Evan (1995). Colour Vision: A Study in Cognitive Science and the Philosophy of Perception. London: Routledge.

Colour theories of, theories of colour make proposals about the nature of the colours that we attribute to physical objects in visual perception. The most common proposals are that these colours are mental properties of perceptual states (subjectivism), they are physical properties of physical objects (physicalism), or they are dispositions of physical objects to produce perceptual states of colour (dispositionalism).

The problem of the constituting nature of colour is typically put in terms of the following question about the intentional content of visual states of colour: what sorts of properties are the colours that we attribute to physical objects in virtue of our visual states of colour? Are attributed colours, for example, physical properties of physical objects? Or are they other sorts of properties, such as mental properties of visual states themselves, or dispositions of physical objects to produce visual states of colour?

The problem of the constituting nature of colour has been largely motivated by concerns about how colour fits into a scientific description of the world. In the seventeenth century, Galileo and Newton undertook a comprehensive description of nature in terms of mathematical physics. Physics requires that if colours are properties of physical objects, then they are describable in physical terms.

However, due to problems with understanding how colours can be describable in physical terms, many philosophers and scientists since the time of Galileo have come to reject the claim that colours are physical properties of physical objects. Most theorists assume that if we reject this claim, then the nature of colours must be characterised—at least in part—in terms of our mental nature.

In addressing the problem of the nature of the colour we attribute to physical objects in visual states we must consider the following question: how do we characterize the nature of these visual states (also commonly called visual experiences). Some theorists claim visual experiences of colour have both intentional pro-perties and mental qualitative properties which I'll call mental colours; other theorists claim they have intentional properties but don't have mental colours. Those who claim that colour experiences have both intentional properties and mental colours include some physicalists (Lewis, Shoemaker), most dispos-itionalists (currently, Peacocke and McDowell; formerly, McGinn and Johnston), and all subjectivists. Those who claim that visual experiences of colour have inten-tional properties but do not have mental colours include some dispos-itionalists (Smart [1961]) and most physicalists (Smart [1975], Arms-trong, Hilbert [1987 and 1992], and Byrne and Hilbert).

Mental colours are mental qualitative properties of colour experiences. Amongst those who characterize colour experiences as having mental colours, there's a controversy as to how todescribe mental colours. The main divide is between those who claim that mental colours are what it's like for a perceiver to be conscious of colour (Peacocke, McGinn, Shoemaker, Block), and those who describe mental colours in terms of causal relations, for example, in terms of functionally described processes of our visual systems (Hardin, Clark, McGilvray, Lewis).

Proponents of the claim that mental colours are what it's like for a perceiver to be conscious of colour hold that mental colours cannot be described in terms of causal relations. Mental colours described as what it's like to be conscious of colour are typically called qualia. According to subjectivism, the colours that we attribute to physical objects in colour experiences are mental colours, which are mental qualitative properties of visual states themselves. Thus subjectivism claims that physical objects are colourless. (Because subjectivism denies the existence of coloured physical objects, it is sometimes called colour elimin-ativism.) Two kinds of argument are offered in support of subjectivism. One kind stresses epistemological and phenomenological considerations; the other is founded on evidence from colour science, in particular, psycho-physics and neurophysiology. Boghossian and Velleman provide arguments of the first kind. In their 1991, they claim against physicalism that qualitative similarity relations among colours, such as that orange is more similar to red than it is to blue, specify essential features of determinate colours. Furthermore, they assert, ordinary experience provides access to these essential features. However, if physicalism were correct, these essential features would be relations among physical properties. They conclude that physicalism is false because ordinary experience doesn't provide access to relations among the relevant physical properties (namely, relations among surface reflectances). Furthermore, in their 1989 they claim against dispositionalism that colours cannot be dispositions to produce visual states of colour, for colours don't look like dispositions in our ordinary experience. However, disputable epistemological assumptions underlie both of these arguments. Against dispositionalism, they assume the very controversial claim that ordinary experience provides access to the constituting nature of colour, a claim that Johnston calls Revelation. Against physicalism, they assume a claim that physicalists deny, namely, that the qualitative similarity relations among colours specify essential features of determinate colours.

Hardin and McGilvray provide arguments for subjectivism founded on evidence from psychophysics and neurophysiology. Psychophysics indicates that objects with different surface reflectances can produce perceptions of the same determinate colour (such as teal); such physically distinct objects are called metamers. Metamerism is explained in terms of neurophysiology, and this neurophysiological explanation shows that for each determinate colour, indefinitely many different surface reflectances look that colour. Also, functionally described processes of our visual systems called opponent processes explain the qualitative similarity relations among perceived colours (such as that orange is qualitatively more similar to red than it is to blue) (see Hurvich). Fu-rthermore, there is no range of physical properties of objects the members of which are related intrinsically in ways that correspond with the qualitative similarity relations. (Members of a range of properties are related intrinsically so long as these relations are don't hold in virtue of relations between members of the range and members of a distinct range of properties.) Rather, physical properties of objects are related extrinsically in these ways, in virtue of relations between these physical properties and properties of the human visual system. Thus the qualitative identity and similarity relations among perceived colours are explained in terms of neuro-physiology. Because Hardin and McGilvray assume that on any tenable proposal of the constituting nature of colour, this constituting nature must explain these qualitative relations, they conclude colour science shows that perceived colours aren't physical properties of physical objects. Rather, Hardin and McGilvray claim colours are neural events of our visual systems. However, physicalists object to Hardin's and McGilvray's assu-mption. Physic-alists propose that we distinguish between the neural properties that explain the qualitative relations among perceived colours and the perceived colours themselves, which are physical properties of objects.

Physicalism claims that colours we attribute to physical objects in colour experiences are physical properties of those objects, or as I'll call them physical colours. There are several versions of physicalism. According to one type of physicalism held by Hilbert (1987 and 1992), physical colours are surface refle-ctances, and are individuated as finely as surface reflectances. How-ever, objects with different surface reflectances can be perceived as the same determinate colour (such physically distinct objects are called metamers). Thus perceived colours are indeterminate with respect to physical colour. And because colour science shows that metamerism is explained in terms of the neuro-physiology of the human visual system, Hilbert calls perceived colours anthropocentric colours. Nevertheless, Hilbert claims that perceived colours are objective, nonrelational properties of physical objects. On another type of physicalism held by Smart, Arms-trong, and Lewis, no distinction is drawn between physical colours and perceived colours. Physical colours just are the colours perceived by standard human colour perceivers in standard viewing conditions. Since the neurophysiological explanation of metamerism shows that for each determinate perceived colour ind-efinitely many different surface reflectances look that colour, physical colours are indefinitely large disjunctions of surface reflectances. Shoemaker proposes a third type of physicalism. He draws a distinction between the intentional contents and the qualitative contents of colour experiences. He claims that physical colours are included in intentional contents. But, he holds, these physical properties aren't perceived colours—the colours included in qalitative contents. Rather, perceived colours are relations between physical colours and visual exper-iences with colour qualia (which are mental qualitative properties which determine qualitative contents). Of course, Shoemaker's proposal depends on the controversial claim that visual states have qualia. Hilbert (1987 and 1992) argues for physicalism largely on the basis of the visual effect called colour constancy. Colour constancy is an effect in which the colour a physical object looks remains fairly constant despite changes in the light illuminating the object. As it turns out, the constant colours that we perceive physical surfaces as having are correlated with surface refl-ectance. Hilbert (1992) argues that colour constancy shows that the biological function of colour vision is to detect physical object surfaces by way of surface reflectance, and that, therefore, the colours we attribute to physical objects in visual states of colour are surface reflectances. However, some dispute Hilbert's characterisation of the biological function of colour vision in physical terms, and rather characterize this function in ecological terms. For example, Thompson and Hatfield object to Hilbert's physicalism from the standpoint of an ecological approach to colour perception, and claim that perceived colours are relations between objects and colour experiences. The Smart/ Armstrong/Lewis view holds that descriptions of relations between physical objects and colour experiences of standard perceivers in standard viewing conditions merely serve to fix the reference of colour terms (for a similar claim, see Kripke). However, the claim that perceived colours are disjunctions of physical properties is controversial. But crucial to a defence of this view is a distinction between properties and universals. Whereas Armstrong denies that universals can be disjunctive, he allows that properties can be disjunctive, where disjunctive properties can be explained in terms of ranges of universals. And perceived colours can be explained in terms of psychophysical laws that quantify the relations between ranges of physical properties of objects and visual states of colour. Since visual science indicates that the qualitative identity and similarity relations among perceived colours are explained in terms of neurophysiology, indepe-ndently of the physical colours themselves, physicalists claim that these qualitative relations don't specify essential features of determinate perceived colours. However, this claim is controversial (Boghossian and Velleman [1991], as well as Hardin and McGilvray assume that it's false; Johnston argues against it).

According to dispositionalism, the colours we attribute to physical objects in colour experiences are dispositions of physical objects to produce perceptual responses. Different versions of dispositionalism characterize perceptual responses differently. Smart (1961) characterizes perceptual responses nonqualitatively, namely, in terms of the discriminatory behaviour of perceivers. But the most common version of dispositionalism characterizes perceptual responses in terms of visual experiences with colour qualia, in particular such visual experiences of standard perceivers in standard viewing conditions (currently, Peacocke and McDowell; formerly, McGinn and Johnston). If the colours we attribute to objects are dispositions to produce visual experiences with colour qualia, then these colours are constituted by relations between some physical property or other of objects and visual experiences with colour qualia. Acco-rding to current versions of this view, even though the colours we attribute to objects are in part constituted by colour qualia, the colours we attribute to objects aren't themselves colour qualia. Rather, colour qualia determine what it's like to experience physical properties of physical objects as colours, and colours we attribute to physical objects are dispositional properties of physical-objects. Proponents of this version of dispositionalism argue that the colours we attribute to objects are in part constituted by colour qualia on epistemological grounds, in particular on the basis of the claim that ordinary experience provides access to essential features of colour. For example, Johnston claims that qualitative similarity relations among colour specify essential features of determinate colours to which ordinary experience provides access, and supports this claim with considerations about scepticism. However, physicalists reject this argument, and it remains controversial as to whether qual-itative similarity relations specify essential features of determinate colours at all.

References: (Note: "*" indicates more central reference) A bibliography of colour and philosophyStanford Encyclopedia entry on colour Armstrong, D. M. (1987). "Smart and the Secondary Qualities" in Metaphysics and Morality: Essays in Honour of J. J. C. Smart, eds. Philip Pettit, Richard Sylvan, and Jean Norman. Oxford: Basil Blackwell, 1-15. Block, Ned (1990). "Inverted Earth" in Philosophical Perspectives, 4: Action Theory and Philosophy of Mind, ed. James E. Tomberlin. tascadero, Cal.: Ridgeview Publishing Company, 53-79. *Bogh-ossian, Paul A. and J. David Velleman (1989). "Colour as a Secondary Quality", Mind, Vol. 98, No. 389 (January 1989): 81-103. Boghossian, Paul A. and J. David Velleman (1991). "Physicalist Theories of colour", Philosophical Review, Vol. 100, No. 1 (January 1991): 67-106. *Byrne, Alex and David R. Hilbert (1997). "colours and Reflectances" in Readings on colour, Vol. 1, The Philosophy of colour, eds. Alex Byrne and David R. Hilbert. Cambridge, Mass.: The MIT Press. *Clark, Austen (1993). Sensory Qualities. Oxford: Clarendon Press. *Hardin, C. L. (1993). colour for Philosophers: Unweaving the Rainbow, Expanded Edition. Indianapolis: Hackett Publishing Company. Hatfield, Gary (1992). "colour Perception and Neural Encoding: Does Metameric Matching Entail a Loss of Information?" in Proceedings of the 1992 Biennial Meeting of the Philosophy of Science Association, Vol. 1, Contributed Papers, eds. David Hull, Micky Forbes, and Kathleen Okruhlik, 492-504. *Hilbert, David R. (1987). colour and colour Perception: A Study in Anthropocentric Realism. Stanford: Center for the Study of Language and Information. Hilbert, David

R. (1992). "What Is colour Vision?", Philosophical Studies, Vol. 68, No. 3 (December 1992): 351-370. *Hurvich, Leo M. (1981). colour Vision. Sunderland, Mass.: Sinauer Associates Inc. Hurvich, Leo M. (1981). colour Vision. Sunderland, Mass. Sinauer Associates Inc. Kripke, Saul (1972). Naming and Necessity. Cambridge, Mass. Harvard University Press. Lewis, David (1995). "Should a Materialist Believe in Qualia?", Australasian Journal of Philosophy, Vol. 73, No. 1 (March 1995): 140-144. *Johnston, Mark (1992). "How to Speak of the colours", Philosophical Studies, Vol. 68, No. 3 (December 1992): 221-263. McDowell, John (1985). "Values and Secondary Qualities" in Morality and Objectivity: A Tribute to J. L. Mackie, ed. Ted Honderich. London: Routledge & Kegan Paul, 110-129. McGilvray, James A. (1994). "Constant colours in the Head", Synthese, Vol. 100, No. 2 (August 1994): 197-239. McGinn, Colin (1983). The Subjective View: Secondary Qualities and Indexical Thoughts. Oxford: Clarendon Press. *Peacocke, Christopher (1984). "colour Concepts and colour Experiences", Synthese, Vol. 58, No. 3 (March 1984): 365- 381. *Shoemaker, Sydney (1996). "colours, Subjective Relations, and Qualia" in Philosophical Issues, 7: Perception, ed. Enrique Villanueva. Atascadero, Cal.: Ridgeview Publishing Company, 55-66. Smart, J. J. C. (1961). "Colours", Philosophy, Vol. 36, No. 137 (April and July 1961): 128-142. *Smart, J. J. C. (1975). "On Some Criticisms of a Physicalist Theory of colours" in Philosophical Aspects of the Mind-Body Problem, ed. Chung-ying Cheng. Honolulu: University of Hawaii Press, 54-63. Thompson, Evan (1995). Colour Vision: A Study in Cognitive Science and the Philosophy of Perception. London: Routledge. See also colour perception theories of Peter Ross.

Combination, 1. A set containing a certain number of objects selected from another set. The number of combinations of r objects chosen from a set of n is where

$$n \mathrm{C} r = n! / ((n - r)!\, r!)$$

"n C r" is normally with n and r as subscripts or as n above r in parentheses. See also permutation.

2. In the theory of combinators, a combination denotes an expression in which function application is the only operation.

Combinatory logic, A system for reducing the operational notation of logic, mathematics or a functional language to a sequence of modifications to the input data structure. First introduced in the 1920's by Schoenfinkel. Re-introduced independently by Haskell Curry in the late 1920's (who quickly learned of Schoenfinkel's work after he had the idea). Curry is really responsible for most of the development, at least up until work with Feys in 1958. See combinator.

Communalism, collectivism or communism on a smaller scale or on a voluntary basis, usually in a utopia or an ideal community, utopianism. For example, there were many communalist utopias in 19th century America which did not really subscribe to what one would call communism. (Reference from collectivism).

Communication system, A system or facility capable of providing information transfer between persons and equipment. The system usually consists of a collection of individual comm-unication networks, transmission systems, relay stations, tributary stations, and terminal equipment capable of interconnection and interoperation so as to form an integrated whole. These individual components must serve a common purpose, be technically compatible, employ common procedures, respond to some form of control, and generally operate in unison.

Communism, political theory according to which the individual's actions should benefit the community or the state rather than the individual himself. It is the most radical kind of political collectivism, and depends on an equally radical form of collectivism or altruism in ethics. In practice, communism has always been a form of authoritarianism or of totalitarianism. When referring to actual political systems, communism is sometimes called Marxism-Leninism because of communism's link with therevolutionary doctrines of Marxism and with countries inspired by the examples of Lenin's revolution in Russia, and Mao's in China. (References from capitalism, collectivism, dialectical materialism, and socialism).

Communitarianism, With the demise of true socialism as a viable intellectual force, communitarianism is now the most active philosophical opposition to libertarianism. Communitarianism is usually presented in vague terms, but it is probably best understood as a moderate form of collectivism or "democratic socialism". Communitarianism has had some influence in the realm of practical politics.

Compatibilism, also known as "soft determinism" and most famously championed by Hume, this theory holds that free will and determinism are compatible. Properly understood, according to Hume, freedom is not an absolute ability to have chosen differently under exactly the same inner and outer circumstances. Rather it is a hypothetical ability to have chosen differently if one had been differently psychologically disposed by some ifferent beliefs or desires. Alternately, Hume maintains that free acts are not uncaused (or mysteriously self-caused as Kant would have it) but aused in the right way, *i.e.*, by our choices as determined by our our beliefs and desires, by our characters. See determinism. Contrast: hard determinism, libertarianism.

Compatibility, compatible

Complement, 1. The other value or values in the set of possible values. See logical complement, bitwise complement, set complement.

2. ***complement of a set***

The complement of a set *A* is the set of elements that are not members of A. Notation: *A* with a single bar over the top, or -*A*, or *A*'.

a. *Absolute complement of a set*

The set of all things whatsoever that are not members of the given set. Standard set theory does not recognize absolute complements. See Russell's paradox

b. *Relative complement of a set*

The set of all things that are not members of the given set, *A*, but that are members of some particular "background" set, *B*. This can be expressed through the notation for set difference: the relative complement of *A* in *B* or relative to *B* (*A* against the background of B) is the set *x*: (*x: B*) o (*x /: A*). The background set is sometimes called the universe or universe of discourse. Notation: *B-A*, or *B\A*.

Complete, See complete theory, negation completeness, omegacompleteness, semantic completeness, syntactic completeness complete graph, complete inference system, complete lattice, complete metric space, complete partial ordering

Complete graph, A graph which has a link between every pair of nodes. A complete bipartite graph can be partitioned into two subsets of nodes such that each node is joined to every node in the other subset.

Complete inference system, An inference system A is complete with respect to another system B if A can reach every conclusion which is true in B. The dual to completeness is soundness.

Completeness,complete theory, negation completeness, omega-completeness,semantic completeness, syntactic completeness com-plete graph, complete inference system, complete lattice, complete metric space, complete partial orde-ring a (logical) language is said to be complete iff all the formulas in the language that must be true (in any world in which the axioms of the language are true) can be proved from theaxioms. Goedel's incompleteness theorem shows that any language in which the truths of basic arithmetic can be formulated cannot be complete (unless the number of axioms is infinite).

Complex number, A number of the form $x+iy$ where i is the square root of -1, and x and y are real numbers, known as the "real" and "imaginary" part. Complex numbers can be plotted as points on a two-dimensional plane, known as an Arganddiagram, where x and y are the Cartesian coordinates.

An alternative, polar notation, expresses a complex number as (r e^it) where e is the base of natural logarithms, and r and t are real numbers, known as the magnitude and phase. The two forms are related:

$$r\, e^{it} = r \cos(t) + i\, r \sin(t)$$
$$= x + i\, y$$

where

$$x = r \cos(t)$$
$$y = r \sin(t)$$

All solutions of any polynomial equation can be expressed as complex numbers. This is the so-called Fundamental Theorem of Algèbra, first proved by Cauchy.

Complex numbers are useful in many fields of physics, such as electromagnetism because they are a useful way of representing a magnitude and phase as a single quantity.

Complex question, the informal fallacy of framing an issue as if it involved genuine alternatives while implicitly assuming the truth of the desired conclusion. Example: "Do you expect Peter to speak for thirty minutes or fifty? In either case, you acknowledge that he will be longwinded." Denying the presumption that lies behind both alternatives (in this case, that Peter will speak for at least thirty minutes) would eliminate the supposed evidence that the conclusion is true.

Component, a proposition that is part of a compound proposition. A component may itself be compound. For example, p is a component in $p => q$, and $p => q$ is a component in $(p => q) \vee r$.

Composite, aggregate.

Composition, One of the simple function-building operations of recursive function theory. Given the one-place functions $f(x)$ and $g(x)$, composition allows us to create function h thus: $h(x) = f(g(x))$. More generally, if f is an m-place, $f(x1...xm)$, and there is a series of n-place functions g, $g(x1...xn)$, then we can create the n-place function h by composition: $h(x1...xn) = f(g(x1...x\ n),...,gm\ (x1...xn))$. Also called substitu-tion.

Composition fallacy of, the informal fallacy of attributing some feature of the members of a collection to the collection itself, or reasoning from part to whole. Example: "Each of the elements in this compound (NaCl) is poisonous to human beings; therefore, this compound is itself poisonous to human beings."

Compositionality, representations may be said to be compositional insofar as they retain the same meaning across diverse contexts. Thus, "kick" means the same thing in the context of "...the ball", "...a rock", "... a dog", although it changes meaning in the context of "...the bucket". One might say that according to the principle of the compositionality of representations atomic representations make the same semantic contribution in every context in which they occur.

The term "compositionality of representations" is also used to refer to a putative psychological regularity that is supposed to support the view that there exists a syntactically and semantically combinatorial language of thought. The locus classicus for this argument is Fodor and Pylyshyn, 1988.

According to Fodor and Pylyshyn, in normal cognitive agents, there exist intrinsic connections between some thoughts and others. Thoughts come in clumps. This putative fact is the systematicity of cognitive representations. The compositionality of representations says something about the nature of the thoughts that are intrinsically connected. It says something about the nature of the clumps of mental thoughts: the thoughts in the clumps are semantically related. The thoughts in the clumps have common terms and predicates, for example. Thus, the thoughts "John loves Mary" and "Mary loves John" are compositional sets of representations since they both represent John, loving, and Mary.

According to Fodor and Pylyshyn, the reason that cognitive represe-ntations are compositional, as well as systematic is that there exists a syntactically and semantically combinatorial language of thought that respects the principle of compositionality, that atomic representations mean the same thing in all contexts in which they occur. The existence of a syntactically and semantically combinatorial language of thought respecting the principle of compositionality explains the compositionality of representations.

A theory that admits mental representations, but rejects combinatorial structure, lacks a genuine explanation of the compositionality of representations. Even if a normal cognitive agent has thoughts that are intrinsically connected to each other, there is no principled reason why it should be the case that these thoughts should be semantically related. Suppose that one thought involves the mental representation that is intrinsically connected to the mental representation. Even if it means John loves Mary, why hould mean Mary loves John, rather than say,

Alfred likes pizza? There seems to be no principled answer to this question.

References: Fodor, J., and Pylyshyn, Z. (1988). "Connectionism and cognitive architecture: A critique." Cognition, 28, 3-71. See systematicity, productivity, symbolicism.

Compound proposition, A proposition made up of two or more simple propositions (components) joined by a connective. A compound proposition has just one truth-value for a given interpretation. Also called "molecules" (by writers who call simple propositions "atoms").

Computability theory, The area of theoretical computer science concerning what problems can be solved by any computer.

A function is computable if an algorithm can be implemented which will give the correct output for any valid input.

Since computer programs are countable but real numbers are not, it follows that there must exist real numbers that cannot be calculated by any program. Unfortunately, by definition, there isn't an easy way of describing any of them!

In fact, there are many tasks (not just calculating real numbers) that computers cannot perform. The most well-known is the halting problem, the busy beaver problem is less famous but just as fascinating. ["Computability", N.J. Cutland. (A well written undergraduate-level introduction to the subject)]. ["The Turing Omnibus", A.K. Dewdeney].

Computable, see computability theory, computable function

Computable function, A total function for which there is an effective method for determining the value (output, member of the range), given the arguments (inputs, members of the domain).

Incomputable function

A function for which there is no such effective method.

Computation, a series of rule-governed state transitions whose rules can be altered.

There are numerous competing definitions of computation. Along with the initial definition provided here, the following three definitions are often encountered:

1) rule-governed state transi-tions
2) discrete rule-governed state transitions
3) rule-governed state transi-tions between interpretable states.

The difficulties with these definitions can be summarised as follows:

(1) admits all physical systems into the class of computational systems, making the definition somewhat vacuous.
(2) excludes all forms of analog computation, perhaps including the sorts of processing taking place in the brain.
(3) necessitates accepting all computational systems as representational systems. In other words, there is no computation without represe-ntation on this definition.

Computer ethics, Ethics is the field of study that is concerned with questions of value, that is, judgments about what human behaviour is "good" or "bad". Ethical judgments are no different in the area of computing from those in any other area. Computers raise problems of privacy, ownership, theft, and power, to name but a few.

Computer ethics can be grounded in one of four basic world-views: Idealism, Realism, Pragmatism, or Existentialism. Idealists believe that reality is basically ideas and that ethics therefore involves conforming to ideals. Realists believe that reality is basically nature and that ethics therefore involves acting according to what is natural. Pragmatists believe that reality is not fixed but is in process and that ethics therefore is practical (that is, concerned with what will produce socially-desired results). Existentialists believe reality is self-defined and that ethics therefore is individual (that is, concerned only with one's own conscience). Idealism and Realism can be considered ABSOLUTIST worldviews because they are based on something fixed (that is, ideas or nature, respectively). Pragmatism and Existentialism can be considered RELATIVIST worldviews because they are based or something relational (that is, society or the individual, respectively).

Thus ethical judgments will vary, depending on the judge's world-view. Some examples:

First consider theft. Suppose a university's computer is used for sending an e-mail message to a friend or for conducting a full-blown private business (billing, payroll, inventory, etc.). The absolutist would say that both activities are unethical (while rec-ognising a difference in the amount of wrong being done). A relativist might say that the latter activities were wrong because they tied up too much memory and slowed down the machine, but the e-mail message wasn't wrong because it had no significant effect on operations.

Next consider privacy. An instructor uses her account to acquire the cumulative grade point average of a student who is in a class which she instructs. She obtained the password for this restricted information from someone in the Records Office who erroneously thought that she was the student's advisor. The absolutist would probably say that the instructor acted wrongly, since the only person who is entitled to this information is the student and his or her advisor. The relativist would probably ask why the instructor wanted the information. If she replied that she wanted it to be sure that her grading of the student was consistent with the student's overall academic performance record, the relativist might agree that such use was acceptable.

Finally, consider power. At a particular university, if a professor wants a computer account, all she or he need do is request one but a student must obtain faculty sponsorship in order to receive an account. An absolutist (because of a proclivity for hierarchical thinking) might not have a problem with this divergence in procedure. A relativist, on the other hand, might question what makes the two situations essentially different (*e.g.* are faculty assumed to have more need for computers than students? Are students more likely to cause problems than faculty? Is this a hold-over from the days of "in loco parentis"?). "Philosophical Bases of Computer Ethics", Professor Robert N. Barger.

Computron, /kom'pyoo-tron"/ 1. A notional unit of computing power combining instruction speed and storage capacity, dimensioned roughly in instructions-per-second times meg-abytes-of-main-store times megab-ytes-of-mass-storage. "That machine can't run GNU Emacs, it doesn't have enough computrons!" This usage is usually found in metaphors that treat computing power as a fungible commodity good, like a crop yield or diesel horsepower. See bitty box, Get a real computer!, toy, crank.

2. A mythical subatomic particle that bears the unit quantity of computation or information, in much the same way that an electron bears one unit of electric charge (see also bogon). An elaborate pseudo-scientific theory of computrons has been developed based on the physical fact that the molecules in a solid object move more rapidly as it is heated. It is argued that an object melts because the molecules have lost their information about where they are supposed to be (that is, they have emitted computrons). This explains why computers get so hot and require air conditioning; they use up computrons. Conversely, it should be possible to cool down an object by placing it in the path of a computron beam. It is believed that this may also explain why machines that work at the factory fail in the computer room: the computrons there have been all used up by the other hardware. (This theory probably owes something to the "Warlock" stories by Larry Niven, the best known being "What Good is a Glass Dagger?", in which magic is fuelled by an exhaustible natural resource called "mana".)

Comte, Auguste (1798-1857), French positivist philosopher, one of the most important early figures in sociology. Comte was born in Montpellier on January 19, 1798. From an early age he rejected his family's Roman Catholicism and royalist political views. He attended the École Polytechnique in Paris from 1814 to 1816, but was expelled for participating in a student rebellion. For several years he was secretary to the noted socialist Claude Henri de Rouvroy, comte de Saint-Simon, whose influence is reflected in much of Comte's work. Comte's last years were, however, marked by periods of mental illness. He died in Paris on September 5, 1857.

In response to the scientific, political, and industrial revolutions of his day, Comte was fundamentally concerned with an intellectual, moral, and political reorganization of the social order. Adoption of the scientific attitude was the key, he thought, to such a reconstruction.

Comte argued that an empirical study of historical processes, particularly of the progress of the various interrelated sciences, reveals a law of three stages that governs human development. He analysed these stages in his major work, the six-volume *Course of Positive Philosophy* (1830-1842; trans. 1853). Because of the nature of the human mind, he thought, each science or branch of knowledge passes through "three different theoretical states: the theological or fictitious state; the metaphysical or abstract state; and, lastly, the scientific or positive state". At the theological stage, events are immaturely explained by appealing to the will of the gods or of God. At the metaphysical stage phenomena are explained by appealing to abstract philosophical categories. The final evolutionary stage, the scientific, involves relinquishing any quest for absolute explanations of causes.

Attention is wholly focused on how phenomena are related, with the aim of arriving at generalizations subject to observational verification. Comte's work is considered the classical expression of the positivist attitude—namely, that the empirical sciences are the only adequate source of knowledge.

Each of the stages, Comte believed, is correlated with certain political developments. The theological stage is reflected in such notions as the divine right of kings. The metaphysical stage involves such concepts as the social contract, the equality of people, and popular sovereignty. The positivist stage entails a scientific or "sociological" (a term coined by Comte) approach to political organization. Quite critical of democratic procedures, Comte envisioned a stable society governed by a scientific elite who would use the methods of science to solve human problems and improve social conditions.

Although he rejected belief in a transcendent being, Comte recognized the value of religion in contributing to social stability. In his four-volume *System of Positive Polity* (1851-1854; trans. 1875-1877), he proposed his religion of humanity, aimed at encouraging socially beneficial behaviour. Comte's chief significance, however, derives from his role in the historical development of positivism.

Comte Auguste M.E.X., French philosopher (1798-1857). As an early exponent of positivism, Comte was a founder of the discipline of sociology. In an early letter to M. Valat, Comte identified a methodological culture of science. His Cours de philosophie positive (Course in Positive Philosophy) (1830-1842) traces the historical development of philosophy from its origins in theological and met-aphysical thought to its culmination in observational science, especially the discipline of sociology. Comte proposed in SystËme de politique positive (System of Positive Polity) (1851) that political development should follow a similar path, resulting in a highly-organized communitarian state. Discours sur l'Ensemble du positivisme (A General View of Positivism) (1848) offers a convenient summary of his views. *Recommended Reading*: Auguste Comte, Introduction to Positive Philosophy, ed. by Frederick Ferre (Hackett, 1988); Auguste Comte and Positivism: The Essential Writings, ed. by Gertrude Lenzer (Transaction, 1998); Comte: Early Political Writings, ed. by H.S. Jones (Cambridge, 1998); and Mary Pickering, Auguste Comte: An Intellectual Biography (Cambridge, 1993).

Concept, a semantically evaluable, redeployable constituent of thought, invoked to explain properties of intentional phenomena such as productivity and systematicity. Applied to an assortment of pheno-mena including mental repre-sentations, images, words, ster-eotypes, senses, properties, reasoning abilities, mathematical functions, etc. See nonconceptual content.

Conceptualism, in philosophy, a theory that is intermediate between nominalism and so-called medieval, or logical, realism. Conceptualism maintains that although universals (abstractions or abstract ideas) have no real existence in the external world, they do exist as ideas or concepts in the mind and are thus something more than mere words. This theory contradicts nominalism, which holds that abstractions (universals) are mere figments of language, without any substantive reality, and that only individual objects have real existence. Conceptualism was espoused by the French scholastic philosopher Peter Abelard. *See* Idealism; Logic.

Conceptualization, The collection of objects, concepts and other entities that are assumed to exist in some area of interest and the relationships that hold among them. A conceptualisation is an abstract, simplified view of the world that we wish to represent. For example, we may conceptualise a family as the set of names, sexes and the relationships of the family members. Choosing a conceptualisation is the first stage of knowledge representation.

Every knowledge base, knowledgebased system, or knowledge-level agent is committed to some conceptualisation, explicitly or implicitly.

Conceptualism, the theory that universals are general ideas, such as the idea of man or of redness, which exist in minds and only in minds, but it is grounded on experience. This view is typically contrasted with—and held as a kind of compromise between—nominalism and realism. In the history of philosophy Peter Abelard (1079-1142) is usually called a conceptualist. He was a logician who opposed both the nominalism and the intrinsicism of his age. Abelard sought a middle position between these two poles of thinking, and ended up with views in epistemology that were quite similar to those of Aristotle or the later Aristotelians namely, that conceptual knowledge consists in an objective relation between reality and the mind (see objectivism and Aristotelianism).

Conceptual role semantics, functional role semantics.

Conclusion, The result of an argument or inference. The wff derived from or supported by premises.

Concomitant variation method of, one of Mill's Methods. If an antecedent circumstance is observed to change proportionally with the occurrence of a phenomenon, it is probably the cause of that phen-omenon. Example: "The more coffee I drink, the more difficult it is to fall asleep at night. Therefore, drinking coffee may be a cause of my insomnia." *Recommended Reading*: John Stuart Mill, System of Logic (Classworks, 1986).

Concrete class, In object-oriented programming, a class suitable to be instantiated, as opposed to an abstract class.

Concretism, the view according to which only concrete things actually exist, and there are no such things as actual universals. Both Aristotle and Abelard are, in this sense of the word, concretists. (References from indivi-dualism and physicalism). [The Ism Book]

Condillac Etienne Bonnot de, French philosopher and clergyman (1715-1780); author of Logique (Logic) (1741), Essai sur l'origine des connaissances humaines (Essay on the Origins of Human Knowledge) (1746), Traité des systémes (Treatise on Systems) (1749), Traité des systémes (Treatise on Sense Perception) (1754), Traité des animaux (Treatise on Animals) (1755), and Langue des calculs (The Language of Numbers) (1777). As one of the Encyclopedists, Condillac was the foremost French popularizer of the empiricist philosophy of Locke. *Recommended Reading*: Philosophical Writings of Etienne Bonnot, Abbe De Condillac, ed. by Franklin Phillip (Erlbaum, 1987) and Jacques Derrida, The Archeology of the Frivolous: Reading Condillac, tr. by John P. Leavey (Nebraska, 1987).

Conditional, any statement of the form: "If (antecedent), then (consequent)." Although conditionals may have several uses in ordinary language, all share at least the truth-functional structure of material implication. *Recommended Reading*: Anthony Appiah, Assertion and Conditionals (Cambridge, 1985); Nelson Goodman, Fact, Fiction, and Forecast (Harvard, 1983); Frank Jackson, Conditionals (Oxford, 1991); H. McLaughlin, On the Logic of Ordinary Conditionals (SUNY, 1990); and Michael Woods, Conditionals, ed. by David Wiggins and Dorothy Edgington (Clarendon, 1997). See implication.

Confirmation, the relationship between empirical evidence and the scientific hypotheses it is used to support. Although abductive reasoning can provide only partial or incomplete support for such hypotheses, their falsification by contadictory evidence can be absolute. Hempel pointed out a systematic paradox regarding the nature of confirming instances. *Recommended Reading*: Karl R. Popper, Logic of Scientific Discovery (Routledge, 1992); Richard Swinburne, An Introduction to Confirmation Theory (Methuen, 1973); Lawrence Sklar, Probability and Confirmation (Garland, 1999); and Induction, Probability, and Confirmation, ed. by Maxwell Grover and Robert Anderson.

Confucianism, Confucianism derives its name from the great sage K'ung Fu Tzu or Confucius (550-480 B.C.), who was in many ways the Chinese equivalent of Socrates(470-399 B.C.). Confucianism is the main stream of Chinese philosophy, just as Western philosophy is mostly in the Socratic tradition. Although his views have been interpreted in various ways throughout history, no one denies that the philosophy of Confucius is a powerful variety of humanism. Herbert Fingarette's book on Confucius is subtitled "The Secular as Sacred". Confucius holds that the most important, indeed sacred, aspect of life is our dealings with other people, so that he puts a great emphasis on virtues like honesty, justice, integrity, and so on. He provides a great many insights about human relationships. Sometimes, when people talk about "Conf-ucianism" they are referring not so much to Confucius' actual views as to the way his writings were used by later interpreters to justify reactio-nary political practices like a large bureaucracy and the strati-fication of society.

Confucianism, major system of thought in Chinese philosophy, developed from the teachings of Confucius and his disciples, and concerned with the principles of good conduct, statecraft, practical wisdom, and proper social relationships. Confucianism has influenced the Chinese attitude towards life, set the patterns of living and standards of social value, and provided the intellectual unde-rpinning for Chinese political theories and institutions. It has spread from China to Korea, Japan, and Vietnam, becoming a constant factor in East Asian culture, and has aroused interest among Western scholars almost from the moment it was introduced to the West.

Although Confucianism became the official ideology of the Chinese state, it has never existed as an established religion with a Church and priesthood. Chinese scholars honoured Confucius as a great teacher and sage but did not worship him as a personal god, though the ancestor worship integral to Chinese religion can confuse Western observers on this point. Nor did Confucius himself ever claim divinity. Unlike Christian churches, the temples built to Confucius were not places in which organized community groups gathered to worship, but public edifices designed for annual ceremonies, especially on the philosopher's birthday. Several attempts to deify Confucius and to preach Confucianism as a cult failed because of the essentially secular nature of the philosophy.

Foundations of Confucianism: The principles of Confucianism are contained in the nine ancient Chinese works handed down by Confucius and his followers, who lived during the Zhou dynasty in an age of great philosophic activity. These writings can be divided into two groups: the Five Classics and the Four Books.

The *Wujing* (Five Classics), which originated before the time of Confucius, consist of the *Yijing* or *I Ching* (Book of Changes), *Shujing* (Book of Documents), *Shijing* (Book of Poetry), *Liji* (Book of Rites), and *Chunqiu* (Spring and Autumn Annals). The *Yijing* is a manual of divination probably first compiled under the Shang dynasty before the 11th century BC; its supplementary philosophical portion, contained in a series of appendixes, may have been written later by Confucius and his disciples. The *Shujing* is a collection of ancient historical documents, and the *Shijing*, an anthology of ancient poems. The *Liji* deals with the principles of conduct, including those for public and private ceremonies; it was destroyed in the 3rd century BC, but presumably much of its material was preserved in the present compilation, which dates from the Han dynasty. The *Chunqiu*, the only work reputedly compiled by Confucius himself, is a chronicle of major historical events in Confucius's home state of Lu and elsewhere in feudal China from the 8th century BC to Confucius's death early in the 5th century BC.

The *Sishu* (Four Books), compilations of the sayings of Confucius and Mencius and of commentaries by followers on their teachings, are the *Lunyu* (Analects), a collection of maxims by Confucius that form the basis of his moral and political philosophy; *Daxue* (The Great Learning) and *Zhongyong* (The Doctrine of the Mean), containing some of Confucius's philosophical utterances arranged systematically with comments and expositions by his disciples; and the *Mengzi* (Book of Mencius), containing the teachings of one of Confucius's great followers.

Confucius's own teachings were passed on as oral traditions and collated in the *Lunyu*. They show him as a self-confessed moral conservative in a turbulent age, appalled at the political chaos and social changes which followed the disintegration of the Zhou kingdom into warring feudal states. This turbulence had forced Confucius and others to start thinking about the lost "Way of the Ancient Kings" of Zhou, and how to restore it, obliging them to become philosophical innovators despite themselves.

For Confucius, social and political order were the same, and the personal virtue of rulers and gentlemen ensured the health of the state. His keys to good order were rites (*li*) and music, for Chinese music of the period was central to religious and official rites, and Confucius valued both its ritual function and its power to move men's hearts. He also valued the poems of ancient Chinese literature (most of which were sung to music) as civilizing and edifying influences. Allied to this was his emphasis on the rectification of names, ensuring that the correct social and other distinctions were maintained by using only the appropriate words for them. A state provided with the most fitting rites and music, selected from the various available traditions, would automatically produce virtuous and happy citizens; laws would be almost unnecessary because disputes would never arise. Confucius roamed China seeking in vain for a sympathetic ruler to adopt his scheme.

The keynote of Confucian ethics is *ren,* variously translated as "love", "goodness", "humanity", and "human-heartedness". *Ren* is a supreme virtue representing human qualities at their best; in Confucius's time it apparently was associated with the ruling class and had a meaning more like "nobility", but its usage soon broadened. In human relations, construed as those between one person and another, *ren* is manifested in *zhong,* or faithfulness to oneself and others, and *shu,* or altruism, best expressed in the Confucian golden rule, "Do not do to others what you do not want done to yourself". Other important Confucian virtues include righteousness, propriety, integrity, and filial piety. One who possesses all these virtues becomes a *junzi* (perfect gentleman). Politically, Confucius advocated a paternalistic government in which the sovereign is benevolent and honourable and the subjects are respectful and obedient. The ruler should cultivate moral perfection in order to set a good example to the people, and to attract subjects to swell his realm. In education Confucius upheld the theory, remarkable for the feudal period in which he lived, that "in education, there is no class distinction".

Confucian Schools of Thought: After the death of Confucius two major schools of Confucian thought emerged: one was represented by Mencius, the other by Xunzi (Hsün-tzu). Mencius continued the ethical teachings of Confucius by stressing the innate goodness of human nature. He believed, however, that original human goodness can become depraved through one's own destructive effort or through contact with an evil environment. The problem of moral cultivation is therefore to preserve or at least to restore the goodness that is one's birthright. In political thought, Mencius is sometimes considered one of the early advocates of democracy, for he advanced the idea of the people's supremacy in the state. This thesis in fact developed from the Chinese religious rationale for kingship, the Mandate of Heaven. In this equ-ivalent of the Western divine right of kings, Heaven (*Tian*) conferred the right of kingship on a virtuous ruler, but could withdraw it from a tyrant. Mencius equated the will of Heaven with the will of the people, who would live happily under a good sovereign but would rise up against an oppressor.

In opposition to Mencius, Xunzi contended that a person is born with an evil (or at least, chaotic and ungovernable) nature, but that it can be regenerated through moral education. He believed that desires should be guided and restrained by the rules of propriety and that character should be moulded by an orderly observance of rites and by the practice of music. This code serves as a powerful influence on character by properly directing emotions and by providing inner harmony. Xunzi was the main later exponent of ritualism in Con-fucianism.

After a brief period of eclipse in the 3rd century BC, when the tyrannical Qin dynasty proscribed all philosophies other than its own orthodoxy of Legalism, Confucianism was revived during the Han dynasty (206 BC-AD 220). The Confucian works, copies of which had been destroyed in the preceding period, were restored to favour, canonized, and taught by learned scholars in national academies. The works also formed the basis of later civil service examinations; candidates for responsible government positions received their appointments on the strength of their knowledge of classic literature. Both the dynastic founder Gaodi and his great descendant Wudi officially supported Confucianism. As a result, Confucianism secured a firm hold on Chinese intellectual and political life, and was also spread by Wudi's armies into Vietnam.

The success of Han Confucianism was attributable to Dong Zhongshu, who first recom-mended a system of education built upon the teachings of Confucius. Drawing on ideas from contemporary cosmology and divination, Dong Zhongshu believed in a close correspondence between human beings and nature; thus a person's deeds, especially those of the sovereign, are often responsible for unusual phenomena in nature. Because of the sovereign's authority, he or she is to blame for such phenomena as fire, flood, earthquake, and eclipse. Since these ill omens can descend on Earth as a warning to humanity that all is not well in this world, the fear of heavenly puni-shment proves useful as a curb to the monarch's absolute power. Dong thus gained a check on imperial authority, at the cost of polluting the original Confucian rationalism.

In the political chaos that followed the fall of the Han dynasty, Confucianism was overshadowed by the rival systems of Daoism and Buddhism, and suffered a temporary setback. Nevertheless, the Confucian Classics continued to be the chief source of learning for scholars, and with the restoration of peace and prosperity in the Tang dynasty (618-906), the spread of Confucianism was encouraged. The monopoly of learning by Confucian scholars once again ensured them the highest bureaucratic positions. Confucianism returned as an orthodox state teaching. Inspired by the example of Chinese civilization, 7th-century Japan introduced a major programme of

Confucian state reform under Prince Shotoku and Emperor Tenji, establishing an imperial bureaucracy and examination system on the Chinese model. However, the new institutions made an unwieldy apparatus of government for a small aristocratic country like Japan, and became chiefly sources of honorary titles for the Fujiwara nobility.

Confucius, in Chinese Kongfuzi (c. 551-479 BC), Chinese philosopher, founder of Confucianism and one of the most influential figures in Chinese history.

According to tradition, Confucius was born in the state of Lu (present-day Shandong [Shantung] Province) of the noble Kong clan. His original name was Kong Qiu. Accounts of his life record that his father, commander of a district in Lu, died three years after Confucius was born, leaving the family in poverty; but Confucius nevertheless received a fine edu-cation, for Lu was famous for preserving the state traditions of the Zhou dynasty. He was married at the age of 19 and had one son and two daughters. During the four years immediately after his marriage, poverty reportedly compelled him to perform menial labours for the chief of the district in which he lived. His mother died in 527 BC, and after a period of mourning he began his career as a teacher, usually travelling about and instructing the small body of disciples that had gathered around him. His fame as a man of learning and character with great reverence for traditional ideals and customs soon spread through the principality of Lu.

Living as he did in the second half of the Zhou dynasty, when central government had degenerated in China and intrigue and vice were rampant, Confucius deplored the contemporary disorder and lack of moral standards. He came to believe that the only remedy was to convert people once more to the principles and precepts of the sages of antiquity. He therefore lectured to his pupils on the ancient classics of Chinese literature. He also stressed the importance of music, for the Chinese music of this time had ceremonial and religious functions important in state functions and worship. He taught the great value of the power of example. Rulers, he said, can be great only if they themselves lead exemplary lives, and were they willing to be guided by moral principles, their states would inevitably attract citizens and become prosperous and happy.

One popular tradition about Confucius's life states that at the age of 50 he was appointed magistrate of Zhongdu, and the next year minister of crime of the state of Lu. His administration was successful; reforms were introduced, justice was fairly dispensed, and crime was almost eliminated. So powerful did Lu become that the ruler of a neighbouring state manoeuvred to secure the minister's dismissal. It is more likely, however, that he was only a minor official in Lu. In any case, Confucius left his office in 496 BC, travelling about and teaching, vainly hoping that some other prince would allow him to undertake measures of reform. In 484 BC, after a fruitless search for an ideal ruler, he returned for the last time to Lu. He spent the remaining years of his life in retirement, writing commentaries on the classics. He died in Lu and was buried in a tomb at Qufu, Shandong.

Confucius did not put into writing the principles of his philosophy; these were handed down only through his disciples. The *Lunyu* (Analects), a work compiled by some of his disciples, is considered the most reliable source of information about his life and teachings. One of the historical works that he is said to have compiled and edited, the *Chunqiu* (Spring and Autumn Annals), is an annalistic account of Chinese history in the state of Lu from 722 to 481 BC. In learning he wished to be known as a transmitter rather than as a creator, and he therefore revived the study of the ancient books. His own teachings became the textbooks of later Chinese generations. Confucius was greatly venerated during his lifetime and in succeeding ages. Although he himself had little belief in the supernatural, he has been revered almost as a spiritual being by millions.

The entire teaching of Confucius was practical and ethical, rather than religious. He claimed to be a restorer of ancient morality and held that proper outward acts based on the five virtues of kindness, uprightness, decorum, wisdom, and faithfulness constitute the whole of human duty. Reverence for parents, living and dead, was one of his key concepts. His view of government was paternalistic, and he enjoined all individuals to observe carefully their duties towards the state. In subsequent centuries his teachings exerted a powerful influence on Chinese philosophy and the history of China.

Conjunctive Normal Form, (CNF) A logical formula consisting of a conjunction of disjunctions of terms where no disjunction contains a conjunction. Such a formula might also be described as a product of sums. *E.g.* the CNF of

(A and B) or C

is

(A or C) and (B or C).

Contrast Disjunctive Normal Form.

Connected graph, A graph such that there is a path between any pair of nodes (via zero or more other nodes).

Thus if we start from any node and visit all nodes connected to it by a single edge, then all nodes connected to any of them, and so on, then we will eventually have visited every node in the connected graph.

Connected subgraph, A connected graph consisting of a subset of the nodes and edges of some other graph.

Connectionism, a computational approach to modelling the brain which relies on the interconnection of many simple units to produce complex behaviour.

Connectionism has a number of important considerations for the philosophy of mind. By positing connectionist models as the best way to model human cognition, philosophers have begun to see high level mental properties as “emergent properties...that depend on lower-level phenomena in some systematic way” (Churchland and Sejnowski, 1992, p.2). These commitments have redefined for many the best way to understand the nature of representation and computation in the human mind. In his well known paper “On the proper treatment of connectionism’, Paul Smolensky forwards a connectionist (or subsymbolic) hypothesis in order to capture these new ideas:

> "The intuitive processor is a subconceptual connectionst dynamical system that does not admit a complete, formal, and precise conceptual-level escription."

This commitment to a "subconceptual" level of description of cognitive processes is a direct rejection of the symbolicist(see symbolicism) or GOFAI approach to human cognition.

Connectionist models can be classified by representational commitments in two categories; distributed and localist. Distributed representations are vectors in a representational state space, and are processed simultaneously by many nodes in a connectionist network. Localist models use individual nodes to represent one entire concept such as "dog". In general, distributed representations are more neurol-ogically realistic that localist repres-entations. However, distributed models are often far more complex and difficult to analyse than localist models.

Critiques of connectionism have been forwarded by dynamic systems theorists (dynamism), symbolicists (symbolicism), and neuroscientists. In particular, dynamic systems theorists claim that connectionist models are unrealistically wedded to ideas of representation and com-putation. Neuroscientists often note the lack of neurological realism in connectionist networks. These networks often have too little recursion, far too much inhibition, unrealistic learning algorithms, simplistic transfer functions, and no analog to the large number of neurotransmitters and hormones which affect human cognition.

Symbolicists have taken a number of lines of argument. Fodor and Pylyshyn (1988) have criticised connectionism as not being able to support the systematic and productive natures of human thought. As well, it is thought that the only role for connectionist work is to provide a method for implementing a symbolicist system in a manner similar to the brain. Thus, the best level of description of human cognition remains at the symbolic level. In recent years, however, a number of connectionist models have been produced which shows these criticisms to be questionable.

References: Connectionist Philosophy Biblio Neural Net Biblio) Neural Parallel Archive Jordan Pollack Computer Science Technical Reports Archive Churchland, P. S. and T. Sejnowski (1992). The computational brain. Cambridge, MA, MIT Press. Fodor, J. and Z. Pylyshyn (1988). "Connectionism and cognitive architecture: A critical analysis" Cognition 28: 3-71. Rumelhart, D. E. and J. L. McClelland, Ed. (1986). Parallel distributed processing: Explorations in the microstructure of cognition. Cambridge MA, MIT Press/Bradford Books.

Connectionism history of, construed broadly, connectionism maintains that cognitive processes are (implemented in) processes taking place in networks of nerve cells. Thus construed, the history of conne-ctionism spans a wide range of research in numerous disciplines over the course of centuries.

A central concern for connectionists is the idea that we must "take the brain seriously" in our psychological theorising. This idea, of course, dates to ancient Greek speculations concerning the action of animal spirits in the nervous system. Later, notable speculations may be found in Rene Descartes" Treatise of Man (composed circa 1633, first published posthumously in 1662) and David Hartley's Observations on Man (1749).

During the 19th Century, histologists developed staining and fixing techniques that enabled them to study the microscopic structure of the brain. With this information, the idea of taking the brain seriously took the form of relating psychological processes to neuronal processes. The existence of the nerve cell came to be widely accepted over the course of the 1890's. At this time, it was widely believed that psychological processes were associative processes. A long tradition of associationism was thus linked to theories of neural networks by the supposition that the biological correlate of the psychological process of association was the formation or strengthening of synaptic connections between neurons. Versions of late 19th Century neural network theorizing may be found in Herbert Spencer's Principles of Psychology, 3rd edition (1872), Theodore Meynert's Psychiatry (1884), William James "Principles of Psychology (1890), and Sigmund Freud's Project for a Scientific Psychology (composed 1895). Neural network theories with an associationist flavour were quite common around the turn of the century, up into the 1930's. Beginning in the 1910's, Karl Spencer Lashley began a series of animal experiments aimed at determining the effects of brain lesions. Lashley supposed that lesions would electively remove the neurons dedicated to specific tasks, hence destroy an animal's ability to perform those tasks. Rather than complete, selective loss of abilities, Lashley found that degradation of task performance was proportional to the amount of tissue removed. (See, for example, Lashley, 1929.) These results led to a decline in the popularity of neural network theories.

During the 1930's, Nicolas Rashevsky proposed to use differential equations and physical concepts, such as energy minim-isation, to describe how the behaviour of nerves and networks of nerves that might be related to psychological processes, such as Pavlovian conditioning. (See, for example, Rashevsky, 1931a, 1931b, 1935). Rashevsky's work was part of a larger project of developing a mathematical biophysics that would mirror the methods of mathematical physics. Rashevsky was instrumental in bringing together Warren S. McCulloch and Walter Pitts, who in 1943 published a seminal cont-ribution to many fields, "A Logical Calculus of Ideas Immanent in Nervous Activity". This work described how networks of binary threshold neurons might be described in terms of sentences of first-order logic. Although popularly remem-bered for having contributed the idea that networks might carry out logical inferences, McCulloch and Pitts were themselves more interested in the description of networks containing closed loops. This interest stemmed in part from McCulloch's work in tracing neural pathways using strychnine neuronography. Neuro-scientific findings by Rafael Lorente de No also increased the interest in closed neural circuits.

In 1949, Donald Olding Hebb, a student of Lashley's, proposed a cell assembly theory of cognition. This version of connectionism was meant to circumvent Lashley's problematic lesion results by supposing that the brain contains numerous redundant neural pathways spatially distributed over relatively broad regions of the brain. In roughly the same years, there was considerable neuroscientific investigation of so-called "post-tetanic potentiation'. It had been found that a large tetanic stimulation of a nerve innervating a muscle would lead to an enhanced effect of the nerve on the muscle. This provided a kind of confirmation of the hypothesis that learning at the psychological level might be realised by facilitation at the biological level. Sir John Eccles, among others, pursued this line of research for over two decades. This research is in some respects a precursor of the current immense interest in so-called "longterm potentiation" and "long-term depression". (See, for example, Baudry & Davis, 1994).

During the 1950's and 60's, Frank Rosenblatt investigated the properties of mathematically described neural networks with modifiable connections, discovering the so-called "perceptron convergence procedure" that could train a two-layer network to compute any two-layer-network-computable function. In 1969, Marvin Minsky and Seymour Papert published Perceptrons, a critique of this sort of neural network model. This work showed that two-layer networks were limited in the functions they could compute, thereby providing a major cause for a decline in neural network research during the 1970's.

During the late 1970's, Geoffrey Hinton, James McClelland, David Rumelhart, Paul Smolensky, and other members of the "Parallel Distributed Processing Research Group" became interested in neural network theories of cognition. Their landmark Parallel Distributed Processing: Explorations in the Microstructure of Cognition, (1986), marks the return of connectionism as a significant theory of cognition. Where previous strains of connectionism were more or less explicitly linked with associationism or logical inference, the new connectionism in PDP guise has been more cognitively eclectic, suggesting that cognitive processes might be constraint satisfaction processes, energy minimisation processes, or pattern recognition processes. It has also been, in large measure, defined, both by its supporters and oppo-nents, in relation to a computational theory of cognition. In this regard, contemporary advocates of connecti-onism often endorse a "subsymbolic paradigm" in contrast to the "symbolic paradigm" of the computational theory of cognition.

References: Baudry, M., Davis, J. L. (1994) (Eds.). Long-Term Potentiation, vol. 2. Cambridge, MA: MIT Press. Descartes, R. (1972, composed 1633). Treatise of man. Cambridge, MA: Harvard University Press. Freud, S. (1895). Project for a scientific psychology. First published in Strachey, J. (ed.). The standard edition of the complete psychological works of Sigmund Freud. London: The Hogarth Press and the Institute of Psycho-Analysis. Hartley, David. (1749). Observations on man, his frame, his duty, and his expectations. London: S. Richardson. Hebb, D. O.

(1949). The organisation of behavior: Aneurops-ychological approach. New York: John Wiley & Sons. James, W. (1890). Principles of psychology. New York, NY: Holt. Lashley, K. S. (1929). Brain mechanisms and intelligence: A quantitative study of injuries to the brain. New York: Dover Publications, Inc. McCulloch, W. S., and Pitts, W. "A Logical Calculus of Ideas immanent in Nervous Activity. Bulletin of mathematical biophysics", 5, 115-133. Reprinted in McCulloch, W. S., Embodiments of mind. Cambridge, MA: MIT Press. Meynert, Theodore (1884). Psychiatry. trans. B. Sachs. New York: G.P. Putnam's Sons. Minsky, M., and Papert, S. (1988). Perceptrons: An introduction to computational geometry, expanded edition. Cambridge, MA: MIT Press. Rashevsky, N. (1931a). "Learning as a Property of Physical Systems" Journal of general psychology, 5, 207-229. Rashevsky, N. (1931b). "Possible brain mechanisms and their physical models" Journal of General Psychology, 5, 368-406. Rashevsky, N. (1935). "Outline of a physico-mathematical theory of the brain" Journal of General Psychology, 13, 82-112. Rosenblatt, F. (1962). Principles of neurodynamics: Perceptrons and the theory of brain mechanisms. Washington, D.C.: Spartan Books. Rumelhart, D., McClelland, J. L., and the PDP Research Group (1986). Parallel distributed processing: Explorations in the microstructure of cognition. vols. 1 & 2. Cambridge, MA: MIT Press. Spencer, Herbert. (1872). Principles of psychology, 3rd ed. London: Longman, Brown, Green, and Longmans.

Connective, A symbol that functions to join two or more propositions into a compound proposition. Sometimes applied to symbols (like "~" for negation) which apply only to one proposition at a time. Sometimes applied to the function denoted by the symbol, rather than the symbol itself. A truth-functional connective is a truth-function; its components are its arguments and the truth-value of the compound it forms is its value.

Truth-functional connectives that apply to only one proposition at a time are monadic; those that join two propositions are dyadic; those that join three are triadic, and so on. Monadic connectives are also called operators. See truth-functional compound proposition

Connotation, the associative meaning of a term, including especially those features in virtue of which the term is properly applied; see denotation / connotation. *Recommended Reading*: Beatriz Garza-Cuaron, Connotation & Meaning (De Gruyter, 1991).

Conscience, inner awareness of the difference between right and wrong in one's own actions, usually understood as a divinely-inspired moral sense. Although Aquinas noted that an individual conscience may err, Butler held that it is the fundamental motive for good conduct. *Recommended Reading*: Joseph Butler, Fifteen Sermons on Human Nature (Classworks, 1986) and James Q. Wilson, The Moral Sense (Simon & Schuster, 1997).

Consciousness, self-awareness. Subjective experience. The way things seem to us. Immediate phenomenological properties. See also phenomenal consciousness, access consciousness.

The subjective phenomenon of self-awareness that normally accompanies human experience. Correct analysis of consciousness is a central goal in the philosophy of mind. *Recommended Reading*: Daniel C. Dennett, Consciousness Explained (Little, Brown, 1992); William G. Lycan,

Consciousness (Bradford, 1995); David J. Chalmers, The Conscious Mind: In Search of a Fundamental Theory (Oxford, 1997); and The Nature of Consciousness: Philo-sophical Debates, ed. by Ned Block and Owen Flanagan (MIT, 1997).

Consciousness access, access consc-iousness

Consciousness objection, an objection to materialism that maintains that, since mentality is fundamentally conscious and consciousness cannot be materialistically explained or reduced, mentality is something (a property or substance that is fundamentally immaterial. Also, an objection to artificial intelligence that maintains that, since consci-ousness cannot be mechanically (or computationally) generated, that machines (or computers) cannot think.

Consequence, semantic consequence, syntactic consequence

Consequent, the element of a conditional statement that states its outcome or result. For example, "You'll see me tomorrow" is the consequent of both: "If you come by the office, then you'll see me tomorrow." and "You'll see me tomorrow, unless I see you first." See implication

Consequentialism, any position in ethics which claims that the moral rightness or wrongness of actions depends on their consequences and therefore that moral decisions should be made on the basis of the expected outcome or consequences of the actions involved. pragmatism and utilitarianism are common forms of consequentialism. Consequentialist theories in ethics tend to be varieties of altruism, although haedonism can be represented as a coherent form of consequentialism. The term has some connotations of subjectivism, of deciding according to what the individual merely thinks is expedient. "Consequentialism" is a technical term in philosophy and is not used in popular discourse, where pragmatism and utilitarianism are more common.

Consistency, feature of any formal system from whose axioms no direct contradiction follows. The customary proof of consistency is to show that there is at least one interpretation of the system upon which all of its axioms are true. *Recommended Reading*: Richard C. Jeffrey, Formal Logic: Its Scope and Limits (McGraw-Hill, 1990). See absolute consistency, m-consistency, omegaconsistency, proof-theoretic consistency, relative consistency proof, simple consistency

Consistently complete, boundedly complete.

Constant, A symbol whose referent has been fixed. An abbreviation or name, as opposed to a place-holder (a variable).

Individual constant

A symbol standing for an individual object from the domain of a system.

Predicate constant

A symbol standing for an attribute or relation.

Propositional constant

A symbol standing for a proposition.

In a system of formal logic, any symbol that—unlike a variable-specifically designates an item. Thus, the propositional calculus employs statement constants, while quanti-fication theory makes use of both individual and predicate constants.

Constraint satisfaction, The process of assigning values to variables while meeting certain requirements or "constraints". For example, in graph colouring, a node is a variable, the colour assigned to it is its value and a link between two nodes represents the constraint that those two nodes must not be assigned the same colour. In scheduling, constraints apply to such variables as the starting and ending times for tasks.

The Simplex method is one well known technique for solving numerical constraints.

The search difficulty of constraint satisfaction problems can be determined on average from knowledge of easily computed structural properties of the problems. In fact, hard instances of NP-complete problems are concentrated near an abrupt transition between under—and over-constrained problems. This transition is analogous to phase transitions in physical systems and offers a way to estimate the likely difficulty of a constraint problem before attempting to solve it with search.

Constructed type, A type formed by applying some type constructor function to one or more other types. The usual constructions are functions: t1 -> t2, products: (t1, t2), sums: t1 + t2 and lifting: lift(t1). See also algebraic data type, primitive type.

Constructive, A proof that something exists is "constructive" if it provides a method for actually constructing it. Cantor's proof that the real numbers are uncountable can be thought of as a 'non-constructive' proof that irrational numbers exist. (There are easy constructive proofs, too; but there are existence theorems with no known constructive proof).

Obviously, all else being equal, constructive proofs are better than non-constructive proofs. A few mathematicians actually reject *all* non-constructive arguments as invalid; this means, for instance, that the law of the excluded middle (either P or not-P must hold, whatever P is) has to go; this makes proof by contradiction invalid. See intuitionistic logic for more information on this.

Most mathematicians are perfectly happy with non-cons-tructive proofs; however, the constructive approach is popular in theoretical computer science, both because computer scientists are less given to abstraction than mathem-aticians and because intuitionistic logic turns out to be the right theory for a theoretical treatment of the foundations of computer science.

Constructive proof, A proof that actually produces an example of that which it proves to exist (which might be a number, *wff*, function, proof, etc. with certain properties). See existence proof constructive.

Container class, A class whose instances are collections of other objects.

Examples include stacks, queues, lists and arrays.

Context, That which surrounds, and gives meaning to, something else.

In a grammar it refers to the symbols before and after the symbol under consideration. If the syntax of a symbol is independent of its context, the grammar is said to be context-free.

Context clash, When a parser cannot tell which alternative production of a syntax applies by looking at the next input token ("lexeme").

E.g. given syntax

C -> *A* | *b c*

A -> *d* | *b e*

If you're parsing non-terminal *C* and the next token is '*b*', you don't know whether it's the first or second alternative of *C* since they both can start with b.

To discover whether a grammar has a context clash:

For each non-terminal, N, with multiple alternatives, look at the first symbol of each alternative's right-hand side, call it s. If s is the empty string, then find the set FOLLOWER(N) otherwise find the set FIRST*(s). If any of the sets for N's alternatives intersect then there will be a context clash when parsing N. If the next input symbol is one of those in theintersection of two sets then you won't know which of the alternatives applies.

FIRST(s) is the set of symbols with which s can start, including s itself. If s is a non-terminal then FIRST(s) also includes the first symbol of each alternative right-hand side of s. The '*' in FIRST*(s) means the "transitive closure" of FIRST which means keep applying FIRST to each element of the result until the result doesn't change. *I.e.* start with just the set R = s, then for each non-terminal x in R, add FIRST(x) to R. Keep doing this until nothing new is added. (We are really only interested in the terminals in FIRST*(s) but some definitions include the non-terminals).

FOLLOWER(N) is the set of symbols which can come after N in a sentence. Find each occurrence of N on the right-hand side of a rule, *e.g.*

M ->... |... N... |...

If there is a symbol s immediately following N then add FIRST*(s) to the result (again, we're only interested in the terminal symbols in FIRST*(s)) if there is no symbol after N in the alternative then add FOLLOWER(M) to the result (*i.e.* if N can be the last symbol in an M then anything that can follow M can also follow N).

If a grammar can generate the same sentence in multiple different ways (with different parse tress) then it is ambiguous. An ambiguity must start with a context clash (but not all context clashes imply ambiguity). The context clash occurs when trying to parse the first token of the phrase with multiple parses—you will not be able to tell which alternative to take. To see if a context clash is also a case of ambiguity you would need to follow the alternatives involved in each context clash to see if they can generate the same complete sequence of tokens.

Context-free, Said of a grammar where the syntax of each constituent is independent of the symbols occurring before and after it in a sentence. Parsers for such grammars are simpler than those for context-dependent grammars because the parser need only know the current symbol.

Continence-incontinence, distinction between modes of human action in the ethics of Aristotle. A continent agent is able to carry out actions that conform to the demands of reason, while an incontinent agent is overcome by desire and said to suffer from weakness of the will. *Recommended Reading*: Nichomachean Ethics, tr. by Terence Irwin (Hackett, 1985); Robert Dunn, The Possibility of Weakness of

Will (Hackett, 1987); and Anthony Kenny, Aristotle's Theory of the Will (Yale, 1979).

Contingency, In truth-functional propositional logic, any proposition that is neither a tautology nor a contradiction, hence any proposition that is sometimes true, sometimes false, depending on the row of its truth table column or the interp-retation.

Contingent, a sentence proposition, thought or judgement is contingent if it is true of this actual world, though it is not true in all possible worlds. Some philosophers claim that contingent a posterori, and synthetic are equiv-alent, holding that the notion of synthetic explains the other two. necessary

Continuous function, A function *f*: *D* -> *E*, where *D* and *E* are cpos, is continuous if it is monotonic and *f* (lub *Z*) = lub *f z* | *z* in *Z* for all directed sets *Z* in *D*. In other words, the image of the lub is the lub of any directed image.

All additive functions (functions which preserve all lubs) are continuous. A continuous function has a least fixed point if its domain has a least element, bottom (*i.e.* it is a cpo or a "pointed cpo" depending on your definition of a cpo). The least fixed point is

fix *f* = lub *f*^n bottom | *n* = 0..infinity

Continuum hypothesis, There is no cardinal, a, such that aleph0 < *a* < *c*, where *c* is the cardinality of the continuum. Proving or disproving the continuum hypothesis was the first problem on Hilbert's famous list of problems in 1900. Goedel (1938) and Cohen (1963) have proved that it is neither provable nor disprovable from standard set theory. Usually abbreviated to CH. Generalized continuum hypothesis

For every transfinite cardinal, *a*, there is no cardinal *b* such that a < *b*2^*a*. Usually abbreviated to GCH.

Contradiction, 1. The conjunction of any 'and its negation,

2. In truth-functional propositional logic, the negation of any tautology, hence any proposition that is false in every row of its truth table or in every interpretation.

Contradictories, a pair of categorical propositions, each of which is true if and only if the other is false. In the traditional square of opposition, an A proposition and its corresponding O proposition are contradictories, as are an E proposition and its corresponding I proposition. Thus, for example: "All dogs are mammals and Some dogs are not mammals" are contradictories, as are "No fish are tuna and Some fish are tuna."

Contraposition, the reciprocal rela-tion-ship between two categorical propositions of the same form such that the subject term of each is the complement of the predicate term of the other. Contraposition is a valid immediate inference for both A and O propositions. Thus, for example: "All voters are citizens and All non-citizens are non-voters", "Some ants are not biters and Some non-biters are not non-ants" are legitimate cases of contraposition.

Contraries, a pair of categorical propositions which (provided that we assume existential import) cannot both be true, but can both be false. In the traditional square of opposition, an A proposition and its corresp-onding E proposition are contraries. Thus, for example: "All cars are green and No cars are green are contraries."

Control flow, (Or "flow of control") The sequence of execution of instructions in a program. This is determined at run-time by the input data and by the control structures (*e.g.* "if" statements) used in the program.

Not to be confused with "flow control".

Conventionalism, technical term for a form of subjectivism (or relativism) which holds that truth, good, and beauty are merely a matter of social convention. Conventionalism is a social kind of subjectivistic theory (the usual understanding is that the word "convention" does not refer to the beliefs or values of individuals, only of groups). In popular meaning, however, conventionalism refers to a person's tendency to adhere to or have regard for what is customary (in thought or action). (References from logical positivism, nominalism, and subjectivism.)

Converse, the truth of a proposition of the form *A* => *B* and its converse *B* => *A* are shown in the following truth table:

A	*B*	*A* => *B*	*B* => *A*
f	*f*	*t*	*t*
f	*t*	*t*	*f*
t	*f*	*f*	*t*
t	*t*	*t*	*t*

Converse accident, the informal fallacy of using exceptional specific cases as the basis for a general rule, omitting reference to their qualifying features. *Example*: "It rained on my birthday this year and it rained on my birthday last year. Therefore, it always rains on my birthday." (a dictum secundum quid ad dictum simpliciter).

Conversion, the reciprocal relationship between two categorical propositions of the same form such that the subject term of each is the predicate term of the other. Con-version is a valid immediate inference for both E and I propositions. Thus, for example: "No snakes are mammals and No mammals are snakes", like "Some carnivors are birds and Some birds are carnivors" are each the converse of the other.

Conway Anne Finch, English philoso-pher (1631-1679); author of Principia philosophiae antiquissimae et recentissimae de Deo, Christo & Creatura (The Principles of the Most Ancient and Modern Philosophy) (1690). A student of Henry More, she engaged in a lengthy correspondence with Leibniz, who borrowed her use of the term, "monad." Conway developed and defended a monistic system in which all beings are modes of god, the one and only spiritual substance. *Recommended Reading*: The Conway Letters: The Correspondence of Anne, Viscountess Conway, Henry More, and Their Friends, 1642-1684, ed. by Marjorie Hope Nicolson (Clarendon, 1992) and Women Philosophers of the Early Modern Period, ed. by Margaret Atherton (Hackett, 1994).

Co-option, being assimilated. Especially, for Herbert Marcuse, the sociopolicticoeconomic assimilation of works of art—and simultaneous subversion of their liberative tendencies—for commercial and control purposes.

Coordinate, One member of a tuple of numbers which defines the position of a point in some space. Commonly used coordinate systems have as many coordinates as there are dimensions in the space, *e.g.* a pair for two dimensions. The most common coordinate system is Cartesian coordinates, probably followed by polar coordinates.

Copernicus Nicolas, (1473-1543) Polish astronomer whose De Revolutionibus Orbium Caelestium (About the Revolutions of the Heavenly Spheres) (1543) proposed a heliocentric view of the universe. Copernicus argued that geocentric astronomies, with their complex appeals to epicyclic motion in the planets, should not be regarded as scientific. His own explanation, in terms of circular motion about the sun, was a much more simple (if somewhat less accurate) way of accounting for the observed facts. *Recommended Reading*: Alexandre Koyre, Astronomical Revolution: Copernicus-Kepler-Borelli (Dover, 1992) and Thomas S. Kuhn, The Copernican Revolution: Planetary Astronomy in the Development of Western Thought (Harvard, 1957).

Copyright, The exclusive rights of the owner of the copyright on a work to make and distribute copies, prepare derivative works, and perform and display the work in public (these last two mainly apply to plays, films, dances and the like, but could also apply to software).

A work, including a piece of software, is under copyright by default in most countries, whether of not it displays a copyright notice. However, a copyright notice may make it easier to assert ownership. The copyright owner is the person or company whose name appears in the copyright notice on the box, or the disk or the screen or wherever.

Countries around the world have agreed to recognise and uphold each others' copyrights, but this worldwide protection requires the use of the c in a circle.

Use of copyright to restrict redistribution is actually immoral, unethical, and illegitimate. It is a result of brainwashing by monopolists and corporate interests and it violates everyone's rights. Copyrights and patents hamper technological progress by making a naturally abundant resource scarce. Many, from communists to right wing libertarians, are trying to abolish intellectual property myths.

Cordemoy, French philosopher and early follower of Descartes (1622-1684). In his efforts to resolve Cartesian difficulties with the unobservable interaction of mind and body in his Le discernment du corps et de l"me (The Mind-Body Distinction) (1666), Cordemoy noted how commonly the two elements of any human being fail to correspond with each other. *Recommended Reading*: GÈraud de Cordemoy, A Philosophical Discourse Concerning Speech (Scholars' Facsimilies, 1999).

Corpuscularianism, seventeenth century physical theory that supposed all matter to be composed of minute particles. Corpuscularians included Gassendi, Boyle, and Locke. *Recommended Reading*: Peter Alexander, Ideas, Qualities and Corpuscles: Locke and Boyle on the External World (Cambridge, 1983); Robert Boyle on Natural Philosophy, ed. by Marie Boas Hall (Greenwood, 1980); and The Concept of Matter in Modern Philosophy, ed. by Ernan McMullan (Notre Dame, 1969).

Correspondence theory of truth, a correspondence theory of truth includes the assertion that a sentence (or proposition) is true if and only if that which the sentence expresses corres-ponds to the 'facts" or to "reality".

The correspondence theory may be analysed into three components (following, *e.g.*, Devitt (1984)). Sentences of a type x are true or false in virtue of:

(i) their structure

(ii) the referential relations between parts of the sentences and some reality, and

(iii) the nature of this reality.

The analysis is restricted to sentences of type *x* so as to allow the correspondence theory to hold of some sentences (*e.g.*, of the type "physics") while not of others (*e.g.*, of the type "ethics"). (ii) concerns the nature of the referential relation, and various theories have been proposed, *e.g.* causal accounts (Dretske, Stampe, Putnam, Kripke), teleo-functional accounts (Millikan), and descriptive accounts. (iii) concerns the nature of the reality to which the parts of the sentences correspond. A realist will hold that this reality is objective and mind-independent. An idealist may hold that it is objective yet not mind-independent. Obviously, many flavours are available. *References*: Devitt, Michael (1984). Realism and Truth. Princeton, NJ: Princeton University Press.

Corresponding argument or derivation, Every conditional statement, *A* =>*B*, can be re-expressed as a derivation, *A* |- *B*, called the corresponding argument or derivation of the conditional.

Cosmological arguments, arguments purporting to prove the existence of God a posteriori from the fact of the existence of the universe or of certain properties of the universe and things. Aquinas' "five ways" include arguments from the existence of, the efficient causal order of, and the motion of the universe, to the existence of a first cause thereof, which he identifies with God. an attempt to prove the existence of god by appeal to contingent facts about the world. The first of Aquinas's five ways (borrowed from Aristotle's Metaphysics), begins from the fact that something is in motion: since everything that moves must be moved by another but the series of prior movers cannot extend infinitely, there must be a first mover (which is god). The second and third of the five ways begin from efficient causation and the existence of contingent beings. *Recommended Reading*: William Rowe, The Cosmological Argument (Fordham, 1998); William Lane Craig, Cosmological Argument from Plato to Leibnitz; and Bruce Reichenbach, Cosmological Argument: A Reassessment (Thomas, 1972).

Countable, A term describing a set which is isomorphic to a subset of the natural numbers. A countable set has "countably many" elements. If the isomorphism is stated explicitly then the set is called "a counted set" or "an enumeration".

Examples of countable sets are any finite set, the natural numbers, integers, and rational numbers. The real numbers and complex numbers are not [proof?]. See also uncountable set.

Countably many,countable.

Counted, A term describing a set with an explicit isomorphism to the natural numbers. See countable.

Counter-example, an example which undermines or refutes the principle or theory against which it is advanced. Note that examples can illustrate, explain and support a theory but not prove it, whereas counter-examples can refute it.

Coupling, The degree to which components depend on one another. There are two types of coupling, "tight" and "loose". Loose coupling is desirable for good software engineering but tight coupling may be necessary for maximum performance. Coupling is increased when the data exchanged between components becomes larger or more complex.

Counterfactual, a conditional statement whose antecedent is known (or, at least, believed) to be contrary to fact. Thus, for example, "If George Bush had been born in Idaho, then he would never have become President." Unlike material impli-cations, counterfactuals are not made true bythe falsity of their antecedents. Although they are not truth-functional statements, counterfactuals may be significant for the analysis of scientific hypotheses. *Recommended Reading*: Igal Kvart, A Theory of Counterfactuals (Ridgeview, 1986) and David K. Lewis, Count-erfactuals (Blackwell, 2000).

Courage, willingness to take reasonable risks in pursuit of a worthwhile goal. According to Plato, courage is vital for both social and personal embodiments of virtue. *Recommended Reading*: Walter T. Schmid, On Manly Courage: A Study of Plato's Laches (Southern Illinois, 1992).

Creativity, creativity is an acid test for artificial intelligence andcognitive science. If computers cannot be creative, then (a) they cannot be intelligent, and (b) people are not machines. However, the standard arguments against machine intell-igence are not convincing.

Issues in computers and creativity include: Can computers be creative? Can they help us understand human creativity? How can they best enhance human creativity? What would the implications be for AI and cognitive science if computers could not be creative? This entry limits itself to two initial questions: Why is creativity important for AI and cognitive science? and How convincing are the standard arguments against machine creativity?

References: Haugeland, J. (1985). Artificial Intelligence: The Very Idea, MIT/Bradford Books, Cambridge. Mass. Dartnall, T. (ed.) (1994). Artificial Intelligence and Creativity: an Inter-disciplinary Approach, Kluwer, Dordrecht. Boden, M. (1990). The Creative Mind: Myths and Mechanisms, Weidenfeld & Nicolson, London. Revised edition, 1992, Cardinal, London. (Precis, with peer reviews, in Behavioural and Brain Sciences, 17.3, 1994.) Chris Eliasmith—[Dictionary of Philosophy of Mind]

Crescas Hasdai ben Abraham, Jewish poet and philosopher (1340-1412). An outspoken opponent of the Aristotelian philosophy of Maimonides and Gersonides, Crescas argued in Or Adonai (The Light of the Lord) (1410) that happiness is to be achieved in mystical union with god rather than through the application of human reason. His work was a significant influence on that of Spinoza. *Recommended Reading*: Hasdai Crescas, The Refutation of the Christian Principles, tr. by Daniel J. Lasker (SUNY, 1992); Harry Austryn Wolfson, Crescas's Critique of Aristotle: Problems of Aristotle's Physics in Jewish and Arabic Philosophy (Cambridge, 1929); and Warren Zev Harvey, Physics and Metaphysics in Hasdai Crescas (Benjamin's, 1999).

Crisp, (Or "discrete") The opposite of "fuzzy".

Criterion, a standard by means of which to judge the features of things. Possession of appropriate criteria necessarily constitutes adequate evidence for our attribution of the feature in question. Thus, as Wittgenstein noted, for example, observation of writhing and groaning are criteria for our belief that someone is in pain. *Recommended Reading*: Ludwig Wittgenstein, Blue and Brown Books (Harpercollins, 1986); Ludwig Wittgenstein, Philosophical Investigations, tr. by G. E. M. Anscombe (Prentice Hall, 1999); and John V. Canfield, Wittgenstein, Language and the World (Massachusetts, 1981).

Critical theory, the theoretical approach of the Frankfurt School of social philosophers. Relying on the work of Hegel and Marx, they tried to exhibit dialectically the contradictions imposed upon modern human beings by varieties of social organization that abuse formal rationality in order to deny power to classes of citizens. Rejecting the detached insularity of traditional efforts at objectivity, critical theorists of any sort generally hope that their explanation of the causes of oppression will result in practical efforts to eliminate it. *Recommended Reading*: Max Horkheimer, Critical Theory, tr. By Mathew J. O'Connell (Continuum, 1975); David Held, Introduction to Critical Theory: Horkheimer to Habermas (California, 1981); Hauke Brunkhorst, Adorno and Critical Theory (U of Wales, 1999); and Ben Agger, Critical Social Theory: An Introduction (Westview, 1998).

Croce Benedetto, (1866-1952) Italian philosopher whose Estetica come scienza dell'espressione e linguistica generale (The Aesthetic as the Science of Expression and of the Linguistic in General) (1902) proposed a non-cognitivist account of artistic intuition as an expression of personal creativity. In Materialismo storico ed economia marxista (Historical Materi-alism and the Economics of Karl Marx) (1914) and Teoria e storia della storiografia (Theory and History of Historiography) (1921), Croce defended an understanding of history akin to that of Hegel. He was also an outspoken critic of the Fascist movement. *Recommended Reading*: Benedetto Croce, My Philosophy, and Other Essays on the Moral and Political Problems of Our Time, tr. And ed. by Raymond Klibansky and E. F. Carritt (AMS, 1977) and Thought, Action and Intuition: A Symposium on the Philosophy of Benedetto Croce (Lubrecht & Cramer, 1976).

CRS, conceptual role semantics.

Cudworth Ralph, English philosopher (1617-1688). His True Intellectual System of the Universe (1678) and Eternal and Immutable Morality (1731) are excellent expositions of Cambridge Platonism in opposition to the mechanistic philosophy of Hobbes. Cudworth's daughter, Damaris Masham, also became an influential philosopher. *Recommended Reading*: Frederick James Powicke, Cambridge Platonists (Greenwood, 1955).

Cultural relativism, moral theory that holds that what's good or bad or right or wrong varies from society to society depending on what each society says to be, or believes to be, good or bad or right or wrong. See:ethical relativism. Compare subjectivism.

Cumberland Richard, English philosopher (1631-1718). Cumberland opposed the ethical egoism of

Hobbes in his De Legibus Naturae Disquisitio Philosophica (Treatise of the Laws of Nature) (1672), arguing that a universal benevolence motivates each human being to seek the happiness of all, leaving no room for the exercise of free will. *Recommended Reading*: Jon Parkin, Science, Religion and Politics in Restoration England: Richard Cumberland's De Legibus Nature (Royal Historical Society, 1999).

Curried function, A function of N arguments can be considered as a function of one argument which returns another function of N-1 arguments. *E.g.* in Haskell we can define:

average:: Int -> (Int -> Int)

(The parentheses are optional). A partial application of average, *e.g.* (average 4), is a function of type (Int -> Int) which averages its argument with 4. In uncurried languages a function must always be applied to all its arguments but a partial application can be repres-ented using a lambda abstraction:

\ x -> average(4,x)

Currying is necessary if full laziness is to be applied to functional sub-expressions.

It was named after the logician Haskell Curry but the 19th-century formalist Frege was the first to propose it and it was first referred to in ["Ueber die Bausteine der mathematischen Logik", M. Schoenfinkel, Mathematische Annalen. Vol 92 (1924)].

David Turner said he got the term from Christopher Strachey who invented the term "currying" and used it in his lecture notes on programming languages written circa 1967. Strachey also remarked that it ought really to be called "Schoenfinkeling".

Stefan Kahrs reported hearing somebody in Germany trying to introduce "scho"nen" for currying and "finkeln" for "uncurrying". The verb "scho"nen" means "to beautify"; "finkeln" isn't a German word, but it suggests "to fiddle". ["Some philosophical aspects of combinatory logic", H. B. Curry, The Kleene Symposium, Eds. J. Barwise, J. Keisler, K. Kunen, North Holland, 1980, pp. 85-101]

Currying, Turning an uncurried function into a curried function.

Cusa Nicolas of, German theologian (1400-1464); author of De docta ingnorantia (Of Learned Ignorance) (1440) and De visione dei (Of the Vision of God) (1554). Cusa's late exposition of neoplatonic philosophy, according to which all contradictions are unified in the infinite divine nature, was greatly influential on major figures of the Renaissance. *Recommended Reading*: Jasper Hopkins, A Concise Introduction to the Philosophy of Nicholas of Cusa (Banning, 1986); Karl Jaspers and Hannah Arendt, Anselm and Nicholas of Cusa, tr. by Ralph Manheim (Harcourt Brace, 1974); and Jasper Hopkins, Nicholas of Cusa's Metaphysic of Contraction (Banning, 1983).

Cybernetics, The comparative study of the internal workings of organic and machine processes in order to under-stand their similarities and differences. Cybernetics often refers to machines that imitate human behaviour. See artificial intelligence, robot.

Cynicism, the word comes from a group of thinkers in ancient Greece who were called Cynics, from the Greek word for "dog". The Cynics held that pure virtue is the only good, and they cultivated an asceticism more rigorous than that of Epicureanism or stoicism. Because of their independence from worldly concerns, they were critical of the rest of society and of conventional morality, somewhat akin to exponents of the skepticism that was arising around the same time. The most famous Cynic was Diogenes (412-323 B.C.), who so faithfully put his ideas into practice that, according to legend, he took to living in a bathtub. It is often reported that, when Alexander the Great came to visit him in search of wisdom, and inquired if there was anything the great leader could do for him, Diogenes replied that, yes, there was: Alexander could move aside and stop blocking his sunshine. It is often forgotten that Alexander replied that, had he not been Alexander, he would have liked to be Diogenes. In common usage, cynicism often denotes a combination of skepticism and pessimism.

Dagger function, The dyadic connective or truth function "neither/nor". One of only two dyadic connectives capable of expressing all truth functions by itself. Notation: p \|/ q. Also called joint denial. See also stroke function

Daly Mary, American philosopher and theologian (1928-). Author of Pure Lust: Elemental Feminist Philosophy (1984) and the autobiographical Outercourse: The Be-Dazzling Voyage: Containing Recollections from My Logbook of a Radical Feminist Philosopher (being an account of my time/space travels and ideas—then, again, now, and how) (1992). Reacting against her early training in neo-Thomist theology, Daly's early work, in The Church and the Second Sex (1968) and Beyond God the Father: Toward a Philosophy of Women's Liberation (1973), noted that the Christian tradition helps to support patriarchal society and explicitly rejected its conception of a supreme male deity. Daly went on to develop an ethical position that regards woman-centered self-creation as the primary means of escaping male domination, and in Gyn/Ecology: The Metaethics of Radical Feminism (1978) she proposed that the life forces embodied in women can achieve their full effect only in a separate women's culture. In an effort to escape the linguistic embodiment of patriarchy, Daly often expresses herself by using inventive neol-ogisms that are playful in tone but serious in purpose; Webster's First New Intergalactic Wickedary of the English Language (1987) offers a delightful glimpse of the advantages of a "gynomorphic" language. *Recommended Reading*: Mary Daly, Quintessence...Realizing the Archaic Future: A Radical Elemental Feminist Manifesto (Beacon, 1999); Feminist Interpretations of Mary Daly, ed. by Sarah Lucia Hoagland and Marilyn Frye (Penn. State, 2000).

Damon and Phintias (often incorrectly Pythias) (4th century BC), philosophers of the Pythagorean school noted for their faithful friendship to each other. Both lived in Syracuse, in Sicily, a city then under the rule of Dionysius the Younger. When Dionysius condemned Phintias to death for plotting against his rule, Damon offered to remain as a hostage while Phintias went home to arrange his private affairs. However, Phintias was delayed and returned just as Damon was about to die in his place. Dionysius was so impressed by this example of fidelity that he pardoned Phintias and asked to share their friendship. The story has been retold in several literary works, notably in a ballad by the German poet Friedrich von Schiller and in a drama by the English playwright Richard Edwards.

Daoism, tradition of Chinese philosophy and Chinese religion, first arising in about the 4th century BC. Among native Chinese schools of thought, the influence of Daoism has been second only to that of Confucianism.

Daoism as now understood consists of two separate streams, a school of philosophical thought originating in the classical age of Zhou dynasty China, and a system of religious belief arising some 500 years later in the Han dynasty. These two are normally termed philosophical and religious Daoism, and the Daoist basis of the latter lies in the revelation from the sage Laozi which a Daoist called Zhang Daoling claimed to have received in AD 142 in the Sichuan mountains. Philosophical Daoism has therefore been preserved beneath a mass of religious accretions derived from native Chinese paganism, shamanism, divination, and superstition; while religious Daoism is now a thriving creed interwoven with Chinese popular culture.

Origins and Basic Tenets: Philosophical Daoism arose out of the intellectual ferment of the Zhou dynasty, in which various philosophical schools competed to advise rulers and others on the correct way to live and govern in a world racked by political and social change. Its likely origins are in the so-called Yangist school, despised by Mencius, who caricatured its doctrines by declaring that Yangists would not pluck a hair from their own heads to benefit the whole world. In fact it apparently preached self-cultivation and withdrawal to private life, drawing on a native Chinese tradition of mysticism and contemplative exercises resembling yoga. This tradition was developed in the late 4th century BC by the philosopher Zhuangzi (Chuang-tzu), who began as a Yangist. Soon after, an anonymous thinker, perhaps a minor official, produced a book of related reflections under the name of the semi-mythical figure Laozi (Lao-tzu), who had allegedly instructed Confucius. Evidence suggests that while Zhuangzi saw his beliefs as purely for private use, Laozi presented his as an explicit manual of government.

The essential Daoist philosophical and mystical beliefs can be found in the *Daodejing* (Classic of the Way and Its Power), a book dating from about the 3rd century BC and attributed to Laozi, and in the *Zhuangzi,* a composite text of parables and allegories also dating from the 3rd century BC but attributed to Zhuangzi. Whereas Confucianism urged the individual to conform to the traditional standards of "the Way of the Ancient Kings", Daoism maintained that the individual should ignore the dictates of society and seek only to conform with the underlying pattern of the universe, the Dao ("way"), which can neither be described in words nor conceived in thought. To be in accord with Dao, one has to "do nothing" (*wuwei*)—that is, nothing strained, artificial, or unnatural. Through spontaneous compliance with the impulses of one's own essential nature and by emptying oneself of all doctrines and knowledge, one achieves unity with the Dao and derives from it a mystical power (*De*). This power enables one to transcend all mundane distinctions, even the distinction of life and death. Later Daoists often took this as some kind of magical force, but it appears that Laozi and Zhuangzi simply used the term for the general strength and competence of the perfectly spontaneous individual. Zhuangzi in particular attacked the claims of the Confucians and the school of Mozi that human reason could uncover the Dao; he regarded the artificial distinctions of conceptual thought to be the essence of human departure from the Dao.

At the socio-political level, the Daoists called for a return to primitive agrarian life. In Zhuangzi's case this was simply distrust of anything which could interfere with the direct participation in life's natural cycles, but for Laozi it had an authoritarian cast. In the *Daodejing*, "do nothing" applies as much to the ruler, who need not act to make his subjects naturally benefit themselves and him, as to the private citizen. As wary of artificial concepts as Zhuangzi, Laozi counselled that the ruler should fill his people's bellies but empty their minds, so that they know and desire nothing. He notoriously compared the common people to the straw dogs used in sacrificial ceremonies, treated with reverence before the rites but thrown away once their usefulness had passed. Laozi's ideal state was clearly a dictatorship by a philosopher-king over an obedient and passive populace. His influence is apparent in the very different totalitarian philosophy of Legalism developed by Han Fei.

History: Daoism survived the persecution of philosophies under the Legalist Qin dynasty, which had unified China, and Laozi's thought was taken up by courtiers of the Han dynasty, who combined it with legends of the primordial Yellow Emperor, Huangdi, and the yin/yang cosmology of the Tai Ji to enhance their philosophy of imperial government. The Later Han dynasty also saw the fusion of aspects of Daoism with Chinese religion, and followers of these new cults such as the Yellow Turbans in Shandong helped bring down the dynasty. After the Han collapse in AD 220, philosophical Daoism grew into the quintessential Chinese creed of private life and irresponsible individualism, in contrast to formal, public-spirited Confucianism. The common people tended to follow religious Daoism, while the educated mandarin class embraced philoso-phical Daoism and associated cosm-ological and scientific speculations.

Daoism has influenced Chinese literature, Chinese art, and Chinese science. A primitive chemistry developed in the course of a search for immortality through magic and the use of various elixirs; for later Daoists took literally the metaphorical references to self-perfection and immortal *xian* which littered Zhuangzi's work. The ideal elixir of immortality was supposedly a red cinnabar pill, and such mercury-based substances poisoned many emperors and others who believed the Daoist myths; but Daoist researches apparently spurred important discoveries in early Chinese science identified by Joseph Needham. Experimentation in alchemy gave way to the devel-opment, between the 3rd and 6th centuries, of various cults that sought to prolong life. These developed into a general health system, still practised today, that stresses regular breathing and concentration to prevent disease and promote longevity. The poetry of Tao Yuanming (T'ao Ch'ien) and Li Bai (Li Po) was heavily influenced by Daoism, while Chinese landscape painting drew considerably on its evocation of natural forces and cult of pastoral retirement.

Daoism and Chinese Buddhism had considerable influence on each other after the proliferation of Buddhism in the 4th century AD. Early translators of Buddhist sutras used Daoist terms to translate difficult Sanskrit concepts. Following Buddhism's example, Daoism developed a pseudo-monastic organization. Some Daoist scholars even claimed that the legendary Laozi had actually left China and become the Buddha, until the Mongol Yuan dynasty emperor Kublai Khan proscribed the myth in 1281. Daoism was implicated in the greatest Chinese persecution of Buddhism in 842-845, by a Daoist emperor of the late Tang dynasty, but Daoist speculations also fused with Buddhist ideas to create the fusion of Zen Buddhism, which has been described as 90 per cent Daoist.

Modern scholarly techniques have revealed the philosophical profundity of much early Daoism, and led to the (perhaps unfair) criticism of religious Daoism for obscuring its underlying philosophy. Martin Heidegger attempted a translation of the *Daodejing*, and ideas reminiscent of Daoism frequently occur in Heideggerian philosophy and its descendants. Philosophical Daoism is now recognized as especially relevant to philosophy of language, antirationalism, structuralism, deconstruction, and many other currents of modern thought.

Darii, name given by medieval logicians to any categorical syllogism whose standard form may be designated as AII-1. *Example*: All logicians are philosophers, and some serious scholars are logicians, so some serious scholars are philosophers. This is one of the fifteen forms in which syllogisms are always valid.

Darwin Charles, English biologist (1809-1882) who recorded his notes from the field in The Voyage of the Beagle (1848). Darwin's Origin of Species by Means of Natural Selection (1859) and The Descent of Man (1871) revolutionized modern science by proposing a non-teleological explanation for the survival of otherwise random variations in animal species. Despite opposition from biblical literalists, a Darwinian version of the theory of evolution became widely accepted within a few decades. *Recommended Reading*: The Portable Darwin, ed. by Duncan M. Porter and Peter W. Graham (Penguin, 1993); Daniel C. Dennett, Darwin's Dangerous Idea: Evolution and the Meanings of Life (Touchstone, 1996); Janet Radcliffe Richards, Human Nature After Darwin: A Philosophical Introduction (Routledge, 2001); The Book of Life: An Illustrated History of the Evolution of Life on Earth, ed. By Stephen Jay Gould and Peter Andrews (Norton, 2001); and Gertrude Himmelfarb, Darwin and the Darwinian Revolution (Dee, 1996).

Dasein, Heidegger's German term for "Being-there," the kind of existence that self-conscious human beings uniquely possess. *Recommended Reading*: Being and Time: A Translation of Sein and Zeit, tr. by Joan Stambaugh (SUNY, 1997) and Hubert L. Dreyfus, Being-In-The-World: A Commentary on Heidegger's Being and Time, Division I (MIT, 1991).

Database, 1. One or more large structured sets of persistent data, usually associated with software to update and query the data. A simple database might be a single file containing many records, each of which contains the same set of fields where each field is a certain fixed width.

A database is one component of a database management system.

See also ANSI/SPARC Architecture, atomic, blob, data definition language, deductive database, distributed database, fourth generation language, functional database, object-oriented database, relational database.

2. A collection of nodes managed and stored in one place and all accessible via the same server. Links outside this are "external", and those inside are "internal".

On the World-Wide Web this is called a web site.

3. All the facts and rules comprising a logic programming program.

Data dictionary, A data structure that stores meta-data, *i.e.* dataabout data. The term "data dictionary" has several uses.

Most generally it is a set of data descriptions that can be shared by several applications.

Usually it means a table in a database that stores the names, field types, length, and other characteristics of the fields in the database tables.

An active data dictionary is automatically updated as changes occur in the database. A passive data dictionary must be manually updated.

In a DBMS, this functionality is performed by the system catalog. The data dictionary is a more general software utility used by designers, users, and administrators for information resource management.

The data dictionary may maintain information on system hardware, software, documentation, users, and other aspects.

Data dictionaries are also used to document the database design process itself and can accumulate meta-data ready to feed into the system catalog.

Data striping, Segmentation of logically sequential data, such as a single file, so that segments can be written to multiple physical devices (usually disk drives) in a round-robin fashion. This technique is useful if the processor is capable of reading or writing data faster than a single disk can supply or accept it. While data is being transferred from the first disk, the second disk can locate the next segment.

Data striping is used in some modern databases, such as Sybase, and in certain RAID devices under hardware control, such as IBM's RAMAC array subsystem (9304/9395).

Data striping is different from, and may be used in conjunction with, mirroring.

Datisi, name given by medieval logicians to a categorical syllogism with the standard form AII-3. *Example*: Since all bookstores are places that sell popular novels and some bookstores are coffee shops, it follows that some coffee shops are places that sell popular novels. This is one of only fifteen forms of syllogism that are always valid.

Davidson Donald, American philosopher (1917-) who, like Quine, applies the methods of logical and linguistic analysis to the study of human nature. On Davidson's view, interpretation of a language should always be governed by a "principle of charity" that maximizes its true statements. Although he regards mental events as irreducibly intentional and denies the possibility of psycho-physical laws, Davidson defends a sophisticated identity theory ("anomalous monism") under which every mental event supervenes upon some physical event, subject to the usual physical laws of nature, even though it cannot be fully described in purely physical terms. Many of Davidson's most influential essays are collected in Essays on Actions and Events (1980) and Inquiries into Truth and Interpretation (1984). *Recommended Reading*: Simon Evnine, Donald Davidson (Stanford, 1991); The Philosophy of Donald Davidson, ed. by Lewis Edwin Hahn (Open Court, 1999); Donald Davidson: Truth, Meaning, and Knowledge, ed. by Urszula M. Zeglen (Routledge, 1999); and Interpretations and Causes: New Perspectives on Donald Davidson's Philosophy, ed. by Mario De Caro (Kluwer, 1999).

Day Dorothy, American social activist (1897-1980). Day combined communist social concern with Christian convictions in the autobiographical From Union Square to Rome (1938). She founded The Catholic Worker magazine in 1933, established a "hospitality house" in New York City, and supported pacifistic resistance to several wars. *Recommended Reading*: Dorothy Day: Selected Writings, ed. By Robert Ellsberg (Orbis, 1992); The Long Loneliness: The Autobiography of Dorothy Day, ed. by Daniel Berrigan (Harper, 1997); Voices from the Catholic Worker, ed. by Rosalie Riegle Troester (Temple, 1993); and June E. O'Connor, The Moral Vision of Dorothy Day: A Feminist Perspective (Crossroad, 1991).

Decidable *wff*, A wff that is either a theorem or the negation of a theorem. Either the wff or its negation is a theorem. Jargon: if wff A is decidable in system S, we often say that "S decides A".

Decidibility, a (logical) language is said to be decidable iff all of its theorems (or logical truths) can be shown to be true through a finite mechanical procedure. Propositional logic is decidable; predicate logic is not.

Decision problem, A problem with a yes/no answer. Determining whether some potential solution to a question is actually a solution or not. *E.g.* "Is 43669" a prime number?". This is in contrast to a "search problem" which must find a solution from scratch, *e.g.* "What is the millionth prime number?".

Decision procedure, an algorithm by means of which to establish, in a finite number of steps, whether a statement form is tautologous or whether an argument form is valid. Drawing Venn diagrams provides a decision procedure for a modern interpretation of categorical logic, and truth-tables give a decision procedure for the propositional calculus, but there is no decision procedure for quantification theory.

Decision theory, A branch of statistics concerning strategies for decision making in non-deterministic systems. Decision theory seeks to find strategies that maximise the expected value of a utility function measuring the desirability of possible outcomes.

Deconstruction, interpretive method that denies the priority or privilege of any single reading of a text (even if guided by the intentions of its author) and tries to show that the text is incoherent because its own key terms can be understood only in relation to their suppressed oppo-sites. Decons-tructionists like Derrida seek to uncover the internal conflicts that tend to undermine (or at least to "decenter") the putative significance of any text. In ordinary language, for example, someone who says, "If I may be perfectly candid for a moment,..." thereby betrays a reluctance—at least in the past and, probably, even in the present case—to do so, and this difference points toward a systematic ambiguity in the very notions of honesty and truth. *Recommended Reading*: Deconstruction in a Nutshell: A Conve-rsation With Jacques Derrida, ed. by John D. Caputo (Fordham, 1997); Deconstruction in Context: Literature and Philosophy, ed. By Mark C. Taylor (Chicago, 1986); and Penelope Deutscher, Yielding Gender: Feminism, Deconstruction, and the History of Philosophy (Routledge, 1997).

De dicto - de re, distinction between ways of understanding the logical necessity or truth of statements, either in terms "of what is said" (de dicto) or in terms "of the thing" (de re). Someone who does not know that the morning star is the planet Venus, for example, could believe the truth, de dicto, of the proposition, "The morning star is larger than Venus," even though no one would believe de re that Venus is larger than itself. *Recommended Reading*: Alvin Plantinga, The Nature of Necessity (Clarendon, 1989) and Saul A. Kripke, Naming and Necessity (Harvard, 1980).

Deduction, an inference in which (when valid) the conclusion contains No information that was not already present in the premises, or whose corresponding conditional is a tautology. See also induction, validity, logic, hypothetical deductive method

Deduction, in logic, the form of reasoning by which a specific conclusion is inferred from one or more premises. In valid deductive reasoning, the conclusion must be true if all the premises are true. Thus, if it is agreed that all human beings have one head and two arms, and that Bertha is a human being, then it can logically be concluded that Bertha must have one head and two arms. This is an example of a syllogism, an argument in which two premises are given and a logical conclusion is deduced from them. Deduction is often expressed in the form of syllogisms.

Deduction-induction, distinction in logic between types of reasoning, arguments, or inferences. In a deductive argument, the truth of the premises is supposed to guarantee the truth of the conclusion; in an inductive argument, the truth of the premises merely makes it probable that the conclusion is true. *Recommended Reading*: Patrick Suppes, Introduction to Logic (Dover, 1999) and Richard L. Wilson, Logic: Deductive,

Inductive and Informal Reasoning (Kendall/Hunt, 1993).

Deduction theorem, When G is a set of wffs, and *A* and *B* are wffs, then if *G, A* |- *B*, then *G* |- (*A* =>*B*). Also called the rule of conditional proof.

Deductive apparatus, The axioms and rules of inference of a formal system.

Formal systems may lack axioms or rules of inference but not both.

Deductive tableau, A theorem proof system consisting of a table whose rows contain assertions or goals. Variables in assertions are implicitly universally quantified and variables in goals are implicitly existentially quantified. The declarative meaning of a tableau is that if every instance of every assertion is true then some instance of at least one of the goals is true.

De facto - de jure, distinction between the grounds for a condition that merely happens to obtain (de facto) and one that holds as a matter of right or law (de jure). The maximum speed at which an automobile may lawfully travel on the highway is 70 m.p.h. de jure, but the de facto speed limit on a busy afternoon is only about 50 m.p.h.

Definite clause, A Horn clause that has exactly one positive literal.

Definite description, an expression that claims to refer to the single being that possesses some unique feature. Russell showed nearly a century ago that the proper analysis of such expressions, as the joint assertion of several distinct propositions, resolves a number of otherwise troubling difficulties. *Recommended Reading*: Definite Descriptions: A Reader, ed. by Gary Ostertag (Bradford, 1998); Stephen Neale, Descriptions (Bradford, 1993); and Jaakko Hintikka and Jack Kulas, Anaphora and Definite Descriptions: Two Applications of Game-Theoretical Semantics (Kluwer, 1985).

Definite sentence, A collection of definite clauses.

Definition, an explanation of the meaning of a word. The five major kinds of definition (distinguished by the functions they may be used to perform) include: stipulative, lexical, precising, theoretical, and persuasive. *Recommended Reading*: Essays on Definition, ed. by Juan C. Sager (Benjamins, 2000); Richard Robinson, Definition (Clarendon, 1950); and Definitions and Definability: Philosophical Perspectives, ed. by James H. Fetzer, David Shatz, and George N. Schlesinger (Kluwer, 1991).

Degrees of freedom, The number of independent parameters required to specify the position and orientation of an object. Often used to classify robot arms. For example, an arm with six degrees of freedom could reach any position close enough and could orient it's end effector (grip or tool etc.) at any angle about the three perpendicular axes.

Deism, the idea that God created the universe but then left it alone to operate on its own principles- principles that human reason and science can discover. Thus, acc-ording to deism, God is not involved in the day-to-day workings of the universe, and there are no miracles. Deism was a creation of the rational, scientific spirit of the Enlightenment, and continues to be held to this day by many people, especially those of a scientific bent. (For other views about the relationship between God and the universe, see theism and pantheism.) (References from naturalism and theism.) belief in god based entirely on reason, without any reference to faith, revelation, or institutional religion. During the seventeenth and eighteenth centuries, advances in the natural sciences often fostered confidence that the regularity of nature reflects the benevolence of a divine providence. This confidence, together with a widespread distrust of the church, made deism a popular view in England and on the continent. Thus, in distinct ways, Toland, Lord Herbert, Paine, Rousseau, and Voltaire were all deists. *Recommended Reading*: John Toland's Christianity Not Mysterious: Text, Associated Works and Critical Essays, ed. by Alan Harrison, Richard Kearney, and Philip McGuinness (Dufour, 1997); Thomas Paine, Age of Reason (Lyle Stuart, 1989); William Stephens, An Account of the Growth of Deism in England (AMS, 1995); and The Radical Rhetoric of the English Deists: The Discourse of Skepticism, 1680-1750, ed. by James A. Herrick and Thomas W. Benson (South Carolina, 1997).

Deism, a rationalist religious philosophy that flourished in the 17th and 18th centuries, particularly in England. Generally, deists held that a certain kind of religious knowledge (sometimes called natural religion) is either inherent in each person or accessible through the exercise of reason, but they denied the validity of religious claims based on revelation or on the specific teachings of any Church.

Deism emerged as a major religious and philosophical view in England. The most prominent 17th-century deists were Edward Herbert, John Toland, and Charles Blount, all of whom advocated a rationalist religion and criticized the supernatural or nonrational elements in the Jewish and Christian traditions. In the early 18th century, Anthony Collins, Thomas Chubb, and Matthew Tindal sharpened the rationalist attack on orthodoxy by attempting to discredit the miracles and mysteries of the Bible.

Although these challenges to traditional and orthodox interpretations of Christianity aroused much opposition, the deists did much to establish the intellectual climate of Europe in the 18th century. Their emphasis on reason and their opposition to fanaticism and intolerance greatly influenced the British philosophers John Locke and David Hume. In France, Voltaire became a particularly effective proponent of deism and intensified his predecessors' rationalist critique of Scripture. Nonetheless, he retained the British deists' view that a deity certainly exists. Versions of deism, some of them approaching atheism, were advocated by many other prominent figures of the European Enlightenment.

Deism was also influential in late 18th-century America, where deistic views were held by Benjamin Franklin, Thomas Jefferson, and George Washington. The most vociferous American deists were Ethan Allen and Thomas Paine.

Deism in Europe and America played an important role both in exposing traditional religion to rationalist criticism and in encouraging the development of rationalist philosophy. Elements of the deists' ideas have been absorbed by Unitarianism, Modernism, and other modern religious tendencies.

De jure, as a matter of law, not merely as a matter of fact. See de facto / de jure.

Delaunay triangulation, (After B. Delaunay) For a set S of points in the Euclidean plane, the unique triangulation DT(S) of S such that no point in S is inside the circumcircle of any triangle in DT(S). DT(S) is the dual of the voronoi diagram of S.

Deleuze Gilles, French philosopher (1925-1995) who used critical interpretations of Spinoza(Spinoza et le problËme de l'expression / Expressionism in Philosophy: Spinoza, 1968) and Nietzsche (Nietzsche et la philosophie / Nietzsche and Philosophy, 1962) as the basis for a profound attack on modernist rationality. Like Foucault, Deleuze was sharply critical of the neo-Freudian psychoanalytic theories of Jacques Lacan. In collaboration with psychoanalyst Fèlix Guattari, Deleuze published L'Anti-Oedipe (Anti-Oedipus: Capitalism and Schizophrenia) (1972), an extended critique of contemporary political structures, and Qu'estce que laphilosophie? (What is Philosophy?) (1981). Deleuze developed his own theories of meaning and interpretation in DiffÈrence et rÈpÈtition (Difference and Repetition) (1968) and Logique du sens (The Logic of Sense) (1969). *Recommended Reading*: Deleuze: A Critical Reader, ed. by Paul Patton (Blackwell, 1996); Dorothea Olkowski, Gilles Deleuze and the Ruin of Representation (California, 1999); Todd May, Reconsidering Difference: Nancy, Derrida, Levinas, and Deleuze (Penn. State, 1997); Tamsin E. Lorraine, Irigaray & Deleuze: Experiments in Visceral Philosophy (Cornell, 1999); and John Rajchman, The Deleuze Connections (MIT, 2000).

Democracy, form of government in which the people rule, either by directly voting on issues (direct democracy), or indirectly through electing representatives to decide issues (representative democracy).

Democritus, presocratic Greek philosopher (460-370 B.C.). As the originator of classical atomism, Democritus maintained in opposition to the Eleatics that the universe comprises a plurality of distinct entities that really do move. The haphazard collisions of these individually indestructible atoms, he believed, account for the formation and dissolution of all observable things. Long before its appropriation by Epicurus, this doctrine produced an attitude toward human life that earned Democritus a reputation as "the laughing philosopher." *Recommended Reading*: Paul Cartledge, Democritus (Routledge, 1999) and C. C. W. Taylor, The Atomists: Leucippus and Democritus (Toronto, 1999).

De Morgan Augustus, British mathematician (1806-1871) who recognized the need to expand the notion of logical validity beyond the narrow confines of Aristotelian syllogistic. His works include Essay on Probabilities (1838), Formal Logic (1847), and Budget of Paradoxes (1872). De Morgan developed the standard statement of De Morgan's Theorems, a pair of logical relationships earlier noted by Ockham and Geulincx. *Recommended Reading*: Robert Adamson, Short History of Logic (Irvington, 1961) and Daniel Davy Merrill, Augustus De Morgan and the Logic of Relations (Kluwer, 1991).

DeMorgan's theorem, A logical theorem which states that the complement of a conjunction is the disjunction of the complements or vice versa. In symbols:

not (x and y) = (not x) or (not y)

not (x or y) = (not x) and (not y)

E.g. if it is not the case that I am tall and thin then I am either short or fat (or both). The theorem can be extended to combinations of more than two terms in the obvious way.

The same laws also apply to sets, replacing logical complement with set complement, conjunction ("and") with set intersection, and disjunction ("or") with set union.

A (C) programmer might use this to re-write thus saving one operator

```
if (!foo && !bar)...
```

as

```
if (!(foo || bar))...
```

application (though an optimizing compiler should do the same, leaving the programmer free to use whichever form seemed clearest).

Dennett Daniel C., American philosopher (1942-); author of Brainstorms (1978), The Intentional Stance (1987), and Consciousness Explained (1991); Co-editor (with Douglas Hofstadter) of The Mind's I (1981). Dennett's careful application of neuroscientific research to the philosophy of mind is characterized by the frequent use of ingenious thought-experiments. Many of Dennet's papers are available on-line at the Center for Cognitive Studies. *Recommended Reading*: Daniel C. Dennett, Elbow Room (MIT, 1984); Daniel C. Dennett, Darwin's Dangerous Idea: Evolution and the Meanings of Life (Touchstone, 1996); Daniel C. Dennett, Brainchildren: Essays on Designing Minds, 1984-1996 (Bradford, 1998); Dennett and His Critics: Demystifying Mind, ed. by Bo Dahlbom (Blackwell, 1995); and Dennett's Philosophy: A Comprehensive Assessment, ed. by Don Ross, Andrew Brook, and David Thompson (MIT, 2000).

Denotational semantics, A technique for describing the meaning of programs in terms of mathematical functions on programs and program components. Programs are translated into functions about which properties can be proved using the standard mathematical theory of functions, and especially domain theory.

Compare axiomatic semantics, operational semantics, standard semantics.

Denotation-connotation, Mill's distinction between the things to which a term refers (its denotation) and the meaning of the term (its connotation). In modern logic, this distinction is often assimilated to the distinction between the extension and intension of an expression. *Recommended Reading*: Ermanno Bencivenga, Logic, Bivalence, and Denotation (Ridgeview, 1991).

Denumerable set, A set whose cardinality is exactly aleph0, for example the set of natural numbers.

Denying the antecedent, *a* formal fallacy of the form:

p -> q
~ p
~ q

Example: "If Rover is a cat, then Rover is a mammal. But Rover is not a cat. So, Rover is not a mammal." Notice the crucial difference between this pattern of reasoning and the valid Modus Tollens.

Deontologism, any ethical position claiming that the rightness or wrongness of actions depends on whether they correspond to our duty or not.

The word derives from the Greek word for duty, "deon". More generally, any kind of ethical theory that puts its emphasis on universal imperatives like moral laws, duties, obligations, prohibitions, and so on (sometimes this is also called "imperativism"). Kantianism is the prime example of a deontological theory, and generally speaking such theories are varieties of altruism. Some thinkers even go so far as to claim that deontology is the extent of ethics, and that any interest in personal happiness or fulfillment is mere egoism and therefore not a matter for ethical theory. (References from altruism, formalism, imperativism, and Kantianism.)

Deontology, study of moral necessity, duty, or obligation. A deontological normative theory holds that moral worth is an intrinsic feature of human actions, determined by formal rules of conduct. Thus, deontologists like Kant suppose that moral obligation rests solely uponduty, without requiring any reference to the practical conse-quences that dutiful actions may happen have. *Recommended Reading*: Immanuel Kant, Grounding for the Metaphysics of Morals, tr. by James W. Ellington (Hackett, 1993); Roger J. Sullivan, An Introduction to Kant's Ethics (Cambridge, 1994); and Philip Stratton-Lake, Kant, Duty, and Moral Worth (Routledge, 2001). See deontologism.

De re, "Of the thing," not "of what is said" See de dicto/de re.

Derivation, A finite, non-empty sequence of wffs in which the last member is the wff derived, and each of the others (the premises) is either an axiom, a member of a set of accepted premises, or the result of applying a rule of inference to wffs preceding it in the sequence.

Notation: Gamma |- *A* (the wff *A* can be derived from the set of wffs *G*). See corresponding argument, proof

Derrida Jacques, French philosopher and leader of the deconstructionist movement (1930-). From the work of Husserl and Heidegger, Derrida derives the view that meaning emerges only provisionally, from an endless process of re-interpretation based on the interaction between reader and text. In La Voix et le phÈnomÈne (Speech and Phenomena) (1967), L'ecriture et la differance (Writing and Difference) (1967), De la Grammatologie (Of Grammatology) (1967), and La DissÈmination (Dissemination) (1972), Derrida argues that all dichotomies between subject and object or appearance and reality are ultimately untenable. *Recommended Reading*: A Derrida Reader, ed. by Peggy Kamuf (Columbia, 1991); Deconstruction in a Nutshell: A Conversation With Jacques Derrida, ed. by John D. Caputo (Fordham, 1997); Deconstruction and Philosophy: The Texts of Jacques Derrida, ed. by John Sallis (Chicago, 1989); Geoffrey Bennington, Interrupting Derrida (Routledge, 2000); Todd May, Reconsidering Difference: Nancy, Derrida, Levinas, and Deleuze (Penn. State, 1997); Christopher Johnson, Derrida (Routledge, 1999); and Feminist Interpretations of Jacques Derrida, ed. by Nancy J. Holland (Penn. State, 1997).

Descartes, René (1596-1650), French philosopher, scientist, and mathematician, often called the founder of modern philosophy. Born in La Haye, Touraine (a region and former province of France), Descartes was the son of a minor nobleman and belonged to a family that had produced a number of learned men. At the age of eight he was enrolled in the Jesuit school of La Flèche in Anjou, where he spent the rest of his schooldays. Besides the usual classical studies,

Descartes received instruction in mathematics and scholasticism, which attempted to use human reason to understand Christian doctrine. Roman Catholicism exerted a strong influence on Descartes throughout his life. Upon finishing school, he studied law at the University of Poitiers, graduating in 1616. He never practised law, however; in 1618 he entered the service of Prince Maurice of Nassau, leader of the United Provinces of the Netherlands, with the intention of following a military career. In succeeding years Descartes served in other armies, but his attention had already been attracted to the problems of mathematics and philosophy, to which he was to devote the rest of his life.

Descartes made a pilgrimage to Italy between 1623 and 1624, then spent the years from 1624 to 1628 in France, where he devoted himself to the study of philosophy and also experimented in the science of optics. In 1628, having sold his properties in France, he moved to the Netherlands, where he spent most of the rest of his life, living in a number of different cities, including Amsterdam, Deventer, Utrecht, and Leiden.

It was probably during the first years of his residence in the Netherlands that Descartes wrote his first major work, *Essais Philosophiques* (Philosophical Essays), published in 1637. The work contained four parts: an essay on geometry, another on optics, a third on meteors, and, lastly, *Discours de la Méthode* (Discourse on Method), which described his philosophical speculations. This was followed by other philosophical works, among them *Meditationes de Prima Philosophia* (Meditations on First Philosophy, 1641; revised 1642) and *Principia Philosophiae* (The Principles of Philosophy, 1644). The latter volume was dedicated to Princess Elizabeth Stuart of Bohemia, who lived in the Netherlands and with whom Descartes had formed a deep friendship. In 1649 Descartes was invited to the court of Queen Christina of Sweden in Stockholm to give the Queen instruction in philosophy. However, the rigours of the northern winter brought on the pneumonia that caused his death in 1650.

Philosophy: Descartes attempted to apply the rational deductive methods of science, and particularly of mathematics, to philosophy. Before his time, philosophy had been dominated by the method of scholasticism, which was entirely based on comparing and contrasting the views of recognized authorities. Rejecting this method, Descartes stated: "In our search for the direct road to truth, we should busy ourselves with no object about which we cannot attain a certitude equal to that of the demonstration of arithmetic and geometry." He therefore determined to hold nothing true until he could be absolutely certain of it. His method for discovering a truth of which he could be absolutely certain was to use scepticism: he attempted to doubt everything that he believed to be true and investigate if it was indeed possible to doubt it. Using this "method of doubt" he found that he could doubt whether he was in fact awake, since it was always possible that he was dreaming. He could also doubt whether the physical world and his own body existed, since it was always possible that a powerful and malicious demon was creating the illusion of these things in his mind. However, try as he might, he could not doubt that he himself existed, since the very act of doubting required a doubter, namely himself. In order to doubt, he had to exist. Descartes expressed this conclusion in the famous words "*Cogito, ergo sum*" ("I think, therefore I am"). He used it as the foundation stone on which to build a complete system of indubitable knowledge. From the principle that thinking proved his own existence, he argued that his essential characteristic was thinking.

Descartes then went on to argue for the existence of God, and to claim that God must have created two kinds of substance that make up the whole of reality. One kind was thinking substance, or minds, entities such as himself whose essential characteristic was thinking, and the other was extended substance, or bodies, for example, rocks or trees or his own body, whose essential characteristic was being extended over a certain amount of physical space. While thinking substances acted in accordance with the laws of thinking, extended substances acted in accordance with the mechanical laws of physics. This division of reality into two kinds of substance, one physical and one mental, has become known as Cartesian dualism. In one form or another it has been extraordinarily influential on Western philosophy ever since Descartes's time.

Descartes Rene, after receiving a sound education in mathematics, classics, and law at La Fleche and Poitiers, Rene Descartes (1596-1650) embarked on a brief career in military service with Prince Maurice in Holland and Bavaria. Unsatisfied with scholastic philosophy and troubled by skepticism of the sort expounded by Montaigne, Descartes soon conceived a comprehensive plan for applying math-ematical methods in order to achieve perfect certainty in human knowledge. During a twenty-year period of secluded life in Holland, he produced the body of work that secured his philosophical reputation. Descartes moved to Sweden in 1649, but did not survive his first winter there. Although he wrote extensively, Descartes chose not to publish his earliest efforts at expressing the universal method and deriving its consequences. The Regulae ad directionem ingenii (Rules for the Direction of the Mind) (1628) contain his first full statement of the principles underlying the method and his confidence in the success of their application. In Le Monde (The World) (1634), Descartes clearly espoused a Copernican astronomy, but he withheld the book from the public upon learning of Galileo's condemnation. Descartes finally presented (in French) his rationalist vision of the progress of human knowledge in the Discours de la mÈthode pour bien conduire sa Raison et chercher la Verite dans les Sciences (Discourse on Method) (1637). In this expository essay, Descartes assessed the deficient outcomes of a traditional education, proposed a set of rules with which to make a new start, and described the original experience upon which his hope for unifying human knowledge was based. The final sections of the Discourse and the essays (on dipotric, meteors, and geometry) appended to it illustrate the consequences of employing this method. A few years later, Descartes offered (in Latin) a more formal exposition of his central tenets in Meditationes de Prima Philosophia (Meditations on First Philosophy) (1641). After an expanded statement of the method of doubt, he argued that even the most dire skepticism is overcome by the certainty of one's own existence as a thinking thing. From this beginning, he believed it possible to use our clear and distinct ideas to demonstrate the existence of god, to establish the reliability of our reason generally despite the possibility of error, to deduce the essence of body, and to prove that material things do exist. On these grounds, Descartes defended a strict dualism, ccording to which the mind and body are wholly distinct, even though it seems evident that they interact. The Meditations were published together with an extensive set of objections (by Hobbes, Gassendi, Arnauld, and others) and Descartes's replies. Descartes later attempted a more systematic exposition of his views in the *Principia Philosophiae* (Principles of Philosophy) (1644) and an explanation of human emotion in Les Passions de L'Ame (The Passions of the Soul). *Recommended Reading*: Primary sources: Oeuvres de Descartes, ed. by C. Adam and P. Tannery (Cerf, 1896-1913); The Philosophical Works of Descartes, tr. by E. S. Haldane and G. T. R. Ross. (Cambridge, 1968); The Philosophical Writings of Descartes: The Correspondence, ed. by John Cottingham, et. al. (Cambridge, 1991); Rene Descartes, Discourse on Method and Meditations on First Philosophy, tr. by Donald A. Cress (Hackett, 1999); The Philosophical Writings of Descartes, tr. by John Cottingham Robert Stoothoff, and Dugald Murdoch (Cambridge, 1985); RenÈ Descartes, Philosophical Essays and Correspondence, ed. by Roger Ariew (Hackett, 2000); RenÈ Descartes, The World and Other Writings, ed. by Stephen Gaukroger (Cambridge, 1998); Rene Descartes, Discourse De La Methode / Discourse on the Method (Bilingual Edition), ed. by George Heffernan (Notre Dame, 1994); Rene Descartes, Meditationes De Prima Philosophia / Meditations on First Philosophy (Bilingual Edition), ed. by George Heffernan (Notre Dame, 1990). Secondary sources: The Cambridge Companion to Descartes, ed. by John Cottingham (Cambridge, 1992); Marjorie Grene, Descartes (Hackett, 998); Anthony Kenny, Descartes: A Study of His Philosophy (St. Augustine, 1993); Margaret Dauler Wilson, Ideas and Mechanism (Princeton, 1999); Feminist Inter-pretations of Rene Descartes, ed. by Susan Bordo (Penn. State, 1999); John Cottingham, Descartes (Routledge, 1999); George Dicker, Descartes: An Analytical and Historical Introduction (Oxford, 1993); Daniel Garber, Descartes Embodied: Reading Cartesian Philosophy Through Cartesian Science (Cambridge, 2001); Martial Gueroult, Descartes' Philosophy Interpreted according to the Order of Reasons, tr. by Roger Ariew (in two volumes) (Minnesota, 1984); E. M. Curley, Descartes Against the Skeptics (Iuni-verse, 1999); Daniel Garber, Desc-artes' Metaphysical Physics (Chicago, 1992).

Descent function, If a recursive function is of the form then d is known

$$f\,x = \ldots f\,(d\,x)\ldots$$

as the descent function.

Descriptive ethics, branch of ethics that non-judgmentally examines the moral tenets of a particular society or tradition, analyzing the logical relations among them and observing the extent of their application in practice. *Recommended Reading*: May M. Edel and Abraham Edel, Anthropology & Ethics: The Quest for Moral Understanding (Transaction, 2000); Hunter Lewis, A Question of Values: Six Ways We Make the Personal Choices That Shape Our Lives (Axios, 2000); and The Book of Virtues: A Treasury of Great Moral Stories, ed. by William J. Bennett (Touchstone, 1996).

Descriptive ethics, branch of ethics that non-judgmentally examines the moral tenets of a particular society or tradition, analyzing the logical relations among them and observing the extent of their application in practice. *Recommended Reading*: May M. Edel and Abraham Edel, Anthropology & Ethics: The Quest for Moral Understanding (Transaction, 2000); Hunter Lewis, A Question of Values: Six Ways We Make the Personal Choices That Shape Our Lives (Axios, 2000); and The Book of Virtues: A Treasury of Great Moral Stories, ed. by William J. Bennett (Touchstone, 1996).

Descriptivism, the view that ethics is purely descriptive and should never prescribe actions or values. The most famous proponents of this view were David Hume and, in the political sphere, Machiavelli. The opposing view is called prescriptivism.

Design, The approach that engineering (and some other) disciplines use to specify how to create or do something. A successful design must satisfies a (perhaps informal) functional specification (do what it was designed to do); conforms to the limitations of the target medium (it is possible to implement); meets implicit or explicit requirements on performance and resource usage (it is efficient enough).

A design may also have to satisfy restrictions on the design process itself, such as its length or cost, or the tools available for doing the design.

In the software life-cycle, design follows requirements analysis and is followed by implementation. ["Object-Oriented Analysis and Design with Applications", 2nd ed., Grady Booch].

Design - argument from, belief that the operation of the universe evidences its providential origin. See teleological argument.

Determinable-determinate, relative terms for general predicates and particular instances that are not (like the species of a common genus) distin-guishible by differentiae. Thus, for example, "red," "yellow," "orange," and "maroon" are all determinates of the determinable "color."

Determinism, philosophical doctrine which holds that every event, mental as well as physical, has a cause, and that, the cause being given, the event invariably follows. This theory thus denies the element of chance or contingency. It is also opposed to indifferentism, or indeterminism, which maintains that, in phenomena of the human will, preceding events do not definitely determine subsequent ones. Because determinism is generally assumed to be true of all events except volition, the doctrine is of greatest importance when applied to ethics. *See also* Fatalism; Free Will; Predestination; Uncertainty Principle.

Determinism, the position according to which all physical events and human actions are determined or settled (by external forces) before they happen. In other words, determinists deny the existence of freely chosen human activity, and the more consistent determinists even deny any personal responsibility for human actions. Determinists are usually, in fact almost exclusively, adherents of materialism although there are social or economic determinists also, especially those influenced by Marxism. Determinism means pretty much the same thing in practice as it does in philosophical theory, except that popularly it has connotations of fatalism. In some technical discussions determinism is called necessitarianism, the opposite of which is libertarianism. (References from automatism, fatalism, historical determinism, indeterminism, libertarianism, materialism, necessitarianism, physicalism, reductionism, and vitalism.)

Deterministic, 1. Describes a system whose time evolution can be predicted exactly.

2. Describes an algorithm in which the correct next step depends only on the current state. This contrasts with an algorithm involving backtracking where at each point there may be several possible actions and no way to chose between them except by trying each one and backtracking if it fails.

Deterministic automaton, A finite-state automaton in which the overall course of the computation is completely determined by the program, the starting state, and the initial inputs. The class of problems solvable by such automata is the class *P* (see polynomial-time algorithm).

Dewey John, educated in his native Vermont and at Johns Hopkins University, John Dewey (1859-1952) enjoyed a lengthy career as an educator, psychologist, and philosopher. He initiated the progressive laboratory school at the University of Chicago, where his reforms in methods of education could be put into practice. As a professor of philosophy, Dewey taught at Michigan, Chicago, and Columbia University. He was instrumental in founding the American Association of University Professors as a professional organization for post-secondary educators. Drawn from an idealist background by the pragmatist influence of Peirce and James, Dewey became an outstanding exponent of philosophical naturalism. Human thought is understood as practical problem-solving, which proceeds by testing rival hypotheses against experience in order to achieve the "warranted assertability" that grounds coherent action. The tentative character of scientific inquiry makes Dewey's epistemology thoroughly fallibilistic: he granted that the results of this process are always open to criticism and revision, so that nothing is ever finally and absolutely true. This approach provides a significant opportunity for progress in morality and education, however. In "Logical Conditions of a Scientific Treatment of Morality" (1903), for example, Dewey tried to show how moral precepts develop and function as confirmable hypotheses. Democracy and Education (1916) describes in detail how an ability to respond creatively to continual changes in the natural order vitally provides for individual and community life. Dewey's social theories shaped during his long association with George Herbert Mead. *Recommended Reading*: Primary sources: John Dewey, Works (Southern Illinois, 1967-); The Essential Dewey: Ethics, Logic, Psychology, ed. by Thomas M. Alexander and Larry A. Hickman (Indiana, 1998); John Dewey, Democracy and Education: An Introduction to the Philosophy of Education (Simon & Schuster, 1997); John Dewey, Experience and Nature (Dover, 1958); John Dewey, How We Think (Prometheus, 1991). *Secondary sources*: The Philosophy of John Dewey, ed. by John J. McDermott (Chicago, 1981); Reading Dewey: Interpretations for a Postmodern Generation, ed. By Larry Hickman (Indiana, 1998); Sidney Hook and Richard Rorty, John Dewey: An Intellectual Portrait (Prometheus, 1995); Jennifer Welchman, Dewey's Ethical Thought (Cornell, 1997).

D'Holbach Paul-Henri-Dietrich, French philosopher (1723-1789). Even among fellow Encyclopedists, d'Holbach was noted for his vigorous materialism and the virulence of his atheistic attacks on revealed religion and deism in Le Christianisme devoile (Christianity Unmasked) (1761) and Systeme de la nature (The System of Nature) (1770).

Dialectic, process of thinking by means of dialogue, discussion, debate, or argument. In ancient Greece, the term was used literally. Parmenides and the other Eleatics used such methods to defend paradoxical claims about the natural world. Dialectic is questioning and conversation for Socrates, but Plato regarded it as a systematic method for studying the Forms of supra-sensible reality. Although he frequently employed dialectical methods in his own writing, Aristotle maintained that it is inferior to the careful logical reasoning that aims at theoretical knowledge. German philosophers of the modern era applied the term "dialectic" only to more narrowly-defined patterns of thinking. Thus, Kant's "Transce-ndental Dialectic" is an attempt to show the general futility of abstract metaphysical speculation, but dialectic is, for Hegel, the fundamental process of development—in both thought and reality—from thesis to antithesis to synthesis. *Recommended Reading*: F. E. Peters, Greek Philosophical Terms: A Historical Lexicon (NYU, 1967); Francisco J. Gonzalez, Dialectic and Dialogue: Plato's Practice of Philosophical Inquiry (Northwestern, 1998); Hans-Georg Gadamer, Dialogue and Dialectic: Eight Hermeneutical Studies on Plato, tr. by P. Christopher Smith (Yale, 1983); Howard P. Kainz, Paradox, Dialectic, and System: A Contemporary Reconstruction of the Hegelian Problematic (Penn. State, 1988); Hans-Georg Gadamer, Hegel's Dialectic, tr. by P. Christopher Smith (Yale, 1982); and Richard Norman and Sean Sayers, Hegel, Marx and Dialectic: A Debate (Humanities, 1980). For Hegel, a logical progression from thesis (established order), through (alienated) antit-hesis, to synthesis (more inclusive order); then the process is repeated, synthesis becomes thesis and gives rise to a new contradiction, or antithesis; ever upward, on to more and more inclusive orders; thus does the Absolute Spirit progress. Hegel's dialectic was "turned off its head, on which it was standing, and placed upon its feet" (Engels, Ludwig Feuerbach and the End of Classical German Philosophy, Part IV) by Karl Marx. Marxian dialectical materialism holds that society progresses through a series of stages—from Feudalism to Capitalism to Communism—by a dialectical progression fueled by class conflict between the owners or ruling class (under Capitalism, the bourgeois) the excluded (ruled or dispossessed) class (under Capi-talism, proletarians).

Dialectic, in philosophy, method of investigating the nature of truth by the criticism of initial concepts and hypotheses. One of the earliest examples of the dialectical method was the *Dialogues* of the Greek philosopher Plato, in which the author shows his predecessor, Socrates, arriving at the truth concerning the good, beauty, justice, or the human soul by persistently interrogating the common-sense views of those with whom he engaged in dialogue, until they find that their views lead to contradictions. Plato's most famous pupil, Aristotle, thought of dialectic as the search for the philosophical basis of science, and he frequently used the term as a synonym for the science of logic.

The German philosopher Immanuel Kant used the term "transcendental dialectic" to describe the method by which he attempted to demonstrate that it is not possible to have knowledge that goes beyond one's experience. The dialectic consisted in showing that to assume otherwise leads to a series of contradictions, such as the contr-adiction between the idea that people are free and the idea that people are determined. Such contradictions can only be resolved by giving up the idea of knowledge that goes beyond experience and making a clear distinction between things as they are "for us", which can be known, and things as they are "in them-selves", which cannot be known.

Kant's successor G. W. F. Hegel famously applied the term "dialectic" to his philosophical system. Hegel believed that the evolution of concepts occurs through a dialectical process—that is, a concept gives rise to its opposite, and as a result of this conflict, a third view, the synthesis, arises, or else a form of consciousness, through reflection on itself, discovers a contradiction within itself, and is thereby forced to transform itself into a new form of consciousness. The synthesis is at a higher level of truth than the first two views. Hegel's work is based on the idealistic concept of a universal mind that, through evolution, seeks to arrive at the highest level of self-awareness and freedom.

In turn, the German social and political theorist Karl Marx famously applied the concept of dialectic to social and economic processes. He conceived historical progress as a matter of the development of technology (of human "productive forces") to the point where this development came into contradiction with the existing system of ownership and exchange of land, labour, and goods (the existing "social relations of production"). At this point the contradiction takes the form of a struggle for power between two classes, one of which represents the development of the productive forces, and the other the maintenance of the existing social relations of production. The former eventually succeeds in overthrowing the latter in a revolution, so that the development of the productive forces can continue. Thus history as a whole has a dialectical movement. Progress towards human mastery over nature, and eventually towards the elimination of all class relations, results from the development and resolution of contradictions. In his later work *Das Kapital* (vol. 1, 1867; vols. 2 and 3, 1885 and 1894 respectively; trans. 1907-1909), Marx applied the idea of dialectic in a different way, in order to give a systematic account of the modern, capitalist system of social relations of production. Starting with the simplest of these relations (the exchange of commodities in the market), Marx attempted to show that, through a process of the development and resolution of internal contradictions, this relation must give rise in turn to all the remaining social relations of production of capitalism.

Marx described Hegel's dialectical method as "idealist" since it was concerned with concepts and forms of consciousness. By contrast he saw his own dialectic as materialist since it dealt with techniques of material production and with the social relations necessitated by those techniques. Marx's collaborator, Friedrich Engels, attempted to generalize Marx's dialectical method into a general philosophy of "dialectical materialism", and to formulate the "laws of dialectics" governing all change in the natural world as well as the social world. In later orthodox Marxist thought, "dialectic" often came to mean nothing more than a relation between two processes in which each act backs on to the other. However, some 20th-century Western European Marxists, such as Theodore Adorno, have attempted to return to the Hegelian notion of dialectic. They have seen it as a process of making explicit contradictions within an existing form of social consciousness in order to criticize it from within, rather than from a standpoint outside it.

Dialectical materialism, the doctrine or theory of history espoused by Marxism. Literally (*i.e.*, in ancient Greek), "dialectic" means dialogue or conversation, but the Hegelian understanding of dialectic posits the progression of history in determined stages. The materialist aspect of Marxism replaced Hegel's collective consciousness (see Hegelianism) with the concept of economic classes. Thus dialectical materialism is the doctrine that history progresses in stages that are based solely on the supremacy of different economic classes: feudalism replaced aristocracy, capitalism replaced feudalism, and socialism or communism will replace capitalism—all according to inexorable, immutable laws (see historical determinism). (References from historical determinism and Marxism.)

Dianoia, Greek term used by Plato to signify understanding or intellectual activity as a discursive process, in contrast with the immediate apprehension characteristic of noesis. In the taxonomy of Aristotle, dianoia includes both the theoretical episteme and the more practical techne. *Recommended Reading*: F. E. Peters, Greek Philosophical Terms: A Historical Lexicon (NYU, 1967).

Diderot Denis, French philosopher who edited the Encyclopedie. Diderot (1713-1784) promoted Locke's thought in France through his Pensees sur l'interpretation de la nature (1746) and Lettre sur le aveugles (Essay on Blindness) (1749). In his later years, Diderot wrote essays and plays expressing favored Enlightenment themes, including atheism and social contract theory. *Recommended Reading*: Denis Diderot, Selected Philosophical Writings (Greenwood, 1987); Denis Diderot, Rameau's Nephew, and Other Works, tr. by Jacques Barzun and Ralph H. Bowen (Hackett, 2001); Denis Diderot, Thoughts on the Interpretation of Nature and Other Philosophical Works (Clinamen, 2000); and

Diderot's Early Philosophical Works (Open Court, 1970).

Difference Engine, Charles Babbage's design for the first automatic mechanical calculator. The Difference Engine was a special purpose device intended for the production of mathematical tables. Babbage started work on the Difference Engine in 1823 with funding from the British Government. Only one-seventh of the complete engine, about 2000 parts, was built in 1832 by Babbage's engineer, Joseph Clement. This was demonstrated successfully by Babbage and still works perfectly. The engine was never completed and most of the 12,000 parts manufactured were later melted for scrap.

It was left to Georg and Edvard Schuetz to construct the first working devices to the same design which were successful in limited applications. The Difference Engine No. 2 was finally completed in 1991 at the Science Museum, London, UK and is on display there.

The engine used gears to compute cumulative sums in a series of registers: $r[i] := r[i] + r[i+1]$. However, the addition had the side effect of zeroing $r[i+1]$. Babbage overcame this by simultaneously copying $r[i+1]$ to a temporary register during the addition and then copying it back to $r[i+1]$ at the end of each cycle (each turn of a handle). Difference Engine at the Science Museum.

Difference equation, A relation between consecutive elements of a sequence. The first difference is

$$D\,u(n) = u(n+1) - u(n)$$

where $u(n)$ is the nth element of sequence u. The second difference is

$$D2\,u(n) = D\,(D\,u(n))$$

$$= (u(n+2) - u(n+1)) - (u(n+1) - u(n))$$

$$= u(n+2) - 2u(n+1) + u(n)$$

And so on. A recurrence relation such as can be converted to a difference

$$u(n+2) + a\,u(n+1) + b\,u(n) = 0$$

equation (in this case, a second order linear difference equation):

$$D2\,u(n) + p\,D\,u(n) + q\,u(n) = 0$$

and vice versa. a, b, p, q are constants.

Difference method of, one of Mill's Methods for discovering causal relationships. If an antecedent circumstance is present only on those occasions when a phenomenon occurs, it may be inferred to be the cause of that phenomenon. Example: "Levi and Jarod lived in the same house and were both exposed to the same children at daycare, but only Levi, who also plays T-ball, caught the measles. So Levi probably caught the measles from one of his teammates." *Recommended Reading*: John Stuart Mill, System of Logic (Classworks, 1986).

Difference of sets, The difference of set B from set A is the set of all members of A that are not also members of B. Notation: A-B, or $A\backslash B$.

$$A\text{-}B =df\ x: (x: A)o(x/: B)$$

Dike, Greek term for legal compensation or justice; the corresponding human virtue of being just is dikaiÙsunÍ. According to Plato, justice in this sense is best exem-plified by harmonious relations in the ideal state.

Aristotle, on the other hand, focussed primarily upon the equitable distribution of goods in a properly-run city. *Recommended Reading*: F. E. Peters, Greek Philosophical Terms: A Historical Lexicon (NYU, 1967); Eric

Alfred Havelock, The Greek Concept of Justice: From Its Shadow in Homer to Its Substance in Plato (Harvard, 1978); and Richard D. Parry, Plato's Craft of Justice (SUNY, 1996).

Dilemma, a difficult choice between equally undesirable alternatives. In a disadvantageous rhetorical position, one is said to be impaled on the horns of a dilemma, but logicians employ Constructive Dilemma as a rule of inference. *Recommended Reading*: Howard Kahane and Nancy Cavender, Logic and Contemporary Rhetoric (Wadsworth, 1997) and Douglas N. Walton, Informal Logic: A Handbook for Critical Argumentation (Cambridge, 1989).

Dilthey Wilhelm, German philosopher (1833-1911) who derived from the thought of Kant a conception of philosophical study as one of the social sciences in Einleitung in die Geisteswissenshaften (Introduction to the Human Sciences) (1883). Metaphysical speculation in particular, Dilthey held in Die Typen der Weltanschauung (1912), is an expression of the world-view of one's culture rather than a timeless expression of perfect rationality. *Recommended Reading*: Wilhelm Dilthey, ed. by Frithjof Rodi and Rudolf A. Makkreel (Princeton, 1996); Rudolf A. Makkreel, Dilthey (Princeton, 1992); and Richard E. Palmer, Hermeneutics: Interpretation Theory in Schleiermacher, Dilthey, Heidegger and Gadamer (Northwestern, 1969).

Ding an sich, German phrase for thing in itself.

Diogenes, Greek philosopher (400-325 BC). As one of the original Cynics, Diogenes both preached and practiced a life of complete self-sufficiency, utter simplicity, and total disregard for the conventional morality of what he took to be a corrupt human society. Diogenes was the teacher of Zeno of Citium. *Recommended Reading*: The Cynics: The Cynic Movement in Antiquity and Its Legacy, ed. by R. Bracht Branham and Marie Odile Goulet-Caze California, 2000) and D. R. Dudley, A History of Cynicism (Ares, 1980).

Diophantine equation, Equations with integer coefficients to which integer solutions are sought. Because the results are restricted to integers, different algorithms must be used from those which find real solutions.

Directed graph, (digraph) A graph with one-way edges. See also directed acyclic graph.

Directed set, *A* set *X* is directed under some relation, <= (less than or equal), if it is non-empty and if for any two elements *x* and *y* there exists an element *z* such that *x* <= *z* and *y* <= *z*. *I.e.* all pairs have an upper bound.

Directive use of language, communication that aims to bring about or to forestall the performance of some action. Example: "Don't forget to take out the trash."

Direct realism, theory of perception according which we perceive material objects directly, without the mediation of ideas or sensory representations. Although it is also called "naÔve" realism, this view often requires a sophisticated defence, especially in its attempts to account for the occurrence of hallucinations and perceptual error. *Recommended Reading*: Thomas Reid, An Inquiry into the Human Mind on the Principles of Common Sense, ed. by Derek Brookes (Penn. State, 2001); H. H. Price, Perception (Greenwood, 1982); and Moltke S. Gram, Direct Realism: A Study of

Perception (Nijhoff, 1983).

Discriminated union, The discriminated union of two sets *A* and *B* is

A + *B* = (in*A*, *a*) | *a* in *A U* (in*B*, *b*)| *b* in *B*

where in A and inB are arbitrary tags which specify which summand an element originates from.

A type (especially an algebraic data type) might be described as a discriminated union if it is a sum type whose objects consist of a tag to say which part of the union they belong to and a value of the corresponding type.

Disjunction, p qp v q

T	T	T
T	F	T
F	T	T
F	F	F

A compound statement that is true whenever either one or both of its component statements (the disjuncts) are true. Disjunctions are symbolized here in the form: *p* v *q* Example: "Either the switch is off or the bulb is burned out."

Disjunctive syllogism, a rule of inference of the form:

p v q
~ p

q

Example: "Either Ellen brought him to the party or Keith did. But Ellen didn't. So, Keith brought him to the party." The validity of this pattern of reasoning is evident from a simple truth-table.

Disjoint sets, Two sets are disjoint iff they share no members, *i.e.* iff their intersection is the null set.

Disjunction, A truth function that is true when one or the other of its components (called disjuncts) is true, and false otherwise. Also the connective denoting this function; also the compound proposition built from this connective. Exclusive disjunction

One or the other of the disjuncts is true, but not both. Notation: no standard symbol, but the concept is accurately captured thus:

p
/<=> q.

(negation of material equivalence). Inclusive disjunction

One or the other or both of the disjuncts is true. Notation:

p
v q.

Disjunctive normal form (DNF), The form of a of truth-functional compound when it is expressed as a series of disjuncts when each disjunct is either a simple proposition or the conjunction of simple propositions and the negations of simple propositions. *E.g.* the DNF of (*A* or *B*) and *C* is (*A* and *C*) or (*B* and *C*).

Disposition, a tendency or propensity to respond in specific ways to particular circumstances. Things are commonly supposed to have dispositional features only in virtue of their possession of intrinsic or non-dispositional properties. Thus, for example, sugar is soluble in water (even when it is not in water) because of its chemical composition. Ryle maintained that mental states can be wholly analyzed as dispositions of human bodies. *Recommended Reading*: Gilbert Ryle, The Concept of Mind (Chicago, 2000).

Distributed memory, The kind of memory in a parallel processor where each processor has fast access to its own local memory and where to access another processor's memory it must send a message via the inter-processor network. Opposite: shared memory.

Distributed representation, a distributed representation is one in which meaning is not captured by a single symbolic unit, but rather arises from the interaction of a set of units, normally in a network of some sort.

The concept of distributed representation is a product of joint developments in the neurosciences and in connectionist work on recognition tasks (Churchland and Sejnowski 1992). Fundamentally, a distributed representation is one in which meaning is not captured by a single symbolic unit, but rather arises from the interaction of a set of units, normally in a network of some sort. In the case of the brain, the concept of "grandmother" does not seem to be represented by a single "grand-mother cell" but is rather distributed across a network of neurons (Churchland and Sejnowski 1992). This method of representation stands in direct opposition to the symbolic representation used by adherents of classical artificial intelligence.

To introduce distributed representations concisely it is helpful to contrast them with the more familiar symbolic representations. Symbolic representations are the easiest for us, as language users, to understand and apply. A symbol, such as a word or a number, is an everyday occurrence for most of humankind. For instance, each word contained in this entry is a symbolic representation of a particular meaning associated with that word. These symbols are joined into propositions based on the rules of a grammar. Of course, symbols are not restricted to being words or numbers, but this is their most common application in classical AI. From computational, psychological, and neurological standpoints, there are a number of shortcomings in using purely symbolic representations in modelling human behaviour. I will briefly examine three of the more important limitations of symbolic representation that serve to distinguish them from distributed representations.

First, symbolic representations are strongly propositional. Thus, when this method of representation is used in non-language based applications such as image proce-ssing it becomes extremely difficult to explain many psychological findings. Similarly, taste, sound, touch, and smell are very awkward to handle with symbolic representations. In contrast, distributed representations are equally well suited to all modes of perception.

Second, symbolic repres-entations are "all-or-none". This means that there is no such thing as the degradation of a symbolic representation, it is either there, or it is not there; this property is referred to as brittleness. The brittleness of symbolic representations is highly psychologically unrealistic. People often exhibit behaviour that indicates partial retrieval of represe-ntations, as in the "tip-of-the-brain" recall, prosopagnosia (loss of face recognition), and image completion. Furthermore, minor damage to a symbolic conceptual network causes loss of entire concepts, whereas a distributed network loses accuracy, as people do, not entire concepts (Churchland and Sejnowski 1992).

Third, symbolic representations are not, in themselves, statistically sensitive. In other words, they are not constructed based on statistical regularities found in the environment. Therefore, symbolic representations are not amenable to modelling low-level perception. This sort of low-level perceptual learning seems to be common to all animals, and is an important part of human development. It is the case, however, that though symbolic representations are not statistically sensitive, they are superbly tructurally sensitive. To many, this had seemed a reasonable trade-off in light of structurally insensitive alternatives. However, with the more recent development of distributed representations that exhibit both structural and statistical sensitivity, this trade-off is no longer as justifiable.

With these limitations in mind, many cognitive scientists have found distri-buted representations very appealing. Though distributed representations are a far less intuitive form of representation, the advantages they provide easily outweigh the difficulty in initially under-standing them. In order to minimize a reliance on a technical description of distributed representations, I have constructed an analogy which will aid in explaining distributed representations in general. The analogy is this: imagine all of your concepts are mapped to the surface of a sphere—a conceptual golf ball, if you will. Each concept is nestled in a dimple on surface of the golf ball. The more similar two concepts are, the closer together they will be on the surface of the golf ball. Also, the distance from the centre of the golf ball to any particular dimple (*i.e.* concept) is approximately the same. The easiest way to identify the position of a concept on the surface of the ball is to provide its coordinates. These coordinates are in the units of "golf ball radii" and are continuous real values. Such a set of coordinates is commonly referred to as a vector. In order for us, as symbol users, to distinguish this vector from others, we assign it a tag *e.g.* "cherub". Thus, the vector (0.5, 0.5, 0.707) may be used to represent the position of the "cherub" dimple on the surface of the conceptual golf ball. Such a representation of "cherub" is a distributed representation, because the "cherub" dimple can only be located through knowing all three values. Thus, the concept of "cherub" is shared, or distributed, across the three dimensions of the golf ball's coordinate system. Notably, a dimple on a golf ball is not a single point, rather it is a collection of points which are in proximity on the surface of the sphere. This makes the dimple particularly appealing as an analog for a concept for the following reasons:

1) A prototype for a concept could be considered to be the centre of the dimple.
2) Multiple vectors define the dimple/concept's boundaries; thus it is a collection of examples. Typically, these "boundary" concepts would be specific examples which the cognizer had observed from its environment.
3) Because of 2, the prototype for a concept would not be defined by one particular example, but rather a superposition of all available examples of the concept.

However, as with any analogy, there are a number of issues which may be obscured or inadequately addressed by thc conceptual golf ball analogy. For instance, when equating concepts to dimples, we must realize that it is misleading to think of concepts as being defined by a static circular boundary as a dimple is. Rather, conceptual boundaries may be dynamic, oddly shaped, "fuzzy", and possibly not even contiguous. Furthermore, such boundaries do not delineate two or three dimensional figures but rather some n-dimensional figures where n is possibly in the thousands or even millions.As we are equating a three dimensional golf ball to an n-dimensional hypersphere, it is important to bear in mind the limitations of such a simplification.

In the introduction to this discussion, I noted that much of the reason researchers were motivated to look for alternate forms of representation was due to the failings of symbolic representations. In particular we discussed the propositional, brittle, and statistical insensitivity nature of symbolic representations. Distributed repre-sentations do not fall prey to these short-comings. Rather, distributed representations:

1) Are the natural result of organisation of statistical input and thus provide a natural means to capturing semantic infor-mation (Smolensky 1995);
2) Have been successfully applied to visual, olfactory, auditory and tactile problems;
3) Have been proved to degrade gracefully with noise and are commonly tested with simulate-d lesions (*i.e.* a removal of part of the representation).

Furthermore, distributed representations have a number of properties which lend significant psychological and neurological plausibility to models employing them. In many instances distributed representations:

1) Represent concepts continuously;
2) Can be processed in parallel (see parallel processing;
3) Can be learned using proven methods (Hinton 1986).

These powerful properties, coupled with the ability of distributed representations to overcome important short-comings of symbolic representation provide a solid foundation for realistic comp-utational models of human cognition.

References: Connectionist Representation Biblio) Churchland, P. S. and T. Sejnowski (1992). The computational brain. Cambridge, MA, MIT Press. Hinton, G. E. (1986). Learning distributed representations of concepts. Eighth Conference of the Cognitive Science Society, Lawrence Erlbaum Associates. Smolensky, P. (1995). Computational models of mind. A companion to the philosophy of mind. Cambridge, MA, Blackwell.

Distribution of terms, a feature that categorical terms come to have by virtue of their use in a specific categorical proposition. The term is distributed if the proposition refers to every member of the class it designates, unidistributed if it does not. Thus, the subject term is distributed in all and only universal propositions; the predicate term is distributed in all and only negative propositions.

Diverge, If a series of approximations to some value get progressively further from it then the series is said to diverge.

The reduction of some term under some evaluation strategy diverges if it does not reach a normal form after a finite number of reductions.

Divine command theory, any ethical position claiming that the rightness or wrongness of actions depends on whether they correspond to God's commands.

Division-fallacy of, the informal fallacy of attributing some feature of a collection to the members of that collection individually, or reasoning from whole to part. Example: "Today's ewspaper has a lot of grocery ads, so each page of today's newspaper has a lot of grocery ads."

Doctrine of pre-established harmony, a view originated by G. W. Leibniz whereby:

1) the mental and the material comprise two different kinds of substance;
2) neither has any direct causal effect on the other and;
3) the coincidence between mental and material events is due to both substances being created to act in concert even though there is no post-creation interaction between the two.

See dualism, occasionalism, parallelism.

Document, A term used on some systems (*e.g.* Intermedia) for a hypertext node. It is sometimes used for a collection of nodes on related topics, possibly stored or distributed as one.

Dogmatism, 1. originally, the position of any philosopher who was not a skeptic.

2. authoritarian approach to ideas which emphasizes rigid adherence to doctrine over rational and enlightened inquiry. The opposite approach is probably best characterized as tolerant humanism or critical rationalism (in the sense of devotion to reason and independent thinking).

Dolors, utilitarian units of pain or displeasure. See also hedons.

Double aspect theory, belief that mental properties and events on the one hand and physical properties and events on the other hand are irreducibly distinct features or aspects of one and the same thing that exhibits them both. Spinoza, for example, maintained that thought and extension are distinct attributes of the one existing substance that is "god or nature." *Recommended Reading*: Keith Campbell, Body and Mind (Notre Dame, 1984); Genevieve Lloyd, Routledge Philosophy Guidebook to Spinoza and the Ethics (Routledge, 1996); and Michael Della Rocca, Representation and the Mind-Body Problem in Spinoza (Oxford, 1996).

Double negation, a rule of replacement of the form: $p = \sim \sim p$

Example: "Alan is clever" is equivalent to "It is not the case that Alan is not clever." Although trivial in ordinary language, this rule is vital for the completeness of the propositional calculus.

Doubt-method of, the starting-point for Descartes's philosophy. He used perceptual illusions, the dream problem, and the possibility of a deceiving god to show the uncertainty of many common beliefs. Only the cogito then survives as an indubitable foundation for knowledge. *Recommended Reading*: Rene Descartes, Discourse on Method and Meditations on First Philosophy, tr. by Donald A. Cress (Hackett, 1999); E. M. Curley, Descartes Against the Skeptics (Iuniverse, 1999); and The Cambridge Companion to Descartes, ed. by John Cottingham (Cambridge, 1992).

Doxa, Greek term for opinion, belief, or judgment, as opposed to systematic knowledge. According to Plato, this limited awareness of the sensible world encompasses the lower portion of the divided line. In Aristotle's works on logic, the same terms are used to distinguish contingent from necessary truths about the world. *Recommended Reading*: F. E. Peters, Greek Philosophical Terms: A Historical Lexicon (NYU, 1967).

Doxastic, pertaining to belief, from the Greek word "doxa", meaning "opinion", "belief". Alternatively, also pertaining to states sufficiently similar to beliefs, such as thoughts, judgments, opinions, desires, wishes, fears.

Often the distinction between doxastic and sub-doxastic states is a way of cashing out the distinction between personal and sub-personal states where instances of the latter include information bearing states not available to awareness (like the information processing going on in the cerebellum). Examples of non-doxastic contentful states would be the numbers of rings in a tree's cross-section: they carry information about the age of the tree, but are neither beliefs (doxastic states), nor states of an entity that has beliefs (sub-doxastic states).

Dual-aspect theory, a view forwarded by Spinoza (also called the dual-attribute theory) in which the unitary substance God is expressed in the distinct modes of the mental and the physical. See dualism.

Dualism, in philosophy, the theory that the universe is explicable only as a whole composed of two distinct and mutually irreducible elements. In Platonic philosophy the ultimate dualism is between "being" and "nonbeing", that is, between ideas and matter. In the 17th century, dualism took the form of belief in two fundamental substances, mind and matter. The French philosopher René Descartes, whose interpretation of the universe exemplifies this belief, was the first to emphasize the irreconcilable difference between thinking substance (mind) and extended substance (matter). The difficulty created by this view was to explain how mind and matter interact, as they apparently do in human experience. This perplexity caused some Cartesians to deny entirely any interaction between the two. They asserted that mind and matter are inherently incapable of affecting each other, and that any reciprocal action between the two is caused by God, who, on the occasion of a change in one, produces a corresponding change in the other. Other followers of Descartes abandoned dualism in favour of monism.

In the 20th century, reaction against the monistic aspects of the philosophy of idealism has to some degree revived dualism. One of the most interesting defences of dualism is that of the Anglo-American psychologist William McDougall, who divided the universe into spirit and matter and maintained that good evidence, both psychological and biological, indicates the spiritual basis of physiological processes. The French philosopher Henri Bergson in his great philosophical work *Mat-*

ter and Memory likewise took a dualistic position, defining matter as what we perceive with our senses and possessing in itself the qualities that we perceive in it, such as colour and resistance. Mind, on the other hand, reveals itself as memory, the faculty of storing up the past and utilizing it for modifying our present actions, which otherwise would be merely mechanical. In his later writings, however, Bergson abandoned dualism and came to regard matter as an arrested manifestation of the same vital impulse that composes life and mind.

Dualism also has an ethical aspect, namely, in the recognition of the independent and opposing principles of good and evil. This is exemplified in Zoroastrianism and in Manichaeism.

Dualism, in metaphysics, the view that reality consists of two disparate parts or that there are only two fundamental things or substances or constituents of things in the world at large or in the human soul. The first influential dualist theory in the West was Platonism, which claimed that there are actually two different worlds: the physical world of ppearances and the higher world of intelligible Forms or Ideas or Essences (thus note the common connection of dualism to transce-ndentalism and idealism), with a similar separation in the human person between mind and body. These ideas were picked up by stoicism and, later, by Christianity. Thus the idea of dualism was current throughout the Christian era—but it received a renewed impetus from Descartes, who held that reality is made up exclusively of Spirit and Matter, and that these two substances can never meet or interact —except in the human soul (which gives rise to the mind-body dichotomy). Aristotelianism, by contrast, holds that mind and body are not two distinct substances but two aspects of the same thing, of the same complete human person (cf. also holism). Even though dualism is a kind of pluralism and is opposed by monism, practically speaking dualists often put their emphasis on the "higher", more spiritual reality that their theoretical separations construct, so that they are often construed as adherents of idealism or transcendentalism, even though this is not strictly the case.

2. In philosophy of mind, the belief that the mental and physical are deeply different in kind: thus the mental is at least not identical with the physical. See occasionalism, doctrine of pre-established harmony-substance dualism, property dualism, Cartesian interactionist dualism, mind-body problem, monism.

Introduction: Dualism is a time-honoured philosophical position which is exemplified by:

1) Pre-Socratics' appearance/reality distinction
2) Plato's forms/world distinction
3) Hume's fact/value distinction
4) Kant's empirical phenomena/transcendental noumena distinction
5) Heidegger's being/time distinction
6) Russell's existence/subsistence distinction
7) Descartes' mind/matter distinction

It is, of course, the last of these which is of most immediate interest to philosophers of mind. There has been a recent revival of interest in the topic of Cartesian dualism amongst modern philosophers of mind and cognitive scientists. Arguments against dualism have been provided on the basis of both empirical evidence and on philosophical grounds, and clearly express the predominant view (*e.g.* Dennett, Damasio, Churchland). However, a number of modern philosophers of mind, though in the minority, have come to the defence of dualism (*e.g.* Hart). The question of dualism is not only of historical interest, it also has important implications for the scientific enterprise. If a convincing rejection of dualism can be formulated, the classic mind-body problem will be solved by its becoming a non-problem and the materialist approach of modern science will be vindicated. If, conversely, dualism can be convincingly maintained, it is by no means obvious that empirical evidence will suffice for a thorough understanding of the mind—in other words, under-standing the brain may not be enough for understanding the mind.

Descartes, Descartes' mind/matter distinction can be found in his Meditations and is a particular kind of dualism Cartesian interactionist. Often, the term "Cartesian dualism" is used to refer to the general class of substance dualist theories. Substance dualists hold that mind and matter are different kinds of substances. Cartesian interactionist dualism is a particular kind of substance dualism in which these two different kinds of substance can causally interact. Thus, mind substance can cause matter substance (*i.e.* the body) to act and matter substance (*i.e.* the body) can cause mind substance to have certain "sensations", most often by itself being acted on by other material objects. For Descartes, the essence of matter is extension (*i.e.* having spatial dimensions and being located, res extensa) whereas that of mind is active thinking (res cogitans). Because Descartes thought these two sorts of substance are essentially different, he held that they are also independent. Thus, matter can exist without minds and minds can exist without matter.

Descartes' position raises an important question: How do mind and matter interact? It is one thing to claim that they do interact, it is another to explain convincingly how, particularly when mind and matter are conceived of so differently. It is this question that must be answered to solve the classic mind-body problem. The Cartesian solution to the problem is to insist that the mental representation, though caused by the physical, does not resemble the physical. However, this does not seem to explain, still, how the mental comes to represent the physical at all. It seems that Descartes' final position is to insist that God, as the only substance in the strong sense (*i.e.* as the only entity that can exist independently of anything else) is responsible for these interactions.

Solving the mind-body problem Subsequent to Descartes, there were a number of attempts to provide dualistic solutions to the mind-body problem.

These included: Occasionalism. Espoused by Clauberg, de la Forge and Malebranche, occasionalism entails the contention that everything is devoid of causal efficacy and that God is the only truly causal agent. So, for example, placing your hand on a hot stove is does not cause pain, but is rather an occasion for God to cause the mental state of pain. So, not only mind/body interactions, but all causal interactions become the work of God. doctrine of pre-established harmony. This doctrine was formulated by Leibniz and is basically Cartesian interactionist dualism without the interaction. Thus, rather than causal interaction, God has provided setup in which the mental and physical are synch-ronised so as to provide this appearance. However, it should be noted that Leibniz himself was not a dualist: for him there were no physical substances, these were just appearances. Nevertheless, this position is often considered a possible dualistic solution to the mind-body problem.

Both occasionalism and the doctrine of pre-established harmony are considered instances of parallelism: the view that the mental and physical realms co-occur but are not causally connected.

Modern dualists: More recently, some philosophers have suggested that the interaction problem is not due to a problem with a dualist ontology, but a problem with our notion of causation (Hart). Indeed, this problem is just as evident in physics as in dualism: a conversion of, say, light to "psychic energy" seems no more a problem than a conversion of energy to matter. Both seem potentially able to contradict a standard notion of causation. Under this view, dualism is at least a viable possibility once we realize the difficulty may lie elsewhere than with a commitment to a dualist ontology.

Another approach to strengthening the dualist position has been to examine critically the claims that our mental lives can be adequately explained by reference to the physical brain. Philosophers of mind have, for the past ten years, begun to question seriously the possibility that science will be able to close the explanatory gap between the brain and our conscious experience, or qualia (termed the hard problem by Chalmers). Clearly, a reason this gap may be unbridgeable is because mind and matter are so different. Those holding this position have been called new mysterians because they insist that mind/consciousness is fundamentally mysterious and can not be explained by standard reductionist scientific means.

References: Dualism Biblio

Chalmers, D. (1996). The conscious mind: In search of a fundamental theory. Oxford, Oxford University Press. Churchland, P. M. (1996). The engine of reason, the seat of the soul. Cambridge, MA, MIT Press. Damasio, A. R. (1994). Descartes' error: Emotion, reason, and the human brain. New York, NY, Grosset/ Putnam. Descartes, R. (1989). Discourse on Method and the Meditations. Translated by John Veitch. Prometheus Books. Dennett, D. C. (1991). Consciousness explained. New York, Little, Brown and Company. Hart, W.D. (1988). The engines of the soul. Cambridge University Press.

Du Bois William Edward Burghardt, American historian and sociologist (1868-1963). After completing his education with a Ph.D. from Harvard, Du Bois embarked on a long and distinguished career as a university professor and social activist. His The

Souls of Black Folk (1903) was a penetrating analysis of the origins, practices, and consequences of racial discrimination in thc United States. Du Bois also participated in efforts at social reform, founding the National Association fot the Advancement of Colored People in 1910 and editing the influential journals Crisis and Phylon. Details of Du Bois's life are to be found in his autobiography, Dusk of Dawn (1940). *Recommended Reading*: The Oxford W. E. B. Du Bois Reader, ed. By Eric J. Sundquist (Oxford, 1996); W. E. B. Du Bois, The Souls of Black Folk: Authoritative Text, Contexts, Criticism, ed. by Henry Louis Gates, Jr. and Terri Hume Oliver (Norton, 1999); W. E. B. Du Bois, Writings: The Suppression of the African Slave-Trade: The Souls of Black Folk: Dusk of Dawn: Essays: Articles from the Crisis (Library of America, 1996); and W.E.B. Du Bois on Race and Culture: Philosophy, Politics, and Poetics, ed. by Bernard W. Bell, Emily Grosholz, and James B. Stewart (Routledge, 1996).

Duhem Pierre M.M., French historian and philosopher of science (1861-1916). In La Theorie physique: son objet et sa structure (The Aim and Structure of Physical Theory) (1906) Duhem maintained that every scientific theory is an exercise in metaphysical speculation, verified or falsified by the predictive power it is shown to have as a systematic whole. *Recommended Reading*: Pierre Duhem: Essays in History and Philosophy of Science, ed. by Roger Ariew and Peter Barker (Hackett, 1996) and R. N. D. Martin, Pierre uhem: Philosophy and History in the Work of a Believing Physicist (Open Court, 1991).

Dummett Michael A.E., English philosopher and logician (1925-). The essays collected in Truth and other Enigmas (1978) and The Seas of Language (1993) defend an intuitionist philosophy of mat-hematics and emphasize the linguistic foundations of epistemology. Dum-mett is also the foremost English interpreter of Frege in such works as Frege: Philosophy of Language (1973), The Interpretation of Frege's Philosophy (1981), and Frege: Philosophy of Mathematics (1991). *Recommended Reading*: Michael Dummett, Frege and Other Philosophers (Oxford, 1996); Michael Dummett, The Logical Basis of Metaphysics (Harvard, 1993); and Michael Dummett, Origins of Analytical Philosophy (Harvard, 1996).

Durkheim Emile, French philosopher and sociologist (1858-1917). Durkheim argued that since society is something more than merely a ollection of individual human beings, it follows that social events cannot be explained wholly in biological or psychological terms. This insight was a significant impetus for the independence of sociology as a science. His major writings include Šlèments de sociologie (1889), Les Regles de la methode sociol-ogique (Rules for Sociological Method) (1895), De la division du travail social (The Division of Labor in Society) (1893), and Le Suicide (Suicide: A Study in Sociology) (1897). Durkheim criticized pragmatism in Pragmatism and Society (1914). *Recommended Reading*: Emile Durkheim, On Morality and Society: Selected Writings, ed. by Robert N. Bellah (Chicago, 1975); Gianfranco Poggi, Durkheim (Oxford, 2000); and Steven Lukes, Emile Durkheim, His Life and Work: A Historical and Critical Study (Stanford, 1985).

Duty, what an individual is obliged to, or ought to do. If an individual has a duty to do X it is not permissible for them not to do X; and if they have a duty not to do X then it is not permissible for them to do it. Kant believed the commands of morality, being categorical, create perfect duties allowing no exceptions. Nonmoral imperatives, on the other hand, being hypothetical, create imperfect duties which allow of exceptions. See categorical imperative, hypothetical imperative.

Duty (philosophy), that which a person is required or obligated to do. What a duty is can be said to be dependent on its foundations or grounds. Thus, duties can be moral, legal, familial, or derived from one's station. A duty can have several grounds—it can be, for instance, both moral and legal. There are many types of duty. Natural duties, for example, are said to be those duties people incur in virtue of being people, that is, simply in virtue of their nature. There are also *prima facie* duties; that is, duties to perform certain acts if and only if there are appropriate reasons for performing such acts. This latter class of duties invites a comparison with "all-things-con-sidered duties", which one incurs if the grounds or reasons which support these duties significantly outweigh any grounds or reasons that count against them. Further to this, there are negative and positive duties. Negative duties are duties not to perform certain acts, such as killing or causing harm, while positive duties are duties to act in certain ways, such as to relieve suffering or to give alms.

Kant's Theory of Duty: While the concept of duty has been the object of philosophical reflection since the time of the ancient Greeks, it is only in modern times that the concept has come into its own. Modern discussion of duty can be traced back to the 18th-century German philosopher Immanuel Kant. For Kant, all moral requirements expressed themselves as duties. Kant contrasted duties to self with duties to others and under these headings distinguished perfect duties from imperfect duties. Perfect duties are complete: they hold unconditionally for all moral agents and require the performance of a determinate act. Examples of perfect duties are refraining from coercion and violence. Imperfect duties, however, are those that do not require a determinate act but exhibit sufficient "latitude" between an aim and the business of bringing about that aim. To explain, the moral requirements that surround the aims of helping others or developing one's talents are imperfect duties, for we cannot help everyone, nor can we develop every talent.

Duty Theories Since Kant: Since Kant, philosophical discussion of the place and importance of duty has mostly taken place in the context of a debate between "deontological" and "consequentialist" theories of morality. A deontological theory is a moral theory which advocates that certain acts can be judged to be right or wrong in themselves. Kant's own views provide an example of such a theory. In contrast, a consequentialist theory holds that the rightness or wrongness of an act is to be judged in terms of the consequences it produces. An example of a consequentialist theory would be the utilitarianism of Jeremy Bentham and J. S. Mill, which argues that every action ought to maximize happiness and minimize bad states of affairs. Thus, contemporary deontologists such as the American philosophers John Rawls and Charles Fried argue that the concepts of right and duty ought to be central to any moral theory, while contemporary utilitarians, such as R. M. Hare and other consequentialists, argue that duties are important only in so far as they indicate those acts which promote good states of affairs.

More recently, however, philosophers in Britain and the United States, influenced by the work of Alasdair MacIntyre and Bernard Williams, have argued that moral philosophy ought to concern itself more with a description of the conditions of human life, and less with traditional concepts of duty and obligation. This has led to a re-evaluation of the place of duty within contemporary moral philosophy, with the consequence that the concept no longer enjoys the pre-eminence and sustained attention it once had.

Dworkin Ronald Myles, American political philosopher (1931-). In Taking Rights Seriously (1977) and Law's Empire (1986) Dworkin defends a version of legal positivism that relies heavily upon the principled adjudicationof disputes by the judiciary. His treatment of concrete legal issues concerning abortion and euthanasia is to be found in Life's Dominion (1993). Objectivity and Truth: You'd Better Believe It" argues that a moderate notion of objectivity secures the objectivity of moral claims. *Recommended Reading*: Ronald Dworkin, Freedom's Law: The Moral Reading of the American Constitution (Harvard, 1997); The Philosophy of Law, ed. by Ronald M. Dworkin (Oxford, 1977); Stephen Guest, Ronald Dworkin (Stanford, 1992); and Ronald Dworkin and Contemporary Jurisprudence, ed. by Marshall Cohen (Rowman & Littlefield, 1984).

Dynamical systems theory, an area of mathematics used to describe the behaviour of complex systems by employing differential and difference equations. Recently, this approach has been advanced by some as the best way to describe human cognition.

Proponents of the dynamical systems theory approach to cognition believe that systems of differential or difference equations are the most appropriate tool for modelling human behaviour. These equations are interpreted to represent an agent's cognitive trajectory through a high dimensional state space. In other words, cognition is explained as a multi-dimensional space of all possible thoughts and behaviours that is traversed by a path of thinking followed by an agent under certain environmental and internal pressures, all of which is captured by sets of differential equations. The terminology of dynamical systems theory is also adapted.. Thus, cognition is spoken of in terms of state spaces; point, cyclic and chaotic attractors; trajectories; and deterministic chaos.

Dynamicists, including van Gelder, Port, Thelen and Smith, believe that they have a mandate to prove that this dynamicist conception of cognition is the correct one to the exclusion of symbolicism and connectionism. Van Gelder has formulated this as the Dynamicist Hypothesis (van Gelder, 1995, p. 4):

> "Natural cognitive systems are certain kinds of dynamical sys-

tems, and are best under-stood from the perspective of dynamics."

Those "certain kinds" of systems are identified as (van Gelder and Port, 1995, p. 5): "state-determined systems whose behaviour is governed by differential equations ...Dynamical systems in this strict sense always have variables that are evolving continuously and simultaneously and which at any point in time are mutually determining each other's evolution."

In sum, van Gelder and Port assign the following criteria to dynamicist explanations of cognition. Dynamicist descriptions must be:

- deterministic
- generally complex (*i.e.* nonlinear)
- described with respect to the independent variable of time
- of low dimensionality
- intimately linked (*i.e.* coupled)

There are also various claims made about the status of computation and representation in such systems. Often, it is claimed that dynamical systems are noncomputational and nonrepresenta-tional.

Criticisms of dynamic systems theory are numerous. Some focus on the rejection of representation and computation. These either claim that the systems are indeed representational and computational or that dynamic systems theory will not be able to explain how cognitive systems are able to be both representational and computational. As well, the similarity between behaviourism and the dynamicist approach is often used to discredit dynamicism because of the numerous and debilitating difficulties faced by early behaviourists.

Another important criticism stems from the relation between dynamic systems theory and connectionist networks. Though many dynamicists feel that connectionism should be replaced by dynamicism, it is not clear why. Connectionist networks exhibit many of the features that behaviours dynamicist note as being central to cognition and incompatible with classical, or symbolicist artificial intelligence. Though many connec-tionist networks do not live up to the expectations of dynamicists, there are a number which do, while not discarding the notions of computation and representation. Though a strong normative claim may be made concerning the importance of dynamical systems theory to connectionist models, it is far from clear that dynamicist cognitive approach will, or should, replace the connectionist approach. *References*: Dynamic Systems Biblio) Eliasmith, C. (1996) The third contender: a critical examination of the dynamicist theory of cognition. Philosophical Psychology, 9(4), 441-463. Van Gelder, T. (1995) "What might cognition be, if notcomputation?" Journal of Philosophy, 91, 345-381. Van Gelder, T. and Port, R. (1995). "It's about time: an overview of the dynamical approach to cognition." in Mind as motion: explorations in the dynamics of cognition. Cambridge, MA: MIT Press.

Dynamicism, dynamical systems theory

Dynamic systems theory, dynamical systems theory.

Dynamis, Greek term for power or force, used by presocratic philosophers in reference to the qualities or features of material elements. Aristotle later used the term to signify potentiality, or the capacity for undergoing change. The neoplatonic tradition, on the other hand, developed a conception of pers-onified causal agents. *Recommended Reading*: F. E. Peters, Greek Philosophical Terms: A Historical Lexicon (NYU, 1967).

Dynamism, the idea that the universe is fundamentally made up of force(s); this idea is often augmented by the notion that much of the stability we perceive is illusory and that everything is constantly changing or in flux (sometimes called a Heraclitean view of the universe, after the ancient Greek philosopher Heraclitus). The most famous dynamists of recent times are probably Whitehead and Bergson, who are also called "process hilosop-hers".

Eckhart Johannes, known as Meister Eckhart (1260-1327). German Dominican theologian whose Von unsagbaren Dingen and other writings and sermons identified the being and intellect of a unified deity that could be appre-hended only through mystical appre-hension of the divine through an inner spark (scintilla animae) of the soul. Condemned as pantheistic in his own time, Eckhart's doctrines were a significant application of neoplatonic thought. *Recommended Reading*: Meister Echkart, Selected Writings, ed. by Oliver Davies (Penguin, 1995); Bernard McGinn, The Mystical Thought of Meister Eckhart: The Man from Whom God Hid Nothing (Crossroad, 2001); and Passion for Creation: Earth-honoring Spirituality of Meister Eckhart, ed. by Matthew Fox (Inner Traditions, 2000).

Eclecticism (Greek, *eklegein,* "to pick out"), in philosophy and art, the formulation of systems of thought by choosing from the doctrines of other, already developed, systems. Eclectic thinkers combine what they regard as the most valid doctrines, although often these doctrines do not make an integral unity.

Eclecticism manifested itself to a great extent among the Greeks, beginning about the 2nd century BC. This period was marked by a decline in the spirit of intellectual inquiry that had motivated the great Greek philosophers, such as Plato and Aristotle, to develop unified cosmologies in their search for truth. Later Greek philosophers, such as Antiochus of Ascalon, who combined Stoicism and scepticism, and Panaetius, who based his thought on Platonism and Stoicism, adopted the doctrines that pleased them most. Roman thinkers, who never deve-loped an independent philos-ophical system, were notably eclectic: Cicero, for example, incorporated elements of Stoicism, scepticism, and Peripatetics in his philosophical works, without regard for their essential disunity.

Among the early Christian philosophers, Clement of Alexandria and Origen developed their systems by selecting elements of Greek metaphysics and combining them with Judaeo-Christian thought expressed in the Old and New Testaments. Later, Meister Eckhart, a German theologian and mystic, formulated a system of Christian philosophy based on Aristotle and his medieval Arabic commentators, on Neoplatonism, and on Jewish doctrine.

The modern school of eclectic philosophy arose in France during the 19th century; its most distinguished figure was Victor Cousin, who tried to unite the idealism of the

German philosopher Immanuel Kant, the philosophy of common sense, and the inductive doctrines of the French philosopher René Descartes.

Eclecticism, approach or way of doing philosophy that does not respect the boundaries of the current or traditional schools, but instead takes whatever seems true from each of them. Eclecticism is usually applied in a negative way, implying a lack of systematic or philosophical consistency, or even implying the presence of subjectivism. (Reference from syncretism.)

Ecofeminism, belief that human violation of the natural world is an extension of the prevalent patriarchy of Western culture. On this view, efforts to protect the environment at large are feminist in spirit, since they challenge systemic male domination of the other. *Recommended Reading*: Ecofeminism: Women, Culture, Nature, ed. by Karen Warren and Nisvan Erkal (Indiana, 1997); Carol J. Adams, The Sexual Politics of Meat: A Feminist-Vegetarian Critical Theory (Continuum, 1999); Ivone Gebara, Longing for Running Water: Ecofeminism and Liberation, tr. by David Molineaux (Fortress, 1999); Ecofeminism: Women, Animals, Nature, ed. By Greta Claire Gaard (Temple, 1993); and Beneath the Surface: Critical Essays in the Philosophy of Deep Ecology, ed. by Eric Katz, Andrew Light, and David Rothenberg (MIT, 2000).

Eco Umberto, Italian novelist, critic, and philosopher (1932-); author of Opera aperta (The Open Work) (1962), Trattato di semiotica generale (A Theory of Semiotics) (1976), and Semiotica e filosofia del linguaggio (Semiotics and the Philosophy of Language) (1984). A serious scholar of semiotics, Eco examines the use of signs, both in literary texts and - as in "Travels in Hyper-reality" (1991) in popular culture. His novels, Il Nome della Rosa (The Name of the Rose) (1980), Foucault's Pendulum (1988), and The Island of the Day Before (1994) offer the kind of postmodern entertainment, eliberately open to re-interpretation at many differentlevels, that he had proposed in Apocalittici e integrati (Apocalyptic Postponed) (1964). *Recommended Reading*: Umberto Eco, The Limits of Interpretation (Indiana, 1994); Umberto Eco, Misreadings (McClelland & Stewart, 1994); Umberto Eco, Six Walks in the Fictional Woods (Belknap, 1995); Reading Eco: An Anthology, ed. by Rocco Capozzi (Indiana, 1997); Michael Caesar, Umberto Eco: Philosophy, Semiotics and the Work of Fiction (Blackwell, 1999); and Out of Chaos: Semiotics: A Festschrift in Honor of Umberto Eco, ed. by William E. Tanner, Anne Gervasi, and Kay Mizzel (Liberal Arts, 1992).

Effect, an event that is taken to result from or to be produced by another event, with which it stands in a causal relationship.

Effective method, An effective method for a class C of problems is a method for solving problems in C when the method (1) is logically bound as opposed to physically bound (2) to give some answer, as opposed to no answer, (3) that is correct, as opposed to incorrect, (4) in a finite number of steps, as opposed to an infinite number, (5) every time, or for all inputs, or for all problems in the class, as opposed to selectively, (6) if the method is followed carefully, as opposed to carelessly, (7) as far as necessary, as opposed to only as far as our resources permit, (8) when each step in the process is "dumb" or "mechanical". The eighth requirement introduces an irreducibly intuitive element into the definition. Some add (9) when given a problem from outside the class for which the method is effective, the method may halt or loop forever without halting, but must not return a value as if it were the answer to the problem. (The wording of this definition was influenced by Geoffrey Hunter.) Also called algorithm; decision procedure. See also Church's Thesis

Efficient cause, the agent or event that produces some change in the accidental features of a thing; one of Aristotle's four causes. *Recommended Reading*: Aristotle, Physics, tr. by Robin Waterfield and David Bostock (Oxford, 1999).

Egalitarianism, the view that equality is a very high, or even the most important, ethical and societal value (sometimes also called qualitarianism). Egalitarians usually focus on equality of results, rather than equality of opportunity or equality before the law, which are ideas associated with classical liberalism or libertarianism. In practical terms, egalitarian policies in political reality usually focus on the equal re-distribution of wealth, often verging on socialism. (Reference from liberalism.)

Ego, in psychoanalysis, term denoting the central part of the personality structure that deals with reality and is influenced by social forces.

According to the psychoanalytic theories developed by Sigmund Freud, the ego constitutes one of the three basic provinces of the mind, the other two being the id and the superego. Formation of the ego begins at birth in the first encounters with the external world of people and things. The ego learns to modify behaviour by controlling those impulses that are socially unacceptable. Its role is that of mediator between unconscious impulses and acquired social and personal standards.

In philosophy, ego means the conscious self or "I". It was viewed by some philosophers, notably the 17th-century Frenchman René Descartes and the 18th-century German Johann Gottlieb Fichte, as the sole basis of reality; they saw the universe as existing only in the individual's knowledge and exper-ience of it. Other philosophers, such as the 18th-century German Immanuel Kant, proposed two forms of ego, one perceiving and the other thinking.

Egoism, belief that human conduct is governed by self-interest. Psychological egoism holds that all human beings are, as a matter of fact, motivated to act only in pursuit of their own (at least apparent) advantage, never for the sake of others. Ethical egoism is the normative theory that right conduct can be defined in terms of (an enlightened notion of) one's own welfare. Though often held jointly, the distinction between fact and value clearly renders the two views distinct: some might argue that human beings ought to act on their own behalf even though they don't always do so, while others could suppose that they invariably do act selfishly even though they ought not. *Recommended Reading*: Robert William Shaver, Rational Egoism: A Selective and Critical History (Cambridge, 1998) and Kim-Chong Chong, Moral Agoraphobia: The Challenge of Egoism (Peter Lang, 1996).

Egoism, the doctrine or attitude that one's own interests are of greater importance than any other consideration or thing. *See* Altruism; Ethics; Hedonism; Utilitarianism.

Eidos, Greek term for what is seen-figure, shape, or form. In the philosophy of Plato, the eidos is the immutable genuine nature of a thing, one of the eternal, transcendent Forms apprehended by human reason. Aristotle rejected the notion of independently existing Forms and understood them instead as abstract universals. By extension, Husserl used the term "eidetic" for the phenomenological apprehension of essences generally. *Recommended Reading*: F. E. Peters, Greek Philosophical Terms: A Historical Lexicon (NYU, 1967).

Eigenvalue, The factor by which a linear transformation multiplies one of its eigenvectors.

Einstein Albert, german physicist (1879-1955). Einstein's combination of imple thought-experiments with complex mathematical formulae transformed twentieth-century conceptions of matter, space, and time and earned him the Nobel Prize for physics in 1921. His special (1905) and general (1915) theories of relativity emphasized the role of the observer in determining the content of our observations of the natural world. Although he assisted the careers of several of the logical positivists, his own philosophical reflections emphasized the independence of theory-formation from empirical evidence. *Recommended Reading*: Albert Einstein, Relativity: The Special and the General Theory (Crown, 1995); Albert Einstein, Out of My Later Years: The Scientist, Philosopher and Man Portrayed Through His Own Words (Outlet, 1993); Richard Feynman, Six Not-So-Easy Pieces: Einstein's Rel-ativity, Symmetry, and Space-Time (Perseus, 1998); and Albrecht Folsing, Albert Einstein: A Biography (Penguin, 1998).

Eleatic School, Greek school of philosophy, which flourished in the 6th and 5th centuries BC. Eleatic thought is opposed to both the materialist philosophy of the Ionian school and the theory of universal flux propounded by the Greek philosopher Heraclitus. According to the Eleatics, the universe is an essentially changeless unity, that, being infinite in time and space, is beyond the cognition of the human sense. Only through philosophical reflection, they asserted, can ultimate truth be known. Sensory observations yield merely a limited and distorted view of reality. The name *Eleatic* is derived from the Greek city of Elea, in southern Italy, the home of Parmenides and Zeno, the leading exponents of the school. Scholars differ as to whether the school was founded by Xenophanes or Parmenides. Many of the Eleatic doctrines were based upon the teachings of Xenophanes, while Parmenides developed the Eleatic doctrines into a system of meta-physics. Eleatic philosophy served as a basis for the metaphysical system of Plato.

Eleatics, (history of philosophy, school) presocratic philosophers, including Parmenides and Zeno, who used dialectical methods to argue that reality is a unified whole within which no motion or change is possible. *Recommended Reading*: The Cambridge Companion to Early Greek Philosophy, ed. by A. A. Long (Cambridge, 1999).

Eliminativism, belief that language should be purged of all reference to the (none-existent) things of a certain kind; the most extreme variety of reductionism. Thus, while a reductive materialist may hold that pains are really just activities of the central nervous system, an eliminative materialist proposes that we speak only of brain-states. the position that folk psychology is a false theory and that corresponding notions such as belief, experience, and sensation are fundamentally mistaken. The alternative most often offered is physicalist and the position is thus often called eliminative materialism. *References*: Churchland, P.S. 1980. "Language, thought, and information processing". Nous 14:147-70. Churchland, P.M. (1981). "Eliminative materialism and thepropositional attitudes." Journal of Philosophy 78: 67-90. Reprinted in A Neurocomputational Perspective. MIT Press, 1989. Churchland, P.M. (1989). A Neurocomputational Perspective: The Nature of Mind and the Structure of Science. MIT Press.

Elizabeth of Bohemia, German princess (Elisabeth von der Pfalz) (1618-1680). In he extensive corres-pondence with Descartes, Elizabeth deftly identified the impossibility of genuine interaction between mental and physical substances as the central difficulty with mind-body dualism.

Emanation, that which inevitably flows outward from the transcendental central principle of reality ("the One") in the neoplatonic philosophy of Plotinus. Individual things, including human beings, are therefore presumed to be nothing more than the faint ripples left by a primordial big splash.

The timeless reality of a central intelligence, Plotinus held, inexorably results in the formation of both soul as an active principle of organization and, eventually, inert matter. *Recommended Reading*: Plotinus, The Enneads, ed. by John Dillon and Stephen MacKenna (Penguin, 1991) and The Cambridge Companion to Plotinus, ed. by Lloyd P. Gerson (Cambridge, 1996).

Emanation (Latin, *emanare,* "to flow out"), in philosophy and theology, an outflowing of the transcendentally divine that accounts for the origin of the universe.

The word *emanation* was first used to describe divine procreation in Hellenistic Jewish works of the 2nd and 1st centuries BC, especially the Wisdom of Solomon in the Apocrypha. The Alexandrian Jewish philosopher Philo Judaeus unsys-tematically employed emanational language in his cosmological speculation, a version of Platonism that was influenced by Pythagorean interpretation.

The systematic application of the concept of emanation in explaining universal origins was the product of speculation in Gnosticism and Neoplatonism. The process is understood in Gnostic works as the overflowing of the highest deity's superabundant greatness. In the succession of emanations such as Mind, Word, and Wisdom, a diminution of the divine essence occurs. In most Gnostic cosmologies, the last emanation, Wisdom, attempts to accomplish a creation on her own. This results in an inferior emanation, a *demiurge* who is ultimately responsible for the creation of the material world, which entraps the divine essence of humanity. This entrapped spirit (*pneuma*) must then be recalled and redeemed to the higher divine order.

Under the influence of Neoplatonic works, emanationist theories were elaborated by later Christian, Muslim, and medieval Jewish philosophers. Orthodox Christian and Jewish theologies, however, emphasize the clear distinction between the divine and the mundane in the creative, as opposed to the emanationist, process.

Emanationism, a doctrine in both gnosticism and especially the Neo-Platonism of Plotinus, who posited that the physical world emanated from a "world soul", which in turn emanated from a divine presence, which in turn emanated from a higher divinity, and so on—the whole process having started with an emanation from the divine God or "One".

Emergence, properties of a complex physical system are emergent just in case they are neither (i) properties had by any parts of the system taken in isolation nor (ii) resultant of a mere summation of properties of parts of the system.

A system exhibits emergent properties when those properties are more than the sum of its parts" properties. Emergence is a notion cherished by those philosophers of mind who are mental realists, and physicalists who nonetheless reject the reducibility of the mental to the physical. Mental emergentists, then, posit that mental properties emerge from certain complex sets of physical properties, for instance, physical properties of human brains. Thus they hold that mental events are not identical to any brain events but instead emerge from them.

Ernest Nagel (1961) and Brain McLaughlin (1992) cite Mill's 'Of the Composition of Causes" chapter of System of Logic (1843) as the locus classicus on the notion of emergence. For Mill, the key to the distinction between emergent and non-emergent properties centres on a distinction regarding two different ways in which conjoint causes can produce an effect: Non-emergent properties are effects that are mere summations of the effects of each of the causal conjuncts, whereas emergent properties are effects that are not sums of the effects of each causal conjunct. hese respective notions might be best conveyed by the following examples.

A paradigmatic example of an effect best construed as non-emergent is the way that multiple force vectors sum to propel a body in a given direction. Mill writes:

> "If a body is propelled in two directions by two forces, one tending to drive it to the north and the other to the east, it is caused to move in a given time exactly as far in both directions as the two forces would separately have carried it; and is left precisely where it would have arrived if it had been acted upon first by one of the two forces, and afterwards by the other.

This law of nature is called, in dynamics, the principle of the Composition of Forces: and in imitation of that well-chosen expression, I shall give the name of the Composition of Causes to the principle which is exemplified in all cases in which the joint effect of several causes is identical with the sum of their separate effects. (1843, p. 428)"

A key determinant of whether a behaviour is emergent on this view is whether removing any of the causal conjuncts prevents the remaining conjuncts from contributing their effects to the remaining system. If not, then the behaviour of the system in question is non-emergent. If so, then it is emergent. Mill offers as examples of emergent effects chemical reactions. Consider the following chemical process: CH4 + 2O2—> CO2 + 2H2O (Methane + oxygen produces carbon dioxide + water). For Mill, the products of such chemical reactions are not, in any sense, the sum of the effects of each reactant (McLaughlin, 1992, p.60).

While the mechanics underlying chemical reactions are understood well enough today to render Mill's point dubious, we can see why the above chemical reaction would impress Mill and his contemporaries as significantly different in kind from the Composition of Forces for moving bodies. In the case of the chemical reaction, the resulting compounds exhibit properties significantly different from those of the reactants. For instance, methane is violently combustible, whereas carbon dioxide and water are not. This contrasts sharply against the case of a northwesterly moving object being propelled by two forces—one towards the north, the other towards the west—insofar as the subsequent motion is so obviously decomposable into the effects of the conjoint causes. A very live possibility to consider in connection with these examples is that an enhanced understanding of the processes that underlie some observed property of a system may show that system not to be an example of emergence. That is, an increase of knowledge about the way certain effects are obtained may reveal that certain effects are decomposable into the effects contributed by subcomponents of that system. Mill's chemical examples fail as properly emergent for just this reason. With the development of quantum mechanical explanation, we have been able to see how chemical reactions are composed of additive properties of individual electrons (McLaughlin, 1992, p.89).

I disagree with the definition of emergent properties. This definition would automatically make the shape of a composite body an "emergent" property. Consider a brick in the shape of a cube. The parts of this object are, let's say, molecules. Now (1) None of the molecules is cubical in shape, and (2) "cubical" is not the "sum" of the shapes of the molecules, nor the sum of anything else. (In fact, only quantities can be sums. Since "cubical" isn't a quantity, it can't be the sum of anything.) Thus, the existence of emergent properties would be trivial. Instead, we should take Broad's definition from The Mind and its Place in Nature. Roughly: a property, P, of a composite object, O, is emergent if it is not metaphysically necessary that an aggregate composed of parts having exactly the (intrinsic) properties that the parts of O in fact have and arranged in the way that the parts of O are in fact arranged, should have P. (Broad says, if you were given all the intrinsic properties of the parts plus their arrangement, you could not predict the properties of the whole. I think this is what he means.)

Michael Huemer: *Reply to the Objection*—While I agree that any good definition of "emergence" should exclude the shapes of bricks from counting as emergent properties, I disagree that my definition fails to do so. Superimpose a coordinate system (such as Descartes') on a brick, and it becomes a simple exercise to see that the particular way that the brick occupies space is a sum of the ways its parts occupy space. Given the techniques of analytic geometry, particular shapes can be converted into particular quantities and summed all day long.

As regards the definition attributed to Broad, the following problem arises. According to that definition, my mental properties would count as emergent if and only if it is metaphysically possible that my microphysical doppleganger lacks (qualitatively identical) mental properties. Thus, Broad's definition of "emergence" is inconsistent with many formulations of psychophysical super-venience, which, I think, would strike many contemporary emergentists as an unhappy result.

References: Emergence Biblio) Lewes, George Henry. (1875). Problems of Life and Mind. Vol 2. London: Kegan Paul, Trench, Turbner, Co. McLaughlin, Brain P. (1992). The rise and fall of British Emergentism. Emergence or Reduction?: Essays on the Prospects of Nonreductive Physicalism. Berlin: Walter de Gruyter. Mill, John Stuart. (1843). System of Logic. London: Longmans, Green, Reader, and Dyer. (Eight edition, 1872). Nagel, Ernest. (1961). The Structure of Science. New York: Harcourt, Brace and Wilson.

Emergent property, an irreducible feature (now commonly called supervenient) of a complex whole that cannot be inferred directly from the features of its simpler parts. Thus, for example, the familiar taste of salt is an emergent property with respect to the sodium and chlorine of which it is composed. *Recommended Reading*: Jaegwon Kim, Mind in a Physical World: An Essay on the Mind-Body Problem and Mental Causation (Bradford, 2000); William Hasker, The Emergent Self (Cornell, 1999); and Benjamin Pinkel, Consciousness, Matter, and Energy: The Emergence of Mind in Nature (DeVorss. 1992). see Emergence.

Emerson Ralph Waldo, American essayist and antislavery activist (1803-1882). Emerson's enthusiastic celebration of the individual person expressed a prominent element of nineteenth-century optimism in his Essays—First Series (1841) and Second Series (1844). Among his best-known philosophical works are "The American Scholar" (1837), a speech on American intellectual values, and the confidently huma-nistic essay, "Self-Reliance" (1841). Influenced by German Romanticism, Emerson helped to establish a lasting American taste for non-theistic spirituality. *Recommended Reading*: Ralph Waldo Emerson: Essays and Lectures, ed. by Joel Porte (Library of America, 1983); The Essential Writings of Ralph Waldo Emerson, ed. by Brooks Atkinson and Mary Oliver (Modern Library, 2000); The Portable Emerson, ed. by Malcolm Cowley (Viking, 1987); and The Cambridge Companion to Ralph Waldo Emerson, ed. by Joel Porte and Saundra Morris (Cambridge, 1999).

Emotion appeal, known also as to argumentum ad populum. The informal fallacy of persuading someone to accept (or reject) a conclusion by arousing favorable (or unfavorable) emotions toward it or by emphasizing its widespread acceptance (or rejection) by others. Example: "Nobody with an ounce of common sense or a single shred of integrity believes that our President is truly an effective leader. Therefore, the President is not an effective leader." *Recommended Reading*: Douglas Walton, Appeal to Popular Opinion (Penn. State,

1999).

Emotionalism, any theory of knowledge that considers emotion to be the basic valid means of knowledge (cf. intuitionism), or more commonly to an ethical theory that is based on emotion rather than reason (often having connotations of nihilism or irrationalism). In popular discource, the word "emotionalist" tends to be used to characterize those who are hyper-sensitive, over-emotional, or even irrational. (References from hedonism, irrationalism, romanticism, and subjectivism.)

Emotive meaning, attitudes and feelings associated with the use of a word, phrase, or sentence, in contrast with its literal significance.

Emotivism, the metaethical theory according to which the meaning of moral language is exhausted by its expression, evocation, or endorsement of powerful human feelings. Thus, for example, saying "Stealing is wrong," is just an especially strong way of reporting that I disapprove of stealing, evoking a similar disapproval from others, and thereby attempting to influence future conduct—both mine and theirs. Although its origins lie in the non-cognitivist morality of Hume, emotivism reached its height early in the twentieth century, with the work of the logical positivists and Stevenson. *Recommended Reading*: Charles L. Stevenson, Ethics and Language (Yale, 1944); J. O. Urmson, The Emotive Theory of Ethics (London, 1968); and Stephen Satris, Ethical Emotivism (Martinus Nijhoff, 1987).

Philosophical theory and movement of the 20th century which holds that mora judgments are simply expressions of positive or negative emotions. For example, when I say "Hitler is evil", all that I can really mean is "I don't like Hitler, he rubs me the wrong way". Obviously, this is an extreme form of subjectivism. (Reference from logical positivism.)

Empedocles, Greek presocratic philosopher (d. 433 B.C.) who supposed that thefour elements are irreducible components of the world, joined to and separated from each other by competing principles. Love invariably strives to combine everything into a harmonious sphere, which Strife tries to shatter into distinct entities. Human beings corrupted by eating animal flesh, Empedocles, supposed, pursue philosophy in an effort to contribute positively to the cosmic cycle. *Recommended Reading*: Empedocles: The Extant Fragments, ed. by M. R. Wright (Hackett, 1995); Empedocles, ed. by Brad Inwood (Toronto, 2001); and Peter Kingsley, Ancient Philosophy, Mystery, and Magic: Empedocles and Pythagorean Tradition (Oxford, 1997).

Empedocles (c. 490-c. 430 BC), Greek philosopher, statesman, and poet, born in Agrigentum (now Agrigento), Sicily, a disciple of Pythagoras and Parmenides. According to tradition, Empedocles refused to accept the crown offered to him by the people of Agrigentum after he had helped to overthrow the ruling oligarchy. Instead he instituted a democracy.

Modern knowledge of Empedocles's philosophy is based on the surviving fragments of his poems on nature and purification. He asserted that all things are composed of four primal elements: earth, air, fire, and water. Two active and opposing forces, love and hate, or affinity and antipathy, act upon these elements, combining and separating them into infinitely varied forms. According to Empedocles, reality is cyclical. At the beginning of a cycle, the four elements are bound together by the principle of love. When hate penetrates the cycle, the elements begin to separate. Love reunites everything; then hate begins the process once again. The world as we know it is halfway between the primary sphere and the stage of total separation of the elements. Empedocles also believed that no change involving the creation of new matter is possible; only changes in the combinations of the four existing elements may occur. He also formulated a primitive theory of evolution in which he declared that humans and animals evolved from antecedent forms.

Empirical, based on experience, or observation—describing knowledge derived from or warranted by sense perception. Compare: a posteriori. Contrast: a priori.

Empiricism, in philosophy, a doctrine that affirms that all ideas and knowledge are a posteriori, that is, derived from and based on experience, and denies that they can ever be a priori, that is, discoverable without having to rely on the senses. In particular, empiricists oppose the view that people are born with certain innate ideas and argue that at birth the mind is a complete blank. Until the 20th century the term "empiricism" was applied to the views held chiefly by the British philosophers of the 17th, 18th, and 19th centuries. John Locke was the first of these philosophers to give it systematic expression, although his compatriot, the philosopher Francis Bacon, had anticipated some of its characteristic conclusions. Other empiricists include David Hume and George Berkeley. Directly opposed to empiricism was rationalism, represented by such thinkers as the French philosopher René Descartes; the Dutch philosopher Baruch Spinoza; and the 17th- and 18th-century German philosophers Gottfried Wilhelm Leibniz and Christian Wolff. Rationalists asserted that the mind is capable of recognizing reality by means of its capacity for reason, a faculty that exists independent of experience. Empiricists generally looked to the experimental natural sciences to illustrate their view of how knowledge is acquired, while rationalists often pointed to pure mathematics to illustrate their own view. Empiricists had particular difficulty in explaining how it is possible ever to acquire pure mathematical concepts and kno-wledge, if all concepts and knowledge had to come from the senses.

The German philosopher Immanuel Kant attempted a synthesis of empiricism and rationalism, restricting knowledge to the domain of experience, a posteriori, and thus agreeing with the empiricists, but attributing to the mind a structure of categories into which all sensations had to be incorporated in order for human beings to make sense of them. This structure could be known a priori without resorting to empirical methods, and in this respect Kant agreed with the rationalists.

In recent years the term "empiricism" has taken on a broader meaning, and is now used in connection with any philosophical system or any method of scientific enquiry that finds all of its materials in experience. In the United States, William James called his philosophy radical empiricism, and John Dewey coined the term "immediate empiricism" for his view of experience.

In its extreme form, empiricism leads to the conclusion not just that all knowledge has to start from experience, but that it can never get beyond experience. That is, it is not possible to know anything other than that which comes from experience. This view is a form of scepticism, according to which, for example, claims about subatomic particles or physical forces are just as doubtful as claims about supernatural entities or ethical truths. Science then has to be seen as nothing more than the discovery of regular relationships between the phenomena of experience. Laws that express such relationships between phenomena, without making any claims about the underlying causes of the phenomena, are called empirical laws.

Empiricism, End, that which is sought, or the object of pursuit. Aristotle maintains that all our pursuits aim ultimately at ends that are sought or desired intrinsically, *i.e.* for their own sakes, and that the greatest of these intrinsic goods is happiness. Things sought not for their own sake but for the sake of something else are desired extrinsically or instrumentally, as means.

Energeia, Greek term for the operation or activity of anything. More technically, in the philosophy of Aristotle, energeia is the actuality characteristic of every individual substance toward some end, in contrast with its potentiality or capacity to change. *Recommended Reading*: George A. Blair, Energeia and Entelecheia: Act in Aristotle (Ottawa, 1992) and F. E. Peters, Greek Philosophical Terms: A Historical Lexicon (NYU, 1967).

Engels Friedrich, German political activist and philosopher (1820-1895). Engels collaborated with Karl Marx on the Manifest der kommunistischen Partei (Communist Manifesto) (1848) and other political works. His own philosophical writing, including Lage der arbeitenden Klasse in England (The Condition of the Working Class in England) (1845), Socialism, Utopian and Scientific (1880), and Ludwig Feuerbach and the Outcome of Classical German Philosophy (1888), provided an excellent exposition of dialectical materialism and signif-icantly influenced the development of the ideology of modern communism. His analysis of bourgeois family life in The Origin of the Family, Private Property, and the State (1884) offers an interesting anticipation of feminist concern with the place of women in society by noting the role of patriarchal oppression in preserving the capitalist order and by urging the elimination of private domestic labor for women. *Recommended Reading*: Terrell Carver, Friedrich Engels: His Life and Thought (St. Martins, 1993); Introduction to Marx and Engels: A Critical Reconstruction, ed. by Richard Schmitt, Keith Lehrer, and Norman Daniels (Westview, 1997); and Engels After Marx, ed. by Manfred B. Steger and Terrell Carver (Penn. State, 1999).

Enlightenment, an eighteenth-century movement that placed great emphasis on the use of reason in the development of philosophical, social, political, and scientific knowledge. Enlightenment philosophers include Bayle, Hume, Wollstonecraft, Kant, and many lesser figures. *Recommended Reading*: The Portable Enlightenment Reader, ed. By Issac Kramnick

(Penguin, 1995); Ernst Cassirer, The Philosophy of the Enlightenment, tr. by J. Pettegrove and F. Koelin (Princeton, 1968); Peter Gay, The Enlightenment (The Rise of Modern Paganism (Norton, 1995) and The Science of Freedom (Norton, 1996); and Age of Enlightenment: The Eighteenth Century Philosophers, ed. by Isaiah Berlin (Plume, 1993).

(1) An intellectual movement in modern Europe during the eighteenth century that believed in the power of human reason to understand the world and to guide human conduct.

(2) For Buddhists, the state of Enlightenment or nirvana is the goal of human existence.

Enlightenment, Age of, term for the trends in 18th-century thought and letters in Europe and the American colonies before the French Revolution. The phrase was often used by writers of the period, convinced that they were emerging from centuries of darkness and ignorance into a new age enlightened by reason, science, and respect for humanity.

Early Influences: The precursors of the Enlightenment can be traced to the 17th century and earlier. They include the philosophical rationalists René Descartes, Gottfried Leibniz, and Baruch Spinoza, the political philosophers Thomas Hobbes and John Locke, and sceptical thinkers in France such as Pierre Bayle. Equally important was the self-confidence engendered by new discoveries in science—by Nicolaus Copernicus and Galileo, for example—as well as the cultural relativism encouraged by the exploration of the non-European world.

A fundamental and widely shared belief of the period was the unshakeable faith in the power of human reason. Thinkers of the age were enormously impressed by the discovery of universal gravitation by Isaac Newton. This is summed up by the Alexander Pope quote: "Nature and nature's laws lay hid in night, / God said, 'Let Newton be', and all was light." The laws governing the rest of nature, the human mind, and society could, it seemed, soon be discovered by applying Newton's method. If the centuries-old medieval view of the physical world had been so decisively overthrown by reason, the antiquity of an idea, or indeed of a law, a privilege, or a form of government, could no longer be seen as a guarantee of its worth. People came to assume that by judicious use of reason, an unending progress would be possible—progress in knowledge, technology, prosperity, and even in moral values.

Development of Enlightenment Thought: Under the influence of Pierre Maupertuis and Voltaire, 18th-century intellectuals abandoned Descartes's belief in innate ideas (implanted in human beings by God) and his deductive, non-experimentalist approach to nature, in favour of the empiricism of Newton and Locke. Truth was to be discovered by the observation of nature, not by deduction from self-evident premises, and still less from venerable authorities such as Aristotle and the Bible. With proper education, humanity itself could be altered, its nature changed for the better. Although they saw the Church—especially the Roman Catholic Church—as the principal force that had enslaved the human mind in the past, most thinkers of the Enlightenment did not renounce religion altogether. They opted rather for a form of deism, accepting the existence of God and of a hereafter, but rejecting the intricacies of Christian theology, especially the dogma of original sin, with its implication that human advancement depends on divine grace. Human aspirations, they believed, should not be centred on the next life, but rather on improving this life. Worldly happiness was placed before religious salvation. Nothing was attacked with more intensity and ferocity than the Church, with all its wealth, political power, and suppression of the free exercise of reason.

More than a set of fixed ideas, the Enlightenment was an attitude, a method of thought. The German philosopher Immanuel Kant proposed as the motto of the Enlightenment "dare to know!". A desire arose to re-examine and question all received ideas and values, to explore new ideas in many different directions—hence the great diversity, and often inconsistency, of 18th-century thinkers. Many proponents of the Enlightenment were not philosophers in the strict sense; they were popularizers engaged in a self-conscious effort to win converts. They liked to refer to themselves as the "party of humanity", and in an attempt to mould public opinion in their favour, they made full use of pamphlets, anonymous tracts, and the new journals and newspapers being created. Because they were journalists and propagandists as much as true philosophers, historians often refer to them by the French word *philosophes*.

The homeland of the *philosophes* as a self-conscious movement was France. It was there that the political philosopher and jurist Charles de Montesquieu published satirical attacks on existing institutions, such as his *Persian Letters* (1721; trans. 1961), as well as his monumental study of political institutions, *The Spirit of Laws* (1748; trans. 1750). In this pioneering work he showed the interconnections between religion, education, geography, and forms of government, and argued that despotism is to be avoided by a "separation of powers", assigning the executive, legislative, and juridical functions of the state to distinct institutions. It was in Paris that Denis Diderot, the author of numerous philosophical tracts, began the publication of the *Encyclopédie* (1751-1772). This work, on which numerous *philosophes* collaborated, was intended both as a compendium of all knowledge and as a polemical weapon, presenting the positions of the Enlightenment and attacking its opponents. The most influential of the French writers was Voltaire. Once the most popular playwright of the day, he is now best known for his prolific pamphlets, essays, satires, and novels, in which he popularized the science and philosophy of his age, and for his correspondence with writers and monarchs throughout Europe. He wrote a series of historical works, notably the *Essay on General History and on the Customs and Character of Nations* (1756; trans. 1759), in which he attempted to trace the unfolding of human reason in every area of culture from the time of Charlemagne to the present. Many other historians of the period—the Marquis de Condorcet, David Hume, Edward Gibbon, for example—took Voltaire as their model. Even more original was Jean-Jacques Rousseau, whose *Social Contract* (1762; trans. 1797), *Émile* (1762; trans. 1763), and *Confessions* (1782; trans. 1783) stressed the social nature of a person, in opposition to the dominant individualism of the age. He also made emotion as fashionable as reason, thus serving—along with Hume and Étienne Condillac, who saw passion as the mainspring of the human mind—to refute the charge that the Enlightenment exalted bloodless reason at the expense of emotion. Rousseau had a profound influence on later political and educational theory, on Kant, and on Romanticism.

The Enlightenment was a profoundly cosmopolitan movement with representatives throughout Europe and the American colonies: David Hume in Scotland; in Italy, Cesare Beccaria (a determined opponent of torture and capital punishment); and Benjamin Franklin and Thomas Jefferson in the American colonies. In Germany, Enlightenment thought was championed by Christian Wolff and Gotthold Lessing, as well as by Kant, who is considered to be the greatest philosopher of modern times. While British and French thinkers tended to regard the human mind as a passive receptacle for external stimuli, German philosophers were more inclined to attribute to it an autonomous imaginative creativity. Hence the Germans made important contr-ibutions to aesthetics: Alexander Baumgarten coined the term "aesthetics" and founded systematic aesthetics. German *philosophes* also took religion more seriously than the French, and their historical criticism of the Bible gave an enormous impetus to historical research as well as theology. The Enlightenment affected every sphere of culture, not simply philosophy: the Mozart opera *The Magic Flute* (1791), a tribute to freemasonry and to German unity, is imbued with the spirit of the Enlightenment, as is the Beethoven work *Fidelio* (1814). French comic opera, too, especially after the French Revolution, acquired a more serious, ethical flavour.

During the first half of the 18th century, the *philosophes* waged an uphill struggle against imprisonment, censorship, and attacks by the Church. Later in the century they began to triumph. By the 1770s, the second-generation *philosophes* were receiving government pensions and taking control of intellectual academies. The proliferation of newspapers and books ensured a wide diffusion of their ideas. Scientific experiments and philosophy became widely fashionable, even among members of the nobility and the clergy. Many European monarchs became champions of the Enlightenment. Voltaire and other *philosophes* admired the so-called enlightened despots, notably Frederick II of Prussia, Catherine the Great of Russia, and Joseph II of Austria, and were welcomed at their courts. *Philosophes*, especially in central Europe with its smaller reading public, depended on state patronage for their livelihood. Many ideas of the Enlightenment were useful to rulers: educational and judicial reform, a trained bureaucracy, the ending of noble and clerical exemption from taxation, tolerance of (often talented and industrious) religious dissidents, and the abolition or amelioration of serfdom, enabling peasants to pay more taxes. However, enlightened despots were more than simple opportunists. Their legislation was marked by Enlightenment influence, even if they often sacrificed Enlightenment to *raison d'état*. The *philosophes*, for their part, were united in support of tolerance, the rule of law, social welfare, secular education, and hostility to privilege. They were not, however, opposed to the state as such: it was a crucial instrument for the realization of their ideals, as long as the ruler respected reason and natural law. Especially in central Europe and Italy, they were more concerned to strengthen the state so that it could do its job properly than to limit its power. The main targets of their hatred were the Church and the nobility. Few *philosophes* shared Montesquieu's belief in the need for representative authorities intermediary between the state and the individual. While they mostly followed Locke in viewing the state as the result of a "social contract", they did not invariably draw democratic or even very liberal conclusions from this. They believed in the need to educate the often deluded and backward masses, and this was not always easy to reconcile with their devotion to tolerance.

Nevertheless, the *philosophes* welcomed the American War of Independence, and the Declaration of Independence, seeing them as the beginning of the realization of their dreams. The Marquis de Condorcet, a moderate revolutionary who died in prison in 1794, argued in his *Sketch of the Intellectual Progress of Mankind* (1795) that the purpose of knowledge of human society can only be to guarantee the basic rights of men and, in his view, women: these are personal security, free enjoyment of property, equality before the law, and the participation of every citizen in government. The American states, he believed, were the first to convert these ideas into action.

End of the Enlightenment: The Age of Enlightenment may be said to have ended in 1789 with the French Revolution, which it helped to bring about. The Revolution embodied many of the ideals of the *philosophes*, but its more violent phase, between 1792 and 1794, discredited these ideals temporarily in the eyes of many contemporaries, such as Edmund Burke. While conservatives found the Enlightenment too radical, Romantics found it soulless, neglecting individual differences and cultural diversity. Yet the Enlightenment left a lasting heritage for the 19th and 20th centuries. It marked a key stage in the decline of the Church and the growth of modern secularism. It served as the model for political and economic liberalism and for humanitarian reform throughout the 19th-century Western world. Karl Marx was influenced by the Enlightenment: if people become rationally aware of the workings of their society, he argued, then they will be able to control their own destiny and free themselves from the blind, irrational forces that have so far governed their lives. So too was Sigmund Freud: he held that people can free themselves of the irrational forces that dominate their psychological lives once they become rationally aware of them. The major ideologies of the 20th century in the West—liberalism and socialism—stem from the Enlig-htenment and share its belief that reason, with freedom as its inevitable accompaniment, will eventually prevail. Science as an undiluted good, popular education, democracy, progress—all these ideals of the Enlightenment have retained their appeal in the 20th century.

Enlightenment ideals have, however, been severely tested in the 20th century, with wars and revolutions as well as technological progress beyond the dreams of the *philosophes*. The rise of totalitarian regimes—in the former Soviet Union under the banner of Enlightenment ideals, and in Germany, seemingly a model of Enlightenment civilization—led Theodor Adorno and Max Horkheimer to conclude, in the *Dialectic of the Enlightenment* (1944; trans. 1972), that the Enlightenment had turned against itself, perverting its own ideals in the very process of realizing them. Pollution of the environment and, in much of the world, unrestricted population growth—a danger indicated by an Enlightenment thinker Thomas Malthus—might also suggest that Enlightenment ideals are self-defeating. If the *philosophes* perhaps underrated human irrationality, and the importance of tradition and authority in keeping human beings on the right track, and if Enligh-tenment reason now has few wholehearted adherents, it is, in its broad outlines, irrevocable and indispensable. For to detect the faults of Enlightenment thought, in the hope of finding solutions for them, it is necessary to invoke enlightened reason.

Entailment, relation between propositions such that one of them is strictlyimplied by the other(s); that is, its falsity is logically impossible, given the truth of what entails it. Thus, the premises of a valid deductive argument entail its conclusion. *Recommended Reading*: Charles F. Kielkopf, Formal Sentential Entailment (U. Press of America, 1986) and Entailment, ed. By Alan Ross Anderson, Nuel D. Belnap, and J. Michael Dunn (Princeton, 1992).

Entelecheia, Aristotle's Greek term for the complete reality or perfection of a thing, as the soul is of the human body. For Leibniz, then, an "entelechy" is the active force resident in every monad. *Recom-mended Reading*: George A. Blair, Energeia and Entelecheia: Act in Aristotle (Ottawa, 1992); F. E. Peters, Greek Philosophical Terms: A Historical Lexicon (NYU, 1967); and The Cambridge Companion to Leibniz, ed. by Nicholas Jolley (Cambridge, 1994).

Enthusiasm, an exaggerated state of religious fervor or reliance on divine inspiration. Enlightenment philosophers such as Locke and Leibniz decried manifestations of enthusiasm as incompatible with the proper employment of rational faculties. *Recommended Reading*: Michael Heyd, 'Be Sober and Reasonable': The Critique of Enthusiasm in the Seventeenth and Early Eighteenth Centuries (Brill, 1995) and Josef Pieper, Enthusiasm and Divine Madness: On the Platonic Dialogue Phaedrus, tr. By Richard and Clara Winston (St. Augustine, 2000).

Enthymeme, a deductive argument (especially a categorical syllogism) from whose ordinary-language expression one or more propositions have been omitted or left unstated. Example: "Since some finches are cardinals, it follows that some birds are cardinals."

Entropy, A measure of the disorder of a system. Systems tend to go from a state of order (low entropy) to a state of maximum disorder (high entropy).

The entropy of a system is related to the amount of information it contains. A highly ordered system can be described using fewer bits of information than a disordered one. For example, a string containing one million "0"s can be described using run-length encoding as [("0", 1000000)]whereas a string of random symbols (*e.g.* bits, or characters) will be much harder, if not impossible, to compress in this way.

Shannon's formula gives the entropy H(M) of a message M in bits:

H(M) = -log2 p(M)

Where p(M) is the probability of message M.

Epictetus (c. 55-c. 135), Greek philosopher, whose philosophy of Stoicism emphasized freedom, morality, and humanity. Epictetus was probably born at Hierapolis, Phrygia (now in Turkey). Although a slave, as a youth he had studied the ideals of Stoicism, and, after being granted his freedom, went on to teach philosophy in Rome until AD 90. In that year the Roman Emperor Domitian, fearful of the dangers engendered by the teachings of the Stoics, exiled Epictetus and several other philosophers. Epictetus settled at Nicopolis, in southern Epirus, where he died.

Epictetus's doctrines have been preserved in two works compiled by his pupil, the Greek historian and philosopher Arrian: the *Encheiridion* (Handbook), the whole of which survives today, and *Discourses of Epictetus,* of which four of eight books still exist. According to these works, Epictetus was chiefly concerned with the problem of morality—that is, of defining *good.* He asserted that humans are basically limited and irrational beings, but that the universe, ruled by God through pure reason, is perfect. Because human beings can neither know nor control their destiny, they must cease striving for the attainment of worldly ends and instead calmly accept the fact of their own powerlessness before fate. As a corollary of this doctrine, Epictetus held that human beings must, because of their own weaknesses, be tolerant of the faults of others.

Epictetus, even though he was born a slave in Hierapolis and endured a permanent physical disability, Epictetus (55-135) held that all human beings are perfectly free to control their lives and to live in harmony with nature. After intense study of the traditional Stoic curriculum (established by Zeno of Citium and Chrysippus) of logic, physics, and ethics, Epictetus spent his entire career teaching philosophy and promoting a daily regime of rigorous self-examination. He eventually gained his freedom, but was exiled from Rome by Domitian in 89. Epictetus's pupil Arrianus later collected lecture notes from the master and published them as the Discourses. The more epigrammatic Encheiridion, or Manual represents an even later distillation of the same material. From a fundamental distinction between our ability to think or feel freely and our lack of control over external events or circumstances, Epictetus derived the description of a calm and disciplined life. We can never fail to be happy, he argued, if we learn to desire that things should be exactly as they are. That the same approach to human life may work for others as well as for a slave is suggested by the persuasive oratory of the Roman statesman Seneca. The Meditations of Roman emperor Marcus Aurelius illustrate the practical value of a Stoic approach even in the best of circumstances. *Recommended Reading*: Primary sources: Epictetus, Enchiridion, tr. by George Long (Prometheus, 1955). Secondary sources: Malcolm Schofield, The Stoic Idea of the City (Chicago, 1999); Adolf Friedrich Bonhoffer, The Ethics of the Stoic Epictetus, tr. by William O. Stephens (Peter Lang, 2000); A. A. Long, Hellenistic Philosophy: Stoics, Epicureans, Sceptics (California, 1986).

Epicureanism, school in ancient ethics founded by the Greek philosopher Epicurus (341-271 B.C.). This school began in the generation after the death of Aristotle and lasted over 500 years. Although Epicurus was an avowed advocate of hedonism, he did not advocate the wanton pursuit of pleasure. In fact, his doctrine was quite strict and was far removed from our sense of the word "hedonism", since he held that the greatest pleasure a person can achieve lies in the absence of all pains and disturbances, and that the pleasures and pains of the mind are of greater importance than those of the body. While Epicureanism was much more individualistic than stoicism, its view of happiness was less "activist" than that of Aristo-telianism and one could even draw comparisons between Epicureanism and Eastern views like Taoism. (References from cynicism, hedonism, pessimism, stoicism, and Taoism.)

Epicureanism, system of philosophy based chiefly on the teachings of the Greek philosopher Epicurus. The essential doctrine of Epicureanism is that pleasure is the supreme good and main goal of life. Intellectual pleasures are preferred to sensual ones, which tend to disturb peace of mind. True happiness, Epicurus taught, is the serenity resulting from the conquest of fear, that is, of the gods, of death, and of the afterlife. The ultimate aim of all Epicurean speculation about nature is to rid people of such fears.

Epicurean physics is atomistic, in the tradition of the Greek philosophers Leucippus and Democritus. Epicurus regarded the universe as infinite and eternal and as consisting only of bodies and space. Of the bodies, some are compound and some are atoms, or indivisible, stable elements of which the compounds are formed. The world, as seen through the human eye, is produced by the whirlings, collisions, and aggregations of these atoms, which individually possess only shape, size, and weight.

In biology, Epicurus anticipated the modern doctrine of natural selection. He postulated that natural forces give rise to organisms of different types and that only the types able to support and propagate themselves have survived.

Epicurean psychology is thoroughly materialistic. It holds that sensations are caused by a continuous stream of films or "idols" cast off by bodies and impinging on the senses. All sensations are believed to be absolutely reliable; error arises only when sensation is improperly interpreted. The soul is regarded as being composed of fine particles distributed throughout the body. The dissolution of the body in death,

Epicurus taught, leads to the dissolution of the soul, which cannot exist apart from the body; and thus no afterlife is possible. Since death means total extinction, it has no meaning either to the living or to the dead, for "when we are, death is not; and when death is, we are not".

The cardinal virtues in the Epicurean system of ethics are justice, honesty, and prudence, or the balançing of pleasure and pain. Epicurus preferred friendship to love, as being less disquieting. His personal hedonism taught that only through self-restraint, moderation, and detachment can one achieve the kind of tranquillity that is true happiness. Despite his materialism, Epicurus believed in the freedom of the will. He suggested that even the atoms are free and move on occasion quite spontaneously; his view resembles the uncertainty principle of quantum mechanics.

Epicurus did not deny the existence of gods, but he emphatically maintained that as "happy and imperishable beings" of supernatural power they could have nothing to do with human affairs, although they might take pleasure in contemplating the lives of good mortals. True religion lies in a similar contemplation by humans of the ideal lives of the high, invisible gods.

So firmly fixed and venerated were Epicurus's teachings that the doctrines of Epicureanism, unlike those of its great philosophical rival Stoicism, remained remarkably intact throughout its history as a living tradition. However, Epicureanism was brought into discredit largely because of a confusion, which still persists, between its tenets and the crudely sensual hedonism advanced by the Cyrenaics. Nevertheless, the Epicurean philosophy found many distinguished disciples, including, among the Greeks, the grammarian Apollodorus and, among the Romans, the poet Horace, the statesman Pliny the Younger, and, most notably, the poet Lucretius. The poem *De Rerum Natura* (On the Nature of Things) by Lucretius is the main source of knowledge of Epicureanism. As an organized school, Epicureanism went out of existence early in the 4th century AD. It was revived in the 17th century by the French philosopher Pierre Gassendi. Since then, Epicureanism has attracted eminent followers in all ages and is regarded as one of the most influential schools of moral philosophy of all time.

Epicurus, Epicurus (341-270 B.C.) was born in the Greek colony on Samos, but spent most of his active life in Athens, where he founded yet another school of philosophy. At "the Garden," Epicurus and his friends lived out their ideals for human life, talking about philosophical issues but deliberately detaching themselves from active involvement in social affairs. Epicurus whole-heartedly adopted the atomism of Leucippus and Democritus, maintaining that all objects and events-including human lives-are in reality nothing more than physical interactions among minute indestructible particles. As they fall toward the center of the earth, atoms swerve from their paths to collide with each other and form temporary compound beings. There is no necessity about any of this, of course; everything happens purely by chance. In his Letter to Menoeceus and Principle Doctrines, Epicurus discussed the consequences of this view for the human attempt to achieve happiness. Since death is a total annihilation that cannot be experienced, in our present lives we need only live a simple life and seek always to avoid physical pain. It is pleasure, understood in this negative sense, that is the highest good for Epicurus. Freedom from mental disturbance is the very most for which one can hope. *Recommended Reading*: Primary sources: The Essential Epicurus: Letters, Principal Doctrines, Vatican Sayings, and Fragments, tr. by Eugene Michael O'Connor (Prometheus, 1993). *Secondary sources*: Howard Jones, The Epicurean Tradition (Routledge, 1992); A. A. Long, Hellenistic Philosophy: Stoics, Epicureans, Sceptics (California, 1986).

Epimenides paradox, liar paradox

Epiphenomenalism, belief that consciousness is an incidental side-effect ("epiphenomenon") or by-product of physical or mechanical reality. On this view, although mental events are in some sense real they have no causal efficacy in the material realm. *Recommended Reading*: D. M. Armstrong, The Mind-Body Problem: An Opinionated Introduction (Westviesw, 1999) and Jaegwon Kim, Mind in a Physical World: An Essay on the Mind-Body Problem and Mental Causation (Bradford, 2000).

Epistemology (Greek *episteme*, "knowledge"; *logos*, "theory"), branch of philosophy that addresses the philosophical problems surrounding the theory of knowledge. Epistemology is concerned with the definition of knowledge and related concepts, the sources and criteria of knowledge, the kinds of knowledge possible and the degree to which each is certain, the limits of knowledge, and the exact relation between the one who knows and the object known.

Greek and Medieval Philosophical Problems: In the 5th century BC, the Greek Sophists questioned the possibility of reliable and objective knowledge. Thus, a leading Sophist, Gorgias, argued that nothing really exists, that if anything did exist it could not be known, and that if knowledge were possible, it could not be communicated. Another prominent Sophist, Protagoras, maintained that no person's opinions can be said to be more correct than another's, because each is the sole judge of his or her own experience. Plato, following his illustrious teacher Socrates, tried to answer the Sophists by postulating the existence of a world of unchanging and invisible "forms", or ideas—such as the forms of equality, beauty, or justice—about which it is possible to have exact and certain knowledge. The things one sees and touches, he maintained, are imperfect realizations of the pure forms studied in mathematics and philosophy. Accordingly, only the abstract reasoning of these disciplines yields genuine know-ledge, whereas reliance on sense perception produces vague and inconsistent opinions. He concluded that philosophical contemplation of the unseen world of forms is the highest goal of human life.

Aristotle followed Plato in regarding abstract knowledge as superior to any other, but disagreed with him as to the proper method of achieving it. Aristotle maintained that almost all knowledge is derived from experience. Knowledge is gained either directly, by abstracting the defining traits of a species, or indirectly, by deducing new facts from those already known, in accordance with the rules of logic. Careful observation and strict adherence to the rules of logic, which were first set down in systematic form by Aristotle, would help guard against the pitfalls the Sophists had exposed. The Stoic and Epicurean schools agreed with Aristotle that knowledge originates in sense perception, but, against both Aristotle and Plato, they maintained that knowledge is to be valued as a practical guide to life, rather than as an end in itself.

After many centuries of declining interest in rational and scientific knowledge, the scholastic philosopher St Thomas Aquinas and other philosophers of the Middle Ages (*see* Medieval Philosophy) helped to restore confidence in reason and experience, blending rational methods with faith into a unified system of beliefs. Aquinas followed Aristotle in regarding perception as the starting point and logic as the intellectual procedure for arriving at reliable knowledge of nature, but he considered faith in scriptural authority as the main source of religious belief.

Reason Versus Sense Perception: From the 17th to the late 19th century, the main issue in epistemology was the role of reasoning as opposed to that of sense perception in acquiring knowledge. For the rationalists, among whom the French philosopher René Descartes, the Dutch philosopher Baruch Spinoza, and the German philosopher Gottfried Wilhelm Leibniz were the leading figures, the main source and final test of knowledge was deductive reasoning based on self-evident principles, or axioms. For the empiricists, beginning with the English philosophers Francis Bacon and John Locke, the main source and final test of knowledge was sense perception.

Bacon inaugurated the new era of modern science by criticizing the medieval reliance on tradition and authority and also by setting down new rules of scientific method, including the first set of rules of inductive logic ever formulated. Locke attacked the rationalist belief that the principles of knowledge are intuitively self-evident, arguing that all kno-wledge is derived from experience, either from experience of the external world, which stamps sensations or ideas on the mind, or from internal experience, in which the mind reflects on its own activities. Human knowledge of external physical objects, he claimed, is always subject to the errors of the senses, and he concluded that one cannot have absolutely certain knowledge of the physical world.

The Irish philosopher George Berkeley agreed with Locke that knowledge comes through ideas, but he denied Locke's belief that a distinction can be made between ideas and objects. The Scottish philosopher David Hume continued the empiricist tradition, but he did not accept Berkeley's conclusion that knowledge was of ideas only. He divided all knowledge into two kinds: knowledge of relations of ideas—that is, the knowledge found in mathematics and logic, which is exact and certain but provides no information about the world; and knowledge of matters of fact—that is, the knowledge derived from sense perception. Hume argued that most knowledge of matters of fact depends upon cause and effect, and since no logical connection exists between any given cause and its effect, one cannot hope to know any future matter of fact with certainty. Thus, the most reliable laws of science might not remain true—a conclusion that had a revolutionary impact on philosophy.

The German philosopher Immanuel Kant tried to solve the crisis precipitated by Locke and brought to a climax by Hume; his proposed solution combined elements of rationalism with elements of empiricism. He agreed with the rationalists that one can have exact and certain knowledge, but he followed the empiricists in holding that such knowledge is more informative about the structure of thought than about the world outside of thought. He distinguished three kinds of knowledge. The first is analytic a priori knowledge, which is knowable independent of experience and therefore exact and certain, but is uninformative or contentless because it only makes clear what is already contained in the meanings of words; an example would be the knowledge that all bachelors are unmarried. The second kind is synthetic a posteriori knowledge, which is informative knowledge about the world gained through experience, but which is subject to the errors of the senses; an example would be the knowledge that the star Sirius is blue. The third kind is synthetic a priori knowledge, which is knowable independent of experience, so that it is exact and certain, but at the same time has content. This type of knowledge is gained by reflecting on the nature of rational experience as such, and it expresses the categories that the mind necessarily has to impose on its sensations in order to organize them into rational experience. An example is the knowledge that every event has a cause, which expresses the fact that the mind has to impose the category of cause-and-effect on all its sensations. According to Kant, mathematics and philosophy provide us with synthetic a priori knowledge. Since the time of Kant, one of the most frequently argued questions in philosophy has been whether or not such a thing as synthetic a priori knowledge really exists.

During the 19th century, the German philosopher G. W. F. Hegel revived the rationalist claim that absolutely certain knowledge of reality can be obtained by equating the processes of thought, of nature, and of history. Hegel inspired an interest in history and a historical approach to knowledge that was further emphasized by Herbert Spencer in Britain and by the German school of historicism. Spencer and the French philosopher Auguste Comte brought attention to the importance of sociology as a branch of knowledge, and both extended the principles of empiricism to the study of society.

Empiricism was carried further by the American school of pragmatism, founded by the philosophers Charles Sanders Peirce, William James, and John Dewey at the turn of the 20th century. They maintained that knowledge is an instrument of action and that all beliefs should be judged by their usefulness as rules for predicting experiences.

Epistemology in the 20th Century: In the early 20th century, epistemological problems were discussed thoroughly, and subtle shades of difference began to divide rival schools of thought. Special attention was given to the relation between the act of perceiving something, the object directly perceived, and the thing that can be said to be known as a result of the perception. The phenomenalists contended that the objects of knowledge are the same as the objects perceived. The neo-realists argued that one has direct perceptions of physical objects or parts of physical objects, rather than of one's own mental states. The critical realists took a middle position, holding that although one perceives only sensory data such as colours and sounds, these stand for physical objects of which they provide knowledge.

A method for dealing with the problem of clarifying the relation between the act of knowing and the object known was developed by the German philosopher Edmund Husserl. He outlined an elaborate procedure that he called phenomenology, by which one is said to be able to distinguish the way things appear to be from the way one thinks they really are, thus gaining a more precise understanding of the conceptual foundations of knowledge.

During the second quarter of the 20th century, two schools of thought emerged, each indebted to the Austrian philosopher Ludwig Wittgenstein. The first of these schools, logical empiricism, or logical positivism, had its origins in Vienna, Austria, but it soon spread to Britain and the United States. The logical empiricists insisted that there is only one kind of knowledge: scientific knowledge; that any meaningful knowledge claim must be verifiable in experience; and hence that much that had passed for philosophy was neither true nor false but literally meaningless. The so-called verifiability criterion of meaning has undergone changes as a result of discussions among the logical empiricists themselves, as well as their critics, but has not been discarded. More recently, the sharp distinction between the analytic and the synthetic, which was maintained by the logical positivists, has been attacked by a number of philo-sophers, chiefly by the American philosopher W. V. O. Quine, whose overall approach is in the pragmatic tradition.

The second of these recent schools of thought, generally referred to as ordinary language philosophy or linguistic philosophy, seems to break with traditional epistemology. The ordinary language philosophers undertake to examine the actual way key epistemological terms are used—terms such as "knowledge", "perception", and "probability"—and to formulate definitive rules for their use in order to avoid verbal confusion. The British philosopher John Langshaw Austin argued, for example, that to say a statement is true adds nothing to the statement except a promise by the speaker or writer. Austin does not consider truth a quality or property attaching to statements or utterances.

Much recent work in epistemology has concentrated not so much on the sources, kinds, and limits of knowledge as on the question, first raised by Plato, of what the concept "knowledge" entails.

Epistemology, one of the major branches of philosophy, also known as philosophy of knowledge. It concerns the forms, nature, preconditions, sources, types and limits of knowledge.

Most of contemporary Anglo-American epistemology concentrates on:

1. the analysis of propositional knowledge (knowing that) as opposed to, *e.g.*, procedural knowledge (knowing how) and knowledge by acquaintance (knowing who);
2. the nature, sources, and justification of its major types, *e.g.* a priori and empirical;
3. the tripartite analysis of knowledge as justified true belief (see Gettier problem;
4. supplying a theory of the justification of empirical knowledge (foundationalism, coherentism, or other).
5. the analysis of sceptical arguments.

Epoché, Greek term for cessation or stoppage; hence, in the philosophy of the skeptics, the suspension of judgment. Only by refusing either to affirm or to deny the truth of what we cannot know, they supposed, can we achieve the ataraxia of a peaceful mind.

E proposition, in the traditional notation for categorical logic, a proposition that is both universal and negative. Example: "No reptiles are insects." This proposition affirms that the designated classes have no common members. Its contradictory is an "I" proposition with the same subject and predicate terms.

Equational logic, First-order equational logic consists of quantifier-free terms of ordinary first-order logic, with equality as the only predicate symbol. The model theory of this logic was developed into Universal algebra by Birkhoff et al. [Birkhoff, Gratzer, Cohn]. It was later made into a branch of category theory by Lawvere ("algebraic theories").

Equivalence, A truth function that returns truth when its two arguments have the same truth-value, and false otherwise. Also the connective denoting this function; also the compound proposition built from this connective. Syntactically: the two propositions imply one another. Semantically: they have the same models. Also called a biconditional, or biconditional statement.

Logical equivalence

A tautologous statement of material equivalence (next).

Material equivalence

A truth function that is true when its two arguments have the same truth-value (not necessarily the same meaning). Notation: $p <=> q$, or p iff q. See also equivalence thesis partial equivalence relation.

Equivalence thesis, the equivalence thesis states that, for any proposed notion of truth, each instance of the schema "S is true if and only if P" resulting from the substitution of a translation of the sentence designated by *S* for *P*, is true. This thesis is often taken to be a minimal requirement on any notion of truth.

Note that the equivalence thesis does not presuppose a correspondence notion of truth. For example, deflationary notions of truth, such as the Quinian "disquotational" notion, satisfy the equivalence thesis. *References*: Dummett, Michael (1978). Truth and Other Enigmas. Cambridge, MA: Harvard University Press. Devitt, Michael (1984). Realism and Truth.

Princeton, NJ: Princeton University Press.

Equivalent sets, Two sets are equivalent iff they have the same cardinality, that is, if they can be put into one-to-one correspondence. Also called equinum-erous sets. Notation: $A =\sim B$; sometimes $A\sim B$.

Equivocal, having more than one meaning.

Equivocation, the informal fallacy that can result when an ambiguous word orphrase is used in different senses within a single argument. Example: "Odd things arouse human suspicion. But seventeen is an odd number. Therefore, seventeen arouses human suspicion."

ER, Entity-Relationship

Erasmus Desiderius, Dutch humanist (1466-1536). Erasmus produced editions of classical texts far superior to those of the medieval period and, in Diatribede libero arbitrio (Discourse on Free Will) (1524) defended the moral freedom of individual human beings. The Ecomium moriae id est Laus stultitiae (Praise of Folly) (1509) satirized the political and religious institutions of his time, and many of his Colloquia (1518) are stinging condemnations of ecclesiastical fraud. *Recommended Reading*: Christian Humanism and the Reformation: Selected Writings of Erasmus, ed. by John C. Olin (Fordham, 1987) and Erasmus: His Life, Works and Influence, tr. by J. C. Grayson (Toronto, 1996).

Erigena John Scotus, Irish philosopher (812-877). In De Divisione Naturae (On the Distribution of Nature) (863), Erigena notoriously combined Greek and neoplatonic elements into a highly rationalized scheme in which everything both emanates from and later is reabsorbed by god. Although the divine is incomprehnsible for Erigena, god may be known indirectly, as manifested in the created order. The views on human freedom he defended in De praedestinatione (On Predestination) (851) earned for Erigena the official condemnation of the church. *Recommended Reading*: Deirdre Carabine, John Scottus Eriugena (Oxford, 2000) and Henry Bett, Johannes Scotus Erigena: A Study in Medieval Philosophy (Hyperion, 1979).

Eros, Greek personification of love; hence, sexual desire or love generally. Plato's Symposium offers a set of speeches on the nature of love in human life. *Recommended Reading*: F. E. Peters, Greek Philosophical Terms: A Historical Lexicon (NYU, 1967); Louis A. Ruprecht, Jr., Symposia:Plato, the Erotic, and Moral Value (SUNY, 1999); and Jamey Hecht, Plato's Symposium: Eros and the Human Predicament (Twayne, 1999).

Esse est percipi, Latin phrase meaning "to be is to be perceived." According to Berkeley, this is the most basic feature of all sensible objects; for spirits, on the other hand, esse est percipere ("to be is to perceive"). Granting this to be the most fundamental principle of idealistic philosophy, Moore argued that it is indefensible. *Recommended Reading*: George Berkeley, Principles of Human Knowledge / Three Dialogues Between Hylas and Philonous, ed. By Roger Woolhouse (Penguin, 1988) and Kenneth P. Winkler, Berkeley: An Interpretation (Clarendon, 1994).

Essence (philosophy), the property or properties an object must have if it is to be what it is. In addition, if being human is the essence of Socrates, it is then a necessary truth about Socrates that he is human.

The thesis that objects have

essences might be motivated as follows. It seems plausible to suppose that an object might not have had some of the properties it actually has. For example, Socrates might not have been executed by the Athenians in 399 BC; he might have died peacefully in his sleep a few years later. However, there seems to be a limit to the properties Socrates could have failed to have while remaining Socrates. Suppose one suggested that Socrates could have been a giraffe rather than a human being. At this point most people will agree that we have simply ceased to talk about a genuine possibility for the historical Socrates. The historical Socrates—that very individual—could not have been anything other than human. Having been human, therefore, unlike having been executed in 399 BC, is part of Socrates's essence.

The essence of an object is often taken to constitute its identity, that is, what makes the object what it is. Its essence may consist in membership of a natural kind, as in the claim that Socrates is essentially human. Alternatively, some have supposed that each object has a unique individual essence. A special, but controversial, case of individual essence is called a "haecceity", which is the property an object has of being that very object. Clearly, if there are haecceities, they are properties an object could not have lacked.

For Aristotle, the definition of something states its essence. A scientific understanding of some-thing is achieved only once one has grasped its essence. Aristotle identifies an object's essence with its substantial form: this is what makes the object what it is. For Aristotle, an object's essence is the kind of thing it is: so, the essence of Socrates is to be human; the essence of a house is to be a shelter for people and goods.

The close connection evident in Aristotle's thought between essence, definition, and the means by which we identify something as a member of a kind was challenged by John Locke. Locke distinguished between the "real essence" of an object, which he identified as the internal constitution of its underlying parts, and its "nominal essence". Its nominal essence is the idea we have in our minds corresponding to the name of the object; this idea is a list, more or less complete, of its known sensible qualities. Since the real essence of an object, according to Locke, is unknown to us, the criteria by which we identify an object are divorced from its underlying nature.

Essence in More Recent Philosophy: In recent philosophy, discussion of essence has conc-entrated on the question of what kind of necessity is involved in the claim that an essential property is a property an object *must* have. Willard Van Orman Quine argued against essences, contending that what makes something necessary is not some feature of the object concerned, but rather some feature of the way we describe the object. For example, the number nine may be referred to by the numeral "9" or, since there are nine planets, by the phrase "the number of the planets". However, while the sentence "9 is necessarily greater than seven" is true, the sentence "the number of the planets is necessarily greater than seven" is false, since there might have been fewer planets than seven.

The necessity, Quine argues, is a function of the way we describe the object concerned.

Against Quine, the American philosopher Saul Kripke argued that the example turns on a feature of descriptions such as "the number of the planets". Kripke calls such a description a "weak designator": it does not designate the same object in all possible worlds, that is, in all possible conditions of the actual world. By contrast, natural kind terms and proper names are "rigid designators". For example, the term "water" designates a substance which is H_2O in all possible worlds. Water is thus necessarily H_2O and this fact is independent of the way we describe water. For Kripke, therefore, natural kinds such as water have empirically discoverable essences. Kripke also argues in defence of individual essences, which he ties to the necessity of something's origins, for example, of an individual person's having come from a particular fertilized egg and sperm consisting of a particular set of atoms.

Modern philosophical discussion of essence is embedded in discussion of a cluster of related problems: these concern modality, theories of naming and reference, natural kinds, and laws of nature.

Essence, that without which a specific thing or substance would not be one and the same (type of) individual it is, those features of an object that make it the kind of object it is as opposed to its accidents (*e.g.* a person's ability to reason is an essential human feature, while hair color would be an accident)—Essentialism is the view that the essence-accident distinction is not arbitrary but rooted in the nature of reality.

Essence-accident, distinction among the attributes, properties, or qualities of substances. A thing's possession of its essential properties is necessary either for its individual existence or, at least, for its membership in a specific kind. Accidental features, by contrast, are those which the thing merely happens to have, even though it need not. Thus, for example, rationality may be part of the essence of any human being, but being able to calculate square roots accurately in one's head is (surely) an accident. The legitimacy of the distinction itself is called into question by philo-sophers ("anti-essentialists") who doubt whether any features are genuinely essential to the things that have them. *Recommended Reading*: Charlotte Witt, Substance and Essence in Aristotle: An Interpretation of Metaphysics vii-ix (Cornell, 1994); Saul A. Kripke, Naming and Necessity (Harvard, 1982); and Garth L. Hallett, Essentialism: A Wittgensteinian Critique (SUNY, 1991).

Essentialism, 1) Platonic idealism

2) the view that all things have essential properties which can be discerned by reason (sometimes attributed to Aristotelianism). See substantialism

Estrangement, withdrawal from things or people; see alienation.

Eternal return, belief that everything that happens has happened before and will happen again, since the universe (or time itself) is fundamentally cyclical. A standard feature of Pythagorean and Stoic thought, this view was more recently adopted as a basis for practical hope by Nietzsche. *Recommended Reading*: Joan Stambaugh, Nietzsche's Thought of Eternal Return (Taylor & Francis, 1988) and Mircea Eliade, Myth of the Eternal Return, tr. by Willard R. Trask (Princeton, 1971).

Ethical relativism, the view that what is morally permissible, obligatory, and forbidden differs among individuals or between cultures. According to ethical relativism nothing is absolutely good or bad or right or wrong: rather, relativists hold, what is right or wrong is so for a given individual or within a given culture or society: the underlying idea is that the individual or society's judging things right or wrong or good or evil makes them so for that individual or society. See cultural relativism, subjectivism.

Ethics, branch of philosophy concerned with the evaluation of human conduct. Philosophers commonly distinguish: descriptive ethics, the factual study of the ethical standards or principles of a group or tradition; normative ethics, the development of theories that tem-atically denominate right and wrong actions; applied ethics, the use of these theories to form judgments regarding practical cases; and metaethics, careful analysis of the meaning and justification of ethical claims. *Recommended Reading*: Lawrence M. Hinman, Ethics: A Pluralistic Approach To Moral Theory (Harcourt, 1997); A Companion to Ethics, ed. by Peter Singer (Blackwell, 1993); D. D. Raphael, Moral Philosophy (Oxford, 1994); James Rachels, The Elements of Moral Philosophy (McGraw-Hill, 2000); and The Blackwell Guide to Ethical Theory, ed. by Hugh Lafollette (Blackwell, 1999).

Ethics (Greek, *ethika,* from *ethos,* "character" or "custom"), principles or standards of human conduct, sometimes called morals (Latin, *mores,* "customs"), and, by extension, the study of such principles, sometimes called moral philosophy. This article is concerned with ethics chiefly in the latter sense and is confined to that of Western civilization, although every culture has developed an ethical system of its own.

Ethics studies human conduct; it is concerned with questions such as "When is an act right?", "When is an act wrong?", and "What is the nature, or determining standard, of good and bad?". In asking these questions, ethical theorists have proposed differing accounts of the nature of ethical knowledge, the measure of it, the source of it, the means of knowing it, and how it ought to be applied.

Ethics, as a branch of philosophy, is considered a normative science, because it is concerned with norms of human conduct, as distinguished from the formal sciences, such as mathematics and logic, and the empirical sciences, such as chemistry and physics. The empirical social sciences, however, including psychology, impinge to some extent on the concerns of ethics in that they study social behaviour. For example, the social sciences frequently attempt to determine the relation of particular ethical principles to social behaviour and to investigate the cultural conditions that contribute to the formation of such principles.

Ethical Principles: Philosophers have attempted to determine goodness in conduct according to two chief principles, and have considered certain types of conduct either good in themselves or good because they conform to a particular moral standard. The former implies a final value, or *summum bonum*, which is desirable in itself and not merely as a means to an end. In the history of ethics there are three principal standards of conduct, each of which has been proposed by various groups or individuals as the highest good: happiness or pleasure; duty, virtue, or obligation; and perfection, the fullest harmonious development of human potential.

Depending on the social setting, the authority invoked for good conduct is the will of a deity, the pattern of nature, or the rule of reason. When the will of a deity is the authority, obedience to the divine commandments in scriptural texts is the accepted standard of conduct. If the pattern of nature is the authority, conformity to the qualities attributed to human nature is the standard. When reason rules, moral behaviour is expected to result from rational thought.

Prudence, Pleasure, or Power: Sometimes principles are chosen whose ultimate value is not determined, in the belief that such a determination is impossible. Such ethical philosophy usually equates satisfaction in life with prudence, pleasure, or power, but it is basically derived from a belief in the ethical doctrine of natural human fulfilment as the ultimate good.

A person lacking motivation to exercise preference may be resigned to accepting all customs and therefore may develop a philosophy of prudence. He or she then lives in conformity with the moral conduct of the period and society.

Hedonism is the philosophy which teaches that the highest good is pleasure. The hedonist must decide between the most enduring pleasures or the most intense pleasures, whether present pleasures should be denied for the sake of overall comfort, and whether mental pleasures are preferable to physical pleasures.

A philosophy in which the highest attainment is power may result from competition. Because each victory tends to raise the level of the competition, the logical end of such a philosophy is unlimited or absolute power. Power-seekers may not accept customary ethical rules, but may conform to other rules that can help them become successful. They may seek to persuade others that they are moral in the accepted sense of the term in order to mask their power motives and to gain the ordinary rewards of morality.

History: For as long as people have been living together in groups, the moral regulation of behaviour has been necessary to the group's well-being. Although morals were formalized and made into arbitrary standards of conduct, they dev-eloped, sometimes irrationally, after religious taboos were violated; out of chance behaviour that became habit and then custom; or from laws imposed by chiefs to prevent disharmony in their tribes. Even the great ancient Egyptian and Sumerian civilizations developed no systematized ethics; maxims and precepts set down by secular leaders, such as Ptahhotep, mingled with a strict religion that affected the behaviour of every Egyptian. In ancient China the maxims of Confucius were accepted as a moral code. The Greek philosophers, from about the 6th century BC onward, theorized intensively about moral behaviour, which led to the further development of ethics as philosophy.

Early Greek Ethics: In the 6th century BC the Greek philosopher Pythagoras developed one of the earliest moral philosophies from the Greek mystery religion Orphism. Believing that the intellectual nature is superior to the sensual nature and that the best life is one devoted to mental discipline, he founded a semi-religious order with rules emphasizing simplicity in speech, dress, and food. Its members observed rituals that were designed to demonstrate the decreed ethical beliefs.

In the 5th century BC the Greek philosophers known as Sophists, who taught rhetoric, logic, and civil affairs, were sceptical of moral absolutes. The Sophist Protagoras taught that human judgement is subjective, and that one's perception is valid only for oneself. Another, Gorgias, even went to the extreme of arguing that nothing exists; that if anything does exist, human beings could not know it; and that if they did know it, they could not communicate that knowledge. Other Sophists, such as Thrasymachus, believed that might makes right. Socrates opposed the Sophists. His philosophical position, as repre-sented in the dialogues of his pupil Plato, may be summarized as follows: virtue is knowledge; people will be virtuous if they know what virtue is; and vice, or evil, is the result of ignorance. Thus, according to Socrates, education as to what constitutes virtue can make people moral.

Greek Schools of Ethics: Most later Greek schools of moral philosophy were derived from the teachings of Socrates. Four such schools originated among his immediate disciples: the Cynics, the Cyrenaics, the Megarians (a school founded by Euclid of Megara), and the Platonists.

The Cynics, notably the philosopher Antisthenes, maintained that the essence of virtue, the only good, is self-control and that it is capable of being taught. The Cynics disdained pleasure as an evil, if accepted as a guide to conduct. They considered all pride a vice, including pride in appearance or cleanliness. Socrates is reputed to have said to Antisthenes, "I can see your pride through the holes in your cloak".

The Cyrenaics, notably Aristippus of Cyrene, were hedonists, postulating pleasure as the chief good (as long as it does not dominate one's life), that no one kind of pleasure is superior to another, and that it is measurable only in degree and duration.

The Megarians, Euclid's followers, posited that although good may be called wisdom, God, or reason, it is "one", and that the Good is the final secret of the universe, which can be revealed only through logical inquiry.

According to Plato, good is an essential element of reality. Evil does not exist in itself but is, rather, an imperfect reflection of the real, which is good. In his *Dialogues* (first half of the 4th century BC) he maintains that human virtue lies in the fitness of a person to perform that person's proper function in the world. The human soul has three elements—intellect, will, and emotion—each of which possesses a specific virtue in the good person and performs a specific role. The virtue of intellect is wisdom, or knowledge of the ends of life; that of the will is courage, the capacity to act; and that of the emotions is temperance, or self-control. The ultimate virtue, justice, is the harmonious relation of all the others, each part of the soul performing its appropriate task and keeping its proper place. Plato maintained that the intellect should be sovereign, the will second, and the emotions third, subject to intellect and will. The just person, whose life is ordered in this way, is therefore the good person.

Aristotle, Plato's pupil, regarded happiness (*eudaimònia*) as the aim of life. In his principal work on ethics, the *Nicomachean Ethics* (late 4th century BC), he defined happiness as activity that accords with the specific nature of humanity; pleasure accompanies such activity but is not its chief aim. Happiness results from the unique human attribute of reason, functioning harmoniously with human faculties. Aristotle held that virtues are essentially good habits, and that to attain happiness a person must develop two kinds of habits: those of mental activity, such as knowledge, which lead to the highest human activity, contemplation; and those of practical action and emotion, such as courage. Moral virtues are habits of action that conform to the "golden mean", the principle of moderation, and they must be flexible because of differences among people and conditioning factors. For example, the amount one should eat depends on one's size, age, and occupation. In general, Aristotle defines the mean as being the virtuous state between the two extremes of excess and insufficiency; thus, generosity, a virtue, is the mean between rashness and meanness. For Aristotle, the intellectual and the moral virtues are merely means towards the attainment of happiness, which results from the full realization of human potential.

Stoicism: The philosophy of Stoicism developed about 300 BC, during the Hellenistic and Roman periods. In Greece the principal Stoic philosophers were Zeno of Citium, Cleanthes, and Chrysippus of Soli. In Rome, Stoicism proved to be the most popular of the Greek philosophies, and Cicero was among the famous Romans who came under its influence. Its principal figures during the Roman period were the Greek philosopher Epictetus and the Roman emperor and philosopher Marcus Aurelius. According to the Stoics, nature is orderly and rational, and only a life led in harmony with nature can be good. The Stoic philosophers, however, also agreed that because life is influenced by material circumstances one should try to be as independent of such circumstances as possible. The practice of certain cardinal virtues, such as practical wisdom, courage, discretion, and justice, enables one to achieve independence in the spirit of the Stoic motto "endure and renounce". Hence, the word "stoic" has come to mean fortitude in the face of hardship.

Epicureanism: In the 4th and 3rd centuries BC, the Greek philosopher Epicurus developed a system of thought, later called Epicureanism, that identified the highest good with pleasure, particularly intellectual pleasure, and, like Stoicism, advocated a temperate and even an ascetic life devoted to contemplative pursuits. The principal Roman exponent of Epicureanism was the poet and philosopher Lucretius, whose poem *De Rerum Natura* (On the Nature of Things), written in the middle of the 1st century BC, combined certain ideas derived from the cosmological doctrines of the Greek philosopher Democritus with others derived from the ethics of Epicurus. The Epicureans sought to achieve pleasure by maintaining a state of serenity—that is, by eliminating all emotional disturbances. They considered religious beliefs and practices harmful because they preoccupy one with disturbing thoughts of death and the uncertainty of life after death. The Epicureans also held that it is better to postpone immediate pleasure in order to attain more secure and lasting satisfaction in the future; they therefore insisted that the good life must be regulated by self-discipline.

Secular Ethical Philosophies: In his *Leviathan* (1651), the English philosopher Thomas Hobbes assigned the greatest importance to organized society and political power. He argued that human life in the "state of nature" (apart from or before the institution of the civil state) is "solitary, poor, nasty, brutish, and short", and that it is "a war of all against all". Consequently, people seek security by entering into a social contract in which each person's original power is yielded to a sovereign, who regulates conduct.

This conservative position in politics assumes that human beings are evil and need a strong state to repress them. None the less, Hobbes argued that if a sovereign does not provide security and order and is overthrown by the people, they revert to the state of nature and may then make a new contract. Hobbes's doctrine concerning the state and the social contract influenced the thought of the English philosopher John Locke. In his *Two Treatises on Civil Government* (1690) Locke maintained, however, that the purpose of the social contract is to reduce the absolute power of authority and to promote individual liberty.

Human reason is the criterion of right conduct in the system developed by the Dutch philosopher Baruch Spinoza. In his major work, *Ethica Ordine Geometrico Demonstrata,* or *Ethica* (Ethics Demonstrated with Geometrical Order, published by his friends in 1677 after his death), Spinoza deduced ethics from psychology and psychology from metaphysics. He asserted that all things are morally neutral from the point of view of eternity; only human needs and interests determine what is considered good and evil, or right and wrong. Whatever aids humanity's knowledge of nature or is consonant with human reason is acknowledged as good. Since it is reasonable to suppose that whatever all people have in common is best for everyone, the good that people should seek for others is the good they desire for themselves. In addition, reason is needed in order to keep the passions in check and to achieve pleasure and happiness by avoiding pain. The highest human state, according to Spinoza, is the "intellectual love of God" derived from intuitive understanding, a faculty higher than ordinary reason. By the proper use of this faculty a person may contemplate the entire mental and physical universe and view it as comprising an infinite substance, which Spinoza terms God.

Psychoanalysis and Behaviourism: Modern ethics has been affected by the psychoanalysis of Sigmund Freud and his followers and the behaviourist doctrines based on the conditioned-reflex discoveries of the Russian physiologist Ivan Pavlov. Freud attributed the problem of good and evil in each individual to the struggle between the drive of the instinctual self to satisfy all its desires and the necessity of the social self to control or repress most of these impulses in order for the individual to function in society. Although Freud's influence has not been assimilated completely into ethical thinking, Freudian depth psychology suggests that guilt, often sexual, underlies much thinking about good and evil.

Behaviourism, through observation of animal behaviour, strengthened beliefs in the power to change human nature by arranging conditions favourable to the desired changes. In the 1920s, behaviourism was broadly accepted in the United States, principally in theories of paediatrics and infant training and education in general.

In his late 19th-century and early 20th-century writings, the American philosopher and psychologist William James anticipated Freud and Pavlov to some extent. James is best known as the founder of pragmatism, which maintains that the value of ideas is determined by their consequences. His greatest contribution to ethical theory, however, lies in his insistence on the importance of interrelationships, in ideas as in other phenomena.

Modern Ethical Philosophy: The British philosopher Bertrand Russell, a vigorous critic of conventional morality, held the view that moral judgements express individual desires or accepted habits. In his thinking, both the ascetic saint and the detached sage are poor human models because they are incomplete human beings. Complete human beings participate fully in the life of society and express all of their nature. Some impulses must be checked in the interests of society and others in the interest of individual development, but it is a person's relatively unimpeded natural growth and self-realization that makes for the good life and a harmonious society. He was often criticized for his advocacy of sexual freedom.

A number of 20th-century philosophers, some of whom espoused the theories of existentialism, have been concerned with the problems of individual ethical choice raised by Kierkegaard and Nietzsche. The orientation of some of these thinkers was religious: for example, the Russian philosopher Nikolay Aleksandrovich Berdyayev emph-asized freedom of the individual spirit; the Austrian-Jewish philosopher Martin Buber was concerned with the morality of relations between individuals; the German-American Protestant theologian Paul Tillich stressed the courage to be oneself; and the French Catholic philosopher and dramatist Gabriel Marcel and the German Protestant philosopher and psychiatrist Karl Jaspers were both concerned with the uniqueness of the individual and the importance of communication between individuals. A different tendency in modern ethical thought characterizes the writings of the French philosophers Jacques

Maritain and Étienne Gilson, who followed the tradition of Thomas Aquinas. According to Maritain, "true existentialism" belongs only to this tradition.

Certain other modern philosophers do not accept any of the traditional religions. The German philosopher Martin Heidegger maintained that no God exists, although one may come into being in the future. Human beings are, therefore, alone in the universe and must make their ethical decisions with the constant awareness of death. The French philosopher and novelist Jean-Paul Sartre was an atheist who also emphasized the awareness of death. In addition, Sartre maintained that people have an ethical responsibility to involve themselves in the social and political activities of their time.

Several other modern philosophers, such as the American John Dewey, have been concerned with ethical thought from the viewpoint of instrumentalism. According to Dewey, the good is that which is chosen after reflecting upon both the means and the probable consequences of realizing the good.

Philosophical discussion of ethics continued with the writings of G. E. Moore, especially his *Principia Ethica* (1903). Moore argued that ethical terms are definable in terms of the word "good", whereas "good" is undefinable. This is so because goodness is a simple, unanalysable quality. Philosophers who disagree with Moore in this regard, and who believe "good" to be definable, are termed naturalists. Moore is called an intuitionist. Naturalists and intuitionists regard ethical sentences as descriptive of the world, and hence true or false. Philosophers who disagree with this belong to a third major school, non-cognitivism, in which ethics is not a form of knowledge, and ethical language is not descriptive. An important branch of the non-cognitive school is logical empiricism, or logical positivism, which questions the validity of ethical statements as compared with statements of fact or of logic. Some logical empiricists argue that ethical statements have only emotional or persuasive significance. American philosophers whose works are concerned with ethical considerations include Sidney Hook in his *Human Values and Economic Policy* (1967) and Mortimer Adler in *The Conditions of Philosophy* (1965).

In Britain, R. M. Hare argued for a prescriptive account of ethics, that is, if a person utters a moral judgement, he or she is prescribing a course of action or inaction. He also argued that moral judgements are universal. When a person makes a moral judgement in a particular situation, therefore, he or she is prescribing a course of action that anyone in similar circumstances should follow. His book *Moral Thinking* (1981) gives a good account of his position. Bernard Williams has also been influential, in his case in terms of the importance he has placed on the role of the emotions and individuality in moral reasoning. His *Morality: An Introduction to Ethics* gives a clear account of his thinking.

Ethnicity, a person's ethnicity refers to that individual's affiliation with a particular cultural tradition that may be national (French) or regional (Sicilian) in character. Ethnicity differs from race in that ethnicity is a sociological concept whereas race is a biological phenomenon.

Ethos, Greek word for custom or habit. the characteristic conduct of an individual human life. Hence, beginning with Aristotle, ethics is the study of human conduct, and the Stoics held that all behavior—for good or evil—arises from the eqos of the individual. *Recommended Reading*: F. E. Peters, Greek Philosophical Terms: A Historical Lexicon (NYU, 1967).

Euclid, Greek mathematician (365-300 B.C.) whose Elementae (Elements) offered an axiomatic system for geometry based only on a few "common notions" and five basic postulates: (1) Any two points can be joined by a unique straight line. (2) A straight line can be extended indefinitely in either direction. (3) From a center point, a circle can be drawn with any radius. (4) All right angles are equal to each other. (5) If two straight lines crossing a third form angles less than two right angles on one of its sides, then indefinite extensions of these lines eventually meet. Although rejection of the fifth postulate eventually led to the development of alternative geom-etries by Lobachevsky and Riemann, Euclid's emphasis on axiomatic structure remained significant for mathematicians like Peano and Hilbert and served as a significant model for such philosophers as Hobbes and Spinoza. *Recommended Reading*: Thomas L. Heath, History of Greek Mathematics: From Thales to Euclid (Dover, 1981).

Eudaimonia, this is the word that Aristotle uses for "happiness" or "flourishing." It comes from the Greek "eu," which means "happy" or "well" or "harmonious," and "daimon," which refers to the individual's spirit. It is a crucial term in virtue ethics. See also eudaimonism.

Eudaimonism, the word eudaimonism comes from the Greek word for happiness (eudaimonia), and refers to any conception of ethics that puts human happiness and the complete life of the individual at the center of ethical concern. This is solely a technical term and has no popular equivalent, though sometimes humanism comes close. Aristotle is the founder of eudaimonism. By contrast, note that existentialism rejects happiness as a bourgeois fantasy, and that even stoicism and Epicureanism may turn their backs on eudaimonism since they don't advocate individual fulfillment but only the lack of emotion or pain. (References from altruism, Aristotelianism, existentialism, individualism, optimism, and pessimism.)

Event, 1. An occurrence or happening of significance to a task or program, such as the completion of an asynchronous input/output operation. A task may wait for an event or any of a set of events or it may (request to) receive asynchronous notification (a signal or interrupt) that the event has occurred. See also event-driven.

2. A transaction or other activity that affects the records in a file.

Event-driven, A kind of program, such as a graphical user interface, with a main loop which just waits for events to occur. Each event has an associated handler which is passed the details of the event, *e.g.* mouse button 3 pressed at position (355, 990).

For example, X window system and most Visual Basic application programs are event-driven. See also callback.

Evidence, support for the truth of a proposition, especially that derivedfrom empirical observation or experience. *Recommended Reading*: Karl R. Popper, Logic of Scientific Discovery (Routledge, 1992).

Evil, that which is morally bad or wrong, or that which causes harm, pain, or misery. In theology, the problem of evil arises if it is accepted that evil exists in a universe governed by a supreme being who is both good and omnipotent. In a formulation of the problem attributed to the Greek philosopher Epicurus, either God can prevent evil and chooses not to (and therefore is not good) or chooses to prevent it and cannot (and therefore is not all-powerful).

Traditional Religious Solutions: The problem of evil has been a central concern of philo-sophers and of all the major religions. Some of the solutions proposed have rested on a denial either of the existence of evil or of the omnipotence of God. In Hindu teaching, for instance, evil has no real existence, being part of the illusory world of phenomena. In the ancient Persian religion Zoroastrianism and the related ancient Middle Eastern sect known as Manichaeism, evil is attributed to the existence of an evil deity, against whom the good deity must struggle. In the Book of Job, on the other hand, after Job's comforters offer dubious expla-nations of Job's undeserved suffering, the demand for an explanation is ultimately made to seem presumptuous, and the scriptural writer suggests that God's ways are mysterious and beyond human understanding.

The 20th Century: The unprecedented scale of the wars and persecutions of the 20th century undermined the secular belief in inevitable progress and confronted philosophers and theologians once again with the problem of evil. In particular, the question of whether extreme suffering can ever be theologically justified was raised with regard to the Holocaust. Some have speculated about the absence of God; others have recalled the idea in the Book of Job of the mysteriousness of God's ways. The problem of evil has thus returned as a major concern of contemporary theology.

Evil problem of, bad things sometimes happen. Whether they are taken to flow from the operation of the world ("natural evil"), to result from deliberate human cruelty ("moral evil"), or simply to correlate poorly with what seems to be deserved ("non-karmic evil"), such events give rise to basic questions about whether or not life is fair. The presence of evil in the world poses a special difficulty for traditional theists, as both Epicurus and Hume pointed out. Since an omniscient god must be aware of evil, an omnipotent god could prevent evil, and a benevolent god would not tolerate evil, it should follow that there is no evil. Yet there is evil, from which atheists conclude that there is no omniscient, omnipotent, and benevolent god. The most common theistic defense against the problem, propounded (in different forms) by both Augustine and Leibniz, is to deny the reality of evil by claiming that apparent cases of evil are merely parts of a larger whole that embodies greater good. More recently, some have questioned whether the traditional notions of omnipotence and omniscience are coherent. *Recommended Reading*: The Problem of Evil: A Reader, ed. by Mark Larrimore (Blackwell, 2000); The Problem of Evil, ed. by Marilyn McCord Adams and Robert M. Adams (Clarendon, 1991); and Richard Swinburne, Providence and the Problem of Evil (Oxford, 1998).

Evolutionary programming, (EP) A stochastic optimisation strategy originally conceived by Lawrence J. Fogel in 1960.

An initially random population of individuals (trial solutions) is created. Mutations are then applied to each individual to create new individuals. Mutations vary in the severity of their effect on the behaviour of the individual. The new individuals are then compared in a "tournament" to select which should survive to form the new population.

EP is similar to a genetic algorithm, but models only the behavioural linkage between parents and their offspring, rather than seeking to emulate specific genetic operators from nature such as the encoding of behaviour in a genome and recombination by genetic crossover.

EP is also similar to an evolution strategy (ES) although the two approaches developed indepe-ndently. In EP, selection is by comparison with a randomly chosen set of other individuals whereas ES typically uses deterministic selection in which the worst individuals are purged from the population.

Evolution strategy, (ES) A kind of evolutionary algorithm where individuals(potential solutions) are encoded by a set of realvalued "object variables" (the individual's "genome"). For each object variable an individual also has a "strategy variable" which determines the degree of mutation to be applied to the corresponding object variable. The strategy variables also mutate, allowing the rate of mutation of the object variables to vary.

An ES is characterised by the population size, the number of offspring produced in each generation and whether the new population is selected from parents and offspring or only from the offspring.

ES were invented in 1963 by Ingo Rechenberg, Hans-Paul Schwefel at the Technical University of Berlin (TUB) while searching for the optimal shapes of bodies in a flow.

Excluded middle, law of, fundamental logical principle that maintains that every proposition (or thought or statement) is either true or false, or that for every statement, either it or its contradictory is true. Compare: Contradiction.

Exclusive premises, the formal fallacy committed in a categorical syllogism that is invalid because both of its premises are negative. Example: "Since no mammals are fish and some fish are not whales, it follows that some whales are not mammals."

Existence, instantiation in reality, or actual being. Kant pointed out that existence is not a predicate, and Frege proposed that it is a second-order property of those first-order properties that happen to be instantiated. The metaphysical question of what kinds of things exist is the subject of ontology, as is the even more general question of why there is something rather than nothing. *Recommended Reading*: Colin McGinn, Logical Properties: Identity, Existence, Predication, Necessity, Truth (Clarendon, 2001); Jean-Paul Sartre, Truth and Existence, tr. by Adrian Van Den Hoven and Ronald Aronson (Chicago, 1995); and Emmanuel Levinas, Existence and Existents, tr. by Robert Bernaeconi (Duquesne, 2001).

Existence proof, A proof that something exists (*e.g.* a number, wff, proof, etc. with certain properties) but that does not produce an example. constructive proof.

Existential fallacy, the formal fallacy committed in a categorical syllogism that is invalid because it has two universal premises and aparticular conclusion. Example: "All inhabitants of another planet are friendly people, and all Martians are inhabitants of another planet. Therefore, some Martians are friendly people."

Existential import, Quantified statements have existential import iff (in the standard interpretation) they are taken to assert the existence of their subjects. Aristotle held that all quantified propositions have existential import. The modern view, due to George Boole, is that existentially quantified statements do and that universally quantified statements do not. Hence in the modern view, (x)(A*x* => *Bx*) ("All

. *A*'s are *B*'s") is non-committal on the existence of any A's; it may be true even for an interpretation whose domain contains no objects to instantiate x, or none that happen to be A's. By contrast, (Ex)(AxoBx) ("Some A's are B's") asserts the existence of at least one *A*, and it would be false for any interpretation whose domain contained no such values for *x*. See predicate logic, quantifier.

Existential instantiation, instantiation

Existentialism, a (mostly) twentieth-century approach that emphasizes the primacy of individual existence over any presumed natural essence for humanbeings. Although they differ on many details, existentialists generally suppose that the fact of my existence as a human being entails both my unqualified freedom to make of myself whatever I will and the awesome responsibility of employing that freedom appropriately, without being driven by anxiety toward escaping into the inauthenticity or self-deception of any conventional set of rules for behavior, even though the entire project may turn out to be absurd. Prominent existentialists include Kierkegaard, Heidegger, Jaspers, Beauvoir, Sartre, and Camus. *Recommended Reading*: Existentialism: From Dostoevsky to Sartre, ed. by Walter Kaufmann (Meridian, 1988); L. Nathan Oaklander, Existentialist Philosophy: An Introduction (Prentice-Hall, 1995); Robert C. Solomon, Existentialism (McGraw-Hill, 1974); Robert Goodwin, An Introduction to Existentialism (Dover, 1962); and William Barrett, Irrational Man: A Study in Existential Philosophy (Anchor, 1962). Influential movement in 20th century philosophy and especially ethics. Historically, existentialism was inspired by the supposed skepticism and nihilism of Friedrich Nietzsche (1844-1900). Existentialism takes its peculiar character from the fact that, even though it is a form of individualism, it is also very much a kind of pessimism, another major influence on existentialism was Schopenhauer. According to Jean-Paul Sartre (1905-1980), one of the leading philosophers of the movement, existentialism takes its name from its guiding phrase, "existence precedes essence". This means that there is no stable human essence or nature and thus that there are no intrinsic or natural human values (so that any attempt at ethical naturalism is misguided and debased). Existentialism teaches that each person must simply live his or her life and by so doing create his or her own values, almost as an afterthought. Although such a process of living can be haphazard and lacking in self-direction, this fact does not seem to be a problem for the existentialists. In fact, some existen-tialists even revel in the unplanned, irrational character of life and therefore could be characterized as proponents of irrationalism or even nihilism. Existentialists are also extreme oppon-ents of eudaimonism, since they think that the quest for happiness is an indication of the "bad faith" of the bourgeoisie. Quite far from the philosophy above presented, yet existentialist, it is to remember Kierkegaard. (References from individualism, irrationalism, naturalism, nihilism, pessimism and stoicism).

Existentialism, philosophical movement or tendency, emphasizing individual existence, freedom, and choice, that influenced many diverse writers in the 19th and 20th centuries.

Major Themes: Because of the diversity of positions associated with existentialism, the term is impossible to define precisely. Certain themes common to virtually all existentialist writers can, however, be identified. The term itself suggests one major theme: the stress on concrete individual existence and, consequently, on subjectivity, individual freedom, and choice.

Moral Individualism: Most philosophers since Plato have held that the highest ethical good is the same for everyone; insofar as one approaches moral perfection, one resembles other morally perfect individuals. The 19th-century Danish philosopher Søren Kierkegaard, the first writer to call himself or herself existential, reacted against this tradition by insisting that the highest good for the individual is to find his or her own unique vocation. As he wrote in his journal, "I must find a truth that is true for me...the idea for which I can live or die." Other existentialist writers have echoed Kierkegaard's belief that one must choose one's own way without the aid of universal, objective standards. Against the traditional view that moral choice involves an objective judgement of right and wrong, existentialists have argued that no objective, rational basis can be found for moral decisions. The 19th-century German philosopher Friedrich Nietzsche contended that there are no moral "facts", only moral "interpretations", which, moreover, are bound to vary according to the types of human beings who make them.

Subjectivity: All existentialists have followed Kierkegaard in stressing the importance of passionate individual action in deciding questions of both morality and truth. They have insisted, accordingly, that personal experience and acting on one's own convictions are essential in arriving at the truth. Thus, the understanding of a situation by someone involved in that situation is superior to that of a detached, objective observer. This emphasis on the perspective of the individual agent has also made existentialists suspicious of systematic reasoning. Kierkegaard, Nietzsche, and other existentialist writers were deliberately unsystematic in the exposition of their philosophies, preferring to express themselves in aphorisms, dialogues, parables, and other literary forms. Despite their anti-rationalist position, however, most existentialists cannot be said to be irrationalist in the sense of denying all validity to rational thought. They have held that rational clarity is desirable wherever possible, but that the most important questions in life are not accessible to reason or science. Furthermore, they have argued that even science is not as rational as is commonly supposed. Nietzsche, for instance, asserted that the scientific assumption of an orderly universe is for the most part a useful fiction.

Choice and Commitment: Perhaps the most prominent theme in existentialist writing is that of choice. Humanity's primary distinction, in the view of most existentialists, is the freedom to choose. Existentialists hold that human beings do not have a fixed nature, or essence, as other animals and plants do; each human being makes choices that create his or her own nature. In the formulation of the 20th-century French philosopher Jean-Paul Sartre, existence precedes essence. Choice is therefore central to human existence, and it is inescapable; even the refusal to choose is a choice. Freedom of choice entails commitment and responsibility. Because individuals are free to choose their own path, existentialists have argued, they must accept the risk and responsibility of following their commitment wherever it leads.

Dread and Anxiety: Kierkegaard held that it is spiritually crucial to recognize that one experiences not only a fear of specific objects but also a feeling of general apprehension, which he called dread. He interpreted it as God's way of calling each individual to make a commitment to a personally valid way of life. The word "anxiety" (German *Angst*) has a similarly crucial role in the work of the 20th-century German philosopher Martin Heidegger; anxiety leads to the individual's confrontation with nothingness and with the impossibility of finding ultimate justification for the choices he or she must make. In the philosophy of Sartre, the word "nausea" is used for the individual's recognition of the pure contingency of the universe, and the word "anguish" is used for the recognition of the total freedom of choice that confronts the individual at every moment.

History: Existentialism as a distinct philosophical and literary movement belongs to the 19th and 20th centuries, but elements of existentialism can be found in the thought (and life) of Socrates, in the Bible, and in the work of many pre-modern philosophers and writers.

Pascal:The first to anticipate the major concerns of modern existentialism was the 17th-century French philosopher Blaise Pascal. Pascal rejected the rigorous rationalism of his contemporary René Descartes, asserting, in his *Pensées* (1670), that a systematic philosophy that presumes to explain God and humanity is a form of pride. Like later existentialist writers, he saw human life in terms of paradoxes: the human self, which combines mind and body, is itself a paradox and contradiction.

Kierkegaard: Kierkegaard, generally regarded as the founder of modern existentialism, reacted against the systematic absolute idealism of the 19th-century German philosopher G. W. F. Hegel, who claimed to have worked out a total rational understanding of humanity and history. Kierkegaard, on the contrary, stressed the ambiguity and absurdity of the human situation. The individual's response to this situation must be to live a totally committed life, and this commitment can only be understood by the individual who has made it. The individual must therefore always be prepared to defy the norms of society for the sake of the higher authority of a personally valid way of life. Kierkegaard ultimately advocated a "leap of faith" into a Christian way of life, which, although incomprehensible and full of risk, was the only commitment he believed could save the individual from despair.

Nietzsche: Nietzsche, who was not acquainted with the work of Kierkegaard, influenced subsequent existentialist thought through his criticism of traditional metaphysical and moral assumptions and through his espousal of tragic pessimism and the life-affirming individual will that opposes itself to the moral conformity of the majority. In contrast to Kierkegaard, whose attack on conventional morality led him to advocate a radically individualistic Christianity, Nietzsche proclaimed the "death of God" and went on to reject the entire Judaeo-Christian moral tradition in favour of a heroic pagan ideal.

Heidegger: Like Pascal and Kierkegaard, Heidegger rejected the possibility of understanding the world and humanity from the standpoint of a detached, rational spectator, such as the one advocated by his teacher, Edmund Husserl, the founder of phenomenology. Heidegger's "fundamental ontology" attempts to uncover the basic structures of human existence—such as concern and mood—in virtue of which knowledge and understanding are possible. He argues that a person's usual understanding is dictated by the anonymous "public" or "Them", and that individual authenticity—the prospect of which is experienced in the state of angst or anxiety—requires distancing oneself from "Them" and "resolutely" forging one's own "projects" and view of things. This sense of potential individuality is reinforced by the sober recognition of mortality, since a person's own death, and the way he or she faces up to it, is something that is uniquely his or her own.

Sartre: Sartre first gave the term "existentialism" general currency by using it for his own philosophy and by becoming the leading figure of a distinct movement in France that became internationally influential after World War II. Sartre's philosophy is explicitly atheistic and, at first glance, pessimistic, for he declared that human beings seek a rational basis for their lives that they are unable to achieve, so that human life is a "futile passion". Sartre nevertheless denied the charge of pessimism, regarding his existen-tialism as a form of humanism: by facing up to radical freedom and responsibility, instead of hiding from them in cowardly "bad faith", human beings are in a position to forge a new, more honest morality. In his later writings, Sartre tried to reconcile a morality of existential freedom with a Marxist analysis of society and history.

Existentialism and Theology: Although existentialist thought encompasses the uncompromising atheism of Nietzsche and Sartre and the agnosticism of Heidegger, its origin in the intensely religious philosophies of Pascal and Kier-kegaard foreshadowed its profound influence on 20th-century theology. The 20th-century German philosopher Karl Jaspers, although he rejected explicit religious doctrines, influenced contemporary theology through his preoccupation with transcendence and the limits of human experience. The German Protestant theologians Paul Tillich and Rudolf Bultmann, the French Roman Catholic theologian Gabriel Marcel, the Russian Orthodox philosopher Nikolay Berdyayev, and the German Jewish philosopher Martin Buber inherited many of Kierkegaard's concerns, especially the belief that a personal sense of authenticity and commitment is essential to religious faith.

Existentialism and Literature: A number of existentialist philosophers used literary forms to convey their thought, and existentialism has been as vital and as extensive a movement in literature as in philosophy. The 19th-century Russian novelist Fyodor Dosto-yevsky is probably the greatest existentialist literary figure. In *Notes from Underground* (1864), the alienated anti-hero rages against the optimistic assumptions of rationalist humanism. The view of human nature that emerges in this and others of Dostoyevsky's novels is that it is unpredictable and perversely self-destructive; only Christian love can save humanity from itself, but such love cannot be understood philosophically. As the character Alyosha says in *The Brothers Karamazov* (1879-1880), "we must love life more than the meaning of it".

In the 20th century, the novels of the Austrian Jewish writer Franz Kafka, such as *The Trial* (1925; trans. 1937) and *The Castle* (1926; trans. 1930), present isolated men confronting vast, elusive, menacing bureaucracies; Kafka's themes of anxiety, guilt, and solitude reflect the influence of Kierkegaard, Dostoyevsky, and Nietzsche. The influence of Nietzsche is also discernible in the novels of the French writer André Malraux and in the plays of Sartre. The work of the French writer Albert Camus is usually associated with existentialism because of the prominence in it of such themes as the apparent absurdity and futility of life, the indifference of the universe, and the necessity of engagement in a just cause. Existentialist themes are also reflected in the theatre of the absurd, notably in the plays of Samuel Beckett and Eugène Ionesco. In the United States, the influence of existentialism on literature has been more indirect and diffuse, but traces of Kierkegaard's thought can be found in the novels of Walker Percy and John Updike, and various existentialist themes are apparent in the work of such diverse writers as Norman Mailer, John Barth, and Arthur Miller.

Expected value, the net return it is reasonable to anticipate as the result of an action or investment. Expected value may be calculated as the sum of the products of each possible outcome and the relative likelihood that it will occur. *Recommended Reading*: James T. Fey, Elizabeth D. Phillips, and Catherine Anderson, What Do You Expect?: Probability & Expected Value (Seymour, 1997).

Experientialism, empiricism

Experiment, a trial or test of a scientific hypothesis or generalization by manipulation of environmental factors to observe whether what results agrees, or disagrees, with what the hypothesis predicts. See: hypothesis.

Experimentalism, empiricism, especially as applied to the methods of scientific inquiry.

Expert system, A computer program that contains a knowledge base and a set of algorithms or rules that infer new facts from knowledge and from incoming data.

An expert system is an artificial intelligence application that uses a knowledge base of human expertise to aid in solving problems. The degree of problem solving is based on the quality of the data and rules obtained from the human expert. Expert systems are designed to perform at a human expert level. In practice, they will perform both well below and well above that of an individual expert.

The expert system derives its answers by running the knowledge base through an inference engine, a software program that interacts with the user and processes the results from the rules and data in the knowledge base.

Expert systems are used in applications such as medical diagnosis, equipment repair, investment analysis, financial, estate and insurance planning, route scheduling for delivery vehicles, contract bidding, counselling for self-service customers, production control and training. [Difference from "knowledge-based system"?]

Explanandum, "that which needs to be explained", plural = explananda

Explanation, that which shows why features of the world are as they are found to be. People constantly ask questions about why things are as they are, and offer explanations, both in science and as part of everyday life. If someone asks, for example, why the sky is blue or why a bridge collapsed, he or she already knows that the sky is blue or that the bridge has collapsed, but does not yet understand why it is the case. A good explanation provides that understanding. It raises the question, however, of what is it to understand a phenomenon, over and above knowing that it occurs, that is, what is the nature of understanding? That is the central question for the philosophy of explanation.

This area of philosophy has been pursued since antiquity, with important discussions in the work of Plato and, especially, Aristotle, whose doctrine of the four causes (matter, form, goal, and source) was particularly influential. Explanation has also been an active area of philosophical research in the 20th century.

Philosophers have offered at least five different answers to this question. They have suggested that a good explanation facilitates an under-standing of a phenomenon: by giving reasons to believe it occurs; by reducing it to more familiar phenomena; by placing it in a unified general scheme; by showing that it somehow had to occur; or by giving its causes. The first two of these answers—the reason and familiarity views—focus on the states of mind that are supposed to constitute understanding. The other three answers—the unification, necessity, and causal views—focus instead on the structures in the world that it is claimed good explanations must reveal.

Reason: All five answers have something to offer, but they also all face various objections. Of the answers that focus on states of mind, the view that explanations provide reasons to believe that the phenomenon in question occurs fails to show how understanding why something happens goes beyond merely knowing that it does happen, since reasons are often already required for knowledge. There are excellent reasons for believing that the sky is blue, for example, but few people understand why it is blue, so giving reasons for belief is not enough for understanding.

Familiarity: The familiarity view is supported by the fact that surprising, unfamiliar phenomena often prompt questions, unlike what is already familiar. Being familiar, however, is not the same thing as being understood, and in science many explanations appear rather to account for very familiar phenomena, such as the colour of the sky, in terms of very unfamiliar entities and processes.

Unification: Among the answers that focus on the structure of the world, the unification view has a distinguished pedigree, going back to the ancient idea that explanations reveal the deep unity that underlies the superficial diversity of phenomena; but philosophers have found it very difficult to analyse the notion of unification. In addition, the unification view cannot readily account for what is known as the "asymmetry of explanation", that is, that causes explain effects but effects do not explain causes. Thus, the ice on the road may explain why the car skidded, but the skid does not explain why there was ice on the road.

Necessity: Like the unification view, the necessity view appeals to a notion that is very difficult to analyse. Necessity also seems to come in different strengths, and proponents of the necessity view differ among themselves over the question of just how necessary a phenomenon must be shown to be in order for it to be understood. Moreover, many everyday explanations seem to work perfectly well without revealing any deep necessity. For example, it is possible for someone to explain why he or she consulted *Encarta* encyclopedia without showing that he or she had to consult it.

Causality: The last of the five is the causal view, according to which phenomena are explained in terms of their causes. Such an account fits many explanations—to say that one thing happened because of another is very often to say that the first was caused by the second—and the causal view of explanation avoids many of the objections to the other views. The notion of causality, however, like those of unification and necessity, has as yet no uncontroversial philosophical analysis. Another difficulty is that there appear to be non-causal explanations. For example, a mathematician can explain why the square of the hypotenuse of a right-angled triangle is equal to the sum of the squares of the other two sides, even though mathematical facts do not have causes. Another likely source of non-causal explanations are those offered by philosophers themselves.

Explanation, a structure, act, or process that provides understanding.

Providing explanations is one of the most important activities in high level cognition. The nature of explanation and its role in thinking have been addressed by philos-ophers, psycho-logists, and artificial intelligence researchers; inference to the best explanation can be understood in terms of maximising coherence among competing hypotheses and evidence. *References*: Chi, M. T. H., Bassok, M., Lewis, M. W., Reimann, P., Glaser, R. (1989). Self-explanations: How students study and use examples in learning to solve problems. Cognitive Science, 13, 145-182. Harman, G. (1986). Change in view: Principles of reasoning. Cambridge, MA: MIT Press/Bradford Books. Kitcher, P., Salmon, W. (1989). Scientific explanation. Minneapolis: University of Minnesota Press. Leake, D. B. (1992). Evaluating explanations: A content theory. Hillsdale, NJ: Erlbaum. Mitchell, T., Keller, R., Kedar-Cabelli, S. (1986). Explanation-based generalisation: A unifying view. Machine Learning, 1, 47-80. Schank, R. C. (1986). Explanation patterns: Understanding mechanically and creatively. Hillsdale, NJ: Erlbaum. Thagard, P. (1992). Conceptual revolutions. Princeton: Princeton University Press.

Explicit memory, those memories which a subject is able to cite as being a memory of a particular event. See also implicit memory.

Exponential, 1. A function which raises some given constant (the "base") to the power of its argument. *I.e.*

$f x = b^x$

If no base is specified, e, the base of natural logarithms, is assumed.

2. exponential-time algorithm.

Exponential-time, The set or property of problems which can be solved by an exponential-time algorithm but for which no polynomial-time algorithm is known.

Expressionism, 1. aesthetics a kind of modernism which holds that the essential function of art is to provide a vehicle for the subjective, emotional expressions of the artist (at its most extreme and anti-representational, this doctrine takes the form of abstract expressionism).

2. in ethics, "expressionism" refers to the view that value judgments are mere expressions of emotion, although this is more commonly called emotivism. (References from abstractionism and modernism.)

Expression tree, The syntax tree of an expression.

Expressive use of language, communication that gives vent to feelings, attitudes, or emotions. Example: "Yeow-hot, hot, hot!."

Extension, 1. extension of a system

A system S' is an extension of S iff every theorem of S is a theorem of S'. It follows that every model of S' is a model of S.

2. finite extension of a system

System S' is a finite extension of S iff S' has all of the axioms of S, and differs from S only by adding a finite number of additional axioms that are wffs but not axioms of S. having spatial dimensions; the characteristic attribute of anything that occupies space, has shape, is tangible, moves, and is divisible into physical parts.

Extensional, having, or presupposing, a use of terms that is wholly determinedby what falls under them (in this actual world). The meaning of a term in the extensional sense is given just by listing, or somehow indicating what things are referred to by the term. The extensional meaning of "Evening Star," "morning Star," and "Venus" is the same because they all refer to one and the same planet, though the sense, or intension, might be different. Some philosphers (nominalists) have hoped that we could describe the world in wholly extensional terms. intension

Extensional equality, (Or extensionality). Functions, f and g are extensionally equal if and only if where "=" means both

$f\,x = g\,x$ for all x.

expressions fail to terminate (under some given reduction strategy) or they both terminate with the same basic value.

Two functions may be extensionally equal but not inter-convertible (neither is reducible to the other). *E.g.* $\backslash\, x.\ x+x$ and $\backslash\, x.\ 2*x$. See also observational equivalence, referential transpare-ncy.

Extensionality, the feature of a formal system in which the meaning of every non-logical term is wholly determined by its extension; this ensures that compound statments of the system will be truth-functional. extensional equality

Extension-intension, distinction between ways in which the meaning of a term may be regarded: its extension, or denotation, is the collection ofthings to which the term applies; its intension, or connota-tion, is the set of features those things are presumed to have in common. *Recommended Reading*: D. Alan Cruse, Meaning in Language: An Introduction to Semantics and Pragmatics (Oxford, 2000).

Externalism, externalists hold that there are mental events that do not supervene merely on physical events internal to the agent's body, but supervene on environmental events as well. Also known as antiindividualism.

For some externalists, mental events, namely those in which concepts are involved, can be seen to be partially constituted by the entities that those concepts are concepts of. This intuition gets pumped by the famous Twin Earth thought experiments of Putnam (1975) and Burge (1979), which I assume are familiar enough to not require recounting. Suffice it to mention that the upshot of the experiments is that the Earthling Pete and his molecule for molecule Twin Earth counterpart Twin Pete have divergent mental characteristics solely in virtue of their divergent environments: Pete's "water" thoughts are about H2O whereas Twin Pete's "water" thoughts are about XYZ.

Externalism does not apply solely to natural kind concepts like "water". Externalist arguments, using Twin Earth style thought experiments, have been advanced for all sorts of concepts. Further, externalist arguments have also been advanced for non-conceptual mental states, so externalism can apply to any contentful mental state. Some have advanced arguments for the ext-ernalist individuation of qualia on the grounds that they are representational in character (Dretske 1995; Tye 1995).

It is important to note that Burge, in formulating his externalist arguments, considered them as arguments explicitly against, among other things, functionalism (Burge 1979). However, the functionalism Burge had in mind was a strictly internalist functionalism—he left as an open issue whether a functionalism that quantified over environmental as well as bodily states of cognizers could be viable. In fact, the dominant reaction in the literature to Burge's arguments has been to retain functionalism, but allow that events in one's environment are part of the causal topology that constitutes mental states. *References*: Dretske, F. (1995). Naturalizing the Mind. Cambridge, MA, MIT Press. Putnam, H. (1975). Mind, language, and reality. Cambridge, Cambridge University Press. Burge, T. (1979). Individualism and the mental. Midwest Studies in Philosophy IV: Studies in Metaphysics. P. French, et al. Minneapolis, University of Minnesota Press. Tye, M. (1995). Ten problems of consciousness: A representational theory of the phenomenal mind. Cambridge, MA, MIT Press. See supervenience, internalism.

Extrinsic, bearing some relation to something else. See intrinsic - extrinsic.

Fact, The kind of clause used in logic programming which has no subgoals and so is always true (always succeeds). *E.g.*

wet(water).
male(denis).

This is in contrast to a rule which only succeeds if all its subgoals do. Rules usually contain logic variables, facts rarely do, except for oddities like "equal (X,X).".

Facticity, The contingent conditions of an individual human life. In theexist-entialism of Heidegger and Sartre, facticity includes all of the concrete details-time and place of birth, for example, along with the prospect of death-against the background of which human freedom is to be exercized. *Recommended Reading*: Martin Heidegger, Ontology: The Hermeneutics of Facticity, tr. by John Van Buren (Indiana, 1999) and Alterity and Facticity: New Perspectives on Husserl, ed. by Natalie Depraz and Dan Zahavi (Kluwer, 1998).

Factor, A quantity which is multiplied by another quantity. See coefficient of X. See also divisor.

Fact-value, Distinction between assertions about how things really are(fact) and how things ought to be (value). Drawn by Hume, but also defended by Stevenson, Hare, and other ethical non-cognitivists, the distinction is usually taken to entail that claims about moral obligation can never be validly inferred from the truth of factual premises alone. It follows that people who agree completely on the simple description of a state of affairs may nevertheless differ with respect to the appropriate action to take in response to it. *Recommended Reading*: David Hume, An Enquiry Concerning thePrinciples of Morals (Oxford, 1996) and Charles L. Stevenson, Ethics and Language (Yale, 1944).

Failure, The inability of a system or system component to perform a required function within specified limits. A failure may be produced when a fault is encountered.

Fallacy, A mistake in reasoning; an argument that fails to provide adequate logical support for the truth of its conclusion, yet appears convincing orpersuasive in some other way. Common examples include both formal fallacies (structural errors in deductive logic) and informal fallacies (efforts to persuade by non-rational appeals). *Recommended Reading*: Nicholas Capaldi, The Art of Deception: An Introduction to Critical Thinking (Prometheus, 1987); T.Edward

Damer, Attacking Faulty Reasoning: A Practical Guide to Fallacy-Free Arguments (Wadsworth, 2000); and Douglas Walton, A Pragmatic Theory of Fallacy (Alabama, 1995).

Fallacy, in logic, an error in reasoning, or more precisely, a mistake made in the process of moving from the premises of an argument to the conclusion. As a result of the fallacy, the premises do not justify the conclusion.

In logic, a distinction is made between formal and informal fallacies. A formal fallacy is one in which the argument violates a rule of the logical system of which that argument is a part. Formal fallacies may be illustrated in a variety of ways. In arguments in which the first premise is a hypothetical statement, one might commit the fallacy of *affirming the consequent.* For example, it may be stated that if a person is an astronaut, then that person is well trained. If, however, this is followed by the statement that if Bob is well trained, then Bob must be an astronaut, the fallacy of affirming the consequent has been committed.

In arguments in which the first premise is a disjunction (an *either-or* statement), one might commit the fallacy of *affirming a disjunct.* For example, suppose it is stated that either Susan or Joan will attend the meeting. Susan will attend (this premise affirms one of the disjuncts in the initial premise); therefore, Joan will not attend. (In order for this to be a valid form of argument, the major premise would have to read "either ... or ..."; *but not both*—thus eliminating the ambiguity of the disjunctive expression by replacing it with a strong disjunction.)

Traditional Aristotelian logic is concerned with syllogistic reasoning. This is a form of deductive argument that consists of a major premise, a minor premise, and a conclusion. An example of a syllogism is as follows: All virtues are praiseworthy; generosity is a virtue; therefore generosity is praiseworthy. Various rules govern proper syllogistic inferences; if any of the rules are violated, a formal fallacy has been committed.

Informal fallacies are not mistakes in the formal structure of an argument; rather, they are rooted either in the failure of the evidence to be relevant to the conclusion or in some linguistic ambiguity. Informal fallacies of relevance include defending a conclusion by appealing to force, pity, authority, or popular belief. Begging the question or assuming in the premises what is to be proved is also an informal fallacy of relevance. Fallacies of ambiguity include erroneous conclusions based on the equivocal use of language. Consider the argument: all laws are the product of legislative activity; Newton discovered several laws; therefore, Newton discovered several products of legislative activity. This erroneous conclusion is rooted in the ambiguous use of the word *law* as it appears in the two premises.

Fallibilism, Belief that some or all claims to knowledge could be mistaken. Although Peirce limited the application of fallibilism to the empiricalstatements of natural science, Quine extended it by challenging the notion that any proposition can be genuinely analytic. Unlike a skeptic, the fallibilist may not demand suspension of belief in the absence of certainty. *Recommended Reading*: Charles S. Peirce: Selected Writings, ed. by Philip P. Wiener (Dover, 1980); Charles S. Peirce and the Philosophy of Science, ed. by Edward C. Moore (Alabama, 1993); Roger F. Gibson, Enlightened Empiricism: AnExamination of W.V. Quine's Theory of Knowledge (Florida, 1988); and Arthur Franklin Stewart, Elements of Knowledge: Pragmatism, Logic, and Inquiry Vanderbilt, 1997). See also probabilism.

False cause, the informal fallacy of affirming the presence of a causal relationship on anything less than adequate grounds. Post hoc, ergo propter hoc is a common variety of this fallacy. *Example*: "After drinking milk for twenty years, Melanie became addicted to cocaine. Therefore, drinking milk caused her cocaine addiction".

Falsifiability, A property of any proposition for which it is possible to specify a set of circumstances the occurrence of which would demonstrate that the proposition is false. According to Karl Popper, falsifiability is thecrucial feature of scientific hypotheses: beliefs that can never be tested against the empirical evidence are dogmatic. *Recommended Reading*: Karl R. Popper, Logic of Scientific Discovery (Routledge, 1992) and Conjectures and Refutations: The Growth of Scientific Knowledge (Routledge, 1992).

Farabi, al- (c. 873-950), also known as Alfarabius, the first-known philosopher in the Islamic world to uphold the primacy of philosophical truth over revelation, claiming that, contrary to the beliefs of various other religions, philosophical truths are the same throughout the world. He was born in Farab, Transoxiana (now Uzbekistan), of Turkish parentage. He studied first in Khorasan (in Iran) and then in Baghdad, where his teachers were Syriac Christians well acquainted with Greek philosophy. He eventually came to the court of Sayf al-Dawla, the ruler of Aleppo in Syria. Al-Farabi was one of the earliest Islamic thinkers to transmit to the Arab world the doctrines of Plato and Aristotle (which he considered essentially identical), thereby greatly influencing such later Islamic philosophers as Avicenna and Averroës.

Influenced in his metaphysical views by the Neoplatonism of Plotinus, Al-Farabi posited a Supreme Being who had created the world through the exercise of rational intelligence. He believed this same rational faculty to be the sole part of the human being that is immortal, and thus he set as the paramount human goal the development of that rational faculty. Al-Farabi gave considerably more attention to political theory than did any other Islamic philosopher, adapting the Platonic system (as developed in Plato's *Republic* and *Laws*) to the contemporary Muslim political situation in *The Perfect City*.

Alfarabius formulated as an ideal a universal religion of which all other existing religions are considered symbolic expressions. Of his 100 or so works, many have been lost, including his commentaries on Aristotle. Many others have been preserved only in medieval Latin translation. In addition to his philosophical writings, he compiled a catalogue of the sciences, the first Muslim work to attempt a systematization of human knowledge. He also made a contribution to musical theory in his "great book of music".

Farabi al-Abu Nasr, Persian Islamic neoplatonist (872-950) who employed Aristotelian logic in support of his arguments for the existence of god and used Plato's Republic as the model for his own description of civil society in Principles of Citizens of the Virtuous City. *Recommended Reading*: Alfarabi: 'Philosophy of Plato and Aristotle', tr. by Muhin Mahdi, Charles E. Butt-erworth, an Thomas L. Pangle (Cornell, 2001) and Ian Richard Netton, Al-Farabi and His School (Curzon, 2000).

Fatalism, Belief that every event is bound to happen as it does no matter what we do about it. Fatalism is the most extreme form of causal determinism, since it denies that human actions have any causal efficacy. Any determinist holds that indigestion is the direct consequence of natural causes, but the fatalist believes that it is bound occur whether or not I eat spicy foods. *Recommended Reading*: Jordan Howard Sobel, Puzzles for the Will: Fatalism, Newcomb and Samarra, Determinism and Omniscience (Toronto, 1998) and Ted Honderich, Consequences of Determinism: A Theory of Determinism (Clarendon, 1990).

Fatalism, doctrine that all events occur according to a fixed and inevitable destiny that is neither controlled nor affected by the individual will. Fatalism is frequently confused with determinism, the doctrine that events are determined by the events that precede them. According to fatalism, however, preceding events have no causal connection with the events that follow. A fated event takes place not according to a natural law but in accordance with some mysterious decree issued by some mysterious power, perhaps ages before. Determinism, in its tenet that every event has its determining conditions in its immediate antecedents, which may include the human will, is consistent with a belief in the efficacy of the human will, but fatalism is not.

Both fatalism and determinism, thus distinguished from each other, should likewise be distinguished from predestination. Predestination is determination plus the belief in a supernatural power that has established a determining natural sequence of causes. Fatalism is a belief in a supernatural power that predetermines without recourse to natural order.

Fatalism appeared among the ancient Hebrews, Greeks, and Romans and is particularly prevalent today among Muslims. In the modern West, though, it has retained a degree of acceptance only where science has not had a controlling influence in developing the doctrine of causality.

Fault, 1. A manifestation of an error in software. A fault, if encountered, may cause a failure. 2. page fault.

Feature, 1. A good property or behaviour (as of a program). Whether it was intended or not is immaterial.

2. An intended property or behaviour (as of a program). Whether it is good or not is immaterial (but if bad, it is also a misfeature).

3. A surprising property or behaviour; in particular, one that is purposely inconsistent because it works better that way—such an inconsistency is therefore a feature and not a bug. This kind of feature is sometimes called a miswart.

4. A property or behaviour that is gratuitous or unnecessary, though perhaps also impressive or cute. For

example, one feature of Common LISP's "format" function is the ability to print numbers in two different Romannumeral formats (see bells, whistles, and gongs).

5. A property or behaviour that was put in to help someone else but that happens to be in your way.

6. A bug that has been documented. To call something a feature sometimes means the author of the program did not consider the particular case, and that the program responded in a way that was unexpected but not strictly incorrect. A standard joke is that a bug can be turned into a feature simply by documenting it (then theoretically no one can complain about it because it's in the manual), or even by simply declaring it to be good. "That's not a bug, that's a feature!" is a common catch-phrase. Apparently there is a Volkswagen Beetle in San Francisco whose license plate reads "FEATURE". See also feetch feetch, creeping featurism, wart, green lightning.

The relationship among bugs, features, misfeatures, warts and miswarts might be clarified by the following hypothetical exchange between two hackers on an airliner:

A: "This seat doesn't recline."

B: "That's not a bug, that's a feature. There is an emergency exit door built around the window behind you, and the route has to be kept clear."

A: "Oh. Then it's a misfeature; they should have increased the spacing between rows here."

B: "Yes. But if they'd increased spacing in only one section it would have been a wart - they would've had to make nonstandard-length ceiling panels to fit over the displaced seats."

A: "A miswart, actually. If they increased spacing throughout they'd lose several rows and a chunk out of the profit margin. So unequal spacing would actually be the Right Thing."

B: "Indeed."

"Undocumented feature" is a common euphemism for a bug.

7. An attribute or function of a class in Eiffel.

Feedback, Part of a system output presented at its input. Feedback may be unintended. When used as a design feature, the output is usually transformed by passive components which attenuate it in some manner; the result is then presented at the system input.

Feedback is positive or negative, depending on the sign with which a positive change in the original input reappears after transformation. Negative feedback was invented by Black to stabilise vacuum tube amplifiers. The behaviour becomes largely a function of the feedback transformation and onlyminimally a function of factors such as transistor gain which are imperfectly known.

Positive feedback can lead to instability; it finds wide application in the construction of oscillators.

Feedback can be used to control a system, as in feedback control.

Feigl Herbert, Austrian-American philosopher (1902-1988). A member of theVienna Circle of logical positivists, Feigl later taught at the University of Minnesota. He defended a materialist account of the human mind in The "Mental" and the "Physical" (1958). *Recommended Reading*: Herbert Feigl: Inquiries & Provocations,

Selected Writings 1929 to 1974, ed. by Robert S. Cohen (Kluwer, 1980) and Wilfrid Sellars, Empiricism and the Philosophy of Mind, ed. by Robert Brandom (Harvard, 1997).

Feminism, Commitment to the abolition of male domination in human society. Feminists differ widely in their accounts of the origins of patriarchy, their analyses of its most common consequences, and their concrete proposals for overcoming it, but all share in the recognition that the subordination ofwomen to men in our culture is indefensible and eliminable. Many feminist philosophers oppose Cartesian dualism, scientific objectivity, and traditional theories of moral obligation as instances of masculine over-reliance on reason. Serious attention to the experiences of women would offer a more adequate account of human life. *Recommended Reading*: The Cambridge Companion to Feminism in Philosophy, ed. by Miranda Fricker and Jennifer Hornsby (Cambridge, 2000); The Second Wave: A Reader in Feminist Theory, ed. by Linda Nicholson (Routledge, 1997); A Companion to Feminist Philosphy, ed. by Alison M. Jaggar and Iris Marion Young (Blackwell, 1999); Seyla Benhabib, Judith Butler, Drucilla Cornell, Nancy Fraser, and Linda J. Nicholson, Feminist Contentions: A Philosophical Exchange (Routledge, 1995); Sandra Harding, Whose Science? Whose Knowledge?: Thinking from Women's Lives (Cornell, 1991); andEva Feder Kittay, Love's Labor: Essays on Women, Equality, and Dependency (Routledge, 1998).

Ferio, Name given by medieval logicians to any categorical syllogism whose standard form may be designated as EIO-1. *Example*: No mendicant friars are wealthy patrons of the arts, but some medieval philosophers are mendicant friars, so some medieval philosophers are not wealthy patrons of the arts.

This is one of the fifteen forms of valid syllogism.

Ferison, Name given by medieval logicians to any categorical syllogism whose standard form is EIO-3. Example: Since no people who admire Marx are political conservatives and some people who admire Marx are South Carolinians, it follows that some South Carolinians are not political conservatives. This is another of the fifteen forms in which syllogisms are always valid.

Festino, Name given by medieval logicians to a categorical syllogism with the standard form EIO-2. *Example*: No people deserving of our admiration and praise are inveterate liars, but some wealthy industrialists are inveterate liars; therefore, some wealthy industrialists are not people deserving of our admiration and praise. This is one of the fifteen forms in which syllogisms are always valid.

Feuerbach Ludwig Andreas, German philosopher (1804-1872). As a follower of Kant and critic of idealism, Feuerbach supposed that Hegel had mistakenly inverted the relationship between individuals and the Absolute. In Das Wesen des Christientums (The Essence of Christianity) (1841) he argued that religion is a projection of human values onto the concept of the divine. Eliminating the vestiges of theological dependence, Feuerbach maintained in Grunds"tze der Philosophie der Zukunft (Principles of the Philosophy of the Future) (1843), will make it possible to avoid alienation and enjoy a thoroughly humanistic life. *Recommended*

Reading: Van A. Harvey, Feuerbach and the Interpretation of Religion (Cambridge, 1997).

Feyerabend Paul, Austrian-American philosopher (1924-1994). An outspoken opponent of Popper's philosophy of science, Feyerabend argued in Against Method (1975) that there is no privileged method for the confirmation of scientific theories. Thus, Feyerabend defended cultural pluralism and "scientific anarchism" in Science in a Free Society (1978), Farewell to Reason (1987), and Three Dialogues on Knowledge (1991). *Recommended Reading*: Killing Time: The Autobiography of Paul Feyerabend (Chicago, 1996); John Preston, Feyerabend: Philosophy, Science and Society (Polity, 1997); and The WorstEnemy of Science: Essays in Memory of Paul Feyerabend, ed. By John Preston and Gonzalo Munevar (Oxford, 2000).

Fichte Johann Gottlieb, German philosopher (1762-1814). In Versuch einer Kritik aller Offenbarung (Critique of all Revelation) (1792) Fichte turned the critical philosophy of Kant into full-fledged idealism by emphasizing the metaphysical reality of the noumenal self as well as its moral autonomy. His amplification of this theme in Grundlage der gesamten Wissenschaftslehre (Foundations of the Science of Knowledge) (1794-95) and Darstellung der Wissenschaftslehre (Outlines of the Doctrine of Knowledge) (1810) greatly influenced Schelling and Hegel. Die Bestimmung des Menschen (The Vocation of Man) (1800) is Fichte's effort to defend himself against the charge of atheism. Fichte encouraged the development of German nationalism in opposition to Napoleonic threats in Der geschlossene Handelsstaat (The Closed Commercial State) (1800) and Reden an die deutsche Nation (Speeches to the German Nation) (1808). *Recommended Reading*: Fichtes Werke, ed. by Immanuel H. Fichte (de Gruyter, 1971); George J. Seidel, Fichte's Wissenschaftslehre of 1794: A Commentary on Part I (Purdue, 1993); Gunter Zoller, Fichte's Transcendental Philosophy: The Original Duplicity of Intelligence and Will (Cambridge, 1998); and Frederick Neuhouser, Fichte's Theory of Subjectivity (Cambridge, 1990).

Ficino Marsillio, (Christian thought, ethics) Italian philosopher (1433-1499), whose translations into Latin made the works of Plato and Plotinus accessible during the Renaissance. Despite his fascination with myth and magic, Ficino endorsed a synthesis of neoplatonic thought with the doctrines of Christianity. *Recommended Reading*: Marsilio Ficino, Commentary on Plato's Symposium on Love (Spring, 2000); Marsilio Ficino, Three Books on Life, ed. by Carol V. Kaske, John R. Clark (Medieval & Renaissance, 1989); Renaissance Philosophy of Man, ed. By Ernst Cassirer, Paul Oskar Kristeller, and John H. Randall (Chicago, 1956).

Fideism, Belief that religious doctrines rest exclusively on faith (Lat. Fides), instead of on reason. In various forms, fideism was maintained by philosophers as diverse as Pascal, Bayle, and Kierkegaard. *Recommended Reading*: Delbert J. Hanson, Fideism and Hume's Philosophy: Knowledge, Religion and Metaphysics (Peter Lang, 1993) and Terence Penelhum, God and Skepticism: A Study in Skepticism and Fideism (Reidel, 1983).

Figure, A systematic way of indicating the position of the middle term in a categorical syllogism.

Filmer Robert, English political philosopher (1588-1653). Filmer's posthumously-published defense of a divinelyordained hereditary monarchy in Patriarcha, or the Natural Power of Kings (1680) was attacked at length in the first of Locke's Two Treatises of Civil Government.

Final cause, the ultimate purpose, end, or goal of a thing; one of Aristotle's four causes. Explanations of how a thing is that rely on reference to its end are often called "teleological;" their use fell into disfavor during the Renaissance. *Recommended Reading*: Aristotle, Physics, tr. by Robin Waterfield and David Bostock (Oxford, 1999).

First-order, Not higher-order.

First-order logic, The language describing the truth of mathematical formulas. Formulas describe properties of terms and have a truth value. The following are atomic formulas:

True False p(t1,..tn) where t1,..,tn are terms and p is a predicate.

If F1, F2 and F3 are formulas and v is a variable then the following are compound formulas:

F1 ^ F2 conjunction - true if both F1 and F2 are true,

F1 V F2 disjunction - true if either or both are true,

F1 => F2 implication—true if F1 is false or F2 is true, F1 is the antecedent, F2 is the consequent (sometimes written with a thin arrow),

F1 <= F2 true if F1 is true or F2 is false,

F1 == F2 true if F1 and F2 are both true or both false (normally written with a three line equivalence symbol)

~F1 negation—true if f1 is false (normally written as a dash '–' with a shorter vertical line hanging from its right hand end).

For all v. F universal quantification—true if F is true for all values of v (normally written with an inverted A).

Exists v. F existential quantification—true if there exists some value of v for which F is true. (Normally written with a reversed E).

The operators ^ V => <= == ~ are called connectives. "For all" and "Exists" are quantifiers whose scope is F. A term is a mathematical expression involving numbers, operators, functions and variables.

The "order" of a logic specifies what entities "For all" and "Exists" may quantify over. First-order logic can only quantify over sets of atomic propositions. (*E.g.* For all p. p => p). Second-order logic can quantify over functions on propositions, and higher-order logic can quantify over any type of entity. The sets over which quantifiers operate are usually implicit but can be deduced from well-formedness constraints.

In first-order logic quantifiers always range over ALL the elements of the domain of discourse. By contrast, second-order logic allows one to quantify over subsets of M. ["The Realm of First-Order Logic", Jon Barwise, Handbook of Mathematical Logic (Barwise, ed., North Holland, NYC, 1977)]. See also predicate logic

First-order predicate logic, predicate logic

First-order theory, A formal system of first-order predicate logic in which (1) there may be countably many new individual constants in the formal language, provided they are effectively enumerable, and (2) there may be countably many proper axioms to supplement the logical axioms.

First-order theory with identity, A first-order theory with $(x)(x=x)$ as an axiom, and the following axiom schema, $[(x=y)$

$\Rightarrow (A$

$\Rightarrow A'))]^{\wedge}c$,

when $B^{\wedge}c$ is an arbitrary closure of B, and when A' differs from A only in that y may replace any free occurrence of x in A so long as y is free wherever it replaces x (y need not replace every occurrence of x in A). See identity, predicate logic with identity

Fiske, John (1842-1901), American philosopher and historian, whose writings on philosophy were responsible for spreading the ideas of the British social philosopher Herbert Spencer and the originator of the theory of evolution, Charles Darwin, in the United States. Originally named Edmund Fisk Green, he was born in Hartford, Connecticut, and educated at Harvard University. In 1864 he was admitted to the bar, but soon gave up his legal pursuits and began writing for periodicals. In 1869 he gave a series of lectures on positivism at Harvard and the following year he was appointed history tutor at the university, going on to become non-resident Professor of American history at Washington University, St Louis, in 1884.

Fiske claimed as his contribution to the doctrine of evolution his detection of the part played by the longer period of infancy in human beings than in animals. His works include *Darwinism and Other Essays* (1879), *Excursions of an Evolutionist* (1884), *The Destiny of Man Viewed in the Light of His Origin* (1884), and *The Idea of God as Affected by Modern Knowledge* (1885).

During his lifetime Fiske was known primarily as a historian. His works in that field constitute a nearly complete colonial history of America.

Five ways, the attempts to prove the existence of god included in Thomas Aquinas's Summa Theologica I, 2, 3. They include three versions of the cosmological argument, an argument from moral perfection, and the teleological argument. *Recommended Reading*: Thomas Aquinas, Selected Philosophical Writings, tr. by Timothy McDermott (Oxford, 1998); Basic Writings of Saint Thomas Aquinas: God and the Order of Creation, ed. by Anton Charles Pegis (Hackett, 1997); and Anthony Kenny, The Five Ways: Saint Thomas Aquinas' Proofs of God's Existence (Routledge, 1991).

Fix, 1. The fixed point combinator. Called *Y* in combinatory logic. Fix is a higher-order function which returns a fixed point of its argument (which is a function).

fix:: (*a* -> *a*) -> *a*

fix *f* = *f* (fix *f*)

Which satisfies the equation

fix *f* = *x* such that *f x* = *x*.

Somewhat surprisingly, fix can be defined as the non-recursive lambda abstraction:

fix = \ *h*. (\ *x*. *h* (*x x*)) (\ *x*. *h* (*x* *x*))

Since this involves self-application, it has an infinite type. A function defined by

f x1.. *xN* = *E*

can be expressed as

f = *fix* (\ *f*. \ x1... \ *xN*. *E*)

= (\ *f*. \ x1... *xN*. *E*)

(*fix* (\ *f*. \ x1... \ *xN*. *E*))

= *let f* = (*fix* (\ *f*. \ x1... \ *xN*. *E*))

in \ x1... \xN. E

If f does not occur free in E (*i.e.* it is not recursive) then this reduces to simply

f = \ *x*1... \ *xN. E*

In the case where N = 0 and f is free in E, this defines an infinite data object, *e.g.*

ones = fix (\ ones. 1: ones)

= (\ ones. 1: ones) (fix (\ ones. 1: ones))

= 1: (fix (\ ones. 1: ones))

= 1: 1:...

Fix *f* is also sometimes written as mu *f* where mu is the Greek letter or alternatively, if *f* = \ *x*. E, written as mu *x*. E.

Compare quine.

2. bug fix.

Flourishing, eudaimonia

Folk-psychology, the common-sense conceptual framework that we, as human beings, employ to understand, predict, and explain the behaviour of otherhumans and higher animals. *References*: Folk Psychology Biblio Horgan, T. & Woodward, J. 1985. Folk psychology is here to stay. Philosophical Review 94:197-225. Reprinted in (W. Lycan, ed) Mind and Cognition (Blackwell, 1990). Jackson, F. Pettit, P. 1990. In defense of folk psychology. Philosophical Studies 59:31-54.

Force-appeal to, (dialectic, logic, rethoric, method, argument), (argumentum ad baculum) the informal fallacy of securing agreement by threatening adverse consequences in case of disagreement. *Example*: "Anyone who believes that the government has exceeded its proper authority under the constitution will be subjected to severe harassment by the provincial police. Therefore, the government has not exceeded its authority." *Recommended Reading*: Douglas Walton, Scare Tactics: Arguments That Appeal to Fear and Threats (Kluwer, 2000).

Formal cause, structural features or attributes of a thing; one of the four causes. *Recommended Reading*: Aristotle, Physics, tr. by Robin Waterfield and David Bostock (Oxford, 1999).

Formal fallacy, induction, demostration, proof, reason, knowledge, aristotelian-ism, Aquinas, scholasticism, proposition, logic of Portroyal, semantics; Invalid arguments that may appear convincing at first glance because they closely resemble legitimate patterns of reasoning. Commonly occurring formal fallacies include: (1) four terms (quaeternio terminorum), (2) undistributed middle, (3) illicit major, (4) illicit minor, (5) exclusive premises, (6) affirmative conclusion from negative premises, (7) existential, (8) affirming the consequent, (9) denying the antecedent, (10) converting the conditional, (11) negating the antecedent and the consequent, and affirming the alternative.

Formalism, the term usually refers to an over-emphasis in ethics or aesthetics on form over content. In this sense, both deontologism in ethics and classicism in aesthetics might be described as varieties of formalism. More recently, formalism has been used to describe a twentieth-century view in aesthetics, art history, and literary criticism that values artistic form over artistic content and that is therefore opposed both to representationalism and realism in the arts.

Formal language, an alphabet and grammar. The alphabet is a set of uninterpreted symbols. The grammar is a set of rules that determine which strings of symbols from the alphabet will be acceptable (grammatically correct or well-formed) in that language. The grammar may also be conceived as a set of functions taking strings of symbols as input and returning either "yes" or "no" as output. The rules of the grammar are also called formation rules. See decidable system, finitary formal system, wff

Forms, for Plato, the ideal Archetypes or patterns according to which all things are constructed. These are grasped by rational insight—which Plato held to be a kind of recollection—and not by sensory perception. The Forms, according to Plato, intelligible realities which are transcend the material world of sensible objects which somehow resemble or participate in them: they are ideals which material or sensible things imitate or aspire to. For Aristotle forms or essences are immanent aspirations—teleological principles of development—in the things themselves.

The pure objects of mathematical and dialectical knowledge. In the vigorous realism of Plato's middle dialogues, necessary truths are taken to involve knowledge of eternal, unchanging Forms (or Ideas). Particular things in the realm of appearance are beautiful, or equal, or good only insofar as they participate in the universal Forms of Beauty, Equality, or the Good. The doctrine of Forms was attacked in Plato's own Parmenides and by Aristotle. *Recommended Reading*: The Dialogues of Plato, ed. by Eric Segal (Bantam, 1986); Gail Fine, On Ideas: Aristotle's Criticism of Plato's Theory of Forms (Clarendon, 1995); and John Malcolm, Plato on the Self-Predication of Forms: Early and Middle Dialogues (Clarendon, 1991).

Foucault Michel, French philosopher (1926-1984). As he explained in Folie etderaison (Madness and Civilization) (1961), Le Mots et les choses (The Order of Things) (1966), and L'Archeologie du savoir (The Archaeology of Knowledge) (1969), Foucault used historical investigations as a method of exposing how the structure of contemporary thought is shaped by conventional social institutions and practices, including especially the forceful marginalization of deviant behavior by discursive rationality. Surveiller et Punir (Discipline and Punish) (1975) and the unfinished Histoire de la sexualite (History of Sexuality: Introduction, Care of the Self, and The Use of Pleasure) (1976, 1984) focus on the use of social power to circumscribe and control subjective human experience. Genuine freedom, Foucault maintained, can be achieved only through detachment from what is expected of us as "normal." *Recommended Reading*: The Foucault Reader, ed. by Paul Rabinow (Random House, 1984); Michel Foucault, The Birth of the Clinic: An Archaeology of Medical Perception (Vintage, 1994); James Miller, The Passion of Michel Foucault (Harvard, 2000); Barry Smart, Michel Foucault (Routledge, 1993); The Cambridge Companion to Foucault, ed. by Gary Gutting (Cambridge, 1994); Hubert L. Dreyfus, Michel Foucault: Beyond Structuralism and Hermeneutics (Chicago, 1983); Feminist Interpretations of Michel Foucault, ed. by Susan J. Hekman (Penn. State, 1996); and Gary Gutting, Michel Foucault's Archaeology of Scientific Reason (Cambridge, 1989).

Foucher Simon, French philosopher

(1644-1696), who offered trenchantcriticisms of Cartesianism, Malebranche, and Leibniz. The skeptical arguments of Foucher's Dissertation sur la recherché de la verite (On the Search for Truth) (1673) influenced the rejection of the primary / secondary quality distinction by Bayle and Berkeley. *Recommended Reading*: Richard A. Watson and Marjorie Grene, Malebranche's First and Last Critics: Simon Foucher andDortous De Mairan (Southern Illinois, 1995).

Foundation, the axiom of foundation states that the membership relation is well founded, *i.e.* that any non-empty collection *Y* of sets has a member *y* which is disjoint from *Y*. This rules out sets which contain themselves (directly or indirectly).

Fourier Jean-Baptiste Joseph, French Egyptologist and mathematician (1768-1830). In his Theorie analytique de la chaleur (The Analytical Theory of Heat) (1822) Fourier demonstrated the use of infinite series for calculation of the conduction of heat. Accompanying Napolean's army into Egypt, he devoted his later years to archaeological research and occasional essays. *Recommended Reading*: John Herivel, Joseph Fourier: The Man and the Physicist (Clarendon, 1984); Who Is Fourier?: A Mathematical Adventure, tr. by Alan Gleason (Blackwell, 1995); Morris Kline, Mathematical Thought from Ancient to Modern Times (Oxford, 1990); M. J. Lighthill, An introduction to Fourier analysis and generalized functions (Cambridge, 1958).

Four terms-fallacy of, (quaternio terminorum)—the formal fallacy committed in a categorical syllogism that is invalid because it employs more than three distinct categorical terms. Example: "All managers are politicians,and all sybarites are administrators, so all sybarites are politicians."

Fragile, brittle

Frankfurt school, A community of German thinkers in the Institut fuer Sozialforschung (Institute for Social Research) who developed the methodology of critical theory. Prominent members include Hork-heimer, Adorno, Benjamin, Marcuse, Fromm, and Habermas. *Recommended Reading*: The Essential Frankfurt School Reader, ed. by Andrew Arato and Eike Gebhardt (Continuum, 1982); Martin Jay, The Dialectical Imagination: A History of the Frankfurt School and the Institute of Social Research 1923-1950 (California, 1996); and Rolf Wiggerhaus, The Frankfurt School: Its History, Theories, and Political Significance, tr. by Michael Robertson (MIT, 1995).

Freedom, (Lat. libertas; Ger. Freiheit)—the human capacity to act (or not to act) as we choose or prefer, without any external compulsion or restraint. Freedom in this sense is usually regarded as a presupposition of moral responsibility: the actions for which I may be praised or blamed, rewarded or punished, are just those which I perform freely. The further question of whether choice-the volition or will to act is itself free or subject to ordinary causality raises the issue of determinism in human conduct. But most modern philosophers have held that (internal) determination of the will by desire or impulse does not diminish the relevant sense of moral responsibility. *Recommended Reading*: Free Will, ed. by Gary Watson (Oxford, 1983); Ilham Dilman, Free Will: An Historical and Philosophical Introduction (Routledge, 1999); Robert Kane, The Significance of Free Will (Oxford, 1998); Laura Waddell Ekstrom, Free Will: A Philosophical Study (Westview, 2000);Graham McFee,

Free Will (McGill, 2001); and Daniel C. Dennett, Elbow Room (MIT, 1984).

Free variable, 1. A variable referred to in a function, which is not anargument of the function. In lambda-calculus, x is a bound variable in the term $M = \backslash x$. T, and a free variable of T. We say x is bound in M and free in T. If T contains a subterm $\backslash x$. U then x is rebound in this term. This nested, inner binding of x is said to "shadow" the outer binding. Occurrences of x in U are free occurrences of the new x.

Variables bound at the top level of a program are technically free variables within the terms to which they are bound but are often treated specially because they can be compiled as fixed addresses. Similarly, an identifier bound to a recursive function is also technically a free variable within its own body but is treated specially.

A closed term is one containing no free variables. See also closure, lambda lifting, scope.

2. In predicate logic, an individual variable at least one of whose occurrences in a wff does not lie within the scope of a quantifier on the same letter. Because other occurrences may be bound, a variable may be both free and bound in the same wff.

3. free occurrence of a variable

Any occurrence of an individual variable not within the scope of a quantifier on the same letter. See bound variable, closure

Free Will, power or ability of the human mind to choose a course of action or make a decision without being subject to restraints imposed by antecedent causes, by necessity, or by divine predetermination. A completely free act is itself a cause and not an effect; it is beyond causal sequence or the law of causality. The question of human beings' ability to determine their actions is important in philosophy, particularly in metaphysics and ethics, and in theology. Generally, the extreme doctrine in which freedom of the will is affirmed is termed libertarianism; its opposite, determinism, is the doctrine that human action is not willed freely, but is rather the result of such influences as passions, desires, physical conditions, and external circumstances beyond the control of the individual.

Philosophical Views: Freedom of the will has necessarily been a concern of metaphysicians, who attempt to formulate theories explaining the nature of ultimate, universal reality and the relationship of human beings to the universe. Some metaphysicians hold that if the universe is rational it must be based on a sequence of cause and effect: every action, or effect, must be preceded by a cause and must form a part of the unbroken chain of causation extending back to the First Cause, that is, God, or the Divine. An act of absolute free will on the part of a person or an animal is, however, an uncaused act outside the causal chain; to accept the possibility of an uncaused act negates such divine, rational order and makes the universe seem irrational. Viewed in this manner, this question has never been satisfactorily resolved. During the Middle Ages, the inexplicability of free will led to intense argument among religious philosophers and to the famous dilemma known as "Buridan's Ass", often attributed, perhaps incorrectly to Jean Buridan.

The validity of free will has also been a subject of considerable debate among ethical philosophers. It would appear that a system of ethics must imply free will, for the denial of the ability to choose a course of action would seem to negate the possibility of moral judgement. A person without moral judgement is not responsible for his or her actions. In an attempt to resolve this problem, ethical philosophers have taken a great variety of positions, ranging from absolute determinism to absolute libertarianism. Socrates and Plato maintained that people could will their own actions, but that only those actions that accorded with the good or harmony of the whole were truly free. Thus, only a wise action is free. Baruch Spinoza, the Dutch philosopher, reinterpreted free will as self-determination, that is, insofar as a person fits into God's nature and the world's own nature. Immanuel Kant, the German philosopher, believed that a person must be free because freedom is a necessary postulate of the moral consciousness; the Kantian categorical imperative is beyond any theoretical analysis. The prevailing philosophical opinion has been that partial self-determination exists, and that, although many considerations other than will are involved in the formation of moral judgments, in certain circumstances a core remains, however small, of creative decision.

Theological Views: Free will is important in theology. One of the basic tenets of traditional Christian theology is that God is omniscient and omnipotent, and that every human action is foreordained by God. The doctrine of predestination, the theological counterpart of determinism, seemingly precludes the existence of free will. Because morality, duty, and the avoidance of sin are also basic elements in Christian teaching, how, it is asked, can people be morally responsible once predestination is accepted? Many attempts have been made by theologians to explain this paradox. St Augustine, the great Father and Doctor of the Church, firmly believed in predestination, holding that only those elected by God would attain salvation; no one, however, knows who is among the elect, and therefore all should lead God-fearing, religious lives. Freedom, for him, was the gift of divine grace. This was opposed by the British monk Pelagius and particularly by the followers of his doctrine, pelagianism, who maintained that Adam's sin conc-erned only Adam and not the whole human race, and that everyone, although helped by divine grace to attain salvation, has complete freedom of will to choose or reject the way to God. Eventually, Roman Catholic theologians stated the doctrine of prevenient grace to explain free will; according to this doctrine, God bestows on individuals the grace to will themselves into a state of grace.

During the Reformation, the question of free will became a religious battleground. Many Protestant sects, notably the Calvinists, emphasized the Augustinian doctrine of predestination and the complete exclusion of free will. Calvinistic predestination was considered a paramount heresy by the Roman Catholic Church; and the Council of Trent in the 16th century condemned all who denied free will. Still the problem was not resolved. The French

Roman Catholic prelate Jacques Bénigne Bossuet offered yet another approach, which became widely held; he stated that free will and divine foreknowledge are certain truths that must be accepted even though they are not logically connected.

Current Attitudes: Psychologists have found it difficult to explain free will; their method of scientific causality predicates determinism. The rational philosophers of the 17th and 18th centuries, who were, in a sense, psychologists, attempted to state mechanistic laws that would include mental phenomena as they did physical phenomena, such as gravity; free will, being anarchistic by definition, could not be patterned into law. In the 20th century, certain psychologists especially the advocates of existentialism—have recognized the element of spontaneity in the human mind that is admitted to lie outside any possible scientific law. This spontaneity can be interpreted to be free will, or at least a measure of self-determination that people feel themselves to possess and by which they make moral judgements.

Free will,liberty of choice or self-determination. On the absolute or libertarian conception, free will is opposed absolutely to causal determination: given a situation, a person could simply have chosen and done otherwise than they did, unconditionally. Choices, on this conception, are uncaused or self-caused causings. On the compatibilist or hypothetical conception, free will is opposed to constraint; a person is free if they could have done otherwise if they'd so chosen; though our choices, like everything else, are effects of antecedent causes. On this conception free acts are not uncaused, they're just caused in the right way, by our own preferences and desires. Acting freely on this "soft determinist" view is doing what you want (because you want to). See also: determinism.

Frege Gottlob, German mathematician and philosopher (1848-1925) who tried to develop effective ways of representing human thought in language and symbols. Frege was an early exponent of the view that arithmetical truth could be established on purely logical grounds. To that end, he developed a formal symbolic language for the expression of truth in Begriffsschrift (Conceptnotation) (1879), which introduced quantifiers as logical operators, and employed this symbolic method in Die Grundlagen der Arithmetik (The Foundations of Arithmetic) (1884) and both volumes of Grundgesetze der Arithmetik (The Basic Laws of Arithmetic) (1893, 1903). In "Đber Sinn undBedeutung" ("On Sense and Reference") (1892), Frege proposed a strict distinction between the sense and the reference of terms as a way of avoiding difficult epistemological paradoxes about informative statements of identity. *Recommended Reading*: The Frege Reader, ed. by Michael Beaney (Blackwell, 1997); Joan Weiner, Frege (Oxford, 1999); Michael Dummett, The Interpretation of Frege's Philosophy (Harvard, 1981); Michael Dummett, Frege and Other Philosophers (Oxford, 1996); Anthony Kenny, Frege: An Introd-uction to the Founder of Modern Analytic Philosophy (Blackwell, 2000); Hans D. Sluga, Gottlob Frege (Routledge, 1999); and Wolfgang Carl, Frege's Theory of Sense and Reference: Its Origins and Scope (Cambridge, 1994).

Fresison, Name given by medieval

logicians to any categorical syllogism whose standard form may be designated as EIO-4. *Example*: Since no fish are mammals while some animals that live in water are mammals, it follows that some animals that live in water are not fish. This is one of the fifteen forms in which syllogisms are always valid.

Freudianism, name for the ideas of Sigmund Freud, and for the tradition of psychological thought (and psychoanalytic practice) spawned by his theories. The philosophical importance and influence of Freu-dianism or psychoanalysis derives from its view of human nature, which emphasizes the importance of unconscious forces in determining the beliefs and actions of human beings.

Freud Sigmund, Austrian physician and psychoanalyst (1856-1939). Freud offered a series of extended accounts of the mechanism of repression, by means of which the motives of human behavior are unrecognizably disguised even from their agents. A series of lectures entitled Vorlesungen zur Einfuehrung in die Psychoanalyse (The Origin and Development of Psychoanalysis) (1917) offer a summary of his methods and results. In Die Traumdeutung (The Interpretation of Dreams) (1900), Freud proposed the analysis of dreams as a method of discovering the substantive content of the individual unconscious. In Die Zukunft einer Illusion (The Future of an Illusion), he offered a naturalistic account of religious belief. *Recommended Reading*: The Basic Writings of Sigmund Freud, ed. by A. A. Brill (Modern Library, 1995); The Freud Reader, ed. by Peter Gay (Norton, 1995); The Cambridge Companion toFreud, ed. by Jerome Neu (Cambridge, 1992); Paul Ricoeur, Freud and Philosophy: An Essay on Interpretation, tr. By Denis Savage (Yale, 1986); Anthony Storr, Freud (Oxford, 1989); and Donald Levy, Freud Among the Philosophers: The Psychoanalytic Unconscious and Its Philosophical Critics (Yale, 1996).

Fuller Sarah Margaret, American journalist and social reformer (1810-1850). In Woman in the Nineteenth Century (1845), Fuller advocated political equality and intellectual opportunity for women. She died in a shipwreck off the coast of New York during her return from work as a newspaper correspondent in Italy. The posthumously-published Life Without and Life Within (1869) includes essays on several key intellectual figures of the nineteenth century. *Recommended Reading*: The Essential Margaret Fuller, ed. By Jeffrey Steele (Rutgers, 1992); The Portable Margaret Fuller, ed. by Mary Kelley (Penguin, 1994); and Bell Gale Chevigny, The Woman and the Myth: Margaret Fuller's Life and Writings (Northeastern, 1994).

Functionalism 1, see also functionalism. A popular way to pump the intuition that all that needs to be kept constant about a subject to keep the subject's mental properties constant is the set of causal relational properties of the subject is what has come to be known as the silicon chip replacement thought experiment.

Ned Block (1980) identifies three senses of functionalism:

a) simple decompositional functionalism. "Functionalism" in this sense refers to a research strategy that relies on the decomposition of a system into its components; the whole system is then explained in terms of these functional parts.

b) computation-representation functionalism is a special case of decompositional functionalism which relies heavily on the "computer-as-mind" analogy. Psychological explanation under computation-representation functionalism is "akin to providing a computer program for the mind" (Block 1980, p.171). Thus, mental processes are seen as being decomposable to a point where they can be thought of as processes which are as simple as those of a digital computer or, similarly, a Turing machine.

c) metaphysical functionalism. This form of functionalism is a theory of mind that hypothesizes that mental states simply are functional states. The metaphysical functionalist claims that mental states are the types of mental state they are because of the causal relations between inputs, outputs and other mental (*i.e.* functional) states of the system, as in the Turing machine. The physical implementation of the set of functions which implement a mind are irrelevant to what makes something a mind, it's the functional relations that count.

In general, proponents of each of these forms of functionalism make the claim that the physical realisation of a given function is not, in some sense, its essence. Metaphysical functionalism identifies causal structures with mental states which are realisable by "a vast variety of physical systems" (Block 1980, p. 173). Metaphysical functionalism often identifies mental states with Turing Machine "table states" (Block 1980, p. 172). Similarly, computation-representation functionalism holds that the information processing mechanism necessary to run the "mind" program could be hydraulic, electric, mechanical, or whatever. Lastly, decompositional functionalism is, superficially at least, more interested in the function of a system than the physical makeup of the system.

However, decompositional functionalism is seldom, if ever, completely divorced from the physical system it is used to explore. While it is true that in decompositional functionalism the function of the system being explored is often abstracted from its physical realisation, it is also the case that that realisation is continuously re-examined in order to better understand and characterize its function. Decomposition is not a simple matter of observing a system, noting the various functions, and constructing a model. It is a complex process that involves examining and re-examining and re-re-examining ad infinitum (or at least until the model is just about right) the original physical system. In other words, decomposition is severely constrained by the system being decomposed (Bechtel and Richardson 1993).

As a theory of mind, functionalism is quite appealing. It is based in mathematical proof and provides a means of constructing analogies to guide our understanding of the mind. Computation-representation functionalism is a clear example of such a "rigorous" analogy. In fact, because both digital computers and people are presumably Turing machine describable, the computer/brain analogy can be supported by direct reference to computational theory. This is how Turing Machine equivalence has played such a central role in supporting functionalist intuitions

(Fodor 1981).

However, what the Turing Machine really provides for cognitive scientists is not a notion of equivalence and a means for justifying purely functional descriptions of the mind, but rather a very general (though sometimes not suffiently powerful) notion of computation. The Turing Machine describes the whole space of classic computational systems (see Super Turing machine), so anything algorithmically computational lies in the Turing Machine delimited space. Since any given real system is subject to many, possibly infinite, computational descriptions, any given real system will lie at many points in this space. Thus, the notion of Turing Machine equivalence provides little information concerning what is "the same" about any two real systems it simply notes the fact the systems share one point in Turing Machine space. Functionalists provide no means of distinguishing one computational description of the brain from another. It is highly unlikely that they are all important to having a mind. Thus, we need a better way of understanding the relationship between real comp-utational systems than that provided by the Turing machine.

The realisation of this underspecification of relevant functional properties also gives rise to the anti-functionalist argument first forwarded by Ryle (1949). Ryle claims that functionalism does not solve the problem of describing a complex system's behaviour. Rather, it makes a system more complex by introducing more functions. What Ryle has noted is that there will be an infinite proliferation of unexplained functional terms since each upper-level function is decomposed into more lower-level functions under this methodology.

However, as Cummins (1983) remarks, Ryle has missed the important fact that each of the newly posited functions is simpler than the one it is intended to help explain. Thus, the decomposition will eventually be simple enough for us to understand and use in explaining the highest-level functioning and that of the whole system.

But, Cummins later makes a serious mistake in his attempt to circumvent "Ryle's Regress". Cummins is correct in noting that each newly posited function will be simpler, but he is incorrect in assuming, as he does, that these simpler functions may be implemented however we see fit (Cummins 1980). Cummins has erroneously assumed that reserving decompositional functionalism preserves computation-representation and metaphysical functionalism. As noted earlier, there is an important distinction to be made between these types of functionalism; the first is a methodology, where the latter two are theories of mind. As a metho-dology, decompositional functionalism provides a means of explaining the behaviour of a system in simpler and simpler theoretical terms, so Cummins is right thus far. As a theory of mind, however, computation-representation and metaphysical functio-nalism wrongly entail that the implementation of a functional story is irrelevant to capturing the various aspects of behaviour. Even though decompositional functionalism gets to simpler components, it only allows us to stop "Ryle's regress" at a sufficiently simple component if that component has a realisation that preserves the functional description exactly. Once we have an implementable simplest function, there are no more questions as to what functions can be realised by that implementation, unlike in the case of a theoretical characterisation. In other words, it is by no means clear that we have any consistent way of constraining the possible functions of a system without reference to an underlying physical mechanism.

What's the logical relation between functionalism and multiple realisability?

In much discussion in the philosophy of mind, the theses of functionalism and multiple realisa-bility get mentioned in the same breath so often that it's not clear that they are separate theses, and, if so, what the logical relations between the two are. In this entry, I approach the issue by discussing what it takes to be functional and multiply realisable kinds in general. I will argue that the two theses are indeed different theses and further,that neither entails the other.

1. *Functionalism does not entail multiple realisability*: Suppose we were to fix the extension of the predicate "*x* is a blorg" as follows. *x* is a blorg just in case when x collides with a hydrogen atom, then *x* is caused to move in a trajectory precisely perpendicular to the hydrogen atom's original trajectory. Given that the reference of "blorg" is fixed in the above way, it seems that blorgs comprise a functional kind: their defining features are causal relations. It might turn out though, that there's only one set of physical properties whose instantiation is sufficient to instantiate a blorg, say, being a molecule of PQR. So, even though blorgs are individuated by causal relational properties, it turns out that it is impossible to physically realize them in any way but one. Thus they are non-multiply realisable functional kinds.

2. *Multiple realisability does not entail functionalism*: A kind can be multiply realisable even though it is not functionally individuated. For examples of multiply realizable but non-functional kinds, we need to look to kinds whose individuating relations are noncausal or to kinds whose individuating properties are not even relational. One example of the former might be: being outside of my light cone. Anything outside of my light cone is too far away from me to be enjoying any causal commerce with me, so the individuating relations in question are non-causal. Another example would be jade. Two chemically distinct materials are sufficient to realize jade: jadite and nephrite. But being a sample of jade isn't individuated by the kind of causal role it plays (in contrast to, say, a mousetrap). Instead, something is a sample of jade just in case it has the chemical composition of jadite or nephrite. Sticking with examples from chemistry, we might say that being a chemical element is realised by diverse physical properties (at least as many as there are chemical elements) but it is not individuated by the kinds of causal relations that samples of chemicals bear to one another. For another class of examples, consider geometrically individuated kinds, like squares, cubes, circles, and spheres. Whether something counts as a sphere depends on

whether it is a three dimensional object whose outermost points are equidisstant from its centre. Something can be a sphere without being causally related to anything else, so spheres are not functional kinds. And spheres can be realised by physically inverse sets of properties: spheres can be made of gold, protein, or wood; they can be solid or hollow; they can have any of a variety of masses and diameters; etc. Thus, we have another example of a multiply realisable kind.

It seems, then, that being functionally individuated and being multiply realisable are logically distinct in that neither entails the other. Therefore, the thesis that mental states are functionally individuated is logically distinct from the thesis that mental states are multiply realisable. *References*: Functionalism Biblio Bechtel, W. and R. C. Richardson (1993). Discovering complexity: decomposition and localisation as strategies in scientific research. Princeton, NJ, Princeton University Press. Block, N. (1980). Introduction: what is functionalism? Readings in philosophy of psychology. Ed. N. Block. Cambridge, MA, Harvard University Press. 1: 171-184. Cummins, R. (1983). The nature of psychological explanation. Cambridge, MA, MIT Press. Fodor, J. (1981). Representations. Cambridge, MA, MIT Press. Putnam, H. (1975). Mind, language, and reality. Cambridge, Cambridge University Press. Putnam, H. (1988). Representation and reality. Cambridge, MA, MIT. Ryle, G. (1949). The concept of mind. London, Hutchinson & Company.

Functionalism 2, see also functionalism.

a. *Introduction*: Functionalism (2) is an explanatory approach to behaviour and cognition that assumes the framework of evolutionary biology. Consequently, functionalism (2) regards specific behaviours and faculties or capacities as playing correspondingly specific and ada-ptive functional roles in the lives of the individuals and/or species that evidence them.

Functionalism (2) differs from the functionalism 1, sometimes designated as "input-output functionalism", that often appears in the literature of cognitive science and philosophy of mind. This latter functionalism may be described as holding that the defining characteristic of a mental state is the set of causal relations it bears to inputs, other mental states, and outputs. Functionalism (2), by contrast, can be described as a quasi-teleological theory of adapted faculties and their functions.

b. *Defining a Function*: Functionalism (2) assumes a definition of function that, following Wright (1973/1995, p. 42), can be stated as: The function of X is Z means (a) X is there because it does Z, (b) Z is a consequence (or result) of X's being there. In other words, for an organism O, the function of faculty or organ X is that particular thing Z that X is good for and that explains why Os have Xs. This conception of a function is meant to capture two central ideas: first, that Z is a function proper of X and not merely an accidental onsequence or by-product of X, and second, that X is selected by virtue of its doing Z. This latter feature is what Wright calls "consequence-selection," or "selection by virtue of resultant advantage" (1973/1995, p. 43).

c. *The Interaction and Isolation of Functions*: Although under ordinary circumstances an orga-nism's various functions can be expected to interact, individual functions are hypo-thesised to have been shaped by the pressures of the specific domains in which the organism is active. It is in terms of such discrete domains that specific functions can be approached, or, as Reber puts, we can only understand a given behaviour or capacity by "recognising the role of the conditions under which it emerged and the functions that it has" (Reber 1995, p. 156). This has a practical consequence in that attempts to study individual functions will be carried out within domains contrived as narrowly as possible, in order that the target function can be brought to the foreground to the greatest extent. One such attempt at the experimental isolation of a given function can be found in the artificial grammar learning experiments carried out by Reber and others. For these experiments the researchers designed situations meant to articulate effects that could be attributed to a single function, that is, the cognitive faculty hypothesised to afford acquisition of a grammar.

It should be emphasised, however, that the isolation of a function under experimental conditions is no more than a pragmatic expedient. A fuller, more natural account of the isolated function would have to locate it within the context of various interacting functions, the sum of which make up an organism's complex repertoire of capacities and behaviours. But functional isolation does buy us a measure of understanding in that it allows us to model the components making up an organism's cognitive and behavioural resources. Admittedly, the models resulting from functional isolation are necessarily idealisations of the actual processes and faculties under consideration. But as with all such idealisations, these models allow us to try to carve an organism's various functions at the joints.

d. *Functionalism and Adaptation*: Like input-output functionalism 1, functionalism (2) is subject to intentionalist criticism of the type found in Searle (1992). According to this critique, ascribing a function to a faculty or organ is always done against a background of the ascriber's intentions (1992, p. 237). The conclusion to be drawn is that the functional ascription is therefore not intrinsic to the faculty or organ, but rather to the teleology imposed on it from the outside by the observer. However, in the case of functionalism (2) it may be argued that consequence selection answers this concern. As Wright notes (1973/1995, p. 43), framing selection in terms of resulting advantage effectively separates selection from any necessary dependence on volition. For if the function is selected on the basis of the relative adaptive advantage it brings its possessor, we need only say that it is adaptive pressure of whatever sort that determines selection. If this is the case, then ascriptions of function can be taken as hypotheses about the intrinsic properties of a faculty or organ, which are in turn necessarily constrained by the best available theory of what counts as adaptive.

It is worth noting, however, that consequence selection can also accommodate functions that are in fact intentionally selected or designed. Consciously designed functions, no less than naturally selected functions, are functions "by virtue of their being the reason the thing with the function 'is there'" (Wright 1973/1995, p. 43). In sum, consequence selection allows intentional design to define functions without mandating it as a necessary condition of function definition.

e. *Implications for Representational Theory and Content Ascription*: Functionalism (2) carries imp-ortant implications for content ascription and for representational theories generally. Specifically, functionalism (2) requires that given limits be placed on exactly what content states can be ascribed to a person. As Reber points out, content ascriptions made under functionalism (2) are constrained less by pure representational theory than by an understanding of what it is for a person to behave in an adaptive manner (Reber 1995, p. 58). While functionalist (2) content ascriptions still will be formulated in terms of what it is possible for a person to represent, the understanding of what "possible" means in any given situation will be characterised in terms of specifically adaptive possibilities. In sum, under functionalism (2), our attribution of a given representational content to a person will be constrained by what it is possible for that person to represent, given that his or her behaviour or cognitive state is an adaptive response to the domain or situation in question. *References*: Reber, A. (1995). Implicit Learning and Tacit Knowledge: An Essay on the Cognitive Unconscious. New York, Oxford University Press. Searle, J. (1992). The Rediscovery of the Mind. Cambridge, MA, MIT Press. Sober, E. ed. (1995). Conceptual Issues in Evolutionary Biology. Cambridge, MA, MIT Press. Wright, L. (1973/1995). Functions. In Sober (1995) pp. 27-48.

Functional role semantics, also known as conceptual role semantics or CRS. The meaning of a representation is the role of that representation in thecognitive life of the agent. It is an extension of the well known theory of meaning as it supplements external use by including the role of a symbol inside a computer or a brain. (The following discussion is published in The Routledge Encyclopedia of Philosophy)

According to Conceptual Role Semantics (CRS) [*i.e.* functional role semantics], the meaning of a representation is the role of that representation in the cognitive life of the agent, *e.g.* in perception, thought and decision-making. It is an extension of the well known use theory of meaning, according to which the meaning of a word is its use in communication and more generally, in social interaction. CRS supplements external use by including the role of a symbol inside a computer or a brain. The uses appealed to are not just actual, but also counterfactual: not only what effects a thought does have, but what effects it would have had if stimuli or other states had differed.

The view has arisen separately in philosophy (where it is sometimes called"inferential," or "functional" role semantics) and in cognitive science (where it is sometimes called "procedural semantics"). The source of the view is Wittgenstein (1953) and Sellars, but the source in contemporary philosophy is a series of papers by Harman (see his 1987) and Field (1977). Other proponents in philosophy have included Block, Horwich, Loar, McGinn andPeacocke (1992). In cognitive science, they include Woods (1981) and Miller and Johnson-Laird (1976). (See references in Block, 1987.)

Further Discussion: Linguistic and Metaphysical Semantics) Motivations for Functional Role Semantics) Two-factor Conceptual Role Semantics) Criticisms of CRS)Framework, Not Theory; Ned Block. *References*: Block, N. (forthcoming) Conceptual Role Semantics)

Fuzzy computing, fuzzy logic

Fuzzy logic, A superset of Boolean logic dealing with the concept of partial truth—truth values between "completely true" and "completely false". It was introduced by Dr. Lotfi Zadeh of UCB in the 1960's as a means to model the uncertainty of natural language.

Any specific theory may be generalised from a discrete (or "crisp") form to a continuous (fuzzy) form, *e.g.* "fuzzy calculus", "fuzzy differential equations" etc. Fuzzy logic replaces Boolean truth values with degrees of truth which are very similar to probabilities except that they need not sum to one. Instead of an assertion pred (X), meaning that X definitely has the property associated with predicate "pred", we have a truth function truth (pred(X)) which gives the degree of truth that X has that property. We can combine such values using the standard definitions of fuzzy logic:

truth(not x) = 1.0 - truth(x)

truth(x and y) = minimum (truth(x), truth(y))

truth(x or y) = maximum (truth(x), truth(y))

(There are other possible definitions for "and" and "or", *e.g.* using sum and product). If truth values are restricted to 0 and 1 then these functions behave just like their Boolean counterparts. This is known as the "extension principle".

Just as a Boolean predicate asserts that its argument definitely belongs to some subset of all objects, a fuzzy predicate gives the degree of truth with which its argument belongs to a fuzzy subset. ["Fuzzy Logic, State of the Art", Ed. R. Lowen, Marc Roubens, Theory and Decision Library, D: System theory, Knowledge Engineering and Problem Solving 12, Kluwer, Dordrecht, 1993].

Fuzzy subset, In fuzzy logic, a fuzzy subset F of a set S is defined by a "membership function" which gives the degree of membership of each element of S belonging to F.

Game of Life, Life.

Game tree, A tree representing contingencies in a game. Each node in a game tree represents a possible position (*e.g.*, possible configuration of pieces on a chessboard) in the game, and each branching ("edge" in graph terms) represents a possible move.

Gaussian distribution, normal distribution.

Gender, a person's gender refers to that individual's affiliation with either male or female social roles. Gender differs from sex in the same way that ethnicity differs from race: gender is a sociological concept, while sex is a biological one.

Generality constraint, constraint on concept possession (and hence on the ability to entertain genuine thoughts) to the effect that a subject has the concept C only if the set of thoughts the subject is able to entertain is closed under recombination of C with all other semantically and categorically appropriate concepts that the subject possesses.

Generalization, To add a quantifier to a *wff* so that it either binds previously free variables, or binds new variables substituted for constants. See bound variables, free variables, instant-iation, quantifier

Existential generalization: To generalize using the existential quantifier. For example to move from propositional functions like Px or propositions like Pa to (Ex)Px; from "x is purple" or "alabaster is purple" to "something is purple". Valid without restriction.

Universal generalization: To generalize using the universal quantifier. For example to move from propositional functions like Px or propositions like Pa to (x)Px; from "x is purple" or "alabaster is purple" to "everything is purple". Valid only under several restrictions.

Genetic algorithm, (GA) An evolutionary algorithm which generates each individual from some encoded form known as a "chromosome" or "genome". Chromosomes are combined or mutated to breed new individuals. "Crossover", the kind of recombination of chromosomes found in sexual reproduction in nature, is often also used in GAs. Here, an offspring's chromosome is createdby joining segments chosen alternately from each of two parents' chromosomes which are of fixed length.

GAs are useful for multi-dimensional optimisation problems in which the chromosome can encode the values for the different variables being optimised.

Genetic algorithms, genetic algorithm

Genetic programming, (GP) A programming technique which extends the genetic algorithm to the domain of whole computer programs. In GP, populations of programs are genetically bred to solve problems. Genetic programming can solve problems of system identification, classification, control, robotics, optimisation, game playing, and pattern recognition.

Starting with a primordial ooze of hundreds or thousands of randomly created programs comp-osed of functions and terminals appropriate to the problem, the population is progressively evolved over a series of generations by applying the operations of Darwinian fitness proportionate reproduction and crossover (sexual reco-mbination).

Gettier problem, a type of counter example to the definition of knowledge as justified true belief. The first examples of the Gettier problem were published in 1963 by Edmund Gettier. In that paper, Gettier makes very clear that the tripartite definition concerns not knowledge per se, but a knowing subject's epistemic state:

S knows that p iff

1) p is true

2) S believes that p

3) S is justified in believing that p Sceptical arguments usually accept (2) and (3) and try to show that, no matter how one reinforces these two conditions, (1) does not necessar-

ily follow. Gettier-type counter-examples concern (3) and are not to be confused with sceptical arguments. They show that even if (1) and (2) are granted, one can always prove that S has merely guessed that p, since circumstances may be such that (3) only appears to apply, but actually does not, or is satisfied only in a sense too week to be satisfactory. This shows that the tripartite definition is incorrect. Suggestions on how to improve it have abunded. Consider the following example, taken from Theory of Knowledge Course). A teacher has two students, Mr. Nogot and Mr. Havit, in her class. Mr. Nogot seems to be the proud owner of a Ferrari (a rare and expensive car). He says he owns one, drives one around, and has papers which state that the car he drives is his. However, he does not actually own a Ferrari.

The teacher, on the basis of this evidence, concludes that someone in her class owns a Ferrari. This is true enough, but only because Mr. Havit, who shows no signs of Ferrari ownership, secretly owns one. So, it seems that the three conditions (truth, belief and justification) of knowledge have been met, but that there is no knowledge.

Another example of a Gettier case can be developed from an example concerning whether an executive's secretary is in his office. Suppose that she looked into the office and saw, sitting behind the desk, a figure who looked to her exactly like her secretary. We may suppose that she would be completely justified in accepting that her secretary is in his office. However, it may be that the person sitting at the desk is her secretary's identical twin brother. The real secretary is hiding behind the desk, waiting to leap up and surprise her. So it is true that the secretary is in the office, the executive accepts that it is true, and she is completely justified in so accepting that he is.

A third example, very simple, is provided by a broken watch. Suppose it is 3.15 pm and that my watch stopped working yesterday exactly at 3.15 pm. Suppose that checking the time on my watch has always been a very reliable and hence strongly justification-affording procedure in the past. I wish to know what the time is and I check my watch. Do I know that it is 3.15 pm? Of course not, I am just extremely lucky, although the procedure followed is reliable by hypothesis, and my belief that it is 3.15 pm is true.

Gettier counter-example are easy to construct by maintaining but decoupling the justification of p from the truth of p. This can happen whenever p is, or refers to, an empirical (*i.e.* contingent) fact. In mathematical knowledge, where p is a theorem and its justification is a logical proof, not "Gettierisation" seems possible.

Ghazali, al- (1058-1111), full name Abu Hamid Muhammad ibn Muhammad at-Tusi al-Ghazali, Islamic philosopher and theologian whose Latin name is Algazel. Born in Tus, near Mashhad, Persia (now Iran), and having gained an excellent reputation as a scholar, al-Ghazali was appointed in 1091 by Nizam al-Mulk, vizier to the Seljuk sultan, to teach at Nizamiya University in Baghdad. In 1095, following a personal crisis of faith, he relinquished his position, left his family, and became an ascetic. After ten years of wandering and meditation, he accepted another teaching position in Neyshabur but left it shortly afterwards and retired to Tus.

Al-Ghazali reported his internal struggle and the religious solution he finally achieved in *The Deliverance from Error*, a work that has been compared to *The Confe-ssions of St Augustine*. In *The Revival of the Religious Sciences* he presented his unified view of religion, incorporating elements from all three sources formerly considered contradictory: tradition, intellectualism, and mysticism. The work has been considered the greatest religious book written by a Muslim, second only to the Koran. After having mastered the methods of philosophy, al-Ghazali set out to refute the Neoplatonic theories of other Muslim philosophers, particularly those of Avicenna, which were opposed to such orthodox religious doctrines as that of the creation, the immortality of the soul, and divine providence. The resultant attack on philosophical theory and speculation, set forth in al-Ghazali's *Destruction of the Philosophers,* was largely responsible for the eventual decline of the element of rationalism in Islam.

Globalisation, internationalisation

God, omnipotent (all powerful), omniscient (all knowing), and perfectly benevolent creator of the universe. Conceived of as transcending the created universe (as in the Christian tradition) God is thought to exist prior to and beyond the universe which he created from nothing or exnihilo. Conceived of as immanent (as on pantheistic and Stoic conceptions) God is in the universe (as its guiding spirit or logos) and coextensive with it, not beyond it or prior to it.

GOFAI, Good Old-Fashioned Artificial Intelligence. see symb-olicism, artificial intelligence.

Grammar, A formal definition of the syntactic structure of a language (see syntax), normally given in terms of production rules which specify the order of constituents and their subconstituents in a sentence (a well-formed string in the language). Each rule has a left-hand side symbol naming a syntactic category (*e.g.* "noun-phrase" for a natural language grammar) and a right-hand side which is a sequence of zero or more symbols. Each symbol may be either a terminal symbol or a non-terminal symbol. A erminal symbol corresponds to one "lexeme"—a part of the sentence with no internal syntactic structure (*e.g.* an identifier or an operator in a computer language). A non-terminal symbol is the left-hand side of some rule.

One rule is normally designated as the top-level rule which gives the structure for a whole sentence.

A grammar can be used either to parse a sentence (see parser) or to generate one. Parsing assigns a terminal syntactic category to each input token and a non-terminal category to each appropriate group of tokens, up to the level of the whole sentence. Parsing is usually preceded by lexical analysis. Generation starts from the top-level rule and chooses one alternative production wherever there is a choice. See also BNF, yacc, attribute grammar, grammar analysis, formal language.

Grammatical inference, Deducing a grammar from given examples. Also known as "inductive inference" and recently as "computational learning".

Grelling's paradox, If an adjective

truly describes itself, call it autological", otherwise call it "heterological". For example, "polysyllabic" and "English" are autological, while "monosyllabic" and "pulchritudinous" are heterological. Is "heterological" heterological? If it is, then it isn't; if it isn't, then it is. Grelling's paradox cannot be expressed in first-order predicate logic, and is difficult to prevent in higher-order predicate logics.

Habermas Juergen, German philosopher (1929-). As a prominent member of the Frankfurt school, Habermas engages in critical study of the historical origins of human knowledge in many disciplines. His Theorie und Praxis: Sozial-Philosophische Studien (Theory and Practice) (1963) and Legitimations probleme in Spaetkapitalismus (Legitimation Crisis) (1973) examine the social conditions under which the uninhibited dialogue of an "ethics of discourse" is possible in the public literary sphere, serving the basic human needs to gain control over the natural world, to explore the character of interpersonal relationships, and to escape the domination of social powerstructures. In Erkentniss und Interesse (Knowledge and Human Interests) (1968) Habermas again emphasized the implications of social context for the development of epistemology. Habermas is also the author of Theorie des komm-unikativen Handelns (The Theory of Communicative Action) (1981) and Der philosophische Diskurs der Moderne (Philosophical Discourse on Modernity) (1985), where he criticizes the more radical views of Foucault and Lyotard. *Recommended Reading*: Jurgen Habermas, Postmetaphysical inking: Philosophical Essays, tr. by William Mark Hohengarten (MIT, 1994); Jurgen Habermas, Moral Consciousness and Communicative Action, tr. by Shierry Weber Nicholsen and Christian Lenhardt (MIT, 1992); Habermas: A Critical Reader, ed. by Peter Dews (Blackwell, 1999); Perspectives on Habermas, ed. by Lewis Edwin Hahn (Open Court, 2000); The Cambridge Companion to Habermas, ed. by Stephen K. White (Cambridge, 1995); John B. Thompson, Critical Hermeneutics: A Study in the Thought of Paul Ricoeur and Jurgen Habermas (Cambridge, 1984); Habermas and the Unfinished Project of Modernity: Critical Essays on the Philosophical Discourse of Modernity, ed. by Maurizio P. D'Entreves and Seyla Benhabib (MIT, 1997); and Jane Braaten, Habermas's Critical Theory of Society (SUNY, 1991).

Hacker ethic, 1. The belief that information-sharing is a powerful positive good, and that it is an ethical duty of hackers to share their expertise by writing free software and facilitating access to information and to computing resources wherever possible.

2. The belief that system-cracking for fun and exploration is ethically OK as long as the cracker commits no theft, vandalism, or breach of confidentiality.

Both of these normative ethical principles are widely, but by no means universally, accepted among hackers. Most hackers subscribe to the hacker ethic in sense 1, and many act on it by writing and giving away free software. A few go further and assert that *all* information should be free and *any* proprietary control of it is bad; this is the philosophy behind the GNU project.

Sense 2 is more controversial: some people consider the act of cracking itself to be unethical, like breaking and entering. But the belief that "ethical" cracking excludes destruction at least moderates the behaviour of people who see themselves as "benign" crackers (see also samurai). On this view, it may be one of the highest forms of hackerly courtesy to (a) break into a system, and then (b) explain to the sysop, preferably by e-mail from a superuser account, exactly how it was done and how the hole can be plugged - acting as an unpaid (and unsolicited) tiger team.

The most reliable manifestation of either version of the hacker ethic is that almost all hackers are actively willing to share technical tricks, software, and (where possible) computing resources with other hackers. Huge cooperative networks such as Usenet, FidoNet and Internet (see Internet address) can function without central control because of this trait; they both rely on and reinforce a sense of community that may be hackerdom's most valuable intangible asset.

Haecceity, thisness; the property that uniquely distinguishes each individual thing from others of its kind. Introduced by Duns Scotus as a name for the individuating essence of any particular, the term has been used more recently in connection with the view that rigidly designated individuals can exist in each of many possible worlds. *Recommended Reading*: John Duns Scotus, Philosophical Writings: A Selection (Hackett, 1987) and Gary S. Rosenkrantz, Haecceity: An Ontological Essay (Kluwer, 1993).

Hamilton William, Scottish philosopher (1788-1856); author of Lectures on Metaphysics and Logic (1860). Hamilton followed Reid in defending common sense against the skepticism of empiricists like Hume Hamilton's thought was subjected, in turn, to sharp criticism by Mill. *Recommended Reading*: James McCosh, Scottish Philosophy: Biographical, Expository, and Critical (AMS, 1980) and John Stuart Mill, An Examination of Sir William Hamilton's Philosophy and of the Principle Philosophical Questions Discussed in His Writings (Classic, 2000).

Hampshire Stuart, English philosopher (1914-) whose careful study of the philosophy of Spinoza in Spinoza (1951) prompted the development of a detailed description of the presuppositions necessary for human behavior in Thought and Action (1959) and Morality and Conflict (1983). Hampshire suggests that the nature of human freedom can best be understood by considering the difference between the declaration of what one intends to do and a prediction of what one is likely to do. *Recommended Reading*: Stuart Hampshire, Innocence and Experience (Harvard, 1991) and Stuart Hampshire, Public and Private Morality (Cambridge, 1978).

Happiness, general well-being in human life, an important goal for many people and a significant issue for theories in normative ethics. Aristotle disagreed with the identification of happiness with bodily pleasure defended by Aristippus and other hedonists. Most utilitarians accept this identification, but emphasize the importance of considering the greatest happiness of everyone rather than merely one's own. *Recommended Reading*: L. W. Sumner, Welfare, Happiness, and Ethics (Oxford, 1999); Aristotle, Kant, and the Stoics: Rethinking Happiness and Duty, ed. by

Stephen Engstrom and Jennifer Whiting (Cambridge, 1998); and Victoria S. Wike, Kant on Happiness in Ethics (SUNY, 1994).

Haraway Donna Jeanne, American feminist (1944-) philosopher of science who proposes a fundamental re-examination of the concepts of human nature and political identity in light of postmodern rejection of stark dualisms. Her "Manifesto for Cyborgs" (1965) suggests that the extent of our reliance ontechnology makes it difficult to understand ourselves independently of mechanical devices. Although we are all fabricated hybrids of organism and machine, Haraway supposes that feminist cyborgs have the opportunity to escape the perils of patriarchal capitalist technology. *Recommended Reading*: Donna J. Haraway, Simians, Cyborgs, and Women: The Reinvention of Nature (Routledge, 1991); Donna J. Haraway, Primate Visions: Gender, Race and Nature in the World of Modern Science (Routledge, 1990); and The Cyborg Handbook, ed. by Chris Hables Gray, Heidi J. Figueroa-Sarriera, and Steven Mentor (Routledge, 1996).

Harding Sandra, American philosopher of science (1935-). In Discovering Reality: Feminist Perspectives on Epistemology, Methodology and Philosophy of Science (with Merrill Hintikka) (1983), The Science Question in Feminism (1986), and Whose Science? Whose Knowledge?: Thinking from Women's Lives (1991), Harding shows that it may be possible to eliminate such basic concepts of traditional Western epistemology as "objectivity," "universality," and "duality." Doing so would create the possibility of alternative ways of thinking, grounded in fundamentally different standpoints,including a feminist perspective borne of women's experience of reality. *Recommended Reading*: Sandra Harding, Is Science Multicultural? Postcolonialisms, Femi-nisms, and Epistemologies (Indiana, 1998).

Hare Richard Mervyn, English philosopher (1919-). In The Language of Morals (1952), Freedom and Reason (1963), and Moral Thinking (1981) Hare defended a noncognitivist ethical theory according to which moral assertions are prescriptive commands whose genuine unive-rsalizability makes them applicable to every moral agent. *Recommended Reading*: R. M. Hare, Essays in Ethical Theory (Oxford, 1993); R. M. Hare, Essays on Political Morality (Oxford, 1998); R. M. Hare, Essays on Religion and Education (Oxford, 1998); and Hare and Critics: Essays on Moral Thinking, ed. By Douglas Seanor (Oxford, 1997).

Hart Herbert Lionel Adolphus, English legal philosopher (1907-1992) who applied the methods of analytic philosophy to the foundations of jurisprudence in The Concept of Law (1961), rejecting the rival claims of modern legal positivism. Hart's Law, Liberty, and Morality (1963) and The Morality of the Criminal Law (1965) offer a classic defence of the view thatprivate sexual conduct ought not to be subjected to public legislation. He is also the author of Punishment and Responsibility (1968) and Essays on Bentham (1982), both of which examine details of the utilitarian moral theory. *Recommended Reading*: Michael Martin, The Legal Philosophy of H.L.A. Hart: A Critical Appraisal (Temple, 1991) Eric J. Boos, Perspectives in Jurisprudence: An Analysis of H. L. A. Hart's Legal Theory (Peter Lang, 1998) N. MacCormick, H. L. A. Hart (Stanford, 1981) Law, Morality, and Society: Essays in Honour of H. L. A. Hart (Oxford, 1996) Michael D. Bayles, Hart's Legal Philosophy: An Examination (Kluwer, 1992).

Hartley David, English physician and philosopher (1705-1759). Hartley's Observations on Man: his Frame, his Duty, and his Expectations (1749) offered a physiological explanation for the association of ideas in purely mechanistic terms. His classification of various types of pleasure experienced by individual human beings was the basis for the later work of Bentham. *Recommended Reading*: Richard C. Allen, David Hartley on Human Nature (SUNY, 1999) and Hartley's Theory of the Human Mind: On the Principles of the Association of Ideas (AMS, 1990).

Hartmann Nicolai, German philosopher (1882-1950) whose early writings, including Grundz‚ge eine Methaphysik der Erkenntnis (Metaphysics of Knowledge) (1921) and Ethik (Ethics) (1926) used the philosophy of Kant as the starting point for idealistic accounts of reality and human freedom. In such later works as M–glichkeit und Wirklichkeit (Possibility and Actuality) (1938), Der Aufbau der realen Welt (Construction of the Real World) (1940), and Neue Wege der Ontologie (New Ways of Ontology) (1949), however, Hartmann employed phenomen-ological methods in defence of a vigorous realism. *Recommended Reading*: Eva Hauel Cadwallader, Searchlight on Values: Nicolai Hartmann's Twentieth-Century Value Platonism (Univ. Press of America, 1985) and W. H. Werkmeister, Nicolai Hartmann's New Ontology (Florida, 1990).

Hayek Friedrich August von, Austrian-British economist (1899-1992).In Economics and Knowledge (1936), The Road to Serfdom (1944), and Individualism and Economic Order (1949), Hayek agreed with Popper, in opposition to Keynes that the limitations of human knowledge subvert rational attempts at social planning, leaving only "free market" forces as the foundations of economic life. Hayek won the Nobel Prize in 1974, and is also the author of The Constitution of Liberty (1960) and the three-part Law, Legislation, and Liberty (1978)—Rules and Order; The Mirage of Social Justice; and The Political Order of a Free People. *Recommended Reading*: John Gray, Hayek on Liberty (Routledge, 1998); G. R. Steele, The Economics of Friedrich Hayek (Palgrave, 1997); and Hayek: Economist and Social Philosopher, ed. by Stephen F. Frowen (Palgrave, 1997).

Hebbian, Refers to the most common way for a neural network to learn, namely supervised learning. Using a training sample which should produce known responses, the connection weights are adjusted so as to minimise the differences between the desired and actual outputs for the training sample.

Hedon, this is a term that utilitarians use to designate a unit of pleasure. Its opposite is a dolor, which is a unit of pain or displeasure. The term "hedon" comes from the Greek word for pleasure.

Hedonism, the view accordin to which the fundamental standard of ethical judgment should be pleasure (see also sensualism). While nowadays hedonism has connotations of total pleasure-seeking and emotionalism, it was not always so. For example, although Epicureanism was one of the original hedonistic theories in ethics, it is quite strict as to what true pleasure really is (being a kind of naturalism), so that it is often described as a variety of "enlightened hedonism". While hedonism is usually a species of individualism, this is not always the case: for instance, the ethical standard of utilitarianism, which is a form of altruism, is "the greatest pleasure for the greatest number"—which could be construed as a kind of universalized hedonism. (References from Epicureanism and sensualism.) *Recommended Reading*: F. E. Peters, Greek Philosophical Terms: A Historical Lexicon (NYU, 1967); The Essential Epicurus, tr. by Eugene Michael O'Connor (Prometheus, 1993); Lionel Tiger, The Pursuit of Pleasure (Transaction, 2000); Fred Feldman, Utilitarianism, Hedonism, and Desert: Essays in Moral Philosophy (Cambridge, 1997); Rem B. Edwards, Pleasures and Pains: A Theory of Qualitative Hedonism (Cornell, 1987); and Kate Soper, Troubled Pleasures: Writings on Politics, Gender, and Hedonism (Verso, 1991). based on:, [The Ism Book]

Hedonistic, of, or pertaining to, pleasure.

Hegel Georg Wilhelm Friedrich, born in Stuttgart (1770-1831) and educated in Tuebingen, Georg Wilhelm Friedrich Hegel devoted his life wholly to academic pursuits, teaching at Jena, Nuremberg, Heidelberg, and Berlin. His Wissenschaft der Logik (Science of Logic) (1812-1816) attributes the unfolding of concepts of reality in terms of the pattern of dialectical reasoning (thesis—antithesis—synthesis) that Hegel believed to be the only method of progress in human thought, and Die Encyclopaedie der philosophischen Wissenschaften im Grundrisse (Encyclopedia of the Philosophical Sciences) (1817) describes the application of this dialectic to all areas of human knowledge, including history. Hegel's Naturrecht und Staatswissenschaft im Grundrisse and Gundlinien der Philosophie des Rechts (Philosophy of Right) (1820) provide an intellectual foundation formodern nationalism. Hegel's absolute idealism is evident even in the early Phaenomenologie des Geistes (Phenomenology of Mind) (1807). There Hegel criticized the traditional epistemological distinction of objective from subjective and offered his own dialectical account of the development of consciousness from individual sensation through social concern with ethics and politics to the pure consciousness of the World-Spirit in art, religion, and philosophy. *Recom-mended Reading*: Primary sources: Georg Wilhelm Friedrich Hegel, Gesammelte Werke (Meiner, 1968-); The Hegel Reader, ed. by Stephen Houlgate (Blackwell, 1998); Hegel's Science of Logic, tr. by A. V. Miller (Humanity, 1998); Georg Wilhelm Friedrich Hegel, Phenomenology of Spirit, tr. By A. V. Miller and J. N. Findlay (Oxford, 1979);Georg Wilhelm Friedrich Hegel, Philosophy of History, tr. by J. Sibree (Dover, 1956); Georg Wilhelm Friedrich Hegel, Elements of the Philosophy of Right, tr. by A. Wood and H. Nisbet (Cambridge, 1991). *Secondary sources*: The Cambridge Companion to Hegel, ed. by Frederick C. Beiser (Cambridge, 1993); Walter Kaufmann, (Notre Dame, 1997); Peter Singer, Hegel (Oxford, 1983); Charles Taylor, Hegel and Modern Society (Cambridge, 1979); Feminist Interpretations of G.W.F. Hegel, ed. by Patricia J. Mills (Penn. State, 1996); Quentin Lauer, Hegel's Idea of Philosophy (Fordham, 1983); Raymond Plant, Hegel (Routledge, 1999); Justus Hartnack, An Introduction to Hegel's Logic (Hackett, 1998); Judith Butler, Subjects of Desire

(Columbia, 1999); Jon Stewart, The Phenomenology of Spirit Reader: Critical and Interpretive Essays (SUNY, 1997); William Maker, Philosophy Without Foundations: Rethinking Hegel (SUNY, 1994); Allen W. Wood, Hegel's Ethical Thought (Cambridge, 1990); Joseph McCarney, The Routledge Philosophy Guidebook to Hegel on History (Routledge, 2000); Herbert Marcuse, Reason and Revolution: Hegel and the Rise of Social Theory (Humanity, 1999);

Also see: the Absolute, concrete universals, German philosophy, Hegelianism, philosophy of history, idealism, master and slave, metaphysics, nationalism, the owl of Minerva, political philosophy, progress, philosophy of religion, philosophical romanticism, the State, Vorstellung, and world-soul. The Bloomsbury Guide to Human Thought on Nationalism.

Hegel, G(eorg) W(ilhelm) F(riedrich) (1770-1831), German idealist philosopher, who became one of the most influential thinkers of the 19th century. Born in Stuttgart on August 27, 1770, the son of a revenue officer with the civil service, Hegel was brought up in an atmosphere of Protestant Pietism and became thoroughly acquainted with the Greek and Roman classics while studying at the Stuttgart Gymnasium (preparatory school). Encouraged by his father to become a clergyman, Hegel entered the seminary at the University of Tübingen in 1788 where he developed friendships with the poet Friedrich Hölderlin and the philosopher Friedrich Wilhelm Joseph von Schelling. Having completed a course of study in philosophy and theology and having decided not to enter the ministry, Hegel became a private tutor in Berne, Switzerland, in 1793. In 1797 he assumed a similar position in Frankfurt. Two years later his father died, leaving a financial legacy that was sufficient to free him from tutoring.

In 1801 Hegel went to the University of Jena, where he studied, wrote, and eventually became a lecturer. In Jena he completed *The Phenomenology of Spirit* or *Mind* (1807; trans. 1910), now thought of as one of his most important works. He remained at Jena until October 1806, when the city was taken by the French and he was forced to flee. Having exhausted the legacy left him by his father, Hegel became editor of the *Bamberger Zeitung* in Bavaria. He disliked journalism, however, and moved to Nuremberg, where he served as headmaster of a gymnasium for eight years.

During the Nuremberg years Hegel met and married Marie von Tucher. Three children were born to the Hegels: a daughter, who died soon after birth, and two sons, Karl and Immanuel. Before his marriage, Hegel had fathered an illegitimate son, Ludwig, who eventually came to live with the Hegels. While at Nuremberg, Hegel published over a period of several years *The Science of Logic* (1812, 1813, 1816; trans. 1929). In 1816 he accepted a professorship in philosophy at the University of Heidelberg. Soon after, he published in summary form a systematic statement of his entire philosophy entitled *Encyclopedia of the Philosophical Sciences in Outline* (1817 rev. ed. 1827, 1830; trans. 1959). In 1818 Hegel was invited to teach at the University of Berlin, where he was to remain. He died in Berlin on November 14, 1831, during a cholera epidemic.

The last full-length work published by Hegel was *The Philosophy of Right* (1821; trans. 1896), although several sets of his lecture notes, supplemented by students' notes, were published after his death. Published lectures include *The Philosophy of Fine Art* (1835-1838; trans. 1920), *Lectures on the History of Philosophy* (1833-1836; trans. 1892-1896), *Lectures on the Philosophy of Religion* (1832; trans. 1895), and *Lectures on the Philosophy of History* (1837; trans. 1858).

Strongly influenced by Greek ideas, Hegel also read the works of the Dutch philosopher Baruch Spinoza, the French writer Jean-Jacques Rousseau, and the German philosophers Immanuel Kant, Johann Gottlieb Fichte, and Schelling. Although he often disagreed with these philosophers, their influence is evident in his writings. In particular, Hegel's philosophy was deeply influenced by Kant's. Although he dedicated himself to overcoming the various oppositions in Kant's philosophy, especially that between the self and the unknowable "thing in itself", he retained Kant's approach of founding all knowledge in the nature of the self-conscious mind.

Philosophical Aims: Hegel's aim was to set forth a philosophical system so comprehensive that it would encompass the ideas of his predecessors and create a conceptual framework in terms of which both the past and future could be understood philosophically. Such an aim would require nothing short of a full account of reality itself. Thus, Hegel conceived the subject matter of philosophy to be reality as a whole. This reality, or the total developmental process of everything that is, he referred to as the Absolute. According to Hegel, the task of philosophy is to chart the development of the Absolute. This involves first making clear the internal rational structure of the Absolute; second, demonstrating the manner in which the Absolute manifests itself in nature and human history; and, third, explicating the teleological nature of the Absolute, that is, showing the end or purpose towards which the Absolute is directed.

Dialectic: Concerning the rational structure of the Absolute, Hegel, following the ancient Greek philosopher Parmenides, argued that "what is rational is real and what is real is rational". This must be understood in terms of Hegel's further claim that the Absolute must ultimately be regarded as pure Thought, or Spirit, or Mind, in the process of self-development. The logic that governs this developmental process is dialectic. The dialectical method involves the notion that movement, or process, or progress, is the result of the conflict of opposites. Traditionally, this dimension of Hegel's thought has been analysed in terms of the categories of thesis, antithesis, and synthesis. Although Hegel almost never used these terms, they are helpful in understanding his concept of the dialectic. The thesis, then, might be a concept that is part of the structure of the Absolute, or else it might be a historical form of consciousness. Such a concept or form of consciousness contains within itself incompleteness that gives rise to opposition, or an antithesis, a conflicting concept or form of consciousness. As a result of the conflict a third concept or form of consciousness arises, a synthesis, which overcomes the conflict by reconciling at a higher level the truth contained in both the thesis and antithesis. This synthesis becomes a new thesis that generates another antithesis, giving rise to a new synthesis, and in such a fashion the process of metaphysical or historical development is continually generated. Hegel thought that the Absolute itself (that is to say, the sum total of reality) develops in this dialectical fashion towards an ultimate end or goal.

For Hegel, therefore, reality is understood as the Absolute unfolding dialectically in a process of self-development. As the Absolute undergoes this development, it manifests itself both in nature and in human history. Nature is the Absolute objectifying itself in material form. Finite minds and human history are the process of the Absolute manifesting itself in that which is most kin to itself, namely, spirit or consciousness. In *The Phenomenology of Sprit* Hegel traced the stages of this manifestation in the various forms of consciousness from the simplest consciousness of objects, through self-consciousness, rational consciousness, and the various forms of ethical and religious consciousness, to "absolute knowledge", the form of consc-iousness in which the subject recognizes itself as fundamentally identical with the Absolute.

Philosophy of History: In the process of analysing the nature of the Absolute, Hegel made significant contributions in a variety of philosophical fields, including the philosophy of history, ethics, and political philosophy. With respect to history, his two key explanatory categories are reason and freedom. As a rational process, history is the "progress of the consciousness of freedom". That is, it is the progressive realization on the part of the human spirit (or "finite spirit") that its own essential nature is freedom, and thereby the realization of that freedom.

For Hegel, every historical civilization expresses a certain underlying conception of the human spirit through the customs, ethical practices, and social and political institutions that it establishes. It is only once these practices and institutions have been established and become familiar that the people of that civilization can go on to make this underlying conception explicit to itself through its art, religion, and philosophy. As Hegel put it, "the Owl of Minerva" (that is, the wisdom of philosophy) "spreads its wings only with the falling of the dusk". However, by so making this und-erlying conception explicit to itself, the people come to experience it as contradictory, and as inadequate to its sense of what the human spirit really is. As a result, people gradually lose their loyalty to the established practices and institutions, and the civilization begins to decay. Eventually a figure appears who leads the way in overthrowing the old instruments and replacing them with a new set that more adequately expresses the real nature of the human spirit as free. Hegel calls such figures "world historical individuals" and gives Alexander the Great, Julius Caesar, and Napoleon I as examples. The whole historical process of the rise and fall of civilizations is then a process through which the human spirit gradually comes to self-knowledge and freedom.

Ethics and Politics: Hegel saw the ethical practices and the social and political institutions of modern society (such as the nuclear family and the market economy) and of the modern state (for example, an impartial system of law, a system of representation, and a constitutional monarch) as effectively the final stage in this evolution of social and political institutions. With their consolidation in Europe in the wake of the French Revolution it appeared that the "end of history" had been reached. Accordingly, Hegel thought of these institutions as fully expressing the freedom that is the defining character of the human spirit. In *The Philosophy of Right* he attempted to show how these institutions embodied freedom in all its aspects, and so to justify them. In particular, he tried to show how they unite two different kinds of ethical outlook, which he called "morality" (*Moralität*) and "ethical life" (*Sittlichkeit*). At the level of morality, right and wrong are matters of individual reason and individual conscience. At the level of ethical life, duty is a matter of allegiance to the social wholes of which one is a member: one's family, one's social class or "estate", and one's country. Since individuals are only complete through their social relationships, morality alone is inadequate and one must move beyond it to the level of ethical life. The state is the expression of the most inclusive social whole to which one can belong, one's own country, and so when there is a conflict of duties, one's duties to the state override all others. Obedience to the general will, which is manifested in the properly constituted state, is the act of a fully free and rational individual. Hegel emerges as a political conservative, in that he supported the basic institutions of the modern state, but he should not be interpreted as sanctioning totalitarianism, for he argued that the state when properly constituted must allow spheres of private property, freedom of conscience, domestic privacy, and choice of economic activity.

Hegelianism, Hegelianism is the name for the philosophical system of G.W.F. Hegel (1770-1831) and for the philosophical tradition he started. Hegel did not have strong positions of his own in ethics, since he was more interested in the great movements of history than in the individual—he probably even thought that individuals don't have independent spiritual existence and that they are just part of the collective consciousness. Hegel's absolute idealism is often contrasted with the subjective or transcendental idealism of Kant (1724-1804), on whose innovations—in addition to the absolutism of Spinoza (1632-1677) Hegel based much of his philosophy. In political theory, Hegel advocated what is called "the organic theory of the state", which is one of the most consistent kinds of collectivism to be found in philosophical literature (Plato is often said to have advocated such a theory, as well). Hegel was probably the first philosopher to think of history in terms of a dialectic, which is what gave Marx (1818-1883) the inspiration for his doctrine of dialectical materialism. Hegel, by contrast, was a fervent believer in rationalism and absolute idealism, almost even to the point of spiritualism. (References from dial-ectical materialism and Marxism.)

Heidegger, Martin (1889-1976), German philosopher, who developed existential phenomenology and is widely regarded as one of the most original philosophers of the 20th century. Born in Messkirch, Baden, on September 22, 1889, Heidegger studied Roman Catholic theology and then philosophy at the University of Freiburg, where he was a student of Edmund Husserl, the founder of phenomenology. After periods teaching at Freiburg and Marburg, he became a professor of philosophy at Freiburg in 1928. He died in Messkirch on May 26, 1976.

Being and Time: Besides Husserl, Heidegger was especially influenced by the pre-Socratics of Greek philosophy, by the Danish philosopher Søren Kierkegaard, and by the German philosopher Friedrich Nietzsche. In his most important and influential work, *Being and Time* (1927; trans. 1962), Heidegger was concerned with what he considered the essential philosophical (and human) question: "What is being?", in other words, "What is it, to *be*?". This could only be answered, he said, by first answering the question of what kind of being (*Sein*) human beings have. Heidegger called this kind of being *Dasein* (literally, "being-there"), existence, or more specifically "being-in-the-world". We are, he said, self-interpreting, deciding entities practically involved along with others in a world that we have not made but that consists of potentially useful things, including cultural as well as natural objects. Thus, a person's being is inseparable from that of other human beings and things, and once he or she sees this, the question of whether the world or other people exist is not one that can sensibly be posed. Because these objects and artefacts come to humanity from the past and are used in the present for the sake of future goals, Heidegger posited a fundamental relation between the mode of being of objects and of humanity and the structure of time.

The individual is, however, always in danger of being submerged in the world of objects, everyday routine, and the conventional, shallow behaviour of the crowd, and of losing touch with his or her own nature as a choosing entity. The feeling of dread (*Angst*) brings the individual out of this state of inauthenticity to a confrontation with his or her own impending death and the ultimate meaninglessness of life, but only in this confrontation can an authentic sense of being and of freedom be attained.

Later Work: After 1930, Heidegger turned, in such works as *An Introduction to Metaphysics* (1953; trans. 1959), to the interpretation of particular Western conceptions of being. He felt that in contrast to the reverent ancient Greek conception of being, modern technological society has fostered a purely manipulative attitude that has deprived being and human life of meaning, a condition he called nihilism. Humanity has forgotten its true vocation, which is to recover the deeper understanding of being that was achieved by the early Greeks and lost by subsequent philosophers.

Influence: Heidegger's original treatment of such themes as human finitude, death, nothingness, and authenticity led many observers to associate him with existentialism, and his work had a crucial influence on the French existentialist Jean-Paul Sartre. Heidegger, however, eventually repudiated existentialist interpretations of his work. His association with the Nazis in the 1930s and during World War II, which he never decisively repudiated, has led to continuing controversy around his name. Despite this, however, his influence has grown throughout the 20th century. Heidegger's work has had an important influence on thinkers such as Hans-Georg Gadamer, Herbert Marcuse, and Theodor Adorno in Germany, and Maurice Merleau-Ponty, Michel Foucault, and Jacques Derrida in France. It has also had an increasing impact on philosophy in English-speaking countries.

Heidegger Martin, after studying with Husserl, Martin Heidegger (1889-1976) undertook an academic career in Germany, teaching at both Marburg and Freiburg. He became Rector of the University of Freiburg in 1933, where he continued to teach until 1944. Because of his public support for the Nazi regime, Heidegger was forbidden to teach after the end of World War II. Heidegger's Sein und Zeit (Being and Time) (1927) applied the methods of phenomenology to ontology, in an effort to comprehend the meaning of "Being" both in general and as it appears concretely. This led Heidegger to a conception of human existence as active participation in the world, "being-there" (Ger. Dasein), despite its inherent limitations and the threat of inauthenticity. Heidegger's most familiar themes are evident in The Basic Problems of Phenomenology (1927) and Einfuehrung in die Metaphysik (Introduction to Metaphysics) (1953). "Hegel and the Greeks" is a sample of Heidegger's reflections on the history of philosophy. *Recommended Reading*: Primary sources: Martin Heidegger Gesamtausgabe (Klostermann, 1975-); Martin Heidegger, The Basic Problems of Phenomenology, tr. by Albert Hofstadter (Indiana, 1988); Martin Heidegger, Being and Time: A Translation of Sein and Zeit, tr. by Joan Stambaugh (SUNY 1997); Martin Heidegger, An Introduction to Metaphysics, tr. by Ralph Manheim (Yale, 1986); Martin Heidegger, The Metaphysical Foundations of Logic, tr. By Michael Heim (Indiana, 1992); Martin Heidegger, On the Way to Language (Harper San Francisco, 1982). Secondary sources: Joan Stambaugh, The Finitude of Being (SUNY, 1992); The Cambridge Companion to Heidegger, ed. by Charles B. Guignon (Cambridge, 1993). Steven Mulhall, Routledge Philosophy Guidebook to Heidegger and Being and Time (Routledge, 1996); George Pattison, Routledge Philosophy Guidebook to the Later Heidegger (Routledge, 2000); Michael Inwood, Heidegger (Oxford, 1997); John D. Caputo, The Mystical Element in Heidegger's Thought (Fordham, 1986); Herman Philipse, Heidegger's Philosophy of Being (Princeton, 1998); Jonathan Ree, Heidegger (Routledge, 1999).

Heisenberg Werner, German physicist (1901-1976) who expressed the uncertainty principle, according to which the position and momentum of a subatomic particle cannot both be determined precisely at the same time, as a crucial element of modern quantum mechanics, described in his Physik und Philosophie (Physics and Philosophy) (1958). Heisenberg won the Nobel Prize for physics in 1932.

Recommended Reading: Werner Heisenberg, Physical Principles of the Quantum Theory (Dover,. 1930); Werner Heisenberg, Philosophical Problems of Quantum Physics (Ox Bow, 1979); and David C. Cassidy, Uncertainty: The Life and Science of Werner Heisenberg (Freeman, 1993).

Held Virginia Potter, American philosopher (1929-); author of Rights and Goods: Justifying Social Action (1984), Feminist Morality: Transforming Culture, Society, and Politics (1993), and Liberalism and the Ethics of Care (1997). Held maintains that the experience of women in our culture promotes the development of ethical practices appropriate in a private rather than in a public sphere of influence. *Recommended Reading*: Justice and Care: Essential Readings in Feminist Ethics, ed. by Virginia Held (Westview, 1995) and Ethics in International Affairs, ed. by Andrew Valls and Virginia Held(Rowman & Littlefield, 2000).

Hellenism, interest in, devotion to, and imitation of the culture and ideals of ancient Greece, especially as developed in Athens in the 5th and 4th centuries BC. The term, implying an unrestricted, pagan love of life, is often used in contrast to Hebraism, which implies an austerely moralistic, less sensuous, way of life. *See* Greek Art and Architecture; Greek Literature.

Helvaetius Claude-Adrien, French philosopher (1715-1771), Encyclopedist, and committed hedonist. Both De l'esprit (Of Mind) (1758) and De l'homme (Of Man) (1773) use empiricist methods to defend a strictly materialist account of human life, according to which ethical egoism is generated y the natural desire to maximize pleasure. *Recommended Reading*: Claude-Adrien Helvetius, Philosophical Works (Thoemmes, 2000) and David W. Smith, Helvetius: A Study in Persecution (Greenwood, 1982).

Hempel Carl Gustav, German-American philosopher of science (1905-1997). In Fundamentals of Concept Formation in Empirical Science (1952) and Aspects of Scientific Explanation (1965) Hempel pointed out that a paradox arises from the supposition that confirming evidence provides equal support for all logically equivalent hypotheses: Since "All swans are white" is logically equivalent to "All non-white things are non-swans" (by contraposition), it follows that observing a brown dog should increase confidence in our belief that swans are white. *Recommended Reading*: Carl Gustav Hempel, Selected Philosophical Essays, ed. by Richard C. Jeffrey (Cambridge, 2000); Carl Gustav Hempel, Philosophy of Natural Science (Prentice-Hall, 1966); and The Philosophy of Carl G. Hempel: Studies in Science, Explanation, and Rationality, ed. by James H. Fetzer (Oxford, 2000).

Henotheism, term used to describe a belief in one god that at the same time does not deny the existence of other gods. This idea or practice is obviously opposed by monotheism, which regards henotheism's tolerance of other gods as patently ridiculous. (Reference from polytheism.)

Heraclitus, Greek presocratic philosopher (540-475 B.C.) who used paradox and riddles to argue that the world is constantly changing in discussions preserved only in fragmentary reports. Although he identified fire as the original stuff of the universe, Heraclitus supposed that its changeable nature results in the formation of all of the traditional opposites. *Recommended Reading*: Fragments: The Collected Wisdom of Heraclitus, tr. by Bruce Haxton and James Hillman (Penguin, 2001); Henry W. Johnstone, Jr., Heraclitus (Bryn Mawr, 1989); and Richard G. Geldard, Remembering Heraclitus (Lindisfarne, 2000).

Herbert of Cherbury Baron, English philosopher (1583-1648). His rationalistic defence of theology in De Religione Laici (The Layman's Religion) (1645) and De Religione Gentilium (On the Religion of the Gentiles) (1663) was an early statement of the principles of seventeenth-century deism. Herb-ert's claim, in De Veritate (On Truth) (1624), that human beings are divinely endowed with "common notions" about god and religion, however, was a primary target of Locke's attack on innate ideas. *Recommended Reading*: John A. Butler, Lord Herbert of Cherbury 1582-1648: An Intellectual Biography (Edwin Mellen, 1990); Eurgen D. Hill, Edward, Lord Herbert of Cherbury (Twayne, 1987); and R. D. Bedford, The Defence of Truth: Herbert of Cherbury and the Seventeenth Century (Princeton, 1987).

Heredity, A property possessed by all the wffs in a set is logically hereditary iff the accepted rules of inference pass it on (transmit it) to all the conclusions derivable from that set by those rules.

Hermeneutics, formal study of appropriate methods of interpretation, first developed as a formal discipline of study by Schleiermacher. Following the work of Dilthey, Gadamer, and Ricouer, the hermeneutical process is often regarded as involving a complex interaction between the interpreting subject and the interpreted object. The task is complicated by the apparent circularity of understanding particular elements in light of the text as a whole, which can in turn be understood only by reference to them. *Recommended Reading*: John D. Caputo, Radical Hermeneutics: Repetition, Deconstruction, and the Hermeneutic Project (Indiana, 1987); John D. Caputo, More Radical Hermeneutics: On Not Knowing Who We Are (Indiana, 2000); Jean Grondin and Hans-Georg Gadamer, Introduction to Philosophical Hermeneutics, tr. by Joel Weinsheimer (Yale, 1997); Paul Ricoeur, Hermeneutics and Human Sciences: Essays on Language, Action, and Interpretation, ed. by John B. Thompson (Cambridge, 1981); Hans Georg Gadamer,Philosophical Hermeneutics (California, 1977); and Gianni Vattimo, Beyond Interpretation: The Meaning of Hermeneutics for Philosophy, tr. by David Webb (Stanford, 1997).

Heterogeneous, Composed of unrelated parts, different in kind.

Often used in the context of distributed systems that may be running different operating systems or network protocols (a hete-rogeneous network).

For examples see: interoperable database, middleware. Contrast homogeneous.

Heterological paradox, Grelling's paradox.

Heteronomy, for Kant, heteronomy is the opposite of autonomy. Whereas an autonomous person is one whose will is self-determined, a heteronomous person is one whose will is determined by something outside of the person, such as overwhelming emotions. Etymologically, heteronomy goes back to the Greek words for "other" and "law."

Heuristic, an informal method for solving problems in the absence of an algorithm for formal proof. Heuristics typically have only restricted applicability and limited likelihood of success but, as George Polya showed, contribute significantly to our understanding of mathematical truths. *Recommended Reading*: George Polya, How to Solve It (Princeton, 1971); Gerd Gigerenzer amd Peter M. Todd, Simple Heuristics That Make Us Smart (Oxford, 1999); and George Polya, Mathematics and Plausible Reasoning (Princeton, 1990).

1. A rule of thumb, simplification or educated guess that reduces or limits the search for solutions in domains that are difficult and poorly understood. Unlike algorithms, heuristics do not guarantee optimal, or even feasible, solutions and are often used with no theoretical guarantee. [What is a "feasible solution"?]

2. approximation algorithm.

Hex, 1. hexadecimal.

2. A 6-pack of anything (compare quad). Neither usage has anything to do with magic or black art, though the pun is appreciated and occasionally used by hackers. True story: As a joke, some hackers once offered some surplus ICs for sale to be worn as protective amulets against hostile magic. The chips were, of course, hex inverters.

3. The hash character, used to introduce hexadecimal constants in some assembly languages.

Hierarchy, An organisation with few things, or one thing, at the top and with several things below each other thing. An inverted tree structure. Examples in computing include a directory hierarchy where each directory may contain files or other directories; a hierarchical network (see hierarchical routing), a class hierarchy in object-oriented programming.

Higher-order logic, predicate logic.

Higher-order predicate logic, predicate logic.

Hilbert David, German mathematician (1862-1943) whose influential lecture at Paris, "Mathematical Problems" (1900), outlined the development of classical mathematics as the application of Kant's notion of a regulative principle. Hilbert's Grundlagen der Geometrie (Foundations of Geometry) (1899), Axiomatisches Denken" ("Axiomatic Thinking") (1917), "Die Grundlagen der Mathematik" ("Foundations of Mathematics") (1926), and Principles of Mathematical Logic (1931) proposed the axiomatic formalization of mathematics in order to demonstrate consistency by syntactical or meta-mathematical methods. *Recommended Reading*: Constance Reid, Hilbert (Copernicus, 1996) and Jeremy Gray and David Rowe, The Hilbert Problems: A Perspective on Twentieth Century Mathematics (Oxford, 2000).

Hippias, presocratic philosopher and mathematician (485-415 B.C.) who emphasized the use of empirical methods in pursuit of knowledge. Although his efforts to trisect the angle geometrically failed, they led Hippias to the discovery of the quadratrix, a curve satisfying the modern algebraic formula $y = x$ tan (py/2a), whose construction would render trisection of acute angles unproblematic.

Historical determinism, the view according to which the movement of history is determined by material or spiritual forces that are not open to human volition or change. Hegel's spiritualized dialectical understanding of history is an example of this doctrine, as is the dialectical materialism that is part of Marxism. (Reference from dialectical materialism.)

Historicism, concept generally associated with the development in the mid-19th century, in Germany in particular, of a "historical sense", that is, the recognition that the past is radically different from the present and can be grasped only in terms of its own context. The term was first widely used in the methodological debates among German-speaking political economists. Gustav Schmoller and his school came under attack for making economic theory overly dependent upon economic history, and this was described as *Historismus*. Here the term "historicism" had a depreciatory sense, and also referred to the attempt to extend history into disciplines where it lacked legitimate authority. The philosopher Friedrich Nietzsche regarded historicism as an anti-quated, uncritical approach to history, that is, the mere accumulation of historical data.

Ernst Troeltsch made the first attempt to characterize historicism in a more objective way. He defined it as the tendency to regard all knowledge and all experience as subject to historical change. For him, historicism was the dominant mode of 19th-century thought, which he contrasted with the generalizing, quantitative study of nature or *Naturalismus*. Historicism stood for a *Weltanschauung,* or world view, fundamentally different from a "naturalistic" or "positivistic" unde-rstanding of reality based on the idea of an unchanging, universal natural law. In another interpretation of historicism the focus was on that which is concrete, unique, and individual (Friedrich Meinecke).

Historicism underwent a shift in meaning when it was adopted in the English-speaking world in the late 1930s. The term took on a methodological dimension once it was associated with issues regarding principles of explanation and evaluation. The historicism which F. A. Hayek and, above all, Karl Popper attacked was the 19th-century doctrine that there exist certain laws of development on which scientific predictions about the future can be based. This definition reflects an attempt to make history "scientific", to model it on the natural sciences. The ideological and the methodological dimensions of the term "historicism" are clearer in the German language, which distin-guishes between *Historismus* and *Historizismus,* respectively.

Since the early 1980s, "new historicism" has emerged in literary studies as a new kind of historically based criticism. The work of Michel Foucault was especially influential to the "new historicists", who attempted to eradicate any distinction between literature and history. In contemporary philosophical thinking historicism has re-emerged as a thesis on the limits of enquiry based on an understanding of scientific concepts being relative to a given tradition (Robert D'Amico).

Historicism, belief that social structures, events, and texts are best to be understood in the context of their historical development. Versions of this view were defended by Dilthey, Lukacs, and Gramsci. More recently, Popper and Hayek criticized the extreme version of this view, according to which the historical outcomes are inevitably determined. In the milder form embraced by Croce, Kuhn, and Gadamer, however, historicism is simply the notion that a purely ahistorical perspective on human affairs would be misleading. *Recommended Reading*: H. Aram Veeser, The New Historicism Reader (Routledge, 1993); Paul Hamilton, Historicism: The New Critical Idiom (Routledge, 1996); Charles R. Bambach, Heidegger, Dilthey, and the Crisis of Historicism: History and Metaphysics in Heidegger, Dilthey, and the Neo-Kantians (Cornell, 1995); Robert D'Amico, Historicism and Knowledge (Routledge, 1992); and Karl Popper, The Poverty of Historicism (Routledge, 1993).

Hoagland Sarah Lucia, American moral philosopher (1945-). In Lesbian Ethics: Toward New Value (1988) Hoagland attributes a host of individual and social evils to their origin in a patriarchal and heterosexualist culture and proposes a moral revolution based on the formation of lesbian communities purposefully separated from the society at large. *Recommended Reading*: For Lesbians Only: A Separatist Anthology, ed. by Sarah Lucia Hoagland and Julia Penelope (Onlywomen, 1992).

Hobbes, Thomas (1588-1679), English philosopher and political theorist, whose mechanistic and naturalistic theories led to suspicion and controversy in political and ecclesiastical circles. Born in Westport (now part of Malmesbury), Wiltshire, on April 5, 1588, Hobbes was educated at Magdalen Hall, University of Oxford. In 1608 he became the tutor of William Cavendish, later Earl of Devonshire; in the following years he made several tours through France and Italy with his pupil and, later, with the son of the latter. During his travels Hobbes met and talked with several advanced thinkers of the time, including Galileo and the French philosophers René Descartes and Pierre Gassendi. In 1637, while in England, Hobbes became interested in the const-itutional struggle between King Charles I and Parliament. He set to work on "a little treatise in English" in defence of the royal prerogative. This work was privately circulated in 1640 under the title *The Elements of Law, Natural and Politic* (published in 1650). Hobbes feared that Parliament might have him arrested because of his book, and he fled to Paris, where he remained in voluntary exile for 11 years.

In 1642 Hobbes finished *De Cive,* a statement of his theory of government. From 1646 to 1648 he was mathematics tutor to the Prince of Wales, later King Charles II, who was living in exile in Paris. Hobbes's best-known work, *Leviathan, or, The Matter, Form, and Power of a Commonwealth Ecclesiastical and Civil* (1651), is a forceful exposition of his doctrine of sovereignty. The work was interpreted by the followers of the exiled prince as a justification of the Commonwealth and aroused the suspicions of the French authorities by its attack on the papacy. Again fearful of arrest, Hobbes returned to England.

In 1660, when the Commonwealth ended and his former pupil acceded to the throne, Hobbes again came into favour. In 1666, however, the House of Commons passed a bill that included *Leviathan* on a list of books to be investigated on charges of atheistic tendencies. The measure caused Hobbes to burn many of his papers and to delay publication of three of his works: *Behemoth: The History of the Causes of Civil Wars of England; Dialogues Between a Philosopher and. a Student of the Common Laws of England;* and a metrical *Historia Ecclesiastica.* At the age of 84, Hobbes wrote an autobiography in Latin verse; over the next three years he translated into English verse the *Iliad* and the *Odyssey* of Homer. He died on December 4, 1679.

Hobbes's philosophy represents a reaction against the liberty of conscience of the Reformation, which, he contended, brought anarchy. He effected the breach of English philosophy with scholasticism, and laid the foundations of modern scientific sociology by attempting to apply to human beings, as both the makers and matter of society, the principles of physical science that govern the material world. Hobbes developed his politics and ethics from a naturalistic basis; he held that all people fear each other and for this reason must submit to the absolute supremacy of the state in both secular and religious matters.

Hobbes Thomas, decades after completing his traditional education as a classicist at Oxford and serving as tutor of William Cavendish, Thomas Hobbes (1588-1679) became convinced that the methods employed by mathematicians and scientists-geometry, in particular-hold the greatest promise for advances in human knowledge. Voluntarily exiled to Holland during the years of Parliamentary Rule, the royalist Hobbes devoted much of his time to the development and expression of a comprehensive philosophical vision of the mechanistic operation of nature. Although he returned to England with the restoration of Charles II, Hobbes was for the remainder of his life embroiled in bitter political and religious controversies. They did not prevent the ninety-year-old Hobbes from completing his English translation of the works of Homer. Hobbes's first systematic statement of a political philosophy, Elements of Law, Natural and Politic (1640), relies heavily upon the conception of natural law that had dominated the tradition from Aquinas to Grotius. But his views had begun to change by the time he reissued portions of his work in a Latin version known as De Cive (1642). The Leviathan (1651) is the most complete expression of Hobbes's philosophy. It begins with a clearly materialistic account of human nature and knowledge, a rigidly deterministic account of human volition, and a pessimistic vision of the consequently natural state of human beings in perpetual struggle against each other. It is to escape this grim fate, Hobbes argued, that we form the commonwealth, surrendering our individual powers to the authority of an absolute sovereign. For Hobbes, then, individual obedience to even an arbitrary government is necessary in order to forestall the greater evil of an endless state of war. *Recommended Reading*: Primary sources: The English works of Thomas Hobbes, ed. by Sir William Molesworth (Oxford, 1962); Thomas Hobbes, Leviathan, ed. by J.C.A. Gaskin (Oxford, 1998); Thomas Hobbes, On the Citizen, ed. by Richard Tuck and Michael Silverthorne (Cambridge, 1998); *Secondary sources*: The Cambridge Companion to Hobbes, ed. by Tom Sorell (Cambridge, 1996); Richard Tuck, Hobbes (Oxford, 1989); Quentin Skinner, Reason and Rhetoric in the Philosophy of Hobbes (Cambridge, 1997); Samuel I. Mintz, The Hunting of

Leviathan: Seventeenth-Century Reactions to the Materialism and Moral Philosophy of Thomas Hobbes (St. Augustine, 1997); Aloysius P. Martinich, Thomas Hobbes (St. Martin's, 1997). Additional on-line information about obbes includes: Bernard Gert's article in The Oxford Companion to Philosophy.

Also see: conservatism, the social contract, English philosophy, the Leviathan, materialism, "nasty, brutish, and short", the people, the persecution of philosophers, political philosophy, and the state of nature.

Hofstadter Douglas, American computer scientist and philosopher (1945). In Goedel, Escher, Bach: an Eternal Golden Braid (1979), Hofstadter offers an insightful account of major developments in the metamathematics of recursive functions, tracing its importance for artificial intelligence research and human self-understanding through metaphorical comparisons with art and music. Hofstadter is also author of Metamagical Themas (1985) and co-editor (with Dan Dennett) of The Mind's I (1981). *Recommended Reading*: Douglas R. Hofstadter, Fluid Concepts & Creative Analogies: Computer Models of the Fundamental Mechanisms of Thought (Basic, 1996) and Douglas R. Hofstadter, Le Ton Beau De Marot: In Praise of the Music of Language (Basic, 1998).

Holism, the view that parts of a system have significance mostly in virtue of their interrelations with other parts. (The following discussion is from The Routledge Encyclopedia of Philosophy)

Mental (or semantic) holism is the doctrine that the identity of a belief content (or the meaning of a sentence that expresses it) is determined by its place in the web of beliefs or sentences comprising a whole theory or group of theories. It can be contrasted with two other views: atomism and molecularism.

Molecularism characterizes meaning and content in terms of relatively small parts of the web in a way that allows many different theories to share those parts. For example, the meaning of "chase" might be said by a molecularist to be try to catch.

Atomism characterizes meaning and content in terms of none of the web; it says that sentences and beliefs have meaning or content indepe-ndently of their relations to other sentences or beliefs.

One major motivation for holism has come from reflections on the natures of confirmation and learning. As Quine (1953) observed, claims about the world are confirmed not individually, but only in conjunction with theories of which they are a part. And typically, one cannot come to understand scientific claims without understanding a significant chunk of the theory of which they are a part. For example, in learning the Newtonian concepts of "force", "mass", "kinetic energy" and "momentum", one doesn't learn any definitions of these terms in terms that are understood beforehand, for there are no such definitions. Rather, these theoretical terms were all learned together in conjunction with procedures for solving problems.

The major problem with holism is that it threatens to make generalisation in psychology virtually impossible. If the content of any state depends on all others, it would be extremely unlikely that any two believers would ever share a state with the same content. Moreover, holism would appear to conflict with our ordinary conception of rea-soning. What sentences one accepts influence what one infers. If I accept a sentence and then later reject it, I thereby change the inferential role of that sentence, so the meaning of what I accept wouldn't be the same as what I later reject. But then it would be difficult to understand on this view how one could rationally—or even irrationally!—change one's mind. And agreement and translation are also problematic for much the same reason.

Holists have responded (1) by proposing that we should think not in terms of "same/different" meaning but in terms of a gradient of similarity of meaning,

(2) by proposing "two factor" theories or (3) by simply accepting the consequence that there is no real difference between changing meanings and changing beliefs.

Homogeneous, (Or "homogenous") Of uniform nature, similar in kind.

1. In the context of distributed systems, middleware makes heterogeneous systems appear as a homogeneous entity. For example see: interoperable network.

Contrast heterogeneous.

2. (Of a polynomial) containing terms of the same degree with respect to all the variables, as in $x^2 + 2xy + y^2$.

3. (Of a function) containing a set of variables such that when each is multiplied by a constant, this constant can be eliminated without altering the value of the function, as in $\cos x/y + x/y$.

4. (of an equation) containing a homogeneous function made equal to 0.

Homogenous, homogeneous

Homological-heterological, distinction between concepts or words. A homological term applies to itself, a heterological term does not. Thus, for example: "short" and "having fewer than ten syllables" are homological terms; "big" and "having more than ten syllables" are heterological terms.

Although "homological" is itself a homological term, a self-referential paradox arises when we consider the word "heterological." If we suppose that it applies to itself (thus being homological), then it is not heterological and does not apply to itself. But if we suppose that it does not apply to itself (thus being heterological), then it does apply to itselfand is homological. What, then, are we to make of an expression such as, "The smallest integer not namable in fewer than twenty syllables?"

Homomorphism, A map f between groups A and B is a homomorphism of A into B where the *s are the respective

If $f(a1 * a2) = f(a1) * f(a2)$ for all $a1, a2$ in A. group operations.

Homonymous-synonymous- paronymous, Aristotle's distinction among different uses of a term: they are said to be homonymous if the uses are entirely distinct, synonymous if they are the same, and paronymous if they are different but related. Thus, for example: In "Colleen is a cat," and "Garfield is a cat," "cat" is used homon-ymously. In "Carter was president in 1978," and "Bush was president in 1990," "president" is used ynonymously. In "Jean was brave," and "What Jean did was brave,"

"brave" is used parony-mously. *Recommended Reading*: Aristotle's Categories and De Interpretatione, tr. by J.L. Ackrill (Oxford, 1975).

Horkheimer Max, German philosopher (1895-1973). Co-founder (with Adorno and Marcuse) of the Frankfurt School, Horkheimer proposed unification of abstract philosophy with social science in the practice of critical theory in Dialektik der Aufklrung (Dialectic of Enlightenment) (1947). Zur Kritik der instrumentellen Vernunft (Critique of Instrumental Reason) (1967), Eclipse of Reason (1974), and other late writings express Horkheimer's growing pessimism about the possibility of genuine progress. *Recommended Reading*: Max Horkheimer, Between Philosophy and Social Science: Selected Early Writings, tr. by G. Frederick Hunter, Matthew S. Kramer, and John Torpey (MIT, 1995); Max Horkheimer, Critical Theory, tr. by Mathew J. O'Connell (Continuum, 1975); and Max Horkheimer: A Bibliography, ed. by Joan Nordquist.

Horn clause, A set of atomic literals with at most one positive literal. Usually written where n>=0. If L is false

L <- L1,..., Ln

or

<- L1,..., Ln

the clause is regarded as a goal. Horn clauses can express a subset of statements of first order logic.

The name "Horn Clause" comes from the logician Alfred Horn, who first pointed out the significance of such clauses in 1951, in the article "On sentences which are true of direct unions of algebras", Journal of Symbolic Logic, 16, 14-21.

A definite clause is a Horn clause that has exactly one positive literal.

Hügel, Friedrich, Baron von (1852-1925), British philosopher and theologian, who exerted a strong influence on Modernism within the Roman Catholic Church.

Born in Florence, Italy, the son of an Austrian diplomat, Hügel lived much of his life in England, where he became a naturalized subject. Although he was a Roman Catholic, Hügel acknowledged the sacred truth of all religions and found the essence of religion in the adoration of God by the individual. He defended the application of critical, scientific methods to biblical scholarship and befriended modernist thinkers such as George Tyrrell and Alfred Loisy, who were trying to reconcile Christianity with the findings of modern science and philosophy. Hügel was also interested in mysticism. One of his major works, *The Mystical Element of Religion as Studied in Saint Catherine of Genoa and Her Friends* (1908), is a classic in the field.

Horney Karen, German-American psychoanalyst (1885-1952) who emphasized the role of social conditions in the formation of personality. In New Ways in Psychoanalysis (1939), Horney showed that Freud's notion of "penis envy" is a misrepresentation of female psychology, generated in fact by phallo-centric resentment of women. Horney was also the author of Our Inner Conflicts: A Constructive Theory of Neurosis (1945), Self-Analysis (1947), and Neurosis and Human Growth: The Struggle Toward Self-Realization (1950). *Recommended Reading*: Karen Horney, The Neurotic Personality of Our Time (Norton, 1994); Karen Horney, Feminine Psychology (Norton, 1993);

The Unknown Karen Horney: Essays on Gender, Culture, and Psychoanalysis, tr. Bernard J. Paris (Yale, 2000); and Bernard J. Paris, Karen Horney: A Psychoa-nalyst's Search for Self-Understanding (Yale, 1994).

Humanism, in philosophy, attitude that emphasizes the dignity and worth of the individual. A basic principle of humanism is that people are rational beings who possess within themselves the capacity for truth and goodness. The term *humanism* is most often used to describe a literary and cultural movement that spread through western Europe in the 14th and 15th centuries. This Renaissance revival of Greek and Roman studies emphasized the value of the Classics for their own sake, rather than for their relevance to Christianity.

The humanist movement started in Italy, where the late medieval Italian writers Dante, Giovanni Boccaccio, and Francesco Petrarch contributed greatly to the discovery and preservation of Classical works. Humanist ideals were forcefully expressed by another Italian scholar, Pico della Mirandola, in his *Oration* on the dignity of man. The movement was further stimulated by the influx of Byzantine scholars who came to Italy after the fall of Constantinople to the Turks in 1453 and also by the establishment of the Platonic Academy in Florence. The academy, whose leading thinker was Marsilio Ficino, was founded by the 15th-century Florentine statesman and patron of the arts Cosimo de' Medici. The institution sought to revive Platonism and had particular influence on the literature, painting, and architecture of the times.

The collection and translation of Classical manuscripts became widespread, especially among the higher clergy and nobility. The invention of printing with movable type, around the mid-15th century, gave a further impetus to humanism through the dissemination of editions of the Classics. Although in Italy humanism developed principally in the fields of literature and art, in central Europe, where it was introduced chiefly by the German scholars Johann Reuchlin and Melanchthon, the movement extended into the fields of theology and education, and was a major underlying cause of the Reformation.

One of the most influential scholars in the development of humanism in France was the Dutch cleric Desiderius Erasmus, who also played an important part in introducing the movement into England. There humanism was established at the University of Oxford by the English classical scholars William Grocyn and Thomas Linacre, and at the University of Cambridge by Erasmus and the English prelate John Fisher. From the universities it spread throughout English society and paved the way for the great flourishing of Elizabethan literature and culture.

See also Education, History of.

Humanism, belief that individual human beings are the fundamental source of all value and have the ability to understand—and perhaps even to control—the natural world by careful application of their own rational faculties. During the Renaissance, humanists such as Bruno, Erasmus, Valla, and Pico della Mirandola helped shift attention away from arcane theological disputes toward more productive avenues of classical study and natural science. *Recommended Reading*: The Cambridge Companion to Renaissance Humanism, ed. by Jill Kraye (Cambridge, 1996); Impact of Humanism, ed. by Lucille Kekewich (Yale, 2000); Rebecca W. Bushnell, A Culture of Teaching: Early Modern Humanism in Theory and Practice (Cornell, 1996); and John C. Olin, Erasmus, Utopia, and the Jesuits: Essays on the Outreach of Humanism (Fordham, 1994).

Although the definition of humanism is somewhat fuzzy, humanistic philosophies focus centrally on human concerns (as opposed to the interests of the gods or the technical issues of phil-osophy—that is, as opposed to theism or logicism). Humanistic philosophies have sprung up in many eras and places, including ancient Greece (Aristotelianism and Epicureanism), China (Confucianism, Taoism, and Buddhism), Renaissance Europe, and in America (some forms of pragmatism, "secular humanism", "humanistic psychology" as advocated by Abraham Maslow, and the thought of people like Thoreau and Emerson). While humanism is often closely tied to secularism and to individualism, these connections are not necessary. In fact, humanism is sometimes thought of as a "religion of humanity" that takes altruism and action for the sake of all humanity as its guiding principle (this is true of the positivism of August Comte, for example). Humanism is often more a state of mind or a certain quality of thought than any definite doctrine, but it is almost universally taken to be a positive quality, except by some 20th century religionists (who seem to hold a special scorn for "secular humanism"). (References from Aristotelianism, behaviorism, Confucianism, dogmatism, eudaimonism, individualism, logicism, Marxism, naturalism, pantheism, positivism, pragmatism, secularism, and Socraticism.)

Human rights, rights

Hume David, soon after completing his studies at Edinburgh, Scottish philosopher David Hume (1711-1776) began writing his comprehensive statement of the views he believed would contribute to philosophy no less than Newton's had to science. But the public reception for the three books of his magisterial Treatise of Human Nature (1739) was less than cordial, and Hume abandoned his hopes of a philosophical career in order to support his family as a librarian, historian, diplomat, and political essayist, a course of action he described in the autobiographical My Own Life (1776). Hume's Essays Moral and Political (1741-1742) found some success, and the multi-volume History of England (1754-1762) finally secured the modest livelihood for which he had hoped. Although he spent most of his life trying to produce more effective statements of his philosophical views, he did not live to see the firm establishment of his reputation by the criticisms of Kant and much later appreciation of the logical positivists. The central themes of Book I of the Treatise receive a somewhat more accessible treatment in An Enquiry concerning Human Understanding (1748), a more popular summary of Hume's emp-iricism. According to Hume, little human knowledge can be derived from the deductively certain relations of ideas. Since the causal interactions of physical objects are known to us only as inherently uncertain matters of fact, Hume argued, our belief that they exhibit any necessary connection (however explicable) can never be rationally justified, but must be acknowledged to rest only upon our acquired habits. In similar fashion, Hume argued that we cannot justify our natural beliefs in the reality of the self or the existence of an external world. From all of this, he concluded that a severe (if mitigated) skepticism is the only defensible view of the world. Hume recast the moral philosophy of the Treatise's Book III in An Enquiry concerning the Principles of Morals (1751). In both texts Hume clearly maintained that human agency and moral obligation are best considered as functions of human passions rather than as the dictates of reason. In the posthumously published Dialogu-esconcerning Natural Religion (1780), Hume discussed the possibility of arriving at certain knowledge of god through the application of reason and considered defense of a fideistic alternative. *Recommended Reading*: Primary sources: David Hume, Philosophical Works, ed. by T. H. Green and T. H. Grose (Longmans, Green, 1874-1875); David Hume, A Treatise of Human Nature, ed. by Ernest C. Mossner (Viking, 1986); David Hume, An Enquiry Concerning Human Understanding, ed. By Anthony Flew (0812690540); David Hume, An Enquiry Concerning the Principles of Morals (Free Press, 1966); David Hume, Dialogues Concerning Natural Religion, ed. By Martin Bell (Penguin, 1990). *Secondary sources*: The Cambridge Companion to Hume, ed. by David Fate Norton (Cambridge, 1993); Feminist Interpretations of David Hume, ed. by Anne JaapJacobson (Penn. State, 2000); Jonathan Bennett, Locke, Berkeley, Hume: Central Themes (Oxford, 1971); Anthony Quinton, Hume (Routledge, 1999); Donald W. Livingston, Hume's Philosophy of Common Life (Chicago, 1984); Barry Stroud, Hume (Routledge, 1981); Terence Penelhum, David Hume: An Introduction to His Philosophical System (Purdue, 1992); George Dicker, Hume's Epistemology and Metaphysics: An Introduction (Routledge, 1998); Harold W. Noonan, Routledge Philosophy Guidebook to Hume on Knowledge (Routledge, 1999); Hume's Moral and Political Philosophy, ed. by Henry David Aiken (Free Press, 1975); James Baillie, Routledge Philosophy Guidebook to Hume on Morality (Routledge, 2000).

Hume, David (1711-1776), Scottish historian and philosopher, who influenced the development of scepticism and empiricism, two schools of philosophy. Born in Edinburgh, on May 7, 1711, Hume was educated at home and at the University of Edinburgh, where he matriculated at the age of 12. His health was poor, and after working for a short period in a business house in Bristol, he went to live in France.

Life and Writings: From 1734 to 1737 Hume occupied himself intensively with the problems of speculative philosophy, writing during this period his most important philosophical work, *A Treatise of Human Nature* (3 vols., 1739-1740), which embodies the essence of his thinking. In spite of its importance, this work was ignored by the public. As Hume himself put it, it "fell dead-born from the press", probably because of its abstruse style. Hume's later works were written in the lighter essay or dialogue forms that were popular at that time.

After the publication of the *Treatise,* Hume returned to his family estate in Berwickshire; there he turned his attention to the problems of ethics and political economy and wrote *Essays Moral and Political* (2 vols., 1741-1742), which attained immediate success. He failed to obtain an appointment to the faculty of the University of Edinburgh, probably because, even early in his career, he was regarded as a religious sceptic. Hume became, successively, tutor to the insane Marquis of Annandale and judge advocate to a British military expedition to France. His *Philosophical Essays Concerning Human Understanding* (afterwards entitled *An Enquiry Concerning Human Understanding*) appeared in 1748. This book, perhaps his best-known work, is in effect a condensation of the first part of the *Treatise*. In 1751 he published *An Enquiry Concerning the Principles of Morals,* which is a similar condensation of the third part of the *Treatise*.

Hume took up residence in Edinburgh in 1751. In 1752 his *Political Discourses* was published, and in the following year, having again failed to obtain a university professorship, he received an appointment as librarian of the Advocates' Library in the city. During his 12-year stay in the city, Hume worked chiefly on his six-volume *History of England,* which appeared at intervals from 1754 to 1762. In the years 1762 to 1765 he served as secretary to the British ambassador in Paris. There he was revered by French literary circles and formed a friendship with the French philo-sopher Jean-Jacques Rousseau. Hume brought Rousseau back with him to Britain, but the latter, plagued by delusions of persecution, accused Hume of plotting against him, and the friendship dissolved in public denunciations between the two men. After serving as Under-Secretary of State in London (1767-1768), Hume retired to Edinburgh, where he spent the rest of his life. He died on August 25, 1776. His autobiography was published posthumously in 1777, as was his *Dialogues Concerning Natural Religion* (1779). Hume had written the *Dialogues* in the early 1750s but had withheld the work because of its sceptical nature.

Hume's Metaphysics and Epistemology: Hume's philosophical position was influenced by the ideas of the English philosopher John Locke and the Irish philosopher and clergyman Bishop George Berkeley. Hume and Berkeley both differentiated between reason and sensation. Hume, however, went further, endeavouring to prove that reason and rational judgements are merely habitual associations of distinct sensations or experiences.

In a revolutionary step in the history of philosophy, Hume rejected the basic idea of causation as a necessary connection between events in the world, maintaining that: "Reason can never show us the connexion of one object with another, tho' aided by experience, and the observation of their conjunction in all past instances." That is, when we think we perceive a connection of cause and effect between two events in the world, in fact we are only projecting on to the world a subjective expectation that the first event will be followed by the second. In turn, this expectation is the result of a mental association between the idea of the first event and the idea of the second, which has been created by our past experience of events like the first one always being followed by events like the second, by a "constant conjunction" between one sort of event and the other.

Hume's rejection of causation implies a rejection of scientific laws, which are based on the general premise that one event necessarily causes another and, predictably, always will. According to Hume's philosophy, therefore, knowledge of any matters of fact that go beyond immediate experience is impossible, although he freely acknowledged that, practically, people had to think in terms of cause and effect, and had to assume the validity of their everyday beliefs, or they would go mad. He also admitted the possibility of knowledge of the relationships among ideas, such as the rela-tionships between numbers in mathematics. Hume's sceptical approach also denied the existence both of the spiritual substance postulated by Berkeley and of Locke's "material substance". Going further, Hume denied the existence of the individual self altogether, maintaining that because people do not have a constant perception of themselves as distinct entities, they "are nothing but a bundle or collection of different perceptions".

Hume's Ethics and Other Works: In his ethical thinking, Hume applied the same scepticism to the idea of an objective rightness or wrongness about actions as he had applied to the idea of an objective causal connection between events. He argued that a belief that an action is right or wrong cannot be a belief about some matter of fact, because it is a belief that always in some degree motivates us to act, and beliefs about matters of fact never motivate us to act. Only desires and emotions can motivate us.

He went on to argue that when we think we are perceiving an objective rightness or wrongness in an action, we are only projecting on to the action the approval or disapproval that we, and other members of society, feel towards that action. The emotions of approval or disapproval in turn result from the fact that, although human beings are mainly self-interested, every person also has a degree of "sympathy" with all others. This is a tendency to resonate with their feelings, to feel happy when one sees that others are happy, to feel pain when one sees that they are in pain, and so on. If one thinks that an action is going to create a lot of happiness in a lot of people, then one's sympathy with those people expresses itself in a positive feeling towards the action, and this is the feeling of approval. It is the same with disapproval. Hume tried to show that all our moral experience and moral concepts could be explained as a result of the workings of sympathy, approval, and disapproval.

Hume's moral theory has been very influential on subsequent discussion of morality and human action. As well as producing arguments that are still used today against the idea that there can be an objective morality, he provided the basis for the development of utilitarianism, and pioneered the attempt to see moral norms as generated by interactions between largely self-interested individuals. In developing his views on morality, he also established a conception of rational action according to which an action is rational only if it is a means of attaining some goals of the agent. This instrumental conception of rational action has since become the dominant one in both social science and philosophy.

As a historian, Hume broke away from the traditional chronological account of wars and deeds of state and attempted to describe the economic and intellectual forces that played a part in the history of his country. In this way he anticipated the theories of history of G. W. F. Hegel and Karl Marx in important ways. His *History of Great Britain* (1754) and *History of England* (1759) were for many years regarded as historical classics.

Hume's contributions to economic theory, which influenced the Scottish philosopher and economist Adam Smith and later economists, included his belief that wealth depends not on money but on commodities, and his recognition of the effect of social conditions on economics.

Hume's argument against causation, how can one know that (sensory event) A is the cause of some (sensory event) B? Since A and B are distinguishable, we do not think of one being the cause of the other until, through experience, we find constant conjunction between A and B (coupled with "continguity" (closeness) of A and B, and the priority of A to B). This constant conjunction gives rise to a superstition that there is a necessary connection between A and B but this notion is just superstition, in that we might have had a long run of coincidences. Since A and B are separable, and we can conceive themexisting apart, there is no purely rational basis for deriving B from A; and appeal to some general principle derived from experience (*i.e.*, the future will be like the past) is not helpful because any such principle suffers from the same problem as "A causes B"—because this too can be coincidental.

Husserl Edmund Gustav Albrech, German philosopher t (1859-1938). Student of Brentano and teacher of Heidegger, Husserl pursued the development of phenomenology as a pure investigation into the nature and content of consciousness in Logische Untersuchungen (Logical Investigations) (1901-13) vol. 1 and vol. 2. This pursuit requires that we 'bracket' our natural beliefs in order to understand their structural sources. Husserl described his methods in Pure Phenomenology, Its Method and Its Field of Investigation (1917), his inagural lecture at Freiburg. As Husserl made clear in Meditations CartÈsiennes (Cartesian Meditations) (1931), only the transcendental self thus remains as both the agent and the object of phenomenological study. *Recommended Reading*: The Essential Husserl: Basic Writings in Transcendental Phenomenology, ed. by Donn Welton (Indiana, 1999); Joseph J. Kockelmans, Edmund Husserl's Phenomenology (Purdue, 1994); The Cambridge Companion to Husserl, ed. by Barry Smith and David Woodruff Smith (Cambridge, 1995); Paul S. MacDonald, Descartes and Husserl: The Philosophical Project of Radical Beginnings (SUNY, 1999); and Victor Velarde, On Husserl(Wadsworth, 1999).

Hutcheson Francis, Scottish philosopher (1694-1746). In his Inquiry into the Original of our Ideas of Beauty and Virue (1725), An Essay on the

Nature and Condúct of the Passions and Affections with Illustrations on the Moral Sense (1728), and A System of Moral Philosophy (1755), Hutc-heson introduced the notion of a "moral sense" by means of which we not only recognize the rectitude of particular actions but are also motivated to perform them, together with a formulation of the greatest happiness principle. These conceptions, also developed (in different directions) by Butler, Hume, and Bentham, became staples of British moral philosophy in the eighteenthand nineteenth centuries. His later work included a set of Remarks (1750) on Mandeville's Fable of the Bees. *Recommended Reading*: Francis Hutcheson, Philosophical Writings, ed. by R. S. Downie (Everyman, 1994) and William R. Scott, Francis Hutcheson: His Life, Teaching and Position in the History of Philosophy (Thoemmes, 1998).

Hyle, greek term for wood or forest; hence, in the philosophy of Aristotle, the term is used for matter considered more generally. Among the four causes, hylí is the material cause that underlies any sort of substantial change. *Recommended Reading*: F. E. Peters, Greek Philosophical Terms: A Historical Lexicon (NYU, 1967).

Hylomorphic, Aristotle's theory that natural objects are irreducible composites of matter (Gk. hyle) and form (Gk. morphí). *Recommended Reading*: Aristotle, The Physics: Books I-IV, tr. By Philip H. Wicksteed and Francis M. Cornford (Harvard, 1986).

Hypatia, Egyptian mathematician, astronomer, and philosopher (370-415).Hypatia was a popular teacher and head of the neoplatonic philosophical community at Alexandria until her torture and death at the hands of a clergyled Christian mob. The Alexandrian intellectual community declined significantly after her death. *Recommended Reading*: Maria Dzielska, Hypatia of Alexandria (Harvard, 1996) and Charles Kingsley, Hypatia (Dent, 1968).

Hypostasization, the variety of reification that results from sup-posing that whatever can be named or conceived abstractly must actually exist. When (in Through the Looking Glass) his Messenger declares "I'm sure nobody walks much faster than I do," the White King hypostasizes "Nobody" by responding that "He can't do that, or else he'd have been here first." Such philosophers as Plato, Hegel, and Heidegger are sometimes accused of similar flights of ontological whimsy.

Hypothesis, in science, a testable assertion—especially a generalization or lawlike assertion, *e.g.*, Newton's law of universal gravitation which states (in part) "All bodies attract each other with a force inversely proportional to their distance." Hypotheses that survive testing come to be confirmed, whereupon they are provisionally accepted as scientific laws. A general principle, tentatively put forward for the purposes of scientific explanation and subject to disconfirmation by empirical evidence. For a more detailed discussion, see Logic. *Recommended Reading*: Karl R. Popper, Logic of Scientific Discovery (Routledge, 1992); Henri Poincare, Science and Hypothesis (Dover, 1952); Errol E. Harris, Hypothesis and Perception: The Roots of Scientific Method (Prometheus, 1996); Larry Laudan, Science andHypothesis: Historical Essays on Scientific Methodology (Reidel, 1982); David Weissman, Hypothesis and the Spiral of Reflection

(SUNY, 1989); and Peter Achinstein and Owen Hannaway, Observation, Experiment, and Hypothesis in Modern Physical Science (MIT, 1985).

Hypothetical deductive method, Heisenberg's uncertainty relations; the scientific method of testing would-be laws (hypotheses) by making predictions of particular observable events, then observing whether the events turn out as predicted. If so, the hypothesis is confirmed. If not, the hypothesis is disconfirmed, or (some would say) refuted.

Hypothetical imperative, a command that applies, not unconditionally, but only under certain conditions, or given certain purposes. *e.g.*,

"If you want to see a good movie rent The Big Lebowski": the command, here, to rent The Big Lebowski applies only on the condition that you want to see a good movie. Similarly, the command to change your oil frequently applies only if you want your car to last; the command to look both ways before crossing only applies if you seek a safe crossing; etc.

According to Kant, nonmoral commandments are all of this hypothetical sort. Compare: categ-orical imperative.

Hypothetical syllogism-HS, a rule of inference of the form:

$p \rightarrow q$

$q \rightarrow r$

$p \rightarrow r$

Example: "If Debbie is promoted, then Gene will be, too. But if Gene is promoted, then Kim will be angry. Therefore, if Debbie is promoted, then Kim will be angry." A truthtable shows the validity of this inference.

Icon, (From miniature religious statues) A small picture intended to represent something.

Ideal, In domain theory, a non-empty, downward closed subset which is also closed under binary least upper bounds, *i.e.* anything less than an element is also an element and the least upper bound of any two elements is also an element.

Idealism, in metaphysics, idealism is a term used to describe the sort of theory which claims that something "ideal" or non-physical or non-material or non-extended is the primary reality. In this sense, Plato, Berkeley, Leibniz and Hegel are among the most significant of the idealists (Leibniz is perhaps the most consistent, since he said that all physical things are actually made up of little bundles of consciousness he called "monads", an idea that is close to panpsychism). Obviously, spiritualism is similar to idealism, but spiritualism tends to be used to refer more to religious, supernatural conceptions of reality, rather than to philosophical theories like those of Plato or Hegel. Plato can be considered the "Founding Father" of idealism in Western philosophy, since he claimed that what is fundamentally real are ideas, of which physical objects are pale imitations. The opposite of idealism is materialism. Just as materialism in metaphysics is often linked with subjectivism in epistemology, idealism is often linked with intrinsicism in epistemology (though epistemological intrinsicism is sometimes also called, confusingly, idealism, since intrinsicism holds that we literally perceive universals or ideas). In popular usage, "idealism" is more of an ethical term, characterizing people who have a strong code of values or a great deal of integrity, though sometimes to an excessive degree (often contrasted with those who are merely or healthily pra-gmatic). (References from absolut-ism, abstractionism, Cartesianism, dualism, essentialism, Hegelianism, intrinsicism, Kantianism, Marxism, materialism, mentalism, monism, Neo-Platonism, Platonism, realism, spiritualism, and transcendentalism.)

Idealism, theory of reality and of knowledge that attributes a key role to the mind in the constitution of the world as it is experienced. Different versions and applications of idealism are discernible in the history of philosophy. In its most radical and commonly rejected form it is equivalent to solipsism, the view that reality is nothing but the activity of one's own mind and that nothing really exists or can be known to exist but one's own mind and its thoughts. The idealist, however, usually gives full recognition to the external, or natural, world, avoiding any claim that it can be reduced to the mere process of thinking. The mind, on the other hand, is active and, indeed, is able to produce and sustain modes of being that would not otherwise exist, such as law, religion, art, and mathematics. Furthermore, the way that natural objects exist in human experience is affected by the activity of the mind, and attention to this influence is essential if inquiries concerning the world are to be scientific.

Plato: Plato, a distant precursor of idealism, postulated the existence of a realm of ideas or "forms" that are imperfectly reflected in the varied objects of common experience. He maintained that these ideal forms are not only more clearly intelligible but also more real than the transient and essentially illusory objects themselves.

Berkeley and Kant: The 18th-century Irish philosopher and clergyman George Berkeley spe-culated that all aspects of everything of which one is conscious are actually reducible to the ideas present in the mind. The observer does not conjure external objects into existence, however; the true ideas of these are caused in the human mind directly by God. The 18th-century German philosopher Immanuel Kant greatly refined idealism through his critical inquiry into the limits of possible knowledge. Kant held that all that can be known of things is the way in which they appear in experience; there is no way of knowing what they are substantially in themselves. He also held, however, that the fundamental principles of science are essentially grounded in the constitution of the mind rather than being derived from the external world.

Hegel: The 19th-century German philosopher G. W. F. Hegel regarded as invalid Kant's theory concerning the inescapable human ignorance of what things are in themselves, arguing instead for the ultimate intelligibility of all existence. Hegel also maintained that the highest achievements of the human spirit (culture, science, religion, and the state) are not the result of naturally determined processes in the mind, but are conceived and sustained by the activity of free, reflective intellect. Further strains of idealistic thought can be found in the works of the 19th-century Germans J. G. Fichte and F. W. J. Schelling, the 19th-century British philosopher F.

H. Bradley, the 19th-century Americans C. S. Peirce and Josiah Royce, and the 20th-century Italian Benedetto Croce.

Ideas, on Locke's conception ideas are the contents with which minds are "furnished" (as he puts it). From "simple ideas" (*e.g.*, or red, of round, of sweet) furnished by sense-perception the mind constructs "complex ideas" (*e.g.*, of apple). Conception being nothing but this compounding of sense based ideas, and reasoning being nothing but tran-sitions between ideas thus compounded, all knowledge—Locke maintains—derives ultimately from sensory experience. See also: empiricism, impressions.

Identity theory, the identity theory of mind is standardly understood to be the claim that every mental property is identical with some physical property.

1. Identity theories of mind (IT) and multiple realisation

The version of physicalism that gained ground in the middle of this century was in the first place committed to the identity thesis, namely, that every property (and thereby every mental property) is identical with some physical property.

IT: Every property is identical with some physical property.

Smart's "Sensations and Brain Processes" (1959) provides the classic statement of this view. At that point, the primary concern of physicalists was to establish the point that two nonsynonymous terms could nonethe-less pick out the same property. Even though "pain" and, say, "C-fibers firing," are not synonymous, the property of being in pain could be identical with theproperty of having one's C-fibers firing. Very soon, however, the predominant concern shifted to what is now famous as the problem of multiple realisability and its implications for identity theories.

It's important to distinguish the problem of multiple realisability from the justification of multiple realisability. The justification stems from functionalism. According to functionalism, each mental property can be defined as a second-order property, the property of having some property or other that plays a certain functional role, defined in terms of other functional properties and physical causes and effects. As a result, it is likely that many different first-order physical properties can play the same functional role. There will (likely) be a very large set of different physical properties such that each can play the functional role, so thatdifferent instances of M may be correlated with various members of that set.

The way in which this constitutes a problem for identity theories is by implying a failure of coextension. Call this the Coextension argument:

There exists at least one mental property *M* such that there is a set of distinct physical properties (*P*1, v *P*2 v... *Pn*), no one of which realizes M on every occasion, while each realizes it on some occasion.

1. If *M* is identical with any physical property, it is identical with one of (*P*1, v *P*2 v...*Pn*)

2. *M* can't be identical with any of (*P*1, v *P*2 v...*Pn*) because there is no member of it with which it is co-

extensive

3. There is no physical property with which M is coextensive, and hence none with which it is identical.

Therefore, IT is false. A property *M* exists which is not identical to any physical property.

The identity theory IT can be saved in light of this argument by rejecting either premise 1 or premise 2. The disjunction option and elimination options discussed below correspond to those moves. If these prove unpalatable, the physicalist can still propose some theses that maintain the spirit, if not the letter, of IT; these are trope theories and second-order definition theories. I address each option in turn.

1.1. ***The disjunction option***

One could deny 2 by finding some further physical property, unrelated to the realizers, which that is indeed in common to all the instances of *M*. But there is no reason to expect there to be any such property. The disjunction option instead locates the common property as the property defined by disjoining the members of (*P*1, v *P*2 v... *Pn*). The property *M* is identical with a physical property after all, namely, *P*1 v *P*2 v... *Pn*.

Advocates of the disjunction option face two important questions. First, is *P*1 v *P*2 v... *Pn* a property? Second, is it in fact identical with M? Many philosophers are suspicious of such disjunctive properties as that allegedly named by "*P*1 v *P*2 v... *Pn*" (Armstrong 1978; Lewis 1983). If one believes that every predicate corresponds to a property or a universal, then this problem cannot arise. But if you reject this presumption, then the question becomes pressing. (For debate, see Fodor 1974, Kim 1989, Kim 1992.)

Even if we decide that *P*1 v *P*2 v... *Pn* is a genuine physical property, the question remains whether it can be identified with *M*. The original problem multiple realisability posed for IT was a failure of coextension, and *P*1 v *P*2 v...*Pn* is supposed to be coextensive with *M*. But this is ambiguous: do we mean coextensive in the actual world, in all nomo-logically possible worlds, or all worlds whatsoever? If *P*1 v *P*2 v...*Pn* is to be identical with *M* then,trivially, we must mean that they are coextensive in all worlds whatsoever. But, in fact, if we are tempted to the disjunctive option because of functionalism, we cannot appeal to a purely physical disjunction for anidentity claim. It's a familiar point that functionalism not only allows variable physical realisation; it also allows nonphysical realisation. In some worlds, nonp-hysical properties will realize the mental. Hence, if *P*1 v *P*2 v... *Pn* is to be coextensive with *M* in all possible worlds whatsoever, it must include some nonphysical properties as disjuncts. In that case, however, it is not a physical property with which we are identifying the physical property (Melnyk 1996).

a. *The eliminative option*

If one is an eliminativist about the mental in general, one is of course unfased by the Coextension argument. However, one could adopt a mild sort of eliminativism by denying, not that any mental properties exist at all, but by denying the more limited claim that is the first premise of the Coextension argument.

The strategy is simple. For each of the members of ($P1$ v $P2$ v...Pn) there is said to correspond a mental property, a species of M. If M is the property of pain, there will be many different kinds of pain, but no such thing as pain, period. Each of those kinds is then identified with its corresponding physical realizer, and IT is re-established.

Unlike a more thoroughgoing eliminativism, this view is not saddled with the implausible claim that people are not conscious, that they have no thoughts, etc. But it does face the charge that its invocation of these kinds of pain, and so on, is arbitrary and misleading. Why call it pain if doesn't have the features common to all pains? We cannot, on this view, say that it has those features, because there is no such thing as the property of pain, period, and hence no such thing as what is in common to each such instance. Perhaps, again invoking the distinction between predicates that correspond to properties and those that don't, the advocate of milder eliminativism could say that each such instance is picked out by the predicate "pain," and that is what they have in common; but this predicate fails to pick out any property (Kim 1992; Hooker 1981).

b. *Identity theories and tropes*

The remaining two responses to the Coextension argument admit that IT is, in fact, false; they propose closely related theses instead, however, that maintain the basic idea of IT.

The first of these switches from an identity theory about properties to one about tropes. A trope is the particular instance of a property, an abstract particular. The Coextension argument is powerless against this thesis:

IT1: Every actual trope is identical with a physical trope.

Even if there are properties—universals—that fail to be coextensive with physical properties, each instance of a nonphysical property could be identical with an instance of a physical property. If that were the case, physicalist intuitions would, it seems, be assuaged.

It's important to see that IT1 is more than a token identity thesis. It's not just that all particular events, or all particular objects, are physical; it's that all particular property instances are physical (Robb 1997).

The primary difficulty with this approach is simply that the nature of tropes is obscure and, as a result, it is nearly impossible to evaluate the claim that we have in certain cases not two tropes but one. Property individuation is puzzling enough; trope individuation is worse yet.

c. *The second-order option*

Finally, if functionalism is adopted, one has already provided an identity theory of a sort. That is, one has already subscribed to the following thesis:

IT2: Every property is identical with a physical property or a second-order property defined in purely physical and logical terms.

IT2 is not, of course, an identity theory in the standard sense. It does not imply that every property is a physical property, unless every physically definable second order property thereby counts as a physical property.

One problem with IT2 is that it requires that one buy into functionalism for every property for which multiple realisability is a problem. This may seem innocuous enough if one is convinced of multiple realisability because of a commitment to functionalism in the first place, but IT2 highlights how contentious a thesis functionalism is in the first place. It is fair to call it a sort of "reductionism," since it claims that every property can be defined using only logical apparatus and physical terms. If IT2 is one's method of saving the spirit of the identity theory, one certainly doesn't dilute its strength at all (Field 1992).

Increasingly, physicalists (see Papineau 1993; Melnyk 1996) have appealed to a related thesis:

> IT3: Every property is identical with a physical property or is realised on every occasion by a physical property.

Depending on exactly how the notion of realisation is cashed out, this may turn out to be identical with IT2. The notion of realisation has, however, been neglected in the philosophical literature, even as its appeal has grown. *References*: (in order of importance) Smart, J. J. C. 1959. "Sensations and Brain Processes." The Philosophical Review 68: 141-156. Putnam, Hilary. 1967. "The Nature of Mental States."Originally appeared as "Psychological Predicates" in W. H.Capitan and D. D. Merrill, eds., Art, Mind and Religion. Pittsburgh: University of Pittsburgh Press. Reprinted (1975) in Putnam, Mind, Language and Reality: Philosophical Papers, Volume 2. Cambridge: Cambridge University Press, 429-40. Fodor, Jerry. 1974. "Special Sciences." Synthese 28: 97-115. Reprinted (1981) in Fodor, Repr-esentations: Philosophical Essays on the Foundations of Cognitive Science. Cambridge, Mass.: MIT Press, 127-146. Armstrong, David. 1978. A Theory of Universals: Universals and Scientific Realism, Volume 2. Cambridge: Cambridge University Press. Lewis, David. 1983. "New Work for a Theory of Universals." Australasian Journal of Philosophy 61: 343-377. Hooker, Clifford. 1981. "Towards a General Theory of Reduction." Parts 1 - 3. Dialogue 20: 38-59, 201-236, 496-529. Kim, Jaegwon. 1989. "The Myth of Nonreductive Materialism." Proceedings and Addresses of the American Philosophical Association 63: 31-47. Reprinted in Kim (1993) Kim, Jaegwon. 1992. "Multiple Realisation and the Metaphysics of Reduction. Philosophy and Phenomenological Research 52: 1-26. Reprinted in Kim (1993). Kim, Jaegwon. 1993. Supe-rvenience and Mind. Cambridge: Cambridge University Press. Melnyk, Andrew. 1996. "Formulating Physicalism: Two Suggestions." Synthese 105, 381-407. Robb, David. 1997. "The Properties of Mental Causation." The Philosophical Quarterly 47: 178-194. Papineau, David. 1993. Philosophical Naturalism. Oxford: Blackwell. Field, Hartry. 1992. "Physicalism." In J. Earman, ed., Inference, Explanation and other Frustrations. Essays in the Philosophy of Science. Berkeley: University of California Press, 271-291.

Identity, A 2-adic predicate, say Ixy, asserting that its two arguments are identical. Customarily symbolized by "=" and written in infix notation, "x=y". While all systems of polyadic predicate logic can express identity as easily as any other 2-adic relation, a system is said to be "with identity" iff it also contains axioms, axiom schemata, and/or rules of inference determining how "=" is to be used. Note that an axiom like "(x)(x=x)" or "(x)Ixx" is not logically valid because there are interpretations of "=" or "I" that do not take the meaning of identity. See first-order theory with identity, predicate logic with identity, interpretation, normal

Ideology, comprehensive system of concepts and beliefs, often political in nature, held by a group or an individual. The term was coined by the French philosopher Antoine Destutt de Tracy, one of the so-called Ideologues, who attempted to reform postrevolutionary French society according to a pragmatic "science of ideas".

Modern Origins: The modern concept of ideology originated in the writings of Karl Marx, who believed that ideologies were false systems of political, social, and moral concepts invented and preserved by ruling classes out of self-interest. According to Marx, religious hierarchies, for example, perpetuate systems of faith that at bottom protect the economic well-being of those in power. As refined by later social thinkers, this pejorative definition of ideology came to dominate modern usage of the term. Following Marx, proponents of a particular sociopolitical system felt free to dismiss arguments offered by opponents as ideologically based, that is, false because they reflect only the ideological biases of the opponent and not the true state of affairs. Because this tactic could be used to argue against every ideology, the clash of modern ideologies became a strident and passionate affair dominated more by propaganda than by rational argument.

Ideology in the 20th Century: Perhaps the chief distinguishing characteristic of 20th-century ideologies has been the almost religious devotion of their adherents to systems of political ideas that are viewed as absolutely incompatible with other systems. This trait has been most pronounced in the two major modern ideologies, communism and fascism. Other political concepts, such as socialism, democracy, and conservatism, while often strongly upheld, have tended to be more diffuse and less exclusive; their proponents differ on some issues while agreeing on others.

The concept of ideology has had a profound effect on world civilization in the 20th century. Almost all modern conflicts, from the "crusade against fascism" in World War II to the various "police actions" of the post-war period, have had ideological overtones. The prime example of an ideological conflict was the cold war, in which the principal antagonists (the United States and the Union of Soviet Socialist Republics) waged a political, economic, and psychological struggle for influence in every part of the world.

Iff, Abbreviation of "if and only if", which designates material equivalence.

Imagination, traditionally, the mental capacity for experiencing, constructing, or manipulating "mental imagery" (quasi-perceptual experience). Imagination is also regarded as responsible for fantasy, inventiveness, idiosyncrasy, and creative, original, and insightful thought in general, and, sometimes, for a much wider range of mental activities dealing with the non-actual, such as supposing, pretending, "seeing as", thinking of possibilities, and even being mistaken. See representation.

Immanent, internal or indwelling as opposed to external or out dwelling: inparticular, what is internal to the material, sensible world as opposed to what is above or beyond it, or transcendent. On pantheistic views (*e.g.*, those of the Stoics or Spinoza) God is held to be an immanent guidingspirit in and of the sensible material world, not existing apart or beyond it. Orthodox Christian views, by contrast hold God be transcendent. Similarly, Plato asserts the transcendence while Aristotle maintains the immanence of the Forms or essences of things.

Immoralism, intellectual stance that involves an outright rejection of conventional morality, of systematic approaches to ethics, or even of ethics as such. Friedrich Nietzsche is famous for having called himself an immoralist. (References from atheism and secularism.)

Immortalism, the view according to which human beings, or their souls at least, survive after death. This idea is sometimes called athanatism (from the Greek word for immortal), the opposite of which is thanatism.

Impartiality, in ethics, an impartial standpoint is one which treats everyone as equal. For many philosophers, impartiality is an essential component of the moral point of view.

Imperative, a command. Philosophers often distinguish between hypothetical imperatives and categorical imperatives.

Imperativism, deontologism

Implementation, 1. execution (the process of carrying out a course of action)

2. effectuation (providing a practical means for accomplishing something)

3. realisation (*e.g.* of a model or blueprint)

4. the outcome of 1-3

Implicans, implication

Implicate, implication

Implication, A statement of the form, "if *A*, then *B*," when *A* and *B* stand for wffs or propositions. The wff in the if-clause is called the antecedent (also the implicans and protasis). The wff in the then-clause is called the consequent (also the implicate and apodosis). As a truth function, see material implication. Also called a conditional, or a conditional statement. See corresponding conditional

Logical implication: A tautologous statement of material implication (next)

Material implication: A truth function that is false when its antecedent is true and its consequent false, and true otherwise. Also the connective that denotes this function; also the compound proposition built from this connective.

Notation: $p \Rightarrow q$ (or a thin right arrow). $A \Rightarrow B$ is true unless *A* is true and*B* is false. The truth table is

A B	*A => B*
F F	*T*
F T	*T*
T F	*F*
T T	*T*

It is surprising at first that $A \Rightarrow B$ is always true if *A* is false, but if $X \Rightarrow Y$ then we would expect that (*X*

& Z) => Y for any Z. This truth function is rarely what implication or "if...then" means in English, but it captures the logical core of that usage and is truth-functional.

Paradoxes of material implication: Two consequences of the formal definition of material implication that violate informal intuitions about implication: (1) that a material implication is true whenever its antecedent is false, and (2) that a material implication is true whenever its consequent is true. These so-called paradoxes do not create contradictions.

Implicit memory, implicit memory is evident when the performance of a subject on a task is improved despite the inability of the subject to consciously recollect memories which facilitate to the task. See also explicit memory.

Impossible, what cannot be the case, under any circumstances, is impossible. What is logically impossible is self contradictory; inconsistent with the basic principles of logic itself (to be both human and nonhuman, *e.g.*, is logically impossible). It is convenient for many purposes to recognize types of impossibility weaker than strict logical impossibility. Natural or nomological impossibility is the next strongest generally recognized type:. what is nomologically impossible, while it may be logically consistent, is inconsistent with the laws of nature: *e.g.*, it's nomologically impossible (current physics tells us) for anything to travel faster than the speed oflight. Practical impossibility is a weaker variety yet: what is practically impossible may be consistent with the laws of nature, but is incon-sistent given the circumstances; *e.g.*, it's nomologically possible for a human being to run a four minute mile but it's not practically possible for most of us (given our ages, physiques, and physical conditions) to do so. Contrast: possible. See also: necessary, contingent, actual.

Impressions, Hume terms the direct experiential deliverances of sensation impressions; simple ideas,for Hume are faint copies (in memory) ofthese sensory impressions, and complex ideas (all the rest) are compounded from these simple ideas, much as they are for Locke. See also: empiricism, ideas.

Inclination, this is the word that Kant used (actually, he used the German word Neigung) to refer to our sensuous feelings, emotions, and desires. Kant contrasts inclination with reason. Whereas inclination was seen as physical, causally-determined, and irrational, reason was portrayed as non-physical, free, and obviously rational.

Inclusive predicate logic, predicate logic

Inclusive quantification theory, predicate logic

Incomparable, Two elements *a*, *b* of a set are incomparable under some relation <= if neither *a* <= *b*, nor *b* <= *a*.

Incremental analysis, Partial analysis of an incomplete product to allow early feedback on its development.

Independence of an axiom, If "*S-A*" denotes system *S* minus axiom *A*, then for many logicians an axiom *A* is independent of system *S* iff neither *A* nor ~*A* are theorems of *S-A*. For some, *A* is independent iff *A* is not a theorem of *S-A*, even if ~*A* is a theorem of *S-A*. The former concept is equivalent to the undecidability of wff *A* in *S*.

Indeterminism, view, similar to accidentalism, according to which at least some events or human actions are not determined by outside causes; bviously this idea is opposed to determinism. Epicurus' idea of the "atomic swerve" is an example of an indeterminist doctrine.

Individualism, 1. while the word individualism usually pertains to ethics, we can also speak of meta-physical individualism (that only particular, individual things exist—see concretism and nominalism), epistemological individualism (that only individual minds can come to have knowledge), political indiv-idualism (respect for individual rights), and methodological indiv-idualism (as in Austrian economics). In ethics, individualism refers to the principle that it is the unique, unrepeatable person who should be the beneficiary of action, not any sort of collective entity (thus individualism is essentially the same as egoism and is opposed to ethical collectivism). Most varieties of ethical individualism are brands of eudaimonism, but this is not true of, for example, existentialism or stoicism. In popular usage, the connotations of "individualism" can be positive or negative, depending on who is using the term. Though it is a positive word for many people, the term can imply a kind of atomism that necessarily puts a low or even negative value on relations with other people. (References from altruism, Aristotelianism, Buddh-ism, egoism, gnosticism, hedonism, humanism, naturalism, stoicism, transcendentalism, and utilitarianism.)

2. see internalism

Individualism, in political and economic philosophy, the doctrine, promulgated by such theorists as the English philosopher Thomas Hobbes and the Scottish economist Adam Smith, that society is an artificial device, existing only for the sake of its members as individuals, and properly judged only according to criteria established by them as individuals. An individualist does not necessarily subscribe to the doctrine of egoism, which regards self-interest as the only logical human motivation. He or she may instead be guided in political and economic thinking by motives of altruism, holding that the end of social, political, and economic organization is the greatest good for the greatest number. What characterizes such an individualist thinker, however, is his or her conception of the "greatest number" as composed of independent units and an opposition to the interference of the state with the happiness or freedom of these units.

Individualist tendencies or theories play a part in all the sciences that deal with a person as a social being. Although individualism would theoretically consider the state as placing an artificial restraint on a person's individual tendencies, practical distinctions between individualism and its antitheses, such as socialism, are often difficult to make. Individualism differs from socialist or collectivist theories not so much in setting a high value upon the well-being and free initiative of the individual as in subordinating the demands of the community as a whole to individual welfare.

Individuals, also called particulars are

single things (*e.g.*, Socrates) as opposed to properties or kinds of things (humanity or humankind). The latter are universals. Individuals are typically the sorts of things named by proper names (*e.g.*, "Socrates") whereas universals are associated withgeneral words such as verbs (*e.g.*, "teaches"), common nouns (*e.g.*, "man"), and adjectives (*e.g.*, "human").

The objects or elements taken as the subjects of the predicates of first-order predicate logic. See constant, domain, variable

Induction, an inference in which the conclusion contains information thatwas not contained in the premises. Or, also, a form of reasoning in which one moves from one or more premisses to a conclusion in such a way that while the conclusion seems to have been given some justification, it is logicallypossible for the premisses to be true and the conclusion false.

Induction (logic), in logic, process of reasoning from the particular to the general as opposed to the inverse process of deduction. The basis of induction is the assumption that if something is true in a number of observed instances, it is also true in similar, but unobserved, instances. The probability of accuracy depends on the number of instances observed. One of the simplest types of induction involves the interpretation of opinion polls, in which the answers given by a small percentage of the total population are projected for the entire country. Inductive reasoning was developed by various philosophers, from Francis Bacon to David Hume, John Stuart Mill, and Charles Sanders Peirce.[1]

Inference, 1. The logical process by which new facts are derived from known facts by the application of inference rules. See also symbolic inference, type inference.

2. A series of *wff*s or propositions in which some (called premises) support another (called the conclusion); also the act of concluding theconclusion from the premises. See deduction, derivation, induction, proof.

Inference rule, A procedure which combines known facts to produce ("infer")new facts. For example, given that we can infer that Socrates is mortal.

1. Socrates is a man and that
2. all men are mortal,

This uses the rule known as "modus ponens" which can be written in Boolean algebra as (if proposition A

$$(A \& A \Rightarrow B) \Rightarrow B$$

is true, and A implies B, then B is true). Or given that,

1. Either Denis is programming or Denis is sad and we can infer that Denis
2. Denis is not sad,

is programming. This rule can be written

$$((A \text{ OR } B) \& \text{ not } B) \Rightarrow A$$

(If either A is true or B is true (or both), and B is false, then A must be true).

Infimum, greatest lower bound

Infinite, 1. Bigger than any natural number. There are various formal set definitions in set theory: a set X is infinite if

(i) There is a bijection between X and a proper subset of X.

(ii) There is an injection from the set N of natural numbers to X.

(iii) There is an injection from each natural number n to X.

These definitions are not necessarily equivalent unless we accept the Axiom of Choice.

2. The length of a line extended indefinitely. See also infinite loop, infinite set.

Infinite-Monkey Theorem, "If you put an infinite number of monkeys at typewriters, eventually one will bash out the script for Hamlet." (One may also hypothesise a small number of monkeys and a very long period of time.) This theorem asserts nothing about the intelligence of the one random monkey that eventually comes up with the script (and note that the mob will also type out all the possible *incorrect* versions of Hamlet). It may be referred to semi-seriously when justifying a brute force method; the implication is that, with enough resources thrown at it, any technical challenge becomes aone-banana problem.

This theorem was first popularised by the astronomer Sir Arthur Eddington. It became part of the idiom through the classic short story "Inflexible Logic" by Russell Maloney, and many younger hackers know it through a reference in Douglas Adams's "Hitchhiker's Guide to the Galaxy".

Infinite set, A set with an infinite number of elements. There are several possible definitions, *e.g.*

(i) ("Dedekind infinite") A set X is infinite if there exists a bijection (one-to-one mapping) between X and some proper subset of X.

(ii) A set X is infinite if there exists an injection from N (the set of natural numbers) to X.

In the presence of the Axiom of Choice all such definitions are equivalent.

Inherence, the relation between individuals or particulars and their attributes or universals: when an individual has an attribute, the attribute is said to "inhere" in the the thing.

Innate ideas, ideas that are inborn rather than acquired through sensory experience. Socrates and Plato taught that such ideas were acquired by direct acquaintance (prior to birth) with the archetypes or Forms or according to which all things are constructed. Descartes, as well as other rationalists (in agreement with Plato) believe such "clear and distinct" innate ideas are the source of all real knowledge. Belief in innate ideas is the distinguishing feature of rationalism.

Instance, An individual object of a certain class. While a class is just the type definition, an actual usage of a class is called "instance". Each instance of a class can have different values for its instance variables, *i.e.* its state.

Instance variable, In object-oriented programming, one of the variables of a class template which may have a different value for each object of that class. Instance variables hold the state of an object.

Instantiate, instantiation

Instantiation, 1. In predicate logic, to remove a quantifier from a wff and either leave the previously bound variables free or replace them with constants. See generalization, quantifier

Existential instantiation: Instantiation from the existential quantifier. For example, to move from statements like $(Ex)Px$ to Px or Pa; from "something is purple" to "x is purple" or "alabaster is purple". Valid only under several restrictions.

Universal instantiation: Instantiation from the existential quantifier. For example, to move fromstatements like $(x)Px$ to Px or Pa; from "everything is purple" to "x ispurple" or "alabaster is purple". Valid without restriction.

2. Producing a more defined version of some object by replacing variables with values (or other variables).

3. In object-oriented programming, producing a particular object from its class template. This involves allocation of a structure with the types specified by the template, and initialisation of instance variables with either default values or those provided by the class's constructor function.

4. In unification, (as used in logic programming, type checking and type inference), binding a logic variable (type variable) to some value (type).

Instrumental, a feature of values or valued things which is extrinsic: had by things insofar as they are not desirable or commendable in and of themselves but rather for the sake of, or as a means to, something else. Money (which gets its value from enabling us to purchase good) and medical treatment (which is valuable for the health it maintains or restores) are classic examples of extrinsic or instrumental goods. Contrast: intrinsic.

Instrumentalism, the view according to which concepts are merely useful instruments, and that the proper way to evalute concepts and propositions is not through the categories of truth and falsity but through judging their effectiveness; the view developed out of, and is somewhat similar to pragmatism. Perhaps the most famous avowal of instrumentalism was opernicus' advertisement of his heliocentric hypothesis as nothing more than an aid to astronomical calculation—a predictive instrument, not purporting to be a true description of astronomical realities. Contrast scientific realism.

Integrationist, any position which attempts to reconcile apparently conflicting tendencies or values into a single framework. Integrationist positions are contrasted with separatist positions, which advocate keeping groups (usually defined by race, ethnicity, or gender) separate from one another.

Integrity constraint, A constraint (rule) that must remain true for adatabase to preserve integrity. Integrity constraints are specified at database creation time and enforced by the database management system.

Examples from a genealogical database would be that every individual must be their parent's child or that they can have no more than two natural parents.

Intellectualism, the first historical figure who is usually called an intellectualist is Socrates (470-399 B.C.), since he enunciated the principle that "knowledge is sufficient for excellence"—in other words, that one will do what is right or best just as soon as one truly understands what is right or best. As an approach to philosophy and to values, the word intellectualism often has the same meaning as philosophical or psychological rationalism and commonly has the same negative connotations of over-reliance on theoretical models to the detriment of practical living. (References from Platonism and Socraticism.)

Intensional, having, or presupposing, a use of terms that relates not to the extension (that is, the individual things that actually happen to fall under these terms in this world) but determines what could or could not fall under the term (in for example any possible world). *E.g.* the extension of "having a heart" and "having a kidney" is the same in this world because in fact all creatures that have one have the other. But the intension is not the same because a creature with one feature might not have the other. extension

Intentionalism, the principle that consciousness is always consciousness of something, that is, of some aspect of reality. This idea is common to most varieties of epistemological realism. A different formulation defines "intentionalism" as the thesis that all mental states are representational states. Specifically, raw feels and qualia, are said to have representational content.

Intentionality, the property of the mind by which it is directed at, about, or "of" objects and events in the world. Aboutness—in the manner of beliefs, fears, desires, etc. Chris Eliasmith.

Intentionality derived, the power of a system (*e.g.* the mind) to be "about"something if that power is derived from that system's connection to another, already intentional system. Language's intentionality is said to be derived from that of the mind.

Intentional state, intentionality

Intention-in-action, the intentional or mental component of an action. The intention in action causes, and is contemporaneous with, the agent's bodily movement or state that is its condition of satisfaction. Introduced by Searle in 1983. See also intentionality, prior intention, Background, phenomenological critique of representationalism.

Interactive, A term describing a program whose input and output are interleaved, like a conversation, allowing the user's input to depend on earlier output from the same run.

The interaction with the user is usually conducted through either a text-based interface or a graphical user interface. Other kinds of interface, *e.g.* using speech recognition and/or speech synthesis, are also possible.

This is in contrast to batch processing where all the input is prepared before the program runs and so cannot depend on the program's output.

Internalism, internalists hold that mental events supervene only on physical events internal to the body of the subject of those mental events. Also known as individualism. See also supervenience, externalism.

Intrinsicism, intrinsicism in epistemology claims that our evaluations of things as true or valuable are not affected by our nature as human beings, but that truth and values exist out there in reality, divorced from human interests and concerns. A classic example is the intrinsic theory of value in the economic thought of the Middle Ages, which held that there is one natural, intrinsically-correct price for each product in the world. This example shows the principle that intrinsicism is frequently the flip side of subjectivism, since the "natural price" was the price that the authorities or the guilds set up for themselves according to their own interests. Forms of objectivism attempt to offer workable alternatives to the false dichotomy of intrinsicism vs. subjectivism. (References from conceptualism, idealism, intuitionism, Kantianism, objectivism, perspe-ctivism, Platonism, realism, and subjectivism.)

Intuition, in philosophy, a form of knowledge or of cognition inde-pendent of experience or reason. The intuitive faculty and intuitive knowledge are generally regarded as inherent qualities of the mind. The term *intuition* has been used in different, sometimes opposing, senses by various writers and cannot be defined except with reference to its meaning in the writings of an individual philosopher. The concept of intuition apparently arose from two sources: the mathematical idea of an axiom (a self-evident proposition that requires no proof) and the mystical idea of revelation (truth that surpasses the power of the intellect).

Intuition was important in Greek philosophy, particularly in the thinking of such philosophers as Pythagoras and his followers, who were trained in mathematics. The concept also had great significance in much of Christian philosophy as one of the basic ways in which a person could know God. The philosophers who relied most on the idea of intuition were Baruch Spinoza, Immanuel Kant, and Henri Bergson.

In Spinoza's philosophy, intuition is the highest form of knowledge, surpassing both empirical knowledge derived from the senses and "scientific" knowledge derived from reasoning on the basis of experience. Intuitive knowledge gives an individual the comprehension of an orderly and united universe and permits the mind to be a part of the Infinite Being.

Kant regarded intuition as the portion of a perception that is supplied by the mind itself. He divided perceptions, or "phenomena", into two parts: the sensation caused by the external object perceived; and the "form", or the understanding of the perception in the mind, which results from intuition. Such apprehension as space and time are types of pure intuition, or *Anschauung*.

Bergson contrasted instinct with intelligence and regarded intuition as the purest form of instinct. Intelligence, he believed, was adequate for the consideration of material things but could not deal with the fundamental nature of life or thought. He defined intuition as "instinct that has become disinterested, self-conscious, capable of reflecting upon its object and of enlarging it indefinitely". Intelligence, on the other hand, can only analyse, and the function of analysis is to produce what is relative in an object, rather than what is absolute, or individual. Only by intuition, Bergson declared, can the absolute be comprehended.

Some ethical philosophers, among them Spinoza, have been called intuitionists or intuitionalists because of their belief that a sense of moral values is intuitive and immediate. This view contrasts with that of the empiricists, who hold that moral values result from human experience alone, and that of the rationalists, who believe that moral values are determined solely by reason.

Intuitionism, 1. in ethics the term refers to the doctrine (popular in Britain around the turn of the century) that all of our moral judgments are made through an appeal to our moral intuitions or "moral sense". This ethical doctrine is derived from a more general idea in episte-mology dating back to Plato: namely, a radical intrinsicism which holds that all of our knowledge is gained through intuition, immediate insight, or spiritual vision of a transcendent higher reality. In addition, the movement of ethical intuitionism picked up on the ideas of the earlier "moral sense theorists" such as David Hume (1711-1776) and Adam Smith (1723-1790). Even though intuitionism is a form of intrinsicism, it ends up being a kind of subjectivism, in which the justification for ethical values is the fact that a certain person or philosopher thinks they are true. Historically, intuitionism has tended to be a kind of deontologism, although the cause may have been simply the beliefs of the intuitionists themselves and not anything about intuitionism in general. (References from emotionalism and mysticism.)

2. in philosophy of mathematics see intuitionistic logic

Intuitionistic logic, Brouwer's foundational theory of mathematics which says that you should not count a proof of (There exists x such that $P(x)$) valid unless the proof actually gives a method of constructing such an x. Similarly, a proof of (A or B) is valid only if it actually exhibits either a proof of A or a proof of B.

In intuitionism, you cannot in general assert the statement (A or not-A) (the rinciple of the excluded middle); (A or not-A) is not proven unless you have a proof of A or a proof of not-A. If A happens to be undecidable in your system (some things certainly will be), then there will be no proof of (A or not-A). This is pretty annoying; some kinds of perfectly healthy-looking proofs by contradiction just stop working. Of course, excluded middle is a theorem of classical logic (*i.e.* non-intuitionistic logic).

Invariant, A rule, such as the ordering of an ordered list or heap, that applies throughout the life of a data structure or procedure. Each change to the data structure must maintain the correctness of the invariant.

Irrefutable, The opposite of refutable.

James, William (1842-1910), American philosopher and psychologist, who developed the philosophy of pragmatism. James was born in New York on January 11, 1842. His father, Henry James, Sr., was a Swedenborgian theologian (a follower of Emanuel Swedenborg); one of his brothers was the great novelist Henry James. William James attended private schools in the United States and Europe, the Lawrence Scientific School at Harvard University, and the Harvard Medical School, from which he received a degree in 1869. Before finishing his medical studies, he went on an exploring expedition in Brazil with the Swiss-American naturalist Louis Agassiz and also studied physiology in Germany. After three years of retirement due to illness, James became an instructor in physiology at Harvard in 1872. After 1880 he taught psychology and philosophy at Harvard; he left Harvard in 1907 and gave highly successful lectures at Columbia University and the University of Oxford. James died in Chocorua, New Hampshire, on August 26, 1910.

Psychology: James's first book, the monumental *Principles of Psychology* (1890), established him as one of the most influential thinkers of his time. The work advanced the principle of functionalism in psychology, thus removing psyc-hology from its traditional place as a branch of philosophy and establishing it among the laboratory sciences based on experimental method.

In the next decade James applied his empirical methods of investigation to philosophical and religious issues. He explored the questions of the existence of God, the immortality of the soul, free will, and ethical values by referring to human religious and moral experience as a direct source. His views on these subjects were presented in the lectures and essays published in such books as *The Will to Believe and Other Essays in Popular Philosophy* (1897), *Human Immortality* (1898), and *The Varieties of Religious Experience* (1902). The last-named work is a sympathetic psychological account of religious and mystical experiences.

Pragmatism: Later lectures published as *Pragmatism: A New Name for Old Ways of Thinking* (1907) summed up James's original contributions to the theory called pragmatism, a term first used by the American logician C. S. Peirce. James generalized the pragmatic method, developing it from a critique of the logical basis of the sciences into a basis for the evaluation of all experience. He maintained that the meaning of ideas is found only in terms of their possible consequences. If consequences are lacking, ideas are meaningless. James contended that this is the method used by scientists to define their terms and to test their hypotheses, which, if meaningful, entail predictions. The hypotheses can be considered true if the predicted events take place. On the other hand, most metaphysical theories are meaningless, because they entail no testable predictions. Meaningful theories, James argued, are instruments for dealing with problems that arise in experience.

According to James's pragmatism, then, truth is that which *works*. One determines what works by testing propositions in experience. In so doing, one finds that certain propositions become true. As James put it, "truth is something that happens to an idea" in the process of its verification; it is not a static property. This does not mean, however, that anything can be true. "The true is only the expedient in the way of our thinking, just as 'the right' is only the expedient in the way of our behaving", James maintained. One cannot believe whatever one wants to believe, because such self-centred beliefs would not work out.

James was opposed to absolute metaphysical systems and argued against monism, a doctrine that maintains that reality is a unified, monolithic whole. In *Essays in Radical Empiricism* (1912), he argued for a pluralistic universe, denying that the world can be explained in terms of an absolute force or scheme that determines the interrelations of things and events. He held that the interrelations, whether they serve to hold things together or apart, are just as real as the things themselves.

By the end of his life, James had become world-famous as a philosopher and psychologist. In both fields, he functioned more as an originator of new thought than as a founder of dogmatic schools. His pragmatic philosophy was further developed by the American philosopher John Dewey and others; later studies in physics by Albert Einstein made the theories of interrelations advanced by James appear prophetic.

Kant, Immanuel (1724-1804), German philosopher, considered by many to have been the most influential thinker of modern times.

Life: Born in Königsberg in Prussia (now Kaliningrad, Russia) on April 22, 1724, Kant received his education at the Collegium Fredericianum and the University of Königsberg. At the college he chiefly studied the Classics, and at the university he studied physics and mathematics. After his father died, he was compelled to halt his university career and earn his living as a private tutor. In 1755, aided by a friend, he resumed his studies and obtained his doctorate. Thereafter, he taught at the university for 15 years, lecturing first on science and mathematics, as well as geography, but gradually enlarging his field of concentration to cover almost all branches of philosophy.

Although Kant's lectures and works written during this period established his reputation as an original philosopher, he did not receive a chair at the university until 1770, when he was made Professor of Logic and Metaphysics. For the next 27 years he continued to teach and attracted large numbers of students to Königsberg. Kant's unorthodox religious teachings, which were based on rationalism rather than revelation, brought him into conflict with the government of Prussia, and in 1792 he was forbidden by Frederick William II, King of Prussia, to teach or write on religious subjects. Kant obeyed this order for five years until the death of the king and then felt released from his obligation. In 1798, the year following his retirement from the university, he published a summary of his religious views. He died on February 12, 1804.

Kant's Philosophy: The keystone of Kant's philosophy, sometimes called critical philosophy, is contained in his *Critique of Pure Reason* (1781), in which he examined the bases of human knowledge and created an individual epistemology. Like earlier philosophers, Kant differentiated modes of thinking into analytic and synthetic propositions. An analytic proposition is one in which the predicate is contained in the subject, as in the statement "birds have wings". The truth of this type of proposition is evident, because to state the reverse would be to make the proposition self-contradictory. Such propositions are called analytic because truth is discovered by the analysis of the subject itself, in this case, of the concept "bird". Synthetic propositions, on the other hand, are those that cannot be arrived at by pure analysis, as in the statement "that bird is blue". All the common propositions that result from experience of the world are synthetic.

Propositions, according to Kant,

can also be divided into two other types: empirical, or a posteriori, and a priori. Empirical propositions can be known only through sense perception, but a priori propositions can be known without the use of such perception. The difference between these two types of proposition may be illustrated by the empirical "that bird is blue" and the a priori "two plus two makes four". Before Kant, it was assumed that only the a priori judgements were analytic ones. Kant's thesis in the *Critique*, however, is that it is possible to make synthetic a priori judgements.

In describing how this type of judgement is possible, Kant regarded the objects of the world as fundamentally unknowable; from the point of view of reason, they serve merely as the raw material from which sensations are formed. Objects in themselves are unknowable, and to think of them as situated in time and space is to apply the ideas of time and space, which are in fact part of the mind, to raw perceptions in order to organize them and make them intelligible.

Kant stated that in addition to the ideas of time and space, which he called "pure forms of intuition", the mind necessarily contains a number of fundamental concepts, which he called "categories". He divided the categories into four groups: those concerning quantity, which are unity, plurality, and totality; those concerning quality, which are reality, negation, and limitation; those concerning relation, which are substance-and-accident, cause-and-effect, and reciprocity; and those concerning modality, which are possibility, existence, and necessity.

We apply the pure forms of intuition and our concepts to our "intuitions", or raw perceptions, in order to make sense of them and to make a posteriori judgements about the world. This is how people gain most of their knowledge. However, we can also reflect on the fact that we must apply these forms of intuition and categories in order for us to have any intelligible experience at all, because these forms of intuition and categories are intrinsic to the self-conscious mind. In the part of the *Critique* called the "transcendental deduction", Kant attempts to prove this for the categories. It follows that any intelligible experience will be organized through the forms of intuition and categories, and this fact can be expressed in a series of synthetic a priori judgements that apply to the world of experience, the only world we can know. For example, the fact that we have to organize all our experience through the category of "cause and effect" can be expressed in the synthetic a priori judgement that "every event has a cause". This judgement is a priori because we can know it simply by reflecting on the fact that the category of cause and effect is essential to intelligible experience as such. We do not have to check whether in our experience every effect does indeed have a cause. However, it is synthetic because the concept "event" does not contain the concept of "caused" in the way that the concept of "bird" contains the concept of "winged". Such synthetic a priori judgements form the fundamental principles of science.

Therefore, for Kant the forms of intuition and the categories belong to the mind, and they are applied by the mind to our raw perceptions in order to gain knowledge. Accordingly, our conceptual knowledge can only be of the world as it is "for us", that is, as we experience it. Kant calls this view "transcendental idealism". The opposite view would be that time, space, and the categories are inherent in the structure of the world as it is "in itself", that is, as it is independently of its being experienced by people. It would then be possible to gain knowledge that goes beyond experience by applying these categories to the world as it is in itself. Kant regards this opposite view as the source of most of the errors of philosophy. In the section of the *Critique* called the "trans-cendental dialectic" he attempts to show that it leads to a series of pairs of contradictory propositions or "antinomies", both of which can be proved true. For example, it can be shown that people are both free and determined. The only way to resolve these contradictions is to adopt the standpoint of transcendental idealism, and to distinguish clearly between things as they are for us—or phenomena, of which we can have knowledge—and things as they are in themselves—as well as noumena, such as the human agent, which can be conceived of through reason but which cannot be known. Thus, the human being as a phenomenon is determined, but as a noumenon is free.

In the *Foundations of the Metaphysics of Morals* (1795) Kant described his ethical system, which is based on a belief that reason is the ultimate foundation of morality. Moral actions, he believed, must be undertaken from a sense of duty ultimately dictated by reason, and no action performed out of inclination, for expediency, or solely in obedience to law or custom can be regarded as moral. Kant described two types of commands given by reason: the "hypothetical imperative", which rationally dictates a given course of action to reach a specific end or goal; and the "categorical imperative", which rationally dictates a course of action independent of whatever goals the agent may have. The categorical imperative is the basis of morality and was stated by Kant in two key formulations: "Act as if the maxim of your action were to become through your will a general natural law"; and "Act so that you treat humanity, whether in your own person or in that of another, always as an end and never as a means only".

Kant's ethical ideas are the logical outcome of his belief in the fundamental freedom of the individual as stated in his *Critique of Practical Reason* (1788), also known as the second *Critique*. This freedom he did not regard as the lawless freedom of anarchy, but rather as the freedom of self-government, the freedom to obey consciously the laws intrinsic to one's nature as a rational being. He believed that the world was progressing towards an ideal society in which reason would "bind every law-giver to make his laws in such a way that they could have sprung from the united will of an entire people, and to regard every subject, in so far as he wishes to be a citizen, on the basis of whether he has conformed to that will". In his essay *Perpetual Peace* (1795), Kant advocated the establishment of a world federation of republican states.

In the second *Critique*, Kant also attempted to demonstrate that although beliefs in God, freedom, and the immortality of the soul cannot be grounded in empirical experience, they are also not refuted by it. In addition, such beliefs are necessary if people are to see their moral actions as having a point, and this justifies them. In this way Kant tried to reconcile religion with a scientific world view.

In the *Critique of Judgement* (1790), also known as the third *Critique*, Kant attempted to deal with the capacity to see history and nature as tending to the realization of inherent goals. He also addressed the capacity to make aesthetic judgements, that is, judgements on whether something is beautiful or not. He argued that the sense of beauty of an object is based on a direct personal intuition, and yet in making an aesthetic judgement, a person feels entitled to judge that the object is objectively beautiful, not just beautiful to him or her, and that everyone ought to find it beautiful. Kant argued that this is because a person making an aesthetic judgement adopts a disinterested attitude whereby he or she abstracts all the particular desires and goals that distinguish him or her from other people.

Kierkegaard, Søren Aabye (1813-1855), Danish religious philosopher, whose concern with individual existence, choice, and commitment profoundly influenced modern theology and philosophy, especially existentialism.

Life: Kierkegaard was born in Copenhagen on May 15, 1813. His father was a wealthy merchant and strict Lutheran, whose gloomy, guilt-ridden piety and vivid imagination strongly influenced Kierkegaard. Kierkegaard studied theology and philosophy at the University of Copenhagen, where he encountered Hegelian philosophy (see below) and reacted strongly against it. While at the university, he ceased to practise Lutheranism and for a time led an extravagant social life, becoming a familiar figure in the theatrical and café society of Copenhagen. After his father's death in 1838, however, he decided to resume his theological studies. In 1840 he became engaged to the 17-year-old Regine Olson, but almost immediately began to suspect that marriage was incompatible with his own brooding, complicated nature and his growing sense of a philosophical vocation. He abruptly broke off the engagement in 1841, but the episode took on great significance for him, and he repeatedly alluded to it in his books. At the same time, he realized that he did not want to become a Lutheran pastor. An inheritance from his father allowed him to devote himself entirely to writing, and in the remaining 14 years of his life he produced more than 20 books.

Philosophical Approach: Kierkegaard's work is deliberately unsystematic and consists of essays, aphorisms, parables, fictional letters and diaries, and other literary forms. Many of his works were originally published under pseudonyms. He applied the term "existential" to his philosophy because he regarded philosophy as the expression of an intensely examined individual life, not as the construction of a monolithic system in the manner of the 19th-century German philosopher G. W. F. Hegel, whose work he attacked in *Concluding Unscientific Postscript* (1846; trans. 1941). Hegel claimed to have achieved a complete rational understanding of human life and history; Kierkegaard, on the other hand, stressed the ambiguity and paradoxical nature of the human situation. The fundamental problems of life, such as the existence and nature of God, he contended, defy rational explanation. Although objective truth is typically impossible to determine, he argued that in connection with such problems, people should aim at "subjective truth", by which he meant personal commitment to a belief.

The Choice of Life: Kierkegaard maintained that systematic philosophy not only imposes a false perspective on human existence but that it also, by explaining life in terms of logical necessity, becomes a means of avoiding choice and responsibility. Individuals, he believed, create their own natures through their choices, which must be made in the absence of universal, objective standards. The validity of a choice can only be determined subjectively.

In his first major work, *Either/Or* (2 vols., 1843; trans. 1944), Kierkegaard described two spheres, or stages of existence, that the individual may choose: the aesthetic and the ethical. The aesthetic way of life is a refined hedonism, consisting of a search for pleasure and a cultivation of mood. The aesthetic individual constantly seeks variety and novelty in an effort to stave off boredom but must eventually confront boredom and despair. The ethical way of life involves an intense, passionate commitment to duty, to unconditional social and religious obligations. In his later works, such as *Stages on Life's Way* (1845; trans. 1940), Kierkegaard discerned in this submission to duty a loss of indi-vidual responsibility, and he proposed a third stage, the religious, in which one submits to the will of God, but in so doing finds authentic freedom. In *Fear and Trembling* (1843; trans. 1941) Kierkegaard focused on God's command that Abraham sacrifice his son Isaac (see Genesis 22: 1-19), an act that violates Abraham's ethical convictions. Abraham proves his faith by resolutely setting out to obey God's command, even though he cannot understand it. This "suspension of the ethical", as Kierkegaard called it, allows Abraham to achieve an authentic commitment to God. To avoid ultimate despair, the individual must make a similar "leap of faith" into a religious life, which is inherently paradoxical, mysterious, and full of risk. One is called to it by the feeling of dread (*The Concept of Dread*, 1844; trans. 1944), which is ultimately a fear of nothingness.

Influence: Kierkegaard's influence was at first confined to Scandinavia and to German-speaking Europe, where his work had a strong impact on Protestant theology and on such writers as the Austrian novelist Franz Kafka. As existentialism emerged as a general European movement in the 20th century, Kierkega-ard's work was widely translated, and he was recognized as one of the seminal figures of modern culture.

Kindi, al-, (c. 801-c. 873), first major Islamic philosopher, born in Kufa and educated at Al Basrah and Baghdad (all in Iraq). He was one of the earliest Muslim students of ancient Greek philosophers and one of the first translators of the works of Aristotle into Arabic. Called the philosopher of the Arabs because he was descended from Arab nobility, he is the author of more than 270 works, most of which are short tracts covering a wide range of topics, including philosophy, medicine, mathematics, optics, and astrology. Some of his works were translated into Latin during the Middle Ages and influenced Christian scholars in Europe.

Al-Kindi's philosophy was strongly influenced by Neoplatonism and medieval Aristotelianism. He attempted to provide a philosophical basis for the speculative theology of the Mutazilis, later adopted by the Imams (*Twlevers*) of the Shiites. Although he claimed the essential conclusions of philosophy and religion to be harmonious, he nevertheless placed revelation above philosophy and prophetic insights above reason. Al-Kindi's influence on Muslim thinkers continued for about a century after his death.

Know how, knowledge how.

Knowledge, 1. see

2. The objects, concepts and relationships that are assumed to exist in somearea of interest. A collection of knowledge, represented using some knowledge representation language is known as a knowledge base and a program for extending and/or querying a knowledge base is a knowledge-based system.

Knowledge differs from data or information in that new knowledge may be created from existing knowledge using logical inference. If information is truthful data plus meaning then knowledge is information plus justification/explanation.

A common form of knowledge, *e.g.* in a Prolog program, is a collection of facts and rules about some subject.

For example, a knowledge base about a family might contain the facts that John is David's son and Tom is John's son and the rule that the son of someone's son is their grandson. From this knowledge it could infer the new fact that Tom is David's grandson. See also Knowledge Level Gettier problem, know how, knowledge tacit Luciano Floridi.

Knowledge argument, an argument from Frank Jackson (1982) purporting to show that physicalism is false on the ground that there exist facts that cannot be known solely in virtue of knowing all the physical facts. See dualism, consciousness.

Knowledge how, epistemically praiseworthy, non-propositional proceduralelements of a cognitive system thought to underlie abilities where performance of a task is consistently better than chance. See knowledge.

Knowledge base, A collection of knowledge expressed using some formal knowledge representation language. A knowledge base forms part of a knowledge-based system (KBS).

Knowledge-based system, (KBS) A program for extending and/or querying a knowledge base.

The related term expert system is normally used to refer to a highly domain-specific type of KBS used for a specialized purpose such as medical diagnosis.

The Cyc project is an example of a large KBS.

Knowledge level, A level of description of the knowledge of an agent that is independent of the agent's internal symbol-level representation. Knowledge can be attributed to agents by observing their actions. An agent "knows" something if it acts as if it had the information and is acting rationally to achieve its goals. The "actions" of agents, including knowledge base servers and knowledge-based sys-tems, can be seen through a "tell and ask" functional interface, where a client interacts with an agent by making logical assertions (tell), and posing queries (ask).

Knowledge representation, The subfield of artificial intelligence concerned with designing and using systems for storing knowledge - facts and rules about some subject.

A body of formally represented knowledge is based on a conceptualisation—an abstract view of the world that we wish to represent. In order to manipulate this knowledge we must specify how the abstract conceptualisation is represented as a concrete data structure. An ontology is an explicitspecification of a conceptualisation.

Knowledge, Theory of. *See* Epistemology.

Knowledge under entailment, See principle of closure of knowledge under entailment, knowledge under known entailment principle of closure of.

Knowledge under known entailment principle of closure of, If *S* knows *p*, and *S* knows that *p* entails *q*, then *S* knows *q*. See Cartesian scepticism, principle of closure of knowledge under entailment.

Language of thought, a phrase coined by Fodor to voice the view that all mental representations are linguistic expressions within an "internal" language which significantly resembles spoken language.

Latency, 1. The time it takes for a packet to cross a network connection, from sender to receiver.

2. The period of time that a frame is held by a network device before it is forwarded.

Two of the most important parameters of a communications channel are its latency, which should be low, and its bandwidth, which should be high. Latency is particularly important for a synchronous protocol where each packet must be acknowledged before the next can be transmitted.

Laws of Nature, pervasive general features of the world or descriptions of those features. Laws of nature are central to scientific investigation, in part because of the role they play in the prediction and explanation of natural phenomena. From antiquity people have considered why there should be regularities in nature. The status of laws has been a central topic in the history of theology because a deity provides a possible source of regularities and because of theological interest in miracles as violations of natural law. Laws of nature are also a central topic in the philosophy of science. There are two main philosophical questions about laws: the epistemological question asks how laws are discovered, while the metaphysical question asks what sort of thing they are.

The Epistemological Question: The epistemological question presents difficulties because scientists cannot deduce laws of nature from their data. For example, no matter how many ravens have been observed to be black, it cannot be deduced that all ravens are black: the possibility always remains that there is an unobserved raven that is not black. The logical gap between data and laws is even wider for scientific laws that concern entities, properties, and processes that are not just unobserved in fact but unobservable in principle. Scientists cannot actually observe that some light is a stream of photons, for example, much less that all light is like this. The evidence for such theoretical laws can thus only be indirect. Much of the philosophy of science is concerned with giving an account of the form such inferences take and of the justification that scientists can have for making them.

The Metaphysical Question: At first glance, the metaphysical question about laws seems easier to answer. Difficult though it may be to state how scientists discover the laws of nature, it seems simple enough to say what sort of thing they are discovering. According to the straightforward answer to the metaphysical question, laws are simply universal patterns in nature or true universal generalizations, such as "all ravens are black", or general mathematical relationships that science describes, such as Boyle's law, which claims that the pressure of a given amount of gas at a constant temperature is inversely proportional to the volume it occupies, so that if the volume is reduced, the pressure is increased.

Such an answer is misleading, however, because not all true universal generalizations are laws. Even if by some extraordinary coincidence it turns out that every philosopher has been right-handed, it would not be a law that all philosophers are right-handed, though this universal generalization would be true. Similarly, even though it is presumably true that all the gold spheres that there will ever be will have a diameter of less than 100 miles (there being only a limited amount of gold in the world), this is not a law. Universal generalizations that would not be laws even if they were true are known by philosophers as "accidental generalizations"; on the other hand, generalizations that are laws if true are known as "law-like generalizations". To understand what it is to be a law of nature requires explaining the difference between law-like and accidental generalizations. Philosophers have not found this an easy task.

Law-like statements appear to say more than accidental generalizations by describing not just how things are, but also how they would have been under different, counterfactual conditions. If it is a law that pressure is inversely proportional to volume, that is not just to state that the pressure goes up when the volume is decreased: even if the volume of a given sample of gas is kept the same, it is still the case that the pressure would have increased, had the volume been reduced. By contrast, even if it is true that all philosophers are right-handed, it is not the case that had a left-handed person taken up the subject, he or she would have suddenly become right-handed.

A second apparent difference between law-like and accidental statements is connected to the way laws are discovered. Only laws seem susceptible to inductive support. For example, if Boyle s law is found to hold wherever it is tested, scientists may infer that it also holds in unobserved cases. By contrast, even if all the philosophers who were asked turned out to be right-handed, it would not be inferred that the same holds for the philosophers who had not been asked. The only way to be confident that all philosophers are right-handed would be to ask every one of them.

There are thus at least two apparent differences between laws and accidents: only laws have counterfactual content and only laws are susceptible to inductive support. It is not clear, however, that these two tests for lawfulness give the same answer for every generalization or that either gives the correct answer for every generalization. In addition, even if these tests were reliable, they only provide symptoms of law-likeness, rather then confirming directly what laws of nature are like. Philosophers have thus attempted to give deeper accounts of laws of nature and of what distinguishes them from accidental generalizations.

Defining Laws: Although there are many different and conflicting accounts of laws, they all fall into two groups. Almost all philosophers of science agree that some universal generalizations are not law-like. However, the accounts of the first group—sometimes known as "regularity views"—all maintain that law-like statements are simply a special class of universal gener-alizations, whereas the accounts of the second group afford law-like statements a different sort of content.

Regularity Views: There are three popular types of regularity view. According to the first, the "attitude" view, what distinguishes law-like from accidental generalizations is nothing in the generalizations themselves: it is instead a difference in our attitudes towards them. Thus, a supporter of the attitude view might say that law-like statements are those that scientists are willing to use for purposes of explanation or prediction. It is not that they are used in this way because they are laws; rather, they count as laws because they are used in this way.

According to the second account, known as the "projectible predicate" view, a generalization only counts as law-like if it contains the right sort of terms: for example, predicates such as "pressure" and "volume" can figure in laws, while perhaps "philosopher" or "right-handed" cannot. Proponents of the projectible predicate view then go on to consider what distinguishes "good" from "bad" predicates. Some proponents hold that good predicates correspond to natural kinds, whose members are fundamentally similar to each other, while bad predicates lump together dissimilar things.

The third type of regularity account is the "best system" view, in which laws of nature are those true generalizations that would feature in an ideal theory of the world. Such a theory could be constructed if everything was known and an optimal balance struck between the conflicting criteria of describing as much as possible while keeping things as simple as possible. Hence, many generalizations would fall within this theory, though many would be left out, since including them would incur too great a loss of simplicity for too small a gain in strength. The universal generalizations within the system are the laws; those without are the accidental generalizations.

Non-Regularity Views: Philosophers who reject the regularity view of laws also offer three different accounts. There is, first, the "property" view, according to which laws do not describe patterns of particular events in nature, but rather give relations between general properties. Thus, the generalization about philosophers being right-handed is not a law, because it is only a claim about particular philosophers; Boyle's law, by contrast, is a law, because it describes a relationship between the general properties of pressure and volume.

A second account is the "necessity" view, according to which the essential difference between accidental and law-like statements is that whereas accidentals only describe what does happen, laws describe what in some sense must happen.

The final non-regularity account is the "capacities" view, in which laws are taken to be radically different from universal generalizations, describing instead the stable tendencies or capacities of physical objects. On the capacities view, laws do not describe patterns of actual behaviour of objects but rather the forces that underlie them, forces that combine in complex ways which preclude simple patterns. This view accounts for the fact that many laws of nature, such as Boyle's law, describe only what happens under ideal conditions, when only a single set of forces is in operation. The aim of this view is to show how simple laws may reveal truths about a complex world.

Liar paradox, A sentence which asserts its own falsity, *e.g.* "This sentence is false" or "I am lying". If it is true, then it is false; if it is false, then it is true. Also called the Epimenides paradox. ["The Liar: an Essay on Truth and Circularity", Jon Barwise and John Etchemendy.]

Liberalism, at least in the classical sense of the word, liberalism is a doctrine or principle in political philosophy that is very similar to modern libertarianism—namely, that what matters in political affairs is the absolute freedom and rights of the individual. Unfortunately, this word has lost its original meaning (at least in the United States), so that it now refers to something akin to egalitarianism or a watered-down version of socialism. (References from anarchism, Aristotelianism, capitalism, egalitarianism, and libertarianism.)

Libertarianism, 1. in metaphysics, the term libertarianism refers the idea that human beings have free will (opposed to necessitarianism and determinism).

2. in political philosophy, libertarianism (sometimes also called classical liberalism) espouses the right of individuals to act in whatever way they please, so long as they do not initiate force or fraud against other people; sometimes libertarianism verges on anarchism. (References from accidentalism, anarchism, capitalism, determinism, egalitarianism, liberalism, necessitarianism, and voluntarism.)

Like this, You weren't supposed to follow that link, it was just an example of what a link looks like.

Linear argument, A function argument which is used exactly once by the function.

If the argument is used at most

once then it is safe to inline the function and replace the single occurrence of the formal parameter with the actual argument expression. If the argument was used more than once this transformation would duplicate the argument expression, causing it to be evaluated more than once.

If the argument is sure to be used at least once then it is safe to evaluate it in advance (see strictness analysis) whereas if the argument was not used then this would waste work and might prevent the program from terminating.

Linear space, A vector space where all linear combinations of elements are also elements of the space. This is easy for spaces of numbers but not for a space of functions. Roughly, this is to say that multiplication by numbers, and addition of elements is defined in the space.

Linear type, 1. An attribute of values which are used exactly once: they are neither duplicated nor destroyed. Such values require no garbage collection, and can safely be updated in place, even if they form part of a data structure.

Linear types are related to the linear logic of J.-Y Girard. They extend Schmidt's notion of single threading, provide an alternative to Hudak and Bloss' update analysis, and offer a practical complement to Lafont and Holmstrm's elegant linear languages.

Locke, John (1632-1704), English philosopher, who founded the school of empiricism and defended the idea of a social contract.

Life: Locke was born in the village of Wrington, Somerset, on August 29, 1632. He was educated at the University of Oxford and lectured on Greek, rhetoric, and moral philosophy at Oxford from 1661 to 1664. In 1667 he began his association with the English statesman Anthony Ashley Cooper, 1st Earl of Shaftesbury, to whom Locke was a friend, adviser, and doctor. Sha-ftesbury secured for Locke a series of minor government appointments. In 1669, in one of his official capacities, Locke wrote a constitution for the proprietors of the Carolina Colony in North America, but it was never put into effect. In 1675, after the liberal Shaftesbury had fallen from favour, Locke moved to France. He returned to England in 1679, but in view of his opposition to the succession of the king's Catholic brother to the throne, he soon found it expedient to return to the Continent. From 1683 to 1688 he lived in Holland, and following the so-called Glorious Revolution of 1688 and the accession of a Protestant monarch, Locke returned once more to England. The new king, William III, appointed Locke to the Board of Trade in 1696, a position from which he resigned because of ill health in 1700. He died in Oates on October 28, 1704.

Empiricism: Locke's empiricism held that all knowledge other than deductive reasoning must be based on sensory experience. Empiricist ideas were put forward by the English philosopher and statesman Francis Bacon early in the 17th century, but Locke gave the doctrine a systematic expression in his *Essay Concerning Human Understanding* (1690). He regarded the mind of a person at birth as a tabula rasa, a blank slate upon which experience imprinted knowledge. He rejected the belief in inate ideas, a concept that derived originally from Plato. *See* Epistemology.

Political Theories: Locke's political ideas were formed through theoretical reflection, practical engagement, and religious commitment. Although he believed that God had designed human beings and given them reason, and thus the ability to know natural laws, he rejected theories of his day that claimed a divine origin for human government as such, or for certain rules in particular. In his *Two Treatises of Government* (1690), Locke attacked the divine right theory put forward by the Anglican theologian Robert Filmer. Instead, he argued that sovereignty resides in the people, and that government gains its authority only from the transfer of individual rights by means of a contract. In developing this social contract argument, Locke in some ways drew upon, but also criticized, the views of Thomas Hobbes. For Locke, individuals must consent to government if it is to be legitimate; their consent can be explicit or tacit.

Because government exists only to further the security and liberty of the people, revolution can be justified if the people collectively come to find the government intolerably oppressive. This aspect of Locke's theory arguably derives from his involvement in Shaftesbury's plots against the accession of a new Catholic ruler. So long as government remains legitimate it must protect individual rights and control its own power through a system of checks and balances. Locke was also a powerful advocate of religious toleration by the state. However, he rejected toleration of atheists, whom he believed had no grounds for loyalty or truthfulness, and of Catholics, whom he believed were loyal to an alien power, the pope.

Locke's influence on modern philosophy has been profound. His empiricism continues to influence many thinkers, and his political theory arguably influenced the American War of Independence and has inspired many liberals since. Among his other works are *Some Thoughts Concerning Education* (1693) and *The Reasonableness of Christianity* (1695).

Logic (Greek *logos,* "word", "speech", "reason"), science dealing with the principles of valid reasoning and argument. The study of logic is the effort to determine the conditions under which one is justified in passing from given statements, called premises, to a conclusion that is claimed to follow from them. Logical validity is the characteristic of an argument that guarantees that if the premises of the argument are true then the conclusion must necessarily be true.

The validity of an argument should be distinguished from the truth of the conclusion. If one or more of the premises is false, the conclusion of a valid argument may be false. Take, for example:

All mammals are four-footed animals

All people are mammals

Therefore, all people are four-footed animals.

This is a valid argument with a false conclusion because its first premise is false. On the other hand, an invalid argument may by chance have a true conclusion. For example:

Some animals are two-footed
All people are animals
Therefore, all people are two-footed.

This happens to have a true conclusion, but the argument is not valid.

Logical validity depends, therefore, on the form of the argument, not on its content. If the argument were valid, some other term could be substituted for all occurrences of any one of those used and validity would not be affected. By substituting "four-footed" for "two-footed" in the second argument, it can be seen that the premises could both be true and the conclusion false. Thus the argument is invalid, even though it has a true conclusion.

Aristotelian Logic: What is now known as Classical or traditional logic was first formulated by Aristotle, who developed rules for correct syllogistic reasoning. A syllogism is an argument made up of statements in one of four forms: "All As are Bs" (universal affirmative), "No As are Bs" (universal negative), "Some As are Bs" (particular affirmative), or "Some As are not Bs" (particular negative). The letters stand for common nouns, such as "dog", "four-footed animal", or "living thing", which are called the "terms" of the syllogism. A well-formed syllogism consists of two premises and a conclusion, each premise having one term in common with the conclusion and one in common with the other premise. A famous example of a well-formed syllogism is:

All men are mortal
Socrates is a Man
Therefore, Socrates is mortal.

In Classical logic, rules are formulated by which all well-formed syllogisms are identified as valid or invalid forms of argument.

Kant and Hegel: Traditional logic was often described as the science of the laws of thought, meaning the laws that thinking must obey if it is to be rational, rather than psychological generalizations about the way that people actually think. The 18th-century German philo-sopher Immanuel Kant relied on this definition in order to introduce a new area of logic. In his *Critique of Pure Reason* (1781), Kant argued that thinking is not just a matter of deriving one proposition from another. In order to make any sense of its sensations, the mind has to organize them through certain general concepts or categories, and this organizing activity is itself a kind of thinking. Kant said that traditional logic, which he called "general logic", was the science of the principles of rational thinking in general. In contrast to this, he introduced the idea of a "transcendental logic" that would be the science of the categories and the structural principles associated with them, through which the mind has to "think" its sensations in order to organize them into rational experience. Kant called these structural principles "synthetic a priori" because they are informative and yet are not derived from experience. Instead, they are intrinsic to the nature of the mind, which has to bring them to its experience in order to make rational sense of it. For example, the mind has to organize its sensations through the category of cause and effect, and accordingly it has to experience the world as governed by the synthetic a priori principle that "every event has a cause", in order to make sense of its sensations.

The science of these categories and synthetic a priori principles is logic, because it elucidates the principles in terms of which the mind must think its sensations in order to make rational sense of them. However, it is also metaphysics, since these categories and principles govern the workings of the world as it has to be experienced, and this is the only world that can possibly be known. Kant also retained the idea of a world of things in themselves, things as they are independent of human experience of them, to which the categories do not apply and about which nothing can be said.

Kant's successor, G. W. F. Hegel, extended the idea of logic as a science of the necessary categories of rational thinking. However, he abandoned Kant's notion of the thing in itself, so that for Hegel there is no world at all apart from the world as it is thought. Thereby, Hegel completed the identification of logic and metaphysics begun by Kant. His *Science of Logic* (1812-1816) is an attempt to expound the complete system of categories that must both govern rational thinking and underpin reality, beginning with the simplest category of all, that of "being" or "is". Hegel tried to show that these categories necessarily arise out of each other through a process of internal reflection and contradiction. For example, in thinking about the category "being", one is led necessarily to formulate the category "nothing", and realizing the contradiction between these two categories must in turn lead one to formulate the category "becoming". Not only thinking but reality itself is supposed to be essentially characterized by this development of new categories out of old ones through internal contradiction.

This kind of logic, in which categories are derived from each other through internal contradiction, has been called dialectical logic. It was subsequently applied to the analysis of material economic structures by the social and political theorist Karl Marx, and Marxists have since tried to combine the idea of dialectical logic with a materialist metaphysics. However, most logicians did not take up the idea of a "logic of categories" initiated by Kant and Hegel, and instead pursued the traditional notion of logic as a science of the principles governing valid arguments.

Modern Formal Logic: In the mid-19th century, the British mathematicians George Boole and Augustus De Morgan opened a new field of logic, now known as symbolic or formal logic, which was further developed by the German mathematician Gottlob Frege and especially by the British mathematicians Bertrand Russell and Alfred North Whitehead in *Principia Mathematica* (3 vols., 1910-1913). The logical system of Russell and Whitehead covers a far greater range of possible arguments than those that can be cast into syllogistic form. It introduces symbols for complete sentences and for the conjunctions that connect them, such as "or", "and", and "if ... then.... ". It has different symbols for the logical subject and the logical predicate of a sentence; and it has symbols for classes, for members of classes, and for the relationships of class membership and class inclusion. It also differs from Classical logic in its assumptions as to the existence of the things referred to in its universal statements. The statement "All As are Bs" is rendered in modern formal logic to mean, "If anything is an A, then it is a B", which, unlike Classical logic, does not assume that any As exist. The basic elements of modern formal logic are called the propositional (or sentential) calculus and the predicate calculus.

Both Classical logic and standard modern formal logic are systems of deductive logic. In a sense, the premises of a valid argument contain the conclusion, and the truth of the conclusion follows from the truth of the premises with certainty. To hold that the premises are true and the conclusion is false would be to contradict oneself. Efforts have also been made to develop formal systems of inductive logic, such that the premises are evidence for the conclusion, but the truth of the conclusion follows from the truth of the evidence only with a certain probability. The most notable contribution to inductive logic is that of the British philosopher John Stuart Mill who, in his *System of Logic* (1843), formulated the methods of proof that he believed to characterize empirical science. This inquiry has developed in the 20th century into the field known as the philosophy of science. Closely related is the branch of mathematics known as probability theory.

Both Classical and modern formal logic in their usual versions assume that any well-formed sentence is either true or false. In recent years efforts have been made to develop systems of so-called many-valued logic, such that an assertion may have some value other than true or false. In some this is merely a third neutral value; in others it is a probability value expressed as a fraction ranging between 0 and 1 or between -1 and +1. Another development in recent years has been the effort to develop systems of modal logic, to represent the logical relations between assertions of possibility and impossibility, nece-ssity and contingency. Still another development is deontic logic, the investigation of the logical relations between commands or between statements of obligation.

Philosophical Logic: The above versions of formal logic continue the attempts begun by Aristotle to formulate the rules governing valid arguments. By contrast, philosophical logic examines the philosophical problems associated with formulating these rules, such as, whether the rules of logic are made true by the way the world is, or by the way thought must operate. Philosophical logic also examines the concepts used in formulating the rules of logic: for example, the concepts of proposition, argument, validity, necessity, possibility, a priori, essence, meaning, and truth. It also studies the conceptual content of basic words such as "the", "is", and "if". The themes of philosophical logic are anticipated by Aristotle and Kant, but in the 20th century the subject has developed rapidly, under the impact of developments in formal logic. The philosophers Bertrand Russell, Peter Strawson, and Michael Dummett in Britain, and Willard Van Orman Quine, Saul Kripke, and Donald

Davidson in the United States, have been especially important in this development.

Logic, A branch of philosophy and mathematics that deals with the formal principles, methods and criteria of validity of inference, reasoning and knowledge.

Logic is concerned with what is true and how we can know whether some-thing is true. This involves the formalisation of logical arguments and proofs in terms of symbols representing propositions and logical connectives. The meanings of these logical connectives are expressed by a set of rules which are assumed to be self-evident.

Boolean algebra deals with the basic operations of truth values: AND, OR, NOT and combinations thereof. Predicate logic extends this with existential and universal quantifiers and symbols standing for predicates which may depend on variables. The rules of natural deduction describe how we may proceed from valid premises to valid conclusions, where the premises and conclusions are expressions in predicate logic.

Symbolic logic uses a meta-language concerned with truth, which may or may not have a corresponding expression in the world of objects called existence. In symbolic logic, arguments and proofs are made in terms of symbols representing propositions and logical connectives. The meanings of these begin with a set of rules or primitives which are assumed to be self-evident. Fortunately, even from vague primitives, functions can be defined with precise meaning.

Boolean logic deals with the basic operations of truth values: AND, OR, NOT and combinations thereof. Predicate logic extends this with existential quantifiers and universal quantifiers which introduce bound variables ranging over finite sets; the predicate itself takes on only the values true and false. Deduction describes how we may proceed from valid premises to valid conclusions, where these are expressions in predicate logic.

Carnap used the phrase "rational reconstruction" to describe the logical analysis of thought. Thus logic is less concerned with how thought does proceed, which is considered the realm of psychology, and more with how it should proceed to discover truth. It is the touchstone of the results of thinking, but neither its regulator nor a motive for its practice.

Logical axiom, axioms

Logical positivism, Logical positivism is a movement in 20th century philosophy that originated as a reaction against nineteenth-century idealism.

The word logical in the name refers to the belief that logic is all-important for philosophy (thus this movement is a sort of logicism), while "positivism" here is really a certain form of empiricism which claims that empiricism is the whole of philosophy and that there is no validity to anything which could be called conceptual experience or conceptual insight. The movement is also a form of conventionalism, since its adherents hold that things are true only by convention. Logical positivists denigrate or ignore ethics, and some have even gone so far as to say that all values are merely expressions of emotion (see emotivism). Thus the logical pos-itivists, while holding a deep respect for reason in the limited context of logic and mathematics, have had such a limited view of what reason is (a process of contraction started by Kant) that they have ended up holding some extremely subjectivistic views, especially in ethics. (References from logicism, nominalism, positivism, and scholasticism.)

Logical empiricist, a term for those 20th century philosophers who maintain that empiricism is right on purely logical (not psychological) grounds.

Empiricism becomes a theory about the meaning of synthetic propositions: namely, that their meaning can be given entirely in experiential, or henomenal terms.

Logical validity For a wff, to be true for every interpretation of the formal language; to have every interpretation be a model. "Every interpretation" here is understood to mean all, but only, those interpretations in which the connectives and/or quantifiers take their standard meanings. In truth-functional propositional logic, logically valid wffs are also called tautologies. In standard predicate logic, logical validity is limited to interpretations with non-empty domains. Logical validity is also called logical truth.

Lower set, A finite non-empty downward closed subset of a partial order.

Marcus Aurelius, full name Marcus Aelius Aurelius Antoninus (121-180), Roman emperor (161-180) and Stoic philosopher.

Marcus Aurelius, whose original name was Marcus Annius Verus, was born in Rome on April 20, 121, the nephew by marriage of Antoninus Pius, later emperor. After the latter succeeded to power, he adopted his nephew and married him to his daughter (145). Marcus Aurelius became emperor in 161, and throughout his reign was engaged in defensive wars on the northern and eastern frontiers of the empire. His legions succeeded in repelling the Parthian invasion of Syria 166, but Rome was again forced into battle in 167 by the Germanic tribes on the Rhine-Danube frontier. Marcus Aurelius returned to Rome intermittently during the German campaign to undertake legal and administrative reforms. Although he was particularly concerned with public welfare and even sold his personal possessions to alleviate the effects of famine and plague within the empire, he ruthlessly persecuted the Christians, believing them a threat to the imperial system. In 176 he returned to the northern frontier, hoping to extend the boundaries of the empire north-eastwards to the Wisla river. He died of the plague in Vindobona (now Vienna) on March 17, 180, before he could begin the invasion. His plan was abandoned by his son and successor, Commodus.

In his domestic policy Marcus Aurelius was a champion of the poor, for whom he founded schools, orphanages, and hospitals and alleviated the burden of taxes. He also tried to humanize criminal laws and the treatment of slaves by their masters.

As a philosopher he is remembered for his *Meditations,* a compendium of 12 books of moral precepts written in Greek while on his various campaigns. The work is an important formulation of the philosophy of Stoicism and reveals his belief that the moral life leads to tranquillity. It stresses the virtues of wisdom, justice, fortitude, and moderation.

Marx, Karl (1818-1883), German political philosopher and revolutionary, co-founder with Friedrich Engels of scientific socialism (modern communism), and, as such, one of the most influential thinkers in modern history.

Marx was born in Trier on May 5, 1818, and educated at the universities of Bonn, Berlin, and Jena. In 1842, shortly after contributing his first article to the Cologne newspaper *Rheinische Zeitung,* Marx became editor of the paper. Although his political views were radical he was not yet a communist. His writings in the *Rheinische Zeitung* criticizing contemporary political and social conditions embroiled him in controversy with the authorities: in 1843 Marx was compelled to resign his editorial post, and soon afterwards the *Rheinische Zeitung* was forced to discontinue publication. Marx then went to Paris. There, as a result of his further studies in philosophy, history, and political science, he adopted communist beliefs. In 1844, when Engels visited him in Paris, the two men found that they had independently arrived at identical views on the nature of revolutionary problems. They undertook to collaborate in a systematic elucidation of the theoretical principles of communism and in the organization of an international working-class mov-ement dedicated to those principles. Their collaboration was to continue throughout Marx's life.

The Communist Manifesto: In 1845 Marx was ordered to leave Paris because of his revolutionary activities. He settled in Brussels and began the work of organizing and directing a network of revolutionary groups, called Communist Correspondence Committees, in a number of European cities. In connection with the consolidation of these committees in 1847 to form the Communist League, Marx and Engels were commissioned to formulate a statement of principles. The programme they submitted, known throughout the world as the *Communist Manifesto*, was the first systematic statement of modern socialist doctrine and was written by Marx, partly on the basis of a draft prepared by Engels. The central propositions of the *Manifesto*, contributed by Marx, embody the theory, later explicitly formulated in his *Critique of Political Economy* (1859), called the materialist conception of history, or historical materialism. These propositions are that in every historical epoch the prevailing economic system by which the necessities of life are produced determines the form of societal organization and the political and intellectual history of the epoch; and that the history of society is a history of struggles between the exploiting and the exploited, that is, between the ruling and the oppressed social classes. From these premises, Marx drew the conclusion in the *Manifesto* that the capitalist class would be overthrown and that it would be eliminated by a worldwide working-class revolution and replaced by a classless society. The *Manifesto* influenced all subsequent communist literature and revolutionary thought generally; it has been translated into many languages and published in hundreds of millions of copies.

Influence: Marx's influence during his life was not great. After his death it increased with the growth of the labour movement. His ideas and theories came to be known as Marxism, or scientific socialism, which constitutes one of the principal currents of contemporary political thought. His analysis of capitalist economy and his theories of historical materialism, the class struggle, and surplus value have become the basis of modern socialist doctrine. Of decisive importance with respect to revolutionary action are his theories on the nature of the capitalist state, the road to power, and the dictatorship of the proletariat. These doctrines, revised by most socialists after his death, were revived in the 20th century by Lenin and, as developed and applied by him, constituted the core of the theory and practice of Bolshevism and the Third International.

Marxism, social and political theory based on the works of Karl Marx and his followers, associated with the socialist and communist movements. Marx's works can be broadly divided into his early philosophical writings (for example, the posthumously published *Ökonomisch-philos-ophische Manuskripte aus dem Jahre 1844/ Philosophic and Economic Manuscripts of 1844, Die deutsche Ideologie/The German Ideology,* 1845-1846), his pamphlets (for example, *Manifest der kommu-nistischen Partei/The Communist Manifesto,* 1848), his analyses of contemporary events (for example, *Der Achtzehnte Brumaire des Louis Napoleon/The Eighteenth of Brumaire of Louis Napoleon,* 1852, and *Der Bürgerkrieg in Frankreich/The Civil War in France,* 1871), and his mature and fundamental works, *Zur Kritik der politischen Ökonomie* (*Contribution to the Critique of Political Economy,* 1859), and, above all, *Das Kapital* (vol. 1, 1867; vols. 2 and 3 published posthumously). To summarize, let alone explain, this vast and complex theoretical system in a few paragraphs is impossible. The ramification of the doctrine have included philosophy, economics, history, politics, and most of the social sciences. No theorist has been as analysed and discussed in the 20th century as Karl Marx. The reason behind this attention is far from being purely academic. No comparable modern thinker has had as much impact on political parties and movements. Prior to the collapse of communism in Europe one-third of humanity was under regimes purportedly inspired by Marx's works.

Marx sought to unveil the inner laws of the development of capitalism. Each historical epoch was said to be characterized by a specific mode of production to which corresponds a particular system of power and, consequently, a ruling class in constant open or hidden conflict with an oppressed class. Thus feudal society is dominated by a feudal mode of production in which the class of landlords extracts a surplus from a rural population bound to the land. Transitions from slavery to feudalism and from feudalism to capitalism occurred when the forces of production (that is, labour power and the actual means of production such as machines) could no longer develop within existing relations of production, that is the relations between classes. For example, the crisis which overcame feudalism when capitalism's need for a growing working class required the elimination of traditional legal and ideological arrangements which tied serfs to the soil.

In capitalism the fundamental relation, the wage relation, is based on a contract between juridically equal parties. The owners of capital (capitalists) pay the workers (the proletariat) wages in return for an agreed number of working hours. This disguises a real inequality: the capitalists "cheat" the workers by appropriating far more than they pay out in wages and other necessary production costs. This special and statistically unquantifiable appropriation, or "surplus value", gives the owners of capital great wealth and control over the economic development of society. They thus appropriate not simply wealth but also power. A complex political supers-tructure, consisting of laws and ideologies of various types, regulates and reinforces these social relations. In effect, by being in charge of the surplus which results from accumulation, capitalists can determine the overall direction of society. The commodities produced by capitalism must possess "use-value", otherwise they would not find buyers, but to the capitalist they must have exchange-value: they are not needed for the capitalist's own consumption but only to be exchanged for money. Thus capitalist production is essentially production for exchange and not for needs. Competition drives inefficient capitalists into bankruptcy and leads to concentration and monopolies. Markets, however, are constantly expanded while techniques of production and forms of exchange are ceaselessly revolutionized.

Crises are central to capitalism. Capitalists are driven to try to increase the length of the working day, its intensity, or the productivity of labour. Workers, if appropriately organized, will offer resistance. Capitalists try to enlarge their markets while paying their workers as little as possible. Yet if they all succeeded, workers' consumption and so their demand would decrease, markets would shrink, and capitalism enter into crisis. Marx's complex and at times obscure writings allowed for disparate interpretations. Before 1914 the dominant orthodoxy was that propounded by Karl Kautsky, who stressed the inevitability of capitalism's collapse. After the Russian Revolution, Vladimir Illich Lenin added to the Marxist canon a theory of imperialism, a theory of the state, and principles of revolutionary organization—hence Marxism-Leninism. The Italian communist Antonio Gramsci stressed the role of ideology in civil society in the construction of political hegemony. The appeal of Marxism was that it gave powerful intellectual backing to the moral outrage arising from the purported iniquities of capitalism and to the hope that a system which ought to disintegrate would eventually do so. The theory was sophisticated enough to appeal to the intellectually minded while being amenable to simplification and diffusion at a mass level by socialist activists. Since 1945 most socialist parties have renounced Marxism, while the study and development of the doctrine has remained largely confined to academic circles.

Materialism, in philosophy, doctrine that all existence is resolvable into matter or into an attribute or effect of matter. According to this doctrine, matter is the ultimate reality, and the phenomenon of consciousness is explained by physiochemical changes in the nervous system. Materialism is thus the reverse of idealism, in which the supremacy of mind is affirmed and matter is characterized as an aspect or objectification of mind. Extreme or absolute materialism is known as materialistic monism.

Philosophical materialism is ancient and has had numerous formulations. The early Greek philosophers subscribed to a variant of materialism known as hylozoism, according to which matter and life are identical. Related to hylozoism is the doctrine of hylotheism, in which matter is held to be divine, or the existence of God is disavowed apart from matter. "Cosmological materialism" is a term used to characterize a materialistic interpretation of the universe.

Anti-religious materialism is motivated by a spirit of hostility towards the theological dogmas of organized religion, particularly those of Christianity. Notable among the exponents of antireligious materialism were the 18th-century French philosophers Denis Diderot, Paul Henri d'Holbach, and Julien Offroy de la Mettrie. The historical materialism of the writings of Karl Marx is of a different kind. The emphasis is not on an explanation of consciousness in terms of matter, but on an explanation of social organization in terms of the production of the material necessities of life. According to Marx, the state of development of the technologies for producing these material necessities in a particular historical epoch determines the economic system under which they are produced. In turn, the prevailing economic system determines the form of societal organization and the political, religious, ethical, intellectual, and artistic history of the epoch. History progresses through the development and resolutions of contradictions between these elements.

Marx's companion and collaborator Friedrich Engels extended this historical materialism into a general philosophical standpoint called dialectical materialism, according to which nature, like history, progresses through the development and resolution of contradictions. Engels thought of dialectical materialism as the inverse of the dialectical idealism of G. W. F. Hegel. In the 20th century, dialectical materialism became the official philosophy of the Union of Soviet Socialist Republics.

In modern times philosophical materialism has been largely influenced by the doctrine of evolution and may, indeed, be said to have been assimilated in the wider theory of evolution. Supporters of the theory of evolution go beyond the mere antitheism or atheism of materialism and positively seek to show how the diversities and differences in creation are the result of natural as opposed to supernatural processes. In particular, sociobiologists attempt to show how the natural processes of evolution can give rise to human phenomena such as altruism, morality, criminality, and authority.

Materialism, the view according to which the only thing that really exists in the world is matter in its various states and movements (commonly atoms or other physical particles). Thus materialism is the opposite of idealism. Note that many philosophers and scientists now use the terms "material" and "physical" interchangeably (for a version of physicalism distinct from materialism, see physicalism. Materialism considers any talk of, say, the soul to be complete nonsense and a throwback to the bad old days of spiritualism and vitalism in philosophy. Note that because matter can be completely known by means of physical laws and mathematical description (see reductionism), materialism tends to be used to lend heavy support to determinism. (References from behaviorism, determinism, idealism, monism, reductionism, and vitalism.)

Maxim, an action guiding principle or policy, *e.g.*, the carpenter's maxim, "Measure twice, cut once." According to Kant, a maxim is the subjective rule that an individual uses in making a decision. For him, all human actions are undertaken under the color of maxims, and the moral character of the act—whether it's right or wrong—depends on the universalizability or nonuniver-salizability of the maxim under color of which it is undertaken. See categorical imperative.

Maximal proof-theoretic consistent set, A set of wffs that cannot be enlarged without becoming p-inconsistent. See proof-theoretic consistency

Mead, George Herbert (1863-1931), American pragmatist, philosopher, and social psychologist, born in South Hadley, Massachusetts. Educated at various universities in the United States and Europe, he taught at the University of Chicago from 1894 until his death.

Influenced by evolutionary theory and the social nature of experience and behaviour, Mead emphasized the natural emergence of the self and mind within the social order. The self, he argued, emerges out of a social process in which the organism becomes self-conscious. This self-consciousness arises as a result of the organism's interaction with its environment, including communication with other organisms. The vocal gesture (language) is the mechanism through which this development occurs. Mind, too, is a social product. The mind, or intelligence, is an instrument developed by the individual to "make possible the rational solution of...problems". Mead emphasized the application of the scientific method in social action and reform.

During his lifetime, Mead published only articles. His books were published posthumously from manuscripts and students' notes and include *The Philosophy of the Present* (1932), *Mind, Self, and Society from the Standpoint of a Social Behaviorist* (1934).

Means, philosophers often contrast means and ends. The ends we seek are the goals we try to achieve, while the means are the actions or things which we use in order to accomplish those ends. A hammer provides the means for pounding a nail in a piece of wood. Some philosophers, most notably Immanuel Kant, have argued that we should never treat human beings merely as means to an end.

Mechanicism, philosophical theory that denies "action at a distance" and holds, that natural systems,including living organisms, are complex machines. Descartes famously held this to be true of all nonhuman animals but not of human minds and their freely willed actions.

Meliorism, the view according to which the universe is getting better all the time—a belief in progress which we could call a kind of optimism.

Mental content, as distinguished from vehicle, mental content is that aspect of mentality which, ideally, refers to an object, property or relation and specifies some properties of that item. Externalism, internalism, sense.

Mentalism, the view according to which only mind or spirit really exists, or that mind or spirit is the fundamental substance in the universe. Mentalism is sometimes called immaterialism, and is usually held to be similar to or equivalent to idealism.

Mereology, branch of logic that studies part-whole formal rela-tionships.

Metaclass, The class of a class. A metaclass is a class whose instances are themselves classes.

Metalogic, The study of formal systems, especially those intended to capturebranches of logic, *e.g.* truth-functional propositional logic, resulting inmetatheorems about those systems. Reasoning about reasoning.

Metaphysics, the study of or branch of philosophy concerned with the ultimate nature of reality and with existence as a whole.

Metaphysics, branch of philosophy concerned with the nature of ultimate reality. Metaphysics is customarily divided into ontology, which deals with the question of how many fundamentally distinct sorts of entities compose the universe, and metaphysics proper, which is concerned with describing the most general traits of reality. Together, these general traits define reality and would presumably characterize any universe. Because these traits are not peculiar to this universe, but are common to all possible universes, metaphysics may be conducted at the highest level of abstraction. Ontology, by contrast, because it investigates the ultimate divisions within this universe, is more closely related to the physical world of human experience.

The term "metaphysics" is believed to have originated in Rome about 70 BC, with the Greek Peripatetic philosopher Andronicus of Rhodes (fl. 1st century BC) in his edition of the works of Aristotle. In the arrangement of Aristotle's works by Andronicus, the treatise originally called *First Philosophy,* or *Theology,* followed the treatise *Physics*. Hence, the *First Philosophy* came to be known as *meta* (*ta*) *physica,* or "following (the) *Physics*", later shortened to *Metaphysics.* The word took on the connotation, in popular usage, of matters transcending material reality. In the philosophical sense, however, particularly as opposed to the use of the word by occultists, metaphysics applies to all reality and is distinguished from other forms of inquiry into reality only by its generality.

The subjects treated in Aristotle's *Metaphysics* (substance, causality, the nature of being, and the existence of God) fixed the content of metaphysical speculation for centuries. Among the medieval scholastic philosophers, metaphysics was known as the "transphysical science" on the assumption that, by means of it, the scholar could make the transition philosophically from the physical world to a world beyond sense perception. The 13th-century scholastic philosopher and theo-logian St Thomas Aquinas declared that the cognition of God, through a causal study of finite sensible beings, was the aim of metaphysics. With the rise of scientific study in the 16th century the reconciliation of science and faith in God became an increasingly important problem.

Metaphysics Before Kant: Before the time of the German philosopher Immanuel Kant, metap-hysics was characterized by a tendency to construct theories on the basis of a priori knowledge, that is, knowledge derived from reason alone, in contradistinction to a posteriori knowledge, which is gained from experience. From a priori knowledge were deduced general propositions that were held to be true of all things. The method of inquiry based on a priori principles is known as rationalistic. The metaphysical theories that were developed using this method may be divided into monism, which holds that the universe is made up of a single fundamental substance; dualism, the belief in two such substances; and pluralism, which proposes the existence of many fundamental substances.

The schools of monism, while agreeing that only one basic substance exists, differ in their descriptions of its principal char-acteristics. Thus, in idealistic monism the substance is believed to be purely mental; in materialistic monism it is held to be purely physical, and in neutral monism it is considered neither exclusively mental nor solely physical. The idealistic position was held by the Irish philosopher George Berkeley, the materialistic by the English philosopher Thomas Hobbes, and the neutral by the Dutch philosopher Baruch Spinoza. The latter ex-pounded a pantheistic view of reality in which the universe is identical with God and everything is an expression of God's substance.

The most famous exponent of dualism was the French philosopher René Descartes, who maintained that body and mind are radically different entities and that they are the only fundamental substances in the universe. Dualism, however, does not show how these basic entities are connected.

In the work of the German philosopher Gottfried Wilhelm Leibniz, the universe is held to consist of an infinite number of distinct substances, or monads. This view is pluralistic in the sense that it proposes the existence of many separate entities, but it is monistic in its assertion that each monad reflects within itself the entire universe.

Other philosophers have held that knowledge of reality is not derived from a priori principles, but is obtained only from experience. This view of knowledge is called empiricism. Still another school of philosophy has maintained that, although an ultimate reality does exist, it is altogether inaccessible to human knowledge, which is necessarily subjective because it is confined to states of mind. Knowledge is therefore not a representation of external reality, but merely a reflection of human perceptions. This view is known as scepticism, or, in respect to the soul and the reality of God, agnosticism.

The Metaphysics of Kant: Several major viewpoints were combined in the work of Kant, who developed a distinctive critical philosophy called transcendental idealism. His philosophy is sceptical in that it denies the possibility of a strict knowledge of ultimate reality; it is empiricist in that it affirms that all knowledge arises from experience and is true of objects of actual and possible experience; and it is rationalistic in that it maintains that it is possible to have a priori knowledge of the structural principles of this empirical knowledge.

These principles are held to be necessary and universal in their application to experience, for in Kant's view the mind by its nature furnishes the archetypal forms and categories (space, time, causality, substance, and relation) to its sensations. These categories are logically prior to and necessary for experience, although manifested only in experience. Their logical priority to experience makes these categories or structural principles transcendental; they transcend all particular experiences, both actual and possible. Although these principles determine all experience, they do not in any way affect the nature of things in themselves, that is, things as they are independent of being experienced by people. The empirical knowledge that is structured by these principles must not be considered, therefore, as providing a revelation of things as they are in themselves. This knowledge concerns things only insofar as they appear to human perception or as they can be apprehended by the senses. For Kant, the description of the system of categories and structural principles governing experience is itself a metaphysics, but it is a metaphysics of reality as it is for human beings, that is, a metaphysics of the only reality that can only ever be known, rather than of reality as it is in itself.

The argument by which Kant sought to fix the limits of human knowledge within the framework of experience and to demonstrate the inability of the human mind to penetrate beyond experience strictly by reason to the realm of ultimate reality constitutes the critical feature of his philosophy, expounded in *Critique of Pure Reason, Critique of Practical Reason,* and *Critique of Judgement.* In the system propounded in these works, Kant also sought to reconcile science and religion in a world of two levels, comprising "noumena", objects conceived by reason although not perceived by the senses, and "phenomena", things as they appear to the senses that are accessible to material study. He maintained that, because God, freedom, and human immortality are noumenal realities, these concepts are understood through moral faith rather than through scientific knowledge.

Metaphysics Since Kant: Some of Kant's most distinguished successors, notably Johann Gottlieb Fichte, Friedrich Schelling, G. W. F. Hegel, and Friedrich Schleiermacher, negated Kant's criticism in their elaborations of his transcendental metaphysics by denying the Kantian conception of the thing-in-itself. They thus developed an absolute idealism in opposition to Kant's critical transcendental idealism.

Since the formation of the hypothesis of absolute idealism, the development of metaphysics has resulted in as many types of metaphysical theory as existed in pre-Kantian philosophy, despite Kant's contention that he had definitely fixed the limits of philosophical speculation. Notable among these later metaphysical theories are radical empiricism, or pragmatism, a native American form of metaphysics expounded by Charles Sanders Peirce, developed by William James, and adapted as instrumentalism by John Dewey; voluntarism, the foremost exponents of which are the German philosopher Arthur Schopenhauer and the American philosopher Josiah Royce; phenomenalism, as it is exemplified in the writings of the French philosopher Auguste Comte and the British philosopher Herbert Spencer; emergent evolution, or creative evolution, originated by the French philosopher Henri Bergson; and the philosophy of the organism, elaborated by the British mathematician and philosopher Alfred North Whitehead. The salient doctrines of pragmatism are that the chief function of thought is to guide action, that the meaning of concepts is to be sought in their practical applications, and that truth should be tested by the practical effects of belief; according to instrumentalism, ideas are instruments of action, and their truth is determined by their role in human experience. In the theory of voluntarism the will is postulated as the supreme manifestation of reality. The exponents of phenomenalism, who are sometimes called positivists, contend that everything can be analysed in terms of actual or possible occurrences, or phenomena, and that anything that cannot be analysed in this manner cannot be understood. In emergent or creative evolution, the evolut-ionary process is characterized as spontaneous and unpredictable rather than mechanistically deter-mined. The philosophy of the organism combines an evolutionary stress on constant process with a metaphysical theory of God, the eternal objects, and creativity.

Contemporary Developments: In the 20th century the validity of metaphysical thinking has been disputed by the logical positivists (*see* Analytic and Linguistic Philosophy) and by the so-called dialectical materialism of the Marxists. The basic principle maintained by the logical positivists is the verifiability theory of meaning. According to this theory a sentence has factual meaning only if it can in principle be verified by empirical observation. Logical positivists argue that metaphysical expressions such as "nothing exists except material particles" and "everything is part of one all-encompassing spirit" cannot be tested empirically. Therefore, according to the verifiability theory of meaning, these expressions have no factual meaning, although they can have an emotive meaning relevant to human hopes and feelings.

The dialectical materialists assert that the mind is conditioned by and reflects material reality. Therefore, speculations that conceive of constructs of the mind, such as the categories of metaphysics, as having any reality of their own are themselves unreal and can result only in delusion. To these assertions metaphysicians reply by denying the adequacy of the verifiability theory of meaning and of material perception as the standard of reality. Both logical positivism and dialectical materialism, they argue, conceal metaphysical assumptions, for example, that everything is observable or at least connected with something obse-rvable and that the mind has no distinctive life of its own. In the philosophical movement known as existentialism, thinkers have contended that the questions of the nature of being and of the individual's relationship to it are extremely important and meaningful in terms of human life. The investigation of these questions is therefore considered valid whether or not its results can be verified objectively.

Since the 1950s the problems of systematic analytical metaphysics have been studied in Britain by Stuart Newton Hampshire and Peter Frederick Strawson, the former concerned, in the manner of Spinoza, with the relationship between thought and action, and the latter, in the manner of Kant, with describing the major categories of experience as they are embedded in language. In the United States metaphysics has been much pursued in the spirit of positivism by Wilfred Stalker Sellars and Willard Van Orman Quine. Sellars has sought to express metaphysical questions in linguistic terms, and Quine has attempted to determine whether the structure of language commits the philosopher to asserting the existence of any entities whatever and, if so, what kind. In these new formulations the issues of metap-hysics and ontology remain vital.

Method of doubt, method of doubting everything conceivably doubtful, proposed by Descartes, with the aim of discovering what—if anything—can be known indubitably, with absolute certainty. Descartes concludes that the "Archimedian point" of certainty he seeks can be found in his unshakable assurance of his own existence as a thinker. See also: cogito argument.

Methodology, 1. An organised, documented set of procedures and guidelines for one or more phases of the software life cycle, such as analysis or design. Many methodologies include a diagramming notation for documenting the results of the procedure; a step-by-step "cookbook" approach for carrying out the procedure; and an objective (ideally quantified) set of criteria for determining whether the results of the procedure are of acceptable quality.

An example is The Yourdon methodology.

2. A pretentious way of saying "method".

Microcosm and Macrocosm, two philosophical terms, opposite in meaning, used to explain the relationship between human beings and the universe. The term *microcosm* denotes the conception of a human being as a complete world, universe, or cosmos, in miniature, within himself or herself. *Macrocosm* refers to the idea of the whole gigantic universe outside human nature. The microcosm concept was utilized by a number of great thinkers ranging from the 5th-century BC Greek philosopher Democritus to the 17th-century German philosopher Gottfried Wilhelm Leibniz.

Mill, James (1773-1836), British philosopher-economist, the father of John Stuart Mill; he expounded and developed the utilitarian doctrine of the British philosopher Jeremy Bentham. Mill was born in Northwater

Bridge, Angus, Scotland, and educated at the University of Edinburgh. In 1803, he became the editor of the London *Literary Journal*, and in 1805 editor of *St James' Chronicle*. From 1806 to 1818 he was engaged in writing his *History of India*.

Although he sharply criticized the East India Company and the British administration in India, in 1819 Mill was appointed to a position in the examiner's office of the India House in London. During this period he became a close associate of Bentham. As one of the leading exponents of *chrestomathic*, or useful, learning on a non-sectarian basis, Mill played a prominent role in the establishment of the University of London in 1825. A British Radical, Mill was also the founder of philosophical radicalism, a system of thought based on the teachings of the British economist David Ricardo and presented by Mill in *Elements of Political Economy* (1821). In his *Analysis of the Phenomena of the Mind* (1829), Mill applied utilitarian doctrines to psychology, basing his theory of the human mind on the principles of associationism.

Mind-body dichotomy, dualism between mind (soul, spirit) and body (brain, matter), see the mind-body problem.

Mind-body problem, most generally, the problem of describing the relationship between the mind and body (or brain). First explicitly raised by Descartes, it is, perhaps, the best known problem in the philosophy of mind. See dualism, epiphenomenalism, monism, and materialism.

Mind, Philosophy of, investigation of mental phenomena, including cognitive and affective (emotional) states and processes, and of the nature of the subject of these—the person, the soul, the brain, or whatever it may be. As a branch of philosophy it is characterized by its a priori method; it is not an empirical science, but an attempt to understand the concepts involved in thinking about the mind. In its present form, the subject dates from the modern period, that is, from the 17th century; but questions of the sort discussed then and since were also explored in the ancient world and during the Middle Ages. Indeed, every great philosopher from Plato to Ludwig Wittgenstein has considered aspects of the mind. The subject is one of the most important branches of philosophy and is among the most widely studied.

The Mind-Body Problem: The principal issue in the philosophy of mind is the place of mental phenomena in nature. The question is whether to suppose that mental states are just physical conditions of a complex material object, as in materialism, or whether there is reason to distinguish mind and body, and view them as belonging to different realms, as in dualism. In the period prior to Plato some philosophers took a materialist stance and held that mental features are distinguishable from other features only by virtue of the size and unpredictable behaviour of the particles that make up the soul. However, materialism soon gave way to dualism, with Plato arguing for a sharp distinction between body and soul, and crediting the latter with existence both prior to and following the life of the body.

The influential view of Aristotle, presented in *De Anima* (*Of the*

Soul), falls somewhere between these two extremes. He agreed with Plato that mental phenomena are not wholly reducible to states of the body; but he rejected the idea that people are unions of two distinct substances, viz. body and soul. Instead, he argued that the mind is a set of higher powers of a living organism, a rational animal, and that the highest of these properties or powers—abstract thought—transcends the capacity of matter.

In antiquity and the Middle Ages philosophers and theologians tended to follow either Plato or Aristotle, and were thus either substance or property dualists respectively. During the Renaissance, however, there was something of a resurgence of materialism, although the influential writings of Descartes re-established a dualism similar to that of Plato. In his arguments, Descartes introduced a style of reasoning that has remained popular ever since. It considers whether two features are separable in imagination ("conception") and concludes that if they are, then they must be distinct in reality also. Since it is possible to imagine having thoughts even without a body, it seems to follow that mental and physical phenomena must be distinct.

This mode of argument was revived in recent times by the American philosopher Saul Kripke who, in a famous series of lectures ("Naming and Necessity"), suggested that the imaginable possibility of feeling pain in the absence of relevant neurological activity (c-fibre stimulation) indicates that the two are not identical. The dualist arguments of Plato, Descartes, and Kripke have been much discussed and criticized. For example, one rejoinder is to argue that from the fact that it is possible to imagine *A* without *B* it does not follow that *A* and *B* are distinct, but only that they are not known to be the same. Nonetheless, there is a perennial appeal in dualism and in the Cartesian style of reasoning, since it is difficult to see how mental states could be "nothing other than" physical states.

Another response by modern-day materialists or physicalists (that is, those who argue that all facts are physical facts) to these arguments for dualism is to concede that what makes a state mental are its psychological features, but at the same time to maintain that it does not follow therefore that it is not a physical state—any more than it follows from the fact that what makes something a portrait are its repre-sentational properties, and that a portrait is thus not a physical object. Every portrait of Queen Elizabeth II, for example, is a physical object, but not every portrait is a physical object of one and the same sort. This subtle form of materialism is associated principally with the American philosopher Donald Davidson, and is known as either "anomalous monism" or "non-reductive phys-icalism".

The Problem of Intentionality: One of the oldest and most troubling questions is that concerning the nature of thinking. By means of thought is seems possible to make some kind of connection with distant and past objects; thought even appears able to relate human beings to objects that have never existed, let alone things that are currently absent from the environment. This raises the question of how all of this is possible. The attempt to answer this question is the basis of the theory of "intentionality" (that is, the "directionality" or "aboutness" of thought).

Some philosophers try to explain intentionality in terms of mental representations (ideas, images, or sentences in the language of thought) to which the thinking subject is related, as a reader is to a text or a viewer is to an image. This theory has the singular disadvantage that it confines mental reference to an inner world of ideas. A radical alternative insists that thought is directly related to external reality. Accounts of this sort are to be found in the writings of the German theologian Meister Eckhart and, much later, in those of Sartre; in Britain and the United States versions of this view are currently in fashion. The main problem faced is that of erroneous and empty thoughts. If to say that to think of X is to be directly related to X itself, what is to be made of cases where X does not exist?

Whatever the difficulties faced by these and whatever the defensibility of other accounts of intentionality, there is the residual question of whether thought is a material process. Arguments for doubting that it can be usually take the form of observing that thought is quite unlike physical processes: for example, in the possible non-existence of its objects; in the fact that thought is often vague and highly abstract; and in its being subject to principles of rationality rather than mere causal regularity. The challenge for the materialist is to explain these features naturalistically, in terms of the causal interaction between material objects—or, failing that, to explain them away.

The Status of Common-Sense Psychology: In recent years some physicalists, specifically those termed "eliminative materialists", have concluded that there cannot be a satisfactory naturalistic explanation of mental phenomena; rather than abandon their physicalism, however, they have argued that what this shows is that it is a mistake to suppose that there are such things as mental states. The error in this respect is rather like that of those who believed in plant spirits, for they, similarly, were trying to explain the behaviour of things by positing certain sorts of entities within them. Certainly plants and human beings do have inner causes of their observable behaviour, but on the present account these do not include plant souls or human minds. For the eliminative materialists, the mental should be eliminated as a category in favour of an exclusively materialist perspective; psychology should be replaced with neuroscience.

Critics of the eliminative materialism position have rejected the charge that common-sense ("folk") psychology—that is, offering everyday descriptions and expla-nations in terms of beliefs and desires—is inadequate or incoherent; they have countered with the argument that the attempt to formulate eliminativist claims proves self-refuting, for thinking that there are no such things as thoughts proves that there are. Needless to say, eliminativists try to avoid this trap, and their formulations and arguments are often very subtle. Nonetheless, their view has attracted few proponents and it is increasingly regarded as another failed attempt to resolve the central questions of the philosophy of mind.

Consciousness: Much has been written about the nature of consciousness, attempting to characterize it and to say how it relates to unconscious mental processes and to physical activity in the brain. To date, no definitive account has been developed, and some fear that human beings may simply be incapable of arriving at one. This might leave the issues forever unresolved, but it could also be that unforeseeable developments in the sciences open up a way to understand the conscious mind.

Model, 1. A description of observed behaviour, simplified by ignoring certain details. Models allow complex syst-ems to be understood and their behaviour predicted within the scope of the model, but may give incorrect descriptions and predictions for situations outside the realm of their intended use. A model may be used as the basis for simulation.

2. An interpretation in which expressions of interest to us (*e.g.* a wff, a set of wffs, a system) come out true for that interpretation. See isomorphism of models, true for an interpretation Cardinality of a model The cardinality of the domain of the model.

Model of a wff or set of wffs An interpretation, I, that makes those wffs true for I.

Model of a formal system An interpretation, I, that makes its set of theorems true for I. A model of a system is a model of its set of theorems.

Non-standard model Weakly, any non-standard interpretation that is a model. Strongly, any model that is not isomorphic with the intended (standard) model. See isomorphism of models

Normal model A normal interpretation that is a model. See interpretation, normal

Modernism, modernism (sometimes called abstractionism) is an aesthetic doctrine and movement of the 20th century that repudiates the traditional purpose of art to represent reality and/or address timeless human values; instead, modernism holds that the purpose of art is to enable the artist to express his or her emotions, often in an utterly non-representational manner (also called abstract expressionism). Modernism is usually an aesthetic variety of subjectivism. (References from abstractionism and expressionism.)

Modus tollens, A rule of inference by which we infer $\sim A$ when given $A \Rightarrow B$ and $\sim B$.

Molecule, In propositional logic, a compound proposition as opposed to a simple proposition or atom

Monad, according to Leibniz, monads are the ultimate indivisible units or "true atoms" of all existence. Monads are not material: each monad is a self-activating, unique, center of "purpose" and "perception." Monads cannot interact, but are in a "pre-established harmony" with each other, by the grace of God.

Monadic predicate logic, predicate logic.

Monism, answer offered to philosophical dualism by adherents of idealism and of materialism. Monism holds that reality is made up of only one type of substance, historically either spirit/mind (according to idealists Berkeley) or matter. See also materialism, idealism, neutral monism, anomalous monism, dualism.

Monism (Greek, *monos,* "single"), in philosophy, doctrine that ultimate reality is composed entirely of one substance. Monism is thus opposed to both dualism and pluralism. Three basic types of monism are recognized: materialistic monism, idealistic monism, and the mind-stuff theory. According to the first doctrine, everything in the universe, including mental phenomena, is reduced to the one category of matter, as in materialism. In the second doctrine, matter is regarded as a form of manifestation of the mind; and in the third doctrine, matter and mind are considered to be merely aspects of each other. Although monistic philosophies date from ancient Greece, the term *monism* is comparatively recent. It was first used by the 18th-century German philosopher Christian Wolff to designate types of philosophical thought in which an attempt was made to eliminate the dichotomy of body and mind.

Although he was not known by the term, the 17th-century Dutch philosopher Baruch Spinoza was one of the most influential monists. He taught that both material and spiritual phenomena are attributes of one underlying substance. His doctrine strongly anticipated the mind-stuff theory.

Monotheism, the belief there is only one god, or that the gods of different religions are really just different manifestations of the one true god. Monotheism is opposed to both henotheism and polytheism.

Moral, morality.

Moral isolationism, the view that we ought not to be morally concerned with, or involved with, people outside of our own immediate group. Moral isolationism is often a consequences of some versions of moral relativism.

Moral Philosophy. *See* Ethics.

Morality, "morality" refers to the first-order beliefs and practices about good and evil by means of which we guide our behaviour. Contrast with ethics, which is the second-order, reflective, critical and normativeconsideration of our moral beliefs and practices.

Moral luck, the phenomenon that the moral goodness or badness of some of our actions depends simply on chance. For example, the drunk driver may safely reach home without injuring anyone at all, or might accidentally kill several children that run out into the street while the drunken person is driving home. How bad the action of driving while drunk is in that case depends in part on luck.

Moral rights, rights

Morphing, The animated transformation of one image into another by gradually distorting the first image so as to move certain chosen points to the position of corresponding pointsin the second image.

Mother, parent

Multiple realisability, the thesis that a mental state is the type it is independent of the physical realisation of that mental state. See functionalism.

Murphy's Law, (Or "Sod's Law") The correct, *original* Murphy's Law reads: "If there are two or more ways to do something, and one of those ways can result in a catastrophe, then someone will do it." This is a principle of defensive design, cited here because it is usually given in mutant forms less descriptive of the challenges of design for lusers. For example, you don't make a two-pin plug symmetrical and then label it "THIS WAY UP"; if it matters which way it is plugged in, then you make the design asymmetrical (see also the anecdote under magic smoke).

Edward A. Murphy, Jr. was one of the engineers on the rocket-sled experiments that were done by the US Air Force in 1949 to test human acceleration tolerances (USAF project MX981). One experiment involved a set of 16 accelerometers mounted to different parts of the subject's body. There weretwo ways each sensor could be glued to its mount, and somebody methodically installed all 16 the wrong way around. Murphy then made the original form of his pronouncement, which the test subject (Major John Paul Stapp) quoted at a news conference a few days later.

Within months "Murphy's Law' had spread to various technical cultures connected to aerospace engineering. Before too many years had gone by variants had passed into the popular imagination, changing as they went. Most of these are variants on "Anything that can go wrong, will"; this issometimes referred to as Finagle's Law. The memetic drift apparent in these mutants clearly demonstrates Murphy's Law acting on itself!

Mutual recursion, recursion

Narcissism, an excessive preoccupation with oneself. In mythology, Narcissus was a beautiful young man who fell in love with his own image reflected in a pool of water.

Natural deduction, A set of rules expressing how valid proofs may be constructed in predicate logic.

A horizontal line separates premises (above) from conclusions (below). Vertical ellipsis (dots) stand for a series of applications of the rules. "T" is the constant "true" and "F" is the constant "false".

"^" is the AND (conjunction) operator, "v" is the inclusive OR (disjunction) operator and "/" is NOT (negation or complement.

P, *Q*, *P1*, *P2*, etc. stand for propositions such as "Socrates was a man". *P*[*x*] is a proposition possibly containing instances of the variable *x*, *e.g.* "*x* can fly".

A proof (a sequence of applications of the rules) may be enclosed in a box. A boxed proof produces conclusions that are only valid given the assumptions made inside the box, however, the proof demonstrates certain relationships which are valid outside the box. For example, the box below labelled "Implication introduction" starts by assuming *P*,which need not be a true proposition so long as it can be used to derive *Q*.

Truth introduction:

–

T

(Truth is free).

Binary AND introduction:

.   .

.   .

*Q*1   *Q*2 |

*Q*1 ^   *Q*2

(If we can derive both Q1 and Q2 then Q1^Q2 is true).

N-ary AND introduction:

..   ..   .

.   ..   .

*Q*1   ..   *Qn*

*Q*1 ^.. ^ *Q*i ^.. ^ *Qn*

Other n-ary rules follow the binary versions similarly.

Quantified AND introduction:

x.

.

Q[x]

For all x. Q[x]

(If we can prove Q for arbitrary x then Q is true for all x).

Falsity elimination:

F

_

Q

(Falsity opens the floodgates).

OR elimination:

*P*1 *v* *P*2

*P*1 *P*2

. .

. .

Q *Q*

Q

(Given *P*1 v *P*2, if *Q* follows from both then *Q* is true).

Exists elimination:

Exists *x*. *P*[*x*]

x *P*[*x*] |

.

.

Q

Q

(If *Q* follows from *P*[*x*] for arbitrary *x* and such an *x* exists then *Q* is true).

OR introduction 1:

*P*1

*P*1 *v* *P*2

(If *P*1 is true then *P*1 OR anything is true).

OR introduction 2:

*P*2

*P*1 *v* *P*2

(If *P*2 is true then anything OR *P*2 is true). Similar symmetries apply to ^ rules.

Exists introduction:

P[*a*]

Exists *x*.*P*[*x*]

(If *P* is true for "a" then it is true for all *x*).,

AND elimination 1:

*P*1 ^ *P*2

*P*1

(If *P*1 and *P*2 are true then *P*1 is true).

For all elimination:

For all *x*. *P*[*x*]

P[*a*]

(If *P* is true for all *x* then it is true for "a").

For all implication introduction:

x *P*[*x*]

.

.

Q[*x*]

For all *x*. *P*[*x*] -> *Q*[*x*]

(If *Q* follows from *P* for arbitrary *x* then *Q* follows from *P* for all *x*).

Implication introduction:

P

.

.

Q

P -> *Q*

(If *Q* follows from *P* then *P* implies *Q*).

NOT *introduction*:

P

.

.

F

/ *P*

(If falsity follows from P then P is false).

NOT-NOT:

$$\frac{//P}{P}$$

(If it is not the case that P is not true then P is true).

For all implies exists:

$$\frac{P[a] \text{ For all x. } P[x] \text{ -> } Q[x]}{Q[a]}$$

(If P is true for given "a" and P implies Q for all x then Q is true for a).

Implication elimination, modus ponens:

$$\frac{P \; P \text{ -> } Q}{Q}$$

(If P and P implies Q then Q).

NOT elimination, contradiction:

$$\frac{P \; /P}{F}$$

(If P is true and P is not true then false is true).

Natural Law, in ethical philosophy, theology, law, and social theory, a set of principles, based on what are assumed to be the permanent characteristics of human nature, that can serve as a standard for evaluating conduct and civil laws. Natural law is considered fundamentally unchanging and universally appli-cable. Because of the ambiguity of the word *nature*, the meaning of *natural* varies. Thus, natural law may be considered an ideal to which humanity aspires or a general fact, the way human beings usually act. Natural law is contrasted with positive law, the enactments of civil society.

Classical Theories: The ancient Greek philosophers were the first to elaborate a doctrine of natural law. In the 6th century BC, Heraclitus spoke of a common wisdom that pervades the whole universe, "for all human laws are nourished by one, the divine". Aristotle distinguished between two kinds of justice: "A rule of justice is natural that has the same validity everywhere, and does not depend on our accepting it or not; a rule is legal [conventional] that in the first instance may be settled in one way or the other indifferently." The Stoics, especially the philosopher Chrysippus of Soli, constructed a systematic natural law theory. According to Stoicism, the whole cosmos is rationally ordered by an active principle, the logos, variously named God, mind, or fate. Every individual nature is part of the cosmos. To live virtuously means to live in accord with one's nature, to live according to reason. Because passion and emotion are considered irrational movements of the soul, the wise individual seeks to eradicate the passions and consciously embrace the rational life. This doctrine was popularized among the Romans by the 1st-century BC orator Cicero, who gave a famous definition of natural law in his *De Republica:* "True law is right reason in agreement with Nature; it is of universal application, unchanging and everlasting; it summons to duty by its commands, and averts from wrongdoing by its prohibitions ... There will not be different laws at Rome and at Athens, or different laws now and in the future, but one eternal and unchangeable law will be valid for all nations and for all times." In the *Corpus Juris Civilis* a compilation and codification of Roman legal material prepared in 534 under Emperor Justinian I, a *jus naturale* is acknowledged, but there is no assertion that natural law is superior to positive law and no vindication of human rights (slavery, for example, was legal).

Modern Theories: The Dutch jurist Hugo Grotius is considered the founder of the modern theory of natural law. His definition of natural law as that body of rules which can be discovered by the use of reason is traditional, but in raising the hypothetical argument that his law would have validity even if there were no God or if the affairs of human beings were of no concern to God, he effected a divorce from theological presuppositions and prepared the way for the purely rationalistic theories of the 17th and 18th centuries. He thus departed from scholasticism in his methodology if not in his content. A second innovation of Grotius was to view this law as deductive and independent of experience: "Just as the mathematicians treat their figures as abstracted from bodies, so in treating law I have withdrawn my mind from every particular fact" (*De Jure Belli ac Pacis;* On the Law of War and Peace, 1625).

The German jurist Samuel von Pufendorf, the first to hold a chair of natural law in a German university, more fully developed the concept of a law of nature. The 17th-century English philosophers Thomas Hobbes and John Locke proposed an original state of nature from which a social contract arose and combined this theory with that of natural law. Locke's doctrine that nature had endowed human beings with certain inalienable rights that could not be violated by any governing authority was incorporated in the American Declaration of Independence.

In the 19th century a critical spirit dominated discussions of natural law. The existence of a natural law was generally regarded as unprovable, and it was largely replaced in legal theory by utilitarianism, formulated by the English philosopher Jeremy Bentham as "the greatest happiness of the greatest number", and by legal positivism, according to which law is based simply on "the command of the ruler", in the phrase of the English jurist John Austin.

The atrocities committed by Nazi Germany during World War II revived interest in a higher standard than positive law. The United Nations (UN) Charter declared the "faith" of that organization in human rights, and on December 10, 1948, the UN General Assembly adopted the Universal Declaration of Human Rights, which, however, is more a moral prono-uncement than a legally enforceable treaty. *See also* Ethics.

Natural theology, knowledge about God that can be obtained by natural means by the exercise of reason and sense perception. Contrast: revealed theology.

Naturalised semantics, the project of explaining semantic notions, such as "means", "refers", "denotes", in terms of non-semantic notions, such as correlation, causation, resemblance, structural isomorphism, or teleological function. Some leading efforts in this area include Dretske's, Fodor's, and Millikan's works.

Naturalism (philosophy), in philosophy, a movement affirming that nature is the whole of reality and can be understood only through scientific investigation. Denying the existence of the supernatural and deemphasizing metaphysics, or the study of the ultimate nature of reality, naturalism affirms that cause-and-effect relationships, as in physics and chemistry, are sufficient to account for all phenomena. Teleological conceptions, which suggest design and metaphysical necessity in nature, while not necessarily invalid, are excluded from consideration. The ethical implication, since the naturalist denies any transcendent or supernatural end for humankind, is that values must be found within the social context. It is impossible to determine what is best in an ultimate context, because the ultimate is beyond discovery. Values, therefore, are relative, and ethics is based on custom, inclination, or some form of utilitarianism, the doctrine that what is useful is good.

Naturalism is rooted in British empiricism, which holds that all knowledge is derived from experience, and in European positivism, the doctrine that denies any validity to metaphysical speculation. It reached its peak in the late 19th- and 20th-century works of the American philosophers George Santayana, John Dewey, and their followers.

Naturalism, 1. in relation to mind, the view that mental phenomena can beexplained as part of the natural order and are empirically accessible features of the world.

2. in metaphysics, the view according to which reality operates according to natural laws, without spiritual intervention (opposed to theism and spiritualism, but compatible with deism).

3. in aesthetics,the view according to which art (and especially literature) should present human experience "as is", without evaluating reality or projecting ethical ideals (historically, naturalism in literature developed in reaction to romanticism).

4. in ethics, the view according to which at least some human values (though not necessarily all) are determined by, and hence can be derived from, the nature of the human organism and our situation on earth —values like food, water, shelter, safety, psychological closeness, actualization of human talent and potential, the attainment of knowledge, and so on. By way of illustration, existentialism could be considered a humanistic form of individualism, but it differs from many other forms of humanism in denying ethical naturalism. Since, according to naturalism, moral values can be derived from facts about the world and human nature, the naturalist holds that "is" can imply "ought."

Naturalistic fallacy, according to G. E. Moore, any argument which attempts to define the good in any terms whatsoever, including naturalistic terms. For Moore, good is simple and indefinable. This is revealed,

Moore thought, by the fact that, after listing any "natural" quality of something (pleasurable, for example), we can always raise the question "but is it good?"

Natural language, A language spoken or written by humans, as opposed to a language use to program or communicate with computers. Natural language understanding is one of the hardest problems of artificial intelligence due to the complexity, irregularity and diversity of human language and the philosophical problems of meaning. See also Pleuk grammar development system, proof.

Natural law, in ethics, believers in natural law hold (a) that there is a natural order to the human world, (b) that this natural order is good, and (c) that people therefore ought not to violate that order.

Natural rights, rights

Natural theology, knowledge about God that can be obtained by natural means by the exercise of reason and sense perception. Contrast: revealed theology.

Necessary, a sentence, proposition, thought, or judgement is necessaryif it is true of any possible world. Some philosophers (*e.g.* A.J. Ayer)maintain that the truths of logic and mathematics are necessary because they are a priori, and a priori simply because they are analytic; similarly maintaining that contigent, a posteriori, and asynthetic are equivalent.

Necessitarianism, determinism applied to human beings: the doctrine that human beings do not have free will but are determined in their actions by antecedent, external causes. Necessitarianism is thus opposed to libertarianism regarding human action. (References from determinism and libertarianism.)

Negation, A truth function that is true when its argument is false, and false when its argument is true (in 2-valued logics). Also the operator or connective denoting this function; also the proposition built from this operator. Notation: ~*p*, also °*p*, also, *p* with a bar on top. (By convention an unadorned propositional symbol, *p*, is the affirmation of proposition *p*.)

Negation completeness, A system is negation-complete when for every closed wff *A* of its language, either *A* or ~*A* is a theorem. That is, all closedwffs are decidable

Negation incompleteness, A system is negation-incomplete when for at least one closed wff *A* neither *A* nor ~*A* is a theorem, or when there is at least one undecidable closed wff.

Negative rights, rights

Neo-Confucianism, variety of Confucianism that survived as a response to the introduction of Buddhism to China from India. While this is strictly a technical or scholarly term, it helps to be aware that philosophical development occurred in the East as in the West (the changes in Confucianism are similar to the changes in Aristotelianism and Platonism in the West), and that the modern understanding of Confucianism is not necessarily true to the original tenets held by Confucius himself.

Neo-Platonism, Neo-Platonism refers specifically to the doctrines of Plotinus (205-270 A.D.) and his followers in the early centuries A.D., and more generally to the tradition of such thought stretching through late antiquity into the Middle Ages and early Renaissance. Neo-Platonism was a revamped Platonism which put greater emphasis on Plato's dualism and idealism, even to the point of a spiritualism which early Christian theologians like Augustine found congenial despite the basic pantheism of Neo-Platonic ideas.

Neorationalist, a term for those 20th century philosophers who wish to revive aspects of rationalism. Specifically, maintaining mentalism, as opposed to behaviourism, in psychology, possibly insisting on innateness in learning theory and on intensional structures in a scientific description of the world.

Neutral monism, the doctrine that

reality, though unified, is neither mental nor physical but rather conglomerations of a neutral entity. See monism, materialism, idealism.

Nietzsche, Friedrich Wilhelm (1844-1900), German philosopher, poet, and Classical philologist, who became one of the most provocative and influential thinkers of the 19th century.

Life and Works: Nietzsche was born on October 15, 1844, in Röcken, Prussia. His father, a Lutheran minister, died when Nietzsche was a young child, and he was raised by his mother in a home that included his grandmother, two aunts, and a sister. He studied Classical philology at the universities of Bonn and Leipzig and was appointed Professor of Classical Philology at the University of Basel at the age of 24. Ill health (he was plagued throughout his life by poor eyesight and migraine headaches) forced his retirement in 1879. Ten years later he suffered a mental breakdown from which he never recovered. He died in Weimar on August 25, 1900.

In addition to the study of Greek culture, particularly the philosophies of Plato and Aristotle, Nietzsche was influenced by the German philosopher Arthur Schopenhauer, by the theory of evolution, and by his friendship with the German composer Richard Wagner.

A prolific writer, he wrote several major works, among them *The Birth of Tragedy* (1872; trans. 1967), *Daybreak* (1881; trans. 1974), *The Gay Science* (1882; trans. 1974), *Thus Spoke Zarathustra* (1883-1885; trans. 1961), *Beyond Good and Evil* (1886; trans. 1973), *On the Genealogy of Morals* (1887; trans. 1967), *The Antichrist* (1895; trans. 1968), *Ecce Homo* (1908; trans. 1968), and *The Will to Power* (1901; trans. 1910).

Central to Nietzsche's thought was the notion that with the development of the modern secular world the traditional values (represented by Christianity) had lost their power in the lives of individuals, which he expressed in his infamous proclamation "God is dead". Modern efforts to ward off the threat of nihilism by transplanting transcendent authority into such ideals as, for example, reason or nature (as in the works of Thomas Hobbes and Jean-Jacques Rousseau respectively), were condemned by Nietzsche as the slavish urge of the "herd" or "mob". In contrast, he held aloft the tragic hero, who affirms life in the face of its meaninglessness. Against modern interpretations of progress as the realization of material goals, Nietzsche argued that the purpose of human life is to encourage the great individual (whom he calls the Übermensch—"overman" or "superman"). Such individuals will heroically construct meaning in the face of a paradoxically meaningless world—hence the subtitling of his work *The Twilight of the Idols* (1889; trans. 1968) as *How to Philosophize with a Hammer.* It is this creative will that for Nietzsche is the "will to power". He was convinced that traditional values represented a "slave morality", a morality created by weak and resentful individuals who encouraged such behaviour as gentleness and kindness because it served their interests. He claimed that new values could be created to replace the traditional ones, and his discussion of the possibility led to his concept of the overman.

According to Nietzsche, the

masses conform to tradition, whereas his ideal overman is secure, independent, and highly individualistic. The overman feels deeply, but his passions are rationally controlled. Concentrating on the real world, rather than on the rewards of the next world promised by religion, the overman affirms life, including the suffering and pain that accompany human existence. He is a creator of values, a creator of a "master morality" that reflects the strength and independence of one who is liberated from all values, except those that he deems valid.

Nietzsche maintained that all human behaviour is motivated by the will to power. In its positive sense, the will to power is not simply power over others, but the power over oneself that is necessary for creativity. Such power is manifested in the overman's independence, creativity, and originality. Although Nietzsche explicitly denied that any overmen had yet arisen, he mentions several individuals who could serve as models, including Socrates, Jesus Christ, Leonardo da Vinci, Michelangelo, Shakespeare, Goethe, Julius Caesar, and Napoleon.

The concept of the overman has often been interpreted as one that postulates a master-slave society and has been identified with totalitarian philosophies. Many scholars deny the connection and attribute it to misinterpretation of Nietzsche's work.

Nihilism, the belief that there is no value or truth. Literally, a belief in nothing (nihil in Latin). Most contemporary discussions of nihilism arise out of a consideration of Friedrich Nietzsche's remarks on nihilism, especially in The Will to Power. Nihilism can also be described as an extreme form of existentialism or pessimism which holds that life has no meaning and that even if you try to achieve your goals, in the end your life must necessarily come to nothing—thus nihilism is similar to fatalism.

Sometimes, nihilism is worse than fatalism because nihilists don't usually say that life comes to zero but to less than zero, since they hold that life really just consists of one thing: pain. Nihilism is popularly taken to refer to wanton destruction for its own sake, a sort of activist irrationalism.

Nihilism (Latin, *nihil,* "nothing"), designation applied to various radical philosophies, usually by their opponents, the implication being that adherents of these philosophies reject all positive values and believe in nothing.

The term was first used to describe Christian heretics during the Middle Ages. In Russia it was applied in the 1850s and 1860s to young intellectuals who, influenced by Western ideas, repudiated Christianity, considered Russian society backward and oppressive, and advocated revolutionary change. The best-known fictional nihilist was Bazarov in the novel *Fathers and Sons* (1862) by Ivan Turgenev. Conservatives claimed that nihilism would destroy all possibility of orderly and purposeful existence and was directly contrary to real human needs and desires, but the novelist N. G. Chernyshevsky and other radicals called it a necessary phase in the transformation of Russia. The Narodniks (Populists), who worked for a peasant uprising in the 1870s, and the Narodnaya Volya (People's

Will) movement, members of which assassinated Tsar Alexander II in 1881, were also considered manifestations of nihilism.

Nominalism, the view (held by Berkeley, among others) that general terms, such as "table," do not express or refer to general concepts, abstract ideas, or any sort of really existing universals; there are just individual words and the individual things they refer to.

Nominalist, 1. in the middle ages, someone who maintained that there where nouniversals above and beyond particular individual things and words (marks on paper) in particular languages. realist

2. today, we tend to call someone a nominalist whose general account of the universe tries to get along without sanctioning things that are not realized completely in our experience. Goodman is often said to be a nominalist, and Quine may be said to have such tendencies (though Quine sanctions sets).

Nonconceptual content, a content, possibly of a non- or sub-doxastic state, whose canonical specification employs concepts which the subject neednot possess in order to entertain the content, but rather might, for instance, be canonically specified in terms of abilities and skills the subject possesses, or in terms of significant though nonconceptualised experience.

Non-contradiction, a fundamental logical principle, first formulated by Aristotle, which maintains that one and the same proposition (or thought or statement) cannot be both true and false or that a statement and its denial or contradictory cannot both be true.

Non-determinism, A property of a computation which may have more than one result. One way to implement a non-deterministic algorithm is using backtracking, another is to explore (all) possible solutions in parallel.

Non-deterministic, Exhibiting non-determinism.

Non-truth-functional, an operator (*i.e.* something which if added to one or more propositions makes a (molecular) proposition) is non-truth-functional iff the truth value of a proposition in which it appears is not wholly determined by the truth value of the subsiduary propositions on which it operates. *E.g.* the truth value of "it is necessary that there are nine planets" and "it is believed that there are nine planets" is not determined by the truth value of "there are nine planets." Hence the operators "it isbelieved that" are non-truth-functional operators. truth-functional

Non-volatile, non-volatile storage

Norm, A real-valued function modelling the length of a vector. The norm must be homogeneous and symmetric and fulfil the following condition: the shortest way to reach a point is to go straight towards it. Every convex symmetric closed surface surrounding point 0 introduces a norm by means of Minkowski functional; all vectors that end on the surface have the same norm then.

The most popular norm is the Euclidean norm; it is calculated by summing up squares of all coordinates and taking the square root; this is the essence of Pythagoras's theorem. In the infinite-dimensional case, the sum is infinite or is replaced with an integral when the number of dimensions is uncountable.

Normal distribution, (Or "Gaussian distribution", "bell curve") The frequency distribution of many natural phenomena such as the height of people of a certain age and sex. The formula looks something like:

$P(x) = e^{((x-m)/s)^2}$

where $P(x)$ is the probability of a measurement x, m is the mean value of x and s is the standard deviation.

Normal form, In reduction systems, the state of a term which contains no reducible expressions. Variants include head normal form, weak head normal form.

Normal interpretation, interpretation

Normalization, 1. A transformation applied uniformly to each element in a set of data so that the set has some specific statistical property. For example, monthly measurements of the rainfall in London might be normalised by dividing each one by the total for the year to give a profile of rainfall throughout the year.

2. Representation of a floating-point number so that its mantissa's left-most digit is non-zero. If the leftmost fraction digit are zeros, the number is said to be unnormalised. Unnormalised numbers are normalised by shifting the fraction left, one digit at a time, until the leftmost digit is nonzero and reducing the exponent by the number of shifts.

Normalized, normalisation

Normal order reduction, Under this evaluation strategy an expression is evaluated by reducing the leftmost outermost redex first. This method will terminate for any expression for which termination is possible, whereas applicative order reduction may not. This method is equivalent to passing arguments unevaluated because arguments are initially to the right of functions applied to them.

Noumenal, a Kantian term that refers to the unknowable world as it is in itself. According to Kant, we can only know the world as it appears to us, as a phenomenon. We can never know it as it is in itself, as a noumenon. Theadjectival forms of these two words are "phenomenal" and "noumenal," respectively.

Noumenon, for Kant noumena or "things-in-themselves" are realities transcending all possible thought and experience. Since the Categories of thought do not apply to things-in-themselves but only "things-for-us" or phenomena, knowledge is possible only of these phenomena.

N-wff, wff, open

"O" proposition, in the traditional notation for categorical logic, a proposition that is both particular and negative. Example: "Some trees are not evergreens." Such a proposition affirms that there is at least one tree that is not also an evergreen. Its contradictory is an "A" proposition with the same subject and predicate terms.

Ob-,/ob/ prefix Obligatory. A piece of netiquette acknowledging that the author has been straying from the newsgroup's charter topic. For example, if a posting in alt.sex is a response to a part of someone else's posting that has nothing particularly to do with sex, the author may append "ObSex" (or "Obsex") and toss off a question or vignette about some unusual erotic act. It is considered a sign of great winnitude when one's Obs are more interesting than other people's whole postings.

Objective, something is objective

insofar as it is independent of either a particular human mind or minds altogether.

Objective-subjective, distinction between propositions or judgments about the way things are and those about how people think or feel about them. The truth of objective claims is presumed to be entirely independent of the merely personal concerns reflected in subje-ctive expressions, even though is difficult to draw the distinction precisely. Thus, for example: "Spinach is green" is objective, while "I like spinach" is subjective. "Seventy-three percent of people in Houston don't like spinach," however, seems to be an objective claim about certain subjects. The legitimacy of this distinction is open to serious question, since it is unclear whether (and how) any knowing subject can achieve genuine objectivity. Nevertheless, because objective truth is supposed to carry undeniable persuasive force, exaggerated claims of objectivity have often been used as tools of intellectual and social oppression. *Recommended Reading*: Richard Rorty, Objectivity, Relativism, and Truth (Cambridge, 1991); Thomas Nagel, The View from Nowhere (Oxford, 1989); Richard J. Bernstein, Beyond Objectivism and Relativism: Science, Hermeneutics, and Praxis (Pennsylvania, 1983); and The Authority of Reason, ed. by Jean E. Hampton and Richard A. Healey (Cambridge, 1998).

Objective truth, objective truths are true regardless of what anyone thinks. Example: The earth revolves around the sun. This was true, a believer in objective truth would say, long before anyone thought so (the earth being long uninhabited) and even despite everyone thinkingotherwise for a long time (prior to Copernicus, for millennia, virtually everyone thought the sun revolved around the earth).

Objectivity, the property of being objective.

Object language, The formal language of a system. The language used to talkabout the object language is called the metalanguage. Outside logic, an object language need not be formal; it is any referent language of any metalanguage.

Object-orientation, object-oriented

Objective-subjective, distinction between propositions or judgments about the way things are and those about how people think or feel about them. The truth of objective claims is presumed to be entirely indepe-ndent of the merely personal concerns reflected in subjective expressions, even though is difficult to draw the distinction precisely. Thus, for example: "Spinach is green" is objective, while "I like spinach" is subjective. "Seventy-three percent of people in Houston don't like spinach," however, seems to be an objective claim about certain subjects. The legitimacy of this distinction is open to serious question, since it is unclear whether (and how) any knowing subject can achieve genuine objectivity. Nevertheless, because objective truth is supposed to carry undeniable persuasive force, exaggerated claims of objectivity have often been used as tools of intellectual and social oppression. *Recommended Reading*: Richard Rorty, Objectivity, Relativism, and Truth (Cambridge, 1991); Thomas Nagel, The View from Nowhere (Oxford, 1989); Richard J. Bernstein, Beyond Objectivism and Relativism: Science, Hermeneutics, and

Praxis (Pennsylvania, 1983); and The Authority of Reason, ed. by Jean E. Hampton and Richard A. Healey (Cambridge, 1998).

Obligation, that which binds us to act in accordance with duty. Obligatory acts are those one is morally, legally, or contractually required to perform. Normative theories usually try to explain the grounds of moral obligation as well as its practical application. *Recommended Reading*: Michael J. Zimmerman, The Concept of Moral Obligation (Cambridge, 1996).

Obscenity, artistic expression which appeals solely to prurient interests and is without redeeming artistic merit or social importance. (As defined under U. S. law.)

Obscurum per obscurius, Latin phrase meaning "the obscure through the more obscure;" hence, the flaw in any account that proves more difficult to understand than what it purports to clarify. In this vein, philosophers reflecting upon each other's work sometimes echo Byron's complaint about Coleridge: "But, like a hawk encumbered with his hood, Explaining metaphysics to the nation —I wish he would explain his explanation."

Obversion, the reciprocal relationship between two categorical propositions of opposite quality such that the predicate term of each is the complement of the predicate term of the other. Obversion is a valid immediate inference for categorical propositions of every form. Thus, for example: All lizards are reptiles and No lizards are non-reptiles. No spiders are insects and All spiders are non-insects. Some fish are birds and Some fish are not non-birds. Some mammals are not dogs and Some mammals are non-dogs. They are all legitimate cases of obversion; either member of each pair can be substituted for the other.

Obversion, the reciprocal relationship between two categorical propositions of opposite quality such that the predicate term of each is the complement of the predicate term of the other. Obversion is a valid immediate inference for categorical propositions of every form. Thus, for example: All lizards are reptiles and No lizards are non-reptiles. No spiders are insects and All spiders are non-insects. Some fish are birds and Some fish are not non-birds. Some mammals are not dogs and Some mammals are non-dogs. They are all legitimate cases of obversion; either member of each pair can be substituted for the other.

Occam's Razor, The English philosopher, William of Occam (1300-1349) propounded Occam's Razor:

> *Entia non sunt multiplicanda praeter necessitatem.*
>
> (Latin for "Entities should not be multiplied more than necessary"). That is, the fewer assumptions an explanation of a phenomenon depends on, the better it is.

For example, some claim that God caused himself to exist and also caused the universe to exist—he was the "first cause"—whereas Occam's Razor suggests that if one accepts the possibility of something causing itself then it is better to assume that it was the universe that caused itself rather than God because this explanation involves fewer entities.

The negation of Occam's Razor would suggest that an arbitrarily complex explanation is just as good as the simplest one. (*E.g.* God and his cat created a robot called Sparky who built the universe from parts bought from a shop in another dimension). See also KISS Principle.

Occasionalism, a view popularised by Nicholas Malbranche whereby:

1) the mental and the material comprise two different kinds of substance;
2) neither has any direct causal effect on the other and;
3) all seeming interactions between the two are due to the continual intervention by God who brings about a change in one on the occasion of a change in the other.

See dualism, doctrine of pre-established harmony, parallelism.

Ockham William of, English philosopher (1285-1349) who defended the logic, physics, and metaphysics of Aristotle in Summa Logicae (The Whole of Logic) (1328) vol. 1 and vol. 2 and the Dialogus. An extreme nominalist, Ockham held that general terms are signs that indefinitely signify discrete (though similar) particulars. Ockham is best known for his statement of the law of parsimony as the ontological principle often called Ockham's Razor: "Frustra fit per plura quod potest fieri per pauciora" ("It is pointless to do with more what can be done with less"). Thus, according to Ockham, we ought never to postulate the reality of any entity unless it is logically necessary to do so. *Recommended Reading*: William of Ockham, Opera Philosophica (Franciscan, 1975); William of Ockham, Philosophical Writings: A Selection, tr. by Philotheus Boehner (Hackett, 1990); The Cambridge Companion to Ockham, ed. by Paul Vincent Spade (Cambridge, 1999); Rega Wood, Ockham on the Virtues (Purdue, 1997); and Five Texts on the Mediaeval Problem of Universals: Porphyry, Boethius, Abelard, Duns Scotus, Ockham, ed. by Paul Vincent Spade (Hackett, 1994).

Oligarchy, literally, rule by the few. Both Plato and Aristotle assumed that the small group most likely to gain control over the governance of a citystate would be those with great wealth. *Recommended Reading*: Plato, The Republic, tr. by Desmond Lee (Viking, 1979) and Aristotle, Politics (Oxford, 1998).

Omega-completeness, A system is omega-complete iff there is no wff W withone free variable such that (1) Wn is a theorem for every natural number n, and (2) (x)Wx is not a theorem. See closure of a system

Omega-incompleteness, There is a wff W with one free variable such that (1) Wn is a theorem for every natural number n, and (2) (x)Wx is not a theorem. Wx is true for every n by instantiation but not by generalization. See k-validity

Ontological argument, an attempt to prove the existence of god by a priori reasoning from the content of the concept of god. As formulated by Anselm, the ontological argument begins with a notion of "that thanwhich nothing greater can be conceived.". Anything that satisfies this concept must exist in reality as well as in thought (since otherwise it would be possible to conceive something greater-one that really exists); hence, god exists. Descartes endorsed a different version of this argument, and Spinoza also relied upon it, but Kant rejected it because of the unintelligibility of comparing the relative greatness of real and merely possible beings. A form of the argument that emphasizes god's possession of the attribute of necessary existence has been defended in recent decades. *Recommended Reading*: Anselm of Canterbury: The Major Works, ed. by Brian Davies and G. R. Evans (Oxford, 1998); Alvin Plantinga, God, Freedom, and Evil (Eerdmans, 1978); and The Ontological Argument, from St. Anselm to Contemporary Philosophers, ed. By Alvin Plantinga (Anchor, 1989).

Ontological commitment, commitment (of a theory) to an existence claim, usually concerning some individual entity. It is often implicit.

Ontology. *See* Metaphysics.

Ontology, 1. A systematic account of what there is, an inventory of what exists.

2. An explicit formal specification of how to represent the objects, concepts and other entities that are assumed to exist in some area of interest and the relationships that hold among them.

For AI systems, what "exists" is that which can be represented. When the knowledge about a domain is represented in a declarative language, the set of objects that can be represented is called the universe of discourse. We can describe the ontology of a program by defining a set of representational terms. Definitions associate the names of entities in the universe of discourse (*e.g.* classes, relations, functions or other objects) with human-readable text describing what the names mean, and formal axioms that constrain the interpretation and well-formed use of these terms. Formally, an ontology is the statement of a logical theory.

A set of agents that share the same ontology will be able to communicate about a domain of discourse without necessarily operating on a globally shared theory. We say that an agent commits to an ontology if its observable actions are consistent with the definitions in the ontology. The idea of ontological commitment is based on the Knowledge-Level perspective.

3. The hierarchical structuring of knowledge about things by subcategorising them according to their essential (or at least relevant and/or cognitive)qualities. See subject index. This is an extension of the previous senses of "ontology" (see 2 above) which has become common in discussions about the difficulty of maintaining subject indices. *Recommended Reading*: Jean-Paul Sartre, Being and Nothingness: A Phenomenological Essay on Ontology, tr. by Hazel E. Barnes (Washington Square, 1993); Herman Philipse, Heidegger's Philosophy of Being (Princeton, 1998); Gustav Bergmann, New Foundations of Ontology, ed. by William Heald and Edwin B. Allaire (Wisconsin, 1992); W. V. O. Quine, Ontological Relativity (Columbia, 1977); and Roger F. Gibson, Jr., The Philosophy of W. V. Quine: An Expository Essay (Florida, 1986).

Open question argument, G. E. Moore's contention that any effort to define the good must fail, since it always remains possible to ask significantly whether or not the proposed definiens is actually good. *Recommended Reading*: G. E. Moore, Principia Ethica (Prometheus, 1988); Brian Hutchinson, G. E. Moore's Ethical Theory: A Reassessment Cambridge, 2001); and Tom Regan, Bloomsbury's Prophet: G. E. Moore and the Development of His Moral Philosophy (Temple, 1986).

Operationalism, belief that the meaning of scientific terms and concepts is wholly captured by a description of the process that determines their applicability in particular cases. On this view, theoretical entities are merely logical constructs. *Recommended Reading*: Charles S. Pierce: The Essential Writings, ed. by Edward C. Moore and Richard Robin (Prometheus, 1998) and Percy W. Bridgman, Logic of Modern Physics (Ayer, 1980).

Operational semantics, A set of rules specifying how the state of an actual or hypothetical computer changes while executing a program. The overall state is typically divided into a number of components, *e.g.* stack, heap, registers etc. Each rule specifies certain preconditions on the contents of some components and their new contents after the application of the rule.

It is similar in spirit to the notion of a Turing machine, in which actions are precisely described in a mathematical way.

Compare axiomatic semantics, denotational semantics.

Opinion, acceptance of a proposition despite a lack of the conclusive evidence that would result in certain knowledge of its truth.

O proposition, in the traditional notation for categorical logic, a proposition that is both particular and negative. Example: "Some trees are not ever-greens." Such a proposition affirms that there is at least one tree that is not also an evergreen. Its contradictory is an "A" proposition with the same subject and predicate terms.

Optimism, otimism is something of a "marginal" term in philosophy, in the sense that it is not really used in technical philosophy (when it is used, it refers to Leibniz's belief that this is "the best of all possible worlds"). The term is useful, however, since it describes a metaphysical affirmation of the possibility of knowledge and happiness in opposition to pessimism. In this sense, for example, eudaimonism can be a form of optimism. The popular usage of optimism is related to the meaning described here, but it is not as fundamental or "metaphysical". See also meliorism *Recommended Reading*: Gottfried Wilhelm Leibniz, Theodicy: Essays on the Goodness of God, the Freedom of Man, and the Origin of Evil, ed. by Austin Marsden Farrer (Open Court, 1988) and The Cambridge Companion to Leibniz, ed. by Nicholas Jolley (Cambridge, 1994).

Organicism, 1. in metaphysics the view according to which the universe is or is like a living organism. The same basic idea is behind the Gaia hypothesis, which claims that the earth is a living thing. Sometimes this is what is meant by holism, especially in popular usage, but holism simply says that all parts of reality are interconnected and does not claim that the earth or the universe is a living thing.

2. in aesthetics, the word organicism is sometimes used in aesthetics to refer to the idea (which goes back at least to Aristotle) that a work of art should be an "organic whole" with all its parts or aspects serving one entral purpose.

Ortegay Gasset Jose, Spanish politician and philosopher who taught at Madrid (1883-1955); author of La deshumanizacion del arte e ideas sobre la novela (The Dehumanization of Art) (1923), Mision de la Universidad (The Mission of the University) (1930), En torno a Galileo (Man and Crisis) (1933), Que est filosofia? (What is Philosophy?)

(1934), and Historia como sistema (History as a System) (1941). Ortega's thought emphasized the unique reality and perspectival independence of each unique person in Meditaciones del Quijote (Meditations on Quixote) (1914): "yo soy yo y mi circumstancia" ("I am myself and my circumstances"). His political concerns, best expressed in La rebeliÛn de las masas (The Revolt of the Masses) (1930), resulted in Ortega's exile from Spain during its Civil War. *Recommended Reading*: Carlos Ramos Mattei, Ethical Self-Determi-nationin Don Jose Ortega Y Gasset (Peter Lang, 1988); Oliver W. Holmes, Human Reality and the Social World: Ortega's Philosophy of History (Massachusetts, 1976); and Antonio Rodriguez Huescar, Jose Ortega Y Gasset's Metaphysical Innovation: A Critique and Over-coming of Idealism, ed. by Jorge Garcia-Gomez (SUNY, 1995).

Orthogonal, Mutually independent; well separated; sometimes, irrelevant to. Used in a generalisation of its mathematical meaning to describe sets of primitives or capabilities that, like a vector basis in geometry, span the entire "capability space" of the system and are in some sense non-overlapping or mutually independent.

In logic, the set of operators "not" and "or" is orthogonal, but the set "nand", "or", and "not" is not (because any one of these can be expressed in terms of the others).

Also used in comments on human discourse: "This may be orthogonal to the discussion, but..." See also orthogonal instruction set.

Ostension, the attempt to provide a non-linguistic definition of a term by pointing at something to which it applies. Although useful enough for some primitive purposes, ostensive definitions are systematically ambiguous, since they poorly discriminate among things and their temporal features.*Recommended Reading*: Ludwig Wittgenstein, Blue and Brown Books (Harper Collins, 1986); Routledge Philosophy Guidebook to Wittgenstein and the Philosophical Investigations, ed. by Marie McGinn (Routledge, 1997); Ludwig Wittgenstein: Philosophy and Language, ed. by Alice Ambrose and Morris Lazerowitz (St. Augustine, 1996); and William H. Brenner, Wittgenstein's Philosophical Investigations.

Other minds problem, the problem of how we know that there are minds other than our own on the assumption that mental life consists, essentially, of private conscious experiences directly accessible only to oneself.

Otto Rudolf, German philosopher of religion (1869-1937). Extrapolating from the philosophy of Kant in Naturalistische und religise Weltansich (Naturalism and Religion) (1904) and Das Heilige (The Idea of the Holy) (1917), Otto tried to identify, describe, and classify the variety of "numinous" feelings that give rise to the cognitive content of religious belief. *Recommended Reading*: Rudolf Otto, Autobiographical and Social Essays, ed. by Gregory D. Alles (De Gruyter, 1996); Philip C. Almond, Rudolf Otto: An Introduction to His Philosophical Theology (North Carolina, 1992); Melissa Raphael, Rudolf Otto and the Concept of Holiness (Clarendon, 1997); and Todd A. Gooch, The Numinous and Modernity: An Interpretation of Rudolf Otto's Philosophy of Religion (De Gruyter, 2000).

Ousia, Greek term for being or substance. Thus, in the philosophy of Aristotle, the most crucial of the categories by means of which to describe a natural object. *Recommended Reading*: F. E. Peters, Greek Philosophical Terms: A Historical Lexicon (NYU, 1967).

Pacifism, the view according to which the highest political or social value is peace, which must be sought at all costs. Another meaning of pacifism—connected with the actions and views of reformers like Thoreau, Ghandi, and Martin Luther King—is the ideal of non-violence in human affairs (akin to the moral aspect of anarchism).

Panpsychism, the view according to which some sort of world soul is present in everything that exists. This idea has similarities to animism, pantheism, and organicism.

Pantheism, the belief that God and the universe are identical; among modern philosophers, Spinoza is considered to be a pantheist. Among the ancients the Stoics were the most notable exponents of pantheism. According to Stoicism, the material universe is the Body of God, and the God's spirit or soul is the Mind (or logos) guiding and governing this universal body. In effect, universal Body and indwelling Mind together comprise the divine Person.

Paradox, Originally, any surprising, puzzling, or counter-intuitive claim, especially a counter-intuitive truth, or an apparently sound argument leading to a contradiction. Most paradoxes stem from some kind of self-reference. In modern logic, a concept or proposition that is not only self-contradictory, but for which the obvious alternatives are either self-contradictory or very costly. See Grelling's paradox, Liar paradox, implication, Russell's paradox, Skolem paradox.

Paradox, in logic and mathematics, an apparently absurd or contradictory conclusion that follows from one or more compelling—at any rate, plausible—statements or premises.

Some of the best-known paradoxes originated with the ancient Greeks (*see* Greek Philosophy). In a famous example from Zeno of Elea, the warrior Achilles is pitched against a tortoise in a race, with the tortoise given a head start. However, by the time Achilles has reached the point from which the tortoise started, the tortoise will have moved on a little; and by the time Achilles reaches *that* position, the tortoise will have moved on a bit further still. No matter how many times this is repeated, Achilles is always behind the tortoise. It apparently follows then that Achilles will never catch the tortoise. This apparent paradox does have a solution, though. It lies in appreciating that the infinite number of time intervals involved actually have a finite sum. The supposed conclusion of Zeno's argument does not therefore actually follow from its true premises, despite initial appearances.

Some paradoxes cannot be solved without fundamental revisions of the human conceptual apparatus, however. One example, again from the Greeks, is the paradox of the liar. The sentence "This sentence is false" seems to be well-formed and meaningful. Yet, it is true if, and only if, it is false, that is, not true. This paradox apparently forces either a restriction of the expressive power of language (so that the liar sentence cannot be formed) or a rejection of the compelling principle that a sentence is true if and only if what it says is true. Over 2,000 years after it was first posed, there is still no agreement among philosophers as to its resolution.

Another, perhaps related, example is Russell's paradox (named after Bertrand Russell), which caused a crisis in the foundations of mathematics. Intuitively, for any property *P*, there is a (possibly empty) set that contains all and only those things that possess *P*. So, for example, the set corresponding to the property *being a female who has been Prime Minister of the United Ki-ngdom within the past 50 years* is *Margaret Thatcher*, while that corresponding to *being a female who has been President of the United States within the past 50 years* is the empty-set, Ø. Consider, though, the set *S*, corresponding to the property *being a set that does not belong to itself*. Presumably, *S* either belongs to itself or it does not. However, if it does, it must be in virtue of its *not* belonging to itself (a contradiction); and if it does not belong to itself, then, by the definition of the set, it *does* belong to itself (again, a contradiction).

Useful discussions of paradoxes are found in the Gilbert Ryle text *Dilemmas* (1960), in R. M. Sainsbury's, *Paradoxes* (1995), and in Timothy Williamson's *Vagueness* (1994).

Paradoxes of material implication, implication

Parallelism, the view that mental and physical phenomena occur in parallel but that these simultaneities never involve causal interactions. See dualism, pre-established harmony, occasionalism

Param, argument

Parameter, argument

Parametric polymorphism, polymorphism.

Parent, (Or "mother", "predecessor") In a tree, a node which points to at least one daughter node.

Particularity, in recent discussions, ethicists have contrasted particularity with universality and impartiality and asked how, if morality is necessarily universal and impartial, it can give adequate recognition to particularity. Particularity refers to specific attachments (friendships, loyalties, etc.) and desires (fundamental projects, personal hopes in life) that are usually seen as morally irrelevant to the rational moral self.

Particulars, individual existents (*e.g.*, Ben Franklin): as to kinds (*e.g.*, inventor) or attributes (*e.g.*, inventiveness), which are universals.

Perceive, to detect or become aware of via the outward senses of sight, hearing, touch, taste, and smell, and also (according to the usage of some)via "reflection" (Locke) or introspection.

Perception, the "how it is" to cognitive systems in the world. A means of distinguishing how things are from how a cognizer thinks they are.

Performatives, sentences (or utterances) that serve more to do (than describe) something. Typically, these sentences are in the first person-present noncontinuous, with a main verb that indicates a speech action. *e.g.* "I promise to come to your party" as opposed to the non-performative (or descriptive) "he promises...," or "I kick him". Performatives are important because they make us realize that many declarative sentences are not so much true or false as they are actions which are well or badly done (orders, appointments, christenings, exorcisms, rulings, sentences, etc.).

Persistence, 2. The length of time a phosphor dot on the screen of a cathode ray tube will remain illuminated after it has been energised by the electron beam. Long-pers-istence phosphors reduce flicker, but generate ghost-like images thatlinger on screen for a fraction of a second.

Persistent, persistence

Perspectivism, the view according to which judgments of truth and value depend on one's "perspective". This view is similar to contextualism and can be a valuable tonic to intrinsicism. However, some "radical" versions of perspectivism (for example some interpretations of Nietzsche's thought) come close to making perspectivism a form of relativism.

Pessimism, doctrine that reality, life, and the world are evil rather than good. Pessimism generally takes one of two forms: that of an entrenched negative state of mind, or a permanent expectation of the worst under all circumstances, and that of a philosophical system. The former instance may arise, depending on the temperament of the individual, from the reaction of a person to the difference between the world as it is and the world as it could be. The existence of evil and the link between suffering and sin have been dwelt upon since ancient times; one example is the ancient Hebrew Book of Job.

In the 19th century, pessimism was elaborated into a system of philosophy by the German philo-sophers Arthur Schopenhauer and his successor Eduard von Hartmann. Each saw life in this world as rooted in misery, pain, and endless struggle. An unqualified pessimism encompasses the idea that all the ends and aims of life are illusory. Opposed to pessimism is optimism, which approves of the world as it is and embraces the feeling of hope.

Pessimism, the view according to which any belief in the possibility of knowledge and happiness is, to say the least, naive (see also fatalism). Pessimism has a long history in Western philosophy, beginning in a mild form with stoicism in Greece and Rome and continuing through to existentialism in the twentieth century (consider the rejection of eudaimonism in both of these philosophies). The arch-pessimist of all intellectual history, and the only major thinker whose philosophy is "officially" said to be one of pess-imism, is Schopenhauer (1788-1860), whose ideas held sway over the young Nietzsche and who had a strong influence on the existentialists (and who is reputed to have been influenced by Indian philosophy). Schopenhauer believed that reality, human nature, existence as such are all positively evil. In contrast to the totalistic pessimism of Schopenhauer, other thinkers are often pessimistic only about this world, and can be quite optimistic about the possibility of happiness in an afterlife—for example, Christianity is, or can be seen as, this kind of pessimism. The popular meaning of pessimism is related to the philosophical one, though not as fundamental.

Phenomena, phenomenon

Phenomenal, noumenal

Phenomenal consciousness, phenomenal consciousness [p-consciousness] is just experience thus, p-conscious states are experiential states. The totality of the experiential properties of a state are p-consciousness, *i.e.* "what it is like" to have it. *References*: Ned Block. On a confusion about a function of consciousness) in Behavioural and Brain sciences, 1995.

Phenomenalism, the monistic view that all empirical statements (such as thelaws of physics) can be placed in a one to one correspondence with statements about only the phenomenal (*i.e.* mental appearances). See monism, idealism, neutral monism.

Phenomenological, phenomenology

Phenomenological critique of representationalism, rejection of the notion that representational states define and explain the most basic kind of human interaction with the environment. See also phenomenology, intention-in-action, bckground.

Phenomenology, 20th-century philosophical movement dedicated to describing the structures of experience as they present themselves to consciousness, without recourse to theory, deduction, or assumptions from other disciplines such as the natural sciences.

Husserl: The founder of phenomenology, the German philosopher Edmund Husserl, introduced the term "phenomenology" in his book *Ideas: A General Introduction to Pure Phenomenology* (1913; trans. 1931). Early followers of Husserl, such as the German philosopher Max Scheler, influenced by his previous book, *Logical Investigations* (1900-1901; trans. 1970), claimed that the task of phenomenology is to study essences, such as the essence of emotions. Although Husserl himself never gave up his early interest in essences, he later held that only the essences of certain special conscious structures are the proper object of phenomenology. As formulated by Husserl after 1910, phenomenology is the study of the structures of consciousness that enable consciousness to refer to objects outside itself. This study requires reflection on the contents of the mind to the exclusion of everything else. Husserl called this type of reflection the phenomenological reduction. Because the mind can be directed towards non-existent as well as real objects, Husserl noted that phenomenological reflection does not presuppose that anything exists, but rather amounts to a "bracketing of existence", that is, it sets aside the question of the real existence of the contemplated object.

What Husserl discovered when he contemplated the contents of his mind were such acts as remembering, desiring, and perceiving and the abstract content of these acts, which Husserl called meanings. These meanings, he claimed, enabled an act to be directed towards an object under a certain aspect; and such directedness, called intentionality, he held to be the essence of consc-iousness. Transcendental pheno-menology, according to Husserl, was the study of the basic components of the meanings that make intentionality possible. Later, in *Cartesian Meditations* (1931; trans. 1960), he introduced genetic phenomenology, which he defined as the study of how these meanings are built up in the course of experience.

Heidegger: All phenomenologists follow Husserl in attempting to use pure description. Thus, they all subscribe to Husserl's slogan "to the things themselves". They differ among themselves, however, as to whether the phenomenological reduction can be performed, and as to what is manifest to the philosopher giving a pure description of experience. The German philosopher Martin Heidegger, Husserl's colleague and most noted critic, claimed that phenomenology should make manifest what is hidden in ordinary, everyday experience. He thus attempted in *Being and Time* (1927; trans. 1962) to describe what he called the "structure of everydayness", or "being-in-the-world", which he found to be an interconnected system of equipment, social roles, and purposes.

Because, for Heidegger, one is what one does in the world, a phenomenological reduction to one's own private experience is impossible; and because human action consists of a direct grasp of objects, it is not necessary to posit a special mental entity called a meaning to account for intentionality. For Heidegger, being thrown into the world among things in the act of realizing projects is a more fundamental kind of intentionality than that revealed in merely staring at or thinking about objects, and it is this more fundamental intentionality that makes possible the directness analysed by Husserl.

French Phenomenology: The French philosopher Jean-Paul Sartre, a leading exponent of existentialism, attempted to adapt Heidegger's phenomenology to the philosophy of consciousness, thereby returning, in effect, to Husserl. He agreed with Husserl that consciousness is always directed at objects but criticized his claim that such directedness is possible only by means of special mental entities called meanings. Another French philosopher Maurice Merleau-Ponty rejected Sartre's view that phenomenological description reveals human beings to be pure, isolated, and free consciousnesses. He stressed the role of the active, involved body in all human knowledge, thus generalizing Heidegger's insights to include the analysis of perception. Like Heidegger and Sartre, Merleau-Ponty is an existential phenomenologist, in that he denies the possibility of bracketing existence.

Phenomenology has had a pervasive influence on 20th-century thought. Phenomenological versions of theology, sociology, psychology, psychiatry, and literary criticism have been developed, and phenomenology remains one of the most important schools of contemporary philosophy.

Phenomenology, a philosophic movement that originated around the turn of the century on the Continent (see Husserl's Cartesian Meditations for example). This movement—like Russell, G. E. Moore, and the analytic movement generally—insisted on divorcing philosophy from (empirical) psychology, thus avoiding something labeled psychologism. The phenomenologists insisted that philosophers could directly study the pure phenomenon of thought (intensional objects) by a bracketing technique which avoided any commitments about empirical psychology.

Phenomenon, for Kant, phenomena

are "things for us"—things as understood &experienced. Phenomena contrast with noumena—the "things in themselves"—which transcend our understanding and experience.

Phenominalism, the view that immediate experience (sensations, thoughts, etc.) is all there might be to reality. B. Russell for example, often took the phenominalist view that talk about the external world of objects is more properly understood as talk about a series of experiences or potentialities of experience.

Philosophy, literally "love of wisdom": the discipline that contemplates and seeks to critically illumine the ultimate grounds of being, knowledge, and value.

Philosophy of mind, the branch of philosophy that is concerned with the nature of mental phenomena in general and the role of consciousness, sensation, perception, concepts, action, reasoning, intention, belief, memory, etc. in particular.

Standard problems include those of free will, personal identity, mind-body problem, other minds, computationalism.

Philosophy of psychology, the branch of the philosophy of science concerneds-pecifically with psychology. It is concerned with the sorts of models, theories and explanations used in psychology to address psychological phenomena. See also philosophy of mind.

Phronesis, according to Aristotle, phronesis is practical wisdom, the ability to make the right decision in difficult circumstances.

Physicalism, the view according to which everything that is real is, in some sense, physical. Since physical entities are the only real existents, mental phenomena like consciousness are illusory or reducible to physical phenomena. Physicalism makes a stronger claim about the specific nature of reality than concretism and in so doing strays from metaphysics or ontology into cosmology. The idea often appears in concert with determinism, reductionism, and epiphenomenalism. See also materialism, physicalism non-reductive,idealism.

Physicalism non-reductive, the claim that functional properties cannot be reduced to physical properties, but that nevertheless all causality is physical. See physicalism, multiple realisability, functionalism.

Plato (c. 428-c. 347 BC), Greek philosopher, one of the most creative and influential thinkers in Western philosophy.

Life: Plato was born to an aristocratic family in the Athenian democracy. His father, Ariston, was believed to be descended from the early kings of Athens. Perictione, his mother, was distantly related to the 6th-century BC lawmaker Solon. When Plato was a child, his father died, and his mother married Pyrilampes, who was an associate of the statesman Pericles.

As a young man Plato had political ambitions, but he became disillusioned with the political leadership in Athens. He eventually became a disciple of Socrates, who had pioneered the search for ethical truth through dialectical questions and answers with anyone claiming to have knowledge. Plato witnessed the execution of Socrates by the Athenian democracy in 399 BC. Perhaps fearing for his own safety, he left Athens temporarily and travelled to Italy, Sicily, and Egypt.

In 387 BC Plato founded the Academy in Athens, the institution often described as the first European university. It provided a comprehensive curriculum, including such subjects as astronomy, biology, mathematics, political theory, and philosophy. Aristotle became the Academy's most prominent student.

Pursuing an opportunity to combine philosophy and practical politics, Plato went to Sicily in 367 BC to tutor the new ruler of Syracuse, Dionysius the Younger, in the art of philosophical rule. The experiment failed. Plato made another trip to Syracuse in 361 BC, but again his engagement in Sicilian affairs met with little success. The concluding years of his life were spent lecturing at the Academy and writing. He died at about the age of 80 in Athens in 348 or 347 BC.

Works: Plato's extant writings are all in the form of dialogues, sometimes framed by a narrator. They depict philosophical ideas being advanced, discussed, and criticized in the context of a conversation or debate involving two or more people. The earliest ancient collection of Plato's work includes 35 dialogues and 13 letters. The authenticity of a few of the dialogues and most of the letters has been disputed. The dialogues are conventionally divided by their presumed dates of composition, based on content, style, and internal references. This yields a useful distinction between the early, middle, and late dialogues.

Early Dialogues: The earliest dialogues seem to depict Socrates as Plato saw him at work, questioning leading citizens of Athens about their beliefs. Several of these dialogues take the same distinctive form. Socrates, encountering someone who seems to know much about a particular ethical topic, professes to be ignorant and seeks enlightenment from the person claiming knowledge. As Socrates questions their definitions, however, it becomes clear that the one reputed to be wise does not really know what he claims to know, and Socrates emerges as the wiser person because he at least knows that he does not know. Such self-knowledge, commanded by the oracle at Delphi by the inscription "know thyself", is regarded by Socrates as the beginning of wisdom. Among these dialogues are *Charmides* (on temperance, also translated as "moderation"), *Lysis* (on friendship), *Laches* (on courage), *Protagoras* (on the structure of the virtues), *Euthyphro* (on piety), and Book I of *The Republic* (on justice).

Another distinctive group of dialogues are those that depict the trial and death of Socrates in dramatic form. These include the *Apology,* which presents Socrates's speech in his own defence at his trial on the charges of impiety and corrupting Athenian youth; *Crito,* in which Socrates examines and rejects his friend Crito's proposal to help him escape prison and death; and *Phaedo,* the death scene of Socrates, in which he discusses the theory of forms, the nature of the soul, and the question of immortality. While the *Apology* and *Crito* seem to be early in the sense of depicting the historical Socrates, *Phaedo* seems to open or at least presage the middle period.

Middle Dialogues: Whereas the

early dialogues seem to depict Socrates as Plato knew him, the middle and late dialogues seem to represent his own philosophical development, even though a character named Socrates often leads the discussions. The middle period is considered the great constructive phase of Plato's thought, distinguished by the central role of the theory of forms (see below). Exemplars of this stage are the *Symposium*, a discussion of love as motivating the search for the forms; *Timaeus*, which uses the forms as models in reconstructing the principles of the cosmos; *The Republic*, Plato's longest, most complex, and ambitious work, on the nature of justice in the soul and in the state; and, arguably, as stated above, the *Phaedo*.

Late Dialogues: The works of the later period seem no longer to treat the theory of forms as a central plank in constructing the true philosophy. Instead they criticize this theory and discuss a number of other philosophical problems, often abstractly. These works include *Theaetetus*, which seeks a definition of knowledge and exemplifies the way discussion can help develop ideas; *Parmenides* (which begins with a critical evaluation of the theory of forms); *The Sophist*, which discusses being and not-being in order to distinguish the sophist from the philosopher; *The Statesman*, which analyses the role of the true statesman in the ideal city; *Philebus*, on the relationship between pleasure and the good; and *The Laws*, Plato's unfinished last work, which proposes the laws needed to mediate between human irrationality and rational knowledge.

Theory of Forms: At the heart of Plato's constructive philosophy is his theory of forms, or ideas. This notion underpins his view of knowledge, his ethical theory, his psychology, his concept of the state, and his perspective on art.

Theory of Knowledge: Plato's theory of forms and his theory of knowledge are interrelated. Influenced by Socrates, Plato sought to understand the nature of the genuine knowledge that his teacher had professed to lack. He held that such knowledge must be correlated with the nature of the real: as the fully real is fixed, permanent, and unchanging, so must knowledge be certain and immune to revision or correction. Only such knowledge can be teachable. In his middle period he identified knowledge with knowledge of certain objects that are most truly real in this sense, and which underlie the mutable and misleading world of appearances. These are the forms.

It follows that sense experience and perception are worthless as routes to knowledge; they inform us only of the appearances or "phenomena", not of the real essences. The sole route to knowledge is reason, the faculty of perceiving intelligible objects as contrasted with the senses, which perceive physical objects. The famous images of Sun, line, and cave that Plato uses in *The Republic* express this understanding of knowledge. The image of the Sun suggests that as the Sun is the condition for the perceptibility of physical objects, so the form of the Good is the condition of the intelligibility of the forms; in other words, he implies that a notion of value is pervasive and fundamental to reality.

Nature of Forms: The theory of forms applies centrally to moral and ethical notions. Nonetheless, the best way to begin to understand the forms is to compare them with mathematical entities, exactly as Plato does in the image of the line in *The Republic*. A circle, for instance, is a plane figure composed of a series of points, all of which are equidistant from a given point, yet none of which occupy any space themselves. No one has ever seen an ideal circle; one only ever sees approximations of the mathematical version, since all physical circles do occupy some space. An ideal circle would be perfect, timeless, and the model for the circularity of all ordinary circles. In the same way, the forms—such as Beauty and Good—are perfect, timeless entities. Ordinary physical objects resemble ("participate in") the forms, and thereby gain whatever reality they have. In this sense, the postulation of forms belongs both to epistemology (the study of knowledge) and ontology (the study of what there is).

Most of Plato's arguments for and about the existence of forms move from the instability and relative qualities of physical objects to the claim that some stable objects must exist as benchmarks for those that are comparative and changing. Occasionally, as in Book X of *The Republic*, he seems to suggest that every universal term (such as "bed" or "table") must correspond to a form. However, this suggestion is out of place in the bulk of the discussion of forms.

Political Theory and Ethics: *The Republic*, Plato's major political work, is concerned with the question of justice. Starting with the question "Does justice pay for the individual, apart from any external rewards?", it argues that justice in the soul is linked to justice in the city. Both soul and city have three analogous parts: a desiring part; a spirited part (something like the will); and a rational part. Justice involves each part carrying out its own proper function; Plato argues that this means that the two non-rational parts must be ruled by the rational part. Far from being a mere analogy, the relation between soul and the city turns out to mean that the two lower classes in the city must be ruled by the highest class, the philosophers. They alone can use their reason to acquire knowledge of the forms.

The political structure of the just city would thus depend on a thorough educational programme, which selects the potential philosophers on the basis of merit, without regard to class or gender, and trains them ultimately to know and love the forms, through which each person progresses to his or her maximal level of ability. Such an education must begin by training the appetites and spirit to accede to the rule of reason, and so the earlier stages involve music and gymnastics, which seek to harmonize the passions. The later stages of education use mathematics as a gateway to the forms.

Once the philosophers are selected, their autocratic rule in the light of reason must be safeguarded from corruption. Therefore, they are to be deprived of private property and families, and forced to pay attention to civic affairs instead of only contemplating the forms. Such drastic measures alone can ensure that their rule is for the sake of the city as a whole and not for their private interests.

Nevertheless, Plato is not sanguine about the stability of such a regime; he foresees a failure of the philosophers to apply their ideal knowledge and the decline of regimes that would then follow. In the absence of an ideal city, the individual can only seek to know the form of the Good and guide his or her actions by that knowledge, which Plato compares to the patterns of the stars.

Platonic realism, view that affirms the existence of universals. Extreme or Platonic realism holds that universals ("forms" or "ideas") exist independently of both particular things and human minds. Moderate or Aristotelian realism holds that universals only exist as inhering in, or being instantiated by, particulars. Also see conceptualism. Contrast: nominalism.

Platonism, The word platonism refers both to the doctrines of Plato (427-347 B.C.) and to the manner or tradition of philosophizing that he founded. While it can be difficult to pin down what Plato actually believed (he often tried things out as hypotheses and changed or criticized many of his earlier views late in life), the term refers centrally to Platonic idealism and dualism—though it also refers to the more debatable portions of his thought, such as his collectivism or totalitarianism (as revealed in his dialogue The Republic), his rationalism or intellectualism, his distrust of art, and so on. Often, in philosophy, "Platonism" is virtually equivalent to idealism or intrinsicism, since Plato was the first Western philosopher to claim that reality is fundamentally something ideal or abstract and that knowledge largely consists of insight into or perception of the ideal. In common usage, the adjective "Platonic" refers to Platonic love, the idea that the best form of love is non-sexual or non-physical (originally put forth in Plato's dialogue The Symposium).

Pleonasm, redundancy of expression, tautology.

Pluralism, 1. in ontology the theory that reality is composed or can be explained in terms of two or more fundamental (types of) substance, energy, or force. In the modern era Cartesian dualism represents the most notable pluralist hypothesis. Among the ancients, the pluralism of Pythagorus and Democritus is usually contrasted to the monism of the Milesians (Thales, Anaximenes, Anaximander) and Eleatics (Parmenides, Miletus, Zeno).

2. in political philosophy the term pluralism is also used to refer to political systems that allow more than one political party (roughly equivalent to democracy as opposed to totalitarianism).

3. in ethics, the belief that there are multiple perspectives on an issue,each of which contains part of the truth but none of which contain the whole truth. Moral pluralism is the belief that different moral theories each capture part of truth of the moral life, but none of those theories has the entire answer.

Polytheism, a kind of theism which holds that there is more than one god. It is compatible with henotheism but incompatible with monotheism, by which it was supplanted in the history of Western religion. Polytheism was the dominant view of the supernatural among the ancients, for example in Greek and Roman religion. By contrast, both Judaism and Christianity are monotheistic world-views.

Positivism, while positivism sounds like it should be synonymous with optimism (as in the power of positive thinking), it isn't. Sometimes the word positivism is equivalent to empiricism (as in logical positivism), since positivism in the philosophy of science holds that we should admit as knowledge only that about which we can be absolutely certain, *i.e.*, what is immediately graspable or "empirical". The first thinker who is labeled a positivist was the nineteenth-century French philo-sopher August Comte. Comte put great stress on science and progress and was interested only in observable phenomena and the laws that determine how they act together, without any investigation of ultimate causes or metaphysics. Another aspect of his thought was a humanism that bordered on a "religion of humanity", in which the object of worship was taken to be humanity as a whole. In more recent usage, positivism usually refers to logical positivism.

Possible, what might be the case, as opposed to what'snecessary (what must be the case) and what's actual (what really is the case).

Practical reasoning, figuring out what to do; reasoning directed towards action (as contrasted with reasoning directed towards arriving at belief).

1. *Introduction*: Practical reasoning is a rapidly changing area of study; this article describes the state of the field as it has shaped up over the 1980s and 1990s. For earlier work, see Raz (1978).

The current debate in practical reasoning focuses on the question: what inference patterns are legitimate methods of arriving at decisions or intentions to act, or other characteristically practical predecessors of actions such as evaluations, plans, policies, and judgments about what one ought to do? The spectrum of competing theories ranges from the very minimal, allowing only one form of practical inference (or even none), to maximal-lypermissive views that "let a thousand flowers bloom." The remainder of this entry surveys the most prominent positions on this spectrum. Other important questions in the field include: What mental states and processes are involved in practical reasoning? Is there a principled distinction to be made between practical and theoretical reasoning (that is, reasoning directed towards belief rather than action)? How can one argue about what putative forms of practical inference are legitimate, *i.e.*, are really inference? Is there a fixed list of forms of practical inference to be discovered, or can methods of practical reasoning be invented?

2. *Nihilism*: Nihilism about practical reasoning is the view that there are no legitimate forms of practical inference, and that co-nsequently there is no such thing as practical reasoning: appearances notwithstanding, there is no mental activitythat counts as figuring out what to do. This position is the most minimal on the spectrum of views about practical reasoning; it suffers from a shortage of contemporary defenders, but was argued for by Hume (1739/1978, pp. 413-418,456-470). (Nihilism is canvassed as a possible form of irrationality by Korsgaard (1986, sec.

3). For discussion of Hume, see Hampton (1995) and Millgram (1995).) Nihilism was probably entailed by early twentieth-century non-cognitivism in metaethics, in particular by emotivism; however, it was not discussed at the time. Nihilism should be regarded as the null hypothesis against which other accounts of practical reasoning must be defended.

3. *Instrumentalism*: Instrumentalism holds that all practical reasoning is means-end reasoning, that is, that figuring out what to do is entirely a matter of determining how to achieve one's goals or satisfy one's desires. Such reasoning may consist in finding causes for the outcomes one wants; but it may also involve—for instance—scheduling, or picking one among the various options that would achieve one's goals. (Instrumentalism in this broad sense—as opposed to the sense in which it is restricted to finding causes for outcomes—has sometimes also been called "internalism about reasons for action" in the last few years, however, usage has been shifting to make internalism a distinct notion.) Because infinite regresses are generally thought not possible in instrumental justification (finite creatures have only finitely many suitably distinct desires), and because circularity in instrumental justification is thought to be unrea-sonable, the instrumentalist position usually has it that practical jus-tification bottoms out in desires one just has: you can reason about how to get what you want, but not about what to want in the first place.

Instrumentalism is the default view in the field, and probably among philosophers in general. However, despite its pervasiveness, there is very little explicit argument for it. Hume (1777/1975, p. 293) is perhaps the locus classicus of the view, which is—despite Hume's apparent commitment elsewhere to nihilism about practical reasoning—often called Humeanism. Smith (1987) attempts to tie instrumentalism to belief-desire psychology (see folk psycho-logy) and to an understanding of beliefs and desires in terms of direction of fit. Williams (1981) argues that reasons for action must invoke desires on the grounds that only desires, broadly construed, can explainactions, and that reasons for action must be able, in suitable circumstances, to explain actions.

The shortfall of argument notwithstanding, there are a number of things to be said for the position. First, means-end reasoning is perhaps the least controversial form that practical reasoning has been alleged to take: we all know what it is like to try to figure out how to achieve a goal, and it is often straightforward to determine whether a mistake has been made. Second, since instrumental reasoning proceeds from desires you have, your stake in theresults of such reasoning seems very clear—the actions it tells you to take promise to get you things you already want. Third, when people do seem to act for reasons, it is generally possible to ascribe to them an appropriate desire. Fourth, non-instrumental practical reasoning would evidently allowone's ultimate desires to be corrected by others; but we are familiar with such attempts at correction, and they as a rule are paternalistic, heavy-handed, dog-matic, and unconvincing. Acco-rdingly, instrumentalists insist that the burden of proof lies with their opponents.

Whether or not instrumental reasoning is the only kind of practical reasoning there is, there is widespread agreement that it is a kind of practical reasoning (Thompson (1998) is a very interesting dissenting voice). But although it is uncontroversial in this respect, it is by no means well-understood. The central problem is the defeasibility of instrumental reasoning, that is, the fact that an apparently satisfactory instrumental inference can be defeated by adding further premises, and that we have no means of specifying the defeating conditions up front. For instance, if my end is to have an espresso, a suitable means might be going to a particular cafe...but I might quite properly retract my decision when I learn that its management donates a percentage of the cafe's profits to a terrorist group. There are obviously indefinitely many defeating cond-itions of this kind, and so we do not know how to say under what circumstances a means-end inference ought to go through. Whether or not instrumentalism is correct, perhaps the most important advance that could be made in the field would be to figure out how means-end reasoning really works.

4. *Satisficing,* In 1976, Jimmy Carter ran for President on the slogan: "Why not the best?" One answer, given some time back by Herbert Simon (1957, chs. 14, 15; see also 1979), is that finding the best choice can be computationally and otherwise too expensive. Another is that choice sets may fail to contain maximal elements; when there is no best, choosing the best is not an option (Landesman 1995, Fehige 1994). The alternative to maximising is satisficing, that is, choosing an option that is, while perhaps not the best, good enough. Satisficing is naturally thought of as instrumentalist in spirit, and defended as a kind of second-level maximising: the best first-level strategy, once typical information costs are taken into account, may be satisficing rather than maximising. However, satisficing has also been defended as simply being in line with our intuitions about the rationality of particular choices (Slote 1989).

5. *Reasoning with maieutic ends:* A standard objection to instrumentalism is that it makes ultimate ends come out arbitrary: your ultimate ends are the things you just happen to want, they are beyond the reach of deliberation and rational control, and we know from experience that this is unrealistic. A response to the objection can stay within the spirit of instrumentalism by appealing to maieutic ends (alsocalled second-order ends or second-order desires), that is, ends that consist in having other ends or desires. For example, you might want to have a career in medicine for entirely financial reasons; in order to have the career, you have to care about the right things, *e.g.*, healing the sick; so you come to want to have the end of healing the sick. As the example suggests, it is possible to reason about the desirability of wanting something, without expanding the repertoire of inference patterns beyond the instrumental. One can (it is held) adopt desires that are ultimate in the sense that their objects are not wanted as means to further

ends; but one can adopt these desires for instrumental reasons, because although the desires' objects are not wanted as means to further ends, the desires themselves are so wanted. This approach is developed and defended by Schmidtz (1995).

6. *Plans and intentions*: On the planning view of rational deliberation advanced by Bratman (1987; see Bratman 1983 for an early but more concise presentation of the view), practical reasoning consists largely in the adoption, filling in, and reconsideration of intentions and plans. (In Bratman's usage, a plan is a more elaborate and developed intention, and an intention is a small plan.) Plans have two important characteristics that distinguish them from desires. First, they are typically incomplete: your plan for flying to Spain may include the intention of getting to the airport, but until the day arrives it may well not include a subplan for getting to the airport *e.g.*, calling a taxi, waiting for it, getting in, and taking it there. Second, plans are stable: normally, one reasons about how to execute and fill in one's plan, but not, unless special circumstances arise, about whether to reject the plan in favour of some other.

Practical reasoning that avails itself of plans has advantages over reasoning that uses only beliefs and desires. Because plans are stable, plans make thepractical reasoning one has to do manageable by framing one's deliberations, and so restricting the number of options that need to be considered. For instance, in considering how to get to the airport, you must weigh the merits of driving, taking a cab, taking the bus, and getting a friend to drop you off; but because the plan to go to Spain frames your deliberations, you need not consider the option of going to Peru instead. Because plans are usually filled in as needed, they can efficiently take account of infor-mation that becomes available later rather than earlier: when you formed the intention ofgoing to Spain, you could not know whether your spouse would want to use the car that day. Because plans are stable, they can facilitate interpersonal coordination: knowing that Joe plans to be at the cafe at 3:00 is an entirely different matter from knowing that he wants to be there at 3:00; I am much more willing to go there to meet him on the former basis than on the latter, because I know he will not reconsider unless special circumstances arise. Because plans are stable, they also facilitate intrapersonal coordination, that is, coordination over different times; knowing that you will finish the paper you have now started to write, because your intention to do so is stable, provides some assurance that the effort spent in starting it will not have been wasted.

Bratman's views regarding when reconsideration of plans is rational have been developing over the last decade. One argument turns on the cons-equences of having the policy that triggers reconsideration: if you must reconsider everytime a new bit of information turns up, your decision making task will swamp your cognitive resources. Consequently, the planning theory of practical rationality can deliver prescriptions for action that differ from those of the traditional instrumentalist theory. For example, suppose you adopt a plan because you believe, rationally, that it will best satisfy your desires; suppose circumstances change so that it no longer does, but your rationally held policy for recon-sidering plans does not take the change in circumstances to warrant reconsideration. Then the instrum-entalist theory may hold that it is rational for you not to perform the actions dictated by the plan, whereas the planning theory may hold that it is rational—even though executing the plan will not satisfy your desires anymore.

7. *Specificationism*: Many of our ends—runs one objection to instrumentalism—are simply too vague or indefinite to serve as starting points for means-end reasoning, so practical reasoning must consist partly in further specifying the overly indefinite ends. For instance, I want to improve my looks; but, before actually making purchases at the makeup counter, I need to figure out just what improvement in my looks would be. (The early pivotal papers are by Kolnai (1978) and Wiggins (1991); Kolnai, who thinks that Aristotle was aninstrumentalist, develops the view as an alternative to Aristotle's, while Wiggins attributes the specificationist view to Aristotle.) Richardson (1994) advances a further reason for specification of ends. Many of our ends conflict, but often those conflicts (whether between one's own ends, or the ends of different people) can be removed by further specification of the ends in question. Since the point of cospecification is to remove conflict between ends, specifications should be chosen that make the ends cohere with one another (and with other background elements of one's evaluative system).

In contrast to the three immediately preceding positions, which remain instrumentalist in spirit, specificationism is (like the further positions we will survey) a full-fledged alternative to the view that all practical reasoning is means-end reasoning: only when supplemented with the rational specification of ends is instrumental reasoning viable at all. The most important item on the specificationist agenda is to make out what distinguishes correct or rational from incorrect or irrational specifications of an insufficiently definite goal.

8. *Practical contradiction resolution*: One important aspect of theoretical reasoning (that is, reasoning directed towards belief) is resolving contradictions in one's system of beliefs. The way in which this is done is not well-understood, but it is nonetheless possible to ask whether it has a practical analog: a form of practical reasoning directed towards resolving (something that would count as) a practical con-tradiction. It has been suggested by Candace Vogler that such contradictions may be generated by practical versions of so-called "evening star-morning star" cases, as when one wants to visit Siam, and to avoid visiting Thailand, but then becomes aware that Siam is Thailand. Korsgaard (1990) has a useful discussion of the notion of a practical contradiction in Kant.

9. *Coherence-driven reasoning*: Practical reasoning is sometimes thought to be a matter of adjusting one's practical take on things, together with one's actions, in the direction of greater coherence. Just what this suggestion comes to will

depend both on what the elements of one's practical take on things are thought to be, and on what the coherence of such elements with one another is supposed to consist in. For instance, if preferences are the relevant items, coherence might be understood to consist in the agent's preferences satisfying the conditions for his having a well-defined utility function. (For the canonical account of utility functions, see Luce and Raiffa, 1957, ch. 2.) However, the expected-utility approach to coherence has the problem that no sense is given to the notion of a set of preferences being more or less coherent; your preferences are either coherent (if they induce—that is, can be represented by—a utility function), or they are not. The expected-utility approach to coherence specifies an ideal that is unattainable for human beings, without saying what it would be to move closer to it, or farther away.

The elements of one's practical take on things might alternatively be thought to consist in goals, subgoals and actions. In this case, coherence-driven practical deliberation would amount to choosing the subset of the goals and actions under consideration that best cohere with one another. Practical reasoning of this kind can be described as "inference to the most coherent plan"—in the event that finding the most coherent plan is impractical, the recommendation is to find as coherent a plan as one can. The most urgent issue in this area is the development of comparative notions of coherence that are precise enough to give clear answers to questions of the form: of these competing plans, which is the most coherent? Without notions of coherence thatare usable in this way, appeals to coherence are empty, and the merits of coherence-driven accounts of practical reasoning cannot be assessed. One such comparative notion has been modeled computationally, by using quasiconnectionist networks to represent the competing plans. (Thagard and Millgram, 1995; Millgram and Thagard, 1996) Another is specified as a constraint satisfaction problem. (Thagard and Verbeurgt, 1998) Coherence-driven accounts are yet another alternative to the instrumentalist paradigm; on the goal-oriented notion, for example, goals can be adopted on the ground that they cohere with other goals that one already has, even if achieving them would not be a means to any end that one already has. If coherence-driven accounts of practical reasoning are to make headway, improved definitions of coherence and further development of techniques for modelling them are necessary.

10. *Universalisability*: Kantian theories of practical reasoning typically require that reasons be universalisable: roughly, that it be possible for everyone in like circumstances to act likewise on the basis of a similar reason. Nell (1975) argues that the requirement imposes substantial constraints on what actions are permissible, and explains how the requirement can be proceduralised. Universalisability acts as a filter through which proposed actions and the reasons for them are passed, but it can also be used to generate reasons on its own, when not acting on a proposed reason would fail the universalisability test. Contemporary interest in

univers-alisability is primarily due to the role it plays in Kantian moral theory, which is today one of the most prominent positions in ethics; Korsgaard (1990) reconstructs Kant's reasons for insisting on the universalisability requirement.

11. *Identity-based practical reasons*: Korsgaard has recently suggested that a theory of practical reasoning should make room for a class of reasons that express one's self-conception or "practical identity," "a description under which you value yourself...find your life to be worth living and your actions worth undertaking" (1996, p. 101), *e.g.*, being a philosophy professor, a Canadian, a "made man," and so on. The appeal to practical identities goes some of the way towards meeting achallenge posed by Williams on behalf of the instrumentalist position, that of showing how the practical reasons of different persons in what are substantially similar situations can vary, without (as the instrumentalist does) simply referring the difference to their differing desires. (Williams 1995, pp. 186-194)

12. *Practical empiricism*: On the views we have seen so far, the source of an agent's reasons for action lies within the agent: in his goals or ends or desires (instrumentalism, satisficing, maieutic ends), in his intentions (the planning view, Kantian universalisability), in the ways all these cohere with one another, or in his practical identity. On the instrumentalist view, for instance, experience can supply the facts needed to determine how to attain one's ends, but the ends themselves are set from inside, by one's desires. Against this, practical empiricism has it that it is both possible and necessary to learn what matters, and what is important, from experience.

There is no reason to think that goals, priorities, evaluations and other like pieces of an agent's cognitive equipment will be useful guides to action if the world is not allowed to have its say in what they look like. The desires and intentions with which one comes to a situation may be simply irrelevant (likely when the circumstances are novel), or their objects may prove disappointing when obtained; successful agency requires an ability to correct one's assessments and agenda on the fly.

For example, perhaps I originally took climate control in a car to be more important than mechanical reliability; after many unpleasant experiences withmechanics, I conclude that I was mistaken, and that a reliable car is generally to be preferred to an air conditioned one. This suggests that the basis for correction will be a practical analog of observation, and that, because learning from experience requires the ability to generalize from past observations to future instances, practical empiricism should be committed to a practical version of inductive inference, one that moves from particular to general practical judgments. A version of practical empiricism along these lines is developed by Millgram (1997).

13. *Redescription as practical reasoning*: In order to draw the right conclusion about what to do, you normally have to proceed on the basis of an adequate description of your situation. Arriving at the description is usually regarded as theoretical rather than practical reasoning; you are reasoning about the facts,

rather than about the values. Murdoch (1970) differs on this point: arriving at the description that is ultimately the basis for action is the important and hard part of practicalreasoning (in part because facts cannot be distinguished from values—or, more interestingly, because the attempt to do so is itself the expression of a particular set of values; on this last point, see Diamond 1996). Although Murdoch's work predates the two-decade period under review, her writing is only now coming to be seen as advancing a view about practical reasoning.

Murdoch's discussion focusses almost entirely on one aspect of the process of redescription, that of overcoming the temptation to see situations inemotionally convenient ways. In her most famous example, a mother conquers her jealousy, and learns to see her daughter-in-law as refreshing, simple, spontaneous, and delightfully youthful, rather than vulgar, rude, undignified, and tiresomely juvenile. Her insight is important but incomplete: even if one agrees that redescribing one's situation is practical reasoning, it will be hard to accept that such redescription is all there really is to figuring out what to do; and it will be as hard to agree that all there really is to successful redescription is getting past the emotionally induced distortions.

14. *Other positions*: There are a handful of other positions that deserve mention but are difficult to place on the spectrum.

First, there is the common idea that expected-utility theory (see Luce and Raiffa 1957) is a satisfactory rendition of practical reasoning; this is hard to place because the formalism is advanced both as a kind of instrumentalism (where the agent's goal is to maximize his expected utility), and as a formalnotion of coherence (see above). What is more, some of the justifications for the coherentist interpretation are meant to be instrumentalist in form and spirit; see, *e.g.*, McClennan (1990). Hampton (1994) contains a recent critical discussion of the instru-mentalist interpretation.

As a matter of fact, the formalism may well be compatible with other positions on the spectrum as well. It is certainly compatible with nihilism,and the wide availability of personal computers has made this easy to see. To the computer-literate, the expected-utility formalism looks like a data compression technique, or perhaps an encryption device, rather than a representation of reasoning, or even of rationality in one's preferences. The formalism gives a way of representing one's preferences—provided that they satisfy a handful of actually quite demanding conditions—by assigning real numbers to outcomes, such that selecting the action with the highest expected utility (the sum of the products of those numbers and the probabilities of the respective outcomes, given that the action is performed) will be choice conforming to one's preferences. That is, it performs a function analogous to those of the popular ZIP and Compress programs: just as these store your information in a file formatted to take up less space on your hard disk than an uncompressed file, so the expecte-dutility formalism allows you to encode unmanageably many preferences as much more manageable real numbers. Of course, there may be as many numbers as there were preferences in the first place, and, if one is unlucky, they may not bemuch more manageable than the preferences had been; in that case, one can think of the encoding as encryption rather than compression. But, thought of in either of these two ways, retrieving your original preferences via an expected-utility calculation would be no more practical reasoning than retrieving your original file by decompressing a "zipped" file (or by decrypting an encrypted file) is theoretical reasoning. And the formalism could be used to encode suitably structured preferences even if there was nothing that counted as practical reasoning at all—that is, even ifnihilism were correct.

Second, Velleman (1989; see 1985 for a shorter and easier-to-read discussion) argues that intentions are self-fulfilling predictions (and so practicalreasoning is in fact a variety of theoretical reasoning). The predictions are self-fulfilling because agents desire to understand what they are doing, and acting on the basis of such a self-fulfilling prediction produces the requisite kind of self-understanding.

Third, Brandom (1994, pp. 243-253) claims that desire ascriptions merely express commitments to the material correctness of practical inferences that do not themselves involve desires. For instance, to say that someone desires not to get wet is to make explicit his commitment to inferring "I will take my umbrella" from "It is going to rain;" the desire is not itself a suppressed premise of the inference. This amounts to an argument against instrumentalism, to the effect that the instrumentalist position radically misconceives the point of desire ascriptions. The omnipresence of desires served by one's actions is not, as it has been taken to be, evidence for instrum-entalism. Rather, that one's practical inferences can generally be recast in a form that invokes desires is entirely neutral with respect to the question: what patterns of practical inference are legitimate?

15. *The state of the field*: Two decades ago, practical reasoning was, in the minds of most professional philosophers, not separable as an area of study from ethics, and it tended to be associated with historical scholarship. Instrumentalism was the clearly dominant position, to which a revived Kantian morality was the most visible alternative. Some strong work was being done on prudential (*i.e.*, future-regarding) reasons as well, since these were regarded as a possible model for a treatment of altruistic reasons (Nagel 1970). But, by and large, the field was stagnant.

It has since come a long way. Practical reasoning is no longer the handmaiden of ethics, and today theories of practical reasoning are not normally advanced merely as components of some favoured moral theory. The fortification and defence of a very small number of entrenched positions inherited from the great dead philosophers has given way to a healthy profusion of competing and largely new views. Important ideas and arguments turn up annually or semi-annually—a rate that marks a philosophical subspecialty as rapidly developing.

Work on practical reasoning has consequences for ethics and philosophy of mind: moral reasoning is practical reasoning concerned with moral subject matter; philosophical ontologies of the mental typically reflect whateverhappens to be the current view of rationality. (*E.g.*, the popularity of belief-desire psychology is partly attributable to the recently widespread acceptance of instrumentalism, a view in which desires loom very large.) So we can expect recent developments in practical reasoning to produce ripple effects in those areas also.

References: Brandom, R. (1994) Making It Explicit. Cambridge, Mass., Harvard University Press. Bratman, M. (1983) "Taking Plans Seriously" Social Theory and Practice 9(2-3): 271-287. Bratman, M. (1987) Intention, Plans, and Practical Reason Cambridge, Mass., Harvard University Press. Broome, J. (1991) Weighing Goods Oxford, Basil Blackwell. Diamond, C. (1996) "We Are Perpetually Moralists":Iris Murdoch, Fact, and Value" M. Antonaccio and W. Schweiker, Iris Murdoch and the Search for Human Goodness Chicago, University of Chicago Press. Fehige, C. (1994) "The Limit Assumption in Deontic (and Prohairetic) Logic" G. Meggle and U. Wessels, Analyomen 1 Berlin: de Gruyter. Hampton, J. (1994) "The Failure of Expected-Utility Theory as a Theory of Reason" Economics and Philosophy 10(2): 195-242. Hampton, J. (1995) "Does Hume Have an Instrumental Conception of Practical Reason?" Hume Studies 21(1): 57-74. Hume, D. (1739/1978) A Treatise of Human Nature Oxford, Clarendon Press. Edited by L. A. Selby-Bigge and P. H. Nidditch. Hume, D. (1777/1975) Enquiry Concerning the Principles of Morals Oxford, Oxford University Press. Edited by L. A. Selby- Bigge and P. H. Nidditch. Kolnai, A. (1978) "Deliberation is of Ends" Ethics, Value and Reality Indianapolis, Hackett. Korsgaard, C. (1986) "scepticism about Practical Reasoning", Journal of Philosophy 83(1): 5-25.Korsgaard, C. (1990) The Standpoint of Practical Reason. New York, Garland Publishing. Reprint of doctoral dissertation (Harvard University, 1981). Korsgaard, C. (1996) The Sources of Normativity. Cambridge, Cambridge University Press. Landesman, C. (1995) "When to Terminate a Charitable Trust?" Analysis 55(1): 12-13. Luce, R. D. and H. Raiffa (1957) Games and Decisions New York, John Wiley and Sons. McClennan, E. (1990) Rationality and Dynamic Choice Cambridge, Cambridge University Press. Millgram, E. (1995) "Was Hume a Humean?" Hume Studies 21(1): 75-93. Millgram, E. (1997) Practical Induction Cambridge, Mass., Harvard University Press. Millgram, E. and Thagard, P. (1996) "Deliberative Coherence" Synthese 108(1): 63-88. Murdoch, I. (1970) The Sovereignty of Good London, Routledge/Ark. Nagel, T. (1970) The Possibility of Altruism Princeton, Princeton University Press. Nell, O. (1975) Acting on Principle New York, Columbia University Press. Raz, J. (1978) Practical Reasoning. Oxford, Oxford University Press. Richardson, H. (1994) Practical Reasoning about Final Ends. Cambridge, Cambridge University Press.Schmidtz, D. (1995) Rational Choice and Moral Agency. Princeton, Princeton University Press. Simon, H. (1957) Models of Man. New York, John Wiley and Sons. Simon, H. (1979) "From Substantive to Procedural Rationality" F. Hahn and M. Hollis, Philosophy and Economic Theory (Oxford, Oxford University Press): 65-86. Slote, M. (1989) Beyond Optimizing. Cambridge, Mass., Harvard University Press. Smith, M. (1987) "The Humean Theory of Motivation", Mind 96(381): 36-61. Thagard, P. and Millgram, E. (1995) "Inference to the Best Plan: A Coherence Theory of Decision" D. Leake and A. Ram, Goal-Driven Learning (Cambridge, Mass., MIT Press): 439-454. Thompson, M. (1998)

"Naive Action Theory" (unpublished manuscript). Thagard, P. and Verbeurgt, K. (1998) "Coherence as Constraint Satisfaction" Cognitive Science 22. Velleman, J. D. (1985) "Practical Reflection", Philosophical Review 94(1): 33-61. Velleman, J. D. (1989) Practical Reflection Princeton, Princeton University Press. Wiggins, D. (1991) "Deliberation and Practical Reason," Needs, Values, Truth. Oxford, Blackwell. Williams, B. (1981) "Internal and External Reasons", Moral Luck. Cambridge, Cambridge University Press. Williams, B. (1995) "Replies", J. Altham and R. Harrison, World, Mind, and Ethics: Essays on the Ethical Philosophy of Bernard Williams. Cambridge, Cambridge University Press.

Pragmatics, the characterization, for a natural or artificial, language or relationships between sentences, the world, and the situation of speaker and hearer. Pragmatics is particularly concerned with indexical words such as "I," "Here," "That," "She," "Now," which are sensitive to the context of utterance or statement.

Pragmatism, philosophical doctrine, developed by the 19th-century American philosophers Charles Sanders Peirce, William James, and others, according to which the test of the truth of a proposition is its practical utility; the purpose of thought is to guide action; and the effect of an idea is more important than its origin. Pragmatism was the first independently developed American philosophy. It opposes speculation on questions that have no practical application. It asserts that truth is relative to the time, place, and purpose of investigation and that value is as inherent in means as in ends. Pragmatism was the dominant approach to philosophy in the United States during the first quarter of the 20th century.

The American philosopher and educator John Dewey developed pragmatism into a new philosophy, instrumentalism. The British philosopher Ferdinand Canning Scott Schiller and the French philo-sopher Henri Bergson contributed to the development of pragmatism. Like the older utilitarianism, pragmatism presents a working philosophy for the natural sciences.

Pragmatism, Pragmatism is generally considered to be the only truly philosophical school and tradition to have emerged in America (mainly because it is more technically rigorous than transcendentalism). While the term itself was originated by C.S. Peirce, pragmatism's most famous exponents were William James and John Dewey, although there were numerous lesser figures involved during its heyday in the late nineteenth and early twentieth centuries (G.H. Mead, F.S.C. Schiller, etc.). The original formulation of pragmatism by Peirce applied to epistemology (the idea that knowledge must be tested by its usefulness), but the concept was quickly extended by James. Pragmatism in ethics is a form of consequentialism, but it differs from utilitarianism in that pragmatism emphasizes action while utilitarianism emphasizes usefulness (Greek pragma = "action" while Latin utilis = "use"). Pragmatism is often said to be a kind of humanism, since it stresses the importance of meeting human needs and the real interests of human beings. Pragmatism rejects any kind of ethical naturalism and tends to be a kind of relativism. In popular usage, to say that a person is pragmatic may indicate that he or she lacks principles, although it can simply be a positive statement that he or she has a "can-do attitude" or "knows how to get things done". (References from altruism, consequentialism, empiricism, humanism, instru-mentalism, realism, and tilitarianism.

Predecessor, parent

Predicate, Intuitively, whatever is said of the subject of a sentence. A function from individuals (or a sequence of individuals) to truth-values. Notation: in "*Px*", *P* is the predicate. See matrix, function, n-adic predicate, predicate logic, prefix, propositional function, relation.

Argument of a predicate: Any of the individuals of which the predicate is asserted. Notation: in"*Pxyz*", *x*, *y*, and *z* are the arguments of predicate *P*. In first-order predicate logic, only terms can be arguments;

Extension of a predicate: The set of all objects of which the predicate is true. Notation: the extension of predicate *P* is *x*: *Px*. See Russell's paradox.

Predicate calculus, predicate logic

Predicate logic, the branch of logic dealing with propositions in which subject and predicate are separately signified, reasoning whose validity depends on this level of articulation, and systems containing suchpropositions and reasoning. Also called quantification theory or predicate calculus. predicate first-order theory First-order predicate logic

Predicate logic in which predicates take only individuals as arguments and quantifiers only bind individual variables.

Higher-order predicate logic: Predicate logic in which predicates take other predicates as arguments and quantifiers bind predicate variables. For example, second-order predicates take first-order predicates as arguments. Order n predicates take order *n*-1 predicates as arguments ($n > 1$). See Grelling's paradox.

Inclusive predicate logic: Predicate logic that does not exclude interpretations with empty domains. Standard predicate logic excludes empty domains and defines logical validity accordingly, *i.e.* true for all interpretations with non-empty domains. Also called inclusive quantification theory. See existential import, logical validity

Monadic predicate logic: Predicate logic in which predicate s take only one argument; the logic of attributes.

Polyadic predicate logic: Predicate logic in which predicates take more than one argument; the logic of n-adic predicates ($n > 1$); the logic of relations.

Predicate logic with identity: A system of predicate logic with $(x)(x=x)$ as an axiom, and the following axiom schema, $[(x=y) => (A => A')]^c$, when *A*' differs from A only in that *y* may replace any free occurrence of *x* in *A* so long as *y* is free wherever it replaces *x* (*y* need not replace every occurrence of *x* in *A*), and when *B^c* is an arbitrary closure of B. See first-order theory with identity, identity

Pure predicate calculus: A system of predicate logic whose language contains no function symbols or individual constants. As opposed to a number-theoretic predicate calculus which contains these things.

Predicate logic with identity, predicate logic

Premise, A wff from which other wffs are derived or inferred. In an argument or inference, all the propositions that support the conclusion. Also spelled "premiss".

Prenex normal form, A wff of predicate logic is in prenex normal form iff (1) all its quantifiers are clustered at the left, (2) no quantifier is negated, (3) the scope of each quantifier extends to the end of the wff, (4) no two quantifiers quantify the same variable, (5) every quantified variable occurs in the matrix of the wff.

Prescriptivism, the view according to which the function of ethics is to tell us what we should do, and not just describe what we actually do; thus it is opposed to descriptivism.

Prima facie, in the original Latin, this phrase means "at first glance." In ethics, it usually occurs in discussions of duties. A prima facie duty is one which appears binding but which may, upon closer inspection, turn out to be overridden by other, stronger duties.

Primary qualities, qualities such as shape, extension, duration, etc. which are perceived by several senses and which are thought to be more or less as much a part of the world as of our perception of it. As opposed to secondary qualities such as color, texture, pitch, odor, etc. which are perceived by particular senses and which are though (by people making the distinction) to correspond to anything outside sensation, being an essentially subjective reaction.

Primitive, A function, operator, or type which is built into a programming language (or operating system), either for speed of execution or because it would be impossible to write it in the language. Primitives typically include the arithmetic and logical operations (plus, minus, and, or, etc.) and are implemented by a small number of machine language instructions.

Primitive recursion, One of the simple function-building operations of recursive function theory. If we are given the functions $f(x)$ and g(x), then we can create a new function $h(x)$ from f and g by primitive recursion thus: when $x = 0$, then h(x) = $f(x)$; but when $x > 0$, then $h(x) = g(h(x\text{-}1))$. (For rigor, the minus sign in the last expression should be replaced by another function, but I leave it this way for informal clarity.) Not to be mistaken for "primitive recursive functions".

Principle of closure, See principle of closure of knowledge under entailment, knowledge under known entailment principle of closure of.

Principle of closure of knowledge under entailment, if *S* knows *p*, and *p* entails *q*, then *S* knows *q*. See Cartesian scepticism, knowledge under known entailment principle of closure of P.

Principle of non contradiction, excluded middle (law of), epis-temology, essence, causality> dating back to Aristotle, this basic logical principle or "law of thought" holds that a statement cannot simultaneously be both true and false or that nothing can at once both have an attribute, like redness, and lack it.

Principle of the compositionality of representations, compositionalilty

Prior intention, intention formed prior to the action that is its condition of satisfaction. The prior intention represents the projected action as a unified whole. Introduced by

Searle in 1983. See also intentionality, intention-in-action.

Privacy, Where only the intended recipients can read a message.

Private language argument, Descartes' arguments (Cartesian Doubt) eventually led many philosophers (especially Logical empiricists) to adopt phenomenalism and solipsism. Wittgenstein argued (against this) that such a view amounts to a belief in an essentially-private language (the language in which the phenominalistsolipsism philosopher states what he know, that is, the contents of his purely private experience). And Wittgenstein argues that a purely private language is really impossible (language is essentially objectual and social in nature).·

Probabilism, the view according to which rational certainty about reality is unattainable; it is similar to fallibilism and can even border on total skepticism.

Probabilistic, Relating to, or governed by, probability. The behaviour of a probabilistic system cannot be predicted exactly but the probability of certain behaviours is known. Such systems may be simulated using pseudo-random numbers. Evolutionary computation uses probabilistic processes togenerate new (potential) solutions to a problem. See also deterministic, non-probabilistic.

Procedure, subroutine

Production system, A production system consists of a collection of productions(rules), a working memory of facts and an algorithm known as forward chaining for producing new facts from old. A rule becomes eligible to "fire" when its conditions match some set of elements currently in working memory. A conflict resolution strategy determines which of several eligible rules (the conflict set) fires next. A condition is a list of symbols which represent constants, which must be matched exactly; variables which bind to the thing they match and "<> symbol" which matches a field not equal to symbol.

Productivity, thought is said to be productive, since, in a sense, normal cognitive agents are capable of having denumerably many distinct thoughts. In other words, to say that thought is productive means that normal cognitive agents have the competence to entertain denumerably many distinct thoughts.

Proletarian, a worker or wage laborer under capitalism. Contrast: bourgeois. See: communism.

Pronunciation, In this dictionary slashes (/../) bracket phonetic pronunciations of words not found in a standard English dictionary. The notation, and many of the pronunciations, was adapted from the Hacker's Jargon File.

Syllables are separated by dash or followed single quote or back quote. Single quote means the preceding syllable is stressed (louder), back quote follows a syllable with intermediate stress (slightly louder), otherwise all syllables are equally stressed.

Consonants are pronounced as in English but note:

chsoft, as in "church" ghard, as in "got" ghaspirated g+h of "bughouse" or "ragheap" jvoiced, as in "judge" khguttural of "loch" or "l'chaim" sunvoiced, as in "pass" zhas "s" in "pleas-ure"

Uppercase letters are pronounced as their English letter names; thus (for example) /H-L-L/ is equivalent to /aych el el/. /Z/ is pronounced /zee/ in the US and /zed/ in the UK (elsewhere?).

Vowels are represented as follows: aback, that ahfather, palm (see note) arfar, mark awflaw, caught aybake, rain eless, men eeeasy, ski eirtheir, software itrip, hit i:life, sky oblock, stock (see note) ohflow, sew ooloot, through ormore, door owout, howoyboy, coin uhbut, some uput, foot *r fur, insert (only in stressedsyllables; otherwise use just "r") yyet, young yoofew, chew [y]oo/ oo/ with optional fronting as in `news' (/nooz/ or /nyooz/) A /*/ is used for the 'schwa' sound of unstressed or occluded vowels (often written with an upside-down 'e'). The schwa vowel is omitted in unstressed syllables containing vocalic l, m, n or r; that is, "kitten" and "colour" would be rendered /kit'n/ and /kuhl'r/ , not /kit'*n/ and /kuhl'*r/.

The above table reflects mainly distinctions found in standard American English (that is, the neutral dialect spoken by TV network announcers and typical of educated speech in the Upper Midwest, Chicago, Minneapolis/St.Paul and Philadelphia). However, we separate /o/ from /ah/, which tend to merge instandard American. This may help readers accustomed to accents resem-bling British Received Pronunciation.

Proof, A finite, non-empty sequence of wffs *F*1, *F*2,... *Fn*, where each *Fi* either is an axiom, or follows by some rule of inference from some of the previous *F's*, and *Fn* is the statement being proved. In short, a derivation in which all premises are theorems. See constructive proof, derivation, existence proof proof theory

Proof-theoretic consistency, (p-consistency) The state of not implying a contradiction See maximal p-consistent set, model-theoretic consistency

Proof-theoretic consistent set of wffs, (p-consistent set) *A* set of wffs is p-consistent there is no wff A such that both *A* and *~A* can be derived from the set. Proof-theoretic inconsistency (p-inconsistency). The state of implying a contradiction.

Proof theory, The study of the deductive apparatuses of formal systems and associated questions of what is provable in a system (hence, consistency, completeness, and decidability (decidable system), even though theseconcepts have a semantic motivation). Broadly, any study of formal systems that makes no reference to the interpretation of the language but describes procedures for combining logical statements to show, by a series of truth-preserving transformations, that one statement is a consequence of some other statement or group of statements. See also model theory.

Proper axiom, axioms

Proper names, the view that proper names simply stand for, or denote, individuals without describing them in any way by philosophers such as J. S.Mill, Russell, and S. Kripke. The contrary view is that proper names are equivalent to (or have the same meaning as) a definite description or a cluster of definite descriptions: *i.e.* that "Aristotle was a student of Plato" is equivalent to "The teacher of Alexander was a student of Plato", or in the cluster version "The individual who was most of the following—teacher of Alexander, born in Stagira, wrote the Metaphysics, etc., was a student of Plato". Proper names, as understood in Mill or Russell's manner aresometimes also called "logically proper names" or "rigid designators".

Proper subset, subset

Property dualism, the view that the mental and the physical comprise two different classes of property that are coinstantiated in the same objects.

According to property dualism, even though mental properties are totally different than physical properties, they are nonetheless all properties of the same kinds of objects. Thus, for example, a single object instantiates the property of my being six feet tall and my believing that the Eiffel tower is in France. Property dualism is compatible with the token identity thesis, but not the type identity thesis. Property dualists are typically, if not unanimously, antireductionists about the mental, which is to say, they deny that it is in-principle possible to translate mental predicates into physical predicates. See dualism, substance dualism.

Proposition, 1. In truth-functional propositional logic, any statement.

2. In predicate logic, a closed wff, as opposed to a propositional function or open wff.

3. In logic generally (for some), the meaning of a sentence that is invariant through all the paraphrases and translations of the sentence. See compound proposition, contingency, contradiction, simple proposition, tautology.

Propositional function, In predicate logic, a function from individuals to truth-values. A wff of predicate logic with at least one free variable.An open wff. A propositional function becomes a proposition when it is closed (see closure of a wff); it is closed either by generalization or instantiation, that is, either by binding free variables or replacing them with constants. See generalization, instantiation, wff, open.

Propositional logic, also called sentence logic and the sentential calculus. Such a logic concerns elementary propositions—*p, q, r, s*, etc.—respecting which the only assumption is that they should individually be either true or false, and operators that form complex propositons whenjoined with appropriate numbers of elementary propositons. The operators include conjunction (&) hence '*p* and *q*'; disjunction (*v*), hence '*p* or *q*'; negation (-), hence '-*p*'; conditional (—>), hence 'If *p* then *q*'; and equivalence (=), hence '*p* is equivalent to *q*'. This logic is concerned with determining which complex propositions are logical truths, or tautologies; this effectively determines what are valid arguments because such can always be treated as complex propositions in which the premisses of the argument appear as the antecedent and the conclusion as the consequence. This logic, as opposed to first, or higher, order predicate logic is complete and decidable.

Protasis, implication

Provably unsolvable, The set or property of problems for which no algorithm at all exists. *E.g.* the Halting Problem. See also provably difficult.

Psychological egoism, in ethics and psychology, the view that in fact all human beings act solely in their individual self-interest (so far as they calculate correctly as to what this is). This view—particularly in the ethical tradition established by Hobbes—is often combined, or confused, with the view, which is labeled "ethical egoism" that all human being ought (whether they do or don't) each to act in their individual self-interest.

Psychologism, the view according to which psychology (orr cognitive science) is the foundation for philosophy. Psychologism tends to hold that the current branches of philosophy will become superfluous or be absorbed by psychology with the development of that science, just as the development of astronomy removed cosmology from the realm of philosophy.

Pythagoras (c. 582-c. 500 BC), Greek philosopher and mathematician, whose doctrines strongly influenced Plato. Born on the island of Sámos, Pythagoras was instructed in the teachings of the early Ionian philosophers Thales, Anaximander, and Anaximenes. Pythagoras is said to have been driven from Sámos by his disgust for the tyranny of Polycrates. About 530 BC Pythagoras settled in Crotona, a Greek colony in southern Italy, where he founded a movement with religious, political, and philosophical aims, known as Pythagoreanism. The philosophy of Pythagoras is known only through the work of his disciples.

Basic Doctrines: The Pythagoreans adhered to certain mysteries, similar in many respects to the mysteries of Orphism. Obedience and silence, abstinence from food, simplicity in dress and possessions, and the habit of frequent self-examination were prescribed. The Pythagoreans believed in immortality and in the transmigration of souls. Pythagoras himself was said to have claimed that he had been Euphorbus, a warrior in the Trojan War, and that he had been permitted to bring into his earthly life the memory of all his previous existences.

Theory of Numbers: Among the extensive mathematical investigations carried on by the Pythagoreans were their studies of odd and even numbers and of prime and square numbers, essential in number theory. From this arithmetical standpoint they cultivated the concept of number, which became for them the ultimate principle of all proportion, order, and harmony in the universe. Through such studies they established a scientific foundation for mathematics. In geometry the great discovery of the school was the hypotenuse theorem, or Pythagoras' theorem, which states that the square of the hypotenuse of a right-angled triangle is equal to the sum of the squares of the other two sides.

Qualia, the "what it's like" character of mental states. The way it feels to have mental states such as pain, seeing red, smelling a rose, etc.

Quality, The totality of features and characteristics of a product or service that bear on its ability to satisfy stated or implied needs. Not to be mistaken for "degree of excellence" or "fitness for use" which meet only part of the definition.

Quantification theory, predicate logic

Quantifier, In predicate logic, a symbol telling us of how many objects (in the domain) the predicate is asserted. The quantifier applies to, or binds, variables which stand as the arguments of predicates. In first-order logic these variables must range over individuals; in higher-order logics they may range over predicates. See bound variable, existential import, free variable, generalization, instantiation, predicate logic

Existential quantifier: The quantifier asserting, "there are some" or "there is at least one". Notation: E, also V. For example, the natural translation of (*Ex*)*Px* is, "There is at least one thing with property *P*."

Universal quantifier: The quantifier asserting, "for all" or "for all things". Notation (*x*). For example, the natural translation of (*x*)*Px* is, "All things have property P." The "all" in the universal quantifier refers to all the objects in the domain of the interpretation (universe of discourse), not to all objects whatsoever.

Vacuous quantifier: A quantifier that binds no variables, *e.g.* "(*y*)" in (*x*)(*y*)(*Ax* => *Bx*).

Quantum bogodynamics, /kwon'tm boh"goh-di:-nam"iks/ A theory that characterises the universe in terms of bogon sources (such as politicians, used-car salesmen, TV evangelists, and suits in general), bogon sinks (such as taxpayers and computers), and bogosity potential fields. Bogon absorption causes human beings to behave mindlessly and machines to fail (and may also cause both to emit secondary bogons); however, the precise mechanics of bogon-computron interaction are not yet understood.

Quantum bogodynamics is most often invoked to explain the sharp increase in hardware and software failures in the presence of suits; the latter emit bogons, which the former absorb.

Quantum consciousness theories of, theories which explore possible connections between quantum mechanical phenomena and consciousness.

Quotient, The number obtained by dividing one number (the "numerator") by another (the "denominator"). If both numbers are rational then the result will also be rational.

Radix, (Or "base", "number base") In a positional representation of numbers, that integer by which the significance of one digit place must be multiplied to give the significance of the next higher digit place. Conventional decimal numbers are radix ten, binary numbers are radix two.

Rational, a fractional number n/d, where n and d are integers, n is the numerator and d is the denominator. The set of all rational numbers is usually called *Q*. Computers do not usually deal with rational numbers but instead convert them to real numbers which are represented (approximately in some cases) as floating-point numbers. Compare irrational. respecting logical principles of validity and cons-istency and answering to the evidence of experience. based on

Rationalism (Latin *ratio,* "reason"), in philosophy, a system of thought that emphasizes the role of reason in obtaining knowledge, in contrast to empiricism, which emphasizes the role of experience, especially sense perception.

Rationalism has appeared in some form in nearly every stage of Western philosophy, but it is primarily identified with the tradition stemming from the 17th-century French philosopher, mathematician, and scientist René Descartes. Descartes believed that geometry represented the ideal for all sciences and philosophy. He held that by means of reason alone, certain universal, self-evident truths could be discovered, from which much of the remaining content of philosophy and the sciences could be deductively derived. He assumed that these self-evident truths were innate, not derived from sense experience. This type of rationalism was developed by other European thinkers, such as the Dutch philosopher Baruch Spinoza, who wrote his *Ethics* (1677) in the form of a geometrical treatise, and the German philosopher and mathematician Gottfried Wilhelm Leibniz.

According to the traditional division of the subject, rationalism was opposed by the British empiricists—John Locke, George Berkeley, and David Hume—who believed that all ideas are derived from sense experience. This traditional division goes back to Immanuel Kant, and has recently come under challenge, as overstating the differences between the two sets of philosophers. Book 4 of Locke's *Essay Concerning Human Under-standing* (1690), for example, expounds a model of scientific knowledge that clearly owes much to Descartes.

Nor, contrary to popular tradition, did the rationalists maintain that sensory experience is irrelevant to knowledge. They thought that the senses provided some test of the principles and postulates of reason. Nevertheless, the rationalists regarded the senses as in themselves a source of mere opinion, rather than of true knowledge. They sought knowledge that was systematic and interconnected. Sense experience could at best establish the regular association of certain phenomena; it could not explain why it should happen, though, or show that it had to happen. The rationalists held that truly scientific knowledge would overcome these deficiencies.

The claim of empiricist philosophers to derive all ideas from experience was challenged by Leibniz, who maintained that, for example, the concept of necessity could not come from that source. Far from being found in experience, that which is necessary holds true regardless of what experiences occur. Whereas the empiricists thought of the human mind as a blank tablet (*tabula rasa*), receptive of and shaped by experiences, the rationalists thought of the mind as predisposed towards certain concepts: experience might be necessary to stimulate those concepts, but they were not to be read off from experience. In this sense the rationalists held them to be innate. Thus, for example, they held that substance and quality are categories into which sensory experience is organized, rather than items to be found in experience. A similar position held for identity. Descartes maintained that as we observe a piece of wax being heated by a fire, it is clear that all the properties given to the senses alter (for example, it becomes soft instead of hard, colourless instead of white). Yet, despite the evidence of the senses, it is clear that it is the same piece of wax that undergoes and survives these changes. Descartes thought that this could only be known through intellectual intuition.

Despite having doctrines in common, the rationalists differed among themselves, particularly in their accounts of substance and the mind. Descartes thought that there were two sorts of substance, mind and body, each capable of existing apart from the other but united in human beings. Spinoza argued that the mental and the physical were two aspects of the same reality, and that that reality consists of one substance, of which human beings and all living things are modes (or modifications). Leibniz believed that fundamentally there exist infinitely many indivisible monads, of which everything was constituted, all in some sense perceiving and striving, though not all fully possessed of consciousness. The rationalists all agreed that a substance had independent existence; Spinoza took the step of identifying his one substance as God.

The question of how there could be free actions in a world in which effects followed necessarily from causes was another issue that taxed the rationalists. Descartes thought that there was freedom in the realm of the mental and necessity in the realm of the physical, but that everything a person does follows necessarily from his or her complete notion, and that God chose to create a world in which that person's complete notion was instantiated. Spinoza maintained that free actions are those determined by the self alone.

The rationalists were keenly interested in science and played an important part in its development; not so much by any discoveries they made as by their willingness to press the importance of the mathematical and geometrical approach in going beyond, and helping to explain, sensory appearances.

Epistemological rationalism has been applied to other fields of philosophical inquiry. Rationalism in ethics is the claim that certain primary moral ideas are innate in humankind and that such first moral principles are self-evident to the rational faculty. Rationalism in the philosophy of religion is the claim that the fundamental principles of religion are innate or self-evident and that revelation is not necessary, as in deism. Since the end of the 1800s, however, rationalism has chiefly played an anti-religious role in theology.

Rationalism, the philosophic approach that holds that reality is knowable by the use of reason or thinking alone, starting with innate ideas, without recourse to observation or experience.

Rationalist, specifically, continental philosopher of the 17th-18th centurysuch as Descartes, Spinoza, Leibniz. These philosophers tended to believe that science abounds in pure, a priori, necessary, rational truths that may be discovered through introspective, rational analysis of concepts or ideas that derive more from innate principles of human though than from our actual sensory experience. empiricist, neorationalist, neoempiricist

Rational numbers, All numbers that are equal to the ratio of two integers.

Realization, a set of properties *P* realize a set of properties *M* just in case the instantiation of the properties in *P* is sufficient for the instantiation of the properties in *M*. See also physicalism, token identity theory, supervenience, and functionalism.

Realism, briefly, a realist about *x* holds that *x* enjoys human-mind-independent existence, that is, *x* exists regardless of whether any human being thinks, hopes or fears that x exists.

Realism (philosophy), in philosophy, a term used for two distinct doctrines of epistemology.

In modern philosophy, the term *realism* is applied to the doctrine which states that ordinary objects of sense perception, such as tables and chairs, have an existence independent of their being perceived. In this sense, it is contrary to the idealism of philosophers such as George Berkeley or Immanuel Kant. In its extreme form, sometimes called naive realism, the things perceived by the senses are believed to be exactly what they appear to be. In more sophisticated versions, sometimes referred to as critical realism, some explanation is given of the relationship between the object and the observer that accounts for the possibility of illusion, hallucination, and other perceptual errors.

In medieval philosophy, the term *realism* referred to a position that regarded Platonic forms, or universals, as real. That position is now usually called Platonic realism. In the philosophy of Plato, a common noun, such as *bed,* refers to the ideal nature of the object, which is conveyed by its definition, and this ideal nature has metaphysical existence independent of the particular objects of that type. Thus, circularity exists independent of particular circles; justice, independent of particular just individuals or just states; and "bedness", independent of particular beds. In the Middle Ages, this position was defended against nominalism, which denied the existence of such universals. Nominalists asserted that the many objects called by one name shared nothing but the name. Compromises between these two positions included moderate realism, which claimed that the universal existed in the many objects of the same type but not independent of them, and conceptualism, which held that the universal might exist independent of the many objects of that particular type, but only as an idea in the mind, not as a self-subsisting metaphysical entity.

Realist, 1. generally, someone who claims that various sorts of things that are not realized completely in our (sensory) experience are real. The things in question might be, *e.g.*: numbers, infinite constructions, material objects, theoretical entities (atoms, the unconscious mind, etc.) and so on.

2. during the middle ages "realist" specifically meant someone who maintained that there are universals (*e.g.* "horsiness", "humanity") corresponding to words such as "horse" and "human" and not just individual things. nominalist

Real-time, Describes an application which requires a program to respond to stimuli within some small upper limit of response time (typically milli- or microseconds). Process control at a chemical plant is the classic example. Such applications often require special operating systems (because everything else must take a back seat to response time) and speed-tuned hardware.

Used to describe a system that must guarantee a response to an external event within a given time.

Reason, the power of grasping concepts and drawing inferences.

Recourse, To perform recursion.

Reduction, (Or "contraction") The process of transforming an expression according to certain reduction rules. The most important forms are beta reduction (application of a lambda abstraction to one or more argument expressions) and delta reduction (application of a mathematical function to the required number of arguments).

An evaluation strategy (or reduction strategy), determines which part of an expression (which redex) to reduce first. There are many such strategies. See graph reduction, string reduction, normal order reduction, applicative order redu-ction, parallel reduction, alpha conversion, beta conversion, delta conversion, eta conversion.

Reductionism, the term refers either to a philosophical approach that attempts to reduce complex phenomena to the simplest possible explanation or to the belief that such reduction constitutes the only valid style of explanation. Physicalism and behaviorism are examples of reductionism. (References from behaviorism, materialism, physicalism, and scientism.)

Reference, a property of a representation which denotes what the representation is about, or "of". See sense, intentionality.

Reflection, according to Locke: the inner perception by which minds are aware of their own thoughts. See apperception.

Refutable, In lazy functional languages, a refutable pattern is one which may fail to match. An expression being matched against a refutable pattern is first evaluated to head normal form (which may fail to terminate) and then the top-level constructor of the result is compared with that of the pattern. If they are the same then any arguments are matched against the pattern's arguments otherwise the match fails.

An irrefutable pattern is one which always matches. An attempt to evaluate any variable in the pattern forces the pattern to be matched as though it were refutable which may fail to match (resulting in an error) or fail to terminate.

Patterns in Haskell are normally refutable but may be made irrefutable by prefixing them with a tilde (~). For example,

(\ (*x*,*y*) -> 1) undefined ==> undefined

(\ ~(*x*,*y*) -> 1) undefined==>1

Patterns in Miranda are refutable, except for tuples which are irrefutable.

g [*x*] = 2 *g* undefined ==>undefined

f (*x*,*y*) = 1 *f* undefined==>1

Thus Pattern bindings in local definitions are irrefutable in both languages:

h = 1 where [*x*] = undefined ==>1

Irrefutable patterns can be used to simulate unlifted products because they effectively ignore the top-level constructor of the expression being matched and consider only its components.

Reify, to regard something abstract as a material thing.

Reinvent the wheel, To design or implement a tool equivalent to an existing one or part of one, with the implication that doing so is silly or a waste of time. This is often a valid criticism. On the other hand, automobiles don't use wooden rollers, and some kinds of wheel have to be reinvented many times before you get them right. On the third hand, people reinventing the wheel do tend to come up with the moral equivalent of a trapezoid with an offset axle.

Relation, 1. A way in which two or more objects are connected, associated, or related, or (at a different level) a polyadic predicate symbolizing such A relation. See attribute, predicate logic

2. A subset of the product of two sets, $R: A \times B$. If (a, b) is an element of R then we write $a\ R\ b$, meaning a is related to b by R. A relation may be: reflexive ($a\ R\ a$), symmetric ($a\ R\ b \Rightarrow b\ R\ a$), transitive ($a\ R\ b\ \&\ b\ R\ c \Rightarrow a\ R\ c$), antisymmetric ($a\ R\ b\ \&\ b\ R\ a \Rightarrow a = b$) or total ($a\ R\ b$ or $b\ R\ a$). See equivalence relation, partial ordering, pre-order, total ordering.

3. A table in a relational database.

Relative consistency proof, The proof that some system S is consistent by appeal to theorems and methods of reasoning from some other system S'. The result is that we know that S is consistent only if system S' is consistent.

Relativism, generally speaking, relativism holds that truth and value are relative to an observer or group of observers. In ethics, there are two main type of relativism.

1. Descriptive ethical relativism simply claims as a matter of fact that different people have different moral beliefs, but it takes no stand on whether those beliefs are valid or not.

2. Normative ethical relativism claims that each culture's (or group's) beliefs are right within that culture, and that it is wrong to judge another culture's values from the outside.

Relativism is often just another word for subjectivism. Popularly, relativism is usually contrasted with some form of ethical objectivism, while subjectivism has connotations of a sort of individualism and, in the extreme, of solipsism.

Religion, Philosophy of, critical scrutiny of the claims of established religions and of religious believers. The principal areas of study within the philosophy of religion include: philosophical proofs for the existence of God; philosophical theology, that is, questions arising from attempts to describe God's nature; and religious epistemology, which is concerned with the status of the belief that God exists. The philosophy of religion is one of the oldest branches of philosophy, and is intimately related to other branches of philosophical inquiry, most notably logic, metaphysics, and epistemology. It has also enjoyed a distinguished history within the three main monotheistic traditions—Judaism, Islam, and Christianity—as well as within other religions, for example, Hinduism and Buddhism.

In the Western tradition, most historically important philosophers have made important contributions to the philosophy of religion. These include: Plato, Aristotle, Avicenna, Averroës, Maimonides, Thomas Aquinas, John Duns Scotus, René Descartes, Gottfried Leibniz, Baruch Spinoza, and Immanuel Kant. Further to this, non-theistic philosophers, such as David Hume, have made important contributions to the subject. The discipline has also been shaped by critiques of theism from

Karl Marx, Friedrich Nietzsche, and Sigmund Freud. In this respect, the philosophy of religion is an inclusive subject that is neither indexed to theism, agnosticism, nor atheism, but is simply concerned with the philosophical analysis of those systems of beliefs and practices that are characterized as religion.

Philosophical Proofs for the Existence of God: Three main proofs are offered for the existence of a god: the ontological argument; the cosmological argument; and the "argument from design". These proofs are of interest not only for their rich philosophical history but also as the objects of on-going discussion among present-day philosophers of religion.

The ontological argument is an a priori argument: that is, it does not make any appeal to the facts of experience, but is solely concerned with the implications that stem from thinking about certain concepts. In this case, the concept under consideration is that of God. Two of the more enduring versions of the ontological argument are the versions posited by the 11th-century philosopher St Anselm and by the 17th-century philosopher René Descartes. Anselm began his argument by defining the concept of God as that "which nothing greater can be conceived of". Therefore, to think of God is to think of something "nothing greater than which can be conceived of". Anselm then proceeded to draw the implications that stem from this. The first point, he noted, is that something exists in our understanding when we think of it. Given that something exists—viz. God, or that "than which nothing greater can be conceived of"—it must be the case that God, being the greatest thing of which there can be a thought, must not just exist in our understanding but must exist in reality as well. Thus God exists. From a different perspective, Descartes advanced an argument that began with him defining God as a supremely perfect being. He then claimed that anything that is supremely perfect has existence. In this respect, a being that is completely perfect must, of necessity, possess all perfections. Thus, Descartes concluded, as God is the most perfect being, he must exist.

The ontological argument, in whichever version, has been the object of a great deal of philosophical criticism. Traditionally, the objection posed by the 18th-century philosopher Immanuel Kant has been thought to be one of the most decisive. Kant argued that the problem with the argument lay in its claim that existence is a predicate. (A predicate term describes something done by a subject; so, in the sentence "John is eating" the predicate "is eating" describes something that the subject, John, is doing.) Kant argued that existence cannot be a predicate because it does not add any new information to an understanding of the subject. To be told that John is bald, that he is eating, and that he is angry is to add three things to the stock of information about him. However, to be told that he exists does not genuinely communicate something about him. Likewise with God. To state simply that God's existence follows from thinking about him is to have said nothing other than that God exists. Kant argued that nothing of philosophical conse-quence has been learnt. It is for this reason that many modern-day philosophers have held the onto-logical argument to be in error.

The other main proofs offered, the cosmological argument and the argument from design, are related. Both are a posteriori arguments, that is, concerned with the objects of experience. Unlike the ontological argument, the cosmological argument always holds what is known as an existential premise; part of the argument asserts that something exists. It then seeks to make clear the view that the reason why there is something rather than nothing is down to the fact that the something in question was caused to come about. The origin of this something, or its first cause, is more often than not claimed to be God. The cosmological argument has enjoyed great appeal among philosophers of widely differing religious traditions. It has been advanced by, for example, the ancient Greeks Plato and Aristotle, the Islamic philosophers Avicenna and members of the Kalam school, the Jewish theorists Maimonides and Spinoza, and Christian philosophers of many denominations such as Aquinas, John Locke, and Leibniz. Despite its broad appeal and historical popularity, the cosm-ological argument has been subject to much criticism. For example, it is thought that the argument's appeal to the notion of a first cause is problematic or that it arbitrarily demands an explanation for everything, where such a request is considered to be unwarranted. In recent times, philosophers such as William Lane Craig and Richard Swinburne have attempted to exempt the cosmological argument from such criticisms.

The argument from design is concerned with arguing for the existence of a god on the basis of noting certain facts about the nature and purpose of the world. Central to the argument is the idea that as the world is characterized by such a degree of order and regularity it must have been designed for some purpose. From there, the argument invites consideration that the order and regularity in the world were bestowed by a "divine craftsman", who created the world for a definite reason. Versions of the argument have been proposed by ancient philosophers such as Cicero, as well as by medieval thinkers, for example, Aquinas. It has also proved popular among philosophers with a strong interest in science: an argument from design can be found in the works of the 18th-century philosopher-scientist Issac Newton and in the work of the 19th-century philosopher-theologian William Paley.

The argument from design's most influential critic was David Hume, who raised four points against it. He said, first, that the argument claims too much; that to infer an effect from a cause is to infer only from what is particular to the effect. Thus, it cannot be inferred that God exists simply from noting that there is regularity and order in the world. Secondly, the universe is unique. On this basis, Hume argued that it cannot be inferred that there is anything like a designer behind it. Thirdly, the very activity of positing a divine designer can lead to an infinite regress, for if a designer—viz. God—designed this world, then who designed God, and so on. Lastly, the universe shows as much evidence of disorder as order, so to seek a cause of the order when such order only partially represents what the universe is like is questionable. Since the time of Hume, supporters of the design argument have attempted to argue against his points with varying success. In recent times, this debate has made frequent appeal to new discoveries in biology and theoretical physics.

Philosophical Theology: Philosophical theology is devoted to the exploration of God and of the claims made about God in the various theological traditions. Its range of topics typically includes what are known as the divine attributes. Philosophical theology is also concerned with questions and issues that centre on God's nature and God's relation to the world.

Historically speaking, the divine attributes have been defined thus: existence, simplicity, omnipotence, omniscience, and perfect goodness. Existence has been discussed above. When Jewish, Islamic, and Christian theologians and philosophers said that God is "simple" they meant by this that certain things that are true of human beings, animals, and other living things are not true of God. In this sense, divine simplicity can be distilled into the following claims: God is unchangeable; God is not an individual; and God is not created. The claim that God is omnipotent is to say that God can do anything; namely, that God possesses every possible power and ability. Related to this is the claim that God is omniscient. This means that God can know everything that has happened, will happen, and is about to happen. God has infallible knowledge of all past, present, and future events. The last of the divine attributes is the claim that God is morally perfect and is the personification or very object of goodness itself.

Two central problems surround discussion of the divine attributes. The first concerns the coherence of individual attributes. Thus, for example, if God is omnipotent, can God create a stone that is too heavy for him to lift? The second problem concerns what is known as the "compossibility" of the divine attributes, that is, whether or not it is logically coherent to say that God possesses all the attributes at any one time. For example, if God can know everything, do everything, and is goodness personified, it is asked why he does not actively intervene in order to prevent evil from coming about in the world. This is what is known as the "problem of evil", something that raises a host of difficult issues when trying to reconcile all the attributes of God's nature.

Another issue which concerns God's relation to the natural world is that of miracles. A traditional claim of monotheistic religions is that God can intervene in the affairs of the world. A miracle is an event that goes against the perceived or expected laws of nature, say, in turning water into wine. The philosophical questions that stem from the claim that miracles occur are many: for example, what is a miracle, what is it supposed to prove, and by what means is it to be known?

Religious Epistemology: Religious epistemology is concerned with the justification of the belief that God exists. Traditionally, philosophers have argued that the belief that God exists has to be justified in a particular way because it is what is known as a non-basic belief. A basic belief, on the other hand, is a belief that is not dependent upon another belief for its truth. Thus, any belief that is self-evident, incorrigible, derived from the senses, or based on memory is classed as a basic belief. The belief that God exists appears not to fit into any of the above categories, and needs to be justified by external evidence in order for it to be judged true or false. Throughout history, many philosophers have therefore attempted to justify the belief that God exists by marshalling evidence that attempts to make the belief credible.

In more recent times, many philosophers have argued that the above approach is incorrect: that is, that the belief that God exists can be a basic belief and therefore requires no external justification. Further to this, some philosophers have argued that belief in a god can be justified on the basis of certain facts about religious experience. These two new approaches to the issues of religious epistemology have done much to stimulate recent interest in the philosophy of religion.

Another topic that receives attention as part of the philosophy of religion is the issue of religious language, which is concerned with the assessment of the meaning and coherence of theological terms. A further prominent issue in contemporary study is the subject of religious pluralism. This derives in part from an intellectual response to the widespread phenomenon of religious diversity and is concerned with assessing the claims of a particular religious tradition to embody the complete truth. Encompassing topics such as these alongside its traditional subjects, the philosophy of religion takes its place within Western philosophy not just in the domain of the history of philosophy but also in having much to offer in terms of more specialized philosophical speculation. *See also* Philosophy, Indian; Philosophy, Islamic; Philosophy, Western.

Representation, 1. *Of a function.*

A function *f* of n arguments from natural numbers to natural numbers isrepresented in a system iff there is a wff A with n+1 free variables Such that *A* is a theorem when its variables are instantiated to the natural numbers *k1...kn*+1 when *f*(*k1...kn*) = *kn*+1, and not a theorem otherwise. Strong representation of a function *A* function *f* is strongly represented in a system iff it is represented in the system by wff *A*, and A is a theorem iff ~*A* is not a theorem.

2. *Of a set*: A set *N* is represented in a system iff there is some prepositional function with exactly one free variable, *Px*, such that *Px* is a theoremwhenever *x* is instantiated to a member of the set, and a non-theorem otherwise. Or if *N* is a set of natural numbers, n is a natural number, and is a numeral for n, then N is represented iff |- *P/x* <=> *n*: *N*.

3. that which stands for, refers to or denotes something or the relation between a thing and that which stands for or denotes it. See distributed representation, symb-olicism, dynamic systems theory.

Representationalism, 1. in epistemology, representationalism is the view that the only things we can know are our representations of the world (*e.g.*, ideas, perceptions, beliefs, etc.), not the world itself. Epistemological representationalism is therefore opposed to realism, especially to direct realism. The term is most often used in discussions of perception, phenome-nalism being the more general term of this sort.

2. in aesthetics, representationalism is the idea that art ought to represent reality. This view is sometimes and especially popularly called realism, at least in the visual arts—in literature, realism is something akin to naturalism. (References from empiricism, formalism, realism, and sensationalism.)

Repression, freudian mechanism by which unacceptable wishes and thoughts are banished from conscious awareness but continue to unconsciously and, thence, find expression in dreams and slips of the tongue, and sometimes in compulsive behavior, obsessive thoughts, and other forms of psychopathology. Herbert Marcuse distinguishes necessary repression (without which civilization could not exist) from surplus repression (which serves to maintain unnecessary forms of economic andpolitical control and oppression). Compare: sublimation.

Requirements, The first stage of software development which defines what the potential users want the system to do. In modern methods these requirements should be testable, and will usually be traceable in later development stages. A common feature of nearly all software is that the requirements change during its lifetime.

Requirements analysis, The process of reviewing a business's processes todetermine the business needs and functional requirements that a system must meet.

Restructuring, the transformation from one representation form to another atthe same relative abstraction level, while preserving the subject system's external behaviour (functionality and semantics).

Revealed theology, truths about God that can only be revealed by supernatural means and cannot be discovered by the unaided exercise of reason and perception. Compare: natural theology.

Rights, rights are entitlements to do something without interference from other people (negative rights) or entitlements that obligate others to do something positive to assist you (positive rights). Some rights (natural rights, human rights) belong to everyone by nature or simply by virtue of being human; some rights (legal rights) belong to people by virtue of their membership in a particular political state; other rights (moral rights) are based on acceptance of a particular moral theory.

Robust, Said of a system that has demonstrated an ability to recover gracefully from the whole range of exceptional inputs and situations in a given environment. One step below bulletproof. Carries the additional connotation of elegance in addition to just careful attention to detail. Compare smart, opposite: brittle.

Romanticism, name for the theory and movement of art and philosophy that developed in the nineteenth century in opposition to classicism. The term is not clearly defined and has different meanings in different disciplines. In art and aesthetics the term usually refers to the various attributes of Romantic art in contrast with classicism and naturalism, including a free-flowing style, expression of emotion, concern with values and personal experience, etc. In philosophy the term is often equivalent to emotionalism. (References from aestheticism, classicism, emotionalism, and naturalism.)

Rule, a theoretical device for the explanation of behavioural regularities and/or cognitive states.

Rules are generally, but not always, characterised in terms of causallyoperative mental representations. See computation, symbolicism, connectionism.

Rules of inference, Explicit rules for producing a theorem when given one or more other theorems. functions from sequences of theorems to theorems. In a formal system they should be formal (that is, syntactical or typographical) in nature, and work without reference to the meanings of the strings they manipulate. Also called rules of transformation, rules of production.

Rousseau, Jean-Jacques (1712-1778), Swiss-born French philosopher, social and political theorist, musician, botanist, and one of the most eloquent writers of the Age of Enlightenment.

Rousseau was born in Geneva on June 18, 1712, and was raised by an aunt and uncle following the death of his mother a few days after his birth. He was apprenticed at the age of 13 to an engraver, but after three years he ran away and became secretary and companion to Madame Louise de Warens, a wealthy and charitable woman who had a profound influence on Rousseau's life and writings. In 1742 Rousseau moved to Paris, where he earned his living as a music teacher, music copyist, and political secretary. He became a close friend of the French philosopher Denis Diderot, who commissioned him to write articles on music for the French *Ency-clopédie.*

Philosophical Writings: In 1750 Rousseau won the Academy of Dijon award for his *Discours sur les Sciences et les Arts* (Discourse on the Sciences and the Arts, 1750), and in 1752 his opera *Le Devin du Village* (The Village Sage) was first performed. In the former, and in his *Discourse on the Origin of Inequality Among Mankind* (1755; trans. 1761), he expounded the view that science, art, and social institutions have corrupted humankind and that the natural, or primitive, state is morally superior to the civilized state (*see* Naturalism). The persuasive rhetoric of these writings provoked derisive comments from the French philosopher Voltaire, who attacked Rousseau's views, and subsequently the two philosophers became bitter enemies.

Rousseau left Paris in 1756 and secluded himself at Montmorency, where he wrote the romance *Julie, or the New Eloise* (1761; trans. 1773). In his famous political treatise *The Social Contract* (1762; trans. 1797) he developed a case for civil liberty and helped prepare the ideological background of the French Revolution by defending the popular will against divine right.

Influence: Although Rousseau contributed greatly to the movement in Western Europe for individual freedom and against the absolutism of Church and State, his conception of the State as the embodiment of the abstract will of the people and his arguments for strict enforcement of political and religious conformity are regarded by some historians as a source of totalitarian ideology. Rousseau's theory of education led to more permissive and more psychologically oriented methods of child care, and influenced the German educator Friedrich Froebel, the Swiss educational reformer Johann Heinrich Pestalozzi, and other pioneers of modern education. *The New Eloise* and *Confessions* introduced a new style of extreme emotional expression, concern with intense personal experience, and exploration of the conflicts between moral and sensual values. In these writings Rousseau profoundly influenced Romanticism in literature and philosophy in the early 19th century. He also affected the development of psychological literature, psychoanalytical theory, and 20th-century existentialism, particularly in his insistence on free will, his rejection of the doctrine of original sin, and his defence of learning through experience rather than analysis. The spirit and ideas of Rousseau's work stand midway between the 18th-century Enlightenment, with its passionate defence of reason and individual rights, and early 19th-century Romanticism, which defended intense subjective experience against rational thought.

Russell's Attic, An imaginary room containing countably many pairs of shoes (*i.e.* a pair for each natural number), and countably many pairs of socks. How many shoes are there? Answer: countably many (map the left shoes to even numbers and the right shoes to odd numbers, say). How many socks are there? Also countably many, we want to say, but we can't prove it without the Axiom of Choice, because in each pair, the socks are indistinguishable (there's no such thing as a left sock). Although for any single pair it is easy to select one, we cannot specify a general method for doing this.

Russell's Paradox, A logical contradiction in set theory discovered by the British mathematician Bertrand Russell (1872-1970). If R is the set of all sets which don't contain themselves, does R contain itself? If it does then it doesn't and vice versa. This contradiction infects set theory when it is permissible to speak of "all sets" or set complements without qualification, or when a set is defined loosely as any collection of any elements, or when every predicate (intension) determines a set (extension). See complement The paradox stems from the acceptance of the following axiom: If $P(x)$ is a property then is a set. This is the Axiom

x: P

of Comprehension (actually an axiom schema). By applying it in the case where P is the property "x is not an element of x", we generate the paradox, *i.e.* something clearly false. Thus any theory built on this axiom must be inconsistent.

In lambda-calculus Russell's Paradox can be formulated by representing each set by its characteristic function—the property which is true for members and false for nonmembers. The set R becomes a function r which is the negation of its argument applied to itself:

$r = \backslash\, x.\ \text{not}\ (x\ x)$

If we now apply r to itself,

$r\ r = (\backslash\, x.\ \text{not}\ (x\ x))\ (\backslash\, x.\ \text{not}\ (x\ x))$

$= \text{not}\ ((\backslash\ x.\ \text{not}\ (x\ x))(\backslash\, x.\ \text{not}\ (x\ x)))$

$= \text{not}\ (r\ r)$

So if $(r\ r)$ is true then it is false and vice versa.

An alternative formulation is: "if the barber of Seville is a man who shaves all men in Seville who don't shave themselves, and only those men, who shaves the barber?" This can be taken simply as a proof that no such barber can exist whereas seemingly obvious axioms of set theory suggest the existenceof the paradoxical set R.

Zermelo Frnkel set theory is one "solution" to this paradox. Another, type theory, restricts sets to contain only elements of a single type, (*e.g.* integers or sets of integers) and no type is allowed to refer to itself so no set can contain itself.

A message from Russell induced Frege to put a note in his life's work, just before it went to press, to the effect that he now knew it was inconsistent but he hoped it would be useful anyway.

Russell, Bertrand Arthur William, 3rd Earl Russell (1872-1970), British philosopher, mathematician, and Nobel laureate, whose emphasis on logical analysis influenced the course of 20th-century philosophy. Born in Trelleck, Wales, on May 18, 1872, Russell was educated at Trinity College, University of Cambridge. After graduating in 1894, he travelled in France, Germany, and the United States, and was then made a fellow of Trinity College. From an early age he developed a strong sense of social consciousness; at the same time, he involved himself in the study of logical and mathematical questions, which he had made his specialist fields and on which he was called to lecture at many institutions throughout the world.

Russell achieved prominence with his first major work, *The Principles of Mathematics* (1902), in which he attempted to remove mathematics from the realm of abstract philosophical notions and to give it a precise scientific framework. He then collaborated for eight years with the British philosopher and mathematician Alfred North Whitehead to produce the monumental work *Principia Mathematica* (3 vols., 1910-1913), which showed that mathematics can be stated in terms of the concepts of general logic, such as class and membership of a class. It became a masterpiece of rational thought. Russell and Whitehead proved that numbers can be defined as classes of a certain type, and in the process they developed logical concepts and a logical notation that established symbolic logic as an important specialization within the field of philosophy.

In his next major work, *The Problems of Philosophy* (1912), Russell borrowed from the fields of sociology, psychology, physics, and mathematics to refute the tenets of idealism, the dominant philosophical school of the period, which held that all objects and experiences are the product of the intellect. Russell, a realist, believed that objects perceived by the senses have an inherent reality independent of the mind.

Socialist and Pacifist: Russell condemned both sides in World War I and for his uncompromising stand he was fined, imprisoned, and deprived of his teaching post at Cambridge. In prison he wrote *Introduction to Mathematical Philosophy* (1919), combining the two areas of knowledge he regarded as inseparable. After the war he visited the Russian Soviet Federated Socialist Republic, and in his book *Practice and Theory of Bolshevism* (1920) he expressed his disappointment with the form of socialism practised there. He felt that the methods used to achieve a communist system were intolerable and that the results obtained were not worth the price paid.

Russell taught at Beijing University in China between 1921 and 1922. From 1928 to 1932, after he returned to the United Kingdom, he conducted the private, highly progressive Beacon Hill School for young children; from 1938 to 1944 he taught at various educational institutions in the United States. He was barred, however, from teaching at the College of the City of New York (now City College of the City University of New York) by the New York Supreme Court because of his attacks on religion in such works as *What I Believe* (1925) and his advocacy of sexual freedom, expressed in *Manners and Morals* (1929).

Russell returned to Britain in 1944 and was reinstated as a fellow of Trinity College. Although he abandoned pacifism to support the Allied cause in World War II, he became an ardent and active opponent of nuclear weapons. In 1949 he was awarded the Order of Merit by George VI. Russell received the 1950 Nobel Prize for Literature and was cited as "the champion of humanity and freedom of thought". He led a movement in the late 1950s advocating unilateral nuclear disarmament by the United Kingdom, and was imprisoned, at the age of 89, after an antinuclear demonstration. Russell spent the rest of his life in Wales and died there on February 2, 1970.

Philosopher and Author: In addition to his earlier work, Russell made a major contribution to the development of logical positivism, a strong philosophical movement of the 1930s and 1940s. The major Austrian philosopher Ludwig Wittgenstein, at one time Russell's student at Cambridge, was strongly influenced by his original concept of logical atomism. In his search for the nature and limits of knowledge, Russell was a leader in the revival of the philosophy of empiricism in the larger field of epistemology. In *Our Knowledge of the External World* (1914) and *Inquiry into Meaning and Truth* (1940), he attempted to explain all factual knowledge as constructed out of immediate experiences. Among his other books are *The ABC of Relativity* (1925), *Education and the Social Order* (1932), *A History of Western Philosophy* (1945), *The Impact of Science upon Society* (1952), *My Philosophical Development* (1959), *War Crimes in Vietnam* (1967), and *The Autobiography of Bertrand Russell* (3 vols., 1967-1969).

Russell's theory of descriptions, roughly, the view that sentences in which phrases of the form the-so-and-so appear can be reduced to more revealing logical forms in which "the" disappears and in which there is no longer anytemptation to think that such phrases are like proper names. *E.g.* "The present king of France is bald" becomes "There exists something which is presently kind of France and there is no other individual who is such and that individual is bald". Russell's theory has been called a paradigm of philosophy.

Sartre, Jean-Paul (1905-1980), French

philosopher, dramatist, novelist, and political journalist, who was a leading exponent of existentialism. Sartre was born in Paris on June 21, 1905, and educated in the city at the École Normale Supérieure, the University of Fribourg in Switzerland, and the French Institute in Berlin. He taught philosophy at various secondary schools from 1929 until the outbreak of World War II, when he was called into military service. In 1938 he published his first novel, *Nausea* (trans. 1949), which describes a provincial intellectual like himself who is progressively appalled at the mere "isness" of things, and the absence of any meaning in nature or human life.

From 1940 to 1941 Sartre was imprisoned by the Germans; after his release, he taught in Neuilly, France, and later in Paris, and was active in the French Resistance. The German authorities, unaware of his underground activities, allowed the production of his anti-authoritarian play *The Flies* (1943; trans. 1946) and the publication of his major philosophical work *L'Etre et le Néant* (1943; *Being and Nothingness*, 1953).

Sartre gave up teaching in 1945. With the philosopher Maurice Merleau-Ponty and the feminist writer Simone de Beauvoir, Sartre's lifelong companion, he founded the political and literary magazine *Les Temps Modernes,* of which he became editor-in-chief. He was active after 1947 as an independent socialist, critical of both the Union of Soviet Socialist Republics and the United States in the so-called Cold War years. Most of his writing of the 1950s deals with literary and political problems. Rejecting the 1964 Nobel Prize for Literature, Sartre explained that to accept it would compromise his integrity as a writer.

Sartre's philosophical works combine influences from the Danish philosopher Søren Kierkegaard and the Germans Immanuel Kant, G. W. F. Hegel, Edmund Husserl, and Martin Heidegger. He later developed this in a social direction, attempting to integrate it into a broadly Marxist outlook. His views, made popular by works such as the short *Existentialism and Humanism* (1946; trans. 1948), related philosophical theory to literature, psychology, and political action. They stimulated enormous popular interest, and at one time existentialism was a worldwide movement. He was the dominant intellectual figure in France in the first two decades after World War II.

Being and Nothingness: In his early philosophical work, *Being and Nothingness,* Sartre distinguished between human beings and the nonhuman world, maintaining that human existence is intrinsically characterized by nothingness—that is, a capacity to negate what is and contrast it with what might be—and by individual freedom and responsibility. Human beings, however, constantly tend to fall into "bad faith". That is, they deny this freedom and deceive themselves into thinking that their actions are determined by their circumstances or their own natures, so that they are not really responsible for them. To achieve an authentic human existence, an individual must overcome the tendency to bad faith, recognize his or her own absolute freedom, and assume responsibility for any decisions made, unaided by society, traditional morality, or a belief in God. Sartre's plays and novels express his belief that freedom and acceptance of personal responsibility are the main values in life and that individuals must rely on their creative powers rather than on social or religious authority.

Critique of Dialectical Reason: Sartre's later philosophical work *Critique de la Raison Dialectique* (1960; *Critique of Dialectical Reason*, 1976) shifted his emphasis from individual freedom to a Marx-influenced theory of the subject as an actor who is always historically and socially conditioned. Sartre argued that the influence of modern society as a whole over the individuals who comprise it is so great as to produce "serialization", a kind of loss of the self. Genuine freedom can only be gained by collective revolutionary action. Whereas in his early work, Sartre had portrayed human relations as an endless struggle to reduce the other person to the object of one's "look", and to escape from a similar objectification by the other, in this and other later writings he held out the possibility of relations of mutual recognition between free individuals.

Despite his support for revolutionary action, especially against colonial regimes, Sartre did not himself join the Communist Party. He condemned the Soviet invasion of Hungary in 1956 and of Czechoslovakia in 1968, as well as French actions in the Algerian War in the late 1950s, and American involvement in the Vietnam War in the following decade. In his last years, Sartre was active in attempts to mediate between Israel and the Palestinians. He died in Paris on April 15, 1980.

Satisficing, a concept, due to Herbert Simon, which identifies the decision making process whereby one chooses an option that is, while perhaps not the best, good enough. See practical reasoning.

A term utilitarians borrowed from economics to indicate how much utility we should try to create. Whereas maximizing utilitarians claim that we should strive to maximize utility, satisficing utilitarians claim that we need only try to produce enough utility to satisfy everyone. It's analogous to the difference between taking a course with the goal of getting an "A" and taking it pass-fail.

Satisfaction, 1. In truth-functional propositional logic, a wff A is satisfied iff at least one row of its truth-table makes it true, *i.e.* iff A is either a contingency or a tautology.

2. In predicate logic, a wff A is satisfied iff there is a sequence of objects from the domain of some interpretation such that A is true for that sequence. What it means for a wff to be true for a sequence is satisfaction defined differently for several distinct kinds of predicate logic wff, *e.g.* quantified wffs, atomic wffs, wffs compounded with the various connectives of the language, and naked propositional symbols. Among atomic wffs, satisfaction is defined differently depending on whether the arguments of the predicate are constants, variables, or functions, and in the last case, whether the arguments of the functions are constants, variables, or functions. Hence the concept of satisfaction cannot be made more precise without giving each of perhaps a dozen precise tests for different kinds of wff. See truth for an interpretation

Satisfiability, A wff is satisfiable iff there is some interpretation in which it is satisfied.

Simultaneous satisfiability: A set of wffs is simultaneously satisfiable iff there is an interpretation in which each member of the set is satisfied. In predicate logic, each member may be satisfied by a different sequence from that interpretation, but all must be satisfied in the same interpretation.

Skepticism, any of a class of views that denies some claim to knowledge. See Cartesian scepticism.

Scepticism (Greek, *skeptesthai,* "to examine"), in philosophy, doctrine that denies the possibility of attaining knowledge of reality as it is in itself. By gradual extension of its meaning, the word "scepticism" has also come to signify any doubt about what is generally accepted as true. All philosophical scepticism ultimately relates to epistemology; that is, it is based on views about the scope and validity of human knowledge.

Greek Scepticism: The Greek sophists of the 5th century BC were for the most part sceptics. Their point of view is reflected in their maxims "man is the measure of all things" and "nothing is; or if anything is, it cannot be known". Thus, the sophist Gorgias declared that all statements conc-erning reality are false and that, even if true, their truth can never be proved. Another sophist, Protagoras of Abdera, taught that human beings can know only their perceptions of things, not the things themselves.

The principles of scepticism were first explicitly formulated by the Pyrrhonists, a school of Greek philosophy deriving its name from its founder, Pyrrho of Elis. Pyrrho, whose primary concern was ethics, maintained that human beings can know nothing of the real nature of things, and that consequently the wise person will suspend judgement on them, thereby gaining peace of mind. Timon of Philius, Pyrrho's pupil, carried scepticism to its logical conclusion by asserting that equally good reasons can be adduced both for and against any philosophical proposition.

The members of the Middle Academy (the school that developed in the 3rd century BC from Plato's Academy) and the New Academy (2nd century BC) of Carneades were more systematic but somewhat less radical in their scepticism than the Pyrrhonists. Carneades maintained that no beliefs can be proved conclusively but that some can be shown to be more probable than others. The most important sceptics of later antiquity were the Greek philosopher Aenesidemus, who classified ten arguments in support of the sceptical position, and the 3rd-century AD Greek physician Sextus Empiricus, who emphasized obse-rvation and common sense as opposed to theory.

Modern Scepticism: During the Renaissance the influence of ancient scepticism was reflected pre-eminently in the writings of the 16th-century French philosophical essayist Michel de Montaigne. The 17th-century French philosopher René Descartes, who is often regarded as the founder of modern philosophy, used an extreme form of scepticism in order to establish secure foundations for knowledge. He began by trying to doubt everything he believed, and found that he could even doubt the existence of the world, but that he could not doubt his own existence, since the very act of doubting required the existence of himself as the doubter. He summarized his conclusion by stating his famous "*Cogito, ergo sum*" ("I think, therefore I am"). He then attempted to use this indubitable truth as the basis for his whole system of knowledge.

Descartes took up a sceptical position as a technique, in order to arrive at truths that it was impossible to doubt. However, since he believed that he could in the end arrive at such truths, and build a whole system of indubitable knowledge on them, he is not himself counted as a sceptic.

The greatest exponent of modern scepticism was the 18th-century Scottish empiricist philosopher David Hume. In his *Treatise of Human Nature* (1739-1740) and *An Enquiry Concerning Human Understanding* (1748), Hume questions the possibility of demonstrating the truth of beliefs about the external world, about causal connections, about future events, about morality, and about such metaphysical entities as the soul and God. The 18th-century German philosopher Immanuel Kant, while attempting to overcome Hume's scepticism, denied the possibility of knowing things in themselves or of achieving metaphysical knowledge. In the 19th century, the German philosopher Friedrich Nietzsche denied the possibility of complete objectivity, and thus of objective knowledge, in any field. The 20th-century American philosopher George Santayana, claiming to have taken Hume's scepticism a step further, maintained, in his work *Scepticism and Animal Faith* (1923), that belief in the existence of anything, including oneself, rests on a natural, but irrational impulse. Elements of scepticism may be found in other modern schools of philosophy, including pragmatism, analytic and linguistic philosophy, and existentialism.

In contemporary analytic philosophy, a variety of particular forms of scepticism have been explored, for example, scepticism about the existence of minds (*see* Solipsism). This is the view that each human being cannot be sure that other human beings have minds like their own rather than being merely automatons. Few philosophers would adopt such forms of scepticism seriously, although they are helpful if used in the way that Descartes did, as a tool. By imagining someone who holds a sceptical position, it is easier to identify the reasons against holding such a position, and to test how strong those reasons are.

Schema, (plural: schemata). See axiom schema, tautology schema, theorem schema.

Scholastic logic, traditional, scholastic, or aristotelian logic.

Schopenhauer, Arthur (1788-1860), German philosopher, who is known for his philosophy of pessimism. Born in Danzig (now Gdansk, Poland) on February 22, 1788, Schopenhauer was educated at the universities of Göttingen, Berlin, and Jena. He then settled in Frankfurt am Main, where he led a solitary life and became deeply involved in the study of Buddhist and Hindu philosophies and mysticism. He was also influenced by the ideas of the German Dominican theologian, mystic, and eclectic philosopher Meister Eckhart, the German theosophist and mystic

Jakob Boehme, and the scholars of the Renaissance and the Enlightenment. In his principal work, *The World as Will and Idea* (1819; trans. 1883), he proposed the dominant ethical and metaphysical elements of his atheistic and pessimistic philosophy.

Schopenhauer disagreed with the school of idealism and was strongly opposed to the ideas of the German philosopher G. W. F. Hegel, who believed in the spiritual nature of all reality. Instead, Schopenhauer accepted, with some qualification in details, the view of the German philosopher Immanuel Kant that phenomena exist only insofar as the mind perceives them, as ideas. He did not, however, agree with Kant that the "thing-in-itself" (*Ding an sich*), or the ultimate reality, lies hopelessly beyond experience. He identified it with experienced will instead. According to Schopenhauer, however, will is not limited to voluntary action with foresight; all the experienced activity of the self is will, including unconscious physiological functionings. This will is the inner nature of each experiencing being and assumes in time and space the appearance of the body, which is an idea. Starting from the principle that the will is the inner nature of his own body as an appearance in time and space, Schopenhauer concluded that the inner reality of all material appearances is will; the ultimate reality is one universal will.

For Schopenhauer the tragedy of life arises from the nature of the will, which constantly urges the individual towards the satisfaction of successive goals, none of which can provide permanent satisfaction for the infinite activity of the life force, or will. Thus, the will inevitably leads a person to pain, suffering, and death and into an endless cycle of birth, death, and rebirth, and the activity of the will can only be brought to an end through an attitude of resignation, in which the reason governs the will to the extent that striving ceases.

This conception of the source of life in will came to Schopenhauer through insights into the nature of consciousness as essentially impulsive. He revealed a strong Buddhist influence in his meta-physics and a successful confluence of Buddhist and Christian ideas in his ethical doctrines. From the epistemological point of view, Schopenhauer's ideas belonged to the school of phenomenology.

Renowned for his hostile attitude towards women, Schop-enhauer subsequently applied his insights to a consideration of the principles underlying human sexual activity, arguing that individuals are driven together not by feelings of sentimental love but by the irrational impulses of the will. The influence of Schopenhauer's philosophy may be seen in the early works of the German philosopher and poet Friedrich Wilhelm Nietzsche, in the musical dramas of the German composer Richard Wagner, and in much of the philosophical and artistic work of the 20th century. Schopenhauer died on September 21, 1860.

Science, Philosophy of, investigation into the general nature of scientific practice. The questions considered in the philosophy of science include: how scientific theories are developed, assessed, and changed; and whether science is capable of revealing the truth about hidden entities and processes in nature. The subject is as old and as widespread as science itself. Some scientists have taken a keen interest in the philosophy of science and a few, such as Galileo, Isaac Newton, and Albert Einstein, have made important contributions. Most scientists, however, have been content to leave the philosophy of science to the philosophers, preferring to get on with *doing* science rather than spending too much time considering in general terms how science *is done.* Among philo-sophers, the philosophy of science has always been a central subject. In the Western tradition, the most important figures before the 20th century include Aristotle, René Descartes, John Locke, David Hume, Immanuel Kant, and John Stuart Mill. Much of the philosophy of science is indistinguishable from epist-emology, the theory of knowledge, a subject considered by virtually every philosopher.

The Problem of Induction: The results of observation and experiment provide the evidence for a scientific theory, but they cannot prove that the theory is correct. Even the most modest empirical generalization, say, that all water boils at the same temperature, goes beyond what can be strictly deduced from the evidence. If scientific theories did not say more than the evidence used to support them, they would have little use. They could not be used to predict the course of nature, and they would have no explanatory power.

The nondemonstrative or inductive link between evidence and theory raises one of the central problems in the theory of knowledge, the problem of induction, given its classic formulation by the 18th-century Scottish philosopher David Hume. Hume considered simple predictions based on past observations, for example, the prediction that the Sun will rise tomorrow, given that it has been observed to rise in the past. Life would be impossible without anticipating the future, but Hume constructed a remarkable argument to show that these inferences are rationally indefensible. This con-clusion may be incredible, but Hume's argument has yet to be conclusively answered. He admitted that inductive inferences have been at least moderately reliable so far, or we would not be alive to consider the problem, but he claimed that we can only have a reason to continue to trust induction if we have some reason to believe that induction will continue to be reliable in future. Hume then argued that no such reason is possible. The nub of the problem is that the claim that induction will be reliable in future is itself a prediction, and so could only be justified inductively, which would beg the question. In particular, to argue that induction will probably work in future because it has worked in the past is to argue in a circle, assuming induction in order to justify it. If this sceptical argument is sound, indu-ctive knowledge appears impossible, and there is no rational argument we can give to dissuade someone who takes the view, say, that it is safer to leave the room by the window than by the door.

The problem of induction applies directly to science. Without some answer to Hume's argument, there is no reason to believe any part of a scientific theory that goes beyond what has actually been observed. The point is not that scientific theories are never absolutely certain: that is or ought to be a truism. The point is rather that we have no reason whatever for supposing, say, that water we have not tested will boil at the same temperature as water we have tested. Philosophers have made a sustained effort to resist this sceptical conclusion. Some have tried to show that scientists' standards for weighing evidence and making inference are somehow rational by definition; others that the past success of our inductive policies can be used to justify their future use without vicious circularity. A third approach is to argue that, while we cannot show that induction will work in future, we can show that it will work if any method of prediction does, so we are rational to use it. More recently, a number of philosophers have argued that the actual reliability of our inductive practices, something that Hume does not deny, is sufficient to yield inductive knowledge without a further requirement that the reliability be justified.

Karl Popper has offered a more radical solution to the problem of induction, a solution that forms the basis for his influential philosophy of science. According to Popper, Hume's argument that inductive inferences are rationally indefensible is simply correct. This does not, however, threaten the rationality of science, whose inferences are, appearances to the contrary, exclusively deductive. Popper's central idea is that while the evidence will never entail that a theory is true, it may refute the theory, entailing that it is false. Thus, no number of black ravens entails that all ravens are black, but a single white raven entails that the generalization is false. Scientists can thus know that a theory is false, without recourse to induction. Moreover, faced with a choice between two competing theories, they can exercise a rational preference, if one of the theories has been refuted but the other not, since it is rational to prefer a theory that might be true over one known to be false. Induction never enters the picture, so Hume's argument is defused.

This ingenious solution to the problem of induction faces a number of objections. If it were correct, scientists would never have any reason to believe that any of their theories or hypotheses are even approximately correct or that any of the predictions drawn from them are true, since these judgements could only be inductively justified. Moreover, it appears that Popper's position does not even allow scientists to know that a theory is false, since, according to him, the evidence that might contradict a theory can itself never be known to be correct. Unfortunately, the inductive inferences that scientists make seem neither avoidable nor justifiable.

The Problem of Description: Although Hume's discussion of the justification of induction is a milestone in the history of philosophy, he only offered a crude description of how, for better or worse, inductive practices actually work. He held that inductive inference is just habit formation. Having seen many black ravens, we tacitly apply the rule of "more of the same" and expect that the next raven we encounter will also be black. This clearly does not do justice to scientists' inferential practice, since they infer from the observation of entities of one sort to the existence and behaviour of entities of a quite different and often unobservable sort. "More of the same" will not take scientists from what is seen in the laboratory to the existence of electrons or electromagnetic fields. How then do scientists test their theories, weigh the evidence, and make inferences? This is the problem of *description* in contrast to Hume's problem of *justification*.

The descriptive problem may seem easy to solve: just ask scientists to describe what they do. This is an illusion. Scientists may be good at weighing evidence, but they are not good at giving a principled account of how they do it. This is no more surprising than the fact that native speakers of the English language are largely incapable of specifying the principles by which they distinguish grammatical from ungrammatical sentences. What is more surprising is how difficult the descriptive problem of induction has been to solve, even for philosophers of science who have devoted their careers to it.

Perhaps the most popular account of how scientific theories are tested is the *hypothetico-deductive* model, according to which theories are tested by checking the predictions they entail. Evidence that shows a prediction to be correct supports the theory, evidence incompatible with the prediction refutes the theory, and any other evidence is irrelevant. If scientists have enough supporting evidence and no refuting evidence, they may infer that the tested theory is correct. This model, rough though it is, seems at first to be a reasonable reflection of scientific practice, but it is beset with difficulties. Most of these show that the hypothetico-deductive model is over-permissive, treating irrelevant evidence as if it provided support. To mention just one problem, most scientific theories do not entail any observable consequences on their own, but only in conjunction with various background assumptions. Without some restriction on admissible assumptions, the model will permit any observation to count as evidence for almost any theory. This is an absurd result, but it is surprisingly difficult to specify the appropriate restrictions.

Given the difficulties facing the hypothetico-deductive model, some philosophers have lowered their sights and attempted to give a better model of inductive support for a more limited range of cases. The simplest case is an empirical generalization such as "all ravens are black". Here it seems clear that black ravens support the hypothesis, non-black ravens refute it, and non-ravens are irrelevant. Yet even this modest account has its problems. Suppose we apply the same sort of account to the slightly odd-sounding hypothesis that all non-black things are not ravens. Non-black non-ravens (white flowers, for example) support it, non-black ravens would refute it, and black objects are irrelevant. The trouble comes when we notice that this hypothesis is equivalent to the original raven hypothesis: to say that all non-black things are non-ravens is just an unusual way of saying that all ravens are black. So surely whatever evidence supports the one hypothesis supports the other? This leaves us, however, with the extremely odd result that the observation of white flowers provides evidence that all ravens are black. This raven paradox seems a logical trick, but it has proved remarkably difficult to resolve.

Explanation: Recent work on the problem of describing inferential practices in science has attempted to avoid the weaknesses of the hypotheticodeductive model by going beyond logical relations to account for the bearing of evidence on theory. Some accounts attempt to describe how the plausibility of theories and hypotheses may vary in advance of testing, and have linked this idea to a formal calculus of probabilities. Others appeal to the specific content of hypotheses under test, especially the causal claims many of them make. In the 19th century, John Stuart Mill gave an account of inferences from effects to causes that can be expanded to provide a model of scientific inference. One way the expansion has been attempted is by appeal to the notion of explanation. The basic idea of the model of "inference to the best explanation" is that scientists infer from the available evidence to the hypothesis that would, if correct, provide the best explanation of that evidence.

If "inference to the best explanation" is to be more than a slogan, however, some independent account of scientific explanation is required. The starting point for most contemporary philosophical work on the nature of scientific explanation is the *deductivenomological* model, according to which a scientific explanation is a deduction of a description of the phenomenon to be explained from a set of premises that includes at least one law of nature. Thus, one might explain why the mercury in a thermometer rose by citing the rise in temperature and a law linking temperature and volume for the metal. One challenge for this account is to question what makes something a law of nature, another central topic in the philosophy of science. Not all true generalizations are laws of nature. For example, the statement that all gold spheres have a diameter of less than ten miles is presumably true but is not a law. Genuine laws of nature appear to have a kind of necessity that the statement about gold spheres lacks. They describe not just how things actually behave but how in some sense they must behave. It is, however, far from obvious how that notion of necessity should be articulated.

Another difficulty for the deductive-nomological model of explanation is that, like the hypothetico-deductive account of testing to which it bears a striking structural similarity, the model is too permissive. For example, the period (the duration of one swing) of a particular pendulum can be deduced from the law that relates to the period and length of pendulums in general, together with the length of that particular pendulum. The length of the pendulum is normally regarded as *explaining* the period. However, the deduction can be carried out in the reverse direction: it is possible to calculate the length of the pendulum if its period is known. But the period is not normally regarded as *explaining* the length of the pendulum. So while the deduction works in both directions, explanation is regarded as going in one direction only. Difficulties of this sort have led some philosophers to develop causal models of explanation, according to which we explain events by giving information about their causal histories. This approach is attractive, but it calls for an analysis of causation, a project that faces many of the same difficulties as that of analysing laws of nature. In addition, more needs to be said about which causes of an event explain it. The Big Bang is presumably part of the causal history of every event, but does not provide an adequate explanation for most of them. Once again, there is a problem of excessive permissiveness.

Realism and Instrumentalism: One of the aims of science is to "save the phenomena", to construct theories that entail a correct description of the observable aspects of the world. Of particular importance is the ability to predict what is observable but not yet observed, since accurate prediction makes possible the application of science to technology. What is more controversial is whether science ought also to aspire to the truth about what is unobservable, for the sake of understanding the world even if not for any practical purpose. Those who claim that science should and does reveal the hidden structure of the world are known as *realists*. For them, theories attempt to describe that structure. By contrast, those who say that the job of science is only to save the observable phenomena are known as *instrumentalists*, since for them theories are not descriptions of the invisible world but instruments for predictions about the observable world. The dispute between realists and instrumentalists has been a constant theme in the history of the philosophy of science.

Scientific realists do not claim that all of current science is correct, but they do typically claim that the best current theories are approximately true, that most of the entities they refer to really exist, and that in the history of science later theories in a given domain have generally been closer to the truth than the theories they replaced. For realists, scientific progress consists centrally in generating increasingly accurate and extensive descriptions of a largely invisible world.

Some instrumentalists deny that theories can describe unobservable aspects of the world on the grounds that meaning cannot be given to descriptions of what cannot be observed. On this view, high-level theories are calculational devices without literal meaning: they are no more descriptions of the world than are the circuits in an electronic calculator. Other instrumentalists have claimed that theories are descriptions, but only of the observable world. Talk of atomic particles and gravitational fields is really just a shorthand for descriptions of pointer readings and observable motion. The most influential contemporary version of instrumentalism, known as *constructive empiricism*, adopts a third approach. The meaning of theories is to be taken at face value. If a theory appears to tell a story about invisible particles, then that is the story it does tell. Scientists, however, are never entitled or required to believe that these stories are true. The most that can or need be known is that a theory's observable consequences—past, present, and future—are true. The truth of the remainder of the theory is as may be: all that matters is that the theory tells a story that yields only true predictions concerning what could in principle be observed.

The debate between realists and instrumentalists has generated arguments on each side. Some realists have mounted a "no-miracle" argument. The realist and the instrumentalist agree that our best theories in the physical sciences have enjoyed remarkable predictive success. The realist maintains that this success would be a miracle if the theories were not at least appr-oximately true. From a logical point of view it is possible that an entirely false story about invisible entities and processes could entail all those true predictions, but this is extremely improbable and hence irrational to believe. Suppose that you are given a highly detailed map, which purports to describe in great detail the forest you are in, including many inac-cessible gorges and mountain peaks. You check the map in many different spots, and in each case what you see is just as the map portrays it. It remains possible that the map is quite incorrect in those areas which you have not checked, but this is not likely. The realist maintains that the situation is analogous for any well-tested scientific theory.

Instrumentalists have raised a number of objections to the no-miracle argument. Some have claimed that it begs the question, much as does the argument considered above, that induction will work in future because it has worked in the past. To infer from the observed success of a scientific theory to the truth of its claims about unobservable aspects of the world is to use precisely the form of inference whose legitimacy the instrumentalist denies. Another objection is that the truth of current science is not in fact the best explanation of its observational success. According to this objection, Popper was right at least to claim that science develops through the weeding out of theories that fail the test of prediction. Small wonder then that the theories we now accept have been predictively successful: if they had not been, we would not now accept them. Thus, it is claimed, the hypothesis that our theories are true is not needed to explain their predictive success. Finally, some instrumentalists appeal to what is known as the *underdetermination of theory by data.* No matter how much evidence is available, we know that there are in principle innumerably many theories, incompatible with each other but all compatible with that evidence. At most, one of those theories can be true. Surely, the objection goes, it is unlikely that the successful theory we happen to have thought of is that one. From this point of view, what would be miraculous is not that the successful theories scientists come up with are false, but that they are true.

One of the most popular of recent arguments for instrumentalism is "pessimistic induction". From the point of view of present science, almost all sophisticated theories more than, say, 50 years old, can be seen to be false. This is often suppressed in the way the history of science is presented in elementary science textbooks, but, for example, from the standpoint of contemporary physics, Kepler was wrong to claim that the planets move in ellipses and

Newton was wrong to claim that an object's mass is independent of its velocity. But if all past theories have been found to be incorrect, then the only reasonable inference is that all or virtually all present theories will be found to be wrong 50 years hence. In contrast to this discontinuity in the history of theories, there has been according to the instrumentalist a steady and largely cumulative growth in the scope and accuracy of their observable predictions. They have become increasingly better at saving the phenomena, their only proper job.

There have been various responses to pessimistic induction. Most realists have accepted both the premise that past theories have been strictly false, and the conclusion that present theories are likely to be false as well. They have, however, insisted that all this is compatible with the central realist claim that later theories tend to be better descriptions of the world than those they replace. Some realists have also accused the instrumentalists of exaggerating the degree of discontinuity in the history of science. The strength of an inference from past to present falsity may also be questioned. According to realists, current theories have replaced their predecessors precisely because they give a much better treatment of increasingly extensive and precise evidence, so it is unclear why the weaknesses of the old theories should count against their successors.

Objectivity and Relativism: Although realists and instru-mentalists disagree over the power of science to describe the invisible world, they almost all agree that science is objective, because it rests on objective evidence. Although some experimental results are inevitably mistaken, the history of evidence is largely cumulative, in contrast to the history of high-level theories. In short, scientists replace theories but add to the data. This view of the objectivity and autonomy of the observational evidence for scientific theories has, however, come under attack, especially in the past 30 years.

The objectivity of evidence has been rejected on the grounds that scientific evidence is inevitably contaminated by scientific theories. It is not just that scientists tend to see what they want to see, but that scientific observation is only possible in the context of particular theoretical presuppositions. Observation is "theory-laden". On an extreme version of this view, theories cannot be tested, since the evidence will always presuppose the very theory it is supposed to test. More moderate versions allow for some notion of empirical test, but still introduce historical discontinuities in the evidence to parallel the disco-ntinuities at the theoretical level. If sense can still be made of scientific progress, it cannot be in terms of the accumulation of knowledge, whether theoretical or observational.

If the nature of the evidence changes as scientific theories change, and the evidence is our only access to the empirical facts, then perhaps the facts change too. This is relativism about science, whose most influential recent proponent is Thomas Kuhn. Like the great 18th-century German philosopher Immanuel Kant, Kuhn holds that the world that science investigates must be a world partially constituted by the minds of those who study it. This notion of the human constitution of the world is not easy to grasp. It is not quite the same as the classic idealist view that particular "physical" objects are really just actual or possible ideas, but it does entail that something counts as a physical object or as an object of a certain type, say a star or a planet, only insofar as people so categorize it. For Kant, the mind's contribution to the structure of the world is substantial and unchanging. It consists of very general categories such as space, time, and causation. For Kuhn, the contribution is equally substantial, but also highly variable, since the nature of the contribution is determined by the particular theories and practices of a scientific discipline at a particular time. When those theories and practices change, for example, in the transition from Newtonian mechanics to Einstein's theories, so does the structure of the world those theories are about. The picture of scientists discovering more and more about a mind-independent reality is here completely rejected.

Although metaphysically radical, Kuhn's account of science is in one respect epistemologically conservative. For him, the causes of scientific change are almost exclusively intellectual and internal to a narrow community of scientific specialists. There are, however, other recent forms of relativism about science that reject this internalist perspective, insisting that the major causes of scientific change include social, cultural, and political factors that extend well beyond the confines of the laboratory. Since there is no reason to believe that these highly variable factors are conducive to the discovery of the truth, this "social constructivist" view of science is perhaps even more hostile to scientific realism than is the Kuhnian position.

Scientific realists have not taken these challenges lying down. Some have accused the relativists of adopting what amounts to a self-refuting position. If, as is claimed, there is no such thing as truth, then that claim cannot be true either. Realists have also questioned the philosophy of language that lies behind Kuhn's claim that successive scientific theories refer to different entities and phenomena, and also argued that the social constructivists have exaggerated the long-term influence of noncognitive factors on the development of science. But the debate over whether science is a process of discovery or invention is as old as the history of science and philosophy, and there is no firm resolution in sight. Here, as elsewhere, philosophers have been much more successful at revealing difficulties than at resolving them. Fortunately, an appreciation of how scientific practice resists explanation may itself illuminate the nature of science.

Scientific law, a general scientific hypothesis that is true or (more weakly understood) well confirmed or established. On realist conceptions the laws of science are generally regarded as expressing the [causal laws according to which all occurs, or by which all is governed. See cause, deter-minism.

Scientific realism, view that holds that reality really is as science describes it or as science ultimately would describe it at the ideal end-point of inquiry. Contrast: instrumentalism.

Scientific theory, a logically closely interconnected set of scientific laws.

Scientism, the view according to which the methods of the natural or phsyical sciences are universally valid, and therefore should apply to the "social sciences" and the humanities as well. Scientism is often roughly equivalent to reductionism, since the outcome for the study of human and social affairs of applying each of these approaches is much the same.

Second-order desire, desire about desires, that is, desire of the form "*S* wants *x*" where *x* is a desire.

Secularism, the view according to which there exist no gods or purely spiritual entities. Sometimes the sense of the word is less strong, connoting something close to humanism, *i.e.*, that affairs of this world should be the most important concerns for ethics and human life (it is in this sense that Aristotelianism and other classical philosophies can be described assecularist). Thus, while atheism is a form of secularism, not every secularist is an atheist. In popular usage, secularism often has the same connotations of immoralism that are imputed more strongly to atheism. (References from atheism, Christianity, humanism, and pessi-mism.)

Semantic, semantics

Semantic completeness, The condition of a formal system in which (1) the formal language has the power to express as wffs all the propositions intended by the maker to be meaningful, and (2) the deductive apparatus has the power to prove as theorems all the propositions intended by the maker to be true. The second condition can be put more succinctly: all logically valid wffs of the language are theorems of the system. The first of these is also called expressive completeness; the second is called deductive complete-ness. Semantic incompleteness

Failure of semantic completeness, but especially when not all logically valid wffs are theorems.

Semantic consequence, 1. In truth-functional propositional logic, *B* is the Semantic consequence of *A* iff there is no interpretation, I, in which *A* is true for I and B is false for I, or in short, if all models of *A* are models of *B*.

2. In predicate logic, B is the semantic consequence of *A* iff for every interpretation, every sequence that satisfies *A* also satisfies *B*. Or, thereis no sequence in any interpretation that satisfies *A* but not *B*. Notation: $A \models B$. See satisfaction

Semantic gap, The difference between the complex operations performed by high-level language constructs and the simple ones provided by computer instruction sets. It was in an attempt to try to close this gap that computer architects designed increasingly complex instruction set computers.

Semantics, 1. the meaning of a string in some language, as opposed to syntax which describes how symbols may be combined independent of their meaning.

The semantics of a programming language is a function from programs to answers. A program is a closed term and, in practical languages, an answer is a member of the syntactic category of values. The two main kinds are denotational semantics and operational semantics.

2. the study of relations between a representation and what it represents. See also naturalised semantics.

Semantic tautology, A wff of truth-functional propositional logic whose truth table column contains nothing but T's when these are interpreted as the truth-value Truth. See syntactic tautology.

Semantic validity, An inference is semantically valid iff it cannot be the case that all the premises are true and the conclusion false at the same time. See syntactic validity.

Sensationalism, radical form of representationalism which posits that all knowledge is constructed from or consists in pure sensations (such as blotches of color, pure tones, etc.). Some adherents go further and claim that we do not have any direct knowledge of reality, only of sensations. The popular meaning is obviously non-philosophical and quite unrelated.

Sensations, what we experience directly—such as shapes, colors, and smells—in perceptual expe-rience. Roughly identifiable, with Locke's "simple ideas" and Hume's "impressions". For Kant these are the "matter" of perception for which time and space are the a priori forms. Among contemporary philosophers, sensations (or their distinctive "felt" properties) are commonly called "qualia." Among the presumed contents of the mind, sensations (being concrete and particular) stand in contrast to (abstract and general, or universal]) concepts: compare the experience of seeing red to the idea of redness.

Sense, the property of representations of a part of the world that captures that part as being a certain way; meaning.

Senses, metaphorically, "the doors of perception" (Wm. Blake): the input channels by which the mind] is affected by the external world. Following Aristotle, traditionally, there are said to be five: taste, touch, smell, hearing, and sight. See perceive.

Sentence, A collection of clauses. See also closure, wff, proposition

Seven Wise Men of Greece, also known as the Seven Sages, Greek sages of the 7th and 6th centuries BC who were active in science, philosophy, and politics. Although their identities differ in some accounts, the seven sages usually appear as Bias of Priene, Chilon of Sparta, Cleobulus of Lindus, Periander of Corinth, Pittacus of Mitylene, Solon of Athens, and Thales of Miletus.

Simple consistency, A system is simply consistent iff there is no wff *A* such that both *A* and ~*A* are theorems.

Simple inconsistency, A system is simply inconsistent if there is some wff *A* such that both *A* and ~*A* are theorems.

Simple propositions, A proposition whose internal structure does not interest us; hence a proposition whose internal structure we do not make visible in our notation. Notation: *p, q, r*, etc.

Simulated annealing, A technique which can be applied to any minimisation or learning process based on successive update steps (either random or deterministic) where the update step length is proportional to an arbitrarily set parameter which can play the role of a temperature. Then, in analogy with the annealing of metals, the temperature is made high in the early stages of the process for faster minimisation or learning, then is reduced for greater stability.

Singleton, singleton variable

Singleton variable, A variable which is only referred to once in a piece of code, probably because of a programming mistake. To be useful, a variable must be set and read from, in that order. If it is only referred to once then it cannot be both set and read.

There are various exceptions. C-like assignment operators, *e.g.* "*x* += *y*", read and set *x* and return its new value (they are abbreviations for "*x* = *x*+*y*", etc). A function argument may be passed only for the sake ofuniformity or to support future enhancements. A good compiler or a syntax checker like lint should report singleton variables but also allow specific instances to be marked as deliberate by the programmer.

Skepticism, the philosophic theory that no knowledge can be attained either in general, or (more commonly) with regard to specific categories of presumed knowledge—*e.g.*, Hume's skepticism about our knowledge of presumed necessary connections between things we judge to be causally related.

Skolemisation, A means of removing quantifiers from first order logic-formulas. See Skolem normal form.

Skolem normal form, A wff of predicate logic is in Skolem normal form iff (1) it is in prenex normal form, (2) it contains no function symbols,and (3) all existential quantifiers are to the left of all universal quantifiers. See prenex normal form

Skolem paradox, The paradox that results from the L"wenheim-Skolem theorem (LST). Does LST mean that the real numbers have the same cardinality as the natural numbers? Does it mean that the difference between the real numbers and the natural numbers that explains the greater cardinality of the reals cannot in principle be described or proved? Does it mean that no set is "absolutely" uncountable but only "relatively" to a given set of axioms and a given interpretation?

Social constructivism, view marked by its rejection of the objectivity of truth, generally, and of scientific truth in particular. Constructivists hold that scientific laws, descriptions, and even observations are social constructs—products or projections of human cultures or communities. As such, they are thoroughly theory laden and vary between cultures. Consequently scientific truth is neither objective nor universal. Contrast: objective truth. Compare theory laden, theory neutral.

Social contract, implied covenant between individuals] by which each foregoes certain freedoms (to prey on others) in exchange for certain rights (not to be preyed on) which social contract theorists (most notably Thomas Hobbes, John Locke, and Jean Jacques Rousseau) propose the legitimacy of government derives. Contrast: anarchism.

Social Darwinism, movement of thought that started in the late nineteenth century as an application of Charles Darwin's insights to human affairs; its most (in)famous exponent was Herbert Spencer. Social Darwinism holds that the principle of "the survival of the fittest" applies to human ethics and politics just as it does to biological evolution. Left-leaning critics often allege that social Darwinism provides an accurate description of—or an inexcusable attempt at justification for—life under capitalism.

Socrates (c. 470-c. 399 BC), Greek philosopher, who shaped Western philosophy, although he left no writings of his own. His pupil Plato wrote dialogues purporting to describe Socrates's views and actions. These are the principal source for Socrates's ideas and influence, though Plato sometimes ascribed his own views to his master. The historian Xenophon also wrote dialogues involving Socrates, and he is mentioned in other Greek works.

Life: Born in Athens, the son of Sophroniscus, a sculptor, and Phaenarete, a midwife, Socrates was reportedly short and unattractive, but extremely hardy and self-controlled. He received a typical education in literature, music, and gymnastics, and later familiarized himself with the rhetoric and dialectics of the sophists, the speculations of the Ionian philosophers, and the general culture of Periclean Athens. He married Xanthippe, an Athenian woman, with whom he had three children.

Initially, Socrates followed the craft of his father. He also served with the other male citizens of Athens in the Peloponnesian War with Sparta, acting bravely as an infantryman at the battles of Potidaea in 432-430 BC, Delium in 424 BC, and Amphipolis in 422 BC.

However, according to Plato's *Apology,* his life was given its guiding purpose when a friend asked the oracle at Delphi whether anyone was wiser than Socrates, to which the oracle answered "no". Socrates then devoted his life to talking at the public places in Athens with people claiming knowledge, and trying to help them understand their ignorance, as he came to understand his own, for the sake of their souls.

Ideas: Although Socrates claimed only to know that he was ignorant, in arguments he developed a number of distinctive ethical views in the form of paradoxes. These included the ideas that virtue was knowledge; that no one does wrong willingly, but only out of ignorance; and that it is better to be wronged than to wrong someone else. These ideas, particularly the last, which bars retaliation, were quite foreign to the conventional public culture of Athens at the time. Socrates emphasized rational argument, concern with one's soul, and the search for definitions of ethical ideas. As important as these ideas was his method of engaging in argument, which often involved an ironic stance towards the claims of his interlocutors, known as Socratic irony.

These concerns profoundly influenced the next generations of philosophers, however much they differed from one another. Socrates's pupil, Plato, and Plato's pupil, Aristotle, sought to extend Socratic dialogue while searching for the definitions Socrates never found and allowing for the irrational elements of the soul that he excluded. Antisthenes, a friend of Socrates, founded the Cynic school of philosophy, which taught life according to nature and not convention.

Another pupil of Socrates, Aristippus, founded the Cyrenaic

philosophy of experience and pleasure, from which developed the philosophy of Epictetus. To such Stoics as the Roman philosopher Seneca the Elder and the Roman emperor Marcus Aurelius, Socrates appeared as the very embodiment of and guide to a life in accordance with wisdom rather than passion.

The Trial: Socrates's self-described role as the public "gadfly" of Athens made him unpopular with many citizens. He may have been seen as being in some way responsible for the aristocratic revolt against the democracy in 404 BC, which led to a brief reign of terror in which some of his students and friends participated. He was certainly ridiculed as one of the sophists by the comic poet Aristophanes in his play *The Clouds*, although Socrates himself saw the sophists as dangerous opponents, willing to teach anything for a fee and argue without sincerity.

Perhaps for these reasons, he was charged in 399 BC with neglecting the established gods and introducing new divinities, a reference to the *daemonion*, or mystical inner voice, which he often claimed guided his actions; and with corrupting the morals of the young. Plato's *Apology* depicts Socrates's own defence at his trial, which sought to vindicate his role in the city and his commitment to philosophy. He was found guilty by only a small majority, and in accordance with Athenian legal practice, was given the chance to propose his own counter-penalty to the death sentence demanded by his prosecutors. However, his proposal that he simply be fined, in view of his value to the city as a philosopher, so incensed the jury that it voted by an increased majority for the death penalty.

Socrates's friends wanted to help him escape from prison, but in Plato's *Crito* he argues with one of them that his commitment to philosophy and his own principles make it better for him to suffer the wrong of execution than to wrong the city. Plato's *Phaedo* describes his last day and the calm way in which he drank the hemlock, which was the customary procedure of execution. The manner of Soc-rates's life and his death both contributed to making him a model of the rational, enquiring, and fearless philosopher for future generations.

Socraticism, Socraticism is not a word that pops up very often (even in philosophy). It refers to either of two things: Socrates' position of intell-ectualism in ethics, or his method of asking questions in order to arrive at universal definitions of concepts such as courage and justice (what's come to be known as the "Socratic method"). His intellectualism has not been very influential, but his methodology forms the foundation of Western philosophy. The legacy of Socrates was transmitted through the works of Plato and Aristotle, who continued on the paths he started and who are sometimes called Socratic phil-osophers. Socrates is also a cent-ral figure of Western humanism, since he insisted that the central concerns of philosophy must be ethics and the good life, not technical issues that are of little or no interest to human beings in general.

Solipsism, subjectivism and relativism taken to the extreme: the solipsist is so consistent about his doctrine that he claims that he cannot know if physical reality or other human beings even exist. The solipsist believes knowledge is so subjective that "all I can really know is myself". (References from relativism, skepticism, and subjectivism.)

Sophists (Greek *sophistes*, "expert, master craftsman, man of wisdom"), originally, name applied by the ancient Greeks to learned men, such as the Seven Wise Men of Greece; in the 5th century BC, a name applied to itinerant teachers who provided instruction in several higher branches of learning for a fee.

Individuals sharing a broad philosophical outlook rather than a school, the sophists popularized the ideas of various early philosophers; but, based on their understanding of this prior philosophical thought, most of them concluded that truth and morality were essentially matters of opinion. Thus, in their own teaching, they tended to emphasize forms of persuasive expression, such as the art of rhetoric, which provided pupils with skills useful for achieving success in life, particularly public life.

The sophists were popular for a time, especially in Athens; however, their sceptical view on absolute truth and morality eventually provoked sharp criticism. Socrates, Plato, and Aristotle challenged the philosophical basis of the Sophists' teaching, and Plato and Aristotle further condemned them for taking money.. Later, they were accused by the state of lacking morality. As a result, the word *sophist* acquired a derogatory meaning, as in the modern term *sophistry*, which can be defined as subtle and deceptive or false argumentation or reasoning.

The sophists were of minor importance in the development of Western philosophical thought. They were, however, the first to systematize education. Leading 5th-century sophists included Protagoras, Gorgias, Hippias of Elis, and Prodicus of Ceos.

Soundness, An argument or inference is sound iff its reasoning is valid and all its premises are true. It is unsound otherwise, *i.e.* if either its reasoning is invalid, or at least one premise is false, or both.

Specialization, A reduction in generality, usually for the sake of increase-defficiency. If a piece of code is specialised for certain values of certain variables (usually function arguments), this is known as "partial evaluation". In a language with overloading (*e.g.* Haskell), an overloaded function might be specialised to a non-overloaded instance at compile-time if the types of its arguments are known.

Spinoza, Baruch or **Benedict** (1632-1677), Dutch rationalist philosopher and religious thinker, who is regarded as the most complete modern exponent of pantheism. Born of Spanish-Portuguese Jewish parents in Amsterdam on November 24, 1632, Spinoza was carefully educated in classical Jewish sources. Later, however, he became alienated from established Judaism as a result of his studies of physical science and the writings of the English philosopher Thomas Hobbes and the French scientist and philosopher René Descartes. He withdrew from the synagogue and in 1656 was excommunicated by the rabbis, who secured his banishment from Amsterdam.

For five years Spinoza remained on the outskirts of the city, supporting himself as a grinder of optical lenses. During this period he wrote his first philosophical work, *Tractatus de Deo et Homine Ejusque Felicitate* (Treatise on God and Man and His Happiness), in which the outlines of his developed philosophical system are foreshadowed. The *Tractatus Theologico-Politicus* (Theologicopolitical Treatise) and the dissertation *De Intellectus Eme-ndatione* (On the Improvement of Understanding) were also probably written during this period, although the former was not published until 1670 and the latter until 1677. In 1661 Spinoza went to Rijnsburg, a town near Leiden, and two or three years later to Voorburg, not far from The Hague. Shortly afterwards, on moving to The Hague itself, he was offered a chair in philosophy at the University of Heidelberg by Charles Louis, elector Palatine. Spinoza declined the post, however, in order to be free from any restrictions on his intellectual activities that might be made by theologians. Spinoza also rejected a pension offered to him by Louis XIV, King of France, on the condition that he dedicate one of his works to the monarch.

Philosophy: Spinoza's fullest expression is his great work *Ethica Ordine Geometrico Demonstrata* (Ethics Demonstrated with Geometrical Order, published by his friends in 1677). According to this treatise the universe is identical with God, who is the uncaused "substance" of all things. The con-ception of substance, which Spinoza derived from the scholastic philosophers, is not that of a material reality but rather of a metaphysical entity, the comprehensive and self-sufficient basis for all reality. Spinoza conceded the possible existence of infinite attributes of substance, but held that only two are accessible to the human mind, namely, extension, or the world of material things, and conscious thought. Thought and extension are considered to depend on and exist in an ultimate reality, that is, God. Causation, in Spinoza's system, may exist between individual objects (that is, between physical bodies) in the attribute extension, or between individual ideas in the attribute thought, but not between objects and ideas. To explain the apparent causal interactions between objects and ideas, Spinoza advanced a theory known as parallelism, according to which every idea has a physical counterpart and, similarly, every physical object has a corresponding idea.

The individuality of things, whether physical objects or ideas, Spinoza explained as particular modes of substance. All particular objects are the modes of God in the attribute extension; all particular ideas are the modes of God in the attribute thought. The modes are *natura naturata,* "nature begotten", or nature in the multiplicity of its manifestations; substance or God is *natura naturans,* "nature begetting", or nature in its creative unity, acting as the determiner of its own modes. The modes are transitory, and their existence assumes temporal form; God is eternal, transcending all modal changes. Particular things accordingly, whether of extension or of thought, are finite and fleeting. Spinoza maintained, nevertheless, that an indestructible world does exist.

This world is not to be found in the realm of existing things but in that of essence. Humanity's intuitive knowledge of God is the source of a spiritual love of God (*amor Dei intellectualis*), which in turn is a part of the love in which God loves himself.

Spinoza's conception of essences is closely related to the scholastic conception of "reals" and to the archetypal ideas that Plato proposed, although it differs from both in certain important respects. Spinoza conceived essences as *hypostatizations* (conceptual entities) of the universal aspect of all things. The fundamental difference between existences and essences in Spinoza's cosmology is that the former have their being in time, but the latter are outside of time. Because mortality can pertain only to things subject to the law of time, the realm of essences, being timeless, must consequently be eternal. Nevertheless, the realm of essences is a realm of immanent being.

Every existence has, as previously indicated, a universal or essential character, although to realize this character the existent thing must transcend its own intrinsic form, that is, free itself from the boundaries of its own structure. The realm of essences thus has a kind of being within the realm of existences (the former being the immanent cause of the latter), although it does not share its temporal limitation. Immanent causation, according to Spinoza's metaphysics, means self-causation, and that which is self-determined is free. From this reasoning Spinoza developed his doctrine of freedom as a good to be won only in the realm of essences. Existence in either attribute (extension or thought) is bondage, for each existent thing is determined by its own causal series; every particular object or idea is subject to other objects or ideas, and the form of its being is determined by them. Only in nontemporal, self-caused being, that is, in the universal and immanent, is complete freedom possible; only by identification with substance, or God, is immortality, and with it peace, obtained.

Rejection of the Traditional: Spinoza rejected providence and freedom of will, and his concept of an impersonal God was hostilely received by many of his contemporaries. His position in the history of philosophy is in many respects unique. He belonged to no school and founded none. Although to some extent his work was based on that of a few of his predecessors, it is too strikingly individual to be regarded as a mere continuation, even of the thought of Descartes. In the depth and grandeur of his conception, and in his remarkable power of synthesis, Spinoza ranks with the greatest philosophical thinkers. It was not until a century after his death, on February 21, 1677, that his thought gained recognition, and although his system gave rise to no organized following, he has had perhaps the most pervasive influence of all modern philosophers with the exception of Immanuel Kant. Not only metaphysicians but poets such as Goethe, William Wordsworth, and Percy Shelley have consulted the works of Spinoza for inspiration, and his thought has influenced the poetic pantheism of many modern interpretations of nature.

Standard semantics, The standard interpretation of a term in some language yields the term's standard denotational semantics, *i.e.* its "meaning". This is usually given by a semantic function which maps a term in the abstract syntax to a point in some domain. The domain is the interpretation of the term's type. The semantic function also takes an environment—a function which maps the free variables of the term to their meaning. We say that a domain point "denotes", or "is the denotation of", a term. A non-standard semantics results from some other interpretation, *e.g.* an abstract interpretation.

State, How something is; its con-figuration, attributes, condition, or information content. The state of a system is usually temporary (*i.e.* it changes with time) and volatile (*i.e.* it will be lost or reset to some initial state if the system is switched off).

A state may be considered to be a point in some space of all possible states. A simple example is a light, which is either on or off. A complex example is the electrical activation in a human brain while solving a problem.

In computing and related fields, states, as in the light example, are often modelled as being discrete (rather than continuous) and the transition from one state to another is considered to be instantaneous. Another (related) property of *a system is the number of possible states it may exhibit.*

This may be finite or infinite. A common model for a system with a finite number of discrete state is a finite state machine.

State transition diagram, A diagram consisting of circles to represent states and directed line segments to represent transitions between the states. One or more actions (outputs) may be associated with each transition. The diagram represents a finite state machine.

Stoicism, school of philosophy, founded in ancient Greece, opposed to Epicureanism in its views of life and duty. The Stoic philosophy was developed from that of the Cynics, whose Greek founder, Antisthenes, had been a disciple of Socrates.

History: The Stoic school was established in Athens about 300 BC by Zeno of Citium. Zeno, who derived much of his philosophy from Crates of Thebes, opened his school in a colonnade known as the *Stoa Poikile* ("painted porch"). Among his disciples was Cleanthes of Assos in the Troad (an area surrounding ancient Troy), whose surviving "Hymn to Zeus" sets forth the unity, omnipotence, and moral government of the supreme deity. Cleanthes was followed by Chrysippus of Soli in Cilicia. These three men represent the first period (300-200 BC) of Stoic philosophy.

The second period (200-50 BC) embraced the general promulgation of the philosophy and its introduction to the Romans. Chrysippus was succeeded by Zeno of Tarsus and Diogenes of Babylonia; then followed Antipater of Tarsus, who taught Panaetius of Rhodes. Panaetius introduced Stoicism to Rome; among Panaetius' pupils was Posidonius of Apamea in Syria, who was the teacher of the orator Marcus Tullius Cicero.

The third period of Stoicism was Roman. In this period outstanding Stoics included Cato the Younger and, during the Roman Empire, the three Stoic philosophers whose writings have survived, namely, Lucius Annaeus Seneca, Epictetus, and the emperor Marcus Aurelius.

Principles: Stoicism was the most influential philosophy in the Roman Empire during the period preceding the rise of Christianity. The Stoics, like the Epicureans, emphasized ethics as the main field of knowledge, but they also developed theories of logic and natural science to support their ethical doctrines. Their most important contribution to logic was the discovery of the hypothetical syllogism. They held that all reality is material, but that matter proper, which is passive, is to be distinguished from the animating or active principle, logos, which they conceived as both the divine reason and as simply a finer kind of material entity, an all-pervading breath or fire, such as the Greek philosopher Heraclitus had supposed the cosmic principle to be. According to them the human soul is a manifestation of the logos. Living according to nature or reason, they held, is living in conformity with the divine order of the universe. The importance of this view is seen in the part that Stoicism played in developing a theory of natural law that powerfully affected Roman jurisprudence.

The foundation of Stoic ethics is the principle, proclaimed earlier by the Cynics, that good lies not in external objects, but in the state of the soul itself, in the wisdom and restraint by which a person is delivered from the passions and desires that perturb the ordinary life. The four cardinal virtues of the Stoic philosophy are wisdom, courage, justice, and temperance, a classification derived from the teachings of Plato.

A distinctive feature of Stoicism is its cosmopolitanism. All people are manifestations of the one universal spirit and should, according to the Stoics, live in brotherly love and readily help one another. They held that external differences such as rank and wealth are of no importance in social relationships. Thus, before the rise of Christianity, Stoics recognized and advocated the brotherhood of humanity and the natural equality of all human beings.

Stroke function, The dyadic truth function "not both". One of only two dyadic truth functions capable of expressing all truth functions by itself. Notation: p|q. Also called the Sheffer stroke, and alternative denial. See dagger function.

Subjective, something is subjective insofar as it is dependent on either a particular human mind or minds in general. See also objective

Subjectivism, an extreme version of relativism, which maintains that each person's beliefs are relative to that person alone and cannot be judged from the outside by any other person.

Subjectivity, the property of being subjective.

Sublimation, the redirection, according to Freud, of antisocial sexual and aggressive impulses into socially constructive activity. Compare: repression.

Substance, technically (for Leibniz, Spinoza, Descartes, et. al.)—a self-subsistent entity or thing, not depending on anything (except, possibly God) for its existence: also, the ultimate bearer of attributes or properties. In a somewhat looser sense (closer to Aristotle's) "sub-stance" is used to refer to the individuals which are the bearers of attributes or havers of properties as opposed to the attributes or properties—universals—that they have or which inhere in them.

Substance dualism, the view that the mental and the physical comprise two different classes of objects: minds and bodies.

Perhaps the most famous proponent of substance dualism was Descartes, who cashed out the distinction between minds and bodies as follows: minds are things that think but lack spatial magnitude, and bodies are things that have spatial magnitudes, but don't think. Different substance dualists may disagree as to how best to define what's essential to being mental and physical, but they do agree that the difference in question is one of objects, not properties. So, for example, my belief that the Eiffel tower is in France and my being six feet tall are properties of different objects, *i.e.*, my mind and my body, respectively. See property dualism

Substantialism, essentialism

Sufficient reason, principle formulated by Leibniz according to which, for whatever is the case, there is a sufficient reason why it is the case. Closely akin to this is the Law of Universal Causation, according to which every event has a cause. See also: Determinism.

Supererogatory, literally, "above the call of duty." A supererogatory act is one that is morally good and that goes beyond what is required by duty. Some ethical theories, such as certain versions of utilitarianism, that demand that we always do the act that yields the most good have no room for supererogatory acts. It is sometimes used negatively, to object that an ethical prescription is too demanding.

Supervenience, a set of properties or facts *M* supervenes on a set of properties or facts *P* if and only if there can be no changes or differences in *M* without there being changes or differences in *P*.

Supremum, least upper bound

Syllogism, an argument—usually deductive—having two premises and a single conclusion.

Synthetic, having factual or emp-irical content; *i.e.* not being true or false by definition. Contrast term: analytic.

Symbolic inference, The derivation of new facts from known facts and inference rules. This is one of the fundamental operations of artificial intelligence and logic programming languages like Prolog.

Inference is a basic part of human reasoning. For example given that all men are mortal and that Socrates is a man, it is a trivial step to infer that Socrates is mortal. We might express these symbolically:

man (X) => mortal (X).

man (Socrates).

("if *X* is a man then *X* is mortal" and "Socrates is a man"). Here, "man", "mortal" and "Socrates" are just arbitrary symbols which the computer manipulates without reference to or knowledge of their external meaning. A forward chaining system (a production system) could use these to infer the simply by matching the left-hand-side of the implication against the new fact mortal (Socrates) fact and substituting Socrates for the variable *X*.

Symbolic logic, The discipline that treats formal logic by means of a formalised artificial language or symbolic calculus, whose purpose is to avoid the ambiguities and logical inadequacies of natural language.

Symmetric difference of sets, The symmetric difference of two sets, *A* and *B*, is the set of objects that are members of either *A* or *B* but not both. No standard notation. The symmetric difference of sets *A* and *B* is the set *x*: (*x*: *A*) /<=> (*x*: *B*). The symmetric difference of sets is the set-theoretic equivalent of exclusive disjunction; for the equivalent of inclusive disjunction.

Synchronous, 1. Two or more processes that depend upon the occurrences of specific events such as common timing signals.

2. Occurring at the same time or at the same rate or with a regular or predictable time relationship or sequence. Opposite: asynchronous.

Syncretism, the word syncretism refers to attempts to unify existing and seemingly inharmonious theories or systems of philosophy. In general, syncretism reflects a more serious intellectual endeavor than eclec-ticism.

Syntactic, syntax

Syntactic completeness, A system is syntactically complete iff there is no unprovable schema *B* that could be added to the system as an axiom schema without creating simple inconsistency.

Syntactic incompleteness, The failure of syntactic completeness; there is at least one unprovable schema that could be added as an axiom schema without creating simple inconsistency.

Syntactic consequence, A is the syntactic consequence of a set *G* of wffs iff A can be derived from *G* (and the axioms). Notation:

G

|- *A*.

Syntactic tautology, A wff of truth-functional logic whose truth tablecolumn contains nothing but T's when these T's are uninterpreted tokens rather than, say, truth-values. The rules for generating the truth table column tell us to use one of these uninterpreted T's in exactly those cases where semantic considerations would have led us to use the truth-value Truth. See semantic tautology

Syntactics, the characterization, for an artificial, or natural, language, ofwhat constitutes a well-formed sentence, or, to put it another way, a grammatical sentence, or a sentence of the language. It is usually assumed that a well-formed, or grammatical, sentence need not be meaningful. semantics

Syntactic validity, An inference is syntactically valid iff the conclusion can be derived from the premises by means of stipulated rules of inference. See semantic validity

Syntax, The structure of strings in some language. A language's syntax is described by a grammar. For example, the syntax of a binary number could be expressed as binary *number* = bit [binary *number*] meaning that a binary

bit = "0" | "1"

number is a bit optionally followed by a binary number and a bit is a literal zero or one digit.

The meaning of the language is given by its semantics. See also abstract syntax, concrete syntax.

Syntax tree, A tree representing the abstract syntax of some tokens in a language.

Synthetic, a sentence, proposition, thought, or judgement is synthetic if it is neither logically (analytically) true, or false; generally, synthetic claims are said to be empirical in that they are discovered through experiment and observation, and in that "a bare conception of the subject" will not make it immediately obvious that the predicate applies to it.

Systematicity, a number of putative psychological properties or regularities go by the name of systematicity. These diverse regularities are meant to constitute explananda that are supposed to support the view that there exists a syntactically and semantically combinatorial language of thought. See productivity of thought, compositionality, symbo-licism.

Tacit knowledge, knowledge that enters into the production of behaviours and/or the constitution of mental states but is not ordinarily accessible to consciousness. See also cognize, implicit memory, background, rules.

Taoism, Taoism is an ancient strand of Chinese philosophical thought, similar in many ways to Platonism in the West (just as Confucianism holds a position similar to Aristotelianism). However, Taoism was a reaction against the conservative and action-oriented thought of Confucius: one of the central Taoist concepts was wu-wei or "non-activity". Taoists stress the necessity of living in accordance to nature (their policy of non-activity could be phrased as "do nothing that is contrary to nature or to your own native character"), and their doctrines can be compared to stoicism in this regard. The Taoist emphasis on lack of emotion and "disturbance"—that is, on inner peace—can also be compared to the doctrines of Epicureanism. Taoist thinkers, foremost among them Lao Tzu and Chuang Tzu (the two great authors of classical Taoism), stressed the inherent untrustworthiness of appearances, the unity of the real world behind the appearances, the necessity of understanding this real unity "spontaneously", and the cultivation of one's character so that one could become a "free spirit". Taoism was and is a strong tradition in China, which accounts for the fact that Chinese forms of Buddhism (*e.g.*, Ch'an or Zen Buddhism) show such a heavy dependence on Taoist concepts. (References from Budd-hism, Epicureanism, and humanism.)

Tautology, a logically valid wff of truth-functional propositional logic.

A compound proposition that is true in every row of its truth table or in every interpretation. contingency, contradiction, logical validity, semantic tautology, syntactic tautology Or also, a non-atomic, or molecular, proposition that is true no matter what the assignment of truth value to the atomic propositions that it contains. Example: "p or not-p". This molecular proposition is true whether we assign "p" the value true or the value false.

Tautology schema, (plural: schemata). A formula containing variables of the metalanguage which becomes a tautology when the variables are instantiated to wffs of the formal language.

Teleological argument, also known as the "argument from design", it argues from the observed well-designedness of the universe and the things in it to the existence of a supremely intelligent and powerful Designer, or God. Compare: cosmological argument, ontological argument. Contrast: argument from evil.

Teleological ethics, it claims that it is the consequences (or goals-fostered-by) of actions that determine their moral worth. Mill's utilitarianism ("act so as to achieve the greatest possible balance of pleasure over pain for all sentient creation") is considered a typical example.

Teleology, purpose or direction.

Temporal logic, An extension of predicate calculus which includes notation for arguing about *when* statements are true. Time is discrete and extends indefinitely into the future. Three prefix operators, represented by a circle, square and diamond mean "is true at the next time instant", "is true from now on" and "is eventually true". *x U y* means *x* is true until *y* is true. *x P y* means *x* precedes *y*.

There are two types of formula: "state formulae" about things true at one point in time, and "path formulae" about things true for a sequence of steps. An example of a path formula is "*x U y*", and example of a state formula is "next *x*" or a simple atomic formula such at "waiting".

> "true until" in this context means that a state formula holds at every point in time up to a point when another formula holds. "*x U y*" is the "strong until" and implies that there is a time when *y* is true. "*x W y*" is the "weak until" in which it is not necessary that y holds eventually.

There are two types of temporal logic used: branching time and linear time. The basic propositional temporal logic cannot differentiate between the two, though. Linear time considers only one possible future, in branching time you have several alternative futures. In branching temporal logic you have the extra operators "A" (for "all futures") and "E" (for "some future"). For example, "A(work U go-home)" means "I will work until I go home" and "E (work U go-home)" means "I may work until I go home".

Term, Grammatically, the type of expression that can serve as the argument of a predicate or fun-ction. The subject of predication; the input of a function. As such (in first-order predicate logic) either an individual constant, individual variable, or a function (with its own arguments) defined for a domain and range of individuals.

Closed term

A term without variables.

Open term

A term with at least one variable.

Texture, A measure of the variation of the intensity of a surface, quantifying properties such as smoothness, coarseness and regularity. It's often used as a region descriptor in image analysis and computer vision.

The three principal approaches used to describe texture are statistical, structural and spectral. Statistical techniques characterise texture by the statistical properties of the grey levels of the points comprising a surface. Typically, these properties are computed from the grey level histogram orgrey level cooccurrence matrix of the surface.

Structural techniques characterise texture as being composed of simple primitives called "texels" (texture elements), that are regularly arranged on a surface according to some rules. These rules are formally defined by grammars of various types.

Spectral techniques are based on properties of the Fourier spectrum and describe global periodicity of the grey levels of a surface by identifying high energy peaks in the spectrum.

Theism, the word theism is used to describe any belief in the existence of a god or divine powers. While the true opposite of theism is atheism, in Western philosophy theism is sometimes contrasted with deism or with pantheism, in which case it refers to the active involvement of God in the world or to the separation of God from his creation. (References from atheism, deism, humanism, naturalism, and polytheism.)

Theory, The consensus, idea, plan, story, or set of rules that is currently being used to inform a behaviour. This usage is a generalisation and (deliberate) abuse of the technical meaning. "What's the theory on fixing this TECO loss?" "What's the theory on dinner tonight?" ("Chinatown, I guess.") "What's the current theory on letting lusers on during the day?" "The theory behind this change is to fix the following well-known screw...."

Theory change, The study of methods used to incorporate new information into a knowledge base when the new information may conflict with existing information. Belief revision is one area of theory change.

Theory laden, the property of observations varying with or depending upon the theoretical commitments of the observer. Insofar as observations are theory laden, your beliefs—as shaped by the theory or paradigm you accept—determines what you observe, so that partisans of different theories (or paradigms) will observe differently.

Theory neutral, the property of observations being uninfluenced by the theoretical commitments of the observer. Insofar as observations aret-heory neutral, your beliefs—as shaped by the theory (or paradigm) you accept—do not color what you observe, so that partisans of different theories (or paradigms) all observe alike.

Theory of definite descriptions, Russells' theory of description

Thomism, term used to describe the doctrines and legacy of Thomas Aquinas, who effected a synthesis between Christianity and Aristotelianism. Thomist philosophers continue to be active today, mostly at Catholic or Jesuit universities (neothomism, neoscholasticism).

Thoreau, Henry David (1817-1862), American writer, philosopher, and naturalist, whose work demonstrates how the abstract ideals of libertarianism and individualism can be effectively instilled in a person's life.

Thoreau was born on July 12, 1817, in Concord, Massachusetts, the son of a businessman, and educated at Harvard University. For some years he worked as a teacher and tutored in Concord, and on Staten Island, New York. From 1841 to 1843 he lived in the home of the American essayist and transcendental philosopher Ralph Waldo Emerson, where he met other American transcendentalists, such as the educator and philosopher Amos Bronson Alcott and Margaret Fuller and George Ripley, both social reformers and literary critics. Two years later he moved to a crude hut on the shores of Walden Pond, a small body of water on the outskirts of Concord. He lived there until 1847, resided again with Emerson during 1847-1848, and spent the years from 1849 with his parents and sister in Concord. During his sojourn at Walden Pond and elsewhere in Concord, Thoreau supported himself by doing odd jobs, such as gardening, carpentry, and land surveying. The major portion of his time was devoted to the study of nature, to meditating on philosophical problems, to reading Greek, Latin, French, and English literature, and to long conversations with his neighbours.

The Transcendentalist magazine *The Dial* published Thoreau's poem "Sympathy" in its inaugural issue of 1840. More of Thoreau's poems were published by the magazine, including "To the Maiden in the East" and "A Winter Walk", as well as the essay "Natural History of Massachusetts", but *The Dial* ceased publication in 1844.

Of the numerous volumes that make up the collected works of Thoreau, only two were published during his lifetime: *A Week on the Concord and Merrimack Rivers* (1849) and *Walden; or, Life in the Woods* (1854). The material for the other volumes was edited posthumously by the author's friends from his journals, manuscripts, and letters. *A Week on the Concord and Merrimack Rivers* is the narrative of a boating trip taken in August 1839; it is a combination of nature study and metaphysical speculation and bears the distinctive impression of the author's engaging personality. *Walden*, Thoreau's most popular work, gives a plain and straightforward statement of the author's reasons for adopting the contemplative life and a graphic account of the principal details of that life. His journal entries and essays have great literary value and reflect Thoreau's pronounced gift for a careful, but refreshing writing style.

Thoreau chose going to jail, even if only for one night, rather than supporting a government involved in slavery and the Mexican-American War by paying his poll tax. He clarified his position in perhaps his most famous essay, "Civil Disobedience" (1849). In this essay he discussed passive resistance, a method of protest that later was adopted by the Indian leader Mohandas Gandhi as a tactic against the British, and by civil rights activists fighting racial segregation in the United States. Thoreau died on May 6, 1862.

Thought, an intentional mental phenomenon which has contents about things in the world. See intentionality.

Total function, A function whose value is defined for all possible arguments (from that domain). See partial function

Totalitarianism, totalitarianism is authoritarianism or political collectivism taken to its logical and physical conclusion—the state in which government possesses total control over the individual. (References from authoritarianism, capitalism, collectivism, communism, Marxism, Platonism, and pluralism.)

Traditional logic, traditional, scholastic, or aristotelian logic traditional, scholastic, or aristotelian logic traditional logic was first developed by

Aristotle and sys-tematized (somewhat differently) by the medieval school persons. It was thought to be all there was to logic by most until the end of the nineteenth century (until G. Frege, for example, came out with a version of modern logic in his Concept-Writing (Begriffsschrift). The assumption of traditional logic was that all propostions (sentences) are of a subje‑‑ predicate form (strictly, SUBJECT TERM + COPULA + PREDICATE TERM: for example, fist + are + backboned mammals). This exclusive empl ›is on the subject - predicate form is though misleading, and the underlying cause of mistaken metaphysics by many modern logicians (vice versa for some recent critics of modern logic). Traditional logic is concerned with immediate and mediate inferences between (subject-predicate) propositons. Immediate inference is from one (premiss) to one (conclusion) with the two terms of the premiss both appearing in the conclusion. Mediate inference involves more premisses with the use of "mediating", or middle, terms that do not appear in the conclusion. The syll-ogism, the primary study of traditional logic, is an argument in which the premisses connect the subject and predicate of the conclusion by means of a middle term.

Transcendent, surpassing or apart from sensible or material reality. For Kant, what is beyond the realm of either outer (perceptive) or inner (apperceptive) experience. In some religious views (on orthodox Christian views, *e.g.*) God is held to be transcendent (beyond the world). On other pantheistic views (*e.g.*, those of the Stoics or Spinoza) God is held to be an immanent guiding spirit in and of the sensible material world, not existing apart or beyond it. Similarly, Plato asserts the transcendence while Aristotle maintains the immanence of the Forms oressences of things.

Transcendental, relating to the grounds of possible experience. *E.g.* Kant thought that most of our pure rational knowledge is synthetic or a priori, or transcendental. Thus Kant believed that geometry expresses the pure form of our intuitive faculty for experienceing things visually as in space: this faculty sets the rules for what can be a possible experience of vision.

Transcendental argument, a type of argument, deriving from Kant, which seeks to establish the necessary conditions of the possibility of something's being the case. For example, we have to believe·that we are free when we perform an action; thus belief in freedom is a necessary condition of the possibility of action.

Transcendentalism, in philosophy and literature, belief in a higher reality than that found in sense experience or in a higher kind of knowledge than that achieved by human reason. Nearly all transcendentalist doctrines stem from the division of reality into a realm of spirit and a realm of matter. Such a division is made by many of the great religions of the world.

Philosophical Development and Applications: The philosophical concept of transcendence was developed by the Greek philosopher Plato. He affirmed the existence of absolute goodness, which he characterized as something beyond description and as knowable ultimately only through intuition. Later religious philosophers, influenced by Plato, applied this concept of transcendence to divinity, maintaining that God can be neither described nor understood in terms that are taken from human experience. The doctrine that God is transcendent, in the sense of existing outside of nature, is a fundamental principle in the orthodox forms of Christianity, Judaism, and Islam.

The terms *transcendent* and *transcendental* were used in a more narrow and technical sense by the advocates of scholasticism late in the Middle Ages to signify concepts of unrestricted generality applying to all types of things. The scholastics recognized six such transcendental concepts: essence, unity, goodness, truth, thing, and something (Latin, *ens, unum, bonum, verum, res,* and *aliquid*).

The German philosopher Immanuel Kant was the first to make a technical distinction between the terms *transcendent* and *transcendental*. Kant reserved the term *transcendent* for those entities such as God and the soul, which are thought to exist outside of human experience and are therefore unknowable; he used the term *transcendental* to signify a priori forms of thought, that is, innate principles with which the mind gives form to its perceptions and makes experience intelligible. Kant applied the name *transcendental philosophy* to the study of pure mind and its a priori forms. Later German idealist philosophers who were influenced by Kant, particularly Johann Gottlieb Fichte, Friedrich Wilhelm Joseph von Schelling, and Edmund Husserl, described their views as transcendental. Consequently, the term *transcendentalism* came to be applied almost exclusively to doctrines of metaphysical idealism.

Transcendental Literature: In its most specific usage, transcendentalism refers to a literary and philosophical movement that developed in the United States in the first half of the 19th century. While the movement was, in part, a reaction to certain 18th-century rationalist doctrines, it was strongly influenced by deism, which, although rationalist, was opposed to Calvinist orthodoxy. Transcendentalism also involved a rejection of the strict Puritan religious attitudes that were the heritage of New England, where the movement originated. In addition, it opposed the strict ritualism and dogmatic theology of all established religious institutions.

More importantly, the transcendentalists were influenced by Romanticism, especially such aspects as self-examination, the celebration of individualism, and the extolling of the beauties of nature and humankind. Consequently, transcendentalist writers expressed semireligious feelings towards nature, as well as the creative process, and saw a direct connection, or correspondence, between the universe (macrocosm) and the individual soul (microcosm). In this view, divinity permeated all objects, animate or inanimate, and the purpose of human life was union with the so-called *Over-Soul*. Intuition, rather than reason, was regarded as the highest human faculty. Fulfilment of human potential could be accomplished through mysticism or through an acute awareness of the beauty and truth of the surrounding natural world. This process was regarded as inherently individual, and all orthodox tradition was suspect.

American transcendentalism began with the formation of the Transcendental Club in Boston in 1836. Among the leaders of the movement were the essayist Ralph Waldo Emerson, the feminist and social reformer Margaret Fuller, the preacher Theodore Parker, the educator Bronson Alcott, the philosopher William Ellery Channing, and the author and naturalist Henry David Thoreau. The Transcendental Club published a magazine, *The Dial,* and some of the club's members participated in an experiment in communal living at Brook Farm, in West Roxbury, Massachusetts, during the 1840s. Major transcendentalist works of the American movement include Emerson's essays "Nature" (1836) and "Self-Reliance" (1841), as well as many of his metaphysical poems, and also Thoreau's *Walden, or Life in the Woods* (1854), which is an account of an individual's attempt to live simply and in harmony with nature.

Truth, in philosophy, correspondence of a statement or concept with reality. In general, a sentence or a concept is true only if the facts contained within it are real. This view of truth is generally described as the correspondence theory of truth, and it corresponds with an everyday linguistic understanding of the truth. In philosophy, however, this definition is often questioned. In the 19th century, for example, the main objection was that it was unclear how the correspondence (the corre-sponding relationship) between the statement and the topic should be understood.

At the centre of philosophical theories on truth stands the search for adequate truth criteria, and the basis for such truth criteria. For example, the following elements may be used in assessing truth criteria: the agreement (consent) of a community (of experts and also of laypeople) that decides at any time what is true or false within the community; or the practical use-fulness of an opinion that claims to be true. In addition, the intuitive evidence of a statement is often appealed to, with the truth of a statement justified if it is directly clear and plausible as, for example, in statements about directly perceptible events (observation sentences) as in mathematical principles (*see* Axiom) and conclusions.

Plausible objections are raised the criteria mentioned above. In the first place, consent between members of a community can be founded on error. Consent says nothing about the objective truth of a statement; it is rather decided on the basis of a corresponding opinion that something is held as true, not on whether the facts are true. Second, the facts speak against the usefulness of truth criteria; mistakes and deceptions can also be useful, and it is not ruled out that incorrect opinions can lead to successful action. Third, with regard to the criterion of perceptible evidence, this may also be a case of deception.

The problem with truth criteria, therefore, is that one must concede to each criterion the possibility of mistakes or deceptions. It is just as unclear how to establish the criteria as it is to apply the concept of truth.

From the difficulties related to a general definition of truth, Gottlob

Frege concluded that the concept of truth is a unique and indefinable basic concept of our recognition.

Truth, a property of statements, thoughts, or judgments. According tocorrespondence theories, a statement (*e.g.*) is true if it corresponds to the facts, and false if it doesn't. (See Universals, below, for further explanation.) According to coherence theories, the truth of thoughts (*e.g.*) consists in their coherence with other thoughts.

Truth for an interpretation, 1. For a wff of propositional logic, to be true under the assignments of a given interpretation.

2. For a wff of predicate logic, to be true for all sequences of some interpretation. Also called true for I. How a wff can be true for an interpretation must be defined separately for each connective in the language. See logical validity, satisfaction.

Truth function, an operator in a logical language (sentence, logic) is said to be truth functional iff the truth value of a proposition in which it appears is wholly determined by the truth value of the subsiduary propositions on which it operates. *E.g.* the truth value of p&q is wholly determined once we know the truth value of p and the truth value of q; hence the operator, &, is truth functional. non-truth-functional conjunction, dagger function, disjunction, equivalence, implication, negation, stroke function.

Truth-functional compound proposition, a compound proposition whose truth-value can be determined solely on the basis of the truth-values of its components and the definitions of its connectives.

Truth-functional connective, a connective that makes only truth-functional compounds.

Truth-functional propositional logic, the branch of logic that deals with the truth-functional connectives and the relations they permit among propositions. The logic of the relations between or among propositions, as opposed to predi-cate logic which covers the structure within propositions.

Truth of fact, as distinguished by Leibniz, these truths could have been otherwise since their denials are possible and noncontradictory: such truths hold only contingently (as a matter of fact), so knowledge of themrequires observation or empirical evidence for its certification. Contrast: truth of reason.

Truth of reason, as distinguished by Leibniz, these are truths which cannot be false because their denials would be contradictory and impossible: suchtruths hold of necessity and can be known to be true by the exercise of reason alone. Contrast: truth of fact.

Truth theories, the correspondance theory of truth insists on the common sense view that what makes a sentence true is its correspondance to something external to language (usually), some state of affairs. The coherence theory emphasizes that truth involves above all a coherence between some sentence we are considering and the rest of our beliefs (rest of the sentences that we hold). semantics

Truth-value, The state of being true or the state of being false.

2-valued logics: Logics in which there are only two truth-values, namely, truth and falsehood.

Many-valued logics: Logics that recognize more than two truth-values. In 3-valued logics, for example, the third truth-value is often "unknown" or "unprovable" or"neither true nor false". Also called n-valued logics.

Turing test, A criterion proposed by Alan Turing in 1950 for deciding whether a computer is intelligent. Turing called it "the Imitation Game" andoffered it as a replacement for the question, "Can machines think?"

A human holds a written conversation on any topic with an unseen correspondent (nowadays it might be by electronic mail or chat). If the human believes he is talking to another human when he is really talking to a computer then the computer has passed the Turing test and is deemed to be intelligent.

Turing predicted that within 50 years (by the year 2000) technological progress would produce computing machines with a capacity of 10**9 bits, and that with such machinery, a computer program would be able to fool the average questioner for 5 minutes about 70% of the time.

The Loebner Prize is a competition to find a computer program which can pass an unrestricted Turing test.

Twin earth, the duplicate planet in a series of thought experiments inspired by Hilary Putnam.

Two-valued logic, (Commonly known as "Boolean algebra") A mathematical system concerning the two truth values, TRUE and FALSE and the functions AND, OR and NOT. Two-valued logic is one of the cornerstones of logic and is also fundamental in the design of digital electronics and programming languages.

The term "Boolean" is used here with its common meaning—two-valued, though strictly Boolean algebra is more general than this.

Boolean functions are usually represented by truth tables where "0" represents "false" and "1" represents "true". *E.g.*:

A	B	A AND B
0	0	0
0	1	0
1	0	0
1	1	1

This can be given more compactly using "x" to mean "don't care" (either true or false):

A	B	A AND B
0	x	0
x	0	0
1	1	1

Similarly:

A NOT A A B A OR B
0 1 0 0 |0
1 0 x 1 1
1 x 1

Other functions such as XOR, NAND, NOR or functions or more than two inputs can be constructed using combinations of AND, OR and NOT. AND and OR can be constructed from each other using DeMorgan's Theorem:

A OR B = NOT ((NOT A) AND (NOT B))

A AND B = NOT ((NOT A) OR (NOT B))

In fact any Boolean function can be constructed using just NOR or just NAND using the identities:

NOT A = A NOR A

A OR B = NOT (A NOR B)

and DeMorgan's Theorem.

Type, (Or "data type") A set of values from which a variable, constant, function, or other expression may take its value.

Types supported by most programming languages include integers (usually limited to some range so they will fit in one word of storage), Booleans, real numbers, and characters. Strings are also common, though they may berepresented as lists of characters in some languages.

If *s* and *t* are types, then so is *s* -> *t*, the type of functions from *s* to *t*; that is, give them a term of type *s*, functions of type *s* -> *t* will return a term of type *t*.

Some types are primitive—built-in to the language, with no visible internal structure—*e.g.* Boolean; others are composite-constructed from one or more other types (of either kind)—*e.g.* lists, structures, unions.

Some languages provide strong typing, others allow implicit type conversion and/or explicit type conversion.

Unconscious the, those mental states of which a human being is unaware and can normally only access and/or alter with great difficulty, if at all.

Undecidable system, A system for which there is no effective method. See decidable system

Undecidable wff, A wff that is neither a theorem nor the negation of a theorem. See decidable wff

Union of sets, The union of two sets, *A* and *B*, is the set of objects that are members of either *A* or *B* or both. Also called the sum of two sets. The union of sets is the set—theoretic equivalent of inclusive disjunction; for the equivalent of exclusive disjunction See symmetric difference of sets.

Universal, pertaining to all, especially all times, all places, and all things.

Universalisability, Immanuel Kant used this term when discussing the maxims,or subjective rules, that guide our actions. A maxim is universalisable if it can consistently be willed as a law that everyone ought to obey. The only maxims which are morally good are those which can be universalised. The test of universalisability ensures that everyone has the same moral obligations in morally similar situations.

Universals, the properties or attributes expressed (or kinds denoted) by abstract or general words or predicates in speech (or concepts in thought). Just as the words (or concepts) apply to many things, properties corresponding to the words (or concepts) inhere in many individuals; in just those same individuals to which the word (or concept) can be truly applied. The relation between the universal corresponding to the word and the things to which the word is applied in speech (or the concept in thought) is supposed to explain the truth of that application. If the universal the word expresses does belong to the thing to which the word is applied then the application (an assertion, or affirmative judgment) istrue; if the universal does not belong to the thing, then the application is false. "Grass is green" is true because grass has the property of being green; "Grass is carnivorous" is false because grass hasn't the property of being carnivorous; etc. See nominalism and realism above.

Utilitarianism, a moral theory originally advanced by Jeremy Bentham according to which the moral character of an act—whether it's good or bad or right or wrong—is entirely determined by its consequences, andlikening moral reasoning to economic calculation Utilitarians maintain the right course of action is always the one that has the most beneficial or least detrimental consequences overall, for all affected. Bentham'shedonistic brand of utilitarianism identifies the benefits in question with pleasure and the costs with pain. John Stuart Mill speaks, instead, of "happiness": according to Mill's greatest happiness principle, our moral aim should be "the greatest happiness for the greatest number." Contemporary utilitarians, like Peter Singer, are more apt to speak of the benefits to be counted as "preference satisfactions" or "interest satis-factions," counting the corresponding dissatisfactions as costs. Rule utilitarians hold that utilitarian calculation should be used to make rules rather than directly applied to evaluate actions.

Universe of discourse. The set of all things under consideration in the-context; the set of things covered by universal quantification. See complement, universal set.

Unmoved mover, the argument from first cause, or the unmoved mover: everything we are familiar with was created by and set in motion by somethingelse. But if we are to avoid an infinite regress, there must be some first cause which is not itself set in motion by anything else; this first cause, or prime mover, is God.

Use theory of meaning, the semantic theory according to which the meaning of a word is determined by its use in communication and more generally, in social interaction.

Utilitarianism (Latin *utilis*, "useful"), in ethics, the doctrine that what is useful is good, and consequently, that the ethical value of conduct is determined by the utility of its results. The term "utilitarianism" is more specifically applied to the proposition that the supreme objective of moral action and the foundation on which all morality should be grounded is the achievement of the greatest happiness or satisfaction for the greatest number. This objective is also considered to be the ultimate criterion for evaluating all social institutions as good or bad. The utilitarian theory of ethics is generally opposed to other ethical doctrines in which the final arbiter of right and wrong is either some inner sense or faculty—often called conscience (as in intuitionist theories of ethics)—or else some fundamental ethical principle based on reason (as in the ethics of Immanuel Kant). Utilitarian ethics is likewise at variance with the theological view that right and wrong depend on the will of God, and with the hedonistic view that it depends on the pleasure produced by an act for the individual alone who performs it. The utilitarian theory of legislation is opposed to natural law theory, which states that the criterion for evaluating laws as good or bad is whether they conform to certain natural laws that are given by God or whether they conform to the principles that would be freely chosen by individuals who were banding together to form a state in the first place.

Work of Paley and Bentham: Utilitarianism was enunciated in its most characteristic form by the British theologian William Paley in his *Principles of Moral and Political Philosophy* (1785) and by the British jurist and philosopher Jeremy Bentham in his *Introduction to the Principles of Morals and Legislation* (1789). In Paley's work, utilitarianism is combined with both individualistic hedonism and theological authori-tarianism, as illustrated in his definition of virtue as the "doing [of] good to mankind, in obedience to the will of God, and for the sake of everlasting happiness". Bentham clarified the utilitarian theory and used it as the foundation, not merely of a moral system, but also of legal and political reforms. He maintained the necessity of sacrificing smaller interests to greater interests, and so posited as the ethical goal of human society the greatest happiness of the greatest number.

Bentham sought to illustrate the doctrine of utilitarianism by comparing it to the doctrine of asceticism on the one hand and to the theory of sympathy and antipathy on the other. Asceticism he defined as the principle that pleasure should be forfeited, and pain incurred, without expectation of any recompense. The theory of sympathy and antipathy he held to be based on the "principle which approves or disapproves of certain actions, not on account of their tending to augment the happiness, nor yet on account of their tending to diminish the happiness of the party whose interest is in question, but merely because a man finds himself disposed to approve or disapprove of them: holding up that approbation or disapprobation as a sufficient reason for itself, and disclaiming the necessity of looking out for any extrinsic ground". In his exposition of the theory of utilitarianism, Bentham sought to devise a scale of pleasures and pains, rating them in terms of their intensity, purity, duration, propinquity or remoteness, certainty, fruitfulness, and the extent to which pleasure and pain are shared among fewer or more people.

After Bentham: Other notable exponents of utilitarianism were the British jurist John Austin and the British philosophers James Mill and his son John Stuart Mill. Austin set forth a strong defence of the utilitarian theory in his *Province of Jurisprudence Determined* (1832). James Mill interpreted and popularized the theory in a number of articles contributed for the most part to the *Westminster Review*. a periodical founded by Bentham and others to promote the spread of the utilitarian philosophy. John Stuart Mill, who made utilitarianism the subject of one of his philosophical treatises (*Utilitarianism*, 1863), is the ablest champion of the doctrine after Bentham.

Mill applied utilitarianism to morality in a far more detailed way than Bentham. In addition, he contributed to the theory by recognizing distinctions of quality, in addition to those of intensity, among pleasures. Thus, whereas Bentham maintained that the "quality of pleasure being equal, push-pin [a child's game] is as good as poetry", Mill contended that some pleasures are "higher" or more valuable than others. The higher pleasures are those associated with activities that realize specifically human capacities, for example, art, science, and philosophy. The lower pleasures are those that human beings share with animals. Mill dramatized this distinction between different kinds of pleasures with his statement that it is "better to be a human being dissatisfied than a pig satisfied; better to be Socrates dissatisfied than a fool satisfied". When Mill spoke, therefore, of the greatest happiness of the greatest number as the criterion of morality, what he meant by "greatest happiness" was not simply the greatest amount of a single kind of pleasure and the least amount of pain, as found in Bentham's works and in his own earlier formulations. In the calculation of the total amount of happiness produced by an action, higher pleasures would weigh much more heavy than lower pleasures.

The British philosopher Henry Sidgwick, a contemporary disciple of Mill, gave a comprehensive presentation of Mill's utilitarianism in his *Methods of Ethics* (1874). Somewhat later, the British philosophers Herbert Spencer and Sir Leslie Stephen, the former in his *Data of Ethics* (1879), the latter in his *Science of Ethics* (1882), sought to synthesize the utilitarian theory with the principles of biological evolution as expounded in the works of Charles Darwin. Both the American philosopher and psychologist William James and the American philosopher, psychologist, and educator John Dewey were influenced by utilitarianism. Dewey substituted intelligence for pleasure, or happiness, both as the supreme value and as the most reliable method of achieving other desirable values.

After a period in the early 20th century when utilitarianism was eclipsed by intuitionist theories of morality, it was revived in the second half of the century. When efforts to found morality or legislation on conscience, pure reason, or God's will run into difficulties raised by scepticism, utilitarianism seems a natural grounding. Versions of utilitarianism are still defended by many philosophers today, in spite of the wide variety of attacks that have been made against it.

One objection to utilitarianism is that happiness is impossible to measure. To avoid this problem, modern utilitarianism is usually formulated in terms of "desire-satisfaction" or "preference-satisfaction" rather than happiness. Another objection is that utilitarianism justifies any action, no matter how seemingly bad, if the action produces more happiness than unhappiness overall. So, for example, it might be argued that the act utilitarian could condone the killing of a terminally ill person in order to transplant that person's various organs into a number of people who might otherwise die slow and painful deaths. A response to this is to distinguish "act" utilitarianism from "rule" utilitarianism. Act utilitarianism holds that the utilitarian criterion is to be applied directly to individual acts: an act is right or wrong depends on whether doing that particular act would create more happiness overall than doing anything else. Rule utilitarianism, on the other hand, states that the utilitarian criterion is to be applied to whole systems of social rules: an act is right or wrong depending on whether it is allowed by a system of social rules that, if conformed to by everyone, would produce more happiness overall than any other system of rules. Rule utilitarianism therefore evaluates a whole system of social rules—a social morality—by how much happiness it produces, whereas act utilitarianism attempts to evaluate each individual action in the same way. It is argued that although act utilitarianism would justify killing the ill person in the example to utilize that person's organs, rule utilitarianism would not, since a system of social rules that condoned such action would lead to widespread insecurity and unhappiness in the long run.

Utilitarianism, form of consequentialism made famous by John Stuart Mill (1806-1873) and continued by (mostly British) philosophers of the 19th and 20th centuries. According to utilitarinism, what is morally right is whatever produces the greatest overall amount of pleasure (hedonistic utilitarianism) or happiness (eudaimonistic utilitarianism). Some utilitarians (act utilitarians) claim that we should weigh the consequences of each individual action, while others (rule utilitarians) maintain that we should look at the consequences of adopting particular rules of conduct.

Utilitarianism's famous creed is "the greatest good for the greatest number", which sounds like and in fact tends to result in a kind of altruism, but which is not necessarily altruistic (for instance, Mill advocated a kind of individualism and individual fulfillment in life, since he thought that the best way for humanity to make progress was through the achievements of individuals). Utilitarianism has never made a deep impression in America, where consequentialism has generally taken the form of pragmatism. Popularly, utilitarianism has the same mild connotations of expediency and lack of principles that pragmatism does, although without the positive emphasis on action.

Utopia, concept of an ideal society.

The word "utopia" was coined by Sir Thomas More in his work *Utopia* (1516), from Greek terms meaning "no" and "place". However, many consider the concept to have been in existence long before More. One example is the biblical Garden of Eden, which represents a natural utopia now lost. Another, *The Republic* of Plato, sees Plato seeming to invite philosophers to establish an ideal state, whereas More describes an imaginary society without the inequalities of money and status which characterized his own Tudor England. These cases illustrate three different functions of utopia in literature and philosophy. An author may intend a utopia as a nostalgic vision, a feasible social experiment, or a form of social criticism. The allure of an ideal society often makes it difficult to tell whether or not it is intended as a genuine possibility.

The inspiration of a utopia has not been confined to the realm of ideas. Actual communities have been founded as utopias throughout history, including the Essene communities, the model industrial towns of Robert Owen, and the Israeli kibbutzim. Few of these communities, however, could withstand the tension between their own ideal principles and the pressures from the unreformed outer world which governed the desires and habits of their inhabitants. The problem of how to found a radically new society from scratch, with people who have grown up in existing societies, has plagued all attempts to establish utopias. Insofar as drastic methods of purging society have seemed necessary for founding utopias, fear of these methods has also inspired recurrent works of anti-utopianism. George Orwell's *Nineteen Eighty-four* (1949) is a classic example of anti-utopianism, condemning a purportedly ideal society in which language itself is twisted for political ends.

Valid, a property of arguments: being such that the truth of the premises guarantees or necessitates the truth of the conclusion.

Validity, 1. For wffs or propositions, see logical validity

2. For arguments and inferences, see semantic validity, soundness, syntactic validity.

Variable, A symbol whose referent varies or is unknown. A place-holder, as opposed to an abbreviation or name (a constant). See bound variables, constant, free variables

Individual variable of a system: Only individual variables and constants can serve as the arguments of functions and first order predicates. A variable in the metalanguage of some system S which ranges over wffs of *S*.

Predicate variable: A variable ranging over attributes and relations in higher order logic.

Vice, an undesirable or despicable personality trait, such as cruelty, or cowardice. According to Aristotle vices are either of excess or defect: *e.g.*, cowardice is is not facing up to danger enough (a vice of defect); rashness is facing up to danger too much (a vice of excess); while courage, the intermediate virtue, is facing up to danger appropriately, at the right time, in the right place, for the right reasons.

Virtue, a desirable or admirable personality trait, such as kindness, or courage. According to Aristotle every virtue is a mean between two vices: kindness a mean between cruelty and softness; courage a mean between cowardice and rashness; etc.

Vitalism, vitalism was a reaction against the currents of materialism and mechanistic determinism in the eighteenth and nineteenth centuries. The vitalists posited that human beings are not purely physical but contain some kind of spiritual component or "vital essence". In practice, since the vitalists could not deny the progress of materialist science, they advocated a kind of dualism of matter and life.

Voltaire, assumed name of François-Marie Arouet (1694-1778), French writer and intellectual, who was one of the leaders of the Enlightenment.

Voltaire was born in Paris on November 21, 1694, the son of a notary. He was educated by the Jesuits at the Collège de Louis-le-Grand. His career may be divided into two periods.

1694-1750: Voltaire quickly chose literature as his career. He became known in the Paris salons as a brilliant and sarcastic wit. A number of his writings, in particular a lampoon against the French regent Philippe II, Duc d'Orléans, led to imprisonment in the Bastille. During his 11 months there, Voltaire wrote his first tragedy, *Oedipe* (Oedipus), which was performed to great acclaim in 1718, and began an epic poem on Henry IV of France, of which an early version was printed anonymously in

Geneva under the title *Poème sur la Ligue* (Poem on the League, 1723). In his poem *Le Pour et le Contre* (For and Against, 1722), Voltaire expressed both his anti-Christian views and his belief in a Supreme Being (deism). After a quarrel with an illustrious nobleman, the Chevalier de Rohan, Voltaire was again imprisoned in the Bastille, before going into exile in England, where he quickly mastered the language and wrote two noteworthy essays in English, one on epic poetry and the other on the history of the French civil wars. After much opposition from the French government, an expanded edition of the *Poème sur la Ligue* was published under the title *La Henriade* (The Epic of Henry IV, 1728).

Voltaire returned to France in 1728. During the next few years he lived in Paris, where he wrote the *Lettres sur les Anglais* (Letters on the English Nation, 1734), republished in the same year, with the addition of a letter on the 17th-century religious writer Blaise Pascal, as *Lettres Philosophiques* (Philosophical Letters). These provided the French reader with object lessons on how intellectual, religious, and political matters should be conducted, and contain an eloquent defence of civil liberty and religious toleration. The work brought Voltaire into conflict with the authorities and he was forced to take refuge in the independent duchy of Lorraine, where he formed an intimate relationship with the aristocratic and learned Marquise du Châtelet, who exerted a strong intellectual influence on him. Voltaire's stay with the marquise at Cirey was a period of intense literary activity. As well as plays, stories, satires, and light verse, Voltaire wrote the *Eléments de la Philosophie de Newton* (Elements of Newton's Philosophy, 1737), in which he continued the pioneering work he had begun in the *Lettres sur les Anglais* of explaining Newton's theory of gravitational attraction to an obstinately resistant French public. He often travelled to Paris and through the influence of the Marquise de Pompadour, the mistress of Louis XV, he became a court favourite. He was appointed historiographer of France, then a gentleman of the king's bedchamber; finally, in 1746, he was elected to the Académie Française (*see* Institut de France). Following the death of the Marquise du Châtelet in 1749, Voltaire accepted a long-standing invitation from Frederick II of Prussia to become permanently resident at the Prussian court. He went to Berlin in 1750 but left after two years as his somewhat acid wit clashed with the king's autocratic temper, and led to frequent disputes.

1750-1778: Voltaire finally settled at Ferney, on the Swiss border, in 1758, where he completed his most ambitious work, the *Essai sur l'Histoire Générale et sur les Moeurs et l'Esprit des Nations* (Essay on General History and on the Customs and the Character of Nations, 1756), in which he maintains his belief in the existence of a God but attacks supernaturalism and denounces religion and the power of the clergy. After settling in Ferney, Voltaire wrote several philosophical poems, including the *Poème sur le Désastre de Lisbonne* (Poem on the Lisbon Disaster, 1756), a bitter protest at the belief, encouraged by the Roman Catholic Church, that the earthquake which had devastated Lisbon the previous year was a divinely inspired punishment visited on the city for its immorality. To this period belong the majority of his *contes philosophiques* (philosophical tales), the most famous of which, *Candide* (1759), rejects specious philosophical attempts (notably by the disciples of the German philosopher Leibniz) to explain away evil. Its often-quoted conclusion, "Il faut cultiver notre jardin" ("We must cultivate our garden"), is not a call for resignation, but for positive action, and was followed by a period in which Voltaire himself led a vitriolic campaign against the "Infamous Beast" of the Church. Voltaire involved other, younger Philosophes (a group of 18th-century writers; *see* French Literature: *The 18th century*) in this campaign, but their overt atheism and materialism repelled him, and he attempted to counter their arguments in works like *Le Philosophe Ignorant* (The Ignorant Philosopher, 1766) and *Histoire de Jenni* (The Story of Johnny, 1775).

Voltaire's lifelong ambition was to be hailed as the legitimate successor to the great 17th-century dramatist, Jean Racine, and throughout his long career he wrote numerous tragedies, including *Zaire* (1732) and *Mahomet* (1741), which were performed at the Comédie-Française. The apotheosis of his involvement with the theatre came when, old and sick, he returned to Paris in order to see a bust of himself crowned with laurels on the stage of that great institution. Voltaire died in Paris on May 30, 1778.

Voluntarism, The word voluntarism in philosophy is usually used to describe the doctrine of Schopenhauer that all the universe is fundamentally or exclusively will. The term is sometimes used as another word for libertarianism with regard to freedom of the will.

Watchmaker argument, the world is an orderly and beautiful structure; we can tell that it must have been made by someone, just as if you found a watch on an empty beach, you would know, even if you had never seen a watch before, that it must have been made by someone.

Wff, Acronym of "well-formed formula", pronounced whiff. A string of symbols from the alphabet of the formal language that conforms to the grammar of the formal language. See decidable wff, formal language.

Closed wff: In predicate logic, a wff with no free occurrences of any variable; either it has constants in place of variables, or its variables are bound, or both. Also called a sentence. See bound varia-bles, free variables, closure of a wff

Open wff: In predicate logic, a wff with at least one free occurrence a variable. Some logicians use the terms, 1-wff, 2-wff,...*n*-wff for open wffs with 1 free variable, 2 free variables,...*n* free variables. (Others call these 1-formula, 2-formula,...*n*-formula.)

Will the, a psychological phenomenon with a force-like character that is evident in our acting or trying to act and is necessary for these types of events.

Yoga (Sanskrit *yuga,* "union"), one of the six classic systems of Hindu philosophy, distinguished from the others by the marvels of bodily control and the magical powers ascribed to its advanced devotees. Yoga affirms the doctrine that through the practice of certain disciplines one may achieve liberation from the limitations of flesh, the delusions of sense, and the pitfalls of thought and thus attain union with the object of knowledge. Such union, according to the doctrine, is the only true way of knowing. For most yogi (those who practice yoga), the object of knowledge is the universal spirit Brahma. A minority of atheistic Yogi seek perfect self-knowledge instead of knowledge of God. In any case, it is knowledge and not, as is commonly supposed, feats of asceticism, clairvoyance, or the working of miracles, that is the ideal goal of all yoga practices. Indeed, yoga doctrine does not approve of painful asceticism; it insists that physical and mental training is not to be used for display but only as a means to spiritual ends.

The Eight Stages: Yoga practice forms a ladder leading to perfect knowledge. One: self-control (*yama*) involves truthfulness, abstinence, avoidance of theft, refusal of gifts, and not doing injury to living things. Two: religious observance (*niyama*) embraces austerity, poverty, contentment, purification rites, recital of the Vedic hymns, and devoted reliance on the Supreme Being. Three: postures (*asana*), of which there are a great many, are regarded as basic to all the stages that follow. Four: regulation of the breath (*pranayama*) includes altering its depth and rhythm, breathing through either nostril at will, and the virtual suspension of breath. Five: restraint of the senses (*pratyahara*) means the withdrawal from external objects and the consequent turning of the mind upon itself. Six: steadying of the mind (*dharana*) narrows attention to some one part of the body, such as the navel, the tip of the nose, or the middle of the brow, and in that way renders the practitioner insensitive to outside disturbance. Seven: meditation (*dhyana*) fixes the mind on the object of knowledge, especially Brahma, to the exclusion of all other thoughts. Eight: profound contemplation (*samadhi*) is the perfect absorption of thought in the object of knowledge, its union and identification with that object. The achievement of *samadhi* liberates the self from the illusions of sense and the contradictions of reason. It is thought that has gone beyond thought, reaching its goal by its own negation. It leads to an inner illumination, the ecstasy of the true knowledge of reality.

Liberation: The final stage, in yoga doctrine, can rarely be attained in one lifetime. It is usually claimed that several births are required to achieve liberation, first from the world of phenomena, then from thoughts of self, and finally from the spirit's entanglement with matter. The separation of spirit from matter is *Kaivalya*, or true liberation.

As adept yogi approach *Kaivalya*, they are supposed to acquire certain remarkable capacities. They become insensible to heat or cold, to injury, to pleasure or pain. They can perform supernatural mental and physical feats and even change the course of nature. They can distinguish the subtlest elements of matter and are able, at the same time, to see the universe as a whole, comprehending both microcosm and macrocosm in the same thought.

Such are the powers claimed or

promised by yoga. Few, if any, of these powers have been successfully demonstrated to disinterested obs-ervers. Nevertheless, extraordinary achievements have been reported by witnesses. Most impressive, perhaps, is the yogi-sleep, in which animation is nearly suspended, enabling the yogi to be buried alive for days. The yogi-sleep has been explained by some authorities as a sort of cataleptic state induced by self-hypnosis and not essentially different from the catalepsy that can be a symptom of some mental illnesses.

Various Systems of Yoga: Aspirants of yoga have a selection of practices to suit their capabilities and environments. Many of the wonder-working yogi and almost all occidental devotees are practitioners of Hatha (physical) yoga, the basic system which is concerned with developing those bodily controls from which all else follows. The other systems differ mainly in the varying emphases placed on the several phases of yoga practice. Perhaps the most popular system in India is Bhakti (devotional) yoga. This system emphasizes the first two stages of yoga discipline, that is, self-control and religious observance. Other important yogas are Mantra yoga, which devotes itself to uttering the name of Krishna and other incantations; Karma yoga, the path of work and service; and Jnana yoga, the way of intellect. The combined form of Bhakti, Karma, and Jnana yogas is called Raya (royal) yoga.

History: The doctrines and practices of yoga date from the period of the Upanishads. The Maitrì Upanishad in particular outlines the essential practices of yoga. These practices were elaborated and given a philosophical foundation in the *Yoga Sutra* of the 2nd-century BC Indian scholar Patañjali, who is traditionally regarded as the founder of yoga. Patañjali derived his doctrine from Samkhya, the oldest of the classic systems of Hindu philosophy. In order to explain evolution, he departed from the system by grafting the concept of God (Ißvara) upon the atheistic outlook of Samkhya. The concept is not an integral part of yoga doctrine; indeed, some authorities actually consider it to be in contradiction with the rest of the system. In any case, yoga, unlike other systems of Hindu philosophy, has subordinated doctrine to the refinement of practice. Systematic study of yoga doctrine has declined in recent centuries.

As a system of practice, Yoga has from the beginning been one of the most influential features of Hinduism. Yoga exerted a powerful attraction upon Hindus because of the wonders attributed to it and because it gives countenance to the performance of austerities, to which Hindus are so strongly inclined. The strong influence of yoga can again be seen in Buddhism, which is also notable for its austerities, and for its spiritual exercises and trance states. As knowledge of yoga spread, it fascinated and won followers among Westerners. Among more recent students of yoga are the British writers Major Francis Yeats-Brown, Aldous Huxley, and Christopher Isherwood; the Romanian-born writer on religion Mircea Eliade; and the British violinist Sir Yehudi Menuhin. In recent years yoga exercises have been recommended by some physical fitness experts as a means of cleansing the body of impurities, of reducing weight, of toning up the nerves and muscles, and, generally, of improving health and prolonging life.

Zen, Buddhism

Zombie, a being that behaves like us and may share our functional organisation and even, perhaps, our neurophysiological makeup without conscious experiences or qualia. See consciousness.